LIBERTY, SOLIDARITY, AND COMMUNITY

How have European countries coped with the challenge of industrial capitalism and the rise of superpowers? Through an analysis of European integration from 1945 to the present day, Laurent Warlouzet argues that the European response was to create both new institutions and an original framework of governance for capitalism. Beyond the European case, he demonstrates that capitalism is not just a contest between free marketeers and their opponents, those in favour of welfare and environmental policies, because there is a third camp that defends protectionism and assertive defence policies. Hence, the governance of capitalism has three foundational principles – liberty, solidarity, and community. The book explores debates among Europeans about how to address global interdependence in political, economic, and environmental terms. It is based on fresh archival evidence collected in eight countries. This title is also available as open access on Cambridge Core.

Laurent Warlouzet is Professor of History at the Paris Sorbonne University. He was a postdoctoral fellow at the London School of Economics and Political Science (LSE), and at the European University Institute (EUI) of Florence.

'Laurent Warlouzet offers an innovative and stimulating analysis of the forms of capitalist governance of European institutions since 1945, which he analyzes through an interesting trinity: freedom, solidarity, and community. He shows that the European Union is an ideal laboratory for understanding how compromises are negotiated between these types of capitalism. This can offer new perspectives on possible regulations for the global capitalist system.'

Sandrine Kott, author of *A World More Equal: An Internationalist Perspective on the Cold War*

'This is a highly sophisticated and very effective analysis of the European Union's historical development. Warlouzet uses his economic expertise to identify some of the key motivations for the European integration process, but is equally at home discussing the complicated blend of political factors that have also played essential roles. Strongly recommended.'

Piers Ludlow, author of *Roy Jenkins and the European Commission Presidency, 1976–1980: At the Heart of Europe*

'This is a very timely, yet deeply historical, book about the interaction between capitalism and European integration since 1945. Timely, first, because it tackles centrally the balance between openness and protection, an issue currently front and center in the politics of liberal democracies, especially as the Liberal International Economic Order is ending and being replaced with a yet unsettled order. Second, the book focuses on the history of European integration at a time when the EU has simultaneously become a renewed beacon of hope for countries at the periphery and a poster child for what is wrong both with too much liberalism and regulation. Warlouzet's *Liberty, Solidarity, and Community* is a must-read to understand the deep roots of the current debates regarding the future trajectory of European integration.'

Sophie Meunier, author of *Trading Voices: The European Union in International Trade Negotiations*

'Laurent Warlouzet brings unmatched insight into European economic and social policies since the 1950s. This impressive book illuminates the complex, often ambiguous relationship between the European Union, market competition, and state intervention. By dispelling the myth that the EU is merely a free trade zone without political or social ambition, Warlouzet not only sets the record straight but also provides an essential guide for grappling with today's political challenges.'

Eric Monnet, author of *Balance of Power: Central Banks and the Fate of Democracies*

'This magnum opus sweeps across 75 years of integration history right up to current crises. Warlouzet's challenging interpretation attributes the EU's unique mix of policies to a specific balance that European capitalism strikes between liberty, equality and community.'

Andrew Moravcsik, author of *The Choice for Europe*

'This book provides a powerful analytical lens to understand the interplay between European integration and various forms of capitalist governance since 1945. It combines intellectual rigor with an analysis of the major developments that have shaped the continent over the past eight decades.'

Kiran Klaus Patel, author of *A Concise History of the European Union*

'This is a highly original book for a global understanding of the European variants of capitalism, and their close relationship to European integration.'

Philipp Ther, author of *Europe since 1989: a history*

LIBERTY, SOLIDARITY, AND COMMUNITY

Capitalism and European Integration, 1945 to the Present

LAURENT WARLOUZET
Sorbonne University

Shaftesbury Road, Cambridge CB2 8EA, United Kingdom

One Liberty Plaza, 20th Floor, New York, NY 10006, USA

477 Williamstown Road, Port Melbourne, VIC 3207, Australia

314–321, 3rd Floor, Plot 3, Splendor Forum, Jasola District Centre, New Delhi – 110025, India

Cambridge University Press is part of Cambridge University Press & Assessment, a department of the University of Cambridge.

We share the University's mission to contribute to society through the pursuit of education, learning and research at the highest international levels of excellence.

www.cambridge.org
Information on this title: www.cambridge.org/9781009682640

DOI: 10.1017/9781009682633

© Laurent Warlouzet 2026

This publication is in copyright. Subject to statutory exception and to the provisions of relevant collective licensing agreements, with the exception of the Creative Commons version the link for which is provided below, no reproduction of any part may take place without the written permission of Cambridge University Press & Assessment.

An online version of this work is published at doi.org/10.1017/9781009682633 under a Creative Commons Open Access license CC-BY-NC 4.0 which permits re-use, distribution and reproduction in any medium for non-commercial purposes providing appropriate credit to the original work is given and any changes made are indicated. To view a copy of this license visit https://creativecommons.org/licenses/by-nc/4.0

When citing this work, please include a reference to the DOI 10.1017/9781009682633

Front cover illustration: Shawshots/Alamy Images

First published 2026

A catalogue record for this publication is available from the British Library

A Cataloging-in-Publication data record for this book is available from the Library of Congress

ISBN 978-1-009-68264-0 Hardback
ISBN 978-1-009-68261-9 Paperback

Cambridge University Press & Assessment has no responsibility for the persistence or accuracy of URLs for external or third-party internet websites referred to in this publication and does not guarantee that any content on such websites is, or will remain, accurate or appropriate.

For EU product safety concerns, contact us at Calle de José Abascal, 56, 1°, 28003 Madrid, Spain, or email eugpsr@cambridge.org

CONTENTS

List of Figures, Tables and Boxes   ix
Glossary/Abbreviations in the Footnotes   x

Introduction   1

1 The Trinity of Capitalist Governance   14

2 The European Union as a Political Hybrid   34

3 A Regulated Market at the Core   48

4 Solidarity: A European Welfare State Flanking the Single Market   78

5 A Community without Communitarianism: Europe's Failure as a Military and Industrial Powerhouse   100

6 European Attempts to Promote Alternatives to Neoliberal Globalisation (1970–92)   126

7 Common Currency and Neoliberal Turn? (1970–92)   152

8 The European Union as a Driver of 'High Neoliberalism' (1992–2015)   173

9 Solidarity: Expanded and Contested Social and Environmental Action   206

10 The Resurgence of the Community Approach in the Twenty-First Century   237

Conclusion: Chronology, Alternatives, and Current Challenges   272

Notes   293
Primary Sources (Archives and Interviews)   365
Acknowledgements   367
Index   370

A full list of references to accompany this book can be found at www.cambridge.org/warlouzet *as well as the author's website (https://histeuropes.hypotheses.org/)*

FIGURES, TABLES AND BOXES

FIGURES

1.1 The three forms of capitalism 18
7.1 Government account balance, 1970–1987 (four countries) 160
11.1 Scenarios for the future of Europe 291

TABLES

1.1 The trinity of capitalism applied to various policies 16
2.1 European share of global GDP as compared with the United States and China since 1913 35
2.2 Types of economic cooperation and international institutions 46
8.1 The four dominant paradigms of European competition policy 194
8.2 Evolution of GNP per population 2009–2019 201
9.1 Convergence within the European Union: Changes in per capita wealth in seven countries 216
11.1 Chronology of post-war European integration and globalisation 279

BOXES

7.1 The benefits of monetary union with respect to the trinity of capitalism 153

GLOSSARY/ABBREVIATIONS IN THE FOOTNOTES

Glossary

CFSP:	Common Foreign and Security Policy
COREPER:	Committee of Permanent Representatives
CSCE:	Conference on Security and Cooperation in Europe
EC:	European Community
ECJ:	European Court of Justice
ECSC:	European Coal and Steel Community (1951)
EDC:	European Defence Community (1952)
EEC:	European Economic Community (1957)
EFTA:	European Free Trade Area
EMS:	European Monetary System
EMU:	Economic and Monetary Union
EPU:	European Payments Union
EU:	European Union (1992)
Euratom:	European Atomic Energy Community
GATT:	General Agreement on Tariffs and Trade
GDP:	Gross Domestic Product
ILO:	International Labour Organization
IMF:	International Monetary Fund
NATO:	North Atlantic Treaty Organization
OECD:	Organisation for Economic Co-operation and Development
OEEC:	Organisation for European Economic Co-operation
SGCI:	Secrétariat general du comité interministériel pour les questions de cooperation économique européenne.
UN:	United Nations
UNCTAD:	UN Trade and Development
UNECE:	United Nations Economic Commission for Europe
WTO:	World Trade Organization

Abbreviations in the Footnotes

AAPD:	Akten zur Auswärtigen Politik der Bundesrepublik Deutschland.
ABB:	Archives of the Bundesbank (Frankfurt-am-Main).
ACBI:	Archives of the Confederation of British Industry (Warwick).
ACFDT:	Archives of the French Trade Union CFDT.
AELEC:	Archives of the European League of Economic Cooperation (Louvain la Neuve).
AEP:	Archives of the European Parliament (Luxembourg).
AETUC:	Archives of the European Trade Union Confederation (Amsterdam).
AFDP:	Archives of the FDP, German Liberalism Archive (Gummersbach).
AFNSP:	Archives of the Fondation nationale des sciences politiques (Paris).
AGATT:	Archives of the GATT (online).
AILO:	Archives of the ILO (Geneva).
ANORMED:	Archives of the shipbuilding company Normed (Roubaix).
AOECD:	Archives of the OECD (Paris).
AUN:	Archives of the United Nations (Geneva, Switzerland).
BR-NA:	British National Archives (London, Kew).
EPA:	European Parliament Archives (Luxembourg).
FR-FAA:	French Foreign Affairs Ministry Archives (Paris, La Courneuve).
FR-NA:	French National Archives (Paris, Pierrefitte).
FRUS:	Foreign Relations of the United States.
GER-BB:	German Archive of the Bundesbank (Frankfurt-am-Main).
GER-FAA:	German Foreign Affairs Ministry Archives (Politisches Archiv des Auswärtigen Amts, Berlin).
GER-NA:	German National Archives (Koblenz).
HAEU:	Historical Archives of the European Union (Florence).
JCMS:	*Journal of Common Market Studies.*
JEIH:	*Journal of European Integration History.*

Introduction

'I love the way capitalism finds a place – even for its enemies'

(Banksy)[1]

Which form of capitalist governance best fosters peace, prosperity, social cohesion, and environmental protection? Finding the right answer has been an elusive quest. Neoliberalism served as the global yardstick at the turn of the century. It was replaced by a more social and environmental agenda with the UN Paris Agreement on climate change in 2015. Most recently we have seen the rise of protectionism, epitomised by the policy of US President Donald J. Trump. In Europe as well, the European Union has sent conflicting messages, being described variously as a neoliberal behemoth, an environmental leader, and as 'Fortress Europe'.

In this book I argue that making sense of this complexity calls for revisiting the three different principles of capitalist governance: *liberty* (freeing the market to unleash growth), *solidarity* (reining in the free market to protect the weak and the environment), and *community* (safeguarding the group through protectionism and military might).[2] For convenience, I refer to these three principles as *liberty* capitalism, *solidarity* capitalism, and *community* capitalism. This trinity signifies that the governance of capitalism goes beyond the stereotypical dichotomy between pro-market liberals (*liberty* capitalism) and anti-market egalitarians (*solidarity* capitalism). The third form of governance, *community* capitalism, is worth highlighting in current times – the most glaring example of which has been promoted by President Donald Trump, who combines radical neoliberalism (low social and environmental standards, attacks on redistributive programmes) with protectionism in the service of an arch-nationalist agenda. Yet Trump is just the most visible example of *community* capitalism, for as the book shows, this form of capitalist governance has always existed to a certain degree, including in Europe.

I contend that studying the European Union helps provide insights into how a compromise between *liberty, solidarity,* and *community* capitalisms is struck, as the Union is in a constant process of negotiation among bickering members. The Union and its predecessors have created a new mix of capitalism from scratch, one that is partially federal.[3] This characteristic is all the more important since the Union has been targeted by nationalists both inside and outside of Europe, by President Trump in particular. The reason for this is that it represents a long-standing attempt to mediate between different countries, as well as the three forms of capitalist governance distinguished here. While the European Union is imperfect and could disappear in the future,[4] its study sheds light on how compromises surrounding the governance of capitalism are achieved. I do not argue that capitalism or European integration are flawless, but rather that the examination of their relationships is tremendously important, and not just for Europeans. By exploring the dynamics of the European supranational governance of capitalism in the past, we gain valuable insights into how the worldwide capitalist system might be regulated, and into alternatives that were not pursued.[5] The European Union is not just a neoliberal entity unable to deal with Trump, Putin, and Xi, but a mix of *liberty, solidarity,* and *community* capitalism.

This book focuses on the interaction between capitalism and European integration between 1945 and 2025, drawing on studies from areas of scholarship that rarely enter into dialogue with one other, as well as through new archival research. It links literature on European integration with scholarship on capitalism over the long-term,[6] and combines the nation-centred 'varieties of capitalism' approach with the more global outlook of international political economy and economic history.[7] It also incorporates European organisation within the broader history of international governance, which often neglects the European Union and its forerunners,[8] by showing why the European Union ultimately (and indeed surprisingly) prevailed.[9] It covers fields that are often treated separately, ranging from monetary policy to the welfare state, from environmental issues to military policy.

This book advances three claims. First, all societies have sought to balance the three types of capitalist governance, namely *liberty, solidarity,* and *community* capitalism. Second, the European Union offers an ideal case study for understanding how polities negotiate compromises between these types of capitalist governance. Third, dealing with *community* capitalism has been one of the most pressing challenges for Europe in the past, and is ever more crucial today with rising protectionist and military tensions. In the following pages these three ideas are discussed in detail, before presenting the cubist perspective of the book, as well as its contribution to the existing literature.

The Trinity of Capitalism: Liberty, Solidarity, and Community

Jürgen Kocka has defined capitalism as an economic system based on decentralisation (the market's role in settling transactions), commodification (market-based rules and the profit motive permeating broad segments of society), and accumulation (the concentration and perpetuation of capital).[10] From the nineteenth century onward, industrial capitalism has created huge upheavals, increasing economic growth and raising life expectancy, but also creating new forms of social domination, in addition to poverty, environmental damage, and international imbalances.[11] Colonialism and unregulated capitalism have fuelled violence and inequality both within and among states. Industrial capitalism has created strong interdependence between communities that previously lived more or less isolated from one another, in the form of massive flows of raw materials, goods, capital, and people.

I argue that in order to manage these tensions, societies have striven to strike the right balance between the three goals of capitalist governance, namely *liberty*, *solidarity*, and *community*. These three goals are ideal types used to describe reality. In any given capitalist society, leaders emphasise *liberty* if they believe that freeing markets will unleash plenty, *solidarity* if they prioritise protecting the weak (the poor, minorities, Nature), and *community* if they emphasise the power of the group to which they belong. In a nutshell, the first group favours free trade, the second redistribution, and the third nationalism and protectionism. All three of these elements are required for a capitalist society to thrive, as each one needs innovators (*liberty*), carers (*solidarity*), and a sense of unity and kinship (*community*). These three ideal types are helpful in understanding how actors organising capitalism (governments, entrepreneurs, trade unions, NGOs, etc.) have endeavoured to find the right balance between these three poles.

This trinity challenges the idea that the organisation of capitalism is predicated on a simple binary opposition between free markets and redistribution. By contrast, for many actors the primary goal of capitalism is actually to increase the power of their own *community* (whether it be a nation, religious or ethnic group, or in the case of the EU a continental group), and not growth through a free market (*liberty*), or protection for the weak (*solidarity*). These actors emphasise borders, a sense of belonging, security concerns, and defending the community's identity against external threats. *Community* capitalism translates into economic policies emphasising protectionism, cartels, high military spending, restrictive immigration policy, and privileges granted to national companies. Entrepreneurs sometimes have a direct interest in this organisation of capitalism, for the surest way to bolster profits, at least in the short term, is to shield one's company from competition via state aid, high tariffs, monopolies, and cartels. Companies often prefer to strike agreements that stifle competition, thereby securing high and stable prices. While some entrepreneurs have accumulated wealth through open competition, others have done it through close and mutually dependent interrelations with members of their own family, diaspora, or nation, or through specific protections granted by political authorities.

The notion of *community* resonates with the contemporary debate surrounding the resurgence of protectionism, which is sometimes referred to as 'geoeconomics', the 'geopolitical turn', the 'weaponisation of capitalism', 'deglobalisation', 'statecraft', the rise of 'homeland economics', or the 'Machiavellian moment'.[12] In the eighteenth century, in his book, *The Wealth of Nations*, Adam Smith described this form of capitalism as 'mercantilism'. Later, the term 'neomercantilist' was coined to describe the economic policies of Japan and China in the late twentieth century.[13] The concept of 'community' used in this book transcends both. Returning to the foundation of such policies, namely the defence of a particular group, the term resonates with the reflections of thinkers such as Max Weber, Albert Hirschman, and Elinor Ostrom, who have approached capitalism through the prism of what this book will call the principle of *community* (see Chapter 1).

The key characteristics of the organisation of capitalism can be captured through the lens of *liberty, solidarity,* and *community*. US monetary policy offers one example (since the trinity works for both European and non-European forms of capitalism). The US pursued an approach firmly rooted in *liberty* after the 1979 Volcker Shock, where it hiked interest rates in order to tame inflation. After the 2007 financial crisis, it briefly adopted an approach emphasising a little bit more *solidarity,* when it injected huge amounts of money into the economy. At the same time, Washington has long pursued a *community*-based approach by regularly weaponising the dollar through international sanctions and extra-territorial action, including massive fines handed over to foreign multinationals.[14] Along the same lines, international relations can be pursued via rules-based liberal internationalism (*liberty*), global programmes for redistribution and environmental protection (*solidarity*), or a purely transactional zero-sum game between inherently rival groups (*community*).

Community capitalism is often paired with *solidarity*, since protectionism and subsidies are frequently justified by the need to save jobs. Yet in many instances, *community* capitalism redistributes wealth (through tariffs and state aid) from the broader population to the lucky few (a small number of well-connected companies), while preserving few jobs and sometimes raising prices. This approach has aptly been described as 'corporate welfare'.[15] Such an approach (*community* without *solidarity*) has been the policy pursued by President Trump (2017–2021, 2025–). His administration has erected trade barriers, cut taxes for the rich, and slashed both social and environmental standards. He has thereby combined *community* capitalism with neoliberalism. An extreme variant of *liberty* capitalism, neoliberalism is defined not only by the promotion of free market rules, but also by direct attacks on the welfare state (see Chapter 1).

The three principles of the trinity are often combined, and frequently overlap. The governance of Western capitalism was largely influenced by *solidarity* and *community* from 1945 to 1980. From the 1980s *liberty* came to the forefront, with the rise of neoliberalism. *Solidarity* capitalism has reinvented itself by expanding to new areas, such as environmental protection and the protection of minorities, while sometimes neglecting more traditional forms, such as the fight against wealth inequality. Since 2016, *community* capitalism has returned with rising protectionist – and even military – tensions.

The power exercised by state authorities differs between the three models. In the *liberty* approach, the state is central to creating a framework for the market, but limits its role to that of a so-called neutral arbiter, allowing entrepreneurs to play a larger role. Of course, market rules are never purely 'neutral', as they are the result of balance of power among regulators, and produce distributional effects.[16] But the overall framework of state intervention is rules-bound. By contrast, in the *solidarity* and *community* approaches, public authorities make discretionary choices explicit, either to protect particularly disadvantaged groups at the expense of the most affluent (*solidarity*), or to favour local actors at the expense of foreign ones (*community*). Trade unions and environmental NGOs play a larger role in *solidarity* capitalism. In *community* capitalism, political authorities organise civil society in such a way as to strengthen the group. Entrepreneurs and trade unions can be influential as well, but generally in more of a national than transnational manner. The shift to *community* capitalism – and notably to more assertive trade, industrial, and military policies – is a challenge for the European Union, as it has often considered itself more of a rules-based organisation than an actor making explicit discriminatory choices.[17]

The Trinity of Capitalism in Europe

To examine how capitalism works, a focus on the EU is illuminating for three reasons. First, since the late 1940s, European integration has created a new kind of hybrid capitalist system from scratch, thereby providing a unique case study. The EU has often been criticised for conflicting reasons, being seen as too neoliberal or over-regulated. European integration has simultaneously generated a radical form of neoliberal capitalism; an ambitious attempt to regulate that capitalism through binding social and environmental rules; and a highly ambitious project to establish a sense of *community* from the top down. These three features have been the subject of intense debate. Is the EU the epitome of a regulated market, following loosely what Keynes envisaged in 1919, or instead a space for absolute, cut-throat competition, as Hayek imagined in 1939?[18] Have Europeans shunned solidarity, or have they built a European welfare state of sorts? Was there ever a genuine and assertive European 'community', or is Europe just a regulated market with a limited sense of self-identity and an imperfect democratic system?[19]

Second, as a relatively transparent international organisation, the EU offers an interesting lens to study how compromises are struck. The Union is relatively transparent in the sense that it is based on open debate, which is often more explicit than in national forums because it involves foreigners who must spell out their ideas more explicitly than they would if addressing a compatriot from the same culture.[20] These debates are also broader than national ones because they involve individuals rooted in very different capitalist traditions, ranging from Scandinavian Social Democracy to German ordoliberalism, from English neoliberalism to French Colbertism. As a result, the options present in Brussels are more diverse than in many other places.

Third, the European Union and its forerunners have been extremely influential in organising capitalism, initially with trade (coal and steel since the 1950s, other goods since the 1960s), somewhat later with regional and environmental policy (in piecemeal fashion from the 1970s), and ultimately with monetary policy and the free movement of people, capital, and services (since the 1990s). The Covid crisis (2020–2021) and the Russo-Ukrainian War (2022–) further broadened the EU's range of intervention. Crucially, however, the EU has not replaced nation states, which have remained the leading source for welfare state funding (health, pensions, schools), and have preserved a monopoly over legitimate violence (police, justice system, military).

European integration represents a new and unique development in contemporary history. Never before have nation states, including some of the world's most powerful, chosen to voluntarily pool their sovereignty in connection with the management of capitalism, involving key areas such as border control and their currencies. Important differences remain among member states about the kind of 'Europe' to which they aspire,[21] but while opinions vary regarding European integration, nobody denies its impact. Even the UK, which applied to join the European Economic Community in 1961 and left in 2020 has remained deeply influenced by the EU. The EU now covers most of the European continent, its trade regulations have global impact, and its experience of regional integration has served as an inspiration for other regional groupings, as well as a symbol of decadent liberal cosmopolitanism for its opponents.[22] In other words, the EU is not perfect, and could ultimately disappear, but it nevertheless provides a useful window into understanding how compromises relating to capitalism can be struck. The EU matters not just for Europeans but for the whole world, an example of how people can (or cannot) organise themselves beyond nation states and empires.

I consider the European Union as a hybrid organisation driven by both nation states and supranational institutions.[23] On the one hand, European member states have voluntarily chosen to engage in European integration to promote their national interest, particularly in economic matters, and have largely retained control over the decision-making process.[24] On the other hand, supranational institutions (the European Commission, Parliament and Court) have played an important role as well. This book will focus on the European Commission, whose leadership has been crucial, especially for policies initially considered as relatively secondary, but that eventually proved crucial.

The interpretive lens of the trinity of capitalism can be combined with an intergovernmental approach (i.e. one based mainly on the power of national governments). For example, British Prime Minister Margaret Thatcher (1979–1990) upheld a vision of the EU that was both intergovernmental and neoliberal. French President Charles de Gaulle (1959–1970) also preferred an intergovernmental model as well, but was more inclined toward *community* capitalism. German Chancellor Willy Brandt (1969–1974) placed more emphasis on *solidarity*, while the Italian politician Altiero Spinelli (1970–1986) was a staunch federalist, as well as a strong supporter of *solidarity* and *community* capitalism.[25]

The Challenges of Community Capitalism

The *liberty, solidarity,* and *community* typology is useful for four further reasons. First, it reveals the very existence of *community* capitalism. It helps deconstruct the discourse of leaders who assert their actions are motivated by a quest for general welfare (under the category of *liberty* or *solidarity*), even though bolstering the *community* remains central to their objectives. Companies rarely acknowledge that they would prefer a cosy cartel rather than free competition. States rarely recognise the regressive effect (when a measure benefits the rich more than the poor) of some state aid to industry or other protectionist measures. *Community* capitalism also sheds light on distributional conflicts. Since expenditure cannot be unlimited, if a public authority spends more to support companies, it must cut other spending, such as social programmes benefiting the poor. 'Corporate welfare' can replace the 'welfare state'. *Community* capitalism has been ubiquitous in Europe (Chapter 5). For example, post-war Germany officially had no industrial policies, but when viewed through the lens of *community,* a discreet but effective German industrial policy is clearly discernible. Some form of *community* capitalism persisted in many countries, even in Thatcher's neoliberal Britain.

Second, the trinity facilitates comparison across time and space. The concept of *community* captures similarities between practices of capitalist governance that have borne different names at different times, from DARPA in the US to regional aid in Germany. The trinity helps underscore how Europeans combined their different national approaches, each based on a peculiar mix of *liberty, solidarity,* and *community*. Since all countries have a different mix, European integration has involved striking the right balance not only between countries, but also between different forms of capitalist governance. Examining the notion of *community* capitalism helps compare different experiences, and to thereby determine the conditions required for the emergence of efficient industrial policy, on both the national and international levels.

Third, the trinity helps uncover alternatives that were discussed and considered before ultimately being discarded. By using ideal types, the trinity underscores the fact that there have always been solutions in keeping with *liberty, solidarity,* or *community* capitalism, even if they were not considered to be reasonable by the *Zeitgeist* of the period. This allows us to move beyond simplistic political discourses, whether they are based on the 'there is no alternative' argument (promoted by Thatcher), or the populist argument that public policy is always the same (with elites forming a conspiracy against 'the people').[26] It also helps overcome the technocratic approach of certain institutions, which sometimes portray themselves as pragmatic non-political entities, a claim sometimes made by European Commission officials. On the contrary, this volume takes the view that all economic decisions are choices for a certain mix of governance of capitalism. The rise of neoliberalism in the late twentieth century, or the resurgence of protectionism today, is not automatic and inevitable – both grew out of a balance of power among actors, one that the trinity can help elucidate. History provides perspective for the current rise of *community* capitalism, as European institutions have grappled with protectionism in the past, and even promoted it (see Chapters 5, 6, and 10).

Fourth, the concept of *community* capitalism helps explain several surprising political convergences. For example, low-income individuals have sometimes favoured *community* over *solidarity*. Nationalism prevented the emergence of a united pacifist workers' movement in Europe in 1914. Similarly, the declining affiliation of the poor with centre-left parties in the West from the 1980s onward may partly be a consequence of rising identity politics, and a decline of the centre-left's focus on class inequality.[27]

The concept of *community* should not be considered as a negative one. Past crises have often been sparked by imbalance among the trinity, such as an overemphasis on *community* capitalism in the 1930s, or on *liberty* capitalism in the 'high neoliberal' early twenty-first century. On the whole, this book does not argue in favour of a particular balance, other than that the most radical paths should be avoided (see Chapter 1). *Liberty, solidarity,* and *community* are goals that leaders pursue in the governance of capitalism, but they are also related to values that are dear to most human beings, the quest for liberty, equality, and identity.[28]

A Cubist Perspective Revealing Alternatives

Cubist painters deconstructed the traditional image by presenting multiple perspectives at the same time. Similarly, albeit in much more modest fashion, this study strives to capture complexity through lenses that are national, supranational (EU institutions), international (international organisations), and transnational (trade unions, environmental NGOs, and employers' organisations).[29] This book places emphasis on social, economic, and environmental issues, all while connecting them to institutional, political, and geopolitical developments. It does not focus on the evolution of ideas relating to capitalism, although their evolutions are taken into account, for they have had a major influence on policies, as stressed by Polanyi.[30] As Keynes remarked in 1936, politicians who claim to be pragmatists are often 'the slaves of some defunct economist'.[31]

To identify the full range of policy choices that were and are available, this book uses the literature, interviews with actors, and original material gathered from archives in eight countries for the period between the 1950s to the 1990s (archives usually become available after a thirty-year embargo). Archives typically provide deeper insights than official discourse, allowing us to partially reconstruct the motivations driving various actors. Without archives, historians are left with the discourses and interviews of decision makers who generally claim to be driven by 'common sense'. Moreover, archives reveal alternatives that were not pursued and that may have disappeared from discourses, the media, and even the memoirs of those who advocated them. They are useful in identifying turning points or 'critical junctures', the moment when decisive choices were made.[32] Nevertheless, it is also important to be aware of the limitations of archives and archival research. Archives are often incomplete, and raise more questions than they answer.[33] I complement them by interviews with key actors, who provide invaluable – albeit often biased – information.

By emphasising the alternatives available to policy makers, this book avoids teleological narratives praising European integration as an inevitable march towards a brighter future.[34] On the contrary, it underscores the many alternatives to the EU that have been seriously considered since 1945 at the national (why cooperate with foreign states if national capitalism is efficient?), European (European organisations such as the OEEC and the Council of Europe predate the European Communities), and international levels (because the UN or the OECD have sometimes appeared to be more effective forums for cooperation). In other circumstances, a greater role could even have been played by postcolonial organisations, such as the British Commonwealth or the short-lived French Community, which covered mainland France and its overseas territories (1958–1960).[35]

States have been central actors in post-war Europe, increasing their influence over the regulation of capitalism in a manner never before seen in peacetime, as is demonstrated by the rising share of government expenditure as a proportion of GDP, and the ever-expanding influence of government policies. Public policies are a major element in the governance of capitalism, alongside others such as the relationship among enterprises, and the role of other non-state actors such as churches, trade unions, NGOs, intellectuals, etc.

This book focuses on the British, French, and German governments because they have been the most influential, and because they represent economic orientations that are often antagonistic, thereby representing the continent's diversity. Italy has often played a lesser role than its size would suggest.[36] Rome has sometimes been a decisive player, for instance during the Milan Council of 1985, but it is first and foremost Italian nationals based in Brussels who have left their mark, including the federalist activist Altiero Spinelli, in addition to the two 'Super Marios' – Commissioner Mario Monti and President of the European Central Bank Mario Draghi. The other large European countries, such as Spain and Poland, were influential in European integration only later on. Smaller states can play an important role as well, but usually in specific circumstances.[37] Hence, the focus remains on Britain, France, and Germany, even if use is made of the secondary literature to capture the most important developments in other states, including countries in Central and Eastern European states which are often neglected.[38]

The Commission of the EC/EU is a fourth player calling for systematic consideration, in light of its seniority – it was created in 1958 – and impact. It has a monopoly over proposing legislation, which it implements in cooperation with national administrations. This book will argue that the Commission can, under certain circumstances and depending on the individuals at its helm, act as a powerful political force in the European integration process.[39]

The study of archives across eight countries also revealed the importance of actors beyond the main four outlined above. The roles of the European Parliament and the Court of Justice are studied in relation to certain debates, especially after they began to expand their presence in the 1970s.[40] Archives from other international organisations that have structured the European continent are explored in specific cases, such as those of the United Nations via the archives of the United Nations Conference on Trade and Development (UNCTAD), the Organisation for Economic Co-operation and Development (OECD), the General Agreement on Tariffs and Trade (GATT), and the International Labour Organization (ILO). Finally, the archives of non-state transnational actors are used to shed light on the balance of power in certain negotiations,[41] especially the European Trade Union Confederation (ETUC), the French trade union CFDT, and the British (CBI) and French (CNPF, later MEDEF) business organisations, with the latter being particularly useful because they compensate for the lack of archives for their Europe-wide counterparts (UNICE, later Business Europe).

I do not consider these actors to be monolithic. Governments are often split between protectionist ministries (agriculture and internal affairs), and others leaning more toward free trade (trade and foreign affairs). A company with a technological edge tends to lobby for more international openness, while an uncompetitive one prefers protectionist measures. Trade unions in export-oriented countries (such as Germany and Sweden) are less protectionist than others. Environmental NGOs prioritise *solidarity*, but to achieve this goal some promote *community* capitalism (such as protectionism), while others call for *liberty* capitalism (with market-based mechanisms).

Bridging the Gap between Capitalism and European Integration Studies

This book bridges the gap between studies on capitalism on the one hand, and studies on European and international organisations on the other. With respect to the former, three strands of the literature on capitalism have contributed to this book.[42] The first of these are the general reflections on the links between capitalism and the socio-economic and political tensions it creates,[43] with special emphasis on studies highlighting globalisation's impact on welfare policies and the social movement.[44] This book contributes to the broader debate on whether it is possible to regulate globalisation, that is, to promote an international governance of *solidarity* capitalism, all while accommodating conflicting forms of *community* capitalism. It provides multiple examples of alternatives that were conceived, considered, and discarded (planning, control of multinationals), and sometimes belatedly adopted in a different guise (carbon tax, European preference). Hence, it also contributes to environmental history, as it provides concrete examples of the opposition between pro-environment and pro-business lobbying, as well as the internal divisions within the business community.[45]

Second, this study is informed by more recent literature devoted to industrial policy, which is more global (or US-based).[46] This book will uncover practices of *community* capitalism that were prevalent throughout Europe, West Germany included, in the form of regional aid and tolerance for certain cartels. It will test the main hypothesis about an efficient industrial policy by exploring various instances of international industrial cooperation, some successful, and others not (Chapter 5).[47]

Third, this book helps bridge the gap between literature on international relations and comparative political economy, notably the 'varieties of capitalism' literature. The latter has developed an important typological approach at the national level, especially in the opposition between 'coordinated market economies' and 'liberal market economies'.[48] Other illuminating studies of international political economy have shed light on recent evolutions in Western capitalism from a comparative national perspective,[49] but rarely in association with European integration.[50] While this questioning of national models is included in this book (Chapter 1), its originality resides in identifying transversal types of capitalist governance (affecting not just public policies but also enterprises, trade unions, and NGOs) that simultaneously concern national, European, and international actors.[51] It links purely economic developments with social, environmental, and geopolitical ones.

This book also contributes to the literature on European integration and international organisations, doing so in three ways.[52] First, it will show why the European Union prevailed compared to other international organisations,[53] and sometimes in association with them.[54] This book will examine why many public policies were 'Europeanised', despite the fact that the actors involved considered and sometimes preferred other forums for cooperation.[55] For example, it will show that trade unions became interested in European institutions in the late 1970s when they understood that the European Communities could provide more effective constraints on multinationals than the UN, the ILO, or the OECD (Chapter 4). It will also explain the convergence of actors towards the Single Market Programme in the mid-1980s (Chapter 3), as well as the later reinforcement of the eurozone (Chapters 8 and 9) after the failure of national and international alternatives. Conversely, it will take into account failures (such as in energy and defence), especially those that led to the risk of disintegration (during the eurozone crisis).

Second, the book will also contribute to an understanding of how European integration actually works by merging national, supranational, and transnational approaches.[56] It will include both the perspective of those that consider nation states to be the main actors,[57] and those that emphasise transnational and supranational actors (such as the Commission, the Court of Justice, and the Parliament).[58]

It will argue that the balance of power within European institutions varies, as it is predicated on legal elements (which differ according to time and place), administrative resources, the context, and the character of leaders. Commissioners such as Etienne Davignon of Belgium, Jacques Delors of France, and Margrethe Vestager of Denmark have had a greater influence than their predecessors due to their greater assertiveness and effectiveness. The same logic applies to national leaders of course, but what is already well-known at the national level must be applied to the European level as well.

Third, while many social scientists consider the European Union to be a neoliberal behemoth,[59] this book recognises the neoliberal tendencies of European integration in certain fields – for example exploring the often neglected importance of competition policy in Europe's neoliberalisation (Chapter 8) – while demonstrating the diversity of European capitalism.[60] To this end, it will apply global histories of neoliberal ideas to actual European public policies.[61] Neoliberal markets are not the same as those governed by a moderate form of *liberty* capitalism.

This book shows the complex interplay of non-state actors in European integration, by drawing a more nuanced picture than the binary opposition between neoliberal companies and anti-market socio-environmental actors. The last decade witnessed an important rise in historical studies focusing on non-state actors within European integration, doing so despite the many difficulties faced by researchers struggling to access company records.[62] This book provides concrete examples of how enterprises have interacted with European integration sometimes by defending cartelisation, by lobbying for favourable legislation, and by fostering mixed feelings about European industrial policy.[63] Business actors were not always aligned with each other, notably with respect to environmental regulation, which could represent costly constraints for some, but business opportunities for others. On the whole, I will emphasise the diversity of the business community, following Bastian van Apeldoorn's pioneering study, where he distinguishes between 'neo-mercantilist' and 'neoliberal' business leaders.[64] Similarly, the book will provide examples to show the challenge of mobilising non-state social and environmental actors such as trade unions and NGOs, both for practical (lack of resources) and ideological reasons (strong internal divisions: see Chapter 4).[65]

Book Outline

This book traces the development of this trinity of *liberty, solidarity*, and *community* capitalism in Europe between 1945 and 2025, doing so in three main sections. The first lays the groundwork by presenting the trinity of capitalist governance (Chapter 1), and by examining the distinctiveness of European institutions (Chapter 2).

The second focuses on the Cold War period (1948–1992), marked by the importance of building a common market based on *liberty* capitalism (Chapter 3). It will clearly distinguish between the dynamism of social policy designed to accompany the market – visible in fields such as regional solidarity, gender equality, and environmental protection – and the failure of more disruptive projects, such as the harmonisation of social legislation, planning, and the democratisation of companies (Chapter 4). *Community* capitalism also affected European integration: internally with various attempts to establish European industrial and defence policies (Chapter 5), and externally with a willingness to promote an alternative to the neoliberal globalisation process (Chapter 6). Following the economic crises of the 1970s, the return of the market was reflected in neoliberal tendencies, which were not hegemonic, especially with the creation of a monetary union (Chapter 7).

A final section reviews developments over the last three decades. Here once again, a distinction is made between liberal and neoliberal trends in monetary, trade, and competition policies (Chapter 8), attempts to regulate globalisation in a more social and environmentally friendly manner (Chapter 9), and the more recent challenge (since 2016) of building Europe as a strong and assertive community within a more protectionist and nationalistic world (Chapter 10).

The conclusion proposes a new chronology of post-war European capitalism in four phases. It establishes the conditions required for changes to the European governance of capitalism. Finally, it will feature the alternatives available both in the past and the present.

1

The Trinity of Capitalist Governance

What is the best form of governance for capitalism? It is often a balance between several different approaches tailored to local conditions. It is therefore useful to distinguish between three types of capitalist governance, namely *liberty* capitalism, *solidarity* capitalism, and *community* capitalism. I will examine these three types of capitalist governance one by one, and then explore how they have applied to Western Europe, as well as in the context of international cooperation.

1.1 *The Typology* of Liberty, Solidarity, *and* Community

Max Weber's 'ideal type' is an effective tool for comparing events across long periods of time and within distinct linguistic spaces. These ideal types identify common characteristics that go beyond the diverse nomenclature used, which can vary depending on the country and the time.[1] As Weber pointed out, ideal types are analytical categories that facilitate understanding. Consequently, they were not necessarily used by actors at the time, and run the intrinsic risk of falling into anachronism. All historians are potentially guilty of this. The French historian Marc Bloch observed that the term 'feudalism' was not coined in the medieval period, but in the early modern period to describe a past reality.[2]

Here ideal types will be used to identify types of capitalist governance according to their main principle, namely the 'trinity' of *liberty, solidarity,* and *community*.[3] These forms of capitalism are driven by economic policies implemented by governments, as well as by patterns of relations between various actors both public (state, international organisations, courts, local authorities) and private (companies, trade unions, associations, experts, etc.).

Instead of focusing on artificial groupings based on political labels, ideological references, or official discourse, this typology instead highlights fundamental convergences or divergences. Indeed, identical terms can have different meanings in different countries. For example, the notion of 'industrial policy' is perceived negatively in federal Germany, but is central to French statist ideology. Yet in comparing the measures implemented to support enterprises, one could conclude that assertive industrial policies existed in most Western European countries at least until the late 1980s, including in West Germany (Chapter 5). Similarly, the connotations (positive or negative) surrounding the terms 'liberal' and 'social-democratic' have differed depending on the country and the time. For instance in West Germany, the term 'liberal' was increasingly used from the late 1960s onwards in association with ideas of reform and modernity, including on the left and by some environmentalists with the notion of *'linksliberal'* ('left-liberal').[4] By contrast, in France the equivalent term for 'left-liberal', *'social-libéral'*, is negative, as it refers to neoliberals falsely disguised as socialists. The term 'communist' is equally imprecise. There is nothing in common between bloodthirsty Stalinist apparatchiks, and the millions of Italians and French voters who choose communist parties (the PCI and the PCF) because of their emancipatory struggles (economic redistribution, decolonisation) and local networks of solidarity.[5] The PCI was under the tutelary figure of Antonio Gramsci, who advocated a less violent approach than the USSR, while the PCF leadership followed Moscow more closely. Similarly, depicting an economic policy by referring to an economist is complicated; for instance, Keynes defended free trade in some of his work, and a more protectionist approach elsewhere.

Hence the importance of using principles such as *liberty, solidarity*, and *community* instead of political or ideological labels. A governance of capitalism based on *liberty* seeks to shape the economy according to the ideal of a market governed by pure and perfect competition, with a view to maximising growth, and thereby collective well-being. *Solidarity* capitalism attempts to reduce the detrimental consequences of capitalism by increasing the welfare of the weak and by protecting the environment. *Community* capitalism occurs when the main objective is to reinforce the group of belonging.

While chiefly socio-economic, this typology has larger political and philosophical underpinnings. It helps avoid the 'state v. market' binary. Markets do not exist in a vacuum, but rather are shaped by institutions, ideologies, and power relationships.[6] Some neoliberals have understood that a strong state is actually necessary to promote radical free market policies, for instance to break up monopolies and oligopolies, to impose regressive taxation, and to resist groups motivated by *solidarity* or *community*. Marxists have long complained that state authorities have often been at the service of the dominant classes. Consequently, what is important is not the level of state intervention, but instead the guiding principle driving it.

Under this trinity, any feature of capitalism can be geared towards one of the principles of *liberty, solidarity,* or *community* (see Table 1.1). For example, antitrust policy can promote *liberty* (by encouraging more competition), *solidarity* (by curtailing undue profits reaped by larger companies dominating the market), and *community* (if competition policy primarily targets foreign companies).

Table 1.1 *The trinity of capitalism applied to various policies*

	Solidarity	Community	Free market	Neoliberal
			\multicolumn{2}{c}{Liberty}	
Guiding principle	Equality, solidarity	Strength of the group	Freedom	Competition
Economic objective	Reducing inequality	Strengthening producers	\multicolumn{2}{c}{Free markets}
Macroeconomic policy	Support for demand and environmental policies	Supply-side	\multicolumn{2}{c}{Stability (low deficits, low inflation), supply-side measures}
Competition policy	Strong against companies	Weak to encourage cartels	Strong against companies	Weak to give companies freedom
Industrial policy	Strong, with emphasis on employment	Strong	Weak, except for limited horizontal measures (R&D, environment)	Non-existent
Social policy	Strong	Producer-oriented (safety net and employability measures)		Weak
Education	Emphasis on worldwide solidarity	Focus on the group's history and values	Emphasis on work-related skills	Exclusive emphasis on work-related skills
Non-state actors	Strong role of trade unions and environmental NGOs	Nation-oriented (notably through cartelisation)	Strong role of multinational companies	
International relations	Peace through intensive international cooperation, including transfers to the poor	Peace through balance of power	Peace through trade	Peace through the primacy of the market over politics (depoliticisation)

1.1 THE TRINITY

Each of these three types of capitalist governance has a radical variant. The extreme version of *solidarity* is the socialist utopia, while that of *liberty* is represented by neoliberals, mostly visible since the advent of Margaret Thatcher in London in 1979, and Ronald Reagan in Washington in 1980. The latter emphasise competition, and systematically attack the welfare state.[7] The term 'ultraliberals' is better suited to describe those radical supporters of *liberty* capitalism, but seldom used. Finally, the extreme version of *community* is the warmongering of Nazi Germany (1933–45), when all economic decisions were completely subordinated to promoting the German community (with the exception of German Jews, communists, etc.) at the expense of other communities.[8] The regime was capitalist but not liberal: Hitler preserved private property and capitalism, except for opponents of the regime, but competition was largely abolished by a general cartelisation of the economy to support the armament effort. The regime's social dimension, eradicating unemployment and offering new leisure activities for the working class (such as the affordable cruises of the *Kraft Durch Freude* organisation, 'strength through joy'), was illusory. Improved economic conditions were already apparent in late 1932, before Hitler came to power. He stimulated the economy through dictatorial mechanisms, such as banning strikes, plundering opponents (and later conquered and subjugated peoples), and forcing loans to be repaid through military conquests. Economic organisation was entirely driven by military concerns. Germans were deprived of everyday consumer goods (food and textiles), because the funds that would have been used to import these goods were primarily allocated for rearmament. Promises of everyday consumer products, such as the *Volkswagen* (the 'people's car'), never materialised, or did so only after the war (the Beetle finally came out in 1946); one exception was the radio, which was widely distributed, but at a higher price than its American equivalent, and mainly for propaganda purposes.

By definition, these ideal types are rarely found in their pure state in reality. Decisions often result from a combination of these approaches (see Figure 1.1 and the Conclusion). In a nutshell, in the West the years between 1945 and the 1973 oil crisis were marked by a balance between *solidarity* (strong and expanding welfare states, with a limited environmental dimension), *community* (ambitious industrial policies), and *liberty* (promotion of international free trade, implemented gradually and primarily from the 1960s onwards).

In the 1970s, emphasis shifted towards *liberty*, with the prevailing system being challenged due to financial difficulties, the failure of alternatives based on *solidarity* and *community* (Chapters 4 and 5), as well as the rising tide of neoliberal ideas. The latter gained ground in the 1980s (Chapters 6 and 7).

In the 1990s and 2000s, Western Europeans strove to reform the social aspect of economic policy through the notion of 'workfare', and through environmental policies combined with free market tools (Chapter 8). This

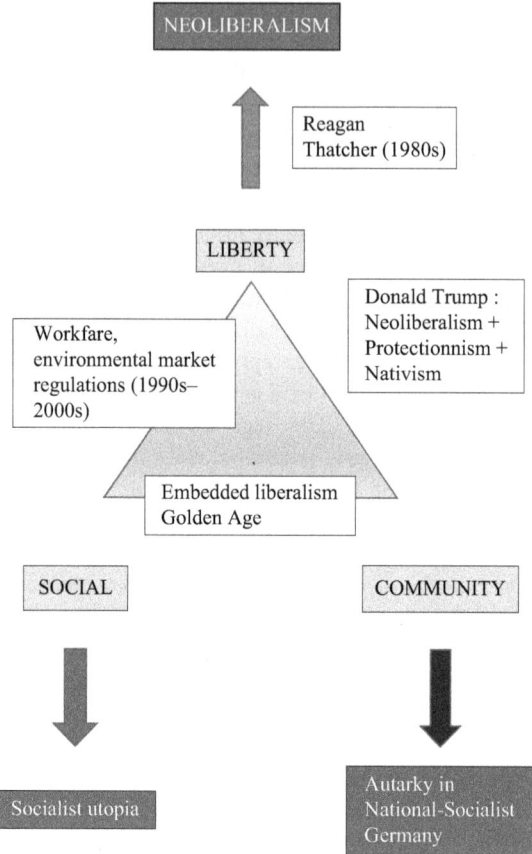

Figure 1.1 The three forms of capitalism

was an attempt to strike a new balance between *liberty* and *solidarity*, but without *community*, for most protectionist measures and industrial policies were dismantled (Chapter 8).

Since the mid-2010s, *community* capitalism has been on the rise again, with more protectionist and nativist policies. Two approaches stand out: the first combines protectionism with socio-environmental measures (Chapter 9), while the second combines protectionism with neoliberalism, for instance under US President Donald Trump (Chapter 10). His supporters are divided between 'national libertarians', who are more neoliberal by virtue of their emphasis on deregulation, and 'national protectionists', who are more in line with a *community* approach via their support for a stronger state.[9]

1.2 Liberty: Market-Oriented Policy and Neoliberalism

Advocates of *liberty* capitalism believe that removing barriers to free competition will lower prices and stimulate growth, employment, and ultimately general welfare. The market is seen as an ideal tool for regulating conflicts at both the national and international level. This approach translates into the promotion of free trade, which provides low-cost imports, export opportunities (through the principle of reciprocity), and increased productivity. The state retains an important role in providing a framework conducive to economic activity, but does so without guiding companies, instead limiting itself to correcting negative externalities (such as pollution), and to managing natural monopolies.

Economic and political liberalism are often associated. Historians of early modern Europe have emphasised the emancipatory ideal of the market, which leads to a certain form of equality of status, in contrast to the practices of the society of privilege.[10] The strong moral dimension in the thought of classical liberal economists such as Adam Smith has also been emphasised, notably by Karl Polanyi. They believed the market is simply a means to a more harmonious society, not an end in itself. The link between the two is nevertheless not automatic, with many dictatorships thriving in the market economy.

As with the two other categories, combinations exist. A moderate form of international free trade has been defended by left-wing globalists to secure peace since the nineteenth century.[11] Some actors blend *liberty* and *solidarity*. For example, among the Swedish Social Democrats, the Rehn–Meidner model of 1951, named after two economists from the most important trade union, postulates that wage increases should be aligned with the productivity of export firms so as not to penalise them.[12] While this system drives underperforming firms out of business, it is backed by a protective welfare state and an effective training system.

In the 1980s, the emergence of a radical form of free market fundamentalism led to a new type of economic policy – neoliberalism.[13] The market and competition became supreme values, with humans reduced to materialistic consumers. This shift translated into a policy of dismantling the welfare state, a regressive fiscal system (with tax cuts mainly for the rich), and extending market logic to all domains of social life. The political framework becomes contingent on the market. Neoliberalism stands in sharp contrast to the emancipatory ideal of Enlightenment liberalism, which challenged authority, and valued critical thinking and autonomy.

Neoliberal policies spread in the 1980s, and especially in the 1990s and 2000s, for several reasons (Chapter 7), including the financial constraints linked to the oil crisis, a cultural shift to a more individualistic ethos, the zeal of neoliberal intellectual networks, and the failure of alternative approaches (Chapter 4).

The term neoliberalism is used here to describe radical free market policies, and not to designate participants in the Colloque Walter Lippmann (a conference of intellectuals organised in Paris in 1938), which is sometimes described as the cradle of neoliberalism because the expression was occasionally used at the time. This event was attended by a disparate group of non-Marxist economists, some of whom were hostile to state intervention (such as Friedrich Hayek), others who supported strong state regulation (such as Alexander Rüstow), and even Keynesian socialists (such as Robert Marjolin).[14] The meaning of 'neoliberal' in the history of ideas is therefore not clear. By contrast, in this book, the concept is used as an ideal type to describe policies aiming to dismantle the welfare state and establish competition (rather than liberty) as the supreme guiding principle.[15]

Neoliberals do not place political liberalism at the heart of their thinking. Both authoritarian and neoliberal thinking converge in their support for inequality, whereas the classical liberals consider that political equality is the precondition for liberty. The first neoliberal state was Pinochet's brutal Chilean dictatorship in the mid-1970s.[16] Many neoliberal activists, such as Hayek and Friedman, along with Thatcher's economic adviser Alan Walters, visited Chile under Pinochet, or cited it as an example of success for the Global South.[17] In 1977, Hayek was critical of the sanctions against the Apartheid regime in South Africa, while Friedman often lamented the inefficiency of democracy versus markets. Within liberal democracies, the association between neoliberalism and social conservatism has often been emphasised, as exemplified by Margaret Thatcher and numerous American economists, although it is not systematic.[18] Ten years before Thatcher, another leading British conservative, Enoch Powell, proposed a neoliberal economic programme in his so-called Morecambe speech on 11 October 1968, in which he called for massive tax cuts financed through privatisation, and the repeal of many social programmes.[19] This statement was overshadowed by his infamous 'rivers of blood' speech, delivered six months earlier on 20 April 1968, in which he predicted chaos if immigration to the UK continued to increase. The subsequent adoption of neoliberal policies by authoritarian regimes such as Russia and China led to the concept of 'authoritarian neoliberalism'.[20] The Chilean dictator Pinochet was even a role model for certain Russian neoliberals, as he demonstrated the possibility of associating authoritarianism with neoliberalism.[21] In 2025, the association of undemocratic arch-libertarian business leaders such as Peter Thiel with US President Donald Trump – who has launched a massive retrenchment of the state – has raised concerns regarding a new link between neoliberalism and authoritarianism.[22]

The case of German ordoliberals is ambiguous. By virtue of their attachment to market mechanisms and their rejection of the welfare state (for some), they can be linked to neoliberals. However, they do not reduce humans to a simple *homo economicus*, instead associating economic liberalism with political liberalism.[23] The first generation of ordoliberals was less neoliberal than subsequent generations influenced by Hayek. Even some radical left-wing German politicians, such as Sahra Wagenknecht today, recognise their debt to original ordoliberalism. It actually began as a reaction against Nazism, which combined political totalitarianism, economic dirigisme, and capitalism. The promotion of ordoliberalism was thus inseparable from the creation of a democratic Germany. As Wilhelm Röpke has argued in *Solution to the German Problem* (1946), by breaking the excessive concentration of big business in Germany and making autarkic policies impossible, free trade would transform the country into a peaceful giant, an 'enlarged Belgium'.[24] Some German ordoliberals included a social and moral component in their approach, and were clearly opposed to the neoliberal second Chicago school when it came to competition policy (Chapter 8). Others argue that ordoliberals are neoliberals through and through, as demonstrated by German policy towards Greece during the eurozone crisis (2010–15).

Neoliberals have had an ambiguous relation to European integration. The project of a neoliberal Europe was presented by Hayek in a short text published in September 1939, at the outbreak of the World War II.[25] He wanted to demonstrate that it was impossible to ensure peace exclusively through political union; it had to be combined with economic union based on the free movement of goods, labour, and capital. This economic union would make social policy superfluous, and even impossible. However, Hayek was less interested in European integration – an idea that was purely theoretical in 1939 – than in criticising state intervention in the economy. He took up the argument in his famous *Road to Serfdom* published in 1944.[26] Many neoliberals have long been sceptical of European integration. Quinn Slobodian has pointed out that in the 1950s and 1960s, many ordoliberals and representatives of radical liberalism, such as Gottfried Haberler, saw the EC as an intolerable protectionist actor.[27] In the 1980s, meetings of the Mont Pelerin Society, a hotbed of neoliberalism, remained highly concerned by the EC's protectionist and dirigiste tendencies.[28] However, many neoliberals gradually came to see some European institutions as being conducive to their policies, especially in the 1990s and 2000s (Chapter 8).

While neoliberalism cannot be combined with *solidarity*, it can integrate elements of *community*. The support of US President Donald Trump (2017–21, and since 2025) for polluting industries goes hand in hand with attacks on the welfare state, an aggressive protectionist trade policy, and tax cuts for the rich. Similarly, Brazilian President Jair Bolsonaro (2019–22) has abandoned the Brazilian forest to such intensive exploitation that the historian Antoine Acker has referred to his policy as 'carbofascism'.[29]

1.3 Solidarity: Social and Environmental Components

Policies based on *solidarity* support the disadvantaged, such as the poor or any groups discriminated against on the basis of gender, sexual orientation, culture, skin colour, and so on. They also include an environmental component, as environmental degradation disproportionately impacts the poor,[30] who are often deprived of access to the greenest and healthiest neighbourhoods, the best-insulated homes, and organic food. They also often perform the most dangerous jobs, as illustrated in *Lowest of the Low* by the German journalist Günter Wallraff, published in 1980.[31] Disguised as an illegal Turkish immigrant working in Germany for two years, he endured a series of jobs that exposed him to health and environmental risks, including nuclear ones.

The *solidarity* approach has an affinity for Marxism, with its supporters being divided between reformists, and revolutionaries defending a more radical path. The former include social democrats and Greens won over by sustainable development. This concept was conceived in 1987 in order to reconcile economic growth and environmentalism.[32] The latter encompasses communists and proponents of the degrowth movement, who are usually not the same people, as environmental movements have a strong anti-authoritarian (and hence anti-communist) element.

Politically, even if *solidarity* is defended by the left, it is sometimes also promoted by right-wing actors for ideological reasons, or to deprive their left-wing opponents of working-class support. The father of the German welfare state was the conservative Otto von Bismarck, while the inventor of the 'welfare state' was the British liberal William Beveridge. Similarly, environmental protection appealed to many conservatives.[33]

Conversely, the combination of *solidarity* and *liberty* produces a synthesis sometimes associated with the Indian economist Amartya Sen and his notion of 'capability'.[34] Sen defined capability as a possible choice and an effective realisation. Similarly, some environmentalists advocate the use of market mechanisms. For example, some German environmentalists have supported liberalising the energy market in order to break up the old oligopolies of fossil fuel companies, with a view to bringing in newer and greener producers.[35]

Those who defend *solidarity* must compensate for the imbalance between dominant capitalist entities and victims of the system, hence the need to build trade unions, non-governmental organisations, and grassroots movements. Large companies and their lobbies can capture the state by imposing lenient social and environmental policies, in addition to regressive taxation (favouring the rich). They can also influence the state through lobbying, sometimes doing so directly, and sometimes more indirectly via the scientific community in order to sow 'doubt' regarding the usefulness of regulation.[36]

1.4 Community: Protection and Assertion

Capitalism is not solely based on a compromise between *liberty* and *solidarity*. *Community* capitalism must also be taken into consideration, which is to say the willingness to organise capitalism in order to defend and promote the group.

Weber noted the importance of communities based on economic, political, or social interests, and not just common residence and/or ethnicity.[37] Humanity has been organised around communities based on a territory, shared feelings of belonging, a common history, cultural elements (such as norms of appropriate behaviour), and sometimes ethnic proximity. As Francis Fukuyama has asserted: 'Natural human sociability is based on kin selection and reciprocal altruism – that is, the preference for family and friends.'[38] Communities are useful in providing a measure of stability and predictability, whereas a world organised entirely according to the principles of *liberty* or *solidarity* capitalism would be more disruptive. A family, tribe, religious group, local network, or nation provides anchors in life. Falling back on these communities is therefore natural.

Contemporary politics have been shaped by a particularly influential form of community: the nation-state. They have interacted with other forms of 'imagined communities', such as subnational regional identity, or as in the case of post-war Europe, with the European identity. For all that, European identity is weaker than national identity, for it is based on the shared but negative memories of the world wars, and the Soviet occupation of Eastern Europe.[39] *Community* capitalism should therefore not be confused with the self-proclaimed European 'communities'. Paradoxically, *community* capitalism has been fairly weak in the European communities, more of a political statement or programme to develop such communitarian feelings in the future rather than an existing reality.

From a philosophical point of view, Rousseau's philosophy supports the idea that the republican political process is based on the existence of natural communities, what he referred to as 'nations' defined by common habits and way of life, and possibly a specific language.[40] The concept of *community* has affinities with the 'communitarian' philosophers, who define the group by a shared history, territory, values, and common action.[41] Beyond the communitarians, Amitai Etzioni, a philosopher influenced by his experience on a kibbutz during his teenage years, has emphasised the importance of community. Commentators on Etzioni's work argue that communitarianism offers a 'third way' between 'excessive liberalism' and 'state-run socialism', and could serve as a 'new paradigm of socio-economic analysis'.[42] Once again we find the trinity of *liberty*, *solidarity*, and *community*.

Foreign policies based on *community* are both defensive and offensive. They include protectionism (high trade barriers), restrictive migration policy, and large military budgets. In terms of foreign policy, they can be either isolationists (refusing any solidarity with other states), or on the contrary imperialistic (acting militarily to gain immediate material advantage instead of upholding international law). The combinaition of European integration and *community* capitalism is aptly described in French by the expression 'Europe puissance'.[43] However, it cannot be translated literally into English, since the notion of 'power' is different. It is present in all three types of capitalist governance. In *liberty* capitalism, companies vie with each other using their market power. In *solidarity* capitalism, social and environmental activists are engaged in a power struggle with their opponents, and sometimes among themselves. Finally, there is no neat opposition between a rules-based *liberty*, *solidarity* capitalism, and law-of-the-jungle *community* capitalism. All forms of capitalist governance can be bound by rules or managed by power struggles.

Community capitalism could also include environmentally friendly policies. Many environmentalists are sympathetic towards the notion of a 'commons' as coined by Elinor Ostrom, winner of the 2009 Nobel Memorial Prize in Economics. She has argued that efficient management of common resources entails a clear identification of who belongs to the community (and has access to the resources), and who does not. Rules for using common resources should be defined by the local community via collective choice, and enforced in the same way. This translates, for example, into quotas given to a particular group for harvesting fishing resources, with no access given to outsiders.

Neomercantilism is an appropriate term for referring to economic policies based on *community*.[44] The notion refers to mercantilism, an early modern policy aimed at protecting domestic producers via protectionism, subsidies, and other advantages. Since 1945, it has been combined with respect for the essential norms of international free trade, which prohibits the most heavy-handed protectionist practices, hence the prefix 'neo'. On the theoretical level, government intervention can be justified to produce externalities (jobs, innovation, security), to correct market failure (limited long-term funding, high barriers to entry), and to provide activity-specific public inputs (infrastructure, health, education, justice, police). It is criticised for its rigidity (information deficit), as well as for political capture. But neomercantilist policies are not inherently effective or ineffective. According to Dani Rodrik and his co-authors, the most successful industrial policies are those that are single-oriented (pursuing one main objective at a time), flexible, based on interaction between public and private actors, and reactive: they can 'pick a winner', but must also 'let the losers go'.[45]

The notion of *community* is useful in moving beyond the public v. private dichotomy. *Community* capitalism concerns both the state and private actors: a cartel of private companies is as efficient in protecting the interest of local producers as is a state-led industrial policy. Enterprises have often forcefully defended protections against the free market, either by obtaining state

1.4 COMMUNITY: PROTECTION AND ASSERTION

measures (banning or taxing imports, monopolies, etc.), or by establishing cartels to avoid a price war or exclude certain competitors. Even some of the most powerful multinationals of the late twentieth century continued to demand public protection, as illustrated by Bastian van Apeldoorn, who used the term 'neo-mercantilism' in the 1980s in reference to one of the two groups in the European Roundtable of Industrialists, a powerful lobby.[46] Neomercantilists therefore oppose the free market in order to boost profits (and the strength of the community), not to promote solidarity.

The best way for an enterprise to maximise profits is not free competition, but rather monopoly, customs barriers, and/or cartels. The most famous is the Organization of the Petroleum Exporting Countries (OPEC), which seeks to fix oil prices worldwide, although many cartels have remained secret (Chapter 5).

The principle of *community* sheds light on the distributional conflicts at the core of public spending: not all public expenditure is directed towards the weak, with some subsidies instead propping up powerful economic actors. Neomercantilism is often justified for social reasons, as it can save jobs, but it does so at significant cost, including higher prices (making affordable imports more expensive) and higher taxes (to fund the subsidies for the protected companies). Sometimes state aid is combined with layoffs and/or factory relocations, while in other instances it is used to protect viable jobs in companies facing short-term threats (such as the Covid-19 lockdown in 2020–21) or unfair competition (everything depends on what qualifies as 'unfair'). All in all, the *solidarity* element of neomercantilist measures is often difficult to gauge without measuring how regressive or redistributive the fiscal system and state expenditure are. Some authors call it 'corporate welfare', which is to say unconditional state aid to business under various forms, including private–public partnerships or quantitative easing.[47] Some state subsidies are inefficient from a social standpoint if they create a windfall effect (an unexpected gain for a company that does not need to change behaviour), or if they artificially prop up a structurally inefficient company by limiting the losses of private shareholders without improving the long-term job prospects of their employees.

Similarly, neomercantilism must be distinguished from free market approaches. The West German approach of stable macroeconomic policy, based on low inflation and favouring investment over consumption, is sometimes described as 'neomercantilist', even though it is textbook 'deflationary' free market policy.[48] The strategy pursued by Gerhard Schröder's government (1998–2005) – to segment the labour market in order to reduce social protection and wages, and to relocate jobs to the East to reduce costs – is neoliberal rather than neomercantilist.

A West German neomercantilism nevertheless existed through: 1) multiple channels of discreet support for firms, such as the long-term financing provided by Landesbanken; 2) an effective vocational training system; and 3) productive social dialogue. This helps explain Germany's long-term export success, as this combination between *liberty, solidarity,* and *community* provides stable working relationships, which encourage high levels of investment in both labour and production, thereby promoting high value-added production.

1.5 Community *Capitalism in History*

'Mercantilism' was originally associated with the policies of Jean-Baptiste Colbert, who held a role akin to that of a minister of economy under Louis XIV of France from 1665 to 1683.[49] Noting that the French economy was lagging behind England and the Netherlands, he encouraged national production through financial aid to royal factories, but also to private factories and shipowners. These were combined with barriers to imports, and sometimes with monopolies. He complemented this action by setting high national standards to improve quality. He sought to unify the domestic market (tackling internal customs and other tolls), and facilitated the import of raw materials. He also sought to attract foreign entrepreneurs and skilled workers. Companies were set up to encourage commercial expansion in the colonies, including through sheer force. Colbert has had an enduring legacy: he founded the glassmaker Saint-Gobain in 1665 (known as the Manufacture des glaces at the time), which has remained a world leader ever since. Outside France, Jürgen Kocka described how the Dutch East India Company (the VoC) embodied mercantilism by merging trade and war:

> The Dutch government had conferred on the VOC the right to operate all Dutch trading business east of the Cape of Good Hope, along with the authorization to wage war, conclude treaties, take possession of land, and build fortresses. ... The distinction between conducting capitalist business and waging war was fluid. There were years in which the company apparently drew the major share of its income from the seizure of competing or enemy ships.[50]

Mercantilism was thus a mixture of dirigisme, militarism, and free market measures primarily designed to maximise the power of the national community.

Many countries adopted this mercantilist approach. The work of the German economist Friedrich List (1789–1846) emphasised the state's crucial role in protecting fledgling industries from foreign competition, notably through customs duties. He influenced numerous German states, with some economic success; the German state (born in 1871) quickly overtook the UK in many industrial sectors. The US political economist Henry Carey was also an influential neomercantilist.[51] On a global scale, colonisation was based on mercantilist logic, for colonising states generally forced open the markets of colonised or dominated states, for example, China, who signed several so-called unequal treaties in the nineteenth century, the first one in 1842. Trade preferences were established to favour metropolitan industrial producers over those from the colonies.

Mercantilism prevailed in the 1930s. After the stock market crash of 1929, the first country to withdraw into trade protectionism was the US with the Smoot–Hawley Tariff Act of 1930, while the first country to practise aggressive currency devaluation was the UK in 1931 (the pound being overvalued since 1925).[52] Both countries benefited from this non-cooperative behaviour, which rewards the first, daring rule breaker. Soon after, Hitler's National Socialist regime embodied the essence of authoritarian mercantilism, combining autarky, social repression, monetary manipulation, and industrial dirigisme, all while preserving capitalism. Albert Hirschmann remarked that interwar international economic relations were marked by an unrelenting 'pursuit of power' in which 'the power of the state [was] the primary aim of economic policy', an apt description of *community* capitalism.[53]

The post-war period saw a shift from mercantilism to neo-mercantilism: since blatant protectionism was seen as disruptive and conducive to nationalism, industrial policies had to be combined with international cooperation. Most Western European countries pursued active industrial policies (Chapter 5), while at the same time avoiding protectionist trade wars. These policies were called into question in the 1970s and 1980s due to their cost and perceived inefficiency. Significantly, at the time German criticism of French industrial policy fell within the lexical field of mercantilism. In 1982, Chancellor Helmut Schmidt stigmatised French 'Colbertist prejudices' in an interview with the British ambassador, while the European Commission's Director-General for Competition, Manfred Caspari of Germany, used the phrase '*Colbertistischer Wahn*' ('Colbertist madness') in connection with the French government in October 1981.[54] In 2004, the Dutch commissioner Frits Bolkestein referred to 'the mercantilist regime of Jean Baptiste Colbert' in the *Financial Times* to criticise French and German projects pursuing industrial policy.[55]

The German case illustrates the interest of the principle of *community*. In their speeches, German leaders constantly affirm their country's adherence to free market rules and their refusal of 'industrial policy'. This has roots in the rejection of communism and Hitler's dirigiste experience. Yet West German public aid to firms reached a level comparable to French aid in the late 1970s (before major structural reforms when French socialists came to power in 1981), and the proportion of nationalised firms was similar as well (Chapter 6). As in France, German investment in Airbus grew out of long-term industrial and strategic calculation (strengthening the national aeronautics industry). German tolerance for certain cartels, especially those dedicated to exports or associated with a period of crisis, are recognised in law. German subsidies have nevertheless been discreet, generally fiscal, and often allocated by the Länder or parallel programmes rather than by the central government.

Outside Europe, *community*-based policy such as neomercantilism has been widespread. Neomercantilism was theorised as a development policy for Latin America by Raul Prebisch, notably through import substitution policies.[56] The most successful example can be found in East Asia, initially in Japan in the 1960s, later in connection with the Tigers (South Korea, Hong Kong, Singapore, Taiwan), and finally with their neighbouring countries and China beginning in the 1980s.[57] They all developed strategies based on powerful national industrial polices, and partial closure of national market to Western products. The approach has been more or less protectionist, with microentities such as Singapore and Hong Kong necessarily adopting a more free trade approach.[58] All of these countries have combined neomercantilism with international free trade to increase productivity, attract investment and expertise, and open foreign markets to their exports.

Even the champion of economic liberalism, the US, has resorted to targeted industrial policy. Washington has helped struggling strategic companies, as shown by the large public loan granted to Chrysler in 1979, as well as during the financial crisis of 2007–10, thirty years later.[59] But these were ad hoc emergency measures rather than long-term industrial policy. On a more structural level, the US also uses certain tools linked to its geopolitical power. Massive funding for the military and space programmes provides a windfall for certain private firms, such as Boeing. This was one of the arguments made by Europeans when the Americans accused them of massively subsidising Airbus (Chapter 6). More generally, Washington has encouraged the emergence of a whole ecosystem of public and parapublic agencies financing innovation, such as the Defense Advanced Research Projects Agency (DARPA), which was created in 1958 by Republican President Dwight D. Eisenhower in the context of a technological war with the USSR (Moscow had launched Sputnik the previous year).[60] In 1982 Ronald Reagan, another Republican president obsessed with technological competition with the USSR, launched the Small Business Innovation Research (SBIR) programmes to award innovation funding to SMEs. These American public institutions helped finance the beginnings of the Internet and GPS in the 1970s, and more recently Apple and the electric car manufacturer Tesla. Washington also used its diplomatic clout to secure contracts. For example, the US expected Bonn to make regular purchases of military equipment to offset the high cost of its military bases in West Germany (which the Germans desperately wanted in order to ensure security against the USSR).[61] The US has also imposed major extraterritorial sanctions through its legal apparatus, a form of legal economic warfare known as 'Economic Lawfare'.[62] The most emblematic case was the €6.45 billion fine imposed on the French bank BNP Paribas in 2014 for violating US embargoes on Sudan, Cuba, and Iran. The fine represented over one year of profits (€4.83 billion in 2013), far more than the sanctions imposed by the European Commission on GAFAM.[63] Finally, illegal means were also used by the US to pursue an industrial policy. The 2010 Wikileaks revelations have shown that the intelligence apparatus was used not only for political purposes, but also to collect economic information potentially useful to American firms.

1.6 The Trinity at National Level: Germany, France, and Britain

Each state has developed a mixed form of capitalism combining the three principles, whose success has depended on many factors such as:

- geography: climate, topographic relief, access to the sea, availability of cheap sources of raw material, and of a wide range of domesticated species;[64]
- the organisation of human society: stable societies with meritocratic leadership are more efficient than those dominated by rent-seeking elites capturing extractive institutions.[65] The 'varieties of capitalism' literature highlights the efficiency of certain 'coordinated market economies', in which various political, financial, economic, and social actors are efficiently coordinated;[66]
- history: notably the detrimental effect of certain episodes of natural disaster, war, or colonisation.

This typology can be applied to Europe's three largest states, Germany, France, and Britain, which have different types of capitalism.

Germany's orientation towards exports is based on the dazzling success of its industrialisation in the late nineteenth century (iron and steel, and later chemicals, automobiles, and electricity).[67] In the absence of a substantial colonial empire, German trade representatives travelled the world in search of new markets. As early as 1896, Edwin Williams published *Made in Germany* to denounce the invasion of German industrial exports, which threatened British pre-eminence.[68]

The centrality of exports has remained a constant regardless of the government, and with it the need for prudent macroeconomic management, since any inflation outpacing that of its neighbours leads to a loss in competitiveness. The aversion to inflation is also rooted in the still-present memory of the hyperinflation crisis of 1923. The latter was caused by the heavy spending of the German government, which resorted to excessive money creation (the famous 'money printing') to finance its massive deficits, linked to the reparations owed under the Treaty of Versailles in 1919. The testimony of Sebastian Haffner, the son of a high-ranking Prussian civil servant, is revelatory in this regard. His family sank into hardship because his father had to spend his entire monthly salary in the hours after being paid, as hyperinflation would have made it worthless within days. The whole family rushed out to buy non-perishable foodstuffs that would last the whole month.[69] This example shows that even middle-class families were ravaged by hyperinflation. The savings of entire generations vanished, while the lucky few who could transfer their capital abroad bought struggling companies for a pittance. Work and savings were no longer rewarded: the Weimar Republic was demonetised in all senses of the term. Germany's first liberal democratic regime was thus deeply unstable. Ten years after this sad phenomenon, Hitler came to power and expanded monetary manipulation in order to conceal inflation and deficits.[70] This explains why the new Federal Republic of Germany created in 1949 chose a completely different path, with a strong Deutsche Mark (the currency was created in 1948 even before the new state), and a commitment to free trade. Debt was low thanks to the cancellation of most internal debt with the monetary reform of 1948, and of international debt with the London Agreement of 1953.[71] Even trade unions have supported this anti-inflationary and export-led consensus, because they have enjoyed a prominent role in this system. The varieties of capitalism literature explains Germany's export success through its 'concerted' approach, in which national and local authorities, trade unions, business representatives, and actors in banking and manufacturing successfully coordinate to pursue long-term objectives.[72]

These factors explain Germany's unwavering post-war support for free trade, except in areas where the country was less competitive (agriculture), or wished to preserve the distinctive features inherent to its model (the special status of regional bank, the Landesbanken, which provides long-term funding for companies, and various rules that protect companies from hostile takeovers).

In contrast, French governments were more protectionist and more keen on industrial policy to make up for the country's industrial backwardness compared with its British and German neighbours. France has long been an export country in a few sectors, notably luxury goods, agricultural products, aeronautics, and cars (until recently), but far less than its German competitors. This was partly due to the dearth of coal (compared with Britain and Germany), and because French companies had little incentive to export, as they benefited from one of the largest internal markets in Europe, as well as a large colonial empire. France also suffered from the destruction of the two world wars. After the war, France waged costly colonial conflicts (between 1945 and 1962), and significantly (but belatedly) increased its socio-economic expenditures to develop its colonial empire.[73]

As a result, Paris supported trade liberalisation, all while preserving numerous protections. In 1945 France led an assertive industrial policy based on nationalisation and indicative planning. Jean Monnet, who shaped the first Plan in 1946, believed that it embodied a 'concerted economy', which is to say a free market economy in which the state plays a major role coordinating enterprises, trade unions, and public actors.[74] When he returned to the helm in 1958, the conservative Charles de Gaulle combined industrial policy with a progressive return to international free trade (Chapter 3). This mix was successful: Paris did better than Bonn during this decade, whereas the opposite was true in the 1950s.

While France has been more protectionist than Germany, it has also always been dependent on its exports to pay for its imports of raw materials, coal and oil in particular. Statistics on the balance of trade in goods and services between 1960 and 2018 indicate surpluses every other year (twenty-nine years out of fifty-eight according to World Bank statistics). On average, France's trade balance was in surplus in the 1960s. It deteriorated after the 1973 oil shock, like all other Western countries bar Germany, before delivering regular surpluses again in the 1990s. The share of exports (goods and services) in national wealth (GNP) was slightly higher in France than in Germany in the 1970s, and equal in the 1980s and 1990s. These statistics demonstrate that France could be considered, like West Germany, as a relatively successfully 'coordinated' economy during the Golden Age (1945–73), albeit with a different organisation. While the French official discourse does not embrace free trade, the country is too small and dependent on exports to avoid international trade.

On the other side of the Channel, the British commitment to free trade has been prominent and enduring. It dates back at least to 1846, when the Corn Laws were abolished, leading to reduced customs tariffs on grains, and ultimately the price of bread. The choice was rational for Britain, an island whose industry dominated the world at the time, but whose agricultural production costs were quite high.

However, the British simultaneously indulged in *community* capitalism. The colonial empire restricted the industrial development of certain overseas territories competing with British production (such as Indian textiles). In 1932, the Ottawa Agreements established imperial preference. When the UK joined the EEC in 1973, it had to lower its customs tariffs, which were higher than those of the Six in the industrial sector, even as the British continued to denounce the protectionist nature of the EC (true for the agricultural sector, but not for manufactured goods).[75]

Thatcher's premiership, which started in 1979, ended this contradiction between a free trade discourse and a more protectionist practice, with London pursuing a radical free market policy ever since. It has supported sectors with a global reach, such as finance, insurance, and legal services for companies, and opened up its traditional manufacturing to foreign direct investment early on, notably to Japanese carmakers.

Of course, these countries have combined long-term preferences with radical changes reflecting their internal diversity. The shifts represented by Thatcher's rise to power in 1979 shows that national strategies are not immutable and univocal, even if long-term structural elements remain. Besides, other national approaches exist. A small country such as Belgium or the Netherlands will be more structurally in favour of free trade than larger states with ample reserves of raw materials, which are more self-reliant.[76] Small countries are also tempted to become tax havens if they struggle to attract foreign capital willing to invest in their small market. Consequently, each country must strike the right balance for itself, and then combine it with that of its neighbours.

1.7 The Trinity in International Cooperation

The trinity can also be applied to international cooperation. In theory, liberal strategies contribute to both prosperity and peace. As the French philosopher Montesquieu emphasised in the eighteenth century, '*commerce*' (often translated as 'trade') fosters interaction and mutual understanding, although he defined '*commerce*' broadly to include a wide range of human contact.[77] Several eighteenth-century philosophers such as Montesquieu, Kant, David Hume, and Adam Smith linked international trade and peace, although not in an automatic way. Since free markets do not emerge spontaneously, international institutions were set up to shape them. International and European trade organisations are predicated on the Kantian ideal in *Perpetual Peace*. In his classical book from 1795, the German philosopher Immanuel Kant argued for developing a peace programmes based on liberal values, non-intervention in each other's communities, and the eventual dissolution of standing armies.[78]

In the final third of the nineteenth century, the first permanent world institutions were created to identify common technical standards, initially for telegraphs with the International Telegraph Union (ITU, 1865), which became the still-extant International Telecommunication Union, followed by the General Postal Union (1874), and the International Union of Railways (1922), among others.[79] After 1919, a more ambitious international organisation aimed at promoting peace was established: the League of Nations (LoN). It strove to promote 'trade disarmament', a revealing term combining both economic and political liberalism (free trade and peace). The Great Crash in 1929 unleashed economic and political nationalism. The LoN was ultimately replaced by the United Nations (UN) in 1944 and the General Agreement on Tariffs and Trade (GATT) in 1947 (in turn replaced by the World Trade Organization or WTO in 1995), all rooted in promoting certain basic liberal norms.

By contrast, the neoliberal view of international relations rests on a Darwinian race to the bottom rather than an enlightened liberalism fostering collective emulation. This can be seen in tax competition with the creation of tax havens, as well as in social and environmental dumping.

The *solidarity* governance of capitalism is naturally cosmopolitan, but difficult to implement on a large scale, as solidarity does not come spontaneously. Marxists strove to promote solidarity through several 'internationals'. The International Labour Office (ILO), which was created in 1919, pursued a more moderate approach. Based on dialogue between trade unions, business interests, and governments, it strove to foster best practices, albeit without binding tools.[80] After 1945, the ILO and the UN tried to develop solidarity in several transnational issues, such as migration and later pollution.

Lastly, *community*-based policies are by nature difficult to internationalise. Since they seek to favour one group at the expense of others, they see international cooperation as a zero-sum game. Colonisation and the autarkic totalitarian regimes of the 1930s are the most radical manifestations of bellicose mercantilism. The post-war years and their 'embedded liberalism' nonetheless saw the emergence of a more cooperative *community* capitalism combining *solidarity* and *liberty*. Some protection is useful in preserving local customs and the social fabric (such as the production of local food). Hence, international organisations are useful in easing conflicts between national forms of *community* capitalism.

1.8 Conclusion

To conclude, the governance of capitalism usually involves a mix of three approaches: *liberty*, *solidarity*, and *community*. This trinity is useful in making comparisons across time and space. This trinity has been applied in various combinations nationally, as well as internationally. Before examining the deployment of those approaches in post-war Europe, it is important to understand the original institutional environment that has shaped them.

2

The European Union as a Political Hybrid

'I have always believed that Europe would be built through crises, and that it would be the sum of their solutions'

(Jean Monnet)

Major crises – the two world wars, the Cold War, decolonisation – forced Europeans to reinvent themselves by creating a hybrid political organisation, the European Union.[1] The EU is more than a traditional international organisation such as the UN, because it has its own budget, currency, and directly applicable law. Yet it is not a state, for it lacks a police force, army, and criminal justice system. Its member states conserve a right of veto for all major decisions, and preserve the 'competence of competence', which is to say ultimate sovereignty. When the British wanted to hold a referendum to leave the EU in 2016, no one denied them that right, unlike the Catalans in 2017. When a corruption scandal involved a vice-president of the European Parliament in 2022, it was the Belgian police and courts that prosecuted her. It is therefore illuminating to explore the EU's unique political and institutional features in order to understand how it has played such a large role in organising European capitalism.

The EC/EU have served as an instrument for member states seeking to reassert their legitimacy and power, as well as an organisation driven by supranational actors such as the European Commission, the Court of Justice, and more recently the European Parliament. This chapter will develop this argument in five stages: (i) on the origins of the EU; (ii) on the centrality of the EU; (iii) on the balance between intergovernmental and supranational dynamics; (iv) on the EU as a compromise between member states; and finally (v) on the EU's compatibility with the three forms of capitalist governance.

2.1 The Three Origins of the European Union

European integration is rooted in a search for peace, prosperity, and freedom. The need for peace was prompted by the industrial-scale destruction of the two world wars, both of which erupted in Europe. That is why the quest for

European integration started in earnest in 1919.[2] This was particularly true for France and Germany, which fought three wars (1870–71, 1914–18, 1939–45), each increasingly lethal. They suffered from deaths (one in four Frenchmen born in 1894 for example), destruction, the payment of reparations (France to Germany during the first war, Germany to France in the final two), and from the cost of occupation (one quarter of French GDP during German occupation in 1940–44).[3] After 1945, the German challenge remained: while the country was occupied and dismembered, the immigration of millions of Germans expelled from Eastern Europe cemented its status as the most populous European country. Despite Allied bombing, Germany's industrial capacity remained the largest on the continent. To break the vicious circle of French–German wars, both countries, along with their immediate neighbours, sought a more innovative approach to international cooperation than the traditional ones (from the Concert of Europe in 1815 to the UN in 1944).

The second motivation was prosperity, and the struggle against decline. Europe was surpassed in economic might first by the US and later by China, and in between lagged behind the Soviet Union and Japan for several decades in terms of economic growth. Western Europe's global economic weight was halved between 1913 and 2008, while the US share remained the same, and China nearly caught up with the US (see Table 2.1).

The third motivation for building the European Union was to defend liberal democracy. Here too, the EC/EU was different from other forms of European cooperation, notably the various projects of authoritarian fascist 'Europe' during the World War II. After 1945, several European institutions, such as NATO and the OEEC, included dictatorships, notably Salazar's Portugal. On the contrary, the EC/EU was founded to bring societies and states together around common values such as liberal democracy and peace. A potent force of unification was anti-communism.[5] Joseph Stalin was a menacing Soviet leader, especially given that Moscow had much more troops than Western European states, and had detonated the Soviet atomic bomb in 1949. The Russo-Soviet threat did not disappear after Stalin, but has remained potent despite a short

Table 2.1 *European share of global GDP as compared with the United States and China since 1913*[4]

GDP percentage estimates by Angus Maddison and his team

	Western Europe (12 countries)	United States	China
1913	30.7	18.9	8.8
1950	24.1	27.3	4.5
2008	14.5	18.6	17.5

period of détente (notably in 1991–2007) and strong cultural links forged between Russia and Europe.

2.2 The Centrality of the European Union

The EU's role gradually became so pivotal that it led to a synecdoche: the part, which is to say the Union, is confused with the whole, the European continent.[6] This result was nevertheless not a preordained outcome: the EC/EU could have failed or remained secondary (and still can).

At the outset, the continent's reconstruction was overseen by the United Nations Economic Commission for Europe, which was quickly marginalised due to the Cold War.[7] The first European organisation was the OEEC, founded in 1948 to manage the Marshall Plan, but its institutions were weak. On the contrary, the European Community, which appeared with the Schuman Declaration on 9 May 1950, was a partially federal Europe of Six intended exclusively for liberal democracies willing to pool their sovereignty in certain areas. What emerged was the ECSC in 1951, and later the EEC in 1957.

However, there was an alternative to the Communities at the time, the free trade area (FTA) proposed by the British in 1956. It was a looser form of European cooperation based on intergovernmental institutions, and encompassed all of Western Europe (including dictatorships such as Portugal). The FTA was rejected by the French in 1958, only to be reborn again in the guise of the European Free Trade Association (EFTA), signed in 1960 by Britain and six other countries: the British press spoke of the 'Outer Seven' as opposed to the 'Inner Six'.

The real breakthrough came in 1961 when the UK submitted its application for membership, thereby recognising the EC's centrality in Europe. The first enlargement eventually occurred towards the north in 1973 (Denmark, Ireland, United Kingdom). Later enlargements can be explained by the return of democracy in both the South (accession of Greece in 1981, Spain and Portugal in 1986) and the East (accession of East Germany with German reunification in 1990, of neutral countries in 1995, and of former Soviet countries along with Malta and Cyprus between 2004 and 2013). These successive enlargements allowed the EU to maintain its share of global population around 5–6 per cent, and of global wealth (GDP) at 15–20 per cent between 1950 and today (approximately 16 per cent in 2024 after Brexit).[8]

All of the EC's competitors faded away. In 1960, the OEEC became the Organisation for Economic Co-operation and Development (OECD). It dropped the adjective 'European' with the membership of the US and Canada, which were followed by Japan in 1964, and later by other non-European countries. While the OEEC organised trade and monetary cooperation in Europe, the OECD became an influential think-tank for the rich countries of the Western bloc.[9] The secretary general of the OECD was unable to secure an invitation for himself to the G7 in 1975, in contrast to the Commission, which gradually imposed itself in this forum.[10] The Commission later extended its prerogatives to fields in which the Council of Europe had been a pioneer, such as education and culture (the Erasmus Programme was launched in 1987), as well as to European symbols (invented by the Council of Europe, and taken up by the EEC in 1985).[11] The Council of Europe nevertheless conserved primacy with respect to human rights.

The Community was strengthened between 1989 and 1992, first by the Maastricht Treaty, which launched the Economic and Monetary Union, but also by the diplomatic initiatives taken by Commission President Delors to fully insert his institution within the post-Cold War world.[12] Delors's support for German reunification and his assistance to former Eastern bloc countries were precocious, dating back to his 17 October 1989 speech at the College of Europe. By contrast, many other European leaders were reluctant to embrace rapid German reunification. At the European summit in Strasbourg in December 1989, all European leaders, except those from countries that had not taken part in the World War II (Spain's Felipe Gonzales and the Irish), expressed reservations about Kohl's failure to give his partners advance notice regarding his ten-point plan to accelerate reunification.[13] On the economic front, Delors's initiatives involving Central and Eastern Europe in 1989 convinced US President George Bush to propose that the Commission coordinate Western aid to these countries.

Still, the enlargement of the Community towards former Eastern bloc countries was not a preordained outcome. In 1990–91, French President François Mitterrand, in keeping with the French preference for a small Europe, supported the creation of a 'European confederation' that would have brought together all European countries, including the USSR but not the US.[14] This vague project was in response to European fears of disorder following an anticipated withdrawal of US troops. Mitterrand promoted the project to the Czech leader Vaclav Havel, who agreed to hold a conference in Prague in 1991. However, when Mitterrand declared in Prague that the EC accession for Central and Eastern European countries could take 'decades and decades', and risked transforming the Community into a free trade area, many leaders realised that Mitterrand's project of what he called a 'European Confederation' was in danger of becoming an alternative to enlargement. The project soon failed.

Enlargement towards the East eventually took place in 2004–13, a few years after the creation of the monetary union in 1999, a project that many actors (notably in the US) considered a chimera when it was launched in 1992. While the EC could have been weakened by the end of the Cold War, it actually morphed into a larger and more influential EU.

The uniqueness of the EC/EU is even greater when compared with other international organisations. For example, the ILO and UNESCO were bogged down by Cold War conflicts, and sometimes by US withdrawal (during the 1970s and 1980s), which strained their finances and hence their capacity to act.[15] The history of the UN Environment Programme (UNEP) shows that it was highly dependent on funding from a few states – generally Scandinavian countries, which allowed them to hold conferences (Stockholm in 1972) or preside over commissions (Brundtland in 1986) – and from private groups as well.[16] The GATT/WTO were not competitors but rather partners, as the Commission has conducted world trade negotiations on behalf of member states (with their close oversight) since the 1960s. A division of labour gradually emerged, with institutions such as the OECD and ILO providing expertise for the EC/EU.[17]

The only real competitor to the Union was NATO, which remains dominant in military matters, and the International Monetary Fund (IMF), which takes the lead in managing monetary crises, although the EU expanded its prerogatives in this area during the euro crisis.[18]

A comparison with other regional organisations further underscores the EEC's institutional distinctiveness.[19] The Council for Mutual Economic Assistance (Comecon) was active in the Soviet Bloc, although archival studies have confirmed the weak powers of this strictly intergovernmental institution. Similarly, studies focusing on Mercosur and other South and Central American organisations for cooperation also reveal their powerlessness. While the EEC eliminated internal customs duties in 1968, customs conflicts still occur frequently in Latin America. Trade integration is much less developed: while share of intra-zone trade has been above 70 per cent in the European Union since its creation in 1992, it has not surpassed 30 per cent in Latin America, and is even significantly lower now with Mercosur. As for ASEAN, it has long remained a partial free trade area undermined by internal divisions, although the dynamism of East Asian countries, China in particular, combined with the rejection of the Trans-Pacific Partnership in 2017 by US President Donald J. Trump, has revitalised Asian regional trade integration.

The EU's central role in organising Europe thus emerged fairly late, and is not permanent. Integration can be followed by disintegration if populations no longer see added value in this type of political configuration, and seek a return to national solutions. After the crises of the 2010s, Euroscepticism became a striking trend in political circles and the media.[20] It was epitomised by Brexit in 2016, and by the confrontational stance of other governments (since 2010 in Viktor Orbán's Hungary, and from 2016 to 2023 in Poland under the Law and Justice Party).

2.3 The Union: Between a Federation and an Association of States

The European Union is a hybrid entity, with federal and intergovernmental aspects.[21] It was launched by the Schuman Declaration of 9 May 1950, which sketched out a new kind of semi-federal organisation by inventing what would later become the European Commission. It was followed by the creation of the ECSC via the Treaty of Paris in 1951, and later the EEC via the Treaty of Rome in 1957. The latter treaty still largely remains the basis for today's EU, which was established in 1992. Some of its articles, in addition to its general philosophy, remained in the Treaty of Lisbon in 2007, which is currently in effect.

This community model was founded on four institutions created by the Treaty of Paris in 1951: the Council of Ministers representing states, the Parliamentary Assembly, the Court of Justice, and a supranational body charged with proposing and implementing legislation. This body was called the High Authority at the ECSC (1952), and the Commission at both the EEC and Euratom (1958). In 1965 they merged into a single Commission.

This institutional setting is partly federal: the absolute sovereignty of member states is challenged by majority voting in the Council of Ministers (a state in the minority must apply the decision adopted), by the Commission's monopoly over initiative (right to propose new legislation), by the existence of federal law, and by the direct election (since 1979) of members of the European Parliament via direct universal suffrage.

But this system does not amount to the United States of Europe. The EU only exists through international treaties that states must accept on a unanimous basis. States designate the leaders of all supranational institutions, with the exception of the European Parliament. The major body for decision-making and (more often) blockage remains the Council.

The Commission is not the equivalent of a government, which is generally united behind a leader and an electoral programme (or at least a coalition), but rather a patchwork of decision-makers from different nationalities with contrasting political, economic, social, and even European orientations. The Commission President is no more than a *primus inter pares*, who can end up in the minority at the College of Commissioners during a formal vote. Besides, while the Commission is tasked with executing the decisions passed by the Council and Parliament, it only has a fairly small administration (32,000 people in 2025), with no independent power of inspection in most fields, and lacks the power of resorting to legitimate violence. It therefore relies heavily on national administrations.

The institutional framework has evolved over time, all while perpetuating this balance between a state-driven and federal logic. The former was strengthened by the Luxembourg Compromise, which encouraged unanimity rather than qualified majority voting at the Council of Ministers between 1966 and 1986, and by the creation of the European Council in 1975. The latter includes heads of government and the Commission, and defines the overall orientation of EC activity. The European Council is more than a purely intergovernmental institution, even though it remains driven mainly by inter-state negotiating.[22]

The federal dynamic was emphasised with the gradual emergence of European federal law, which is to say law that is directly applicable, and takes precedence over national law. This began with the *Van Gend & Loos* (1963) and *Costa v. ENEL* (1964) decisions, which grew out of mobilisation by groups of pro-Community jurists.[23] The federal dynamic continued with the gradual reinforcement of the European Parliament in the 1980s. It also depends on the personality of the Commission President, with the most influential being Walter Hallstein (1958–67) of Germany, who established the supranational basis for institutions, and Jacques Delors (1985–95) of France, who transformed an essentially trade-related community into a budding monetary, economic, and social union.

There is a great deal of internal diversity within the EC. The procedures are not the same for all public policies. The most regalian sectors such as defence, foreign policy, and justice remain in the hands of states. Unanimity is often given primacy over qualified majority voting, intergovernmental agreements over federal law, and the Council of Ministers over the Commission or Parliament. On the contrary, in the most Community-based sectors, the procedures gradually became more federal: for foreign trade and agriculture in the 1960s; for competition in the 1980s; and for monetary policy and a growing number of economic and environmental regulations (excluding taxation and social law) beginning in the 1990s.[24] As a result, according to the economic historian Kevin O'Rourke, 'there has surely never been a more tightly integrated group of economies in human history than the [twenty-seven] member states of the EU'.[25]

Diversity is also territorial, as all of the EU's spaces are not concerned by the same policies.[26] This notion has its origins in the agreement that created the European Monetary System in 1978. The latter included an exception for the British, the only member state not to take part; London subsequently secured exemptions from the Schengen Agreement, the euro, and the Maastricht Social Charter as well. Denmark and Sweden followed suit. The temptation of a 'multi-speed Europe' naturally emerged to reconcile varying commitments to European integration. For example, in 1984, the French Minister of Foreign Affairs Roland Dumas – and later French President François Mitterrand himself – proposed launching a Europe of Eight (the Six plus Spain and Portugal, which would soon be joining the Community) in the event that budgetary negotiations with the British failed.[27] Their German counterparts politely avoided the subject, for Bonn feared the constitution of a small Europe subject to strong French influence. In June 1985, just before a meeting of the European People's Party (EPP), the president of this group of Christian Democratic parties, Piet Bukman of the Netherlands, explicitly envisioned a multi-speed Europe as a working assumption: 'An initiative that would keep the Community moving and would allow progress towards the European Union, namely to advance with the Inner Six (+ Ireland) while waiting for Great Britain to join them.'[28]

2.3 THE UNION AS A COMPROMISE

National and European institutions are intermingled. Kalypso Nicolaïdis has characterised this system as a 'demoicracy', a system in which 'sovereignty' is 'exercised concurrently by several rather than just one demos'.[29] The hybrid nature of the Union's political system generates its complexity and hence its 'democratic deficit': most European citizens struggle to understand how its institutions work. They do not feel part of a fully-fledged European public sphere, for lack of continent-wide media, parties, and grassroot mobilisation.[30] This complexity is also a function of the urge to avoid any strong leadership within the European system, a liberal reflex that has been prevalent in post-war Europe.[31] The democratic deficit has also been fuelled by the tendency of member states to shift the blame on European institutions. Besides, they have devolved to the Union their most unpopular tasks, such as setting standards and managing monetary policy. It is therefore logical that European institutions are seen as being aloof and technocratic. At some point, the European Parliament discussed the noise level of lawnmowers, probably not the best way to elicit public interest![32] By contrast, member states have kept more popular policies to themselves, including providing health care, pensions, schools, police, justice, and the military.

All in all, three main dynamics can explain the EC/EU institutional developments. First, the European institutions represent an opportunity for member states to promote their nation-interest and to get credible commitments from their partners.[33] Second, supranational institutions, the European Commission, the Court of Justice, and later the European Parliament, have managed to progressively increase their power, sometimes stealthily as in the case of the Court relying on the 'integration-through-law' dynamic.[34] More precisely, historical institutionalism has shown that the ability of member states to master the decision-making process is hampered by 'path-dependencies' and 'unintended consequences'. This is particularly true for low salience issues such as competition policy, whose decisive reinforcement in the late 1980s was informed by 'path-dependencies' of the 1960s, which led to 'unintended consequences' for France: Paris underestimated the European Commission, which gained major power in competition policy in 1962 (for cartels), but was unable to implement them in the subsequent years.[35] Yet, Commissioner Brittan drew on this legacy to get major power for the Commission again in 1989 (this time for mergers), only to use them much more forcefully, including against France.

Third, the European integration process is supported by an elusive European federal identity. It is visible in the successive elections of pro-European governments, and in polls, with often a sizeable number of respondents being in favour of vague federal aspiration such as the 'United States of Europe' in the post-war years, or a 'common defence and security policy' today.[36] Europeans are split, most of them considering the nation states as their main anchor, but refusing the return to a jingoistic Europe of aggressive nations, unable to regulate their conflicts by rule-bound institutions.

2.4 The EU as the Intersection of Contrasting National Strategies

'France seeks reincarnation as Europe; Germany hopes for redemption through Europe' said Zbigniew Brzezinski, the National Security Advisor to US President Jimmy Carter (1977–81).[37] As a matter of fact, states developed contrasting European strategies. In Germany, due to the National Socialist past, foreign policy rhetoric is more modest than in Britain and France, which ruled over colonial empires, are both nuclear powers, and have a veto right as permanent members of the UN Security Council. German political discourse has been more federal, in keeping with its history (aside from the Hitler period). Practice was nevertheless more often intergovernmental than the discourse, as demonstrated by the regular criticism of EC institutions by the Federal Constitutional Court in Karlsruhe.[38] Administrative practice has been less unitary than in France or the UK, due to the strong degree of decentralisation (which left many powers to the Länder), and to divisions between ministries, that were more visible than in Paris or London.[39] As Germany depended on the US for its defence, and on the world market for its exports, it has always been favourable to enlargements.

In Paris, the priorities were practically the opposite of those in Bonn; the rhetoric was ambitious, especially under Charles de Gaulle (1958–69). The preferred geographic scale was a small Europe where French influence could be maximised (hence without the British), supplemented by strong ties with Africa (in keeping with a post-imperial logic). This translated into two rejections of British accession in 1963 and 1967, and later unease over enlargement towards the East. The relationship with the US evolved. At the outset of European integration, French governments were highly Atlanticist, and insisted that Washington be actively involved in Europe. However, starting with US opposition to the French–British expedition against Nasser in Suez in 1956, and especially de Gaulle's return to power in 1958, there emerged a discourse of Europe as a power, one that was allied with but independent from the US. Paris withdrew from the NATO integrated command from 1966 to 2009. In terms of institutional preference, French governments have often associated a voluntarist and idealist discourse with an intergovernmental practice. For example, French President Valéry Giscard d'Estaing (1974–81), known for being pro-European, nevertheless sought to curtail the powers of the Court of Justice of the European Communities, which he found overly intrusive.[40]

The British stance towards European integration was encapsulated by the term 'awkward partner', which appeared often in the literature, and was used by British diplomats from 1980 onwards.[41] The British were awkward because they never supported idealist pro-European rhetoric. London proceeded with European cooperation primarily for economic reasons, with no desire to alter its national political model, which was characterised by its striking success during the World War II. The other major European countries suffered various military failures, making them more predisposed towards the delegation of sovereignty to supranational institutions after the war. In his famous speech delivered in Zurich on 19 September 1946, Winston Churchill called for European integration, but without the UK. Studies focusing on European economic cooperation before 1939 also show that British actors (companies in particular) were proportionally less involved in international and continental cooperation than their German, French, Belgian, and Dutch counterparts.[42] This was certainly due to the imperial heritage, as well as the physical interdependence (in the form of rivers, coal mining areas, migrant populations) that united countries in Charlemagne's Europe.

After joining the Community in 1973, following twelve years of difficult negotiations punctuated by two vetoes by Charles de Gaulle, relations between London and Brussels remained strained. The abrasive style of Margaret Thatcher (1979–90) sustained a permanent debate regarding the UK's possible exclusion from the EC, even among the Germans. The archives reveal that in 1980, during an interview with Roy Jenkins (President of the Commission) and Peter Carington (Foreign Secretary) of Great Britain, the German Chancellor Helmut Schmidt asked them if their country wanted to create a situation where other EEC members asked it to leave the EC due to its intransigence on budgetary matters.[43] A few months later, in a discussion with Schmidt regarding Britain's stance, the French president Giscard d'Estaing wondered whether admitting the UK in the EC had not been an error.[44] Schmidt rejected the prospect, but admitted the major problems arising with Thatcher. Around the same dates, in an interview with his counterpart, the German Minister for Foreign Affairs, Hans-Dietrich Genscher, Lord Carington threatened that the British could withdraw from the EEC if the budgetary problem was not resolved, with a veiled threat to pull out British troops from West Germany, which the Germans needed as a buffer against the Soviet Union.[45] Already in late 1958, amid the conflict surrounding the British proposal for a free trade area (FTA), Prime Minister Harold Macmillan threatened the Six with the withdrawal of the British military presence in Germany in the event its proposal for an FTA failed.[46] This explicit linkage between trade and geopolitical issue was typical of Britain. For example, Thatcher reiterated the same threat to Kohl in 1984.[47]

With the EEC membership referendum of 1975, the UK became the only state to demand new concessions immediately after its accession, and to submit them to a referendum. Great Britain was also the only country not to participate in the EMS in 1979, thereby paving the way for additional exceptions. Other countries subsequently secured exceptions, but the UK was the country that initiated and accumulated them, before its ultimate isolation (along with Hungary) over its refusal to elect Jean-Claude Juncker as Commission President in 2014. During the most severe crises, especially those involving the British contribution to the budget (1980–84) and 'mad cow' (1996), it threatened to withdraw, or at a minimum not to adhere to European obligations.

Still, the UK was often central to European cooperation, firstly by playing a major role in many different European organisations (such as the OEEC, the Council of Europe or NATO), and secondly by strongly influencing the EC after joining in 1973, especially with respect to competition policy.[48] Brexit, which was passed in 2016 and implemented in 2020, represents a sharp break with the past, as it was the first time that a fully European state left the EU.

All in all, European states and citizens have nurtured different political ambitions for European integration. Various factors have played a role, such as geopolitical allegiance (neutrality or NATO membership, relationship with Russia), the colonial past (including within Europe), the strength of institutions, and, of course, the national mix of capitalism.

2.5 European Institutions and the Trinity of Capitalism

International economic organisations are not conducive to all forms of capitalism. Many experts have estimated that the European Union is compatible only with *liberty* capitalism. Its decision-making process is complex as it is designed to avoid the domination of any single actor. Its institutions seem to be more effective at promoting free trade by removing obstacles, what is known as 'negative integration', than in creating new instruments expressing *solidarity* or *community*, or 'positive integration'. The German political scientist Fritz Scharpf has deplored the Court of Justice's bias towards negative integration, and the Council's inability to promote positive integration due to the 'joint decision trap' (the difficulty of taking action as a result of unanimity requirements or obstructionary coalitions).[49] The Union is considered exclusively as 'regulatory state', rather than an actor making discriminatory choices.[50] Moreover, only a strong sense of shared identity can justify painful redistribution measures or difficult choices to 'pick the winner' in industrial policy. The steady development of neoliberal policies in Europe since the late twentieth century, particularly at the European level, appears to support this argument.

However, this book will complement this narrative by arguing that the European institutional system, while being easier to combine with the *liberty* aspect of capitalism, is also compatible with moderate forms of *solidarity* and *community* capitalism. Three factors call for consideration. First, from a theoretical point of view, Scharpf's argument can be reversed. 'Negative integration' is easier than 'positive integration' only if the negative redistributive effects of free trade are ignored. All economic rules, even those considered the most neutral, create winners and losers. Pure and perfect competition never exists, as all markets are imperfect, and hence dependent on artificial rules (Who can access the market? How are prices set? etc.). Similarly, the

2.5 THE EU AND THE TRINITY

seemingly depoliticised nature of neoliberal policies, which are supposed to be neutral, is illusory. For example, the politics of deregulating markets are based on discriminatory decisions: most of the time, they tend to discriminate against incumbent monopolies and oligopolies (Chapters 7 and 8). This creates distributional effects, some positive, such as lower prices if the deregulation is well managed, others negative, such as weaker social and environmental protection.

Second, the ensuing chapters will show that, for most of their history, capitalist European states have remained fairly protectionist, as powerful constituencies (starting with farmers) have prevented any liberalisation measures. The role of European institutions was to facilitate the combination of various national forms of *solidarity* and *community* capitalism in Europe.

Third, the historical account developed below shows that the legal framework of the European treaties, while firmly anchored in free market rules, can accommodate *solidarity* and *community* forms of capitalist governance. For example, trade rules have been used to liberalise trade with the US in manufactured goods, but also to support protectionist policies in agricultural and textile products (Chapter 6). The competition policy rules that were defined in the 1957 Treaty of Rome, at a time when hardly any competition policy existed in Europe, are flexible and have accommodated many different approaches, including German ordoliberalism, the second Chicago school in the US, and the public interest criterion (Chapters 5 and 8).[51]

Traditionally, economists have distinguished between several forms of international trade cooperation.[52] In turn, each type of cooperation required a specific set of international institutions, as shown by Table 2.2.

Five steps of integration can be identified. Step 1 is the free trade area, which is based exclusively on the removal of trade barriers. It is compatible only with the principle of *liberty*; intergovernmental institutions are sufficient for managing it. In step 2, the Common Market, a minimal amount of semi-federal rules and institutions are needed to implement the common external trade policy. The EEC went through this stage in the 1960s, by liberalising trade in goods and implementing a protectionist agricultural policy. It then morphed progressively into the Single Market with common rules (step 3), which necessitates more federal procedures in order to adopt such legislation (with qualified majority voting for certain decision taken by the Council of Ministers since 1987) and monitor it (with federal law since the 1960s). Such cooperation is conducive to *liberty* capitalism, but also to moderate forms of *community* capitalism (if cartels and mergers are tolerated or even encouraged, and if standards for domestic companies are adopted at the expense of foreign competitors) and *solidarity* capitalism (if high social and environmental rules are adopted). At the same time, the European Communities implemented redistribution (step 4), initially with regional policy (starting in 1975, reinforced in 1988: see Chapter 4), and later with monetary policy. The latter

Table 2.2 Types of economic cooperation and international institutions

Type of international economic cooperation	Forms of capitalism	Economic policies	Institutions
1. Free trade area (OECE for quotas, 1948, EFTA 1960)	Liberty	Removal of trade barriers (quotas and custom duties)	Intergovernmental agreements
2. Custom Union or 'Common Market' in EEC parlance (EEC 1957, implemented 1968)	Liberty and community	Common external tariff free trade orientation for goods (*liberty*), protectionist for agriculture (*community*)	Common external trade policy with a common authority to implement it
3. Regulated market or 'single market' in EEC parlance (1986, implemented 1992)	Liberty, possibility of integrating moderate forms of *community* (standards favouring domestic companies) and *solidarity* (high standards)	Unification of internal trade rules (norms) towards high or low standards	Common internal trade and competition policy; federal law to ensure homogeneous implementation
4. Redistributive market (1975–88: EEC regional policy; 1992–99: EMU)	Liberty and/or solidarity capitalism	Redistribution through regional and monetary policies, usually based on non-discriminatory rules	Federalisation of monetary policy and some budgetary transfers
5. Assertive Community (not implemented)	Liberty, solidarity, and bolder community capitalism	Assertive policies in industry ('pick the winner'), trade, defence, and foreign policy	More politicised to take explicit discriminatory decisions

created important redistributive effects, for better or for worse, as shown by the eurozone crisis (Chapter 8). Redistribution makes *solidarity* capitalism possible, but only on a limited scale, as the European budget is modest and based on rules deemed to be neutral, and therefore avoids explicit discriminatory choices.

With the return of community capitalism since 2016, the challenge has been to create a more assertive community (step 5), one able to make explicit discriminatory choices in industrial policy ('picking the winner', i.e. concentrating subsidies on a few major projects), trade (reacting to protectionist threats), foreign policy, and defence.[53] The move to step 5 has been under discussion over the past ten years. It does not require a fully-fledged federal union, as the current institutional framework – defined by the 2007 Treaty of Lisbon – is conducive to bold initiatives if there is political willingness to face international challenges together.

Table 2.2 should not be read as a pathway that automatically leads to a more integrated European Union. Stages are partially overlapping: there was no clean break between the Common Market and the Single Market for example, as some elements of social and environmental policies date back before the 1986 Single Market programme (Chapter 4). The neofunctionalist dynamism described by Ernst Hass, which is to say the 'spillover' effect – according to which the pooling of sovereignty in one area of economic policy triggers pooling in another related area – is not automatic. It can be stopped or even reversed, as demonstrated by the threat of a shrinking eurozone in 2010–15, or with the Brexit vote in 2016.

2.6 Conclusion

The European Union is a peculiarity in world history. It is a hybrid actor, both intergovernmental and federal, and based on a complex decision-making process designed to accommodate the fact that each member state has a different relationship to it. The European Union's dominant role in regulating capitalism emerged quite late, after the failure of numerous alternatives in both European and international organisations. As Brexit has shown, it is perfectly possible for the Union to shrivel, potentially due to nationalistic pressures applied by a new group of leaders. The following chapters will explain why Europeans haven chosen to pool together an increasing number of instruments for managing capitalism. They will also argue that the European institutional system, while being easier to combine with the *liberty* aspect of capitalism, is also conducive to *solidarity* and *community*. The role of European institutions was to facilitate the combination of various national forms of *solidarity* and *community* capitalism in Europe.

3

A Regulated Market at the Core

'A free trade union should be established [in Europe] ... By the proposed free trade union some part of the loss of organisation and economic efficiency may be retrieved which must otherwise result from the innumerable new political frontiers now created between greedy, jealous, immature, and economically incomplete, nationalist states'.

(Keynes)[1]

Keynes's words from 1919 captured the main interest of establishing a free market area across the European continent, 'economic efficiency', with a view to overcoming the bickering of 'nationalist states'. Keynes primarily had in mind the new states of Central and Eastern Europe, but he also advocated for France and even Great Britain to join this union. The idea of pacifying Europe by creating a large market is therefore a long-standing one, dating back in its contemporary form to at least 1919.

Supporters of a large market in Europe believed it would bring peace and prosperity. Peace would result from intertwined economies, and prosperity from the removal of obstacles to free trade. Critics, on the other hand, stressed that free markets also increase inequality, pollution, and the domination of certain companies. To avoid these shortcomings, European integration developed a regulated market, one that is more than a simple free trade area (see Table 2.2 in Chapter 2), for it seeks to address the negative externalities of free markets, as well as to avoid unfair competition.

This chapter examines the paradoxical success of the most demanding form of market integration, the Single Market established in 1992. It is surprising that twelve European states, among the richest in the world, felt the need to link their markets so closely, even though they could have perfectly well continued alone. The creation of a unified market gradually became the central aspect of European cooperation between 1919 and 1957. In a second phase, the countermodel of the British-style free trade area (FTA) emerged as a major alternative. In a third step, the Common Market of the six continental European countries was established in the 1960s, but its practical regulation remained challenging, as demonstrated by the difficult emergence of a common competition policy. It was not until the revival of Europe in 1984–86 that a genuine Single Market was pursued for the vast majority of the continent's non-communist states. It had three striking features. First, it was put in place quickly between 1987 and 1992, enabling the unprecedented opening of the Union's internal borders. Second, liberalisation was accompanied by enhanced regulation, in accordance with the oxymoron 'freer market, more rules', including a surprising rise of federal competition policy. Third, this move was opposed by several neoliberal figures, such as British Prime Minister Margaret Thatcher in the late 1980s.

3.1 The Market as an Organising Principle for the Continent (1919–57)

The idea of using the market to foster peaceful European cooperation originated with the economist John Maynard Keynes in his *The Economic Consequences of the Peace*.[2] The book has become famous for its criticism of the Treaty of Versailles, but its prospective passages offering policy solutions are usually ignored. Due to the multiplication of European borders arising from the dismantling of the central empires, as well as the exemplary economic success of the US, Keynes, who was a senior civil servant in the British Treasury at the time, proposed creating a 'free trade union' under the auspices of the League of Nations. It would be complemented by the cancellation of war debts, the elimination of reparations, and an international loan by the US. Keynes's plan largely announced the choices of 1947–48, with the Marshall Plan and the creation of the first European organisation that accompanied it.

The idea of a European market remained a moot point during the interwar period, despite the League's efforts to promote free trade. During the World War II, the idea of reorganising Europe around a regulated market persisted, creating an intellectual bridge across the two wars.[3] For example, Jean Monnet of France, who had already taken part in international economic cooperation in the Inter-Allied Board during the World War I, served as deputy secretary general of the League of Nations from 1919 to 1923, during which time he intervened in several areas of economic and financial cooperation. He once again contributed to Inter-Allied cooperation in 1939, and in 1943 became a member of the Comité de Français de Libération Nationale (Free France) in Algiers, under the leadership of Charles de Gaulle. That same year, he wrote a memorandum on post-war Europe in which he envisioned solving the German problem by forming a large European free trade market. This struck him as the best tool for preserving peace and supporting 'economic and social development', including necessary 'social reforms'.[4] After the war, Monnet promoted this idea once again when he drafted the Schuman Declaration of 9 May 1950, which launched the first European Community. Monnet's example, which is not an isolated one, shows that the idea of integrating Europe through the market predated the Cold War.

After 1945, these European ideas adhered to the world economic order promoted by the US, which was based on immediate financial assistance, combined with a gradual return to economic liberalism. War-battered Europe was condemned to scarcity and protectionism in the immediate post-war period, and was heavily dependent on the US, which represented roughly half of global GDP in 1945. American aid was provided in 1945–46 through bilateral agreements and the United Nations Relief and Rehabilitation Administration (UNRAA). The Cold War convinced the Americans to step up their efforts by establishing the multilateral and multi-year Marshall Plan, announced in 1947.

But the Marshall Plan was more than just a Cold War programme, as it marked the beginning of European integration through the creation of a common market. Anxious to avoid the mistakes of the post–World War I period, as well as to consolidate the Western camp in the Cold War, American leaders made their aid multilateral by requiring the debtor states of the Marshall Plan to join the Organisation for European Economic Cooperation (OEEC) created in 1948. The first European organisation, it was based on the idea of gradually creating a large European market driven by the progressive removal of trade restrictions (quotas in particular). Furthermore, the European Payments Union (EPU), created in 1949 with primarily US funding, enabled fluid capital movements in connection with this trade in goods. Although American aid did not rebuild Europe on its own, it provided undeniable support.[5]

However, the same ambiguity that plagued the League persisted with the OEEC: Was it a first step towards a united Europe, or simply a transitional step towards international free trade? For many observers, and especially the British, the OEEC was a transitional body that would disappear once reconstruction was complete.[6]

In this respect, the Schuman Declaration of 1950, and the resulting European Coal and Steel Community (ECSC), marked a real breakthrough as the market clearly became an effective lever in the quest for a permanent and ambitious European organisation, not a simple tool for reconstruction.[7] For the German Chancellor Adenauer, it allowed his country to rejoin the concert of nations on equal footing – at least in the economic sphere – as well as to strengthen both European construction and the cohesion of the Western bloc. The same logic was true for Italy. For the small free trade nations of Benelux (Belgium, the Netherlands and Luxembourg), it was a guarantee that their neighbours would keep their markets open. Lastly, France suffered from a lack of coal, which at the time was the main source of energy as well as a raw material for producing steel. For Paris, the ECSC was useful for gaining access to German coal at the same price as its German competitors, otherwise

German steelmakers would enjoy a major advantage. To achieve this, Paris had to ensure that an efficient market was created, with rules and procedures aimed at preventing German companies from colluding with each other.[8] The US supported this logic of regulated liberalism because it feared the reconstitution of German interwar cartels, which usually supported the National Socialist regime, and were therefore affected by the decartelisation process imposed at the 1945 Potsdam Conference. While based on a liberal principle (using state action to promote pure and perfect competition), 'antitrust' policy and later 'competition' policy were also defended by some left-wing leaders. The British Labourite Hugh Gaitskell, the French Socialists Léon Blum and Guy Mollet, and the German Social Democratic Party all called for more ambitious competition policies at the time.[9]

To ensure this market oversight, the Schuman Declaration invented supranational institutions: a High Authority and a court independent from member states were created to implement the ECSC Treaty, in conjunction with a Council representing the governments. The supranational principle thus emerged, with a view to ensuring neutral regulation of the market. The Community's objective was to achieve an integrated market by combining: 1) free movement of goods via the elimination of customs duties (and not just quotas as with the OEEC); 2) facilitated movement for workers (mainly Italian immigrants); 3) competition policy (oversight of cartels and mergers); and 4) limited elements of industrial and social policy.

However, this first community did not become an embryonic federal state. When a major crisis struck the Belgian coal industry in 1958, the High Authority asked member states to declare a 'state of manifest crisis', which would have given it broad authority over industrial policy, but the governments refused.[10] The Belgian crisis was solved by the national government. Industrial policies relating to coal and steel remained national. Similarly, in terms of competition policy, the High Authority pursued a cautious but moderately useful policy to bring together the French and German points of view, with Paris refusing a renewed concentration that Bonn sought to encourage.[11] While the ECSC disappointed the federalists, it fulfilled its role as a mediator between the Six.

The ECSC's legacy fuelled a debate in the 1950s regarding the launch of other sectoral organisations, such as in health ('white pool') and agriculture ('green pool'). The Netherlands promoted another path forward: the creation of a large integrated market for all products. This solution was launched by the Dutch government in late 1952 as the Beyen Plan, named after the Dutch Minister of Foreign Affairs, Johan Willem Beyen.[12] His ambitious 'common market' project was based on four elements: 1) the elimination of customs duties for all products (not just coal and steel); 2) the harmonisation of external tariffs; 3) the common regulation of serious problems through safeguard clauses implemented after a common procedure (rather than safeguard clauses implemented unilaterally by member states); and 4) a 'European fund' to pay for modernisation projects. The memorandum insisted on coordinating national economic policies, and envisaged the common market as an area for the free movement of goods, capital, and people. As a small, outward-looking country that had lost most of its colonial empire, the Netherlands was keen to promote free trade. Beyen was inspired by the Ouchy Convention in 1932, which had liberalised trade between this country and its two small neighbours to the south, Belgium and Luxembourg, as well as by the Benelux agreement of 1943.

How did the Beyen Plan of 1953 turn into the so-called Common Market treaty signed by the Six in 1957, which created the European Economic Community (EEC)? This result may seem surprising given the modest size of the Netherlands, the existence of many other European or international organisations for trade cooperation (OECE, ECSC, GATT), and reluctance on the part of more protectionist countries such as Italy and France. The latter accepted the Common Market because they secured specific concession in the Treaty of Rome, with French and Italian negotiators focusing on safeguard clauses, the harmonisation of specific social legislation, special arrangements for agriculture and French overseas territories, and free movement of workers and aid for poor regions for Italy. However, these two countries were also convinced of the centrality of free trade: as importers of raw materials (especially energy), they had to export in order to finance their development. There was also the pressure to return to international free trade (especially from the Benelux countries, West Germany, the US, and the UK). Even outside the West, the steady economic development of the Soviet Union (which pioneered the launch of satellites with Sputnik in October 1957) also seemed to vindicate the efficiency of large markets.[13]

The Benelux countries played a crucial role in striking a compromise around a regulated market.[14] The Six decided to launch negotiations for a Common Market in June 1955 in Messina, Italy. The first discussions were held among seven countries – the Six plus Britain – but the British soon withdrew. After a difficult initial phase, Paul-Henri Spaak, the Belgian Minister of Foreign Affairs, proposed a compromise in an April 1956 report that envisioned a highly integrated market. The Spaak Report was accepted as a basis for negotiations by the Six in May 1956. It was subsequently amended by intergovernmental negotiations in 1956 and 1957, but its general philosophy was kept largely intact in the Treaty of Rome in 1957. As stated in Article 2, the Community aimed to establish a 'common market' combined with a 'progressive approximation of economic policies'. The logic was therefore twofold. On the one hand, an ambitious common market was envisaged, based on the four freedoms of movement for goods, services, people, and capital. However, the clauses were automatic and detailed only for goods, with national barriers being largely maintained for the other three categories.

In addition, external trade policies were unified, with the establishment of a common external tariff, and common or harmonised policies were planned for agriculture, competition and specific social issues. Nation-states were left free to act in social and industrial policy. The Treaty of Rome was therefore based on the constitution of a large integrated 'common market' compatible with national policies, and based on the principles of *solidarity* and *community*.

3.2 The Countermodel of the British Free Trade Area

The main European power, the UK, long remained on the sidelines during these discussions, due to its hostility towards supranationality. However, the Spaak Report of April 1956 forced it to counterattack by launching a project for a 'Free Trade Area', which was limited to the gradual abolition of customs duties on industrial goods between its members (whereas the OEEC focused only on quotas and not on tariffs).[15] As a minimalistic trade agreement, it was aimed at all OEEC countries. Considered as a logical complement to the EEC, the British project for a free trade area enjoyed strong support in Western Europe, especially because it would have strengthened the latter in the context of the Cold War. After Stalin's death in 1953, the Soviet Union appeared less threatening under Khrushchev, but remained a brutal dictatorship nevertheless, as demonstrated by the repression of the Hungarian Revolution in the autumn of 1956 and by the Berlin crisis that began in the autumn of 1958. Continental Europeans were still eager to strengthen ties with their British ally, the great European victor of the World War II. When he met the British Prime Minister Harold Macmillan in late 1956, as part of discussions regarding the secret military operation in Suez, the head of the French government, Guy Mollet, even proposed that France join the Commonwealth! While the British took this proposal seriously, and considered several scenarios, it appears to have been a witticism more than anything.[16] In any case, it demonstrated the Anglophilia of both Guy Mollet (who was an English teacher by training) and more generally that of many French leaders.

The FTA nevertheless suffered from a number of technical flaws compared with the Common Market. The Spaak Report made it clear that reducing internal tariffs would not create an integrated market on its own, as this would trigger trade diversions. For example, if France and Belgium were to abolish tariffs between them, then France's high tariffs towards a third party such as the UK would be useless because British imports into France could be channelled through Belgium, a country with a low tariff towards Britain. To avoid such a phenomenon, the solution would be for all EC members to have the same tariffs towards non-EC members (such as the UK or US). In 1957–58, when the FTA was being actively negotiated, French negotiators (sometimes supported by the Italians and the European Commission) emphasised many other technical shortcomings, such as the absence of an arbitration institution to settle disputes, and of specific regimes for agriculture and overseas territories. Even the European League of Economic Cooperation (ELEC), a business association, was divided regarding the FTA, between those who believed the priority was to avoid the 'disturbances that the implementation of the Common Market could cause ...' (i.e., a British perspective), and the secretary general of the League, Lucien Sermon of Belgium, who tried to find a compromise solution alleviating French concerns.[17] Several British businessmen were also critical of the future FTA's inability to protect against 'unfair competition'.[18] This shows that the FTA was a project crafted to address specific British preferences: London had no interest in an agreement beyond the liberalisation of industrial goods in Western Europe, because it used the Commonwealth to import agricultural products. This also vindicated the rationale of the Spaak Report and the Treaty of Rome, namely the need to balance liberalisation with regulation, and to create efficient institutions to uphold the rules.

Besides, from the political point of view, the purpose of the FTA was ambiguous: was it designed to promote European cooperation, thereby complementing the Common Market of the Six? Or was it aimed at diluting the Common Market 'like sugar in tea' (an expression from the time), thereby preparing for a worldwide liberalisation of trade?[19] British archives show that most British decision-makers sought to win over the most liberal EEC members, such as the German Minister of Economics Ludwig Erhard, who was sceptical of a Treaty of Rome that he considered too protectionist.[20] The establishment of an FTA would have convinced Erhard and other EEC sceptics to support the former instead of the latter, condemning the Common Market to oblivion, or at least to a minor role like the ECSC. In 1958 the British negotiator Reginald Maudling, explicitly cited the global liberalisation of trade as the major objective, casting doubt on London's interest in specifically European cooperation.[21]

French doubts prompted the British to consider implementing the agreement without Paris. At the time France was facing a serious financial and political crisis due to the Algerian War of Independence. Budget and trade deficits had drained its coffers. Paris suspended all of its OEEC trade liberalisation commitments in June 1957: the share of liberalised French foreign trade fell from 82 per cent to 0 per cent, while all other Common Market countries hovered around 90 per cent. In the winter of 1957–58, Paris had to beg for funds from the US, and in a supreme humiliation, from West Germany as well.[22] As a result, serious doubt was cast over France's ability to abide by its EEC obligation of trade liberalisation, namely the first 10 per cent reduction in customs duties among the Six scheduled for 1 January 1959. It appeared that France would have to use the various escape clauses it had insisted on including within the Treaty of Rome. France risked being the only European country unable to implement both its OEEC and EEC trade liberalisation

3.2 THE COUNTERMODEL OF THE BRITISH FREE TRADE AREA 55

obligations. The Common Market would have been seriously hampered if one of its main partners did not implement it, thereby paving the way for the British FTA to organise trade in Western Europe. If France kept its market closed due to a shortage of foreign currency resulting from external deficits, then the Common Market would become far less interesting for the Five (the Six minus the French).

Charles de Gaulle's return to power in June 1958 changed the situation by strengthening the French position. Taking advantage of Reginald Maudling's exasperation – the British negotiator suspended discussions on 14 November 1958 – France declared that the discussions had been broken off definitively. In parallel, the new conservative French leader implemented a stern austerity and trade liberalisation plan, the Rueff Plan (named after the liberal economist Jacques Rueff, who advised de Gaulle), despite near general opposition from politicians, civil servants, and members of the business community. This move allowed de Gaulle to honour all French commitments to liberalisation, both within the EEC and the OEEC. This restored French authority, as well as the Common Market's interest for the Five, as France eventually accepted opening up its markets to their products. De Gaulle subsequently implemented all trade liberalisation measures without delays during his leadership (1958–69). Yet he was not a federalist; he primarily saw the EEC as 'a trade treaty' that could stimulate French industry and secure foreign markets for French agricultural products. As a result, despite being an ardent adversary of federalists, de Gaulle can still be seen as a 'Father of Europe', for without him the Common Market would most likely not have won out over the FTA.[23]

The British then retreated to a less ambitious substitute, the European Free Trade Association (EFTA), a mini free trade area between seven countries surrounding the European Community, but not wishing to join it out of hostility to federalism: the UK, Switzerland, Denmark, Sweden, Norway, Austria, and the Portuguese dictatorship. It was the 'Europe of the Seven' against the 'Europe of the Six', or, according to observers at the time, the 'Outer Seven' against the 'Inner Six'. This demonstrates the centrality of the young EEC, even for the Europeans that were not part of it. Intra-EEC trade increased more quickly than trade between EEC member states and the outside world.[24] However, supporters of the free trade area were not defeated. In his *International Order and Economic Integration* published in 1959, the ordoliberal Wilhelm Röpke called for abandoning the Common Market in favour of a free trade area.[25] In 1960–61, German officials close to the ordoliberals, such as Alfred Müller-Armack, the Secretary of State for European Affairs, launched a project for a customs union between the EEC and the EFTA, albeit to no avail.[26]

The British FTA quickly became a countermodel for European decision-makers attached to the Community. In 1979, the French Ministry of Foreign

Affairs denounced the risk of the Community becoming a 'free trade area' under British influence.[27] Even on the other side of the Channel, there were sometimes negative references to the FTA from pro-European voices. In 1984, just before the Fontainebleau Council, Thatcher's European adviser David Williamson recommended that she conclude her presentation with the incisive phrase: 'We are arguing for radical progress, far beyond the concept of a free trade area.'[28] In 1985, a famous report by a former member of the Thatcher government, Lord Cockfield, asserted that 'a well-developed free trade area offers significant advantages ... But it would fail and fail dismally to release the energies of the people of Europe.'[29]

The EFTA also failed because the Six supported a gradual liberalisation of global trade. A common external tariff was introduced to replace national customs duties, as states delegated their external trade policy to the Community. They defined a common position, with the Commission representing them in international negotiations at the GATT. It was the Commission that negotiated on behalf of the Six during most of the Kennedy Round (1964–67), the first major post-war multilateral trade negotiation, albeit doing so in close contact with the six member states. The EEC was therefore a power multiplier, as its individual members would have carried much less weight with the Americans if they had negotiated alone. As a result, even a leader hostile to supranationality such as Charles de Gaulle supported the Commission in these negotiations, even during the empty chair crisis.[30] The negotiations were successful, as customs duties were reduced by about one-third on both sides of the Atlantic, and the Six preserved the Common Agricultural Policy (CAP) created in 1962. Trade liberalisation negotiations continued despite the oil crisis with the Tokyo Round conducted between 1973 and 1979. While there was a consensus for a further reduction in tariffs of around 35 per cent, the problem of non-tariff barriers to trade remained, namely the technical barriers that multiplied in the 1970s. This shows that removing custom duties was not sufficient on its own to create a unified market.

3.3 Establishing a Unified Market through Competition Policy

Removing trade barriers could not in and of itself ensure fair competition. Setting up a common competition policy was essential not only to maximise market efficiency, but to also alleviate protectionist tensions among the Six by ensuring that the same rules applied to all actors. It would be pointless to abolish custom duties among the Six if companies were allowed to split markets among themselves thanks to cartels, dominant position, or state aid. It was all the more important for the French in particular – as demonstrated by the example of the ECSC – since mighty German companies remained extremely powerful actors.

The Treaty of Rome (1957) therefore established common rules to monitor practices such as cartels (an agreement between companies remaining independent), abuse of dominant position, and state aid (a public subsidy to a company).[31]

However, establishing a common European competition policy was far from obvious in 1957. First, the Six were not ready to grant the Commission broad powers over economic regulation. Second, there was hardly any national competition policy in Western Europe at this stage. Among the Six, only West Germany had a genuinely independent competition policy, but the German law was passed only in July 1957, a few months after the signing of the Treaty of Rome in March. The *Gesetz gegen Wettbewerbsbeschränkungen* (GWB) was the first law in Europe to create an autonomous 'competition policy', applied by an independent authority, the Bundeskartellamt. The Germans were influenced by the ordoliberal approach, which postulated the need for the authorities to institute a liberal order because it was not spontaneous, and to apply its rules to both the state and private actors through the creation of independent authorities (hence the Bundeskartellamt, or in the monetary realm the Bundesbank, also created in 1957).[32] France and the Netherlands also had competition policy provisions, but they were weaker. A common European competition policy had already been established for coal and steel within the framework of the ECSC, but it remained quite limited. The High Authority played a useful role in mediating between French and West German interests, without being able to enforce an ambitious policy. In other words, the European Community had to invent a public policy from scratch.

The Treaty of Rome bears the hallmark of the French–German compromise. Paris had two objectives. First and foremost, it wanted stringent provisions to control large companies, otherwise the larger German conglomerates would have dominated their smaller French counterparts. Second, it requested strict rules against restrictive practices in distribution. France was suffering from high inflation, which the government sought to reduce by increased competition in distribution, notably through the creation of supermarkets. West Germany was more interested in fighting cartels and preserving the GWB, which was adopted immediately after the Treaty of Rome following a long debate.[33] As a result, the provisions of the Treaty of Rome encompassed both the German emphasis on combatting cartels (Article 85 EEC), and the French insistence on monitoring large companies through 'abuse of dominant position' (Article 86 EEC). However, it did not include merger control (as the ECSC experience had been disappointing in this respect). The treaty's provisions were both ambitious and vague, leaving much leeway as to the institutional framework of the future competition policy, in addition to its substance.

It was not until 1962 with 'Regulation 17/62', the first regulation (a European law) implementing the Treaty of Rome, that a specific ordoliberal interpretation took shape.[34] Under the influence of the first European

Commissioner for Competition, Hans von der Groeben of Germany, it was a fairly German interpretation of the treaty that took hold, with priority given to fighting cartels and establishing a cartel notification system. Von der Groeben also secured the centralisation of decisions at the Commission, which was not evident in the Treaty of Rome. During the negotiations surrounding the Treaty of Rome, he had proposed creating a strong institutional framework to enforce competition rules.[35] French influence persisted through the Commission's particularly repressive approach towards exclusive distribution agreements, mirroring French legislation, which was stricter than its German counterpart in this area. Bonn opposed von der Groeben when the latter wanted to prohibit an exclusivity agreement between the German firm Grundig and the French distributor Consten.[36] For Bonn, certain distribution agreements were useful for penetrating foreign markets. However, from the European Commission's point of view, von der Groeben believed that this type of agreement limited competition and intra-European trade. The Commission subsequently prohibited the agreement in 1964, contradicting the German government's position. The latter attempted to have the Commission's decision overturned by the Court of Justice. Ulrich Everling, a senior official at the Ministry of Economics (who later became a judge at the Court of Justice), met with the Court's Advocate General, Karl Roemer.[37] Roemer asked for the annulment of the *Grundig–Consten* decision in his official opinion, but he did not have the support of the Court, which broadly confirmed the Commission's decision (albeit with a reduced impact).[38] This pressure from the German government reflected Commissioner von der Groeben's independence – he was not Bonn's puppet.

However, beyond this first decision, the Commission struggled to apply Regulation 17/62, as it was swamped with over 36,000 cartel notifications, which were handled by only sixty-eight senior (class A) officials in 1964. In addition, the Commission had to pursue unnotified illegal agreements, but companies became increasingly adept at hiding their cartels. Using the archives of Scandinavian and Finnish companies in the paper industry, a historian has successfully reconstructed how they took greater precautions to hide their agreements due to the growing threat of prosecution by European and Community authorities (despite the fact that Sweden and Finland were outside the Community).[39] Before the war, cartels were quasi-public; after the war, they were concealed behind inter-professional bodies. Officials were later forbidden from carrying compromising documents during their travels in Europe. The surprising transparency of these archives shows how the constraint of competition policy became more pressing, thereby forcing the business world (including some established outside the Community) to change its habits.

The situation was even worse with respect to state aid. The provisions of the Treaty of Rome, which are still in force today, are ambiguous: state aid affecting free competition in intra-EC trade was prohibited, but with broad exceptions. In 1960, Competition Commissioner Hans von der Groeben launched studies on national public interventions. He used experts such as the German ordoliberal Ernst-Joachim Mestmäcker, and focused especially on France. He promoted a global 'competition order' based especially on the principle of strict equality of treatment between private and public companies.[40] He nevertheless failed to implement this programme, as member states resisted the Commission. Even the German government was much more cautious than von der Groeben: in 1958, the official instructions to German permanent representatives concentrated on defending German regional aid schemes.[41]

The ordoliberal offensive resumed in May 1978 via the German Minister of Economics Otto Graf Lambsdorff. He released a German memorandum calling for increased monitoring of state aid.[42] The debates were bogged down by hostility from countries granting massive state aid, such as the UK and Italy. This discussion was linked to an ongoing reflection at the OECD regarding 'positive adjustment policies'.[43] According to the OECD, aid that delayed the structural adjustments demanded by the market should be rejected. Instead of such 'defensive' sectoral aid, general measures to improve the economic environment (infrastructure, environment, research and development, labour mobility, etc.) should be favoured. However, while the intellectual debate evolved, the Commission remained largely powerless in 1980, as admitted by national administrations themselves.[44]

The situation changed from 1981 onwards due to three reasons: an ideological context less favourable to neo-mercantilist ideas; the difficulties generated by the vigorous French stimulus plan of 1981–82, which was characterised by massive aid to companies; and the arrival of new leaders seeking to apply the rules for monitoring aid. In Brussels, the new Competition Commissioner, Frans Andriessen of the Netherlands, increased the number of procedures, and became more proactive in monitoring public shareholding in companies.[45] The debate within the Commission became tense, with French Commissioner François-Xavier Ortoli calling for more tolerance, and the German Commissioner Karl-Heinz Narjes advocating a tougher approach. In 1984, the Commission struck a compromise by defining its position more precisely than in the Treaty of Rome: it would not consider equity investments as aid if the state behaved like a long-term private investor.[46]

All member states had 'skeletons in the cupboards' with respect to state aid, as one British official remarked in 1980,[47] but they reacted differently to the Commission's offensive, with cooperation in London and Bonn, and confrontation in Paris. In London, the first Thatcher government continued to provide massive aid to several ailing companies (shipbuilding, automobile) at the start of the 1980s, but Whitehall was open to negotiation with the European Commission.[48] The British government negotiated an exemption from the

Commission to resume its massive aid to the Harland & Wolff shipyard, which launched the Titanic in 1912. The neoliberal Thatcher willingly allowed massive subsidies to a company that played a crucial role for the 'Protestant community' in Northern Ireland, according to one of her advisors.[49] However, another Whitehall official recognised that 'even if all the employees worked for nothing, the company would still not be viable'.[50]

In Bonn, the attitude was twofold. On the one hand, the Germans were on the offensive, pleading for a tougher line against excessive state aid. The German government complained to the Court of Justice about the Commission's decision in November 1981 not to initiate proceedings against a major Belgian aid plan to the textile industry.[51] In 1984 the Court ruled that the Commission should have established a procedure allowing each state to comment on the aid in question.[52] The German mobilisation was linked to pressure from German textile organisations, which sought to use Community competition policy to enforce discipline in Europe. On the other hand, Bonn was targeted by the Commission for its regional aid, especially its specific schemes designed for areas bordering East Germany, for which Bonn had obtained an exemption in the Treaty of Rome.[53] The Volkswagen factory in Wolfsburg, the manufacturer's largest factory, was located in this area, which provided it significant advantages (infrastructure aid, tax provisions, etc.). In response to the Commission, Bonn redirected its aid scheme to emphasise criteria compatible with the Treaty of Rome, such as specific support for SMEs, energy saving, environmental protection, and research and development.[54]

The Commission's relationship with France was more problematic. French aid was more visible than German aid, since the latter was largely distributed through regional channels and tax breaks rather than national subsidies.[55] Above all, the French administration was still marked by a principled hostility to the Commission's powers in this area. While German officials used the Court, the French were more subdued: when a French company complained about specific Dutch aid in 1983, the French government advised it to lodge a complaint on its own, without official backing, for fear of triggering a counter-offensive by the Dutch government against Paris in other cases.[56] While the British tried to negotiate with the Commission, officials at the French Ministry of Industry deliberately ignored it, much to the chagrin of diplomats. For example in 1982, talks were held between the office of French Commissioner Ortoli and the Ministry of Foreign Affairs to adapt a future aid scheme for textiles.[57] But the new scheme was published by the Ministry of Industry without taking into account the opinions of diplomats, who had advocated for more pro-European wording (like the Germans did when they adapted their regional aid schemes). Finally, the Commission referred the matter to the Court of Justice, which condemned France on 15 November 1983. In November 1984, it was the Minister of Foreign Affairs himself, Roland Dumas, who had to remind his colleague Pierre Bérégovoy, the Minister of

Economy and Finance, of the need to send complete information without delay to the Commission.

Under centre-right President Valéry Giscard d'Estaing, France was relatively favourable towards EC competition policy, because it was still fairly weak, and its level of state aid was within the EEC average (on a par with Germany). Paris became much more hostile when the Socialists came to power in 1981.[58] The French government asked for a relaxation of EC competition policy in 1982-83, with respect to both state aid and cartels. However, attitudes later evolved with the 'single market' project.

3.4 The 'Relaunch of Europe' around the 'Single Market'

The 'relaunch of Europe' was an expression coined in 1984 and used widely across the Common Market, including in London, to describe the optimistic mood during the period 1984-86, which saw the launch of the 'single market' programme.[59] While the Common Market was based on the removal of custom duties (which was effective in 1968), the Single Market sought to remove all obstacles to trade that triggered border controls. It translated into the harmonisation of broad swaths of legislation touching on standards, as well as some specific taxes. It was therefore a much more political project, with concrete implications for European citizens, not just companies.

During the early 1980s, European institutions were largely paralysed by the so-called British Budget Question (BBQ) or British Budgetary Dispute (or more colloquially the 'Bloody British Dispute'). The British were paying much more than they were receiving (due to the huge weight of agriculture in European expenditure), while they were relatively poor in the Europe of Nine at the time.[60] This dispute was linked to reforms targeting the CAP, which many actors, including French ones, supported because it represented almost 80 per cent of Community expenditures, generated overproduction and created tensions with third countries due to its protectionism. Another issue was that of Iberian enlargement, which raised competition issues for French agriculture. These three major, interconnected disputes were eventually solved in 1984, when Mitterrand accepted Iberian enlargement for 1986. At the Fontainebleau summit in June 1984, Paris and Bonn conceded a significant reduction in CAP expenditure and the British budget contribution. In exchange, London accepted a 'relaunch' of Europe. This took the form of the Single European Act, a treaty concluded in February 1986 that enacted the Single Market programme. In the meantime, the EEC had expanded to twelve members with the entry of Spain and Portugal on 1 January 1986.

The birth of the Single Market programme has sometimes been presented as the result of pressure from neoliberal groups, business organisations in particular.[61] But this interpretation captures only part of the reality, which actually included five stages. First, as early as 1957-58, both the French and the German governments supported a progressive harmonisation of all trade legislation relating to the Common Market. In Paris, government officials had called for the parallel development of liberalisation and harmonisation since 1955.[62] Thereafter, the French largely abandoned this stance, thanks to the good results of the trade balance in the 1960s, in addition to de Gaulle's intergovernmental vision. In Bonn, the government's official instructions pleaded for the gradual harmonisation of all commercial legislation needed to fulfil the Treaty's objectives.[63] It did not mean that both Paris and Bonn had already planned the internal market programme as early as the late 1950s, but rather that the idea of removing non-tariff barriers was present from the beginning.

Then in a second step, the Commission took over the project. In 1968, when the removal of custom duties was complete, it presented a global programme to remove non-tariff barriers to trade in accordance with several principles, such as the mutual recognition of conformity checks. Adopted in 1969, this programme remained a dead letter for a lack of political will of the part of member states. Unanimity was required at the Council, so a single state could block harmonisation. In London, a 1974 Whitehall note was particularly scathing: it targeted Ivo Schwartz of Germany, the Commission official in charge of harmonisation:

> His approach to company law is theoretical rather than pragmatic. Exponent of the 'man in Palermo' theory i.e. that the unsophisticated Sicilian investor has a right to the same safeguards when he invests in a Company registered in Milan or in Edinburgh. Taken to its extreme this would mean a uniform company law throughout the Community.[64]

London rejected this 'Man in Palermo' approach, out of hostility to supranationality. The same reluctance was present in Paris, tinged with protectionism at the beginning of François Mitterrand's term (1981-83).[65] The Commission still promoted the project throughout the 1970s and 1980s, but with little success before 1985.

Thirdly, the European Court of Justice (ECJ) supported harmonisation. The opinion of the judges is difficult to discern, because the ECJ's internal debates remain secret. Some were in favour of supranational integration, but not all, such as Ulrich Everling of Germany.[66] On the whole, however, it seems that a market-based approach hostile to any form of national protectionism was present in the academic publications of Pierre Pescatore of Luxembourg (judge 1967-85), René Joliet of Belgium (judge 1984-95), Verloren van Theemaat of the Netherlands (Advocate General, 1981-86), and Ulrich Everling of Germany (judge, 1980-88).[67] In the *Cassis de Dijon* case from 1979, the Court defined the principle of mutual recognition (automatic recognition of foreign law without harmonisation), but limited it with four broad exemptions: the effectiveness of tax controls, 'fair trading', consumer protection, and public health. The *Cassis de Dijon* ruling was considered a turning point by many observers,[68] but other analysts have pointed to its limitations.[69] A study of the Commission's archives confirms the second interpretation: Paolo Cecchini, the future author of the famous report on the cost of 'non-Europe', who at the time was the Deputy Director General for the Internal Market, considered the *Cassis de Dijon* ruling interesting but not revolutionary.[70] In other words, the Court could not create a single market *ex nihilo*.

Fourthly, various European circles were active. In the European Parliament, which had grown in standing since its election by universal suffrage in 1979, many parliamentarians called for the removal of customs barriers to trade.[71] Jacques Delors, then a simple Member of the European Parliament, related an anecdote during the plenary session of 14 October 1980 about the Belgian cyclist Jean-Luc Vandenbroucke, who was accused of illegal imports during a custom check because he transported his bicycle in the trunk of his car to train on the other side of the border in northern France, a few kilometres away from his home. The most dynamic members of the European Parliament formed the 'Kangaroo Group', named for its ability to jump barriers, to lobby in favour of removing border controls. The European Parliament exerted significant influence over the intellectual debate by commissioning a report on the relaunch of Europe, drafted by the French civil servant Michel Albert and the British economist Albert Ball. Their report popularised the notion of the 'cost of non-Europe', which is to say the excessive expenditure caused by national barriers to trade within the Community. The Commission subsequently sought to scientifically estimate this 'cost of non-Europe' by commissioning the Cecchini Report in 1988, named after Paolo Cecchini, the former Deputy Director General for the Internal Market.[72] It concluded that the potential gain would be 5 per cent of European GNP. The process was also supported by certain economic circles, such as the European Round Table for Industry (ERT), an employers' organisation made up solely of CEOs from the largest European multinationals, such as Fiat, Shell, and Philips. But many companies did not support the creation of a vast integrated European market, with some adopting a 'reluctant' or 'defensive' posture.[73]

Finally, the main obstacle remained member states, in addition to unanimous voting at the Council. The conversion of member states to the internal market project took place around 1982–83. The Benelux countries tabled a memorandum calling for the elimination of technical barriers in October 1983.[74] In Bonn, the programme seemed useful in limiting the protectionist temptations of its neighbours, which were recurrent in Paris.[75] Some Germans were reluctant, as demonstrated in 1982 when Commissioner Narjes received his compatriot Dieter von Würzen, who was the German State of Secretary for Economic Affairs, and hesitant towards the project. Von Würzen pointed out the risk of promoting lower standards, which would lead to poor quality products.[76] Moreover, German regions (Länder) were reluctant to harmonise standards, because they had confidence in the national DIN system.[77]

In London, support for the internal market agenda grew cautiously.[78] At a meeting in September 1981, Thatcher requested studies on potential new trade agreements, either European or global. She did not express any preference for the Community. In response, the studies conducted by the administration highlighted the protectionism of Britain's main partners, France and Germany: 'German industry also benefits from the most effective "non-tariff barrier" in Europe, DIN standards. Thus, the French for example have made several hundred applications in the past few years for particular French standards to be recognised as equivalent to DIN, but so far not even one has been approved.' Even the Americans were in the line of fire: 'The US government, while formally eschewing specific support to companies for export projects, nonetheless is a past master at using political clout and the leverage of civil/military aid to establish a presence for US exporters for major projects.' Most of the policymakers involved in this debate stressed the interest of the EEC in solving this challenge as compared to the GATT. The Community offered a legal arsenal to combat non-tariff barriers to trade, especially if the internal market programme was adopted. Moreover, 1982 was marked by difficult discussions in the GATT between the US and the UK, in connection with President Reagan's offensive against British steel, as well as the Soviet gas pipeline issue (see Chapter 6), both of which demonstrated the value of European cooperation. In November 1982, Whitehall defined a position that was on principle favourable towards the programme for completing an internal market.

In the meantime, in Paris, the new Socialist President François Mitterrand pursued a more protectionist strategy in 1981–82, dubbed 'the reconquest of the domestic market', and marked by the so-called Battle of Poitiers (the original battle was fought in 732 against the Umayyad). In 1982, the French government faced a new invasion, but this time in the more benevolent form of Japanese videocassette recorders. On 21 October 1982, the Ministry of the Economy, headed by Laurent Fabius at the time, mandated that all video recorders imported to France transit through Poitiers in order to undergo formalities. This became the 'Poitiers Video Recorder' affair. The undeclared aim was to discourage imports of what was a highly sought-after and innovative product, namely through lengthy customs procedures in a town in central France, far from harbours (where they arrived from Japan) and from the biggest cities (where they were sold).

This was followed by a formal negative opinion from the European Commission condemning these measures and inviting France to abandon them, which happened within a few months. Besides, France's trade balance continued to deteriorate, and isolation loomed in Europe. At the EC Council of Ministers meeting in January 1982, almost all member states were concerned about these French measures, and asked the Commission to monitor them.[79]

Faced with this failure of the unilateral protectionist approach, the French government changed its strategy and went on the European counter-offensive.

At the Copenhagen European Council in December 1982, President Mitterrand pointed to the many non-tariff barriers to trade present in other countries, especially the German beer law. The Reinheitsgebot (Beer Purity Decree), issued in Bavaria in 1516, limited the number of ingredients in beer to four – malt, hops, yeast, and water – hindering imports, notably of certain French beers. The Commission's plans for European harmonisation allowed more ingredients, but German producers mobilised against 'chemical beer'. This thorny issue was solved only after a 1987 court ruling that forced West Germany to open up its beer market unless there was a proven health risk for a specific product.

German Chancellor Helmut Kohl accepted Mitterrand's proposal to create an ad hoc group to study these issues.[80] In a sign of its importance, this technical effort was often mentioned during bilateral political conversations, such as during the French–German consultations of May 1983 in Paris.[81] The results were nevertheless modest, as the French were unable to establish that German protectionism existed. The bilateral path was thus seen as not promising in addressing non-tariff barriers.

The failure of the unilateral and bilateral paths led French decision-makers to consider the Community path. At the Fontainebleau European Council in 1984, Paris agreed to the idea of a Single Market after obtaining concessions (adoption of the Esprit programme to fund research, a 'new trade policy instrument' that was actually a protectionist tool, advantages for its farmers, and resolutions in the social field).[82] In return, Paris and Bonn granted budgetary concessions to the UK, thereby strengthening the CAP.[83] According to President Mitterrand's advisor Jacques Attali, this was an essential agreement, otherwise the UK could have suspended its payments to the Community budget, thereby jeopardising aid to French farmers.[84] He estimated that 40 per cent of French agri-food exports were connected to European aid.

After Fontainebleau, the new president of the Commission, Delors, organised the relaunch around the Single Market project. He presented his programme to the European Parliament on 14 January 1985, beginning with an economic issue, namely the crucial importance of 'completing the single market' with a 'harmonisation of rules'.[85] Delors politicised this issue by denouncing a 'feudal Europe', announcing the goal of a market with no internal borders by 1992 (the time of two four year-long Commissions), and by making it central to a citizen's revival of Europe: 'We would ... like to see the people of Europe, your electors, enjoying the daily experience of a tangible Europe, a real Community where travel, communication and trade are possible without any hindrance.' The institutional consequence was the call to adopt qualified majority voting in the Council of Ministers for legislation relating to the unification of the internal market. Delors's speech also touched on other aspects, both social and neomercantilist, all of which revolved around the Single Market.

The Commissioner for the Internal Market, Arthur Cockfield of the UK, transposed this objective into a memorandum listing 300 pieces of legislation to be harmonised, along with several methods of harmonisation.[86] Instead of discussing lengthy directives in the Council, which were bogged down by technical details, Cockfield proposed that Community institutions concentrate on essential principles, with technical specifications being drawn up by international sectoral bodies. By way of example, the Commission mentioned the European Conference of Postal and Telecommunications Administrations (CEPT), an intergovernmental body of national experts including nineteen European countries (see Chapter 6). The Commission wanted to systematise this approach, because the involvement of these standardisation bodies relieved the Council of time-consuming tasks.

This project was then transposed in the Single European Act, signed by all twelve EC members in February 1986. It states that by 31 December 1992: 'The internal market shall comprise an area without internal frontiers in which the free movement of goods, persons, services and capital is ensured in accordance with the provisions of this Treaty' (Article 13). Qualified majority voting prevailed for issues relating to the Single Market, except in three areas: taxation, free movement of persons, and the 'rights and interests of employed persons'. Article 18 completed the system by providing for qualified majority voting for provisions on 'health, safety, environmental protection and consumer protection'. Delors would have liked to go further by obtaining qualified majority voting for indirect taxation, which was one of the major causes of border controls.[87] Article 18 states that harmonisation 'will take as a basis a high level of protection', which apparently satisfied the social demands of Kohl, who emphasised German fears of seeing its standards lowered.[88]

3.5 The Rapid Opening of the Internal Market: 'Freer Market, More Rules'

The deadline to complete the internal market by 1992, which was announced by Delors in 1985, was met. This institutional success resulted from two factors: the extent of the legislative work carried out between 1987 and 1992; and the hybrid nature of the Single Market.

The Single Market was gradually implemented between July 1987, when the Single European Act took effect, and late 1992, when internal borders and the controls that went with them were abolished. A second phase began from 1993 onwards, marked by ongoing efforts towards harmonisation. Community institutions thus acted very quickly, since the 300 pieces of legislation provided for in the Cockfield White Paper had to first be proposed by the Commission, and then adopted by the Council, not to mention consideration of the European Parliament's opinion under the new cooperation procedure. Paradoxically, the deepening of the market required more regulation, as captured by the paradox: 'Freer Markets, More Rules'.[89]

A couple of major laws stand out amid this flurry of legislation.[90] In 1988, the directive on public procurement liberalised the awarding of public contracts, one of the main sources of the 'cost of non-Europe' identified in the Albert Ball Report. This played a key role in driving down the price of certain services and breaking up local cartels. In 1989, the 'Television without Frontiers' Directive was adopted. It responded to the technological changes arising from the growing number of frequencies resulting from the sector's liberalisation, as well as the establishment of minimum standards for broadcast programmes (concerning advertising, decency, European preference, etc.) at the insistence of the French government.[91] This directive exemplifies the balance between the principles of *liberty*, *solidarity*, and *community*.

With respect to taxes, discussions were more difficult, particularly because of the opposition between Margaret Thatcher and her former minister Arthur Cockfield, who became European Commissioner. The departure of the intransigent British prime minister in late 1990 broke the deadlock. Private individuals were subject to border controls relating to VAT, as well as restrictions on products subject to particular taxes (known as 'excise duties'), such as petrol, alcohol, and tobacco. The removal of physical barriers within the Community thus depended on an agreement regarding these taxes, which was finally reached in October 1992.[92] A partial harmonisation of VAT rates and excise rules was agreed upon, but states kept a certain amount of leeway in these sensitive areas. Finally, by late 1992 the Community had adopted over 90 per cent of the measures identified in the White Paper, with a transposition rate (into national law) over 75 per cent on average.[93]

The free movement of persons was extended from workers, the main category originally covered by these provisions, to other groups such as students (with the start of the Erasmus Programme in 1987) and pensioners, who obtained a right of residence in 1990. In addition, the intergovernmental Schengen Agreement – first concluded in 1985 outside the EC by five states (the Six minus Italy) before being incorporated into Community law in 1997 – allowed for the further reduction of border controls for individuals.[94] Here too, the idea was quite old, being first promoted officially at the Paris European Council in 1974; but it led to a political agreement only in 1985, thanks to the 'relaunch of Europe'.

Lastly, the external counterpart of the Single Market was the GATT Uruguay Round, which ran from 1986 to 1994. It led to a further reduction in customs duties, and for the first time extended the logic of liberalisation to the services and agricultural sectors (see Chapter 6).

3.6 The Surprising Rise of Competition Policy

The European Community is a global exception, as it is the only space in which supranational competition policy exists.[95] This means that one of the most basic prerogatives of the state, cartel control – dating back to kings, who granted privileges to certain merchants and market places – has been federalised, as has the power to control mergers and subsidies to companies (in the 1980s). This surprising development is sometimes explained by sheer technical logic: if Europeans wanted to build a borderless area, they had to harmonise their rules on subsidies to companies. However, this functionalist reasoning is insufficient: if the technical need to harmonise was so pressing, then why did Europeans fail to harmonise corporate taxation? It is surely illogical, from a purely technical point of view, to establish a common market that encompasses tax havens and high-tax countries, but this was nevertheless the case. Besides, the legal framework did not change, as the treaty articles on competition policy (cartels and state aid) have remained the same since 1957. The 1986 Single European Act, which established the Single Market programme, did not change the provisions on competition policy. In others words, a Single Market without a powerful and supranational competition policy could easily have emerged. Archives show that the origin of enhanced control over state aid control was actually the initiative of two energetic Competition Commissioners, Peter Sutherland and Leon Brittan, who were supported by a majority at the College of Commissioners, as well as the Court of Justice.

In 1985, a new Competition Commissioner, Peter Sutherland of Ireland, took the helm in Brussels. The former captain of a rugby team during his studies at Trinity College, he brought a more confrontational stance to the Commission informed by his stay in the US, where he was impressed by the possibility of advancing law through legal cases that were subsequently upheld by the Supreme Court, which he called 'integration through constitutional law'.[96] Upon his arrival at the Commission, he established an inventory of existing state aid, and adopted a more aggressive attitude towards industrial policies.

Member states were divided by this offensive. In France, many officials from the Ministry of Industry were hostile, as they wanted to keep their industrial policy intact.[97] Conversely, officials from the Ministry of Finance's Budget Directorate were interested in reduced subsidies for financial reasons. The Department for European Affairs (SGCI), the Department for Regional Policy (DATAR), and even the Ministry of Industry saw a potential interest in Sutherland's new assertiveness, namely controlling discreet German regional aid. The most interested French official was Alain Madelin, one of the French pioneers of neoliberalism, who became the Minister of Industry in March 1986. As early as April 1986, Madelin wrote to Sutherland to explain the new market-oriented French industrial policy.[98] For example, in June 1986 the French government decided to stop aid to shipbuilding for three of the four large yards, leading to their rapid closure.[99] However, French officials still kept a confrontational stance towards Brussels in many other cases. In the UK, Sutherland imposed halving British aid for the Rover takeover (by British Aerospace).[100] Sutherland's offensive extended to other areas.

3.7 Liberalisation and Europeanisation of New Sectors

In the West, many sectors formerly dominated by monopolies and oligopolies moved to free competition in the 1980s and 1990s, starting with telecommunications and air transport.[101] This was combined with extensive Europeanisation, which was quite surprising since these sectors were governed by strong national policies coupled with long-standing international agreements. Besides, the Single European Act did not touch upon this area. Hence, this Europeanisation was driven by the activism of the Commission, in particular Commissioners Sutherland and Brittan.

Liberalisation was driven by ideological reasons – such as the conviction that the free market would provide services with a better quality-price ratio – as well as by growing financial constraints after 1973. Technological reasons also played a role, with prices falling due to technical progress. For air transport, this was reflected in new types of aircraft, such as the large Boeing 747 and the small 737, which entered service in 1970 and 1968 respectively, and in the growing competition from Airbus from the 1970s onwards. Technical progress was accompanied by marketing innovations, with the development of charter flights and low-cost airlines. In the telecommunications sector, the shift to digital communications, the launch of numerous satellites, and convergence with information technology led to both massive growth in traffic and plummeting prices.

This posed a challenge to the earlier neomercantilist regulations. In a market where supply is scarce and expensive, it is natural for states to protect a small number of players from foreign competition. National postal and telecommunications giants, as well as national flag carriers, had to serve unprofitable destinations and customers for reasons of territorial cohesion or political prestige. As a result, only national airlines were allowed to operate on most routes, and prices were set by intergovernmental agreements. But when supply became more abundant because of technological innovation, neomercantilism appeared unduly restrictive.

Liberalisation started in the US, where President Carter launched the deregulation of air transport in 1978. Later on, two European countries were liberalising their own national rules: the Netherlands (with Nelly Kroes, the liberal transport minister and future competition commissioner), and the UK (especially beginning in October 1983 with the new Secretary of State for Transport, Nicholas Ridley).[102] The latter signed a first bilateral liberalisation agreement with the Netherlands in June 1984, and then with West Germany in December 1984. The deregulation of air transport could therefore have occurred through a web of intergovernmental agreement, rather than through European integration.

In the Common Market, Lord Bethell, a Conservative Member of European Parliament from the UK, ran the Freedom of the Skies campaign. He wrote to the Commission in 1981 requesting that the free competition articles of the Treaty of Rome be applied to air transport.[103] But Commissioner Frans Andriessen was reluctant to attack the traditional organisation of air transport, which was based on a combination of bilateral and multilateral intergovernmental agreements, conducted within the framework of the nineteen-member European Civil Aviation Conference (ECAC) and the International Civil Aviation Organisation (ICAO). Lord Bethell then brought a complaint before the European Court of Justice, only to have it dismissed.[104] The European Parliament ultimately took up the case, and filed its own action for failure to act in 1983, which resulted in the Council being condemned for failing to act, although the judgment was not very constraining.[105]

When Sutherland arrived at the Commission in 1985, he used a new tool to foster and Europeanise this nascent effort at liberalisation: a direct attack on airlines even in the absence of Community regulation, with a view to pushing for a favourable interpretation of the articles from the Treaty of Rome. In 1985 he attacked the Greek company Olympic Airways for abuse of dominant position, and the two national flag carriers Air France and British Airways for their domination of the Paris–London route.[106] This activism caused a stir at the Commission because the Commissioner for Transport, Stanley Clinton-Davis of the UK, a member of the Labour Party, was much more reluctant than Sutherland. In the *Nouvelles Frontières* case of 30 April 1986, the Court reaffirmed the Commission's prerogatives, while recalling the need to work with the Council. Finally, in December 1987 the Council of Ministers adopted the regulation introducing a first breach of governmental prerogatives in setting airfare.[107] Liberalisation was supported by the UK and the Netherlands – and with less enthusiasm – even by West Germany and France under Jacques Chirac's centre-right government.[108] Liberalisation continued in the 1990s, with a second package in 1990, and a third in 1992.

The same combination of factors was at work in telecommunications, except that the UK preceded the US.[109] In 1981, Thatcher separated postal and telecommunications activities. In 1982, a second operator, Mercury, was allowed to do business alongside the national company British Telecom, which was subsequently privatised in 1984. An independent regulatory authority for the sector, the Office of Telecommunications (Oftel), was created to regulate the market, paving the way for many similar reforms in various sectors and countries. At the same time, deregulation also affected the US, where an antitrust lawsuit dismantled the telecommunications giant AT&T (the heir to the prestigious Bell Laboratories) into seven companies.

Here too, Sutherland was the driving force behind the Europeanisation of regulation in sectors that could otherwise have been regulated exclusively by states, or by other international organisations. Sutherland threatened to sue the companies in order to pressure the Council to legislate. In 1988 he successfully issued a first directive opening up terminal equipment such as telephone sets to competition.[110] France, supported by Italy, West Germany, Belgium, and Greece, challenged the 1988 directive, but the Court of Justice ultimately ruled in the Commission's favour in 1991.[111] This lawsuit demonstrates the controversial and assertive nature of Sutherland's policy.

Liberalisation had an impact on another area less affected by technical progress, but essential to completing the Single Market programme: road transport. It was liberalised in 1987 with the progressive lifting of numerous restrictions designed to protect national operators and railway companies.

Liberalisation and Europeanisation were then strengthened when Leon Brittan of the UK became Competition Commissioner in 1989. A former minister of Margaret Thatcher and the brother of Samuel Brittan, one of the journalists who spread the neoliberal gospel across the UK, Leon Brittan was explicitly guided by neoliberal ideology.[112] He took the fight against state neomercantilism in another direction, namely merger control, a provision that was missing in the Treaty of Rome. In 1973, the Commission proposed a draft merger regulation to the Council, but member states refused it. Brittan managed to break the deadlock and secure a regulation in December 1989, after sixteen years of negotiations. This law gave the Commission a monopoly over merger control above a certain threshold.

The adoption of the Merger Regulation in 1989 was partly linked to internal market dynamics. If a single market is created, then the number of mergers of European companies can of course multiply; to avoid contradicting national decisions, it is logical to create a single European regulator. This neofunctionalist argument is not enough to explain the adoption of this regulation, otherwise many areas would be federalised. What explained the adoption of the merger regulation was the specific role of European supranational entrepreneurs. The first salvo came from the Court with the so-called *Philip Morris* judgment on 17 November 1987.[113] It gave the Commission limited power to directly control mergers by using the existing legal arsenal (Article 85 of the Treaty of Rome), but it created legal uncertainty, which motivated member states to act.

It is clear from the archives that this Court ruling was insufficient, as many member states were still ready to block the adoption of a merger regulation in 1988–89. The shrewdness of Commissioner Brittan was decisive in bringing about the decision.[114] Bonn was still divided, for the official position was ordoliberal, and there was fear that European merger policy would be too lenient. Yet certain members of the government, such as the Minister of the Economy Helmut Haussmann and his deputy Otto Schlecht, discreetly defended a neomercantilist vision, believing that German competition authorities were sometimes too restrictive regarding mergers, because in his opinion companies needed to grow.[115] In 1988, the German Ministry of Economics authorised the merger between Daimler-Benz and MBB in the aeronautics sector, despite strong reservations from the German competition authority.

In Paris, the French wanted to use the merger regulation to counter what they called German 'protectionism', in this case the refusal by German competition authorities to allow the takeover of the German company Grundig by the French company Thomson-Brandt in 1983.[116] As German archives show, German competition policy made the decision independently from the government, but the latter was also hostile to this French takeover for reasons relating to industrial policy.[117]

Brittan also exploited a favourable political context in December 1989. The French were anxious to conclude negotiations before the end of their Community presidency on 31 December 1989. In Bonn, the Germans wanted at all costs to avoid appearing as the veto wielder, because this symbolic negotiation took place amid high tensions arising from a potentially quick German reunification (the Berlin Wall fell on 9 November 1989). In Paris, the political imperative not to cut itself off from the Germans also frequently appeared in the archives. The few voices advising caution (such as Jean-Claude Trichet, the Director of the Treasury at the time and the future President of the ECB) due to the project's lack of social or neomercantilist clauses were rapidly overshadowed.[118]

Brittan exploited this institutional success by launching a crusade against neomercantilism. In 1990, he proceeded with a spectacular merger prohibition to set an example. He took a specific interest in France and Italy, two countries favouring staunch neomercantilist industrial policies.[119] He seized an opportunity in 1991 when he convinced the Commission to ban a merger between the French–Italian aircraft company ATR (which produced turboprop aircraft), and its Canadian competitor De Havilland. This triggered hostile reactions at the Commission (from Delors) and in France (see Chapter 5). However, beyond this spectacular case, merger prohibitions were rare.

3.8 The Failure of Neoliberal Thatcherite Europe

Thatcher was strongly invested in promoting a neoliberal Single Market, and was quickly disillusioned by its failure. It is important to remember that a pro-European orientation took shape in London in 1984.[120] The main motivation, which appears repeatedly in the archives, was political: the UK had to participate in the 'European relaunch' for fear of being isolated from the French–German motor. As one official put it, Thatcher 'does not want to leave the French making the running'.[121] What is more, trade discussions in 1981–82 showed the interest that Community institutions had in promoting British interests. Additionally, the overriding of the 1982 British veto showed the fruitlessness of a purely hostile stance. At that time the British Minister of Agriculture, Peter Walker, tried to block a decision on the CAP by invoking the Luxembourg compromise, but his opposition was overcome by his partners, who agreed that the clause did not apply in this case (because London's real opposition was towards the budget and not agriculture).

3.8 THE FAILURE OF NEOLIBERAL THATCHERITE EUROPE 73

In early 1984, after a conversation with Kohl, Thatcher announced that a British memorandum was being tabled as a contribution to 'relaunch the Community'. Thatcher's initial aim was to focus the British memorandum on the European contribution to defending the West. In internal discussions, however, Geoffrey Howe (Foreign Secretary) and Michael Butler (Permanent Representative to the EEC) insisted on including economic aspects in order to avoid a negative reaction on the part of Germany. Thatcher accepted this and asked for specific proposals relating to the internal market, as well as the liberalisation of the transport and insurance markets.

The draft memorandum met with Euroscepticism at Whitehall, demonstrating that Thatcher's European voluntarism was disturbing. At the Treasury, the note was introduced by a sceptical comment: 'The paper seeks to match the kind of unrealistic rhetoric about the future of the Community on which Kohl is currently campaigning in the European elections. I must confess that this is not to my taste.'[122] The British memorandum was completed just before Fontainebleau.[123] Entitled 'Europe – the Future', it emphasised the need to create a 'genuine common market for goods and services', which was essential to 'meet the American and Japanese technological challenge'. Qualified majority voting in the Council remained taboo, but the memorandum concluded with a pro-European formula, referring to the Treaty of Rome's principle of 'ever closer union among the peoples of Europe'.

However, the memorandum was largely ignored due to London's procrastination. Initially intended for Kohl, it was completed too late, and was not circulated to Community members until the G7 meeting in London on 9 June 1984. As only four of the ten Community countries were members of that forum, a copy was also sent to the other governments. Howe then wondered about the best way to spark discussion regarding the memorandum without publicising it in the press, as 'it could have caused embarrassment in the last week of the European elections campaign' (in June 1984).[124] In the end, the memorandum was not discussed at the Fontainebleau summit.[125]

In 1985 London sought once again to promote a positive vision of European integration, this time in a more explicitly neoliberal way. At the Council of Ministers meeting of 11 February 1985, the Dutch government of Rudd Lubbers issued a memorandum on deregulation, aiming to remove legislative obstacles to entrepreneurial activity.[126] This issue perfectly fit the Thatcher agenda. The British prime minister requested a British initiative 'to stem the flow of legislation from Brussels',[127] and strove to create a common front with the Benelux countries around this deregulatory agenda. When she met the Belgian Prime Minister Wilfried Martens, she congratulated him on his austerity programme, and lamented the situation in Europe: 'We have lost the spirit of enterprise and we are faltering under the burden of the welfare state.'[128] She proposed using the successive Dutch, British, and Belgian presidencies in 1986–87 to push these ideas through.

However, Whitehall was sceptical about building this common front because Thatcher was more intergovernmental, neoliberal, and abrasive.[129] She insisted on denouncing the excessive cost of welfare states, even as her aides advised her to be cautious on this point.[130] Similarly, when Thatcher requested a list of examples of European legislation hindering business, Whitehall had no concrete examples to offer;[131] the 'burdens on business' survey of British companies did not cite an example of European law until its thirteenth bullet point. The administration also pointed out that most European regulation was adopted unanimously, which is to say with a British vote. The stifling of entrepreneurial initiative by Brussels legislation thus appeared to be a myth.

London finally presented its memorandum entitled 'The Creation of Wealth and Employment in the Community' to the European Council in Brussels on 29–30 March 1985.[132] More neoliberal than the 1984 memorandum, it insisted on the liberalisation of services and the need to conduct studies on 'the burden imposed on businesses by existing Community legislation and the way to reduce it'. It targeted welfare states by calling for measures to 'ensure that the social protection available to the unemployed does not act as a disincentive to their seeking jobs'. In very intergovernmental fashion, the British representative met with Pascal Lamy, Delors's chief of staff, and asked him to initiate a programme to review existing European legislation, with a view to identifying any excessive barriers to the activity of small and medium-sized enterprises.[133] He ended his dispatch with a revealing statement: 'I also spoke to Cockfield and urged him to take an interest.' London thus treated the Commission as a subordinate, one that was at the service of its deregulatory agenda.

Thatcher's offensive continued in 1986. Her priority remained the rapid establishment of a neoliberal Single Market, one based on repealing legislation rather than upwards harmonisation (hence 'deregulation'), extending the liberal logic to new areas such as air and road transport, and refusing any social reform.[134] The targets clearly identified by Whitehall were not just the draft Vredeling directive, but also a new law defended by the Delors Commission on parental leave.

Thatcher was disappointed, however, as she told her foreign secretary Howe in October 1986: 'I suspect that deregulation is *not* working very well.'[135] She chafed at Cockfield's sustained legislative activity, and refused to extend his tenure as Commissioner. He was eventually replaced in Brussels by a closer ally, Leon Brittan. Neoliberals at the Commission were also angered by the excessive legislative activism associated with the Single Market programme, which they associated with French dirigisme and intellectualism.[136] The other looming spectre was that of a social Single Market, as Delors grew closer to trade unions, including British ones (see Chapter 4).

Thatcher's scathing response came in her famous Bruges speech of 20 September 1988, in which she argued in favour of an intergovernmental,

Atlantic, and neoliberal Europe. She attacked excessive legislation, which she opposed to 'deregulation'. Against Delors's Social Europe, she asserted: 'We in Britain would fight attempts to introduce collectivism and corporatism at the European level.' The speech was nevertheless not Europhobic. Thatcher reaffirmed her government's community ambition: 'Britain does not dream of some cosy, isolated existence on the fringes of the European Community. Our destiny is in Europe, as part of the Community.' The style of her speech contradicted this assertion, especially her comparison between the EEC and the USSR: 'It is ironic that just when those countries such as the Soviet Union, which have tried to run everything from the centre, are learning that success depends on dispersing power and decisions away from the centre, there are some in the Community who seem to want to move in the opposite direction.' This practice of 'Community bashing' was well described by her personal adviser Charles Powell in a 1986 note approved by Thatcher: 'There seem to me good reasons for continuing the tactic of "Community bashing" both because it is necessary in its own right to get some sense into the institution, and because you will be a much more convincing exponent of it than the Opposition and will therefore cut the ground from under their feet.'[137]

The neoliberal opposition to a Single Market, seen as overly dirigiste and social, was not limited to Thatcher. In the UK, the Bruges Group, an influential Eurosceptic think-tank, was created in 1989, and marked the beginning of an intensifying dynamic of Tory Euroscepticism. The very same year in France, the Club de l'Horloge and the Club 89, which brought together various elements of the right and extreme right hostile to socialist rule, published a joint memorandum that vilified attempts to create a European welfare state, and explicitly aligned itself with the Bruges speech.[138] In London, this speech marked a radicalisation of Thatcher, who became increasingly bitter against the European integration process. It was her obstructionist attitude to European affairs that led to her downfall in 1990.

3.9 Conclusion

European integration began and largely revolved around establishing a regulated market. The idea is an old one, and predated the Cold War. It was already expressed in vague form by Keynes in 1919. While the neoliberal temptation of the unregulated free trade area always loomed, especially thanks to British influence, more regulated forms of market integration have prevailed, first as a customs union, then as a common market with a European competition policy, and finally as a Single Market with the harmonisation of most trade rules. The strong regulatory framework disappointed most neoliberals, such as Thatcher, as voiced in her famous Bruges speech from 1988.

This choice of an integrated market, which is surprising at first sight, can be explained by the desire to form the most efficient market possible, and the need to establish shared rules and arbiters to avoid and mediate conflict. For pro-Europeans, it was also a way to foster the irreversible rapprochement of European states and populations. This dual motivation explains the driving role of free trade states, such as federal Germany and the Benelux countries, with the latter playing a major role in the emergence of the common market via the Beyen Plan of 1952-53 and the Spaak Report of 1956. To protect themselves from protectionism from their neighbours, these states supported enhanced market unity through common regulation. Similarly, the most protectionist states, such as France and Italy, also helped strengthen the unity of the market: the French demanded access to Ruhr coal under the same conditions as the Germans, and then opposed what they saw as German protectionism, while the Italians requested the free movement of workers. Similarly, most states found an interest in limiting the state aid provided by their neighbours. It is this desire to secure credible commitments from their partners over the long term – for both economic reasons (fair competition) and geopolitical ones (anchoring Germany in liberal Europe) – that drove this effort to gradually and cumulatively strengthen the market.

The transition to the Single Market stage was fundamental, because it involved nothing less than eliminating border controls in the space of six years. It was around this project that a convergence of the main actors took place during the 'relaunch of Europe' in 1984-86. The impetus behind this project was long-standing, and was implemented thanks to convergence between member states and the European Commission. London and Bonn abandoned their plans for international liberalisation, and instead supported a European solution. In Paris, the government ended its attempts at protectionism, and instead sought to use the Single Market to tackle German standards, exemplified by the law on the purity of beer. Ironically, the free movement of alcohol was a powerful driver of market integration, with the *Cassis de Dijon* ruling (1979) serving as a milestone in this quest. It nevertheless took the convergence of member states and the Commission to trigger the institutional reforms of 1985-86 in order for a borderless market to open in 1992. In Brussels, the Commission was driven both by Delors's balanced vision of a Single Market, complemented by *solidarity* and *community*, and by two energetic neoliberal Competition Commissioners, Peter Sutherland and Leon Brittan. In the meantime, the Community has established itself as the major player in regulating trade on the continent, overseeing a series of technical certification bodies that previously operated independently.

This result was not inevitable, especially if other choices had been made: a protectionist approach by the French in 1983, a different leader in Bonn (with Kohl remaining relatively unpopular in the CDU for a long time), or less proactive commissioners than von der Groeben, Sutherland, and Brittan. New fields of public policy were Europeanised (cartels, mergers, state regulation, the liberalisation of air transport and telecommunications), but without the ordoliberal and neoliberal zeal of the commissioners mentioned above, these areas could very well have been mostly regulated at the national and international level, without any significant role for the Community.

Finally, the main reason for the growing importance of the Common Market lies in the flexibility of the Treaty of Rome, which proved open enough to accommodate both pro-Europeans and Eurosceptics such as De Gaulle and Thatcher, who both strongly supported the Common Market, the former to promote regulated liberalism, and the latter in a neoliberal vein. The *liberty* dimension of capitalism therefore prevailed in European integration, but not exclusively.

4

Solidarity: A European Welfare State Flanking the Single Market

The 1942 Beveridge Report famously defined the welfare state as comprehensive protection 'from the cradle to the grave'.[1] Social policies had existed beforehand, but they consisted of an uneven network of laws on working conditions, along with partial social insurance. By contrast, the post-war Western European welfare state has sought to mitigate the detrimental effects of capitalism via three sets of comprehensive measures: a) regulations protecting the weak, or compensating for the negative externalities of capitalism (working conditions, gender, and later environmental issues); b) redistributive policy (benefiting the elderly, the sick, etc.); and c) macroeconomic policies focusing on full employment (which sometimes include a form of indicative planning).[2]

On the European level, the *solidarity* element in the governance of capitalism took the form of a growing number of social and environmental policies.[3] This welfare state arguably did not develop at the same pace across the three components of regulation, redistribution, and macroeconomic policy. It was influential in the regulatory arena, especially with emerging issues such as gender and environmental policy. However, national actors remained prevalent in the other two components: redistribution was ensured through the national health, pension, and education systems, and macroeconomic policy remained almost exclusively under the purview of nation states (until the formation of the monetary union in 1999).[4]

A targeted European welfare state emerged, one that was referred to in the late 1980s as the 'social flank to the internal market', which is to say a 'flanking policy' designed to accompany the Single Market Programme. This chapter will begin with a chronological overview, including a first section on the slow development of this European social policy between 1945 and 1985, and a second one its heights under Delors. It will then proceed with a topical exploration of European measures in this area (protecting the weak, environmental policy, regional solidarity), before concluding with an analysis of the two most important alternatives that were later abandoned: planning, and comprehensive social and fiscal harmonisation.

4.1 The Slow Emergence of European Social Regulation (1945–85)

Social policy was long confined to the national level. The most important actor internationally was the International Labour Organization (ILO), founded in 1919.[5] Driven by a dual focus on free markets and social protection, the ILO sought to harmonise national social legislation upward, although its powers were limited by its intergovernmental structure. It could act only through non-binding recommendations, and conventions that had to be ratified by member states. The ILO monitored the application of conventions, but did so primarily on the basis of reports drafted by the governments themselves.

The European Communities largely replaced the ILO in Europe. The Schuman Declaration of 9 May 1950 provided for the 'equalisation and improvement of the living conditions of workers', a clause that was later included in the ECSC Treaty (Article 3). In 1952, two unionists were appointed to the ECSC's executive body, the nine-member High Authority.[6] It was chaired by Jean Monnet of France, who was accustomed to tripartite dialogue – between the government, employer's associations, and unions – in the context of the Commissariat général au Plan (French Planning Commission), over which he presided. Basing its activity on the ILO's work, the High Authority sought to facilitate labour mobility, especially support for labourers from Southern Italy going north to work in coal mining or steel plants. The ECSC implemented targeted action of uneven scope in different areas: it built housing for workers, provided assistance for mobility and professional training, and conducted studies on occupational safety, especially in mines after the Marcinelle mining disaster in Belgium in 1956 (in which 262 coal miners died, including 136 Italians).[7]

From 1958 onwards, the EEC developed action that was both wider in scope (involving all sectors, not just coal and steel) and more targeted in terms of mechanisms. The social dimension of the Treaty of Rome was limited to an article laying out the principle of social progress (EEC Article 117), and to three specific provisions: the social security of migrant workers (taken from ILO conventions); the creation of a European Social Fund (ESF) to promote the mobility of workers in need of retraining; and a handful of targeted harmonisation measures for social legislation to limit market distortion. The latter were adopted at France's request, and concerned equal pay for men and women, 'equivalence' in paid holidays, and overtime pay. The French government subsequently took little interest in their application; the initially expected problem of competitiveness did not materialise, and Gaullist officials were less attached to it than the socialist government of Guy Mollet, which had negotiated the Treaty of Rome.[8] This outcome is logical, for those who supported the Treaty of Rome were mostly Christian Democrats, along with Atlanticist socialists such as Mollet of France and Spaak of Belgium.[9] For these socialists, the preferred framework for developing social policy was the nation, as illustrated in France by the Mollet government's reforms in 1956–57 (third week of paid holidays, substantial increase for low pensions, etc.). The high growth of the 1950s allowed for the continuous expansion of the welfare state.

The measures adopted in the 1960s primarily involved the implementation of the ESF for professional training and the free circulation of workers, along with social security for migrant workers in 1968–71. Italy was highly reliant on it, for it had high structural unemployment in the country's south.[10]

The years between 1969 and 1974 were marked by a broadening of European social action, driven notably by the Social Democratic German Chancellor Willy Brandt.[11] European social policy was declared an EEC priority at the Paris Summit of 1972, despite hesitation on the part of conservative leaders, such as French President Georges Pompidou and British Prime Minister Edward Heath. Emphasis was placed on professional training and coordinating employment policies, but also included new topics such as the environment and regional policy. This movement unfolded in a post-1968 ideological context favourable towards the emergence and renewal of social policies; the social movement also began to show greater interest in Europe. Non-communist trade unions created the European Trade Union Confederation (ETUC) in 1973.[12]

Moreover, the *solidarity* coalition remained divided. Some organisations, such as the British TUC, remained fiercely opposed to the EC. In addition, Communist trade unions (which were very powerful in France and Italy) were not part of the ETUC, and most communist parties were hostile to European integration (the Italian PCI being a partial exception).[13] The issue of communism divided the European left. This is reflected in the tense relations between Mitterrand and Schmidt. The former supported an anti-German campaign in 1972 when the FRG, under a Social Democrat government, adopted harsh legislation targeting radical communist civil servants. In 1977, a tense meeting was held between Chancellor Schmidt and Mitterrand, who at the time was the opposition leader of the French left.[14] Schmidt expressed his surprise at Mitterrand's alliance with the communists (at a time when the communist East German government was killing those who tried to cross the Berlin Wall); Mitterrand responded by asking him what he would do if there were 8 million communist voters in West Germany.

When, in the late 1970s, Brussels initiated tripartite dialogue by inviting representatives for workers and employers – the ETUC and the Union of Industrial and Employers' Confederations of Europe (UNICE) – to consultations, they had little success.[15] Social partners were not interested in EC-based action, but rather in European coordination of national action. For instance, the ETUC supported a 35-hour working week, which it adopted at its 1976 Congress, but the Community did not have competence in this matter.

These discussions nevertheless led to limited but significant legislation, especially in comparison to the ILO, which was experiencing difficulty in the late 1970s.[16] The US unilaterally withdrew from the organisation from November 1977 until 1980, prompting its Governing Body to institute budget cuts of $36 million, or 22 per cent.[17] There were even plans to reduce delegate speaking time from 15 to 10 minutes, in order to reduce the cost of verbatim transcripts and the length of conferences! These examples give an idea of the ILO's financial challenges, as well as its limited means. The organisation was also caught in the crossfire of the Cold War, with a debate on multinationals rendered impossible due to ideological opposition between Moscow, which believed it was not concerned by this problem, and London, which insisted on the inclusion of major Soviet companies active abroad.[18] In short, the Community slowly emerged as a continent-wide actor for *solidarity*, but did so on modest terms.

4.2 The Social Ambition of the Delors Period (1985–95)

The years between 1985 and 1995 were auspicious for social Europe, due to convergence between the Commission presided by Jacques Delors (1985–95), which had unmatched power owing to his strong leadership, the French socialist President François Mitterrand (but whose proposals for social Europe were fairly modest),[19] and other actors from Germany, Belgium, Italy, and Spain.[20] Delors was a renowned European expert, as he was one of the primary authors of the Maldague Report in 1978, which proposed European planning. As President of the Economic and Monetary Affairs Committee in the European Parliament (elected for the first time via universal suffrage in 1979), he made numerous proposals for a targeted European relaunch, with strong monetary, industrial, and social aspects.[21]

The archives reveal that in 1981, Delors was already known and praised for his expertise by both Chancellor Schmidt and British diplomats.[22] As Minister for the Economy and Finances in the French government between 1981 and 1983, Delors supported a proposal for a social Europe that was more ambitious than the 1981 French memorandum, emphasising coordinating macroeconomic policy in support of employment, a revival of social dialogue, and strengthened social norms. In 1983, while still serving as a French minister, he affirmed: 'How can we imagine proceeding further with the Single Market without a minimum of coherence for the social aspects of each country or enterprise ... The European social sphere is what allows competition between enterprises and people to occur legitimately, without one of them being handicapped because they are more socially advanced than the other. This does not amount to asking for total unification.'[23]

Once at the head of the Commission, he announced his programme during a speech at the European Parliament on 14 January 1985, in which he emphasised the need for 'rules harmonisation' to avoid 'social dumping'. He proposed developing a social Europe by reviving European social dialogue, concluding collective conventions, and professional training (which he had strengthened in France as social advisor to Prime Minister Chaban-Delmas between 1969 and 1972).

A former unionist, Delors sought to revive tripartite social dialogue on a more effective basis than previous attempts in the 1970s and in 1984. He aimed to steer clear of general debates on economic policies, instead limiting discussions to a few subjects that could culminate in concrete EC legislation. The first 'Val Duchesse' meetings, named after the Brussels château where they were held, began in 1985 with representatives from the ETUC and UNICE.[24] Trade unions were generally supportive, but not always: Ernst Breit from the DGB believed that European collective agreements were only a distant prospect.[25] He also mentioned the need to take competitiveness into account, which is logical considering that his country, West Germany, relied heavily on exports from manufacturing companies in which the DGB had numerous members.

With regard to member states, Paris was generally favourable to Delors's ambitions, but French decision-makers refused any excessive concentration of powers at the Commission. Via its Minister of Labour, the Socialist Gianni de Michelis, Rome communicated its support for numerous legislative proposals of a social nature (training, parental leave, democratisation of enterprises) during the Italian Presidency of the Council during the first quarter of 1985.[26] In contrast, London was firmly opposed to any advances in the matter. This configuration led to the inclusion, within the Single European Act of 1986, of the principle of upward social harmonisation for legislation involving occupational health and safety. The harmonisation of social laws was nonetheless hampered by unanimous voting at the Council, where the veto of a single member state (usually Thatcher's Britain, but not exclusively) could block the decision-making process. The Single European Act imposed qualified majority voting, but only for legislation directly connected to creating the Single Market (non-tariff barriers preventing the smooth flow of goods from one country to another). This did not cover most social legislation, with the exception of those touching on non-tariff barriers and slated for harmonisation in connection with the Single Market Programme, such as some environmental, health, and safety regulations.[27] For instance, adoption of the Occupation Health and Safety Framework Directive 89/391/EC in 1989 was followed by twelve sector-specific directives between 1989 and 1993, which improved standards by establishing more protective norms.

Trade unions became more interested in European integration.[28] Beginning in 1988, the ETUC explicitly accepted advancing social Europe through both traditional legislation (at the Commission, the Council, and the Parliament) and tripartite dialogue. Even the British TUC abandoned its opposition to the EC, which it now saw as a counterweight to Thatcherism. Delors gave a speech to the TUC Congress in Bournemouth on 8 September 1988, to which

4.2 THE SOCIAL AMBITION OF THE DELORS PERIOD (1985-95)

Thatcher responded twelve days later with her famous Bruges speech.[29] Delors proposed adopting a law that would establish a 'basis of guaranteed rights for workers ... [with] the creation of a society of European law including participation by workers or their representatives' (see Chapter 6 for the debate on regulating multinationals). He also supported 'extending a right to permanent training to all employees'.

At the same time in Belgium, the Minister of Labour Michel Hansenne, a Christian Democrat (and future Director General of the ILO from 1989 to 1999), proposed 'EC social standards' during the Belgian presidency in 1987.[30]

Another debate arose surrounding an ambitious charter laying out the general principles of social Europe, building on the Council of Europe Social Charter concluded in 1961 (which was non-binding). Paris sought to adopt a bill during the French presidency of the European Council in 1989, but the internal debates were difficult, and not solely due to British reluctance.[31] French decision-makers believed that the Commission, represented at the time by the Commissioner for Social Affairs Vásso Papandréou, a Greek Social Democrat, was too supranational. Another difficulty emerged in West Germany, where the Minister for Labour, the Christian Democrat Norbert Blum, wanted a more binding charter focused exclusively on certain workers' rights (annual vacation, sick pay, pregnant workers, and young mothers). Chancellor Kohl generally supported the process, but was concerned about a possible challenge to German social standards, which he believed to be higher than French ones. He refused any major delegation of sovereignty that could lead to a new 'Social Democrat bureaucracy'.[32] Several members of the German government insisted on extending the German system of co-determination, a return to the debates of the Vredeling directive. Finally, Denmark was always reluctant because it wanted to preserve its social model from foreign interference. It insisted on including the mention of 'equal treatment with employees of the host country' for subcontractors working in another country; this was opposed by Spain and Portugal, most likely to preserve their low paying jobs, which gave them a competitive edge. Thatcher remained adamantly opposed, declaring that the Council of Europe Social Charter was more than sufficient.

In the end, the Charter was adopted by the Twelve minus the UK during the European Council Summit held in Strasbourg on 9 December 1989. The Commission subsequently moved to implement it by proposing forty-seven laws between 1989 and 1991, despite British opposition.[33] Tellingly, a senior German diplomat referred to the Charter as an 'important milestone on the road [to creating] a social flank to the internal market'.[34] It horrified some parts of the business community.[35]

The same configuration was present with the Maastricht Treaty (1991). The French and Italian governments were unable to form a common front, as Mitterrand prioritised the relation with Germany and monetary union, while

Rome allied with London in a joint declaration on NATO's role in European defence.[36] The new treaty had numerous articles addressing social policy, but without the rule of unanimity being lifted for the most significant decisions. In addition, the social protocol appended to the Treaty – the commitment to apply the Social Charter – was not signed by the UK. It nevertheless offered the possibility of transforming agreements emerging from European social dialogue into binding laws if approved by the Council.

In 1993, Delors published an ambitious communication in which he envisioned a socio-environmental and neomercantilist Europe based on European social dialogue, training, and targeted investment, especially in advanced technology. The objective was to relaunch activity in Europe, which had been in the midst of a severe crisis since 1992. This proposal was inspired by research conducted earlier by European unionists and Social Democrats, notably in Sweden.[37] It was not accepted by member states, and ultimately proved to be the high point of Delors's ambitions. Even if Delors wanted to go further in terms of *solidarity*, his years were marked by a balanced understanding of the Single Market as a compromise between *liberty* and *solidarity*, through three elements that will be further elaborated below: socio-environmental regulation, social dialogue, and regional policy.

4.3 Supervising the Market to Protect the Weak

Social Europe concentrated on four especially vulnerable categories: migrant workers, poorly trained workers, women suffering from the gender pay gap, and workers affected by weak labour laws, especially in the fields of health and safety.

'Migrant workers', as they were called at the time, were transnational actors, and therefore required international legislation. In the 1950s and 1960s, the Europeans concerned by this phenomenon were primarily Italian workers from Southern Italy. In 1968, Rome secured the free circulation of workers within the Community, and in 1971 mutual recognition between social security systems, which made it easier to establish the rights of migrant workers and their families from one EC country to another.[38] Thanks to EC laws and a favourable interpretation by the Court of Justice, the portability of workers' rights expanded gradually from the 1950s to the 1980s.

Mobility later extended to new categories, such as students with the Erasmus Programme created in 1987 as part of the 'relaunch of Europe' (a expression widely used in those days). It provided students with a framework for the mutual recognition of education, along with financial aid. The programme was adopted despite reluctance from multiple member states, especially Germany, France, and the UK, regarding the financial cost of mobility aid, as well as the possible influx of students from the south.[39] It was promoted within the Commission by both left-wing civil servants, such as Hywel Ceri

Jones of the UK, and by the Irish neo-liberal Commissioner Peter Sutherland.[40] However, the Council allocated less than half of the funding initially proposed by the Commission, which sought to provide study abroad for 10 per cent of the student population by 1992, as part of its objective to forge a Europe of citizens.

Equal pay for men and women became a Europe-wide issue in the late 1960s. In 1956, the French government asked for the insertion within the Treaty of Rome of Article 119 on 'equal pay for male and female workers for equal work or work of equal value'. It did so for reasons of competitiveness, but quickly dropped the issue, with feminist actors stepping in to revive it, especially in 1966 with the worker strike at the Fabrique Nationale (FN) in Herstal, Belgium. For the first time, Article 119 was invoked to demand equal treatment, a departure from its initial function.[41] This is an example of the 'unexpected consequences' of the Treaty of Rome, as its negotiators did not foresee how some of its articles would be interpreted later on.[42] One of the leaders of the Herstal strike, Charlotte Hauglustaine, learned about Article 119 as part of union training during a presentation by the Belgian feminist lawyer Eliane Vogel-Polsky, who mobilised the Action Committee for equal rights for women in the workplace. This prompted accusations of a takeover from certain strikers, especially since feminism 'still had a connotation as a "bourgeois movement" in worker circles'.[43] While the strike ended with a slight pay raise, its memory remains vivid within the Belgian labour and feminist movements. On the EC level, the struggle continued in the legal arena, with Vogel-Polsky supporting the airline hostess Gabrielle Defrenne in her case against the Belgian airline Sabena, which fired her in 1968 because she had turned forty years old. Her employment contract permitted this, without requiring the company to keep her on as a member of ground staff. Discrimination was explicit, as men had the right to continue working for the airline until fifty-five years of age. On 8 April 1976, in the landmark *Defrenne II* decision, the European Court of Justice decided in her favour. Finally, in its *Defrenne III* decision on 15 June 1978 (case 149/77), the court found that eliminating gender discrimination fell under the general principles of EC law. Gender equality became, almost by accident, one of the leading issues of social Europe.

Three directives were adopted between 1975 and 1978 to broaden application of Article 119.[44] After 1979, the rise to power of Margaret Thatcher, the first woman to lead a major European country, paradoxically represented a handicap to adopting new legislation. In keeping with her conservative standpoint, she complained to Delors that her country was being hampered by implementation of the equal pay directive.[45]

During the same period, protection for the weak extended to certain elements of labour law. A directive on employee consultation in the event of layoffs was adopted in 1975. For some experts, it helped temper the economically liberal bent of the centre-right French government under Jacques Chirac, who wanted to simplify redundancies in 1986.[46] Sometimes harmonisation grew out of a disaster that sparked heightened awareness. For instance, in July 1976, the city of Seveso in Lombardy (near Milan) was the site of a massive dioxin leak from a factory producing highly toxic chemicals, such as the defoliant Agent Orange used during the Vietnam War.[47] It led to the mass death of plants and small animals, as well as skin conditions among local inhabitants. The issue became European for two reasons. First, from the environmental point of view, the cloud of toxic chemical could have spread abroad. As shown by the example of the Rhine, pollution is by its very nature transnational within a European continent consisting of relatively small states. Second, from the economic point of view, if costly security measures were imposed only in one country, this would create market distortion. Henk Vredeling, the new Commissioner for Social Affairs appointed in 1977, prioritised this issue, but discussions proved difficult. The British government (despite being Labour) preferred discussing this issue within the less constraining frameworks of the Council of Europe and the World Health Organization (WHO).[48] It was worried about the cost of additional protection measures adopted after the disaster. The Seveso Directive – bringing national legislation for the risk of major accidents from certain industrial activities closer together – was finally adopted after a lengthy debate on 24 June 1982 (directive 82/501).

The debates often got bogged down with technical and financial issues, the need to preserve industrial interests, and reluctance on the part of member states to give more power to the EC. For instance, the 1983 debate on asbestos opposed the British Minister Norman Tebbit, who was pushing for a low limit value (in keeping with proposed British legislation), and the German minister, who wanted a higher limit to preserve German industrial interests.[49] The dangers of asbestos were clearly established in the early twentieth century, and its causal link with lung cancer in the 1930s.[50] The Commission began to signal the dangers of the substance in 1962, but legislation did not come until 1983, and was still only partial in nature. Such constraints were also in effect with respect to environmental protection.

4.4 The Slow Rise of Environmental Policy

While environmental concerns dated back before the 1970s, it was during that decade when the issue took shape as an independent public policy. It is not mentioned in the European treaties concluded during the 1950s. The emergence of influential non-state actors such as Greenpeace (1971), in addition to the first UN Conference on the Human Environment held in Stockholm in 1972, reflect the issue's sudden appearance in public discourse. In popular culture, disaster movies such as *Smog* and *Soylent Green* (both released in

1973) depicted the overexploitation of nature. This long-standing international awareness regarding the detrimental environmental impact of human activities translated into the creation of dedicated state ministries or agencies (1967 in Sweden, 1970 in the US, 1971 in France).[51] The 1973 oil crisis further reinforced this orientation, by concretely demonstrating the 'Limits to Growth' emphasised in the famous Meadows Report published the previous year. It argued that since natural resources are limited, economic and population growth should be limited as well.[52] Immediately after the crisis, the car culture was challenged by drastic measures such as the cancellation of car races and 'Sundays without cars' in Germany and the Netherlands, while the United States experienced episodes of 'panic at the pump'.[53] The oil crisis raised awareness regarding the intense energy consumption needed for productivity gains. For example, increasing corn yields in the US – which rose 238 per cent between 1945 and 1970 – came at the cost of an even greater spike in energy consumption (+ 313 per cent), with corn's energy yield ultimately decreasing by 24 per cent over the same period.[54]

Pursuing international regulation was logical given that pollution and biodiversity loss are cross-border by nature. The Council of Europe played a pioneering intellectual role by adopting non-binding conventions that defined the major principles for protection, doing so for water pollution and animal transportation in the late 1960s. The OECD also took part in these reflections, creating a group in 1972 to study the Long-Range Transport of Air Pollutants (LRTAP), especially at the instigation of Scandinavian countries.[55] The latter managed to expand the group to include communist Eastern Europe, because the major powers in the West (France, the UK) were not particularly mobilised, and figures from the Soviet bloc were seen as suspect. Finally, the East–West dialogue connected to the Conference on Security and Co-operation in Europe (CSCE) between 1973 and 1975, known as the 'Helsinki process', also had an environmental component. It led to the creation, under UN patronage, of the European Monitoring and Evaluation Programme (EMEP) in 1977, in addition to the Convention on Long-Range Transboundary Air Pollution in 1979, whose application was left up to each state.

How did the European Community emerge in a landscape dominated by national governments and international organisations? Paradoxically, the European Commissioner Sicco Mansholt – who had supported the development of a highly productivist agricultural policy in the Netherlands, and later in the EC with the CAP – championed environmental issues late in his career, praising the Meadows Report in 1972. He even sparked controversy with another commissioner, Raymond Barre of France, who was convinced that technological innovation would maintain high growth rates for many years to come.[56] On the EC level, the Dutch were often pioneers in promoting environmental protection measures, probably because they lived in one of the densest and most artificial and polluted spaces on the planet. The polluting of the

Rhine by the Germans (with massive dumping of chemicals by Hoechts in Frankfurt in 1969) and the French (by the Mines de Potasse d'Alsace) raised concerns for European Member of Parliament Jacob Boersma of Holland, who drafted a report on this subject at the European Parliament in 1970.[57] It pointed to the incapacity of existing institutions, especially the International Commission for the Protection of the Rhine created in 1815, and called for EC legislation, which would be binding.

A first EC environment action programme was adopted in 1973 at the instigation of Italian Commissioner Altiero Spinelli, who had been influenced by the Boersma Report. The latter laid out major principles (such as the precautionary principle and the polluter pays principle), established key goals, and created an initial core group of civil servants to work on these issues. The Commission, which was looking for contacts and expertise (to relay cases of pollution and later of non-compliance with the rules), began to support environmental associations.[58]

Some laws were adopted, but on a modest scale. In the early 1980s, the Parliament, which had just been elected by direct universal suffrage, used its enhanced legitimacy to raise the profile of environmental issues.[59] It took part in the mobilisation, under the leadership of Hanja Maij-Weggen of Holland, to protect baby seals, leading to a resolution adopted on 11 March 1982 asking for an import ban on their pelts. Following the media attention garnered by this cause, which notably had the support of French movie star Brigitte Bardot, on 28 February 1983 the Council adopted a directive banning the import of pelts and derivative products.[60] In those days, the most ardent supporters of environmental protection measures were the Danes, the Dutch, and the Germans, whereas the Thatcher government's objectives were much more modest: 'to agree [to] guidelines for Community environmental policy that take account of cost-effectiveness'.[61]

Taking note of this growing awareness, the Single European Act of 1986 included environmental protection within EC competence. It opened the way for qualified majority voting on the issue if the legislation in question was connected to implementation of the Single Market. The deadly pollution resulting from the Indian Bhopal disaster in 1984 (a chemical accident) and the Soviet Chernobyl disaster in 1986 (the explosion of a nuclear reactor) further enhanced this awareness and international mobilisation. The Brundtland Report of 1987 popularised the concept of 'sustainable development', which combines economic growth and environment protection. The report was drafted by an international commission convened by the UN and presided over by Gro Harlem Brundtland of Norway. It also included the German expert Volker Hauff, a supporter of EC industrial policy in advanced technology.[62] The report emphasised specific efforts to be carried out by the wealthiest countries to moderate their unchecked consumption.[63] Green parties made progress at the 1989 European elections. The Maastricht Treaty

4.4 THE SLOW RISE OF ENVIRONMENTAL POLICY

of 1991 extended qualified majority voting to all matters in this area. There was also intense international action at the time, with the Montreal Protocol of 1987 banning CFCs harmful for the ozone layer. Finally, the Rio Earth Summit in 1992 also marked a first peak in environmental awareness.

However, aside from a few exceptionally influential examples, such as the Montreal Protocol, these international institutions had relatively minor impact, because they could not rely on law that was directly applicable and controlled by an administration. What is more, certain companies were funding the cash-strapped UN Environment Programme (UNEP), thereby giving them influence over its activities.[64] These weaknesses made EC institutions all the more interesting for environmentalists, as it had directly applicable law that was overseen by the European Court, even if it depended on national administrations for inspection.

Unleaded petrol clearly illustrates the difficulties of legislative action, especially as it concerned two of Europe's major economic sectors: automobile manufacturing and power plants.[65] In the early 1980s, a major public campaign named CLEAR (Campaign for Lead-free Air) was conducted in London targeting the harmful health effects of air pollution, lead in particular. On the continent, Germans also mobilised against air pollution, but did so out of despair at the rapid spread of 'forest dieback' from acid rain. In both cases, emissions from cars (and power plants) were one of the main culprits. The US had already solved these problems by passing legislation in the early 1970s mandating catalytic converters, which reduced emissions of nitrogen oxide (NOx, one of the two substances behind acid rain) and lead (since lead damaged catalytic converters, unleaded petrol had to be adopted).

The adoption of unleaded petrol was costly, and was proportionally more substantial for small cars due to loss of power and the price of catalytic converters relative to that of the vehicle. French car manufacturers opposed this bill originating in Northern Europe, for they produced many small vehicles, and had invested little in this technology. In contrast, German manufacturers, which exported in large volumes to the US and mostly produced larger cars (except Volkswagen), quickly adopted catalytic converters. Moreover, some German industrial actors, notably the catalytic converter manufacturer Bosch, actually benefited from stricter environmental legislation.[66]

The German government tried to go it alone with unleaded petrol, but this risked dividing the European market. The Commission therefore pushed for EC-wide legislation. The French government was divided. The Ministry of Industry under Laurent Fabius used the traditional strategy pursued by 'merchants of doubt', affirming that the 'harmful consequences of lead gasoline on the environment and health have not been demonstrated'.[67] There was particular concern about the measure's cost for the French industry. Peugeot CEO Jacques Calvet conducted a very intense lobbying effort against European regulation, while Minister of the Environment Huguette

Bouchardeau, who had a background in environmental and feminist activism, defended the gradual abandonment of leaded gasoline. She commissioned an expert to provide counter-expertise showing the industrial feasibility of quickly abandoning lead, as well as the Roussel Report (jointly with the Minister of Health) emphasising the harmful health effects of car emissions (notably diesel particulates).[68] This expertise enabled Bouchardeau to prove that the cost of automobile pollution was higher than the cost of adapting French industry, thereby rebutting the 'merchants of doubt'. She also called directly on President Mitterrand, who imposed a compromise with West Germany in order to bolster the 'relaunch of Europe'. The French–German agreement paved the way for the Council's adoption, on 28 June 1984, of a first general orientation for the gradual introduction of unleaded petrol. However, it was not until the adoption of the Single European Act in 1986 that more binding laws were passed in 1988–89 thanks to the new procedure for qualified majority voting. The CEO of Peugeot Jacques Calvet was still opposed to the European regulation, but Renault – the other French car-maker – was not, despite the fact that both of them generally had the same product range.[69] Calvet's Euroscepticism probably played a role in this stance, and shows that business lobbying on environmental issues was not homogeneous.

The need to unify the internal market with similar regulations – including environmental ones – put intense pressure on member states to converge, especially since the decision was made at the Council via qualified majority voting under pressure from the European Parliament.

The battle surrounding each piece of legislation was intense not only between governments, but also among non-state actors. Civil society organisations defended stricter regulations for various reasons (protecting health, reducing pollution, fostering biodiversity), while certain companies mobilised against costly measures. The opposition of business was not systematic, as some companies began to pay greater attention to their environmental footprint, while for others environmental regulations even represented a business opportunity.[70] To sum up, environmental protection emerged as an independent public policy in the 1970s, and underwent a first peak in mobilisation in 1992, both in Europe and internationally.

4.5 Regional Solidarity

European integration started with a redistributive programme, albeit a short-lived one: the Marshall Plan (1947–52). Some historians have argued that its impact depended as much on implementing a cooperative framework combining free trade, the welfare state, and a Fordist productivist consensus as it did on the grants. Yet even a historian as sceptical towards the Marshall Plan as Alan Milward estimated its impact in 1949 as approximately 6–8 per cent of British and German GNP, 10 per cent of French and Italian GDP, and 23 per cent of Dutch GDP.[71]

4.5 REGIONAL SOLIDARITY

Once Western reconstruction was complete in the mid-1950s, Europeans no longer depended on American funds, except when experiencing financial crises (such as France in 1957–58). Strong economic growth and expanding welfare states transformed redistribution into a purely national issue for most countries.

Italy put discussions for Europe-wide redistribution on the agenda in the 1950s. Rome sought to secure financial transfers to increase the standard of living in Southern Italy, the Community's poorest region. In 1953 the Beyen Plan, presented by Minister of Foreign Affairs Johan Willem Beyen, envisioned creating a European Adaptation Fund to 'facilitate adaptation to Common Market conditions', and to 'strengthen economic solidarity between participating countries'.[72] However, in the Treaty of Rome Italy was only able to secure a European Social Fund (ESF) granting mobility aid to workers, and a European Investment Bank (EIB) providing funding for economic development projects.[73] These mechanisms were conditional, and the sums allocated modest.

The UK's accession in 1973 was a game changer, for Prime Minister Edward Heath insisted on adopting regional policy during the negotiations preceding enlargement.[74] In 1972, the Paris Summit decided to create the European Regional Development Fund (the future ERDF). It was followed by difficult negotiations between beneficiary countries supporting the creation of the fund (the UK, Ireland, Italy), and contributing countries, chief among them West Germany, which were reluctant. The negotiations lost momentum in 1974 with the arrival of a new Labour government in the UK, which was much less interested in European integration.[75] The ERDF ultimately created in 1975 was fairly modest: the Commission reimbursed national programmes already in effect, over which it had little control, and granted aid based on an allocation key for member states. This modest redistribution policy was in line with the preferences of major countries, with London and Paris both being moderately favourable.[76] As the leading contributor to the EC budget, West Germany was in principle opposed to any significant increase in EC spending, but it accepted regional policy so as not to be seen as obstructing the EC.[77] In 1983, Bonn insisted on a review of European policies, with a view to cutting costs.[78] After 1979, Thatcher also insisted on cuts in certain expenditures in regional policy.[79]

The issue became more pressing with enlargement towards the south (Greece in 1981, Spain and Portugal in 1986), as the new members, notably the Spanish government of Felipe González, wanted an increase in funding. In 1987, Delors proposed a comprehensive reform in February 1987 seeking to massively increase funds, and to combine regional actions divided across multiple intervention tools under a single policy known as 'cohesion policy'.[80] At the College of Commissioners, Delors's proposal was supported by the Commissioners Grigoris Varfis of Greece and Manuel Marín of Spain, but opposed by the commissioners from Germany and the Netherlands.[81] The support of German Chancellor Helmut Kohl at the European Council proved decisive. Kohl acted out of both political conviction and the need to support European integration, as this issue sparked scepticism within the German cabinet, ever focused on cutting costs.[82] What was later called the 'Delors I Package' was ultimately adopted in February 1988. The share of expenditures related to cohesion policy in the EC eventually tripled between the start (1985) and end (1995) of the Delors period, to the detriment of the CAP.[83] Expanded redistribution proceeded in parallel to the Single Market Programme, with the Commission explicitly referring to cohesion policy as a 'joint flanking policy' designed to accompany the Single Market Programme.[84] Some Europeans would nonetheless have preferred going further in the direction of *solidarity*.

4.6 The Twilight of European Planning

It is often forgotten that developing planning on a Europe-wide scale had already been pursued several times. Within a democratic country, planning refers not to an authoritarian process, but rather to a multi-year development framework offering flexible coordination for public and private actors. This approach became more popular after the Great Depression, when laissez-faire capitalism was seen as incapable of self-regulation.[85] European economic cooperation informed by a planning-based logic drove the first projects during the immediate post-war period. When the OEEC was set up in 1948, several decision-makers considered using it to coordinate national reconstruction plans, but this project was never implemented.

Despite this setback, many ambitious projects were envisioned. In 1958, the French socialist Robert Marjolin became the Commission's first Vice-President for Economic Affairs. A former Deputy Commissioner of the French Planning Board, and former general secretary of the OEEC, Marjolin wanted to implement Community-wide economic planning. In order not to scare the Germans, who associated planning with the Soviet-style East German dictatorship, the project was launched in 1962 under the name 'European programming', and later referred to as 'medium-term economic policy'.[86] The intellectual context was favourable, as French planning was cited at the time as an example by numerous observers, such as the British economist Andrew Shonfield in his famous book, in which he identified seven additional European countries that used planning.[87] The debate even spread to the US, as *Business Week* wondered whether the US needed planning, and Harvard University launched a programme to study French indicative planning to understand the sources of French economic growth (which was higher in the 1960s than West German, British, and US rates).[88] More generally, the theory of a long-term convergence between capitalism and the Soviet model enjoyed a certain audience. The famous economist Paul Samuelson even predicted in 1970 that Soviet GDP would catch up with that of the US between 1990 and 2000.[89] After all, the USSR was the first country to launch a satellite into space (Sputnik in 1957) and to send a man into orbit (Yuri Gagarin in 1961).

Marjolin sought to gradually transpose this process onto the European scale.[90] His aim was for the European planning process to gradually Europeanise the practices of European decision-makers by prompting them to regularly compare and coordinate medium-term economic and social policy. The socialist Marjolin clearly approached European programming with the goal of prioritising funding for collective consumption (education, health, etc.), as well as avoiding counterproductive or socially pointless private investments. He used a broad European planning network to create the Medium-term Economic Policy Committee in 1964, but its role was drastically limited by the Empty Chair Crisis in 1965 (triggered by Gaullist France in opposition to an expanded role for the Commission), in addition to West German reluctance towards planning.

The European left did not forget planning during the 1970s. The 'Theses for a Social Europe', adopted by the European Socialist and Social Democratic parties during their meeting in Bonn in 1973, mentioned planning.[91] The most influential document was the 1976 Maldague Report,[92] which originally began as a report on inflation commissioned by the European Commission. While it respected free market rules (emphasis on free trade and limiting inflation), the working group made planning central to its thinking, much to the despair of some at the Commission.[93] This new form of planning was based on a vast democratic consultation (involving sectoral and regional tripartite negotiations), which would have identified targets by sector and region based on wealth, income level, and social indicators. Investment had to be redirected to the priorities defined by planning. There were even plans for an 'investment notification' procedure for private companies in order to avoid 'excessive investment'.

The sections of the report emphasising planning were drafted by three left-wing experts: Franco Archibugi, Stuart Holland, and Delors. Archibugi was a planning expert who had experience as a civil servant in European organisations, as well as within the trade union movement. Holland was a personal assistant to Labour Prime Minister Harold Wilson between 1966 and 1968. An influential Labour intellectual, his reflections on the EEC were widely discussed by Whitehall in 1977.[94] Delors was an official at the Banque de France who belonged to the moderate Christian trade union CFTC. He served as the Head of the Department for Social Affairs at the French Planning Board (1962–69), as well as a social advisor to the moderate Gaullist Prime Minister Chaban-Delmas (1969–72), before joining the socialist party in 1974. He was critical of the decline of French planning,[95] and defended decentralised planning based on contractual relations between social partners, the government, enterprises, and local actors. Public enterprises would enjoy relative autonomy under planning, in order to avoid the risk of management being driven by politics; the requirement of international competitiveness would also be taken into account.[96] In 1978 the three authors published their reflections on planning in the collective book entitled *Beyond Capitalist Planning*, which sought, according to its editor Stuart Holland, to show the convergence of reflections across the European left around modernised planning.[97] He cited the thinking of British Labour, French and Italian socialists, and German Social Democrats. The SPD programme adopted in Mannheim in 1975 included planning components that were included at the insistence of the party's left wing,[98] with the goal of using better information to strengthen public control over private investment.

In 1977, a note from the ETUC preparing a European meeting endorsed 'more medium-term programming or planning', echoing Marjolin's vocabulary.[99] In a nod to the Maldague Report, it called for greater investment coordination to prevent 'wasting rare resources, as well as situations involving private consumption of non-essential and fairly pointless goods driven by factors such as advertising, which occurs at the expense of producing more essential goods and services'. The 1981 ETUC manifesto for a European relaunch emphasised coordinating European economic policy.[100] Holland continued his effort to coordinate thinking on the European left with a new book in 1983 entitled *Out of Crisis*, which also explored the notion of planning.[101] For all that, most planners were not ready to accept the delegation of power to the EC that was inherent in these ideas. Incidentally, in 1980 Holland was one of the leaders of the Labour party's shift towards rejecting participation in the EEC. In the end, planning persisted only in massive investment projects for pan-European infrastructure – promoted by the ETUC in 1986, and taken up by Delors at the Commission – and partially implemented via cohesion policy.[102]

4.7 The Illusion of Well-Developed Social and Fiscal Harmonisation

The idea of supplementing the market with legislative harmonisation in social and fiscal matters was a long-standing one. The French government made it a prerequisite to accepting the Common Market at the beginning of negotiations in 1955–56.[103] Demands for total harmonisation nevertheless receded when French experts realised that the five other EEC countries had comparable welfare states. The 1956 Ohlin Report (commissioned by the ILO and drafted by the Swedish expert Bertil Ohlin) concluded that it was futile to pursue social harmonisation, and instead recommended targeted measures.[104] Studies by the ILO, the ECSC, and the French government diffused during the negotiations underscored the minor difference in labour costs between France and its partners.[105]

4.7 THE ILLUSION OF EXTENSIVE HARMONISATION 95

The quest for harmonisation from above was paradoxically revived by the German Commissioner Hans von der Groeben, who was influenced by ordoliberal ideas. In the 1960s he defended harmonisation for direct taxes on companies based on the principle of 'fiscal neutrality', with a view to avoiding what is today referred to as 'fiscal dumping'.[106] In 1969 the Commission affirmed that its 'ultimate goal' was to centralise a company's taxation in the country where it is headquartered (global profits), stating that 'such a solution entails a fairly extensive convergence of corporate taxes, so that they do not tend to set up in countries where the tax burden is lighter'.

Von der Groeben had to yield due to a lack of will among member states, and obstruction on the part of Gaullist France. On 28 June 1965, the German government supported a major fiscal harmonisation plan including direct taxation – most likely in keeping with von der Groeben's objectives – but the Empty Chair Crisis sparked by Paris two days later hampered this effort. The French Minister Michel Debré took a more intergovernmental stance, calling in 1966–68 for a fight against the most flagrant instances of 'distortion', notably those linked to Luxembourg's very low taxation, all while refusing 'harmonisation'. Debré, who was adamantly opposed to supranationality, also saw his initiative fail. Corporate taxation remained wholly national, a growing problem with the development of Euromarkets in the late 1960s, which increased both the mobility of capital and fiscal competition.[107]

In the 1970s, the economic crisis prompted several left-wing actors to promote a concerted reduction in working time in Europe. This issue was regularly broached by the ETUC in the late 1970s during tripartite conferences between trade unions, employers' representatives, and European institutions.[108] The new Commissioner for Social Affairs, the former trade unionist Henk Vredeling, prioritised it upon his arrival at the European Commission in 1977.[109] The centre-left German government reacted negatively, probably because it believed such a measure to be inappropriate both economically, as it compromised competitiveness, as well as socially, as working time arrangements were managed via agreements between social partners. The British Labour government was also opposed, but chose to adopt a prudent position so as not to clash with the unions supporting it.[110]

Paradoxically, the centre-right French government was more open. It decided that social Europe, energy, and monetary cooperation would be the three priorities for the European summit to be held in Paris in March 1979.[111] The French initiated a discussion on working time since studies showed that annual working time in France was among the highest in the EC (according to French figures for 1977: 1,900 compared with 1,940 in the Netherlands, 1,820 in the UK, 1,750 in the FRG and Belgium, 1,540 in Italy, and by comparison 1,700 in the US). Paris accepted a reduction in wages, otherwise productivity would decrease, ultimately eliminating jobs. The aim was not to impose binding European measures, but to conceive incentive-based mechanisms discouraging recourse to overtime and encouraging the adoption of part-time work (following the model of a French law from 1976). This could increase both flexibility and productivity. The meetings held during the first quarter of 1979 provided the French Labour Minister, the moderate Gaullist Robert Boulin, with an opportunity to promote his vision: 'We can imagine that a framework directive could be developed to establish the outlines, with social partners jointly studying how it would be applied, notably by sector, within the limits fixed by the directive.'[112] The debate soon came to an end due to reluctance from Germany, as well as from the French Ministry of Finance and the French Commissioner Ortoli.[113] According to a French official, the Germans were 'somewhat surprised by the relatively open position taken by M. Boulin', and were especially irritated by the maximalist proposals of Commissioner Vredeling with respect to the 35-hour workweek.[114] This episode shows the obvious lack of coordination among actors defending a European reduction in working time (notably between Boulin and Vredeling).

In May 1979 the Conservatives rose to power in the UK, bringing an end to the debate. Whitehall produced a fairly moderate memo on the topic, which Thatcher marked up with emphatic annotations including exclamation points and a resounding 'No'![115] The discussion concluded with a modest resolution from the Council on working time, adopted on 22 November 1979. In a bilateral interview with Thatcher, the German Social Democratic Chancellor Helmut Schmidt broached the idea for a European reduction in working time, but to no avail.[116]

The unions belatedly took to the offensive. During its discussions with the European Commission, Wim Kok of Holland, who presided over the ETUC from 1979 to 1982, regularly insisted on the need for European stimulus and working-time reductions.[117] Since the Munich Congress of 1979, the ETUC called for adopting a 35-hour workweek, a demand that was included in the platforms of numerous trade unions and left-wing parties (especially in France, Belgium, and West Germany).[118] However, there was no unanimity for defending this objective in 1979, especially due to opposition from Nordic unions, which were attached to their national models.

In Paris, the new socialist president, François Mitterrand, cut the workweek from forty to thirty-nine hours in 1981, but the goal remained thirty-five, along with a fifth week of paid holiday and retirement at sixty instead of sixty-five. The new socialist government sought to transpose these reforms to the European level. At the European Council Summit of 29 June 1981, Mitterrand asked for a European 'social space' devoted to reorganising working time and promoting union participation.[119] Even the French communist minister Marcel Rigout, who was in charge of professional training, proposed relaunching ESF reform.[120] But the French government was divided: while the Minister of the Economy and Finances, Jacques Delors, supported creating tripartite

4.7 THE ILLUSION OF EXTENSIVE HARMONISATION

sectoral committees, the Ministry for Industry (led by the Eurosceptic Jean-Pierre Chévènement), and even the Ministry for Labour showed little interest.[121] The French memorandum of December 1981 was ultimately modest: unemployment would be combatted by creating 'competitive' jobs, for 'anything that causes Europe to fall behind would quickly threaten its independence and standing in the world'. French delegates pressed for reducing working time during EC meetings in 1982 and 1983, but did little more than suggest Boulin's project for EC-level 'proposal frameworks'.

There was strong opposition from Thatcher, as well as scepticism from Chancellor Kohl.[122] West Germany was in the grips of an internal debate regarding the reduction of working time, with mobilisation by the DGB in support of a 35-hour workweek. In 1984 IG Mettall initiated one of the largest strikes in the country's history, and obtaining a 38.5-hour workweek in late June. In a meeting with Thatcher in May 1984, Kohl identified this as his primary domestic political problem (after the ebb of the pacifist movement connected to the Euromissile crisis).[123] Scepticism was rising even in Paris. During a meeting held by the ETUC in May 1983, Minister for Industry Laurent Fabius, who was close to President Mitterrand, stressed that the unilateral French reduction in working time from 1981 was economically problematic. Further reductions would be accepted only in exchange for greater flexibility and a European agreement.[124] The French Presidency of the Council during the first quarter of 1984 provided an opportunity for the new Minister of Social Affairs, Pierre Bérégovoy, to propose an initiative for a 35-hour European workweek in June 1984.[125] A resolution on the reduction and reorganisation of working time was finally adopted by nine member states (ten EEC members minus the UK) via the Council of Ministers for Social Affairs. It stressed that a reduction in working time should 'help facilitate structural changes, enhanced competitiveness, and greater flexibility in the labour market'. The tone was cautious, in keeping with the debates launched by Boulin in 1979.

ETUC, under the presidency of George Debunne (1982–85) of Belgium, advocated for ambitious EC policies, such as targeted public investment programmes, social laws (Noise directive, Vredeling directive, creation of a European fund), and a project to identify an 'EC framework instrument that would lead to negotiation on the national level' for reducing working time.[126] But it was too late, for neo-liberal reforms had already taken hold in many governments. Besides, the ETUC struggled to establish European-wide mobilisation: even when a common position was agreed on, the cost of transporting trade unionists to Brussels was simply too high.[127] As a result, and despite the ambitions of some left-wing pro-European actors, Delors chief among them, the harmonisation of social and fiscal legislation was ultimately limited to a few laws directly linked to establishing the Common Market (see earlier).

4.8 Conclusion: The Success and Failure of a Solidarity-Based Europe

The *solidarity* dimension of the governance of European capitalism was real, but was primarily implemented nationally. A broad exploration of the archives reveals alternatives that were largely ignored, and subsequently left in silence. While Marjolin and Delors spoke very little of their European planning project in their memoirs,[128] probably due to its failure, close examination of debates from the 1960s and 1970s shows its importance at the time. Other major projects that were not pursued include social and fiscal harmonisation, the control of multinationals (see Chapter 6), and Europe-wide stimulus (see Chapter 7).

In the late 1980s, the terms 'flanking policy' and 'social flank' were occasionally used in reference to certain European social efforts. Social and environmental action proceeded via the upward harmonisation of legislation protecting the weak, and targeted redistributive action for poor regions. While European action was initially limited to purely transnational issues such as migrant workers, it later spread to other areas, especially those that were relatively new, such as gender equality and the environment. The European 'flanking' welfare state had a weak redistributive component. In theory, transferring redistributive policies to the federal level is appropriate only when addressing cross-border issues – especially those producing negative externalities such as pollution or unfair competition – or when generating economies of scale.[129] As a result, a European redistributive policy was developed only in connection with regional policy, whose primary aim is to correct the imbalances generated by the Common Market.

This relative weakness of social Europe can be explained by its late development (international action in the social sphere firstly took place within global organisations such as the ILO and the UN), by the sheer difficulty of organising a transnational social movement, as well as by divisions among its supporters. Numerous centre-left leaders in Northern Europe, notably in Scandinavia, Germany, and the UK, were attached to their national models (often co-managed by extremely powerful unions), and did not want to include a distant Brussels bureaucracy. Even when the ETUC became involved in tripartite dialogue in the 1970s, it saw the EC first and foremost as a forum for coordinating national policies.[130] It was not until the mid-1980s that approaches were oriented towards the EC level, in connection with the Delors Commission. However, the high water mark for social Europe under the ambitious Delors (1985–95) coincided with the greatest influence for the most radical British neoliberalism under the Thatcher (1979–90) and Major (1990–97) governments. Examination of the archives from three centre-left governments (UK 1974–79, FRG 1974–82, France 1981–86), in addition to the ETUC, shows no attempt to create a united front on social Europe.

4.8 MIXED RESULTS OF A SOLIDARITY-BASED EUROPE

Thatcher was a formidable obstacle, one that Delors sought to circumvent through greater use of qualified majority voting via the Single European Act and the Maastricht Treaty (for social and environmental matters). He did so by making decisions without London regarding tripartite dialogue, the Social Charter, and the working time directive. Delors was supported by Kohl, Mitterrand, and González among others. But the debate surrounding the harmonisation of most social and fiscal laws was stalled by the veto right at the Council (except for legislation directly related to the Single Market).

Effective social and environmental action was nevertheless taken with key support from national leaders on both the centre-left (Mollet in 1956, Brandt in 1970, and Mitterrand in the 1980s) and the centre-right, with Heath in the case of regional policy, and Boulin for the reduction of working time. European actors also played a major role, such as Delors at the European Commission. The Parliament served as a soundbox for new environmental subjects such as pollution and protecting animal species, for instance baby seals. Other important actors were European trade unions, activist lawyers such as Eliane Vogel-Polsky in connection with gender equality, and defenders of the environment. They successfully established the central role of the market in European integration via a 'flanking' welfare state.

5

A Community without Communitarianism: Europe's Failure as a Military and Industrial Powerhouse

In 1957 the Europeans created the European Economic Community, which is the basis for today's European Union. Despite its name, this Community has not been able to promote communitarianism in the sense used in this book, namely a policy seeking to bolster the group at the expense of others, for example through protectionism, or through assertive foreign and military policy. As a liberal and peaceful project, European integration has thrived as a market governed by rules that are supposed to be neutral. However, agreeing on more discriminatory policies has proven difficult. Creating a European organisation based on *community* has involved grappling with complex questions: Who is a European and who is not? Who is a partner and who is a foe? Should Europeans be favoured or not? Should Europeans be capable of defending themselves independently, or through the US alliance? This includes questions about industrial policy (Which company should receive a grant?), protectionism (Which sector should be protected?), foreign policy (What are European diplomatic interests and how to promote them), and defence (Should a European army be created, and who would it be used against?).

This chapter will show first that during the Cold War defence and diplomacy were largely coordinated on a North Atlantic scale through NATO, despite numerous attempts to create a 'European power'. Second, some form of European protectionism nevertheless thrived in specific areas, such as agriculture and later aeronautics, but surprisingly not in energy, and this in spite of multiple attempts. Third, and most importantly, the ubiquity of national industrial policies led European institutions to counterbalance these policies through free market rules rather than the creation of Europe-wide industrial policy.

5.1 National and Atlantic Approaches to Foreign Policy and Defence

Promoting a governance of capitalism based on *community* entails considering the European Community not just as a market, but also as a superpower in the making. To achieve this, Europeans must: 1) clearly identify allies, partners, and enemies; 2) determine when and how to intervene (diplomatically or militarily); and 3) be willing to intervene on their own (not just in concert with the US) and decide who will produce weapons.

These three issues often proved insoluble during the Cold War. Europe was dominated by the two superpowers, the US and the Soviet Union, in terms of nuclear weapons. Western Europe has been divided between countries attempting to influence international affairs, often former colonial powers and/or those victorious during the World War II (UK, France,), and countries that were neutral or defeated during the war (Germany, Italy, Ireland, Switzerland, Sweden, and Austria). The former are more inclined to intervene in their former colonial empires, or at least to assert their interests explicitly, while the latter are often more pacifist. A second division concerns the relationship with the US: almost all Western European countries considered the US to be indispensable to defending the continent against the Soviets, and as a counterweight against the possible rise of a new German threat. But Paris developed a more distant relationship with Washington after de Gaulle's return to power in 1958.[1] He replaced the old imperial discourse with a post-imperial one marked by France's '*grandeur*'. Its influence in the world was no longer based on its colonial empire (largely dismantled by de Gaulle himself), but on a message of emancipation for all peoples. This involved criticising America's involvement in Vietnam, securing the withdrawal of US troops from France in 1966 (with NATO's European Headquarters being moved from Paris to Brussels), and attempting limited rapprochement with the Eastern bloc. De Gaulle nevertheless did not call into question the Western Alliance. Other European countries, such as Italy, whose Communist Party peaked at 34 per cent of the vote in 1976, or Spain, which hesitated to join NATO after its return to democracy in 1975, also showed occasional outbursts of anti-Americanism, or had powerful anti-American constituencies.

Despite these deep divisions, the project of transforming Europe into an assertive community was promoted through three different projects: the federal and Atlanticist European Defence Community (1950-54), a more Eurocentric intergovernmental project for nuclear cooperation (1957-58), and a French project to transform Europe into an independent geopolitical actor (1961-62). In the end it was a fourth project that prevailed: intergovernmental cooperation dominated by national and North Atlantic dynamics.

5.1.1 *The Federal Ambition of the European Defence Community (1950-54)*

In a striking development, a genuinely European army was almost created in the early 1950s.[2] The project was born out of the Korean War, triggered in June 1950 by the surprise attack of communist North Korea on its capitalist neighbour to the south. The conflict created a stir in Europe, where fears of an imminent invasion by Soviet troops resurfaced. Eastern conventional forces were much more numerous than Western ones, and the detonation of the Soviet atomic bomb in August 1949 wiped out the American technological advantage. This prompted the Americans and British to pressure France into accepting rapid German rearmament; German divisions had to be created quickly to fill the vacuum in Central Europe.

The French had fought three wars with Germany in seventy years (1870–71, 1914–18, 1939–45), and were therefore reluctant to accept. The solution of Europeanisation, already explored for coal and steel after the Schuman Declaration, became a possible avenue, especially since the leader of the French government, René Pleven, was a convinced Europeanist. He was a close associate of Jean Monnet, and Robert Schuman was still the Minister of Foreign Affairs. On 24 October 1950, Pleven proposed to the French National Assembly the creation of a European army, under the control of common political institutions. The project was presented as an extension of the coal and steel initiative to the military sphere, and was fully integrated within the recently created NATO.

The French government played a leading role (with the British one) in the birth of the North Atlantic Alliance in 1949, as it desperately wanted US troops to be permanently stationed in Europe to protect against Germany and the USSR. This was the so-called American 'empire by invitation'.[3] It also played a leading role in this effort to build a European army between 1950 and 1952 (this time without the British, who were opposed to federalism), despite deep divisions among French leaders. Negotiations among the six countries of the ECSC (France, Germany, Italy, Belgium, Luxembourg, the Netherlands) led to the signing, on 27 May 1952, of the treaty establishing the European Defence Community (EDC). The EDC's institutions were relatively similar to those of the ECSC. Additional declarations linked the EDC to the UK and NATO. The treaty was a compromise: France's partners conceded this integrated army, and in exchange France had to accept German rearmament and the creation of an EDC in which it was not an undisputed leader.

But how could a common army exist without a common government? To fill this gap, federalists mobilised to create a European authority. To this end, Article 38 of the EDC treaty stipulated that the future assembly, shared by both the ECSC and the EDC, should draw up a project for a 'federal or confederal structure'.[4] The foreign ministers of the Six agreed to entrust the ECSC Assembly with this task. On 10 March 1953, it adopted a fairly federalist project to create a European Political Community.

Numerous opponents mobilised against this federalist dynamic. French President Charles de Gaulle, who had supported the Atlantic Alliance because Soviet troops were stationed just 'two stages of the Tour de France' away (speech on 22 July 1947), criticised the EDC.[5] It was based on multiple contradictions: a European army was created, but without a genuine government; a European Political Community was hastily negotiated in 1953, but its leadership and doctrine of intervention were unclear; France instigated the EDC to prevent the creation of an autonomous German army, but paid the price of diluting its own army in a common structure where it would wield less influence than the FRG (as French troops committed to the EDC would potentially be less numerous than West German ones). The context had also changed, with the USSR appearing somewhat less threatening after Stalin's death in 1953. Furthermore, France was focused on decolonisation, admitting defeat in the First Indochina War in July 1954. One month later, on 30 August 1954, the French Assembly refused to ratify the EDC, which came as a shock since the initiative had originated in Paris, and had been ratified by most European countries.

The problem of German rearmament was settled within an intergovernmental and Atlantic framework. West Germany joined NATO, and could reconstitute its military (limited to twelve divisions as in the EDC, and without nuclear weapons). On the initiative of British Prime Minister Anthony Eden, the 1948 Brussels Pact was extended to Italy and Germany via the Paris Agreements of 23 October 1954, which created the Western European Union (WEU). The French head of the government, the anglophile Pierre Mendès-France, hoped it would serve as a crucible for armament cooperation, but London soon lost interest, preferring NATO instead. The Europeans were seemingly not genuinely willing to establish a common defence – whether federal (EDC) or intergovernmental (WEU) – instead preferring to remain under the American nuclear umbrella. This situation both strengthened and frustrated Washington. In an internal meeting held in 1958 with his Secretary of State and other collaborators, President Eisenhower complained about European dependence on the US:

> The President recalled that when he first went to SHAPE [the NATO headquarters in Europe], there had been talk that the United States assistance to the NATO countries' defence efforts would be for a 'maximum' of five years. Since then, the NATO countries have come to depend overly on the United States; the President reiterated that it is time for us to begin to wean our allies from overdependence upon us and to encourage them to make better efforts of their own.[6]

5.1.2 The French–German–Italian Project for Nuclear Cooperation (1957–58)

Some Europeans nevertheless envisioned ambitious but discreet military nuclear cooperation in 1957–58.[7] This semi-secretive project originated for several reasons. In France, the nuclear programme had been in full swing since 1954. Guy Mollet, the French president of the Council, wanted to foster European cooperation in this area, with a view to helping fund the French nuclear industry. Mollet had been disappointed by the American stance at Suez in November 1956, when Washington supported Moscow in denouncing the neo-colonial French–British expedition against Nasser. The Euratom Treaty signed on 25 March 1957 fostered civil nuclear cooperation, but preserved the independence of the military nuclear industry.[8]

In addition, the launch of Sputnik in October 1957 sparked what would become the 'missile gap' theory in 1958, since the technology needed to build a satellite rocket launcher and a ballistic missile were one and the same. This led some Western Europeans to fear US military disengagement from Europe: Washington might not want to defend Europe with its nuclear arsenal if it was afraid of being massively targeted by the Soviets. The spectre of US isolationism resurfaced.[9] In West Germany, Chancellor Adenauer was also eager to rebuild a true German power that was both Atlantic and fully supportive of European integration, and had access to non-German nuclear weapons.

Following the failure of the Suez expedition in November 1956, Paris held exploratory talks with Bonn on military nuclear cooperation. This discreet project became the subject of public debate in Germany, with scientists publishing an open letter in 1957 protesting Adenauer's attempt to secure nuclear weapons for Germany.[10] Cooperation was later extended to Italy with an agreement concluded in November 1957, although it was solely between Ministers of Defence, and therefore not binding on member states. The agreement provided for producing nuclear weapons on French soil, giving Paris control over operations. This secret agreement was intended to be announced to NATO partners.

The project faltered in December 1957, when the US became more open to nuclear cooperation with Europe. Meetings between the French, German, and Italian defence ministers continued until the return to power of de Gaulle in June 1958, who put an end to these discussions. In the early 1960s, US Presidents Dwight D. Eisenhower and John F. Kennedy launched a complex project for a multinational European nuclear force under the NATO umbrella dubbed the Multilateral Force (MLF).[11] It also failed. In the end, the two preferred levels for defence cooperation remained the nation state – France detonated its A-bomb in 1960 – and NATO, through which West Germany, Italy, and other Western European countries gained access to American atomic weapons under US control.

5.1.3 The Ambition of a French European Power

France has been tempted to use European integration as a lever to recapture past international clout for two reasons. First, France was the dominant power in Europe between Louis XIV and Napoleon (1643–1815). It lost this dominance, but went on to acquire the world's second-largest colonial empire. However, it was crushed by humiliating defeat in 1940, and lost wars of decolonisation in Indochina (1945–54) and Algeria (1955–62). The Cold War imposed a bipolar logic that clearly relegated France to a secondary role despite its global prerogatives (permanent membership on the Security Council since 1945, the nuclear bomb since 1960, widespread use of the French language in international institutions).

The small Europe of Six that was created with the Schuman Declaration of 1950 was valuable from a strategic perspective, as France was clearly the greatest diplomatic power in this grouping. This ambition began to emerge after the Suez fiasco in November 1956, and appears to have been fairly popular: a French newsreel from 23 January 1957 presenting the Common Market (the future EEC) ended with a map depicting the Europe of the Inner Six sliding in between the US and the USSR, and growing to match the size of the two bigger superpowers.[12] While the discourse was mainly economic, the geopolitical dimension was clearly present.

The ambition to develop Europe as a superpower led by France was more evident under the outspoken de Gaulle (1958–69). He clearly articulated his willingness to develop what he called a 'European Europe', not just an 'Atlantic' one.[13] In July 1960, he explained to Adenauer his desire to create a political Europe based on organised state collaboration, particularly in the diplomatic and military spheres. At the time, both de Gaulle and Adenauer feared partial American disengagement from Europe.[14] De Gaulle was firmer against the Soviet Union than British and US leaders during the Berlin Crisis, which was sparked by Khrushchev in 1958 in a bid to extend his influence over West Berlin. The French leader toyed with the idea of including the French atomic bomb, which had been detonated in 1960, within a European framework (with Paris keeping complete independence over its use).[15]

De Gaulle's project for a powerful Europe was linked to other objectives. First, he sought to reform NATO in order to strengthen France's influence in the Alliance. In September 1958, De Gaulle sent a memorandum to Eisenhower and Macmillan requesting (to no avail) the creation of a NATO tripartite Directorate, in which France would be put on an equal footing with the US and the UK. De Gaulle had a second, more discreet objective: to create a European intergovernmental organisation that would limit the Community and prevent any federal drift. Third, in 1961 de Gaulle accelerated discussions because of the UK's bid to accede the Community. For France, it was important to solidify this Community of Six against its possible dilution in the event of enlargement towards Britain.

The Six agreed to establish a commission to study political Europe, chaired by the French Gaullist Christian Fouchet. On 19 October 1961, he presented the Fouchet Plan to create an intergovernmental union distinct from the EC dealing with issues not connected to the Common Market, such as diplomacy, defence, culture, and human rights. For the first time, European identity was defined, quite broadly, around notions of 'democracy', 'human rights', and 'justice in all areas of social life'. This clearly demonstrates the link between the notions of *community*, power, and identity: to wage an assertive diplomatic policy, it is necessary to define who belongs to the group, and what it stands for.

The other five EC members remained cautious. On 18 January 1962, de Gaulle radicalised the proposal with a second Fouchet Plan making no reference to the Atlantic Alliance, and posing a more direct threat to the EC by giving economic power to the new union. The project quickly failed, because it aimed above all to build a French Europe rather than promoting an independent Europe.

After the creation of European Political Cooperation (EPC) in 1970, diplomatic cooperation was limited to regular dialogue between the diplomatic services of EC member states. It helped bring the positions of EC members closer together at the Helsinki Conference (1973–75), an East–West forum.[16] European police cooperation, known as Trevi, also emerged in the 1970s on a purely intergovernmental basis, at a time when several European countries were struck by terrorist attacks.[17]

Diplomatic cooperation was generally characterised by profound disagreement on most issues in the 1970s and 1980s (the Arab–Israeli conflict, Euro-Arab dialogue, the invasion of Afghanistan). In 1982, the Falklands conflict led to a short demonstration of European unity, before Ireland and Italy condemned the fighting. This episode reinforced British interest in the EPC, as it was purely intergovernmental in nature.[18]

In 1992, the Maastricht Treaty created the Common Foreign and Security Policy (CFSP), which quickly proved ineffective due to divisions between European countries with respect to the civil war in former Yugoslavia (1992–95). The Minister of Foreign Affairs at the time, Jacques Poos of Luxembourg, famously claimed at the start of the conflict in May 1991 that it was 'the hour of Europe, not the hour of Americans. If one problem can be solved by Europeans, it is the Yugoslav problem.' However, the bloody civil war was, in the end, only solved by US military intervention.[19]

5.1.4 *The Military Dimension: The Dominance of National and Atlantic Logic*

The national and Atlantic dimension also prevailed in arms manufacturing. While the arms industry has remained essentially national, the rising costs of its development prompted international cooperation in the post-war era. US technological and economic leadership has generated a considerable pull effect, as it has often proven more cost-effective to buy US products (which are cheaper because they have already been sold in the large US market) than to create a European weapon from scratch.

The best example is probably the emblematic field of combat aircraft. On the one hand, Europeans have cooperated in American programmes, co-constructing some aircraft or parts, such as the F-104 Starfighter in the 1960s (nicknamed the 'widowmaker' in Germany due to its frequent accidents), the F-16 in the 1980s, and the F-35 in the 2010s.[20] This dynamic further reduced investment in European aircraft. The other type of cooperation has been with programmes rolled out on a European scale, but with no connection to the EC: the French–German Transall transport aircraft was launched in 1963, and the German–Italian–British Tornado combat aircraft was launched in 1974.[21] French–German aircraft cooperation, envisaged during a 1984 meeting between President Mitterrand and Chancellor Kohl, did not prevent France's decision in 1985 to go it alone in developing its new fighter aircraft.[22] The result was the French Rafale launched in 2002, and the German–Italian–British Eurofighter Typhoon, which made its maiden flight in 2004.

Lastly, in terms of military cooperation, NATO kept the upper hand during the Cold War, both in terms of strategic planning and tactical cooperation. NATO standards in arms manufacturing and military procedures facilitated the interoperability between European armies as well as with their North Atlantic allies, as did NATO exercises. In addition, NATO's London Summit in 1990 considerably expanded its missions, paving the way for it to play a leading role in the post-Cold War era.

To conclude, European cooperation failed in diplomacy and defence, where national and North Atlantic logic has been dominant due to considerable US influence, as well as Europe's willingness to be comfortably shielded under the American umbrella. The project for a European army collapsed due to hostility towards federalism, while de Gaulle's vision fell victim to the ambiguity between what he referred to as 'European Europe', and what others saw as a French Europe. Nevertheless, a little-known project for European cooperation in nuclear weapons shows that a more voluntarist approach did exist. Combining European integration and the principle of *community* has been envisaged in diplomacy and defence on multiple occasions, but has not yet materialised.

5.2 A Protectionist Europe in Specific Areas

Europe as a protectionist community has existed in very specific fields, characterised by robust state intervention and a strong incentive for European cooperation, namely in agriculture, aeronautics, and aerospace, but not in energy.

5.2.1 *The Common Agricultural Policy (CAP)*

The Common Agricultural Policy (CAP), Europe's most important redistributive policy, was very protectionist from its inception in 1962 to its reform in

1992. It was based on European preference: imports of non-EC agricultural products were heavily taxed, while exports were subsidised. It favoured producers by creating a single price throughout the EC, backed by European subsidies.

This led to far-reaching and enduring Europeanisation in agricultural policy, but one that was not inevitable, as two other schemes were devised beforehand.[23] The first involved bilateral agreements, such as the one concluded between France and West Germany in agriculture in 1954. The second was an international agreement without federalisation that came immediately after the Schuman Plan of May 1950 (dubbed the 'coal–steel pool'), when French Minister of Agriculture Pierre Pflimlin launched a project for a 'green pool' on 12 June 1950, with a view to organising European agricultural markets within the intergovernmental framework of the OEEC, not just the Six.

The three most influential players in the CAP's emergence in 1962 – the two major agricultural exporters France and the Netherlands, and the European Commissioner for Agriculture Sicco Mansholt, himself a former farmer and Dutch Minister of Agriculture – supported its orientation towards maximising food production.[24] Memories of the food shortages of the 1940s were still vivid in the 1960s. The CAP also had a social objective. After the crisis of the 1930s, which devastated agriculture and weakened democracies, all states, including the most liberal, increased aid to farmers. In 1957, even the famous Swedish economist Gunnar Myrdal (who went on to win the Nobel Memorial Prize in Economics) considered the agricultural policies of rich countries to be striking manifestations of the welfare state.[25] This was a crucial objective for Gaullist France, which faced violent rural demonstrations in 1960–61, described by Gordon Wright as a 'rural revolution': 'railways and roads were blocked, towns invaded by tractor-borne demonstrators, telephone lines sabotaged'.[26]

West Germany was divided on the issue. The ordoliberal-inspired Ludwig Erhard (Minister of Economics from 1949 to 1963, Chancellor from 1963 to 1966) was opposed, while the Minister of Agriculture insisted on high prices to satisfy the agricultural lobby. Bonn subsequently became 'Veto Player No. 1' according to Kiran Klaus Patel, which is to say the most reluctant country in the Six-Party negotiations, particularly those held in 1964 to determine the price of wheat (the first product covered by the CAP).[27] Bonn demanded a higher price than all other major EU producers because the average productivity of German farmers was lower. Since this first negotiation in 1964, a ratchet effect has maintained high agricultural prices ever since.

European protectionism had negative consequences, including overproduction, trade tensions (due to the subsidies needed to export this overproduction), and enormous expenditure. On average, Community agricultural prices were higher than world prices (except during certain periods such as the food crisis of the early 1970s). This led to redistribution from consumers and taxpayers to farmers, especially the richest among them, such as grain growers. The CAP regularly gave rise to institutional tensions, and was partly behind the Empty Chair Crisis in 1965. Price fixing led to the ritual agricultural 'marathon' of long price negotiations requiring unanimity, against a backdrop of farmer demonstrations. In 1971, farmers interrupted the Ministers of Agriculture Council meeting with their cows. On 23 March 1971, a massive demonstration in Brussels led to the death of the Belgian farmer Adelin Porignaux after he was struck by a tear gas grenade.[28]

Criticism of the CAP was voiced even within the French government, albeit discreetly, as this policy represented a massive financial transfer to French farmers. The Minister of Economy and Finance Michel Debré (1966–68) criticised the CAP's financial excesses, while the Minister of Agriculture remained in favour of high prices.[29] Advisors to President Giscard d'Estaing (1974–81) stressed that the CAP was less and less favourable towards France, and more and more towards Germany, which had increased its production considerably.[30] By 1987 West Germany had become the world's fourth-largest exporter of agricultural products, behind the US, France, and the Netherlands.[31] French and British studies in 1979 confirmed that because France benefited less from the CAP than before, it had become a net contributor to the Community budget (albeit much less than Britain and Germany).[32] Giscard d'Estaing advocated cautious reform of the CAP. He supported the Commission's proposals to reduce milk surpluses, but in a selective manner, focusing the effort primarily on large industrial farms rather than small farmers, as he explained to Commission President Roy Jenkins in 1979:[33]

- GISCARD D'ESTAING: *We have to tackle this problem [milk overproduction] from both ends. We cannot apply the same treatment to massive, artificial units as to traditional farms. There is no reason to give financial support to purely speculative and artificial production, made primarily from imported raw materials, to the huge soy factories in Northern Europe. On the other hand, we must support normal farming activities.*
- JENKINS: *It's hard to define this last category.*
- GISCARD D'ESTAING: *These are family farms with a few helpers, using the usual techniques.*
- JENKINS: *I find it hard to see this principle being applied to sugar; I don't know any poor beet growers.*

Jenkins's ironic comment clearly illustrates the CAP's productivist logic favouring large-scale farms, such as French beet producers. Under French President Mitterrand (1981–95), the financial difficulties increased opposition between certain diplomats and experts in the Ministry of Finance, who supported reducing CAP expenditure, and the Minister of Agriculture, who remained on the defensive.[34] These developments explain why the French government accepted the reforms of 1984 and 1992, aimed at reducing CAP expenditure all while maintaining its overarching productivist and protectionist architecture.

On the other side of the Rhine, the German Ministry of Agriculture remained strongly committed to high prices in the 1980s.[35] This explains Chancellor Schmidt's contradictory discourse in European forums. While he generally advocated budgetary rigour, he explained to Jenkins and Giscard d'Estaing that he could not accept lower income for German farmers.[36] Under Chancellor Kohl, support for high prices expanded, no doubt because the CDU-CSU was more dependent on the rural vote.[37] At the German cabinet meeting on 11 May 1983, Finance Minister Stoltenberg, who favoured spending cuts, and Agriculture Minister Kiechle, a defender of German farm incomes, continued to clash.[38] At the Council of Agriculture Ministers on 12 June 1985, the German Minister Kiechle even vetoed a cut in grain and rapeseed prices, citing vital interests.[39] Surprisingly, it was Germany that revived the veto at a time when consensus was building around abolishing its use in connection with the Single Market. The Milan European Council meeting held a few days later (on 28–29 June 1985) paved the way for the Single European Act of 1986, which curtailed use of the veto.

Far-reaching reform occurred in 1992.[40] It was linked both to internal pressure – the need to limit spending and surpluses (for instance 700,000 tonnes of beef went unsold in late 1990) – and an external factor, namely that dismantling the CAP's protectionist apparatus was a stumbling block in GATT negotiations. The Americans had threatened the Europeans with 200 per cent tariffs on a wide range of products. A note from the Commission acknoweldged that EEC aid to its farmers was 2.5 times higher than US aid to its farmers. However, the average amount of aid for farmers was higher in the US than in the EEC, as US farms were nearly ten times the size of European ones.[41] The 1992 Blair House Agreement between the US and the EU broke the deadlock. It was based on a reduction in European export subsidies and price support. In Brussels, the Commissioner for Agriculture, Ray MacSharry of Ireland, transformed price support into a subsidy based on past production and compliance with good practices, including social and (modest) environmental standards. Delors considered promoting a differentiated CAP reform, with the brunt of reform falling on large farms. The UK opposed this approach, being a country of large farms (with Queen Elizabeth II one of the main beneficiaries of the CAP at the time). The story of the CAP is therefore not simply a French–German dispute, but rather one between the large farming lobby, which successfully influenced Agriculture Ministries to secure high prices and protectionism, and other socioeconomic interests.

5.2.2 *Airbus and Ariane: Isolated Success*

In the post-war period, the high cost of developing new jet aircraft and rockets prompted small and medium-sized countries to pursue international cooperation. This was the only solution for pooling costs and securing a larger

5.2 A PROTECTIONIST EUROPE IN SPECIFIC AREAS

domestic market to launch the product, but it requires sharing the production process among various contributors, which can prove inefficient. This is the 'fair return' principle, according to which sums invested in an international programme must be returned to the country of origin in the form of industrial activity. In addition, every country strives to maintain strategic military production on its soil.

The first major European programme to launch a commercial aircraft ultimately failed. In 1962, London and Paris signed an intergovernmental agreement to produce the first supersonic commercial aircraft, the Concorde, which made its maiden flight in 1969. It was an aesthetic and technical success but a commercial failure, since the programme was dominated by an approach emphasising political prestige and technological demonstration (it was the first passenger aircraft to fly above Mach 2, and to have a fly-by-wire flight control system) rather than financial profitability.[42] External events such as the oil crisis, new US environmental standards, US protectionism, and the crashes of the Tupolev Tu-144 (a Soviet equivalent of the Concorde) admittedly affected sales, but the programme's architecture was also to blame.

In contrast, Airbus, which was born of a working group set up in 1965, pursued a commercial approach from the outset: airlines were consulted regarding future demand, industrial leadership was unified, technological innovation was restricted, and the role of governments in operational management was limited.[43] The project was initially French–German–British, but the latter left the consortium in 1969 when industrial leadership was awarded to Paris. The British returned in 1978, when Spain's Casa also joined the consortium. The industrial process was shared mainly between these four countries, with final assembly in Toulouse. The project enjoyed strong political support, although it incurred losses during its first two decades. British archives reveal that the British were well aware of the programme's high cost when they rejoined in 1978.[44] They were reassured by the fact that all governments opposed the Commission's efforts to penetrate the sector since the 1970s.[45] At the time sales of the first Airbus (A300, maiden flight in 1972) began to increase, with forty aircraft sold by 1980, which is to say the same number as its direct competitor, the McDonnell Douglas DC10, but still well below Boeing's figures.

Building on this success, the French government proposed developing a range of aircraft by launching the smaller A320, but West Germany was reluctant, as Lufthansa had already chosen the Boeing 737. This is where political power came into play, for in February 1984 Kohl finally agreed to finance the programme after intense lobbying by Mitterrand.[46] The debates remained complicated even in 1989, for within the liberal FDP party, Minister of Foreign Affairs Hans-Dietrich Genscher and former Minister of the Economy Martin Bangemann had to defend Airbus's political and industrial interest against colleagues sceptical about the project's high cost.[47] More generally, the German state played an important role in supporting the rebirth of the German aeronautics industry, after the ban on aircraft production from 1945 to 1955. Bonn subsidised the industry and backed mergers, such as the one that created MBB in 1969, and the one between MBB and Daimler in 1988. The German industrial base was smaller than its French and British counterparts due to the aforementioned ban. Airbus played an important role in this quest for rebirth.[48]

Surprisingly, subsidies to Airbus were justified even from a free market perspective. In 1987, the American economists Richard Baldwin and Paul Krugman argued that without subsidies, it would have been impossible to enter a market with such high development costs, especially as Boeing's competitors Lockheed and McDonnell Douglas had abandoned the market for the largest aircraft by the mid-1980s.[49] Without Airbus there would have been less competition, and hence higher costs for aircraft and consumers.

Airbus turned an operating profit in 1991. A 1992 agreement with the US limited Airbus subsidies to reimbursable grants of up to 33 per cent of programme development costs. This advantage was not perceived as being undue, since Boeing benefited from funding from the Pentagon and NASA, in addition to various indirect subsidies. Negotiations between the Americans and Europeans were conducted by the European Commission, which played the role of honest broker not only between France (always slightly more protectionist) and its partners, but also between Airbus countries (Britain, France, Germany, Spain) and non-Airbus countries (in particular Italy), which did not want to antagonise the US.[50] Despite being purely intergovernmental at the start, Airbus was later included under the EU umbrella.

The Airbus approach was emulated in the space sector. The imperative was also to create a profitable business in an expanding sector (satellite communications), and to provide participating countries with autonomous capacity for action in a strategic field that the American ally wanted to reserve for itself. In 1967 the French and German industries agreed to build the telecommunications satellite Symphonie. Since no reliable European launcher existed at the time, the two countries had to use American rockets, but NASA insisted on only launching a research satellite rather than one for commercial retransmission.[51]

The creation of an independent European space agency divided the Europeans. Some West Germans were tempted by the American proposal to participate in the Apollo programme, which had already taken the Americans to the moon. France, on the other hand, argued for strategic independence. In the end the European Space Agency was created in 1975, with ten European countries (including Switzerland and Sweden). As with Airbus, the Community was not involved in this effort. France played a leading role thanks to its experience with the nuclear-tipped missile programme, and its launch sites in French Guyana near the equator, from where it costs less to launch a satellite, since it reaches orbit more quickly. The French company Aérospatiale was the primary contractor for the Ariane programme, and the first Ariane rocket was launched in 1979. As with Airbus, a commercial approach was favoured from the outset, with the creation of the limited company Arianespace for marketing purposes. Commercial operations started in 1984. The difficulties experienced by the American shuttle, coupled with the dramatic explosion of the *Challenger* shuttle in 1986, allowed Ariane to establish itself as a commercial success.

A European comparison helps to better grasp the successes of Airbus and Ariane.[52] The ESA was created after the failure of numerous European space cooperation projects in the 1960s, notably ESLO and ELDO. On the aeronautical front, two other European passenger jets made their first flight in 1971, around the same time as the A300: the Mercure and the VFW-Fokker 614. The Mercure was a 150-seat aircraft produced by a consortium led by France's Dassault, and included companies from Belgium, Spain, Italy, Switzerland, and Canada. The VFW-Fokker 614 was a 40-seater built by the German VFW and the Dutch Fokker. Fewer than twenty of each were sold, making them commercial failures.

The Europeans were always eager to cooperate with the Americans, even in Paris. In 1974, the French state-owned Snecma created CFM, a joint venture with General Electric to produce jet engines, with considerable commercial success. That same year, France launched a major programme to build nuclear power plants based on American Westinghouse technology. In computer technology, France had launched a European partnership called Unidata in 1971 to compete with IBM, via cooperation with the German company Siemens, and the Dutch company Philips. It proved to be such an industrial failure that French President Giscard d'Estaing, a liberal concerned with sound financial management, put an end to it in 1974. Most European electronics companies were not particularly interested in a purely European venture, as they had strong links with leading US companies.

The failure of these programmes demonstrates both the exceptional industrial success of Airbus and the ESA, as well as the difficulty of replicating their approach. These two European ventures share a number of common features: they involved a new sector, in which none of the European countries had a dominant position, thereby requiring high development costs; they were developed on an intergovernmental basis, with strong and steady state financial support, along with unified industrial and commercial management; they involved only a select number of countries, thereby limiting the problem of fair return, and facilitating the emergence of political leadership, often French or French–German.

5.2.3 Paradoxical Failure in Energy

Energy is a sector where successful European cooperation was logical, as the continent's energy resources are unevenly distributed, and often based in coal or hydrocarbon basins straddling several countries. Moreover, energy was at the foundation of the European Communities, with the European Coal and Steel Community in 1951, and Euratom in 1957.

Paradoxically, no common energy policy emerged. When the High Authority of the ECSC tried to obtain a declaration of manifest crisis to manage the Belgian coal crisis in 1959, member states refused.[53] Managing the decline of the coal industry remained a national effort. It combined subsidies to attract alternative industries such as car manufacturing to coal-mining areas (Opel opened a factory in Bochum in 1962, Renault in Douai in 1970), as well as aid for worker retraining and early retirement for miners.

Regarding nuclear energy, high hopes had been placed in Euratom, which in 1956–57 was considered more important than the EEC by many Frenchmen, especially Jean Monnet. At the time oil shortages threatened France and Great Britain after the Suez fiasco (1956), but the low price of oil in the 1960s and a lack of interest from de Gaulle limited Euratom to research activities.

The 1973 and 1979 oil crises put European cooperation back on the agenda, this time in the oil sector.[54] Reactions nevertheless remained purely national: France supported Euro-Arab dialogue, and did not participate in the International Energy Agency created in 1974, while the UK and the Netherlands concentrated on exploiting their oil and gas deposits in the North Sea.[55] This discovery prompted Norway to remain outside the Community, even though it had been admitted in 1972. When the topic of coordinating oil policy was raised at the Council by France in 1976 and Germany in 1980, London and The Hague refused to commit.[56] Hydrocarbons were managed by national policies supporting national oil companies (the majors), and bilateral agreements between producer countries and a consumer country, with no European dimension.

National paths diverged. West Germany strove to make the most of its extensive coal resources, and applied unsuccessfully for EC aid for coal production. Throughout the 1980s, Bonn continued to pay close attention to the coal issue, as miners remained numerous and influential, particularly in the SPD. In contrast, France, which lacked such natural resources, embarked on a fast-track nuclear power programme in 1974, becoming the world's second-largest producer of nuclear electricity. Equally lacking in abundant energy resources, Italy followed the nuclear option for a time, until a referendum after the 1986 Chernobyl Accident halted the nuclear programme. Nuclear energy actually represented much more than a source of electricity. As Gabrielle Hecht has shown, from the 1960s onwards nuclear power was an essential element of a modern, ambitious French identity, which was

5.3 TAMING NATIONAL PROTECTIONISM

contrasted in public discourse with backward-looking Vichy France.[57] The French civil and nuclear programme enjoyed enduring support as part of a newly assertive France after the humiliating defeat of 1940. One particularly sad episode is illuminating: in 1985 the Rainbow Warrior, a Greenpeace ship, embarked on a campaign to monitor French nuclear testing in the Pacific. The French secret service wanted to sink it without causing any casualties, so they placed two bombs in the ship when it was docked in Auckland, New Zealand: a first small bomb to warn the crew, and a second one to sink the ship. After the first bomb exploded, a photographer rushed to retrieve his equipment and was subsequently killed. The French spies were arrested, and the government was forced to make amends. However, surveys of the French population showed that while 78 per cent condemned the disastrous operation, 60 per cent supported the French nuclear testing programme. Greenpeace was forced to close its French office for a few years due to a lack of membership![58] A certain Europeanisation of energy policy later took hold from the late 1980s onwards due to the growing impact of environmental and competition regulations (see Chapters 3 and 4), albeit without an industrial dimension.

To conclude, protectionism was organised on a European level for certain sectors, ranging from agriculture and traditional manufacturing (Chapter 6) to Airbus, but no overall European protectionist approach emerged, let alone European industrial policy. On the contrary, it was in taming national protectionism that European integration was the most active.

5.3 The European Quest to Tame National Protectionism

Since European integration has depended on the creation of a Common Market (Chapter 3), it has always been important to ensure a level playing field. Yet all of the continent's states, including those that consider themselves paragons of free trade, such as the UK and West Germany, intervened massively to support their industries during the Cold War; the risk of protectionist tit-for-tat was quite real. European policy subsequently endeavoured to tame national protectionism, thereby complicating the emergence of a European industrial policy.

5.3.1 The Omnipresence of Industrial Policy in Europe (1945–80)

Western Europe was marked by widespread industrial policies between 1945 and 1980, in an effort to rebuild the continent and catch up with the US. This policy took various forms, adapting to social and institutional structures (centralised in France and the UK, more federal in Germany).

French industrial policy was, in the words of Vivien Schmidt, characterised by 'formulating heroic policies, announced with great fanfare' by the government.[59] State interventionism was part of the Colbertist heritage, as well as a modern industrial response to the agrarian and dictatorial Vichy regime. Most politicians and civil servants were convinced that they had to shake up a business world seen as 'Malthusian' (in other words too timid and France-centric), to use the expression of the time referring to the British economist Thomas Malthus, who in the context of a stagnant economy advocated birth restrictions. After 1945, this dirigisme was expressed through the nationalisation of numerous companies in strategic sectors, control over credit (many banks were public or semi-public), and indicative planning. Chronologically, French industrial policy experienced two peaks: reconstruction with the Monnet Plan (1946-52), and the revival of planning and industrial policy under the de Gaulle and Pompidou presidencies (1959-74), revolving around the twin imperatives of modernisation and international competitiveness. Major high-tech projects were launched by the government in IT (the Plan Calcul in 1966 and Unidata, both failures), energy (with nuclear power plants), and transport (Concorde and Airbus, followed by the high-speed train TGV in the 1970s).

In 1974 the new liberal president, Giscard d'Estaing, initially considered curtailing support for 'lame ducks', but the oil shocks forced him to revert to dirigisme. The 1979 oil crisis further increased state aid to industry, despite the concerns privately expressed by Giscard d'Estaing and his prime minister Raymond Barre regarding the ineffectiveness of those subsidies.[60] President Mitterrand's industrial policy between 1981 and 1984 was even more dirigiste, since it launched a second wave of nationalisation, followed by a massive injection of public funding. At the time, public sector employment accounted for over 10 per cent of total employment. The state reconfigured and recapitalised these nationalised groups. According to Vivien Schmidt, between 1982 and 1984, the five largest groups received 'ten times more capital than private shareholders had provided them in the eight years between 1974 and 1981'.[61] Paradoxically, the nationalisations of the socialist and communist governments helped restructure and even save part of French capitalism.

By contrast, West Germany offered a contrasting example of an unstated but equally effective industrial policy. The German government's archives are enlightening in this respect. The term *Industriepolitik* is used in a 1976 document from the German Ministry of Economics, which stresses that even if this expression is not used, Germany did intervene a great deal, as proven by a long list of interventions in the economy.[62] European surveys show that the level of state aid and the role of the nationalised sector were comparable in Germany and France before the major socialist reforms of 1981.[63] In 1980, a British study comparing industrial policy in the electronics industry estimated that the programmes created in West Germany and France in the 1970s were equivalent in terms of public funding.[64]

West Germany's industrial policy had two major differences compared to that of France.[65] Firstly, while direct intervention was permitted in certain sectors (such as the 1968 law on adapting coal mines), most measures were more discreet, taking the form of tax subsidies, support for research and development, or merger incentives (notably in the aeronautics industry). The second difference was the much weaker role played by the central government, to the benefit of the German states (the Länder) and banks, especially the regional banks (Landesbanken) that provided long-term financing often backed by public guarantees.[66] Trade unions were also much more influential and sensitive to the need for international competitiveness than their British or French counterparts.[67]

The crisis of the 1970s gave rise to debates within the government coalition, between the Social Democrats of the SPD and the Liberals of the FDP, regarding the advisability of launching a policy to support high-tech sectors. While the FDP Minister of Economics Friedrichs maintained an orthodox line of limited support for companies, the State Secretary to the German Minister for Research and Technology, the Social Democrat Volker Hauff, was in favour of much more active support for high-tech investment, in line with the book he published with the academic Fritz Scharpf in 1975.[68] The controversy widened in 1977 as Otto Schlecht, State Secretary at the Ministry of Economics, and Hans Tietmeyer, a senior official at the Ministry of Economics (and future president of the Bundesbank), defended the orthodox liberal line against the more proactive SPD Minister of Research and Technology, Hans Matthöfer.[69] In 1977 the Schmidt government ultimately decided to launch a massive high-tech investment programme.[70] Matthöfer, who became Minister of Finance in 1978, sought to use the public sector to pursue industrial policy objectives.[71]

German opponents to industrial policy launched a counter-offensive. In July 1979, Tietmeyer called for a *Subventionsordnungsgesetz* (Law on the Order of Subsidies) to regulate state aid in Germany.[72] The very same year, the Land (State) of North Rhine-Westphalia (which encompasses the Ruhr region) discussed adopting a 'framework law for economic aid', which Tietmeyer described as 'bureaucratic'.[73] In contrast, Lower Saxony's Economics Minister Birgit Breuel was in favour of greater restrictions over aid, especially to bring it in line with the principles of '*ordnungspolitik*'.[74] Breuel was a close associate of Minister-President Ernst Albrecht, himself a pioneer in developing EU competition policy in the 1960s (and father of current Commission President Ursula von der Leyen).[75] The debate was rekindled in July 1982 by the Minister of Economics, the neoliberal FDP Otto Graf Lambsdorff, who was determined to limit both the 'exuberant' subsidies of the Länder and their 'mutual rivalry', which produced a subsidy race incompatible with the 'social market economy'.[76] The aim was to increase transparency and control, and eliminate subsidies designed solely to safeguard unprofitable jobs. Once again the Länder were divided between Lower Saxony, which favoured binding legislation, and those supporting aid for employment purposes, including North Rhine-Westphalia (for coal and steel), along with Bremen and Hamburg (for shipbuilding).

The debate took a political turn with the famous Lambsdorff paper of 9 September 1982, which called for limiting the government's involvement in the economy in addition to *Entbürokratisiereung* (debureaucratisation).[77] It played a role in the fall of the Schmidt government a few weeks later, which was replaced by the Kohl government, with Tietmeyer as State Secretary for Finance. West Germany then embarked on a policy of gradual liberalisation, but Bonn remained vigilant when it came to strategic sectors. The government willingly encouraged the merger of Daimler-Benz and MBB in 1988, against the advice of its competition authorities. Foreign takeovers were still hampered by the peculiar structure of German capitalism.

The majority of European countries were situated somewhere between these two poles of France and West Germany. Italy followed the French dirigiste model.[78] The UK had taken a similar path to France in 1945, but to a lesser extent; there was no indicative planning, and trade unions were more powerful. As in France, the early 1970s saw an abortive attempt at a liberal turnaround under Prime Minister Edward Heath. When Labour returned to power in 1974, London reinforced its industrial policy in response to the crisis, with the introduction of sectoral dialogue involving unions. Two companies in difficulty were nationalised in 1977, British Leyland and British Shipbuilders, which accounted for the majority of car and shipbuilding companies respectively. But as the crisis persisted, relations between the government and unions soured, leading to the Winter of Discontent protests of 1978–79.

In 1979 Margaret Thatcher came to power and imposed a radical break with the past. Initially, the change was slower in industrial policy than in the macroeconomic sphere, where the Iron Lady pursued a policy of radical austerity.[79] State aid to ailing industry continued during the first three years, while the privatisation and liberalisation movement got off to a slow start, taking off only with the privatisation of British Telecom in 1984.[80] A more selective industrial policy was gradually put in place, concentrating credit on high-tech companies to the detriment of 'lame ducks'.[81] Large public companies were entrusted to energetic managers, who imposed painful industrial restructuring.[82] Thatcher passed laws gradually restricting union power in 1980, 1982, and 1984, before successfully confronting coal miners head-on in 1984–85, followed by print workers in 1986 (Wapping Dispute). Thatcher's reform heralded a new era of declining neomercantilist policies.

5.3.2 Decline of National Industrial Policies and Liberal Europeanisation (1980s)

From the 1980s onwards, industrial policies began to weaken in Western Europe for three reasons. Firstly, neoliberal ideas gained ground. They theorised the inefficiency of public intervention (Virginia School, second Chicago school, monetarism), reinforced by the discrediting of the Soviet system. Second, industrial policies were expensive, and financial constraints increased in Europe with the crisis of the 1970s, as demonstrated by the IMF's interventions in the UK in 1976 and Italy in 1977, and by the French financial crisis in 1983 (Chapter 7). While some state-owned companies were associated with modernisation, particularly in France (SNCF with the TGV, EDF with nuclear power plants), in other countries they were increasingly criticised when managers and employees were hired due to their political connections rather than their competence.[83] This led to the disillusioned testimony of the Belgian Social Democratic leader Karel van Miert in his memoirs: 'In the days of the RTT [Régie des Télégraphes et Téléphone] monopoly in Belgium, getting a telephone connection was a favour ... unless you knew someone who had a long arm: if you had a political or trade union connection.'[84] The final reason was technical progress, which overturned old monopolies and oligopolies. In 1945, state intervention was necessary in sectors such as air transport and telecommunications, because resources and jobs were scarce. In the 1980s, with the multiplication of producers and products, the coordinating role of public authorities was more difficult to maintain.

Developments followed an uneven chronology in Europe, with Thatcher's UK acting as a pioneer, and Mitterrand's France as a laggard. Indeed, according to OECD and Commission figures, French state aid to business increased massively between 1981 and 1983, exceeding the European average.[85] Prior to this, aid to French and German companies was at roughly the same level, and below that of the UK. Similarly, while before 1981 the weight of the public sector was roughly the same in France and the UK, and considerably lower than in Italy (where the IRI conglomerate employed almost half a million people), the balance changed after the French nationalisations.[86] In 1984, even Mitterrand's France changed course due to financial pressure. At an internal government meeting on industrial policy on 11 January 1984, Mitterrand justified economic layoffs: 'Why should companies pay employees who are no longer needed?'[87] When Communist Minister Marcel Rigout pointed out that 'the number one problem is employment', Mitterrand replied: 'The number one problem is unprofitable companies. There will be no guaranteed jobs with companies that don't work.' Finally, on 29 March 1984 the French government switched to a more selective industrial policy in terms of aid.[88]

Privatisation accelerated everywhere in the mid-1980s – in London in 1984 (British Telecom), in Paris in 1986 (with the return of the centre-right), as well as in Rome (with Alfa Romeo) and with small steps in Kohl's Germany. In addition to privatisation, measures to promote competition were launched to prevent private monopolies from replacing public ones. Sectors previously managed directly by the government were now guided by the market, with public authorities relegated to the role of neutral regulator. Here too the UK was a pioneer, opening up bus transport to competition in 1980, and telecommunications in 1981 and 1984.

The government kept a role as an arbiter and sometimes as a coordinator. For example, in 1982 Chancellor Schmidt refused to intervene to prevent AEG from filing for bankruptcy, but he did encourage creditors to mobilise, sometimes granting state guarantees on certain loans.[89] In 1984, the French state actively intervened to find buyers for the various components of the steelmaker Creusot-Loire and the textile giant Boussac, while granting indirect aid at the same time.[90] The French privatisations of 1986–87 preserved public influence, as the French state created 'hard cores' of stable French shareholders, and placed former senior civil servants in management positions at public companies. British privatisations, on the other hand, often led to foreign takeovers, because the government was less drawn to neomercantilism.

The role of the Community expanded with the creation of the Single Market and the expansion of competition policy, notably in regulating state aid and liberalising new sectors (Chapter 3).

5.3.3 European Neomercantilist Temptation and Minimal Industrial Policy

European industrial policy was an old project: it was broached during the 1949 Westminster conference of the European Movement.[91] The 1951 ECSC entrusted the High Authority with numerous prerogatives in this area, but member states did not allow it to use them. In 1967, the debate was revived when the French journalist Jean-Jacques Servan-Schreiber published his famous book entitled *The American Challenge*.[92] It began with an exhortation to react to the American offensive: 'War, for it is a war, is not being waged with dollars, oil, tons of steel or even modern machines, but with creative imagination and organisational talent.' It denounced the danger of American hegemony in high-tech sectors (aeronautics, aerospace, electronics, and computers), and called for a European response. Written with the collaboration of Michel Albert, at the time a French civil servant at the Commission (in charge of various Community industrial policy projects), it called for developing a federal Community industrial policy, with the creation of European companies and the joint definition of major industrial programmes.[93]

The various projects launched between 1965 and 1974 by the most proactive players – the French, Italian, and British governments and the Commission, often without effective coordination between them – came to nothing.[94] In Paris, the Gaullist government was eager to promote European industrial cooperation on an intergovernmental basis. In early 1965, it initiated an effort in Brussels to coordinate national scientific and technical research policies, as well as to create a European company statute that would facilitate European mergers. This effort was scuttled by the Empty Chair Crisis triggered by de Gaulle. In 1966, Italian Foreign Minister Amintore Fanfani proposed a Technological Marshall Plan based on transatlantic cooperation, while in 1966 British Prime Minister Harold Wilson launched the idea of a European Technological Community. Underscoring Britain's lead over the continent in a number of high-tech fields, Wilson wanted to demonstrate that enlarging the EEC to include the UK would bring new, tangible benefits to member countries. De Gaulle's second rejection of Britain's application in 1967 interrupted these reflections. At the same time, French and Italian commissioners in charge of industrial policy mobilised in Brussels, first under the guidance of Robert Marjolin of France (1958–67), and then under the Italians Guido Colonna di Paliano (1967–70) and Altiero Spinelli (1970–76). In 1974 the fiery federalist Spinelli challenged his president, the cautious François-Xavier Ortoli, to propose an integrated industrial policy: 'I'm also sending you a photocopy of Schuman's speech, which shows how a statesman who really wants to do something expresses himself.'[95] This anecdote serves as eloquent testimony to Spinelli's style, the reluctance of member states, and the caution of President Ortoli, a French Gaullist. Only European projects of an intergovernmental nature, such as Airbus or the ESA, managed to endure.

In 1983, a new American challenge emerged with the relaunch of the arms race under US President Ronald Reagan with the Strategic Defence Initiative (SDI). Nicknamed 'Star Wars', in reference to the trilogy by George Lucas released between 1977 and 1983, it sought to create a shield against the USSR's nuclear missiles by using new technologies, with one of the avenues being the development of laser-armed satellites.

This new American challenge provoked a European reaction, initially on an intellectual level with the Ball–Albert report of 1984 commissioned by the European Parliament.[96] A former co-author of the 1967 *American Challenge*, Michel Albert wrote the report's most neomercantilist chapters. It echoed the ideas of *The American Challenge*, but with a slightly less federal approach. Albert emphasised the importance of the Single Market, envisaged from a neomercantilist perspective with the creation of sectoral agencies defining European standards and rationalising industrial cooperation, along with reciprocity in trade.

France's position, however, remained ambiguous.[97] Centre-right governments (1958–81) opposed any industrial policy out of hostility to the delegation of sovereignty. When the Socialists returned to power in 1981, their first reflections on international cooperation in industrial policy were aired not within the Community, but during the 1982 G7 summit in Versailles.[98] From 1983 onwards, the pro-European fringe of the French government prevailed (Foreign Minister Claude Cheysson, a former European Commissioner, and Elisabeth Guigou, an advisor to François Mitterrand). They recognised the failure of both the purely national route and the purely global one (with discussions stalled at the G7). They drew inspiration from Albert's report to issue a French memorandum calling for a European industrial policy in September 1983. It advocated for standardisation, agreements between European firms, and developing European research policy and infrastructure. It called for European preference in public procurement for high-technology, which meant discriminating against non-EC companies, American and Japanese firms in particular. Moreover, following a long-standing French tradition of opposition towards the Commission meddling in industrial affairs, it called for agencies of variable geometry to be created outside the EC framework, with a shifting number of countries. The aim was to duplicate the success of Airbus, namely by circumventing a potential veto by a Community member such as the UK, and by limiting the Commission's role.

Finally, a minimalist industrial policy emerged in Brussels in 1984 with the creation of the ESPRIT programme (European Strategic Programme for Research and Development in Information Technology), which allocated 1.5 billion ECU (half of which was provided by the EEC) over five years for IT and communication research. The aim was to create profitable high-tech products and impose a European standard. Even Bonn and London supported this highly targeted industrial policy, whose funding was provisional, and limited to the pre-competitive sector.[99] Counter-intuitively, Thatcher strongly supported this initiative against her sceptical technology minister.[100] ESPRIT, like Airbus, was cited as an example in the 1984 British memorandum entitled 'Europe: The Future'.[101] London also actively supported the European standardisation effort, particularly in mobile telephony (Chapter 6).[102]

When the US offered to involve Europeans in the SDI, Paris counter-attacked by proposing an intergovernmental European scheme outside the Community. It was named Eureka, after the Greek interjection ('I discovered (it)') attributed to Archimedes in his bath. It was meant to promote European cooperation between companies in research and development, but outside the Community framework.[103] The Commission could participate, but only as a member. In discussions with his Italian and German counterparts just before the Milan European Council, Mitterrand's advisor Attali insisted that Eureka must not be discussed in depth within the framework of the EEC.[104] This intergovernmental approach met with approval from Thatcher, who supported Eureka.[105] She explicitly asked her administration to produce notes supporting Eureka just before the Milan European Council.[106] Thanks to London's backing, the project was launched after a key meeting in Paris on 17 July 1985. It brought together seventeen countries, plus the Commission. The organisation largely escaped its French public sponsors, despite the involvement of French companies.[107] The Eureka project appears to have been partly a political stunt designed to undercut the Americans; the venture was planned by the French presidency and diplomats, and not by the Ministry of Industry.[108] The latter was more focused on responding to Jacques Delors's

5.3 TAMING NATIONAL PROTECTIONISM 123

industrial policy proposals to the European Commission, but it was soon forced to abandon this task.

In Brussels, Delors looked unfavourably on this attempt to promote a non-EC industrial Europe.[109] He wanted to go further than the ESPRIT programme. As early as the spring of 1985, he made Community industrial policy one of his priorities, along with the Single Market.[110] In the spirit of *The American Challenge*, he proposed EC aid to encourage European companies to cooperate, as well as to fund European infrastructure (notably pan-European transport and communications networks) and industrial projects. This idea goes back a long way. In the interwar years, the Director General of the ILO, Albert Thomas of France, proposed a European plan to build a pan-European communications infrastructure to boost the economy, without success.[111]

Delors's ambitions met with opposition from liberal states, led by Germany and the UK, in addition to intergovernmental scepticism in France. In the end, the pan-European infrastructure was rather limited: the Single Market fostered a massive increase in transport by car and plane, but not by train, due to a lack of international connections (with exceptions such as the Channel tunnel, opened in 1994, but without public subsidies, as Thatcher had insisted on a purely private partnership).

Moreover, European companies were not necessarily seeking European cooperation. For example in 1990–91, the Commission President, in cooperation with the Minister for Industrial Affairs, Martin Bangemann of Germany, prepared an industrial strategy for the electronics industry in conjunction with a number of firms in the sector.[112] The plan was to mobilise European funding to encourage companies to work together beyond R&D – by creating an Airbus of semiconductors – and linking this industrial project to a demand for reciprocity in opening up American and Japanese markets. But this project was doomed due to the reluctance of European companies such as Siemens, Bull, and Olivetti, which were allied with American and Japanese firms.

Delors also faced opposition from within the Commission. In 1989, the Competition Commissioner Leon Brittan of the UK used the newly acquired power of merger control (Chapter 3) to wage a neoliberal crusade. In late 1991, Brittan secured a majority at the College of Commissioners against the planned takeover of Canadian aircraft manufacturer De Havilland by the French–Italian company ATR.[113] The Commission's economic reasoning was contested, and not just in France, as the relevant market was defined narrowly, disregarding the presence of other competitors.[114] This decision was debated even within the Directorate General for Competition, with pure ordoliberals not necessarily convinced by its economic reasoning.[115] Brittan was attacking a symbol of industrial policy, the strengthening of a European champion in a cutting-edge sector (the construction of propeller-driven passenger aircraft). At the College of Commissioners, the Commissioner for

Industry Martin Bangemann and President Jacques Delors voted against Brittan or abstained.

In the end, discussions surrounding Community led exclusively to measures accompanying the Single Market Programme (aid for pre-competitive research, standardisation, and ad hoc financing for infrastructure). National industrial policies, which had been prevalent throughout Europe (including West Germany, where it was more discreet), declined in the 1980s without being Europeanised.

5.4 Conclusion

The development of *community* capitalism at a European level was impossible as national industrial policies dominated, even in supposedly liberal countries such as the UK and West Germany, at least until the early 1980s. An international solution was devised in defence and diplomacy, but it was a North Atlantic (NATO) rather than a European one that ultimately prevailed. As early as 1958, Eisenhower had complained about Europe's passive reliance on the US umbrella.

European integration was useful in easing the tensions caused by national protectionism and European protectionism in specific fields, mainly agriculture, aeronautics, and aerospace. But it failed in the most strategic areas such as energy, diplomacy, armament, and defence. Airbus and Ariane were developed outside the European Communities. The CAP was a success at first, but it made the Community system more cumbersome. It pitted not just states against each other, but also ministries, with those for finance favouring lower prices, and those for agriculture defending high prices in Paris and Bonn. It also created imbalances between small and large farmers, to the advantage of the latter.

The Europeanisation of industrial policy remained an arduous task for three reasons. First, states did not want to relinquish control over strategic sectors (energy, diplomacy, armament). Second, they insisted on the principle of fair return (receiving a share of the production corresponding to the investment). Third, it was difficult to defend European preference without compromising the US alliance, from both a geopolitical and economic point of view. Companies were not necessarily eager to pursue European cooperation, as demonstrated by French enterprises gravitating towards American partners in spite of the government's official Colbertism.

The answer to these three dilemmas was found in the Airbus and Ariane programmes. They shared four common features: 1) a new sector in which no European countries had a dominant position, thereby requiring high development costs; 2) a blend of intergovernmental features (interstate projects with no EC intervention) and federal ones (integrated industrial and commercial structure); 3) a limited number of countries, thereby curtailing the problem of fair return and facilitating the emergence of political leadership, often French or French–German; and 4) long-term state support due to the strategic nature of the project, but without interference in management. Even Bonn supported Airbus with massive subsidies for decades, doing so to forge closer ties with France, and because it was deemed strategically important to rebuild its aeronautics industry. This model has proven difficult to reproduce. The book *The American Challenge* proposed the ideal solution from a technical point of view, even though it was politically unfeasible: federalising all high-tech programmes, thereby eliminating the problem of fair return (as financial costs in one programme could be compensated by gains in another). This would entail a major surrender of sovereignty, as most countries would have to specialise in particular products, thereby abandoning some sectors altogether, and renouncing certain national industries.

The project to transform Europe into a genuine geopolitical power often bore France's hallmark, and resulted in failed projects – such as the European army with the EDC, French–German–Italian nuclear cooperation, the political Europe of the Fouchet Plan, European industrial policy – as well as genuine achievements such as the CAP, Airbus, and Ariane. Paradoxically, Paris has often supported affirming Europe as a *community* in the sense of this book's trilogy, but not affirming the European Community as an organisation. In other words, it has generally favoured an intergovernmental approach (with the exception of the EDC). This was obvious under de Gaulle as well as Mitterrand to a certain extent, as Paris was wary of Delors's ambitions for a Community industrial policy, preferring intergovernmental approaches such as Eureka.

France was not the only country interested in industrial policy. Britain before Thatcher (and under Thatcher for limited ventures such as Airbus or Eureka) and even Germany pursued active industrial policies. Bonn supported aeronautical cooperation to rebuild its aeronautical industry, and defended high agricultural prices. Both London and Bonn supported the Commission's defence of Airbus against the US. There were hesitations about the relationship with the US, but these also affected France. The same dilemmas apply to asserting Europe's power vis-à-vis the outside world.

6

European Attempts to Promote Alternatives to Neoliberal Globalisation (1970–92)

'Of course the Community was protectionist: that was the point of it.'

François Mitterrand, 1990

Protectionism was clearly asserted as being positive by French President François Mitterrand. This is how he responded to British Prime Minister Margaret Thatcher in 1990 when she complained about the European Community's restrictive position on international trade negotiations.[1] This exchange neatly encapsulates the relation between European integration and globalisation: Should European organisation protect Europeans from the excesses of international free trade through some form of protectionnism, or on the contrary foster unregulated free trade? To return to the trinity of capitalist governance – *liberty, solidarity,* and *community* – would the European community be conducive to *community* capitalism or not?

The answer is not that simple, as globalisation has often entailed a compromise, even for the most ardent free traders such as Thatcher. Protectionism dominated the world in the 1930s and 1940s. The Havana Charter signed in 1948 established an international trade organisation combining free trade with clauses protecting certain vulnerable areas of economic activity (such as farming).[2] However, the treaty was not ratified by the US Congress, and the planned organisation never saw the light of day; only the GATT survived, an exclusively free trade agreement. Free trade resumed gradually in the 1960s and 1970s. The European Community played a considerable role, especially with the unification of the trade policy of member states from the 1960s onwards. The Commission represented European countries in the GATT negotiations, with close oversight by experts from member states. An essential element of European capitalism – its relation to trade globalisation – was subsequently Europeanised.

In 1973 the degree of 'trade openesss' reached that of 1913,[3] but this time non-Western producers had a more important role (from Japan to the Arab oil exporting countries that triggered the oil shock). A new era unfolded in the 1990s, one that would be later referred to as 'neoliberal globalisation', namely an unregulated expansion of free trade potentially threatening welfare states. However, before this era of neoliberal globalisation, numerous Europeans promoted alternatives. The European Community launched three oft-forgotten projects combining *liberal, solidary*, and *community* capitalism: the control of multinationals, industrial policy in ailing sectors, and 'European preference'. They for the most part failed, with Europe ultimately emerging only as a 'normative power'.

6.1 Controlling Multinationals

While multinational firms were not specific to the twentieth century, as demonstrated by the powerful East India Company, which conquered and administered the vast Indian colonies until 1858, their importance grew considerably beginning in the 1960s.[4] The opening of international markets for goods and capital, in addition to the collapse of colonial empires, lent them greater weight in the economy. This evolution occurred at a time when state intervention in the economy was at a historical peak during peacetime, and when social emancipation movements were especially active. The confluence of these two dynamics led to a movement to control multinationals. It was coupled with another parallel project that drew on the social movement of the late 1960s to democratise companies by increasing worker power, notably by including union representatives on the boards of enterprises. Since the democratisation of the political sphere appeared to finally be complete, with the elimination of the last discriminatory voting policies, it seemed archaic to preserve an outdated and inefficient authoritarianism within enterprises. This debate was simultaneously launched on the national, international, and European scale.

6.1.1 National Debates in Europe

The democratisation of major companies was the most advanced in West Germany with its system of 'codetermination' (*Mitbestimmung*), in which employee representatives were involved in major decisions.[5] This system did not concern all companies, as the first such law in 1951 only applied to companies in steel or coal with over 1,000 employees. It stipulated that nearly half of supervisory board members must be employee representatives, and provided a right of examination over a wide range of decisions. This was a far cry from worker power, since German enterprises have a two-tier board system – a supervisory board and a management board – with shareholders remaining dominant in the latter. The Social Democratic government sought to expand codetermination in the 1970s, but the law of 1976 led to difficult discussions. The German trade union DGB was disappointed by the 1976 law, which it saw as being too limited, while the employers' association BDI challenged it before the Constitutional Court in Karlsruhe, albeit without success. Some companies circumvented the law by creating subsidiaries, or by transferring divisions to foreign subsidiaries with a view to remaining under the 2,000 employees threshold. Mannesmann, a powerful steel conglomerate from the Ruhr, wanted to benefit from the 1976 law, which was less restrictive than that of 1951. It argued that the share of steelmaking activity in its overall turnover had fallen below 50 per cent, hence the enterprise should be subject to the lighter obligations of the 1976 law. The case sparked a new and tense political debate that ended with the adoption of a law in 1981 establishing specific provisions for firms such as Mannesmann. German codetermination was quite extensive, and strongly supported by unions, but also increasingly challenged.

In contrast, there was no codetermination in Britain, France, and Italy, and no unanimous union support for this project. Some in left-wing parties and trade unions associated codetermination with shameful 'class collaboration', as workers would be cooperating with representatives of capitalism.[6] In Britain, Harold Wilson's Labour government established a committee in 1975, led by the history professor Alan Bullock, to study the extension of 'industrial democracy' via employee representation on management teams. The ambitious report envisioned giving significant powers to unions, but it did not pass. In 1974, the new French President Valéry Giscard d'Estaing revived this issue by appointing a committee led by the centrist Pierre Sudreau.[7] The committee published its fairly prudent report in 1975, but the effort was ultimately abandoned due to negative reactions from both employers and unions.[8] The idea was not abandoned by Minister of Social Affairs Robert Boulin, who established a working group including experts such as Martine Aubry, the daughter of Jacques Delors and a senior civil servant at the Ministry for Social Affairs. The French socialists advocated for some form of codetermination in the 1970s.[9] When they came to power in 1981, the socialists strengthened the rights of employees with the Auroux laws of 1982–83 (with Aubry serving as Deputy Chief of Staff for Minister Jean Auroux), albeit without giving them genuine codetermination powers.

The democratisation of enterprises was widely discussed in Europe.[10] In 1979 it was included in the platform of the two Belgian socialist parties, while in Stockholm a series of laws were passed in 1973 and 1976 strengthening employee rights with respect to occupational health and safety, and establishing employee representation on supervisory boards. In 1976 the Swedish Trade Union Confederation (LO) adopted a project, developed by a group of union economists led by Rudolph Meidner, that provided for the socialisation of profits, which would be transformed into funds controlled by employee unions. A watered-down version of this proposal was adopted in 1983, with the funds in question representing approximately 3.5 per cent of the Stockholm stock exchange's market capitalisation in 1990.

Outside of Western Europe, the Yugoslav model based on decentralised planning and worker participation in management was cited as a model by a growing number of experts in Western Europe in the late 1960s and early 1970s, and this despite the country's fragile economic situation. Paradoxically, the president of the European Commission, Sicco Mansholt of Holland, cited the Yugoslav model for industrial democracy as an example during his official visit to the country in 1972, even though the purpose of his visit was to provide assistance for its sputtering economy.[11] The idea of democratising enterprises was even raised in the US under the Carter administration, albeit in a more modest fashion. Exchanges took place between Americans and European civil servants from the Commission in 1976–77 to study worker participation measures on both side of the Atlantic.[12] The debate was revived after the appointment, in 1980, of a union representative to the board of directors of the financially struggling Chrysler, but Reagan's rise to power profoundly changed the dynamic.

6.1.2 The Global South for a Social and Neomercantilist Globalisation

The debate also spread to international circles in support of mobilising the Global South – once referred to as the 'Third World' or 'the South' in those days – in the effort to promote a more social and neomercantilist approach to globalisation. The Global South acted via the United Nations Conference on Trade and Development (UNCTAD) created in 1964. It developed a comprehensive set of economic ideas thanks to the work of its first secretary general, the famous Argentinian economist Raul Prebisch. The aim was to revamp the international economic order not to diminish free trade, but to make it work in the interest of poorer countries.[13] These ideas translated onto the world stage in a programme called the New International Economic Order (NIEO), which was passed by the UN General Assembly in 1974.[14] This important manifesto emphasised the full sovereignty of the Global South against abuses of power by multinationals from the Global North, which was particularly evident in some Latin American countries whose governments were destabilised by American enterprises (which sometimes supported military coups). It called for organising markets to avoid sudden fluctuations in commodity prices (many poor countries were highly dependent on exporting one or two agricultural or mining products), and to redistribute funds from wealthier countries (both Western and oil-exporting countries). The NIEO explicitly sought to increase exports from the Global South to the Global North, by increasing both public and private foreign investment on the part of wealthy countries in the export industries of poorer countries. The NIEO was therefore not Marxist, but rather a combination between the approaches of *liberty*, *solidarity*, and *community*.

Paradoxically, it was the European Community that implemented some elements of the NIEO with its STABEX programme in 1975 (see Section 6.2.2). In 1974, the IMF created a fund financed by petroleum exporting countries, but it remained fairly modest, as the OPEC surplus was largely recycled on the private Eurodollar market.[15] Solidarity among countries in the Global South thus remained very hypothetical.

In 1976, the fourth session of UNCTAD called for the systematic consultation of countries in the Global South regarding the purchasing policy of the Global North, as well as the regulation of their own exports of raw materials and agricutural products (through control over stock which would have given them leverage over prices). At the Conference on International Economic Cooperation (CIEC) in 1977, countries from the Global South created a Common Fund for Commodities, a major objective of the fourth UNCTAD in May 1976.[16] The agreement was ultimately concluded in 1980, although delays in its ratification pushed its implementation back to 1984. In the end, no systematic organisation of trade emerged.

With respect to controlling multinationals, the Global South believed that multinationals in the Global North often colluded to sell their products, licences, and services via export agreements or market sharing. This allowed them to raise prices in poorer countries, all while hampering local industrial development. This concern sparked a debate at the UN.[17] It translated into a first international report drafted in 1969,[18] which revealed numerous restrictive agreements by Western multinationals. In 1972, Chilean President Salvadore Allende admonished foreign multinationals at the UN. At the Algiers Conference of Non-aligned Countries in 1973, the Chilean representative proposed creating joint enterprises among the non-aligned.[19] Allende's tragic death during Pinochet's coup d'état in 1973 changed Chile's position, but not that of UNCTAD, which established a 'special group of experts on restrictive business practices', and passed a resolution in 1976 calling for negotiations to establish a code of conduct for multinational corporations. A large number of issues still being discussed today were raised at the time, notably surrounding the practice of 'transfer pricing', or internal transactions by major corporations – especially between subsidiaries and the parent company – designed to artificially reduce the profits made in some countries in order to reduce taxes.[20] UNCTAD also denounced international cartels at the time. One of these studies revealed how electrical equipment multinationals from the West (Siemens, General Electric, etc.) had come to an agreement to share the Brazilian market, avoiding direct competition among themselves, and refusing to sell high value-added equipment to their Brazilian competitors, thereby stunting their development in the 1960s. The report concluded: 'the electrical equipment industry that has been established in Brazil by the mid-1960s was decimated systematically by the early 1970s. Local manufacturers, not members of the cartel, were weakened financially, and either they were taken over by the cartel members or they went bankrupt.'[21] This demonstrates how markets were organised according to the neomercantilist logic of *community* (the community here being the West and its multinationals), as opposed to *liberty* (free market) or *solidarity*.

In 1980 UNCTAD succeeded in having the UN adopt the Set of Multilaterally Agreed Equitable Principles and Rules for the Control of Restictive Business Practices (known as 'The Set'), which was created to oversee multinational activity connected to cartels. UNCTAD nevertheless found the application of this non-binding policy disappointing, as reflected in its internal communications during the 1980s.[22]

The same process was at work at the OECD, which established a first working group on multinational control in 1970, and adopted guidelines for multinational enterprises in 1976, although they were non-binding and part of a broader declaration whose objective was to strengthen international investment.[23] According to the guidelines, multinationals should not interfere with local political life. They also required the disclosure of fairly detailed information, such as the enterprise's property, the geographic distribution of its activity (income, number of employees), accounting methods, and pricing policy. The declaration also encouraged worker representation within enterprises. None of these commitments were mandatory, and the results were consequently quite meagre. In response to an ILO study, the French employers' association CNPF affirmed in 1983 that it was in full compliance with the OECD code, and underscored the non-binding nature of this legislation.[24]

6.1.3 Europe as the Only Solution for Controlling Multinationals?

All of these failures led supporters of democratising enterprises to shift their attention to the European Community, the only international body with binding federal law. In the early 1970s, the German Chancellor Willy Brandt was open to the idea of Europeanising this debate, while the conservative British and French leaders, Edward Heath and Georges Pompidou, were much more sceptical.[25] The Belgian Prime Minister Léo Tindemans, a Christian Democrat, raised the issue in his 1975 report on the European Union commissioned by the European Council.[26] The European Trade Union Confederation (ETUC) revived the issue in 1974–76, and it was also mentioned in the Maldague Report.[27]

In Brussels, the issue was revived by Henk Vredeling of the Netherlands, the new Commissioner for Social Affairs appointed in 1977. A former unionist, he played an important role promoting a social Europe and organising the left at the European Parliament in the 1960s and 1970s. He was known at the Commission for asking many questions, and was therefore nicknamed 'Vrageling', from the Dutch verb '*vragen*' (to ask a question).[28] However, like most European unionists, Vredeling's priority was to combat unemployment through macroeconomic action such as 'work-sharing' rather than to democratise companies. When he presented his priorities in 1978, it was the French Minister Robert Boulin who raised the issue of worker participation, which the commissioner had forgotten.[29]

Finally, the proposal for a directive, which in the ensuing public debate became the famous Vredeling directive, was sent by the Commission to the Council on 23 October 1980.[30] It was adopted after a complicated debate at the Commission, with conservative and liberal commissioners such as Davignon, Ortoli, Brunner, and Tugendhat expressing their doubts.[31] The directive was ambitious in three respects. First, it involved all multinationals employing at least 100 workers in the EC. Second, it imposed requirements to disclose information and to engage in consultation (but not codecision) for a wide range of strategic decisions, not just those relating to working conditions. Third, the directive had extraterritorial application via a 'bypass' clause: if a subsidiary did not provide the required information, workers' representatives could initiate consultations with the parent company even if it was based outside the EEC. This provision seemed necessary from a social point of view, otherwise non-European multinationals, American and Swiss ones in particular, could avoid their obligations. This provision raised the issue of the extraterritoriality of EC legislation: to what extent could the young Commission in Brussels impose its standards on powerful foreign conglomerates? Another issue was that the directive was imperfect from a technical point of view, with a weak presentation of its arguments in the introduction; apparently the commissioner's office rushed to present it before the end of his term.

Among member states, Thatcher's neoliberal British government was adamantly opposed.[32] France under centre-right President Valéry Giscard d'Estaing was not enthusiastic (with the Sudreau report failing to garner backing).[33] Surprisingly, Paris offered little support even after socialist President François Mitterrand came to power in 1981.[34] In 1983, French representatives did not discuss it in European meetings, instead emphasising the organisation of working time (the socialist government had reduced working time but had not imposed codetermination).[35] The archives of the French trade union CFDT show that Jacques Delors, who was the French Minister of the Economy and Finances at the time (and a former unionist at the CFTC, which split from the CFDT in 1964), took an interest in 1981. He found little support,[36] probably because the CFDT-CFTC had a more decentralised vision of social policy than other French unions as well as the French Socialist and Communist Parties.

In Bonn, the government was divided. The Ministry for the Economy, led by the liberal Otto von Lambsdorff, was strongly opposed to the project.[37] It did not want Europe to serve as inspiration for the debates unfolding at the OECD and the UN. This reluctance led to a conflict surrounding the instructions given to German representatives in 1981, with the Ministry for Labour emphasising a positive but prudent position (due to potential conflict with German law). There was the potential risk that a lax EC codetermnation law would be used by many West German companies to avoid their national obligations (similar to Mannesmann with the 1976 German codetermination law). Both ministries ultimately agreed on the need to wait for a better proposal from the Commission, a sign that it was deemed to have technical flaws.[38]

The proposal for a directive led to a broad transnational mobilisation, with Vredeling choosing to begin negotiations with a consultation of the European Parliament, despite the institution's lack of binding powers in the matter. Both European and American employers exerted intense pressure on European leaders to sink the project, Members of European Parliament (MEP) in particular.[39] The official position of the European employers' association UNICE and the International Chamber of Commerce was to draw on the non-binding guidelines of the OECD and ILO. The archives of the Confederation of British Industry (CBI) offer an illuminating record of the various levels of employer lobbying. Beginning in 1980, the CBI developed a strategy to influence European commissioners (such as Commission President Roy Jenkins of the UK) and MEPs, sometimes in conjunction with UNICE's efforts (targeting the powerful Belgian commissioner Etienne Davignon).[40] In February 1981, British and German employers' representatives met with MEPs from the European Democrats group, essentially consisting of British conservatives, to explain the flaws of the proposed directive. An expert on the German situation explained the differences between the Vredeling proposal and German legislation. The British government and employers' associations worked together to undermine the EC proposal. In 1982, UNICE formally asked for each national federation 'to lobby' their national MEPs before the July 1982 plenary session. The German trade union DGB published an official protest against this massive mobilisation, in which it opposed the 'destructive campaign led by Capital (in the Marxist sense) on both sides of the Atlantic to stop this directive'.[41]

The European Trade Union Confederation (ETUC) was too weak to thwart this offensive, especially since its main priorities were working-time reductions and stimulus policies to combat unemployment.[42] The Vredeling directive was rarely the subject of discussions in high-level meetings between ETUC President Wim Kok and members of the Commission working on the issue. Even when it was mentioned, as in March 1982, it did not appear in the final communiqué.

Another weakness of the ETUC was the fact that it was not accustomed to European lobbying. The meetings in December 1980 and January 1981 focusing on this issue had a positive view of the proposed directive, but ETUC representatives did not develop a coherent mobilisation strategy. The debate became tangled up in questions connected to ongoing international discussions at the OECD, the UN, and the ILO.[43] The ETUC did not prioritise the EC, failing to tailor its lobbying to the EC's specific institutional features (such as influencing the European Parliament or Commission, as the CBI did).

Instead, it conflated the EC with other international organisations whose institutional power was much weaker. The only measures envisioned were the creation of an ad hoc group, information campaigns, and demonstrations. Only the DGB, which also strongly supported the legislation, tried to establish an influence strategy at the European Parliament via certain German MEPs close to unions, such as Heinz Oskar Vetter, a DGB leader and former ETUC president.[44] The Germans were most likely more mobilised because they were accustomed to difficult German debates connected to codetermination.

The fight was nevertheless too one-sided. The Parliament, which was dominated by the centre-right, ultimately requested a number of amendments limiting the directive's scope.[45] At the Commission, the conservative Commissioners Haferkamp, Narjes, and Ortoli requested changes to preserve the competitiveness of European enterprises.[46] The issue remained at a standstill until the new Commissioner for Social Affairs, the British Labourite Ivor Richard, proposed a new and watered-down version of the directive in July 1983.

In Paris, the socialist government was not particularly committed. France held the rotating presidency of the Council during the first semester of 1984, but its socialist government did not present the law for discussion at the Council of Ministers until June, at the very end of its presidency, nearly one year after it was presented by the Commission. The text was then sent to a committee of national experts for further study, with the debate once again becoming bogged down.[47] The only outcome was an agreement paving the way for voluntary agreements, which was ultimately included in the directive establishing European Works Councils in 1994.

Despite strong national, European, and global mobilisation, the effort to control multinationals largely failed. This was primarily due to lack of support among member states, including opposition from Thatcher, and tepid backing from France and Germany. The left-wing transnational coalition wielded less influence than the business community, which was more effective in its lobbying. Vredeling arrived at the Commission in 1977, but proposed a directive only in 1980. The ETUC was unable to set a coherent campaign for mobilisation, despite the effort of its German leader Oskar Vetter. The Commission did not solve the first directive's technical flaws until 1983, which is to say eight years after the debate's high-point in major European countries in 1975–76. In the meantime, Thatcher had risen to power, and henceforth wielded her country's veto.

6.2 Protecting Struggling Industries

European industry in the early 1970s faced three new threats. First, Europe was weakened by rising unemployment and strong inflation, mostly arising from the 1973 and 1979 oil crises. Second, the Fordist model of growth was exhausted, as productivity gains peaked. Third, Europe had to face new industrial competitors, namely Japan, the recently industrialised countries of East Asia, and communist countries subsidising their exports. Faced with these new competitors, protectionist temptations arose in Europe. European institutions endeavoured to stem this dynamic via global negotiations, especially between Europe and Africa, and by negotiating specific agreements in the textile, automotive, and steel industries.

6.2.1 The European Protectionist Temptations of the 1970s

The European Community was divided between supporters of free trade, such as West Germany and the Benelux countries, and somewhat more protectionist countries, such as France, Italy, and the UK (before Thatcher's rise to power in 1979 shifted the UK back to free trade). Despite the sharply rising price of imported energy-related products, West Germany continued to strongly support international free trade throughout the 1970s due to its regular trade surplus. In contrast, when the UK joined the EC, British customs tariffs were on average higher than the EC's Common External Tariff, requiring London to lower them in 1973.[48]

Divisions broke out into the open during the first summit meeting of leaders from industrialised countries (the future G7), held in Rambouillet in 1975. The British Prime Minister Harold Wilson affirmed that he 'could not rule out action to protect industries threatened with or suffering from serious injury by increased imports'.[49] He was opposed by the German Chancellor Helmut Schmidt, who asserted that some European industry, textiles in particular, should disappear, and that it was illusory to 'build a kind of zoo' around it. Schmidt was also scathing towards the global project to reorganise North–South trade (in particular through the NIEO): 'Less developed countries should be shaped according to market logic rather than count on gifts from industrialized countries.' In 1976, as Schmidt ranted against the Global South: 'Who absorbed the oil crisis? Who provided additional financial facilities for developing countries? We did. So today, we are no longer able to transfer resources, while the USSR provides no aid, and instead sells them weapons. We are transferring our resources to the benefit of the USSR. We are paying for its military interventions.'[50]

Giscard d'Estaing defended North–South dialogue, if only to avoid a new spike in oil prices. In 1977, Paris defended 'organised liberalism' and a 'sensible organisation of global markets', notably for traditional manufacturing (declining industries) and cutting-edge sectors.[51] In London, Callaghan cited the economic nationalism of the 1930s to convince members of his government to adopt a budget reduction programme.[52]

The German Chancellor was contradicted in 1980 by another Social Democrat, his predecessor Willy Brandt in an international report known as the 'Brandt report'. It recommended that the Global South be better integrated within international trade movements by stabilising commodities markets, and more specifically by eliminating restrictive business practices and reducing the North's protectionist barriers. He included environmental concerns, as well as an ambitious proposal to tax some international flows and use the funds for developmental aid. Brandt drew inspiration from the project to tax international transactions, which had been proposed by the economist James Tobin in 1978 (what would later be called the Tobin tax).[53] The report clearly conveyed Brandt's idealism, which stood in sharp contrast to the pragmatism of his successor Schmidt. When asked about Brandt's vision, Schmidt famously replied: 'When you have a vision, you go to the doctor!'[54]

In the end, the main European response to these protectionist tensions was to preserve the free trade agreements, notably via the Commission's closer monitoring of obstacles to free circulation within the Common Market. In 1976 for example, the Commission faced a surge in protectionist measures and had to increase its staff to deal with more than 300 cases. The tide reversed in 1977, but was nevertheless still worrying.[55]

6.2.2 Managing Trade in Eurafrica

As its name suggests, Eurafrica is a concept combining Europe and Africa. In the second half of the twentieth century, it denoted attempts to combine European integration and decolonisation, namely through strong links between the EC and the former colonies of European countries. In 1957, Paris imposed the principle of an agreement between the future EEC and 'associated countries and territories' (colonies and protectorates) as a prerequisite to accepting the Common Market.[56] Since most of those territories were located in Africa (excluding the Maghreb), this decision marked the beginning of what was called Eurafrica, although it established only a limited form of cooperation. France and Belgium, the only two remaining colonial powers, secured the creation of a European Development Fund (EDF), which would allow the Six to fund economic development projects for the benefit of the territories that were largely under French and Belgian influence. The Yaoundé Convention in 1963 codified ties between the EEC and associated territories, which included free trade between the two groups, as well as financial transfers via the EDF. However, many EC members, Germany chief among them, were suspicious of the agreement, as it appeared neocolonial, and was also costly and not economically advantageous, since most African markets were tiny. Bonn supported it only as a concession to Paris, although German enterprises did secure a few occasional markets in Africa.[57]

Paradoxically, even the Algerians were interested in Eurafrica, for while they had won their independence by arms in 1962, they were careful to maintain good relations with the EC, notably to secure funds and facilities for the circulation of Algerians.[58] However, as negotiations between Paris and Algiers quickly grew tense, the European discussions came to a halt. The Algerian government had no agency whatsoever, in what was a completely unbalanced relationship. This shows the limits of Eurafrica.

During the 1970s, the Yaoundé Convention was broadened to include some former British colonies (with the UK's accession to the EC in 1973). In 1975, the Lomé Convention was concluded between the EC and forty-six French- and English-speaking countries in Africa, the Caribbean, and the Pacific (known as 'ACP'). Paris and London conserved broad room for manoeuvre in managing relations with their former colonial empires, notably on the cultural and geopolitical level, although trade relations were henceforth part of an EC framework.

The Lomé Convention was innovative, as it included STABEX, a system to stabilise the export revenues of associated countries.[59] This neomercantilist tool was created at the request of countries from the Global South to compensate for high volatility in commodity prices, notably by providing additional aid when prices were low. Numerous countries in the Global South were highly dependent on exporting one or two unrefined products. Aid was granted to ACP countries if their export revenues fell below a certain level; the transfers amounted to $400 million during Lomé I (1975–79), two-thirds of which were allocated to the poorest countries (Senegal, Sudan, and Mauritania, due to the falling price of peanuts). The volumes were substantial, but modest in relation with developmental needs. The Lomé II Convention in 1979 added the SYSMIN aid system for mining, and this grew out of German concerns regarding the supply of strategic commodities. These neomercantilist tools were abandoned in the 1980s.

6.2.3 A Protectionist Trade Framework for the Textile and Automobile Industries

Protectionism took hold in the automotive and textile industries during the 1970s. In both cases the EC stepped in to negotiate compromises between protectionist and free trades states, as well as to implement a gradual liberalisation during the 1980s.

In the automotive sector, competition from Japanese cars was the primary destabilising element in the 1970s and 1980s, along with the macroeconomic context. States reacted to this challenge on a national level, with the most protectionist – the US, the UK, and France – negotiating Voluntary Export Restraint (VER) agreements with Japan during the 1970s. In short, VERs established quotas – imports could not pass a certain level. In West Germany, an informal 'agreement' apparently existed in the 1980s to limit

Japanese penetration, without anything being official.[60] The Commission was passive at first, before strongly pushing for these VERs to be eliminated in the late 1980s, as they clashed with the negotiations underway during the Uruguay Round of the GATT. The UK under Thatcher simultaneously adopted a free trade discourse, all while defending quotas and seeking to spare the Japanese factories located on its territory. Finally, following a mandate given by member states, the Commission negotiated an agreement with Japan, which was concluded in 1991, and provided for the gradual lifting of quotas during the 1990s.[61] In the meantime, European car manufacturers improved their quality to compete with the Japanese (by adopting the new production procedures precisely referred to as 'Toyotism'). The end of quotas therefore did not translate into a massive increase of Japanese car imports.

Another important sector was textiles, which was once Europe's leading employer. At the time it was severely affected by mechanisation and foreign competition, and employment in the sector shrank by 33 per cent between 1975 and 1985 in the EC.[62] The textile sector included myriad companies, and its workforce was often weakly unionised, thereby complicating a coordinated policy. As a result, the primary action conducted on the European level was trade-related. On the global scale, the EC negotiated its participation in the Multi-Fibre Arrangement in 1973, which granted the textile sector an exemption from the GATT's liberal rules. A quota system protected European producers from imports by new producers based in Southeast Asia, India, Brazil, and Southern Europe. The first MFA covered the period between 1973 and 1977. Since imports continued to rise, the French and British asked for a more restrictive agreement.[63] The second MFA (1977–81) was therefore protectionist, even though the Germans, the Danes, and the Dutch emphasised that it was only a temporary agreement designed to facilitate the restructuring of the European textile industry.[64] European mediation was once again important to easing tensions arising from protectionist temptations. The conclusion of the Uruguay Round in 1994 imposed a return to liberalisation.

European action was different in the sub-sector of synthetic fibres, which underwent rapid expansion during the 1960s with the success of fibres such as polyester, often based on hydrocarbons. Oil crises consequently had a strong negative impact on this sector, which employed 100,000 people in Western Europe in 1979.[65] European coordination was facilitated by the sector's higher level of concentration compared to traditional textile production, with one or two national leaders per country. Private companies sought to establish a European crisis cartel,[66] a type of anti-competitive agreement in theory forbidden by European anti-cartel legislation. In addition, the massive aid granted by Italy to extend production in the country's south threatened the cartel. In 1978 industrial actors asked Commissioner Davignon of Belgium to find a solution. He acted as a go-between in negotiations surrounding a crisis cartel for European and American companies operating in Europe, which consisted of a production discipline agreement involving quotas.[67]

This European crisis cartel immediately sparked a hostile response from the German government. The solution of the crisis cartel as such was not rejected – it was actually provided for under German law as a possible exemption to the rules of free competition – but Bonn feared that the Commission's intervention would lead to dirigisme.[68] This refusal was paradoxical, for many German enterprises were calling for intervention, with 35,000 German jobs in the sector under threat from 'cutthroat competition' from the Italians, to use the words of a German business leader.[69]

The agreement between the companies was concluded on 20 June 1978, and submitted to the Commission for approval.[70] It carefully avoided the term 'cartel', stressing the need to regulate aid on an EC level. There was intense debate at the Commission as to whether the agreement should be accepted. Davignon defended it, and even asked for additional measures, whereas Vouel, the Commissioner for Competition, sought to prohibit it.[71] The Commission dithered, but eventually tolerated the cartel. It is probable that many other crisis cartels existed, without being revealed to the public eye.

6.2.4 A Genuine EC Steel Policy (1980–88)

Steel was always central to European integration because it is the raw material for building weapons, and is produced in coal basins that are by nature transnational, and not bound by state frontiers.[72] In 1926, the Luxemburger steel magnate Emile Mayrisch set up the *Entente internationale de l'acier*, a major steel cartel with his German, Belgian, and French counterparts. He explicitly linked the cartel's creation to the need for increased coordination among European countries, with a view to promoting peace. This attempt was shattered by the nationalistic tensions of the 1930s. After 1945, member states took the place of companies in organising the European steel market. In 1951, the first semi-federal European organisation was the ECSC. However, when the ECSC High Authority sought to intervene in the Belgian coal crisis in 1959, member states refused, as they wanted to preserve their prerogative. This situation changed in the early 1980s. Since the crisis was massive and affected the entire EC (production fell by 23 per cent and staff by 44 per cent between 1974 and 1984), member states decided to coordinate their action with the Commission. The steel industry crisis began in 1975, driven by rising international competition (including from new Asian producers), oil crises, and technological innovation that reduced the need for labour. Private attempts at cartelisation, the industry's traditional solution during the interwar period, failed because enterprises could not agree, and because anti-competitive agreements were in theory banned by competition law.

Since the Merger Treaty of 1965, the EEC Commission assumed the prerogatives of the ECSC High Authority. Davignon, who became the Commissioner for Industrial Affairs, promoted European action with respect to steel. He was unsuccessful at first, as the crisis only involved the French (Usinor, Sacilor) and British (BSC) giants, along with the Walloon and Saarland steel industries. However, all producers were affected after the 1979 oil crisis, including those in Flanders, the rest of Germany, and Italy. For the first time, the Nine voted unanimously on 31 October 1980 to implement Article 58 of the ECSC Treaty on 'manifest crisis', through which they granted sweeping powers to the Commission to regulate the steel industry. It devised a system of quarterly production quotas, required disclosure of deliveries, and imposed minimum prices, including for imported products. The Commission would oversee application of the agreements as well as the subsidies granted by governements, thanks to two increasingly strict aid codes adopted in 1980 and 1981. The Council agreed on the principle of a return to profitability by 1985, which meant that all aid would be prohibited after that date, with a few exceptions (research and development, environment, retraining). At the same time, the Commission strove to protect the EC market from Japanese and American offensives. The Europeans clearly pursued a policy based on the principle of *community*, seeking firstly to preserve the production capacity and competitiveness of European industry rather than to save jobs in the short term. Dismissals continued, and were eased by essentially national social measures.

This was the only instance of EC-level sectoral industrial policy. The exceptional decision resulted from the fact that the crisis impacted the entire EC, as well as the institutional specificities of the ECSC Treaty (which was more neomercantilist than the EEC Treaty) and Davignon's personality. Schmidt, who was often critical of the Commission, nevertheless confided to Thatcher his esteem for the Belgian commissioner: 'Viscount Davignon is a little too pro-French and protectionist. But he is one of the best European diplomats.'[73] In 1984, Thatcher supported Davignon's candidacy for Commission President. In Paris, the French government also supported Davignon, who since 1977 had been advocating for EC discipline with respect to aid, which the Italians were using to expand their production capacity. Paris and London opposed any supranational drift, but supported the Commission's steel policy, for it ensured the same discipline for all.

West Germany was the most reluctuant state, due to its hostility towards EC industrial policy. In 1978, the Minister of the Economy, the neoliberal Lambsdorff, sent his EEC partners an official memorandum emphasising strict control over state aid, and a refusal of both protectionism and state intervention. Bonn's ultimate acceptance of the manifest state of crisis in 1980 can be explained by the weakening of the German steel industry after the 1979 oil crisis, and by the failure of its preferred solution, the private crisis cartel. The most competitive producers, such as Thyssen and Krupp in Germany, and the Bresciani in Italy, did not want to lower production. The least cooperative enterprise was Klöckner, which suspended its participation in the Eurofer cartel because it deemed its quota to be too low.

Lambsdorff, who was isolated, ultimately accepted recourse to the 'state of manifest crisis' procedure during the Council meeting on 30 October 1980. In internal debates, the German Ministry of Foreign Affairs stressed the political impossibility of a German veto. It would call into question all of West Germany's pro-European policy, while exacerbating the considerable difficulties already faced by the EEC due to tensions surrounding the CAP and the British budget. French President Giscard d'Estaing and Prime Minister Barre also pressured Schmidt.

Lambsdorff nevertheless remained committed to limiting national subsidies to ailing firms. In the winter of 1980–81, he threatened unilateral protection measures: West Germany would no longer import massively subsidised steel unless greater oversight over state aid was implemented, thereby calling into question the Common Market. This extreme position sparked opposition from the German Ministry of Finance, out of its commitment to free trade, as well as from the German Ministry of Foreign Affairs, as it threatened European integration. In the end Schmidt's intercession helped secure an agreement to strengthen aid control in the spring of 1981. In opposition to Belgium, Luxembourg, and Italy, West Germany was supported by the Netherlands, France, and the UK under Thatcher (despite London's massive aid to BSC).

Bonn was very vigilant with respect to the application of the aid code. In 1983, Bonn filed a complaint against the Commission's authorisation of aid for the steel industry in France, Italy, the UK, and Belgium. The German government's complaint was supported by the steel industry employers' association, which deemed the amount of aid granted excessive, and Germany's quota too low. The Court ultimately rejected the complaint in October 1985. As the steel crisis worsened in Germany, Bonn asked for a certain amount of clemency in aid control and production cuts. Everyone now had an interest in Europe-wide control of state aid.

Liberalisation came only in 1988 with the end of aid for production, and the lifting of the quota system made possible by improved circumstances. Another problem arose at the time, namely the increase of low-cost and highly subsidised steel imports from communist Europe: the Commission concluded voluntary export reduction agreements with these countries in 1990, before concluding an association agreement in 1992.[74] This brought to a close an exceptional period running from 1980 to 1988, in which Brussels implemented EC-wide sectoral industrial policy in response to the widespread crisis. Davignon was nicknamed 'Stevie Wonder',[75] but was unable to reproduce this approach in other sectors, such as shipbuilding.

6.2.5 The Failure of Comprehensive Regulation in Shipbuilding

In his *Wealth of Nations* from 1776, the famous economist Adam Smith complained about the disruptive effects of British aid for shipbuilding, which he likened to a kind of 'bounty'.[76] Two centuries later, aid remained widespread in Europe, all the more so with intensifying competition from Japan in the 1960s, and South Korea in the 1970s. The 1973 and 1979 oil crises drastically depressed the market: between 1976 and 1984, global production fell by a third, with the decline reaching 50 per cent in France and Germany, and even 70 per cent in the UK, long the world's leading producer.

European states tried to solve this predicament with subsidies, but their amounts increased exponentially without solving the problem. Companies attempted to form a cartel. In 1976 the Association of European Shipbuilders offered the Japanese to divide the global market in three (one-third for each of them, and one-third for the rest of the world), but they declined the offer.[77] After this failure, enterprises asked their governments to support an equivalent agreement within the framework of the OECD – of which Japan was a member – but to no avail, as the rapidly expanding South Koreans were not yet members of this organisation.

Employers tried to constitute national cartels. In France, the shipbuilding employers' association proposed in 1978 to adopt a 'survival charter' based on coordinated production, which was a cartel in all but name.[78] It was refused by profitable companies. Finally, in 1981 the left nationalised part of the sector, and brought the remaining private companies together under a single enterprise, Normed. The latter soon received an infusion of public money, and was entirely dependent on orders negotiated by public authorities. The sector was thus de facto nationalised. The UK and Sweden had already nationalised their shipbuilding industries in 1977. For lack of a private cartel, there was massive public intervention in Europe.

In the face of this failure, Davignon tried to develop a Europe-wide approach similar to the one later implemented in steel. In 1977, the Commissioner of Industrial Affairs met with companies to propose making national aid conditional on restructuring, and to emphasise the principle of European preference (subsidies would be directed only to EC ships). To enhance his expertise, Davignon initiated operational cooperation with the shipbuilding employers' association, from which he recruited an expert in 1980 to gather statistics. These attempts nevertheless met with failure, for member states refused any binding cooperation. Another solution would have been a protectionist policy towards Japan, a solution broached by French leader Giscard d'Estaing at the European Council meeting held in Rome in March 1977. But here too the Nine were divided. Even the British, who were among the more protectionist Europeans at the time, refused, as clearly expressed in a memorandum drafted for the prime minister: 'Because of voluntary restraint arrangements on British imports from Japan (more extensive than those affecting imports of other member states), and the Japanese initiative to increase imports from the UK, we stand to lose a good deal more from the ending of cooperation with Japan than we would gain from a relationship of retaliation and counter-retaliation.'[79] The UK was not ready to launch an offensive against Japan on shipbuilding if it stood to lose in other sectors.

In the end, the only European action came in the form of competition policy, with increased regulation of national subsidies by Brussels. EC action in this area was justified on the grounds of a specific Treaty of Rome article on shipbuilding aid (Article 92-3c), which reflected its prevalence. Even the UK under Thatcher requested and received European authorisation in 1983 to provide massive aid for the Harland & Wolff shipbuilders located in Northern Ireland (which launched the Titanic in 1912). An internal British governement note justified national subsidies by the yard's importance to the Northern Irish Protestant community, although according to one of Thatcher's advisors, 'even if all the employees worked for nothing, the company would still not be viable'.[80] Overall, the chronology for regulating shipbulding subsidies was the same as that of state aid control in general: weak before 1980, more ambitious under Commissioner Andriessen (1981–85), and much more robust with Sutherland (1985–89).[81] In the end, this was the only industrial policy led by the European Commnuity, and it was based on *liberty* capitalism rather than *community* capitalism.

6.3 Rising up to Globalisation: From European Preference to Normative Power

The context evolved radically in 1979–80 with the advent of what was called 'globalisation'.[82] Understood as the internationalisation of trade and the interpenetration of economies, it was not a new phenomenon, but it certainly accelerated in the 1980s. Europeans reacted by regulating protectionist tensions: they devised a project for 'European preference' that was ultimately shelved, and instead opted to transform Europe into a normative power.

6.3.1 A More Neoliberal Globalisation

Globalisation took a more neoliberal turn after 1979–80, shattering any projects to organise international free trade around a *community*-based approach. Two influential neoliberal leaders, Reagan and Thatcher, came to power in 1979–80, while the Volcker Shock increased interest rates and the value of the dollar. Indebted countries of the south had to contend with a large increase in their debt (often issued in dollars), as well as lower prices for commodities. The conference held in Cancun, Mexico in 1981 was a turning point, the last major North–South Summit of the Cold War. It was marked by the non-cooperative stance of US President Ronald Reagan.[83] That same year, the Berg report from the World Bank sanctioned a free-tradist transformation of development policy, recommending cuts in state expenditures, and an emphasis on free trade. During the sixth session of UNCTAD in 1983, the West was divided between those supporting the regulation of commodities markets (France, Italy, Belgium), and those defending free trade (the US, the UK, West Germany).[84]

Reagan and Thatcher wanted to further liberalise international trade. The former wanted to expand liberalisation to new sectors such as agriculture, services, and investment, while the latter insisted upon a discourse based on free trade at the G7 meeting in 1980, and worried about François Mitterrand's protectionism in 1981–82 (Chapter 3).[85] Paris could not afford to walk away from the GATT talks, because France needed to export. It also relied on its European partners to defend the CAP against the US.[86] In 1985, EEC member states adopted a declaration expressing their acceptance of a new round of GATT negotiations only after including, at the request of Paris, the need to preserve the CAP, as well as the link between trade and monetary talks (the erratic fluctuations of the dollar irritated the French government).[87] In London, internal reflections emphasised securing concessions from 'newly industrialized countries' – in other words countries in the South – whose exports expanded to the detriment of traditional producing countries in the North.[88] The EEC also highlighted its competitive advantages, indicating it was ready to discuss new subjects such as the liberalisation of services and intellectual property, and denouncing the closure of the Japanese domestic market.

The Uruguay Round was launched a year later at Punta del Este in September 1986. The negotiations were very difficult, especially in connection with the CAP. They did not progress until 1992, with a decisive compromise between the US and the EU, concluded simultaneously with a reform that weakened the protectionist nature of the CAP.[89] The countries that benefited the most from the CAP, such as France and the Netherlands, accepted this reform in order to preserve its key features, and because the GATT presented trade opportunities for industrial products and services, as well as better protection for industrial property rights.

The final agreement of the Uruguay Round was concluded in Marrakesh in 1994, expanding liberalisation for the exchange of merchandise, and gradually extending this to agricultural products and services. All sectoral exceptions to free trade (notably in textile and in cars) were slowly reduced.

6.3.2 Regulating Protectionist Tensions with the US and Japan

The liberalisation of international trade always came with protectionist tensions. This was true even between Western Europe and its closest ally, the US.

In the 1950s, Washington supported European integration, but trade conflicts erupted as early as 1964, with the 'chicken war' over European poultry subsidies.[90] Conflicts occurred regularly over agricultural products. US President Richard Nixon (1969–74) was more assertive, and oversaw a major conflict over steel. The Trade Act passed in 1974 facilitated the adoption of sectoral protectionist measures, and was massively used by the US government under pressure from the most influential sectors in Washington (textiles, steel industry, automobile industry). President Reagan (1981–89) also conducted an aggressive trade policy, with regular conflicts with Europe over agriculture and steel.[91] A deep rift opened between the EEC and the US regarding the construction of a Siberian gas pipeline, in which European enterprises were taking part.[92] The contract was negotiated in 1980–81, at a time of great tension between the US and the USSR following the Soviet–Afghan War. The West Germans, who had closely cooperated with the USSR in energy since the first agreement in 1970, were the ones primarily involved. Despite American pressure, the agreement was concluded between the Soviets and Ruhrgas AG in November 1981. On 18 June 1982, the US government imposed sanctions on all European firms participating in the construction of the gas pipeline. Washington also imposed extraterritorial sanctions by prohibiting equipment produced in Europe under American licence from being exported. This reaction particularly irritated German Chancellor Schmidt, but he wanted to avoid protectionist escalation, which some of his European partners such as the French could have used to their advantage.[93] The British were also involved, but did not want to engage in open conflict with the US.[94] Finally, all European actors had an interest in coordinating Community action in order to maximise pressure on the US and avoid protectionist escalation. Brussels transmitted a joint memorandum to the Americans on 12 August 1982. In the end, the US government lifted the sanctions on 13 November 1982.

The same phenomenon occurred with Airbus when the Reagan administration launched an offensive against European subsidies to the consortium before the GATT. Airbus was an intergovernemental venture, but it was defended by the European Commission, in relation with member states.[95] The Commission played a useful role in balancing the position of the 'Airbus countries', which were keen on defending Airbus agains the US (notably by accusing Boeing of receiving massive indirect subsidies through its military contracts), and non-Airbus countries such as Italy, who wanted to avoid a trade war with Washington.

Japan represented another a challenge for Europeans from the 1970s onward. The Japanese government actively supported industrial development thanks to massive state aid and the protection of its domestic market. It also had higher productivity than Europe. At first it was primarily the British and French governments that mobilised. In 1976 they secured the dispatching of a

European Commission delegation to negotiate agreements with Tokyo, with a view to preserving European industrial capacity.[96] However, the Europeans were divided, with Germany being more supportive of free trade, and numerous other countries (Benelux, the UK, Italy) being chiefly preoccupied by the bilateral trade contingents they were negotiating with Japan in multiple sectors.[97]

Later on, Thatcher proposed initiating legal proceedings against Japan at the GATT in November 1982, and establishing a common European-American front against the country.[98] However, the UK also sought to attract Japanese investment, especially in the automotive sector.[99] Thatcher adopted a robust industrial strategy, convincing Nissan to establish a factory in Sunderland with large amounts of state aid, proposing five times the amount usually granted (according to the British Treasury), thereby sparking conflict with the Chancellor of the Exchequer Nigel Lawson. The Iron Lady saw it as an opportunity to reindustrialise the country, increase the productivity of British enterprises (which would emulate their Japanese competitors), and offer a new type of union relations, since Nissan imposed a single union in its factories, based on the Japanese model. Thatcher also insisted on a typical neomercantilist clause, namely that the Japanese firm include a percentage of local parts (above the 45 per cent required by EC legislation for the product to be considered European), with a view to boosting British industry in the process. The UK and Japan thus took advantage of British membership in the EC, which allowed the Japanese to circumvent the import restrictions established by certain European countries by producing directly within the Common Market. In Brussels, the Commissioner for Industry Etienne Davignon expressed his disapproval of the British strategy, which would lead to distortions in the Common Market, especially given the struggling position of European car manufacturers.

In 1983 it was ultimately decided to have the Community conduct friendly negotiations with Japan, and to abandon all legal proceedings.[100] Tokyo quickly accepted voluntary agreements (especially with the UK and France) to limit exports of cars, video recorders, machine tools, colour tubes, and televisions.[101] For cars, the bilateral VER agreements with Japan were on an EC-wide basis. The Japanese challenge was thus mitigated via targeted and temporary protectionism.

6.3.3 Two Chimeras: European Preference and 'Fortress Europe'

Translating the principle of *community* into European economic policy involved a preference for European products over non-European ones. This was the principle of 'European preference', which was sometimes evoked in the 1970s and 1980s. Commissioner Davignon mentioned it in connection with ailing sectors. The French government strongly supported it, but the principle's application came up against practical difficulties, as demonstrated by Nissan in the UK: Were Nissan cars produced in Sunderland British or Japanese? The example of aircraft cooperation demonstrated that many European companies were enmeshed in a complex web of agreements with their US partners. Defining what represented a purely European product was therefore difficult, and risked triggering protectionist tensions.

An example of this dilemma is the European action against IBM. During the 1970s, IBM dominated the global computing market.[102] US antitrust authorities targeted Big Blue (as it was nicknamed) for allegedly abusing its position as market leader. IBM won all of the trials against it in the US during the 1970s, but this did not prevent the modest Commission in Brussels from attacking the American giant. The offensive was launched in 1973-74 with the support of the Commissioner for Industrial Affairs, Altiero Spinelli. He used EEC Article 86, which prohibited abuse of dominant position, on the grounds that IBM did not allow peripheral devices manufactured by other companies to connect to its computers. Big Blue pressured the European institution, and even issued threats regarding its factory in Montpellier, France.[103] IBM enjoyed strong support from the US government; in January 1982, after dropping its charges against IBM, the Department of Justice advised the Europeans to do the same, and the US government defended IBM before Helmut Kohl (leader of the German opposition at the time) and the British House of Lords. In the words of the Commissioner in charge of the case, Frans Andriessen of the Netherlands, 'it was truly David [versus] Goliath'.[104] The Commission ultimately accepted negotiating with IBM, all while preserving the threat of issuing an adverse decision. An agreement was finally concluded in 1984, under which the Commission was tasked with monitoring whether IBM effectively followed through on its commitment to allow peripheral devices from other brands. European firms were divided on the matter, but were generally favourable towards a compromise with IBM as long as it opened up its interfaces.

Another form of European preference was to give priority to EC firms in public procurement for high-technology products. Public authorities played a considerable role in launching technological innovation, as they were often the first buyers, and helped establish standards that could shape the market for decades to come. In 1968-70, the EC broached the topic of limiting public procurement for new technologies exclusively to European firms.[105] Discussions always faltered due to two problems: a technical one regarding what constitutes a 'European' enterprise, namely whether firms such as IBM and Nissan, which produced in the EC, should be included; and a political one, namely the desire not to encourage protectionism. There was also an ongoing risk of incompatibility with the GATT.

In 1982-83, as the possible opening of national telecommunications markets was being discussed, West Germany explored the idea of granting preference to 'suppliers established in the EEC', while France wanted to reserve it for European producers.[106] Bonn would accept favouring American enterprises established in the EC, something that was unacceptable for Paris. Archival records on the French government's internal reflections regarding 'EC producers' show the difficulties in identifying a European enterprise, as numerous criteria could be taken into account (headquarters, nationality of shareholders, location of jobs, etc.). The note concluded: 'it is practically impossible to find a legal definition for a producer that fulfils this goal [of being a genuine European producer]'.[107] Even multinationals discussed European preference in high-technology. Wisse Dekker, who served as the president of the multinational Philips as well as of the European Round Table, an association of large European enterprises, evoked opening up high-technology markets in 1985 on the basis of reciprocity.[108] In 1988, French Prime Minister Jacques Chirac asked French negotiators to promote 'Community preference' in implementing the Single Market programme.[109]

However, the rare pieces of legislation that contained a modicum of European preference were quickly attacked by third countries. In 1988, a vigorous press campaign swept across the US and the UK against the 'Fortress Europe' being designed in Brussels.[110] They feared EC legislation based on reciprocity, and singled out a single draft directive defining what type of banks could operate in the Single Market. Under the influence of the neoliberal Commissioner Leon Brittan, the final directive in 1989 included no reciprocity clause. Similarly, with respect to the free circulation of capital, the 1988 directive provided for lifting restrictions on all financial movements regardless of their origin, but even the British wanted to conserve a few restrictions for non-Europeans.[111] In this case it was the West Germans, guided by the absolute imperative of depoliticising the currency, who imposed this neoliberal conception.

The debates at the Commission in 1990 pitted Delors, who defended 'Community interest', especially to avoid technological dependence, against Leon Brittan, who refused such a principle, which he associated with protectionism. Brittan's rejection in 1991 of the merger between the aviation companies ATR and De Havilland – counter to Delors – prevented the creation of a truly European leader in the sector (Chapter 5). 'Fortress Europe' never existed (except in agriculture), as European preference was never implemented.

6.3.4 Europe as a Normative Power: The 'Brussels Effects'

The only tool used by Europeans to promote its industry based on the principle of *community* was norms. The idea of using the EC as a 'civil power' was suggested in 1971 by François Duchêne (a former journalist at *The Economist* close to Jean Monnet): to compensate for lack of military power, Europe had to exert its influence in the economic sphere.[112] The idea spread to official circles. When Delors spoke of 'Europe as a power' during his speech in Bruges on 17 October 1989, he did not mention military aspects, but instead the promotion of European values in the East. More specifically, the notion of 'normative power' associated with the Single Market emerged with Zaki Laïdi in 2008, and with Kazuto Suzuki in 2009 with his evocation of a 'regulatory empire'.[113] Anu Bradford later coined the term 'Brussels Effect' to depict this phenomenon, an expression which had a major impact.[114] For these actors, the EC's normative power was connected to its domestic market and regulatory clout, which stemmed from the federal nature of its law, in addition to the origin of European standards. Since European norms emerge from compromises between very different European states, they can serve as an acceptable compromise for numerous actors across the globe.

This assertive stance generated friction, for the Americans asked to be consulted regarding European standardisation efforts. The Commissioner for the Internal Market, Arthur Cockfield of the UK, categorically refused this request in 1988.[115] In 1991, US Secretary of State James Baker went on the offensive, asking for 'active dialogue with the EC on EC-92 [the name of the Single Market Programme] and related trade problem ... We also need to ensure that harmonization of EC standards does not discriminate against US firms.'[116] This call was not heeded, as the EC legislated on its own without consulting the US.

European normative capacity expressed itself in fields as diverse as agriculture, culture, and telecommunications. In agriculture, countries in the south (France, Italy, Spain, Portugal, Greece) supported adopting standards to protect the geographical origin of products. The French presidency of the European Community in 1989 resulted in a compromise during a meeting of agriculture ministers held in Beaune, in the heart of the Burgundy winemaking region.[117] A 1992 regulation established 'protection of geographical indications and designations of origin' for agricultural products (with the exception of wines, which were protected later). The EU sought to include this protection for the geographical indication of products in its trade agreements, causing numerous conflicts with its partners in the ensuing years, with the US in particular. Regarding cultural products such as films, in 1993 the Commission negotiated a 'cultural exemption', which is to say the exclusion of cultural products from the GATT Uruguay Round. France pressured Brussels to grant such an exemption in order to protect its film industry from the aggressiveness of Hollywood.[118] Paris managed to build an alliance with several countries in Southern Europe, and convinced Commissioner Brittan to support it during tense negotiations with his US couterpart, the trade negotiator Mickey Kantor. In the end, the 'cultural exemption' allowed European countries to maintain quotas and subsidies for their film industries.

In telecommunications, norms were needed for the new products that emerged in the 1980s, and as national and even international calls became cheaper. In the US, the dismantling by antitrust authorities of AT&T, the world's largest industrial actor, intensified competition as earlier market-sharing agreements prohibiting AT&T from penetrating the international market were abolished. In 1982, the US pressured Europeans to open their markets for telephone terminals, which was generally reserved for national industrial actors, arguing that they had concluded an agreement of this type with the Japanese in 1981.[119] Washington pursued bilateral negotiations with the UK (which was liberalising its market) and West Germany, before the Commission asked these two countries to suspend discussions in order to adopt a European-wide approach. In 1984, the German government supported active EEC participation in international standardisation efforts, given the risk of Europe's marginalisation before the Americans and Japanese.[120] That same year saw the adoption of the ESPRIT programme to strengthen intra-European cooperation in research and development, as well as through the development of European standards. During the UK's European Council presidency in 1986, Thatcher successfully included the adoption of common telecommunication standards within EC priorities. The project was initiated by her Minister of Industry Geoffrey Pattie, who pointed out in a letter to the prime minister: 'The next generation of digital systems, coming into operation in the early 1990s, offers an opportunity to create a unified European system ... But if they [European producers] are to do this against Japanese and American competition, they must have the economies of scale which a unified European market will bring.'[121] The initiative led to the definition of a European mobile standard in 1987, the GSM, which was adopted by EC institutions as part of the Single Market programme, and took hold globally.[122] Even Thatcherite Britain could support modest European industrial policy as long as it took the form of standards.

6.4 Conclusion

Alternatives to neoliberal globalisation were developed by European leaders during the 1970s and 1980s. They proposed approaches more in tune with *solidarity* capitalism and *community* capitalism. The organisation of free trade through protectionism, industrial policy, and cartels was a major bone of contention during the 1970s, and not just in the Global South with the NIEO. Cartels were usually secret and hidden, but archival study nevertheless reveals they were widespread, and could be based on logic that was public (steel, shipbuilding), mixed (synthetic textiles), or fully private and secret (electrical equipment manufacturers in Brazil).

The Europeans promoted a vision of globalisation that was a compromise between *liberty* capitalism, *solidarity* capitalism, and *community* capitalism with its STABEX programme in 1975, which aimed to stabilise export revenue for some associated countries in the Global South. Protectionism was also

6.4 CONCLUSION

present in certain sectors until the early 1990s, such as agriculture, steel, automobiles, and aerospace (see Chapter 5 on Airbus and Ariane). Thatcher's policy with Nissan or the shipyards shows that even a neoliberal leader could practice neomercantilism, but in a much less systematic and showy manner than in Colbertist France. For all that, there was no common promotion of 'European preference', despite numerous talks. A minimal promotion of *community* capitalism emerged through the notion of 'normative power', which ultimately proved highly successful.

The most ambitious project of European *community* capitalism failed. Commissioner Davignon wanted to reproduce the EC-centred approach adopted for steel in other sectors, but with little success. The convergence towards a European solution in steel was linked to exceptional factors: the existence of a legal basis in the ECSC Treaty, a widespread crisis, and the possibility for all states to delegate important powers to the Commission on a time-limited basis. This failure can be linked to multiple structural problems: hostility to federalism, intra-European competition, the risk of a trade war, the interconnection of European and non-European firms, and the division of the left-wing coalition. The case of the Vredeling directive to control multinationals is exemplary: the social coalition was divided regarding the law, which was proposed quite late, when Thatcher had already risen to power. The late mobilisation of unions can also be explained by the fact that the ETUC was created only in 1973, two decades after the first EC-wide employers' associations.[123] This was logical, as unions long concentrated on national and international spheres of action. They realised only late that the EC offered a more conducive institutional environment for social norms, as opposed to the weaker international organisations (UN, ILO, OECD). The coalition supporting the Vredeling directive subsequently did not have an effective lobbying strategy. The organisation of a European worker's movement, such as the decision to hold a strike, came up against both political obstacles (where and when to protest?) and practical obstacles (how to cover the considerable cost of transportation?). In contrast, employers enjoyed more substantial financial resources than workers to organise and promote their action. They became familiar with the EC system earlier, thereby allowing them to conduct effective lobbying during the debate on the Vredeling directive.

The failure of the most ambitious projects should not obscure the weight of (often EC-level) protectionist regulations in numerous international markets during the 1970s and 1980s. This came in sectors such as agriculture, steel, textiles, and automobiles, before the advent of a more neoliberal form of globalisation after the completion of the Uruguay Round of the GATT (1986–94).

7

Common Currency and Neoliberal Turn? (1970–92)

In an exceptional phenomenon in world history, eleven European countries, among the richest in the world, freely decided to create a monetary union in 1992, doing so during a powerful neoliberal shift. How should we explain this, and what connection is there between European monetary integration and neoliberalism? This chapter argues that monetary union cannot be reduced exclusively to its neoliberal dimension, as forging such a union was devised by European leaders before the neoliberal turn, and had numerous justifications including ones more consistent with the *solidarity* and the *community* governance of capitalism.

While the literature on the history of the European Monetary Union is extensive and convincing,[1] additional archival research conducted for this book has shed new light on two neglected factors: the importance of projects for monetary cooperation devised in the 1950s and 1960s within the framework of the EEC (before the neoliberal turn); and the crucial importance of concerted stimulus in 1978, followed by German balance of payment difficulties in 1980–81, which explain the convergence towards stability-oriented policy.

This chapter will first present the theoretical argument supporting European monetary integration, in order to explain why such an original choice was made. It will then proceed chronologically, starting with the first plans devised in the 1950s and working up through the Maastricht Treaty in 1992, which created what became the eurozone.

7.1 Justifying European Monetary Union

The European Monetary Union is a surprising phenomenon. Usually, monetary unification has occurred after military conquest or national unification. For instance, the Zollverein, a customs union launched by Prussia in 1833, was supplemented by near-complete monetary union, and later by national union after the victory against France in 1871. To understand this striking phenomenon, it is important to return to the theoretical justifications for such unions (see Box 7.1). Politically, the aim was to foster European integration.

> **BOX 7.1: THE BENEFITS OF MONETARY UNION WITH RESPECT TO THE TRINITY OF CAPITALISM**
>
> **Liberty**
> - Eliminates the time and costs associated with foreign exchange transactions.
> - Removes the uncertainty linked to the exchange rate.
> - Avoids non-cooperative monetary policies such as devaluation.
> - Ensures a minimum convergence of economic policies.
>
> **Solidarity**
> - Facilitates transactions and travel, especially for the most mobile populations (tourists, students, cross-border workers, residents abroad).
> - Ensures effective solidarity if transfer mechanisms exist.
> - Provides lower interest rates for weaker countries.
>
> **Community**
> - Asserts European interests in relation to other important currency areas, notably the dollar.

Economically, the creation of a monetary union was in keeping with a market-oriented logic, according to which reducing barriers to trade boosts growth. Advocates of a *solidarity* approach can support a monetary union if it includes elements of redistribution (through market interventions in the event of attacks on the currency, budgetary transfers, or lower interest rates). Creating a monetary union is also consistent with the *community* approach, especially for the French, for whom it was important to assert a European monetary identity in the face of international competitors, the dollar in particular. The latter was the source of many problems, symbolised by the famous words of John Connally, the Treasury Secretary under US President Richard Nixon, who told Europeans worried about the fluctuations of the greenback in 1971 that 'the dollar is our currency, but it is your problem'. The 'exorbitant privilege' of the dollar denounced by French Minister of Finance Valéry Giscard d'Estaing in 1964, was rooted in US geopolitical dominance. A common monetary identity would allow Europeans to influence the international monetary system, and to be more independent from the US.

The main economic disadvantage of a monetary union is the impossibility of conducting an independent exchange rate or interest rate policy suitable to every country. Central bank rules on financing government expenditure are also harmonised. This discrepancy is evident in the European Community, which includes strong-currency countries generally located in Northern Europe (except for the UK), and weak-currency countries in Southern Europe. Similar differences also exist within the same country, between highly competitive Northern Italy and less productive Southern Italy, for example. Another issue was that the Community was not an 'optimal currency area' as defined by Robert Mundell in 1961, because the mobility of labour and capital was too low. Such mobility is important to compensating for geographical differences in economic dynamism in the event of asymmetric shocks; for instance, Americans can easily emigrate to another state in the US in case of economic hardship. However, in this oft-quoted article, Mundell did not deny that the Community was an optimal currency area, he was merely citing arguments in both directions.[2]

7.2 An Old Debate on Monetary Cooperation

After 1945, the dollar's domination pulled monetary issues into the Atlantic framework, which explains the quasi-absence of these matters in treaties involving the European communities (ECSC, EDC, EEC). In 1950, monetary exchanges were managed by the European Payments Union (EPU) associated with the Marshall Plan and the OEEC. The resumption of convertibility for European currencies in 1959 also took place within this Atlantic framework.

Monetary projects were nevertheless devised within the EEC as early as 1958.[3] The Commissioner Robert Marjolin of France wanted to take advantage of the French financial crisis to strengthen the mechanisms of European solidarity, which were practically absent from the Treaty of Rome.[4] His plan failed because member states were reluctant, and because the French financial recovery rendered the plan redundant. Marjolin continued to work on this project throughout the 1960s, combining his thinking with that of the Belgian-American economist Robert Triffin and Jean Monnet. Marjolin, Triffin, and Monnet developed several projects to set up a European Monetary Fund, with a view to reinforcing the mechanisms of monetary solidarity. A more intergovernmental project based on *community* capitalism was launched in 1966 by French Minister of the Economy and Finance Michel Debré.[5] He asked the Six to form a common front against the US in connection with reforms to the international monetary system, which he accused of unduly favouring the US and facilitating money creation. He defended a purely intergovernmental vision sidelining the Commission, but his Gaullist offensive eventually lost momentum. Several Western European countries experienced monetary and financial crisis throughout the 1960s, both inside (Italy) and outside (UK) the EEC. These crises were resolved within the framework of the IMF and the Bretton Woods system, with no role for European authorities.[6]

The French crisis of May 1968 transformed the French franc into a weak currency again. From that point onward, France, like other weak-currency countries (Italy), demanded monetary solidarity from strong-currency countries, primarily West Germany. In the event of a crisis, Paris wanted the Bundesbank to have to buy French francs and grant credit to the Banque de

France. Conversely, Bonn wanted to avoid any obligations to provide assistance to neighbours that it considered poorly managed, unless they made efforts to respect the rules of good management.[7] In the 1970s, this opposition was referred to as a debate between the 'economists' (the Germans, who insisted on the convergence of economic policies) and the 'monetarists' (the French, who favoured monetary solidarity above all). The latter term was specific to this debate on monetary union, and has nothing to do with the heirs of Milton Friedman.

The debate between 'economists' and 'monetarists' started in 1969, when the Six officially began discussions on European monetary cooperation, notably at the initiative of the new German Social Democrat Chancellor, Willy Brandt.[8] In early 1970, the Council asked Pierre Werner, the prime minister of Luxembourg, to draft a report on deepening monetary cooperation.[9] The Werner Report, presented in October 1970, was the first to call for creating an economic and monetary union in several stages, leading to a monetary union within ten years. It reconciled the standpoints of weak-currency countries (France and Italy) that prioritised solidarity with those of strong-currency countries (Germany and the Netherlands) focused on convergence towards stability-oriented policies.

Beginning in 1971, the crisis in the international monetary system triggered two opposing effects. The monetary instability generated by the transition from fixed exchange rates to floating ones (between 1971 and 1973) made European monetary cooperation even more attractive. However, it further increased divergence among the Six, with Paris arguing for maintaining fixed exchange rates, and Bonn accepting floating rates. The latter created problems for the CAP, which was based on the same prices for all European countries. Consequently, monetary instability jeopardised a flagship European policy. To address this issue, a first monetary agreement emerged in 1972, the European Monetary Snake. It was based on a commitment to limit fluctuation margins between European currencies, and on very short-term credit agreements between central banks to implement this agreement. All member states were opposed to significant delegations of sovereignty.[10] The currency turbulence following the 1973 oil crisis forced two weak currencies (the French franc and Italian lira) to leave the Snake, which was transformed into a small mark zone, resulting in the failure of European cooperation in this field.

7.3 The Impossible Concerted Recovery of 1978

In 1975–78, international monetary cooperation among Western countries was once again on the agenda. Since the oil crisis increased unemployment and lowered growth, the governments of countries in financial difficulty (the UK and Italy) and the European Trade Union Confederation (ETUC) called for a 'concerted recovery' among the richest Western countries. The aim was to convince the wealthiest countries to reflate (by spending more) in order to pull the weakest countries out of the crisis.[11] Failing that, isolated stimulus by a single country would only result in more imports, and hence in a widened trade deficit rather than more growth. The idea was an old one: Keynes himself had visited the US in the spring of 1931 to promote concerted international action in order to combat the Great Crash.[12]

In 1975–77, British prime ministers, Wilson and Callaghan, pressured West Germany to revive this idea, because its balance of payments was in surplus, whereas London and Rome were at the IMF begging for financial help (the IMF rescued the UK in 1976 and Italy in 1977). Chancellor Schmidt nonetheless remained hostile to any European financial solidarity. He believed that the way out of the crisis was not to 'print money', since that would only encourage inflation, but to adopt stability-oriented national policies.[13] The British note on the exchange between Schmidt and Callaghan ended with this ironic comment: 'Mr Crosland [the British Foreign Secretary] commented that Chancellor Schmidt was apocalyptic in tone, bordering on bullying, and advocating a far more right-wing view than that of [opposition leader] Mrs Thatcher.'[14] Schmidt presented the German example as a model in the field.

Even the French president suffered from Schmidt's intransigence. While the French–German 'couple' of Valéry Giscard d'Estaing and Helmut Schmidt is often celebrated, their rapprochement on monetary issues only emerged in 1978, with profound differences prior to that. At the Luxembourg European Council in April 1976, when the weak French franc had just left the Snake, the French president asked for an expression of European solidarity in the form of a declaration.[15] Schmidt refused. In early 1977, Giscard d'Estaing supported the project of concerted recovery, in which West Germany would have to make the greatest effort, although he was more moderate than Callaghan.[16]

In 1977, international pressure on West Germany increased as the new US President, Jimmy Carter, favoured better coordination between the three poles of North America, Western Europe, and Japan.[17] He advocated the 'locomotive' theory, according to which West Germany and Japan should stimulate consumption to boost growth in developed countries. At the same time, the British Chancellor of the Exchequer, Denis Healey, pointed out to Schmidt that the IMF had also criticised West Germany for having too large a trade surplus, which was causing international disturbances.[18] In the summer of 1978, documents from the OECD and the Commission recommended concerted economic action.

Finally, an agreement on macroeconomic policy coordination was reached at the G7 summit in Bonn on 16–17 July 1978.[19] The US agreed to fight inflation and reduce its oil consumption, an important issue for Schmidt. In return, Japan and West Germany would stimulate demand (up to 1 per cent of GDP for West Germany). France had to contribute somewhat less to this stimulus, and the UK and Italy much less. Bonn accepted these concessions to ensure the success of the Bonn G7, and to support the international free trade system.

Initially the concerted recovery seemed to work, as German growth was strong in the first half of 1979. The 1979 oil shock, however, broke the momentum. It is often forgotten that West Germany ran a current account deficit for a couple of quarters around 1980. Its budget deficit widened, and became larger than that of France, while its debt was much higher.[20] At the European Council, and again at the G7 meeting in Venice in June 1980, Schmidt complained that this deficit was due not only to the oil crisis, but also to the concerted recovery.[21] The Bundesbank even had to resort to emergency measures to stabilise the Deutschmark on 19 February 1981.[22] The bank's archives provide a pessimistic report from its Board of Directors, which noted at its meeting on the same day that there was a 'crisis of confidence' in the Deutschmark because 'Federal Germany had become a deficit country'.[23] Finance Minister Hans Matthöfer attended the next meeting of the Bundesbank's Governing Board a month later, and noted that its high interest rate policy was hampering economic expansion. However, he could not criticise it directly, due to the Bundesbank's independence.[24] The German situation was not dramatic, because its deficits were linked to cyclical causes (the oil crisis and spending by German tourists abroad), but this crisis convinced the German leader that concerted stimulus was too risky. These evolutions took place against the background of a profound cultural shift to market mechanisms.

7.4 A Cultural Shift to Market Mechanisms

In the 1970s and 1980s, norms based on free competition and private enterprise gradually took precedence over those focusing on public general interest and collective organisations. The ideological movement that structured this transformation is familiar. It originated in the growing influence, from the 1970s onwards, of neoliberal ideas, which is to say those of Hayek, Friedman, the second Chicago school, and the Virginia school. The influence of these economic thinkers was channelled through long-standing transnational networks, from the Mont Pelerin Society to transatlantic think tanks circulating ideas between Reaganites and Thatcherites.[25] These networks used various intermediaries such as international institutions (like the OECD) and national leaders, with the pioneer being the dictator Augusto Pinochet of Chile and his 'Chicago Boys' (economists who had spent time at the University of Chicago). In 1979 Thatcher followed suit with policies that reduced taxes on companies and the highest incomes, and retrenched the welfare state, with Reagan embarking on the same path in 1981.[26]

This change was accentuated by the discrediting of the Marxist system. The Soviet model had already been criticised because of the violent repressions that occurred in Eastern Europe even after Stalin's death (Berlin 1953, Budapest 1956, Berlin Wall 1961–89, Prague 1968, and Poland 1980–81). Criticism grew in the 1970s with the dissident movement, embodied by Alexander Solzhenitsyn. In the 1980s, the Soviet economy looked more inefficient than before, while in China the death of Mao in 1976 led to a successful experiment in economic liberalisation beginning in 1979. In many southern countries, the economic failure of socialist experiments also had a negative impact on Marxism.[27]

In the West, criticism of state inefficiency acquired a popular dimension. Antitax agitation gained a wider audience, as witnessed by the troubles with tax authorities experienced by French musicians in the 1970s, such as Michel Polnareff, Charles Aznavour, and Johnny Halliday, in addition to the Swedish actress Ingrid Bergman, who left her country in 1976 after a humiliating police investigation for tax evasion, for which she was finally acquitted.[28] The actress Astrid Lingren warned of the risk of Sweden drifting towards a 'bureaucratic dictatorship'. The Social Democrats, who had been in power since 1932, lost the elections in 1976. During those same years, the Progress Party – Mogens Gilstrup's antitax movement in Denmark – became the second-largest political force in the country for a time, before its leader was finally sent to prison, ironically for tax evasion.[29] In countries with the highest income tax brackets such as Sweden, the UK, and the US (where the top rates in 1975 were 85 per cent, 83 per cent, and 70 per cent respectively compared with 60 per cent in France), tax protests increased in the 1970s.[30]

Long-standing class divisions declined. In 1985, the left-wing intellectual Stuart Hall explained the success of Thatcherism by the fact that part of the working class had been severed from the left by a discourse emphasising the traditional values of order and security through 'authoritarian populism'.[31] Conversely, the traditional working class and trade union culture, sometimes driven by a masculine ethos, was less appealing to left-wing voters, who were more drawn by rising post-materialist values such as the defence of women, ethnic minorities, the environment, and human rights.[32] There was also the persuasive power of neoliberal discourse. The British political economist Mark Blyth said as much when he explained how his father, a butcher by profession, told him that he would not vote Labour in 1987, because their policies were creating inflation, whereas the Conservatives' tax cuts were going to boost growth.[33]

7.5 Growing Economic and Financial Constraints

The adoption of stability policies (based on low inflation and deficit targets) in the 1980s was also a response to two objective constraints: the ineffectiveness of uncoordinated Keynesian policies in the face of inflation, and financial crises. During the 'Golden Age' (1945–74), decision-makers could arbitrate between employment and inflation: in the event of a price spike, spending was tightened, which limited inflation but slightly increased unemployment. If unemployment rose too high, all that was needed was stimulus, which slightly increased inflation. However, after the 1973 crisis, stimulus policies often led to much higher inflation, with only a very modest rise in growth. This phenomenon of low growth and high inflation was known as 'stagflation'. Inflation was persistent due to a fourfold rise in the price of oil in 1973, in addition to US deficits.[34] Conversely, stimulus plans were hampered by the liberalisation of trade, as they tended to increase imports rather than national production. Western decision-makers gradually came to see the fight against inflation as an essential prerequisite for recovery, and therefore for reducing unemployment.

In theory, inflation is negative because it leads to uncertainty among economic agents (thereby discouraging investment and savings), poverty traps (for those whose income is not indexed), and decreased competitiveness (if trading partners have lower inflation). The only way to compensate for this deterioration in competitiveness is to devalue the currency, but that renders external financing more complicated. Money creation, or 'money printing', can be a way to compensate for this, but that may also revive inflation. The ultimate fear is runaway inflation, as witnessed by the hyperinflation in Germany in 1923. The German's anti-inflationary mentality even spread to groups on the political left, including the Social Democratic Party of Germany (SPD) and the German Trade Union Confederation (DGB). In 1979, a note from the French trade union CFDT emphasised this culture of anti-inflationary 'stability' in the DGB.[35]

This concern regarding inflation went beyond elites in the 1970s. Surveys showed that it affected many segments of the Western population, which was worried about the erosion of their income and savings.[36] On the left, the ETUC regularly called for intensifying the fight against inflation after 1973.[37] Left-wing politicians often accused employers of creating inflation in order to increase profits.[38] As a result, in the 1970s the fight against inflation was not just the prerogative of the most conservative, but also concerned a growing number of Europeans.

Financial crises played a major role in the turn towards a macroeconomic approach rejecting Keynesian stimulus. Financial difficulties were caused by several factors: the rising cost of energy (the price of oil increased tenfold due to the two oil shocks) and low growth led to reduced tax revenues and increased spending; the ageing population created additional burdens on the health and pension systems (even if the phenomenon remained measured at the time); and finally, the welfare state extended its prerogatives. The four major countries of Western Europe all experienced a marked deterioration in their public finances following the 1973 and 1979 oil crises (Figure 7.1).

These external financing problems were not unique to Western Europe in the 1970s. Dependence on external financing had already manifested itself

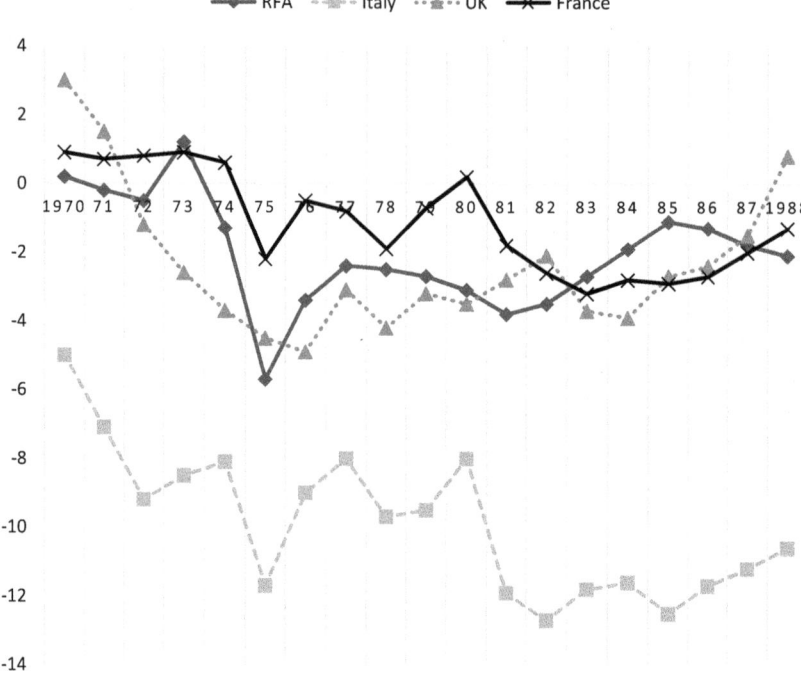

Figure 7.1 Government account balance, 1970–87 (four countries) France, UK, FRG, Italy. Deficit or surplus as % of GNP/GDP.[39]

there during post-war reconstruction, and again in France during the financial crisis of 1957–58, which prompted French negotiators to secure credit from the US and France's European partners.[40] Other countries also experienced monetary and financial difficulties in roughly the same period, such as Italy in 1964 and the UK in 1967.

This financial constraint was also visible in communist countries in the East, whose elites could hardly be accused of complacency with liberalism. In Poland and East Germany, the governments chose to take advantage of the abundant international financing made possible by the recycling of petro-dollars after 1973. They borrowed massively in order to finance industrial development (exports would be used to repay the loans) and to support domestic consumption via subsidies. However, the low productivity of their industry condemned this strategy to failure.[41] Faced with repayment difficulties and rising interest rates, Warsaw was forced to cut back on spending, which played a role in the massive protest movements of 1980.[42] In East Berlin, Erich Honecker was determined to avoid this situation. To stem inflation, the East German state subsidised prices at exorbitant cost to state finance, accounting for up to 25 per cent of national expenditure in 1987, precipitating the system's bankruptcy.[43]

The chronology of the turn towards stability policies varied geographically. It occurred first in West Germany, a country traumatised by inflation and possessing a limited Keynesian tradition. Chancellor Schmidt (1974–82) pursued a macroeconomic policy that combined the imperative of stability with targeted stimulus packages.[44] This policy caused a stir within his Social Democratic Party. While on vacation in Marbella in January 1977, Schmidt explained to SPD leaders Brandt and Wehner in his Marbella Paper that the 1974 crisis differed from that of 1930. While the latter was a deflationary crisis calling for a Keynesian stimulus response, the former was an inflationary crisis. This 'inflationary mentality' therefore had to be destroyed in order for the recovery to proceed.[45] In September 1982, the Minister of Economics Otto von Lambsdorff published a memorandum, the Lambsdorff paper, calling for the liberalisation of economic policy through deregulation, reduced government intervention, and the 'adaptation of the social welfare system to the new conditions of growth'. These tensions led to the collapse of the SPD/FDP government and the rise to power of the Kohl government, which led a new CDU/CSU-FPD coalition. Lambsdorff once again was appointed Minister of Economics and pursued a gradual neoliberal policy (with a reduction in social benefits and civil servant salaries in real terms, corporate tax cuts, labour market flexibility, and privatisation).[46] In 1983, Oskar Vetter, the former leader of the DGB, called it 'sado-monetarism'.[47]

In France, the evolution was more uneven, marked by alternation between an austerity approach (1974, 1976–81) and vigorous stimulus packages (1975–76 under Jacques Chirac's right-wing government, 1981–83 under Pierre Mauroy's left-wing government). The Mauroy stimulus one was predicated on permanent spending increases, including a reduction in working time and a vast nationalisation programme for companies facing difficulty, which required massive injections of capital. The prospect of a financial crisis in 1983 prompted the French government to more fully convert to stability policies.

In the UK, inflation rose to an annualised rate of 24 per cent in early 1975, far higher than in continental Europe, while deficits grew. The country was named the sick man of Europe in the famous 1975 Trilateral Commission report.[48] The ultimate humiliation came in 1976, when London had to turn to the IMF, which granted a loan in December of that year.[49] The Callaghan government then tried to pursue a policy combining fiscal discipline, inflation control, and dialogue with unions. This high-wire act finally came crashing down when unions abandoned the government, with massive strikes during the Winter of Discontent in 1978-79.

Margaret Thatcher's rise to power in 1979 brought a massive change in macroeconomic policy. The priority given to fighting inflation led to drastic budget cuts and credit restrictions. This policy resulted in massive protests, especially from employers who complained about high interest rates, in addition to 364 economists who signed a manifesto in 1981.[50] Even within the Conservative Party, serious doubts emerged, thus explaining Thatcher's defiant statement at the 1980 Conservative Party conference: 'The lady's not for turning.' With regard to housing, the government granted long-time tenants the right to buy social housing at reduced prices and with loan facilities. This policy popularised neoliberalism while depriving the welfare state of one of its essential levers of action. In the areas of industrial and trade union policy, the change was more gradual, taking place over several years (see Chapter 5).

The evolution was similar elsewhere in the West. In the US, the turning point came with the Volcker Shock in 1979, when the new governor of the central bank, Paul Volcker, sharply raised interest rates. Ronald Reagan assumed power in 1981 and implemented a full-fledged neoliberal policy with massive tax cuts (especially for the rich) and reductions in social spending. Reagan combined this with *community* capitalism through increased military spending and a more aggressive trade policy. In Italy, the financial crisis of 1977, combined with the IMF intervention, led to a neoliberal shift between 1978 and 1981.[51] In Northern Europe, two conservative leaders came to power in 1982 – Rudd Lubbers in the Netherlands and Poul Schlüter in Denmark – with both replacing social democratic governments and pursuing more free market policies. In the Netherlands, the Wassenar Compromise of 1982 between unions and employers established the principle of wage moderation, especially in exchange for working time arrangements. In Japan, Yakuhiro Nakasone became prime minister in 1982, and adopted Reagan's rhetoric of government withdrawal through tax cuts and privatisation. In Canada, the neoliberal turn was prepared by the 1985 Macdonald Commission. Economic conditions improved after 1983, but growth and employment were still far below the Golden Age. This convergence towards stability-oriented policy facilitated the conclusion of the European Monetary System.

7.6 The Voluntary Constraint of the European Monetary System

In the absence of a concerted international recovery, macroeconomic policy coordination was provided by the European Monetary System (EMS), created in 1979 within the European Community. It marked a break with the past, not so much on the institutional level, since the EMS was an intergovernmental agreement (like the Snake), but on the political level, by demonstrating a desire for convergence in economic policy.

Both French President Giscard d'Estaing and Commission President Roy Jenkins had been eagerly awaiting a revival of monetary cooperation since 1977, but Chancellor Schmidt remained reluctant.[52] The creation of the EMS was decided in late 1978 thanks to French–German convergence arising from three factors. The first was the good relationship between the two leaders, although their frequent clashes on numerous economic issues (see Chapter 6) shows that their good rapport was not enough on its own. Two other factors were needed to convince Schmidt and especially the (independent) Bundesbank to engage in extensive monetary cooperation in Europe: distrust in President Carter, who allowed the dollar to devalue, and Schmidt's confidence in the anti-inflationary policies of the new French prime minister appointed in 1976, the austere Raymond Barre.[53]

Like the European Monetary Snake created in 1972, the EMS was a monetary stability area based on a voluntary commitment by each of its eight members (the UK refused to participate). Each country retained its currency, but had to maintain that currency's value within a limited band of divergence from other currencies. Under the Snake, the pressure to remain within the fluctuation band fell primarily on weak currencies. Paris tried to establish a more symmetrical system by placing the adjustment burden on both countries whose currency was too weak (France and Italy) and those whose currency was too strong (West Germany).[54] The French wanted to benefit from automatic German solidarity in the event of crisis, and sought assurances that the powerful Bundesbank would rescue the French franc if it was attacked on the markets.

German opposition, particularly from the Bundesbank, prevented any major institutional change. The adoption of a new unit of account, the ECU (an acronym for European Currency Unit, as well as a nod to 'the ecu', a medieval French currency), to serve as a reference for the exchange rate divergence indicator did not entail any obligation to intervene, nor did it prevent the Deutschmark from remaining at the centre of the system.[55] If the German currency appreciated, weak-currency countries (France and Italy) bore the burden of adjustment: they had to converge with Germany's economic policy, or their currency would risk leaving the EMS. As Chancellor Schmidt said to the Bundesbank on 30 November 1978, the EMS was a 'bathing suit' or 'make-up' used to hide the fact that France was returning to the Snake; it did not force the Bundesbank to intervene indefinitely in support of the franc.[56] The EMS nevertheless created political pressure on Germany to cooperate more closely with its European partners (as the 1983 French financial crisis would eventually prove).

Similarly, for French and Italian leaders, joining the EMS would serve as a voluntary constraint, forcing them to intensify their fight against inflation in exchange for the promise of German solidarity in the event of monetary crisis. President Giscard d'Estaing's advisor for international economic affairs was emphatically clear on the matter: 'Our entry into the EMS is tantamount to a return to a fixed exchange rate system ... It is therefore necessary to ensure, through internal money creation (treasury and credits to the economy), the adjustment needed to respect the growth objectives of the money supply. In particular, control over changes to public finances is absolutely essential.'[57]

The approach remained one based on *liberty* rather than *solidarity*. A solidarity mechanism was not included in the EMS due to German opposition and French reluctance. In late 1978, when the Italian Prime Minister Giulio Andreotti called for imposing rules on countries with problematic surpluses and not just those with deficits, Giscard d'Estaing did not support him.[58] Similarly, the agreement creating the EMS provided for creating the European Monetary Fund (EMF) after two years (Article 1.4), but this provision remains unimplemented. Giscard d'Estaing opposed any major delegations of sovereignty, and Prime Minister Barre was not particularly interested, especially since the French franc was strong in 1979-81.[59] Furthermore, Paris doubted that Italy, with its permanent financial difficulties, could join the EMS, which shows the absence of a common policy between France and Italy.[60] After the change of majority in May 1981, the new socialist government in France was not interested in creating this fund either.[61] The reference to 'strengthening the instruments of European monetary solidarity', in the draft version of the 1981 French memorandum on Europe did not appear in the final version.[62]

In Germany, opposition to creating the fund was even stronger, since it would have been the main contributor. A conversation between Chancellor Schmidt and Bundesbank President Pöhl in July 1980 is revelatory in this regard.[63] Pöhl believed that the creation of a 'European IMF' would pose serious sovereignty issues. Schmidt recognised that it would be very difficult to envisage such an institution with the high inflation rates in France and Italy.[64] The EMF was dead on arrival.

7.7 The 1983 French Financial Crisis: A European Turning Point

The problem of European solidarity was not theoretical, as demonstrated by the French financial crisis narrowly averted in the spring of 1983.[65] The economic stimulus provided by the socialist government in 1981-82 was massive and isolated (all of France's neighbours were still reeling from the 1979 oil shock). It soon led to a sharp increase in the trade deficit. In 1977 and 1980, the ETUC considered any attempt at a unilateral Keynesian revival in an open world to be illusory, except for targeted measures (especially for low-paid jobs).[66]

The French stimulus increased the budget deficit and debt, in a context in which high interest rates made borrowing expensive. The French government was one of the world's largest borrowers on the international capital market in 1982 and 1983.[67] The fall of the franc made borrowing foreign currency more

7.7 THE FRENCH FINANCIAL CRISIS

expensive. Paris had to borrow from Saudi Arabia, and risked having to call on IMF assistance, as the UK had done in 1976, and Italy in 1977. Robert Lion, the Chief of Staff to Prime Minister Pierre Mauroy, summed up the general impression after a cabinet meeting in March 1982: 'It is important that we do not give the French, or the outside world, the impression that we are going down the "British road": that of complacency and the least effort.'[68]

In early 1983, the situation deteriorated with the depletion of reserves. Mitterrand was having difficulty deciding between two possible responses. The first, defended by the 'Albanians' (in reference to the autarchic and communist European country of Albania) and multiple ministers – including Bérégovoy (Social Affairs), Jean-Pierre Chevènement (Industry), and Laurent Fabius (Budget) – was to devalue the franc by leaving the EMS.[69] It would have made French exports cheaper, but would also have increased inflation, potentially offsetting any advantage from the more favourable exchange rate. The drop in the franc's value would likely have resulted in higher interest rates, thereby making industrial expansion more difficult.

The alternative was to pursue a policy of stability and to negotiate a measured devaluation within the framework of the EMS, with a view to gaining support from European partners in defending the parity of the franc. The main objective was to obtain Germany's commitment (from both the government and the central bank) to defend the franc. This solution was advocated by Prime Minister Mauroy – who in 1981 had already expressed his desire to pursue a policy combining social justice and budgetary 'rigour'[70] – and by the Minister of Economy and Finance, Jacques Delors.

Mitterrand chose the second option, but the negotiations were tense, as he was asking for German solidarity in the form of a German stimulus package, monetary support, and the revaluation of the mark.[71] On 18 March 1983, the German cabinet met in Bonn. The participants included: Helmut Kohl (Chancellor), Hans-Dietrich Genscher (Foreign Affairs), Jens Stoltenberg (Finance), and Karl-Otto Pöhl (Bundesbank). Stoltenberg, who had recently returned from a secret trip to Paris to meet with French officials, insisted that Germany pledge its support for France, because he was afraid that the French threat to leave the EMS was genuine.[72] Delors confirmed that, for political reasons, there was a risk of protectionist measures by France if German support measures did not materialise. However, Stoltenberg ruled out the Deutschmark bearing the cost of monetary realignment alone. Kohl and Lambsdorff agreed, and supported keeping the franc in the EMS. Pöhl, the head of the Bundesbank, was more hesitant: he believed a French exit from the EMS would not be especially tragic, and in any event it was hardly in Paris's interest to pursue a protectionist policy. Kohl finally imposed German support for the French devaluation. On 21 March 1983, the Chancellor sent a letter of support to Mitterrand.[73] Kohl emphasised the link between German solidarity and French measures combatting inflation and protectionism.

The monetary operation that was finally decided upon on 21 March 1983 was a European one, since all EMS currencies were involved.[74] The Bundesbank lowered rates slightly and sold Deutschmarks to limit the revaluation of the German currency. In addition, the European Community granted a loan of 4 billion ecus to France in May 1983.

France could very well have ended up before the IMF. The decisions of 1983 were not really neoliberal, since most of the welfare state reforms of 1981–82 were preserved. The Delors Plan of 1983 also included tax increases for the rich. The Communists even remained in government until 1984. The primary neoliberal measure was the end of wage indexing, but according to Thomas Piketty, the minimum wage (and the share of wages in GDP) rose much faster than productivity between 1968 and 1983.[75] The policy of austerity and financial market liberalisation, which aimed to lower interest rates, was implemented by the new Prime Minister Laurent Fabius and the Minister of Economy and Finance Pierre Bérégovoy (1984–86), both of whom had been in favour of leaving the EMS in 1983. The conversion of French leaders to a stability-oriented policy also involved the opposition: when he met Chancellor of the Exchequer Nigel Lawson in November 1983, the centre-right leader Jacques Chirac praised Thatcherite policies, but criticised them for not going far enough in cutting taxes.[76] London was now a model for some French leaders.

Overall, for France the choice made in 1983 was one of European and international influence rather than national withdrawal, because this policy of stability meant that the humiliation of an IMF intervention in France would be avoided.

7.8 Convergence towards a Federal Monetary Union

Despite this conversion to stability policies, the transition from an intergovernmental agreement on monetary cooperation (the EMS of 1979) to a federal monetary union at Maastricht in 1992 represented a considerable leap. It resulted from convergence among three actors: the Delors Commission, weak-currency countries (especially France), and the most powerful and reluctant actor, Germany.

In Brussels, Commission President Delors wanted to strengthen monetary cooperation right from the start, probably because he was a former Banque de France official, and as he served as the French Minister of Finance during the 1983 financial crisis.[77] In early 1985, he asked Kohl and Genscher to deepen European monetary cooperation, but had no success.[78] In his request Delors underscored three central ideas: reinforcing the EMS (with an obligation for strong-currency countries to intervene, and a convergence towards mixed policy combining stability and solidarity); the creation of a reserve fund to implement European solidarity and show unity in negotiations with the US;

7.8 CONVERGENCE TOWARDS A FEDERAL MONETARY UNION 167

and lastly harmonisation of financial market regulation in order to facilitate the free movement of capital all while avoiding speculation. He was already thinking of giving central banks a major role. Delors therefore combined all three approaches of *liberty*, *solidarity*, and *community*.

During the 1985 negotiations for the Single European Act, Delors proposed creating a monetary fund, once again unsuccessfully.[79] The Commission then entered the intellectual fray in order to justify monetary union as the necessary crowning achievement of the Single Market: it published several reports between 1987 and 1990, including one by the Italian economist Tommaso Padoa-Schioppa.[80] The Commission had to convince Europeans that reinforcing the EMS was not sufficient (even if it involved creating a parallel currency instead of a common currency, as the British envisaged in the late 1980s). Only a fully federal monetary union would provide growth and solidarity.

In Paris, the French government felt that it had lost all monetary independence despite its stability-oriented economic policy. In Frankfurt, the Bundesbank maintained interest rates that were too high for France, but the Banque de France had to increase its rates each time its German counterpart did, otherwise devaluation would have been inevitable (creating additional challenges to funding the French economy). In September 1987, Paris and Bonn struck a compromise in the Basel–Nyborg Agreement: the French accepted the liberalisation of capital movements (leading to a European directive adopted in 1988), in exchange for an agreement in principle by the Germans to intervene in the foreign exchange market to assist weak currencies. But doubt remained in Paris over the extent of German solidarity. At the time, in 1990, Jacques de Larosière, the Governor of the Banque de France, remarked: 'Today I am the governor of a central bank that has decided, along with his nation, to fully follow German monetary policy without voting on it. At least as part of a European central bank, I'll have a vote.'[81] Multiple French Ministers of the Economy and Finance (Balladur in 1987, Bérégovoy in 1988) had asked the Germans to consult with them more systematically over monetary matters, but the sacrosanct independence of the Bundesbank prevented any coordination. The loss of the French franc was not seen as a major loss of sovereignty by pro-Europeans. Similarly, the ban on monetary financing of the national debt, which was included in the Maastricht Treaty, was only a small concession, since this method of debt financing represented only 3 per cent of French debt in 1993.[82]

A major step was taken in December 1987 when the French Minister of Economy and Finance, Édouard Balladur, argued in a memorandum that the freedom of movement for capital put the prospect of a common currency managed by a common central bank back on the agenda.[83] This perspective was echoed in memoranda issued the following year by the Italian Finance Minister Giuliano Amato and by the German Minister Hans-Dietrich Genscher (who spoke in his own name and not that of the German government).

Across the Rhine, the conversion was more difficult. West Germans did not want to abandon the Deutschmark, a currency that was created in 1948 even before the Federal Republic (1949), and a symbol of the new democratic Germany's success. Nor did they wish to waste their resources by supporting countries accused of mismanagement. In 1985, Helmut Kohl justified his reluctance to strengthen monetary cooperation to the prime minister of Luxembourg, Jacques Santer. He cited past experiences of currency manipulation, especially by Hjalmar Schacht, the president of the Reichsbank during the first half of the Nazi period (1933–39).[84]

The key change came when Bonn secured the 1988 directive on the liberalisation of capital movements (strongly supported by the UK and the Netherlands).[85] This measure was intended to both lower the cost of capital within the Community (by creating a larger market) and create indirect pressure for economic policy convergence towards the most virtuous country, otherwise capital flight would ensue. It was this agreement that convinced Kohl, during the Hanover European Council in 1988, to accept establishing a committee chaired by Delors to reflect on a future economic and monetary union. The result was the Delors Report of April 1989. It largely prefigured the economic and monetary union that was eventually adopted in the Maastricht Treaty, and implemented ten years later in the eurozone. The president of the Commission obtained the agreement of the Bundesbank president, Karl-Otto Pöhl, by accepting some of the German's ordoliberal demands, such as the independence of the future central bank, in exchange for the single currency. Delors wanted to go even further by developing the idea of a common intervention budget, but it was shelved.[86] He believed that in the long run, the European budget would reach 3 per cent of GDP (it has never exceeded 1.2 per cent) through expanded structural policies to help the poorest regions adapt to monetary union. Delors also included in his report the need to 'coordinate the banking oversight policies of supervisory authorities'. In the end, it took the eurozone crisis (2010–12) to make this a reality.

The pressure of German reunification in 1989–90 facilitated the adoption of these ideas, especially in Bonn, where Kohl enjoyed a commanding stature that allowed him to marginalise internal opposition, and in Paris, where there was looming fear that Germany could reunify and turn away from Europe.[87] The German cabinet accepted monetary union provided that it would adopt certain ordoliberal features. While this latter term was not used, German leaders consistently referred to *Ordnungspolitisch*, a concept denoting stability-oriented policy (low deficits, fiscal discipline, central bank independence, and free competition).[88] The German cabinet's official position on European monetary matters in 1989 also referred to the objective of a 'high level of employment'.

At the European Council in Strasbourg held on 8–9 December 1989, Kohl agreed to initiate negotiations on a monetary union. This agreement came immediately after a meeting between Tyll Necker, the president of the employers' association (the BDI) and Foreign Minister Genscher. Necker asked the minister to refuse monetary union, while Genscher insisted on Germany's political duty to accept such a prospect, especially at a time of upheaval in the East.[89] Once Kohl gave his own agreement and overcame internal opposition, the road to the federal monetary union was open.

7.9 Monetary Union at the Maastricht Treaty

The Maastricht Treaty, concluded in early 1992 by eleven countries (all EU members save the UK), created an economic and monetary union (known as the EMU) based on a fundamental asymmetry: while the monetary union was federal, the economic union remained intergovernmental. Member states remained free to determine their own economic policies. The Union was to be implemented in three stages between 1992 and 1999, culminating with the introduction of a single currency managed by a European Central Bank (ECB) independent of the states. To join the EMU, states had to meet stability criteria (low inflation, contained deficits and debts) as well as convergence criteria (with an inflation level and interest rates close to the eurozone average). The Treaty established multilateral monitoring, but the sanction procedure was difficult to apply because it required a two-thirds majority in the Council (not counting the votes of the state involved). The central bank was independent, and guided primarily by a 'stability' objective of low inflation.

An ordoliberal shift therefore occurred between the Delors Report (1989) and the Maastricht Treaty (1991). Two elements present in the former – solidarity and banking oversight – disappeared from the latter, despite appearing in the initial draft treaty presented by the Commission in 1990.[90] These drafts were rejected by most European states out of opposition to the delegation of sovereignty. Moreover, for the Germans it would have been more difficult for the ECB to concentrate on price stability if it also had to take financial stability into account. This would run the risk of recapitalising weak banks.

Maastricht was the result of a compromise. Weak-currency countries such as France and Italy obtained a monetary union with the powerful Deutschmark, which allowed them to lower interest rates.[91] French archives show that the negotiation was considered a success at the time, particularly because it was the Council that defined the 'broad economic policy guidelines': France could then benefit from more favourable financing conditions, while retaining full budgetary autonomy. What is more, while the ECB's mandate focused primarily on inflation, Article 2 of the Protocol on the ECB also referred to the EU's general objectives, which include 'a high level of employment and of social protection, the raising of the standard of living and quality of life, economic and social cohesion and solidarity among Member States'.

Most importantly for some French negotiators, monetary union warded off the spectre of the Community being replaced by an unregulated free trade area, a daunting but realistic prospect with the end of the Cold War.[92]

Germany had to abandon the Deutschmark, but in return obtained a monetary union designed to create a strong currency: the central bank was independent and oriented primarily towards the objective of low inflation, no common solidarity fund was created, no common responsibility for national debt existed, and financial assistance to a state in crisis required unanimity.

The features of the Maastricht Treaty should not be seen as an expression of German ordoliberalism alone, but rather as a consensus among governments on various ideas, such as the refusal to strengthen EU institutions beyond a certain degree (by increasing their budget), and the independence of central banks (an idea that had been gaining ground in the West throughout the 1980s). Member states opposed expanding the EU's role in times of financial crisis.[93] Incidentally, the prospect of providing financial assistance to Greece had already arisen in 1989.[94]

However, there was a debate regarding how to put the independence of the Central Bank into practice. In April 1989, just after the Delors Report, the socialist group at the European Parliament believed that while the future ECB should be independent in its choice of instruments, it should also be subject to the general objectives defined by the Council of Ministers in conjunction with the European Parliament. In addition to monetary stability, the group also felt that the ECB's mandate should promote convergence in economic development.[95] Similarly, during the negotiations on the Maastricht Treaty, Delors tried unsuccessfully to include provisions for some form of political control by European institutions over the ECB, while preserving its independence.[96]

As we have seen, the Maastricht Treaty provided for a transition towards a federal monetary union with a distinctly ordoliberal tinge, combined with an intergovernmental economic union. *Solidarity* was present thanks to the very existence of a monetary union that would allow the most fragile countries to benefit from low interest rates and avoid monetary crises. *Community* was inherently present, as a European monetary identity could be asserted vis-à-vis the dollar if the Europeans so wished. Delors used this argument in 1985, during a period of intense monetary discussions with Washington.[97] The most neoliberal, such as Thatcher in London and certain North American economists, were very critical of this project, which they considered utopian. Such a surprising outcome – a federal monetary union among such powerful and differing nation states – was a bold political choice on the part of European leaders. For them, the fall of the Berlin Wall represented both an opportunity and a threat: the EU was in danger of being replaced if not consolidated. Pressure from structural economic forces, such as the internationalisation of financial movements or the Single Market programme, also played a role, but could not explain how a federal monetary union emerged as the solution, because other solutions (such as the strengthening of the EMS) could have been pursued.

7.10 Conclusion

The birth of the European Monetary Union largely based on *liberty* capitalism can be explained by three factors (in addition to long-term dynamics such as Europeanism). First, the conversion to more market-oriented and even neoliberal ideas was deep and influential across large segments of the population. However, these ideas were not dominant until the 1979 oil shock, and so the situation could have been different with Carter's re-election in the US, combined with a successful concerted recovery in 1978, or even a European campaign by trade unions for shorter working hours (see Chapter 4).

Second, major economic and financial constraints resulted from the oil crises. Many European states found it more difficult to finance themselves and export goods. They came to see the lowering of inflation as a priority, so that they could later reduce unemployment. Inflation and budgetary constraints also began to affect the countries of Eastern Europe under communist rule. Even the communist government of China at the time was very sensitive to inflation, since it was aware of the role that hyperinflation played in the demise of Guomindang China in the 1940s.[98] These examples from communist countries demonstrate that post-1973 financial and inflationary constraints were real, and not just the result of an ideological choice.

Third, the choice for a federal monetary union came late, since it emerged only after other avenues had failed. For a long time, ideas for monetary cooperation focused on creating a European fund that would reinforce solidarity. Such proposals were therefore not linked to a neoliberal dynamic. In the end, this idea was adopted by European leaders in the 1970s, notably with the EMS's European Monetary Fund, but it was never fully implemented.

European solutions became more interesting after the failure of purely national approaches during financial crises or near-crises (UK in 1976, Italy and Portugal in 1977, France in 1983), as well as the limitations of the international approach, with the failure of the concerted recovery in 1978 (due to the 1979 oil shock, and to a German balance of payment crisis in 1980 that was largely ignored). In the 1980s, intergovernmental solutions such as the EMS were considered insufficient by weak-currency countries such as France and Italy, which were suffering from the Bundesbank's high interest rate policy. Federal monetary union was paradoxically seen as a way of regaining lost international influence. Its predominantly ordoliberal features were accepted as a condition for a recovery that could include elements of *solidarity*. The fall of the Berlin Wall in 1989 helped to overcome opponents of this bold solution, because a federal monetary union was seen as a way to keep Germany firmly anchored in the peaceful project of European integration.

There is consequently no automatic link between monetary union and neoliberalism. The surprising birth of the euro can ultimately be explained by a combination between an old pro-European project of monetary cooperation (which had existed since at least the 1960s), rising monetary and financial constraints beginning in the 1970s (which had reinforced the West German model), the limited success of alternatives (the Snake and later the EMS), and geopolitical upheavals (in 1989–92).

More generally, the Maastricht Treaty was dominated by the principle of *liberty*. Social Europe was present in the form of the Social Charter, social dialogue, and the broadening of competence to include environmental protection, whereas the *community* form of capitalism was only present in language mentioning large trans-European networks. Neoliberal Europe was expressed in certain ordoliberal clauses of the Economic and Monetary Union. For weak-currency countries, the single economic and monetary union also represented *solidarity*: a promise that Germany would assist them in the event of financial crisis, and an assurance of lower interest rates. Above all, many clauses of the Maastricht Treaty remained open to different interpretations, as confirmed by the ensuing decades.

8

The European Union as a Driver of 'High Neoliberalism' (1992-2015)

According to Aristotle, tragedy aims, 'through pity and fear', to achieve the 'purgation of these emotions'.[1] The Greek tragedy that unfolded during the eurozone crisis (2010-15) was the height of a period of 'high neoliberalism' that has been particularly prevalent since 1992. The European Union has been one of the driving forces behind a neoliberal dynamic that has unfolded in many areas, particularly between 1992 and 2015. However, European capitalism has always been of a mixed nature. Therefore, even within the most neoliberal policies, elements of *solidarity* and *community* capitalism have persisted.

This chapter will examine the global rise of neoliberalism, and three European policies, the development of the Single Market, competition policy, and the monetary union, especially during the eurozone crisis.

8.1 The Global Rise of Neoliberalism: From the Internet to China

Neoliberalism gained ground worldwide after 1992, spreading to numerous sectors and countries. For example, market logic became prevalent in 1992 in basketball (in the US) and football (starting in the UK).[2]

Neoliberalism also spread to Internet regulation. While the World Wide Web has often been hailed as an emancipatory libertarian enterprise by celebrity entrepreneurs sometimes drawing on the progressive ideals of the 1960s (Steve Jobs, the founder of Apple, went to an ashram in India in 1974), in some respects it has turned out to be a neoliberal jungle, with limited concern for preserving individual freedom, decency, or the soundness of democratic debate.[3] The neoliberalisation of the Internet was not preordained, but rather the outcome of three dynamics. First, some of its promoters are libertarian, and verge on neoliberal. For example, one of the founders of Wikipedia, Jimmy Wales, was explicitly influenced by Hayek.[4] Second, political authorities refused to regulate the content circulating online. Section 230 of the US Communication Decency Act passed in 1996 exempts Internet 'providers' and 'users' from any liability for potentially harmful publications. This means that web-based publication has an intrinsic competitive advantage over traditional media, whose regulation is much more constraining. Other governments, such as those in Europe, followed suit by establishing similar lax rules, although they are slightly more constraining in some countries than others (racial hatred is more strictly regulated in Germany, for example). Third, US antitrust authorities have been very tolerant, allowing monopolistic or oligopolistic Big Tech companies to flourish. The World Wide Web has undergone several phases of centralisation and decentralisation, with the most recent phase – marked by the rise of GAFAM in the US and its equivalent in China – has brought increasing centralisation, and sometimes collusion with political authorities. Even technologies that were used to skirt state regulation (such as crypto-currencies) are now encouraged by some states, such as the US under the second Donald Trump administration. As Helen Margetts, a specialist on the politics of IT, has observed: 'past (Hayekian) confidence that centralized micro-control of complex economic markets by the state is impossible has been challenged by digital era developments'.[5]

With regard to the trinity of capitalism, the World Wide Web has certainly brought certain elements of *solidarity* and *liberty*: by decreasing the cost of information and translation, it has given access to much more information than at any time in history. What was once reserved for the lucky few, who could afford to pay for encyclopaedias and newspapers subscription, is now more widely available. The organisation of protest movements has also become easier. The fight against Covid-19 has certainly been facilitated by the availability of data, as well as user-friendly apps and softwares. However, the almost complete absence of regulation over information has been a bonanza for radical opinions, fake news, and somewhat later the manipulation of democratic debate by dictatorships.[6] Similar to the Cold War, during which the ideological confrontation between the US and the USSR also took place in the media, current geopolitical confrontations have also played out on the web, as shown by the leaks connected to the presidential elections in the US in 2016 and in France in 2017. In other words, the neoliberalisation of the Internet has favoured a radical *community* approach, namely by fuelling fake news and hate speech. All technologies have dual effects, both positive and negative, depending on how they are regulated.

Neoliberalism has also spread geographically. At the global level, the protectionist agreements from previous decades (agricultural protectionism, multi-fibre textile agreements, voluntary export restraint agreements by the Japanese) were gradually abandoned at the end of the Uruguay Round of the GATT in 1992–94.[7] In 2000, the Cotonou Agreement dismantled part of the neomercantilist apparatus that linked the EU and its partner countries in the Global South (the so-called ACP countries). As tariffs have largely disappeared, trade negotiations have subsequently focused on more sensitive areas of public action, such as social and environmental rules, or on dispute settlement mechanisms between states and multinationals, often to the benefit of the latter.

Even core areas of social policy have been affected. While social spending has often remained relatively high (as a percentage of GDP), a stabilisation or even increase in public expenditure may actually conceal a decline in concrete social benefits, because the need for solidarity has structurally increased over time due to an ageing population, rising education levels, and increasing environmental risks.

In Europe, even centre-left strongholds have been affected: Gerhard Schröder, the Social Democratic Chancellor of Germany, made deep cuts to unemployment benefits with the 2004 Hartz IV legislation, while Sweden adopted the radical idea of liberalising the education market, an idea once touted by the neoliberal grandee, Milton Friedman.

EU enlargement to the former countries of the Eastern Bloc was a long-awaited reunification, as well as a massive political and economic shock. Eastern European leaders converted to neoliberalism for both economic and geopolitical reasons. Gradualism, or the policy of gradually adopting liberal capitalism, was not considered viable due to the failure of Perestroika and Yugoslav reform strategies in the late 1980s.[8] The predicament faced by these countries, which included excessive debt, high inflation and unemployment, insufficient productivity, and a massive decline in national wealth, empowered those arguing for 'shock therapy', a brutal conversion to unregulated free markets (by contrast with China which 'escaped shock therapy').[9] While some countries tried a more cautious transition towards a market economy in the 1990s, they all converged in the 2000s towards a development model fuelled by foreign direct investment and a limited welfare state.[10] This model was also encouraged by the EU. The massive transfer of funds provided by the Union gave Brussels leverage that it primarily used to ensure Western investment would proceed unhindered. As there was no private capital in these former communist countries, companies were often bought by Western firms. Foreign investment was sought by both the elite and employees, who were seeking more flexible and efficient working methods. Hence, the neoliberal dynamic went further in the East than in the West.[11]

Geopolitics also played a role: Lech Walesa, the leader of the Polish trade union Solidarnosc, explained in 1991 that Western investment also served as security against Russian influence: 'We need foreign investment because it also gives us security. Having a Frenchman or an Englishman here with his factory is like having a division of troops.'[12] Even during Russia's most liberal period in the 1990s, the threat of the giant bear loomed large over Eastern Europe. In 1993, Estonia faced a Russian embargo in protest of its citizenship laws that were considered discriminatory against the ethnic Russians living there: the distribution of vouchers in connection with popular privatisations was indexed to seniority of residence, with a view to excluding Russians.

In the rest of Europe, these changes also had an impact through massive competition from low-cost countries. Destabilisation affected both the West, which faced relocations, and the East, which saw massive emigration by the young, who sometimes had to leave their children behind in the care of grandparents, giving rise to the Polish term *Eurosieroty* ('European orphans').[13] The process proved destabilising even in mighty Germany. While Bonn expected to reap a substantial benefit from the privatisation of the former GDR's companies, the introduction of Western standards, environmental ones in particular, proved so costly that many of them were liquidated. East Germans either had to go into exile in the West, or remain in a country experiencing industrial collapse and the arrival of new elites from the West. In return, West Germans accepted higher taxes to finance massive transfers to the East, as well as liberalisation of the labour market. The reunification costs contributed to the Bundesbank's high interest policy, which further depressed not only the German economy, but also Europe's entire economic outlook in the early 1990s.

Beyond Europe, neoliberalism spread as far as China, with a peculiar mix of *community* capitalism (strong industrial policy, protectionism, strict control of migration) and neoliberal features (stingy safety net, harsh working condition). *Solidarity* capitalism has certainly been present, with massive success in reducing poverty for hundreds of millions of Chinese. But the *solidarity* dimension of Chinese capitalism, and of East Asian capitalism in general, has remained limited considering their current level of development.[14] This has created a massive competitive pressure from China, which has developed the infrastructure and know-how of rich countries, all while keeping social expenditure and wages relatively low on average. Skilled workers in Shanghai have Western-style education and wages, but much higher working times (dubbed the '996' regime: working from 9:00 am to 9:00 pm six days a week), and with menial workers receiving very low pay. Besides, Chinese companies can still tap into the vast pool of cheap unskilled labour. Lastly, China possesses a vast territory blessed with multiples resources, making it less dependent on strategic imports than other East Asian countries, such as Japan or Singapore.

The global economic crisis of 2008–10 called neoliberal ideas into question. The financial crisis that sparked it grew out of an unquestioning belief in the self-regulating nature of financial markets, as well as rising global inequality since the 1980s, which fuelled excessive indebtedness among the working class (notably in the US, where subprime mortgages triggered the crisis). The crisis was resolved by massive spending from governments and central banks. Neoliberal practices nevertheless continue to dominate the agenda, combined with populism, as demonstrated by cuts to taxes as well as social and environmental protections in the US under Donald Trump (2017–21, 2025 to present), and in Brazil under Jair Bolsonaro (2019–23).

8.2 The Single Market and Its Liberal Dynamics

The Single Market is at the heart of the *liberty* dimension of European capitalism, and of European identity itself, as it is a genuinely political project. By contrast, in the US the legislative unification of the domestic market is not a political project, and the market is less economically unified than the EU's in terms of trade.[15] Local protectionist rules abound (such as favouring US products, or products from a particular US state), unlike in Europe where national preference is banned. Another large market, that of India, was also very fragmented until a recent wave of unification initiated by Prime Minister Narendra Modi, although the internal mobility of workers across Indian states remains quite low due to different rules, languages, and customs.[16]

The European Single Market is therefore quite unique, for it almost comprehensively harmonises trade rules across twenty-seven different independent countries. Driven by European institutions as well as companies and consumers seeking harmonisation, the Single Market has grown steadily, expanding to new countries (including outside the EU) and sectors. It has sometimes exhibited neoliberal features, in particular with the Bolkestein directive, certain decisions of the Court of Justice, and the drift towards legislative Darwinism.

8.2.1 The Momentum of the Single Market

The Single Market opened on 31 December 1992 with the removal of physical borders for the circulation of goods.[17] It firstly involved conventional goods, and slowly expanded to highly regulated goods (such as medicine or energy) and services, which were gradually included from the 1990s onwards. It has spread across the European continent through EU enlargement and the creation of the European Economic Area (EEA) in 1992, which encompasses Norway, Iceland, and Lichtenstein. Norway must apply all EU legislation pertaining to trade in goods in order to benefit from the Single Market, but without taking part in the decision-making process, a situation derided by the term 'fax democracy' (a democracy reduced to applying EU standards sent by fax). In exchange, Oslo retains complete freedom over fishing and hydrocarbons. Switzerland has refused the EEA, but remains bound to the EU by multiple ad hoc agreements that make it an informal member of the Single Market, even if recurrent tensions surface regarding Bern's intentions to limit the free movement of people but not of goods and services, with Brussels insisting on linking them. Only the UK has left the Single Market, but must accept most EU legislation in Northern Ireland in order to preserve free movement with the Republic of Ireland. More generally, UK producers have an interest in avoiding excessive divergence from the Union, which remains its largest market (42 per cent of UK exports in 2021).

If the Single Market was a compromise for Delors between the approaches of *liberty, solidarity*, and *community*, it subsequently took on a more neoliberal bent through the activism of certain actors at the European Commission in the 1990s and 2000s. The key player was Leon Brittan, initially as Commissioner for Competition (1989–93, see Chapter 5), and later as Commissioner for Trade (1993–99), during which time he promoted the idea of an unregulated transatlantic free trade area including all services.[18] Brittan's former colleagues include John Mogg, who led a career as a senior civil servant between London and Brussels. He became Director General of the Internal Market between 1993 and 2002, defending a minimalist approach emphasising self-regulation, and rejecting most of the binding legislation proposed to him.[19] In 1994 the Commission requested a report on simplifying legislation from a group chaired by Bernhard Molitor, known internally as 'Demolitor' for his propensity to deregulate.[20] Finally, in 1996 the Commission adopted the SLIM approach, standing for Simpler Legislation for the Internal Market. The laudable objective of reducing red tape has sometimes been interpreted as encouraging laissez-faire policies.

This neoliberal pressure to deregulate was opposed at the Commission by officials in charge of environmental, health, and labour regulation.[21] The same opposition was present at the Council. In 1999, during a debate on the internal market, the French government, which was led at the time by the socialist Lionel Jospin, issued a note stating that 'the objectives set by the Commission in this document to achieve the Single Market should take greater account of European social policy'. Conversely, the document of his British counterpart, whose Labour government was led by Tony Blair, refused to include any objectives relating to social protection.[22]

8.2.2 Football: Between Protectionism and Europe-Led Liberalisation

The liberalisation of the football market offers a striking example of the expansion of this neoliberal logic. The famous *Bosman* ruling of 1995 completely liberalised and Europeanised the market for football players, whereas regulators – chief among them the European football association UEFA – had previously imposed restrictions in order to maintain national pre-eminence in the recruitment pools for each championship, a typically protectionist approach.

The archives provide a clearer picture of the conflicting models of Europe that have presided over the liberalisation of the football market. The issue was discussed at the Commission as early as 1986. The Commissioner for Competition at the time, Peter Sutherland of Ireland, was in favour of liberalising this sector to comply with the dynamics of the Single Market, but President Delors, who was a football enthusiast, was opposed,[23] perhaps because he was drawn to the *community* component of the public policy trilogy: football clubs were often embedded in a strong local identity, for instance in mining towns with Shalke 04 in Germany, and Lens in France.

The UEFA ultimately agreed to a compromise in 1990: the 3+2 rule, which limited the number of foreign players on each first division team to three, plus two who had continuously played in the host country for five years, including three years as a junior. This compromise combined *liberty* (more foreign players) with *solidarity* (emphasis on training) and *community* (limited number of foreigners). It did not satisfy the new Commissioner for Competition Brittan, who was considering extending competition rules to the football sector.[24]

The Court of Justice annulled the 3+2 Rule in its *Bosman* ruling in 1995. Jean-Marc Bosman, an FC Liège footballer, filed a complaint against his Belgian club for preventing his transfer to French clubs in 1990.[25] In 1995, on the grounds of Article 48 of the Treaty of Rome, which provided for the free movement of workers and prohibited discriminating between nationalities among Community nationals, the Court supported Bosman and annulled the UEFA's 3+2 clause. As a result, the number of foreign players in each club increased considerably, thereby facilitating the emergence of a unified European market in this field.

Archives reveal the Commission's role in promoting an expansive interpretation of that judgment. The Commissioner for Competition, Karel Van Miert of Belgium – in association with several liberal and conservative commissioners such as Brittan, Padraig Flynn, and Marcelino Oreja – believed that the Court had not gone far enough, as it decided the case solely on the basis of the free movement of workers (Article 48 EEC), and not on competition (Article 85 EEC).[26] Van Miert pressured the UEFA by threatening to use the procedures against it. He succeeded in having the 3+2 rule lifted for all competitions (whereas the UEFA only wanted to do so for certain matches), and for non-discrimination to apply to all nationalities, not just European nationals.

This neoliberal interpretation sparked resistance. Among member states, the German government intervened in the *Bosman* ruling to emphasise that sport is not an economic activity like any other due to its similarity with culture. It also argued that the principle of subsidiarity called for respecting the freedom of organisation of sports associations.[27] When the action following the judgment was discussed at the Commission, the Commissioner Yves-Thibault de Silguy of France expressed his reluctance towards liberalising the sector.[28] In other words, a group at the Commission imposed a neoliberal interpretation of the *Bosman* ruling, even denying any notion of European identity, since no difference was made between Europeans and non-Europeans.

8.2.3 The Battle Surrounding the Bolkestein Directive

The Bolkestein directive symbolised this neoliberal approach. Fritz Bolkestein, a former executive of the major Anglo-Dutch oil company Shell, served as minister under Ruud Lubbers and later as leader of the Dutch Liberal Party. According to Neil Kinnock, he spoke 'Dickensian English' and defended an 'ideological free market orientation'.[29] The Bolkestein directive, which was adopted in 2004 and liberalised the services market without prior harmonisation, was named after him.[30] While the directive excluded certain sectors such as finance, it included others staples of the welfare state, such as health services. It stipulated that short-term services could be provided by European nationals in accordance with the regulatory conditions of their country of origin (rather than their country of destination, thereby creating a risk of social dumping). At first the neoliberal nature of the draft directive went relatively unnoticed at the Prodi Commission, which was in its last months, and focused on enlargement towards the east (in 2004 the EU's membership increased from fifteen to twenty-five countries). In contrast, the new president of the Commission, José Manuel Barroso of Portugal, made the adoption of this draft directive a priority. Opponents mobilised, and the Bolkestein directive became central to the debate on the Constitutional Treaty in France. In protest, electricians at the French public utility company EDF even cut off power to the Dutch commissioner's country house, located in northern France. The directive crystallised the spectre of the 'Polish plumber', a recurrent negative symbol in several European countries for low-cost workers threatening local jobs. Beyond this hostile reaction, there was fear of the looming threat to national welfare states; a genuine European movement emerged, with large European demonstrations in Brussels and Strasbourg in 2005.

In the end, the anti-Bolkestein movement proved somewhat effective, as the Services Liberalisation Directive adopted in December 2006 was largely amended. These protests challenged the 2004 Constitutional Treaty, whose Article I-3 included the establishment of an 'internal market where competition is free and undistorted' among the objectives of the European Union. By contrast, in the Treaty of Rome, this notion did not appear as an objective (Article 2), but instead as one of the actions needed to achieve those objectives (Article 3). After the defeat of the draft treaty in 2005, French President Nicolas Sarkozy, who came to power in 2007, succeeded in having this mention removed from the Treaty of Lisbon of 2009, although it reappeared in Protocol No. 27, an integral part of the Treaty, as pointed out in Article 36 of the TEU. Moreover, Article I-3 of the Constitutional Treaty included many other social objectives, as did Articles 2 and 3 of the Treaty of Rome. The French president's intervention is indicative of how the very definition of Europe was at stake.

8.2.4 The Court of Justice: A Neoliberal Actor?

The Court of Justice of the European Union also displayed a neoliberal orientation in some cases. The Court has always defended a proactive interpretation of European rules for both functional reasons – the efficiency of the internal market – and political reasons, namely the promotion of federal European law based on non-discrimination between Europeans.[31] Its logic has always been market-oriented, but not necessarily neoliberal. For example, in the *Keck and Mithouard* case from 1993, the Court rejected a complaint targeting a national law on resale at loss, arguing that it was not discriminatory since it applied to all actors, both national and not.[32] In 1996, the Court promoted a broad interpretation of the article on health and workplace safety in order to accept the Working Time Directive.[33]

However, between 2006 and 2008 the Court issued several rulings considered to be neoliberal. In 2006, *Cadbury Schweppes* limited national measures combatting the tax optimisation of multinationals.[34] In *Viking* (2007), the Court condemned an action by a Finnish trade union to deter the Viking Line ferry company from relocating its business by registering its boats in Estonia, with a view to hiring staff at lower cost.[35] The Court therefore gave precedence to freedom of establishment over the right to strike if it resulted in market partition. In *Laval* (2007), the Court allowed a Latvian construction company operating in Sweden not to comply with Swedish collective agreements.[36] The result was similar in the judgment issued in *Rüffert* (2008), involving the German State of Lower Saxony and a German service provider, whose contract was terminated because it worked with a Polish subcontractor suspected of not complying with the collective agreement.[37] Finally, in *Luxembourg* (2008), the Court supported the Commission, which had challenged the Luxembourg government by finding that its transposition of the Posted Workers Directive imposed too many obligations on enterprises.[38] It is nevertheless difficult to interpret the intent of the judges. On the basis of Advocate General Miguel Poiares Maduro's argument in *Viking* (which is more explicit than the final ruling), some believe he issued a balanced judgment, while others estimate that his opinion was negatively biased towards trade unions.[39]

The European Trade Union Confederation (ETUC) formally protested after the *Viking* and *Laval* judgments and called for corrective legislation, including a revision of the Posted Workers Directive of 1996, which liberalised the dispatching of foreign workers by multinationals within the Union with few social strings attached. Faced with the resulting outcry, President Barroso asked Mario Monti, the former Commissioner for the Internal Market, to draft a report, which in 2012 inspired a Commission proposal for a regulation to protect trade union prerogatives. According to its opponents, this draft regulation enshrined a restrictive view of trade union rights. Finally, following the first use of the Yellow Card procedure newly created by the Treaty of Lisbon of 2009, in which one third of Parliament can urge the Commission to withdraw a law under debate, the proposal was withdrawn even before it was discussed.[40]

However, it would be excessive to equate the Court with a neoliberal federalist body. This is demonstrated by its positive action for protection against discrimination, respect for human rights, consumer protection, and the application of social and environmental legislation.[41] The Court seems to recognise that the European Union is a social market economy with economic as well as social aims, even if it tends to give precedence to the logic of market integration (in particular through the freedom of establishment and the freedom to conduct a business).

8.2.5 The Slope of Legislative Darwinism

Legislative Darwinism denotes the tendency to adopt neoliberal legislation in the face of growing international competition. It was inspired by Friedrich Hayek's application of Social Darwinism to institutions.[42] This is particularly true in tax matters, where unanimity among all states is necessary at the Council. Some European countries have adopted provisions so favourable to the wealthy and businesses that they can be considered tax havens. In 2017, the European Parliament's PANA (Panama Papers) Committee requested that four EU countries – Ireland, Luxembourg, Malta, and the Netherlands – be added to the list of tax havens, albeit in vain.[43]

While the Commission may seem all-powerful, it is actually a small administrative body, and must therefore rely on national administrations and sometimes even private bodies financed by industrialists themselves in order to ensure compliance with its own standards. This entails a risk of 'regulatory capture', through which companies ensure lenient implementation of the rules.[44] In an extreme case it could lead to massive fraud, epitomised by the Dieselgate scandal in 2015. The US Environmental Protection Agency (EPA) revealed widespread fraud by the German carmaker Volkswagen with respect to NOx emissions controls (there are different emissions limits on both sides of the Atlantic). In both Europe and the US, standards are overseen by manufacturer-funded organisations; however, in the US the public body EPA purchases vehicles at random to carry out additional checks.[45] It was ultimately revealed that Volkswagen also committed fraud in Europe, but the Union was too weak or naive to detect it. Standard controls were tightened as a result.

More generally, many national administrations are suspected of being lax in verifying the application of European standards among their domestic producers. The example of the mad cow crisis of 1996 bears witness to this.[46] The British government originally denied there was any risk of bovine spongiform encephalopathy (BSE) being transmitted to humans, despite the Commission's initial suspicions. London eventually had no choice but to declare a health crisis in the face of rising deaths. Agriculture Commissioner Franz Fischler of Austria (an agriculture specialist) quickly adopted a series of emergency measures, including a ban on exporting all bovine products from the UK, with compensation measures for affected farmers. Shortly thereafter, a report accused the British government and the Commission of underestimating the risks, and a number of other governments of not complying with all of the embargo's clauses. In the end, it was not until a second mad cow crisis erupted that the Prodi Commission created a European Food Safety Authority in 2002. Other instances of national mismanagement include the Greek government's statistical fraud, which was recognised in 2009, and the many instances of fraud relating to the Posted Worker Directive of 1996, which led to the creation of a European Labour Authority, but only in 2019.

To sum up, the Single Market has been a resounding success from a pro-market perspective: growth has been promoted through the removal of borders, and barriers to trade have largely disappeared for goods.[47] Economic studies show that the Single Market has been more effective than a free trade area – or the maintenance of national trade policies – in terms of boosting trade and productivity, and thereby growth. However, integration remains limited for services, particularly in banking and regulated professions, as well as in certain sectors, such as energy or rail transport. The Single Market is still contested, as part of its implementation has drifted towards a neoliberal crusade threatening major components of the welfare state, such as national labour law or trade unions. The same dynamic applies to competition policy.

8.3 Competition Policy: Between Neoliberalism and Multinational Control

Since the 1990s, European competition policy has reigned triumphant. Because competition policy is probably the most centralised of all European policies, with member states and the European Parliament playing only a minor role in its implementation, the character of the various commissioners has proven decisive. There are substantial differences between the messianic neoliberal Leon Brittan (1989–93) and his more moderate successor, the Belgian Social Democrat Karel Van Miert (1993–99). The Italian economist Mario Monti succeeded him (1999–2004) and completed the 'modernisation' of procedures and economic thinking. His two successors, Neelie Kroes (2004–10) of the Netherlands and Joaqim Almunia of Spain, had a slightly more modest record, while the liberal Margrethe Vestager of Denmark has been more offensive and innovative (2014–24).

Four main developments should be underscored: first, the neoliberal offensive has primarily targeted national protectionism in terms of mergers and state aid; second, this offensive has also proceeded via the liberalisation of new sectors; third, the free marketeers were divided between ordoliberals and 'modernisers' partially inspired by US neoliberalism; and fourth, the recent Vestager offensive (since 2014) has been rather original, for it has included a (modest) social dimension.[48]

8.3.1 Controlling Mergers and State Aid against National and European Champions

The Commission's action to control mergers and state aid directly targeted the policy of establishing national champions. After Delors left the Commission in 1995, the doctrine evolved towards explicit condemnation of promoting European champions, a policy that Delors had previously encouraged.[49] In the field of aluminium, the Commission blocked the proposed three-way merger between the French national champion Péchiney, the Canadian Alcan, and the Swiss Algroup in 2000, but it accepted Alcan's acquisition of Alussuisse that same year, and Alcan's acquisition of Péchiney in 2003.[50] Péchiney, the French 'national champion' in aluminium, thus came under a foreign flag. In 2001, the Commission prohibited a merger between two French electrical equipment manufacturers, Schneider Electric and Legrand. The decision was later reversed by the Court of First Instance due to economics errors and breach of the defence's rights.[51] In 2019 the ban on the merger between two railway giants, Alstom of France and Siemens of Germany, seemed more logical, as the dominance of the two firms in the European market was clear, and foreign competition was weak in the short term, unlike with ATR/De Havilland. However, the rejection of the merger neglected Chinese competition over the long term, and was therefore strongly opposed by the French and German governments. More generally, beyond these various examples, the Commission has accepted most mergers. A longitudinal survey of all decisions made by the Commission shows a clear negative bias towards mergers between two companies in the same country (as opposed to European mergers), especially in sectors with a strong tradition of state intervention, such as telecommunications and air transport.[52] The Commission has therefore prioritised the fight against national neomercantilism, especially in its own backyard.

The same approach has prevailed in state aid. Commissioner Neelie Kroes explicitly stated in her 2005 action plan that the objective was to reduce state aid, whereas the Treaty only provided for banning those subsidies that are incompatible with European rules, not reducing them in absolute terms.[53] The French and Italian 'usual suspects' were particularly targeted. In 1993, the Italian government had to pour state aid into its hugely indebted state holding IRI, but the Commission intervened to limit the amount. Negotiations were conducted between Commissioner Karel Van Miert and Italian Foreign Minister Beniamino Andreatta, and between the Director General of Competition, Claus-Dieter Ehlermann, and the Director General of the Italian Treasury, Mario Draghi (the future governor of the ECB).[54] The Commission imposed conditions such as massive deleveraging, with Rome accepting and privatising in order to finance this deleveraging. Consequently, even if European law cannot impose privatisation (according to Article 222 of the Treaty of Rome), the constraints imposed by competition policy can encourage such a solution. In France, recurrent conflict between Paris and Brussels continued in the early 1990s, notably in connection with state aid to Renault and Air France. The French government gradually learned how to contend with competition zealots. In 2004, when it purchased a stake in the capital of the electric equipment manufacturer Alstom, which was facing bankruptcy, Nicolas Sarkozy, the French Minister of the Economy at the time, negotiated a compromise directly with Commissioner Neelie Kroes, thereby avoiding conflict.

Even Germany was targeted by the Commission because of the massive aid granted to the former East Germany. For example, in 1996 the Commission prohibited aid from the State of Saxony (located in the east) to establish a Volkswagen plant, prompting the company's CEO to threaten moving its investments further east, outside Germany. The Commission ultimately agreed to a compromise.[55] The French government, among others, had urged the Commission not to exempt the new German States in the east from state aid discipline. In 1995, Brussels initiated thirty-seven aid examination procedures in Germany, compared with four in France, and none in the UK. Similarly, Bonn was the only country that opposed the Commission's plans for regional aid. Ten years later, the Commission annulled the 1960 Volkswagen Act, which gave the German government and the State of Lower Saxony a privileged role in the ownership of Volkswagen.[56]

At the same time, Brussels was accused by the US of protectionism when it banned the merger between the two US aircraft giants Boeing and McDonnell Douglas in 1997. It was only authorised after obtaining concessions from the two firms, particularly to avoid exclusive supply agreements that would have significantly limited the penetration of Airbus in the North American market. Commissioner Van Miert complained about the intense lobbying of powerful US companies, while the only European company to write to the Commission to defend the merger was the Scandinavian SAS.[57] Similarly in 2001, when US antitrust authorities approved the merger between the giant General Electric and Honeywell, an aeronautical component supplier, Commissioner Monti banned the merger despite pressure from the highest levels in Washington, including US President George W. Bush, Jr. In 2004, the same Monti condemned Microsoft for abuse of dominant position, because it linked the sale of its Windows operating system with other software, including the Internet Explorer browser. The fine totalled almost $500 million, and was even increased as a result of the company's failure to comply with the measures. The decision had an impact, as the Firefox browser dethroned Internet Explorer shortly thereafter, probably in part because of Community action. Commissioner Kroes then targeted Intel with a $1 billion fine in 2009. The offensive resumed under Vestager against the new generation of US giants: Apple, Google, and Amazon (see below). However, these decisions cannot be labelled as protectionist, because the fines were tiny compared to the size of the companies, and because there are few European competitors to those US giants. Moreover, studies carried out on all merger cases handled by the Commission do not reveal any anti-American bias.[58] State aid rebounded after 2008 because of the economic crisis, the Covid-19 crisis (2020–21), and the Russo-Ukrainian War (2022–present) (see Chapter 10).

In short, European control over state aid, mergers, and abuse of dominant position helped create a level playing field within the Single Market, sometimes at the cost of reinforcing certain European companies. It especially targeted France and Italy, but free market bastions such as Germany and the US were not spared. In other words, European competition policy supported *liberty* capitalism but not *community* capitalism. It also, to some extent, included a *solidarity* dimension, as it targeted 'corporate welfare' by reducing state aid to companies, thereby avoiding a costly subsidy race (since state aid represents a transfer of funds from taxpayers to companies).

8.3.2 Liberalisation of New Sectors: A Contested Process

The liberalisation of new sectors that began in the late 1980s accelerated, further increasing the neoliberal dynamic at the expense of other approaches. Proponents of *solidarity* insist that some sectors must be tightly regulated to ensure access to basic services at a low cost for the entire population (including in the most remote areas). Supporters of *community* aim to preserve national (or European) industrial potential in the face of foreign competition through discriminatory measures. The conflict between these approaches is particularly evident in three areas: telecommunications, energy, and the debate surrounding 'service of general economic interest' (SGEI).

In telecommunications, a sector marked by technological innovation (the rise of mobile telephony, international communication, and the World Wide Web), the Commission initiated four changes from 1987 onwards: liberalisation via the phasing out of old monopolies; opening up networks to competition; applying competition policy to these areas; and regulating them through the establishment of independent national regulators.[59] After a first set of directives in 1990, the Telecom package of 1996–98 completely opened up the former national monopolies for telephony services, and restricted state aid to a limited number of social obligations. As a result, universal service – a public service operator's obligation to provide minimum telephone service at a basic cost irrespective of the consumer's geographical distance – has been maintained. At the same time, to ensure that these directives are transposed into national law, the Commission used competition law via the control of state aid and mergers. In 1996 the Commission authorised the creation of Atlas, a joint venture between the French and German national giants France Telecom and Deutsche Telecom, provided that national networks were quickly liberalised.[60]

Both France and Germany were divided over the liberalisation, with some lamenting the decline in terms of social and industrial policy. However, in many cases privatisation was supported by consumers, company management, and most political elites, as it brought several advantages: an influx of revenue for the government, the ability to form international alliances more easily, the prospect of increasing productivity, and lower prices. Taking the helm of France Telecom in 2002 in a difficult context, Thierry Breton (the future European Commissioner) argued that the company's excessive indebtedness was due to the absence of privatisation, because the company had to make international acquisitions through debt rather than an exchange of shares, which would have been less expensive.[61]

In energy, the liberalisation of the electricity market proved more difficult, since the national energy mix is different from one country to another, and because it is a strategic sector. The process was initiated by Nicolas Mosar of Luxembourg, the Energy Commissioner from 1985 to 1989. In 1971, Mosar had previously served as the complainant's lawyer in one of the first cases involving the electricity sector adjudicated by the Court of Justice.[62] He estimated the 'cost of non-Europe' (see Chapter 3) in this sector to be 0.5 per cent of GDP in 1987. The torch of liberalisation was later taken up by Commissioner Antonio Cardoso of Portugal, with laws enacted in 1990 on the transparency of prices for industrial consumers, and on the transit of electricity in high voltage grids. Member states prevented this effort from proceeding further until 1996, when the governments of France and Germany accepted a gradual liberalisation directive under pressure of direct action by the Commission against their national monopolies under competition law. In 2005, the Commission launched investigations into the infringement of competition rules by energy giants, including 'dawn raids', surprise early-morning inspections to seize documents. This ratcheting up of pressure facilitated the adoption of a new liberalisation package in 2009.[63]

Many national champions were largely preserved. As early as 1991, Jean Bergougnoux, the CEO of the French giant EDF, asked for more freedom over prices in the name of European competition, as it could lead to higher prices in France.[64] Similarly, the 1996 directive was implemented in restricted fashion in France, with a very gradual liberalisation process (involving a small number of eligible customers), and recognition of social obligations. According to the press agency Europe, Commissioners Monti, Brittan, and Van Miert wanted to proceed further with liberalisation. French neomercantilist interests were partly preserved, with the national champion EDF initially facing little competition at home, and taking advantage of the opportunity to expand towards France's more open neighbours.

Other sectors either followed the steady pace of liberalisation in telecommunications, where innovation created a supply shock (such as postal services), or that of energy, where structural constraints are strong, with a single costly network (such as railways). In railways, liberalisation was encouraged by the British, leading to four 'rail packages' adopted between 2001 and 2016, but the position of the former national monopolies has remained predominant.

The liberalisation dynamic met with a counter-offensive from supporters of *solidarity*, who defended the notion of 'services of general economic interest' (SGEI).[65] This concept did not originally exist in the Treaties of the European Union. It emerged from the mobilisation of various actors, including the French who were eager to defend the notion of 'public service', and the Germans seeking to preserve subsidiarity, as many local actors are entrusted with social missions. The notion of 'service of general interest' refers both to sectors where non-market logic is predominant (such as health, poverty reduction, and education), as well as those dominated by free market logic, but where social obligations exist, for instance serving the most remote populations at a reasonable cost, and providing reduced rates for the poor. A coalition of actors thus emerged, bringing together the ETUC, the employers' union of public employers (Centre Européen des Entreprises Publiques, CEEP), MEPs from various countries, and some governments, especially but not exclusively the French one. The debate emerged in 1995–96 during the negotiations surrounding the Treaty of Amsterdam. In 1995, the Director General for Competition, Claus-Dieter Ehlermann, feared that the Intergovernmental Conference would lead to the creation of sectoral agencies, thereby depriving the Commission of some of its prerogatives.[66] In Berlin, Kohl requested that protections for the German system of guarantees in the Landesbanken be included in the future Treaty.[67] In Paris, the government supported the adoption of a law recognising the role of public services.[68] In the end, a compromise was reached in the form of Article 7D of the Treaty of Amsterdam, which recognised the existence of these 'services of general economic interest'.

The European Parliament and the ETUC called for a European Charter of Services of General Interest, in addition to their inclusion in binding legislation to protect them from the zeal of the Commission's DG Competition. However, it was not included in the Treaty of Amsterdam, much to the satisfaction of DG Competition.[69] In the absence of a clear political settlement, it was the Court of Justice that clarified the relationship between competition and public service in the *Altmark* ruling in 2003, which defined the four eligibility criteria for state aid allowed in compensation for a public service: the public service obligations must be clearly defined; the financial compensation must be transparent; the latter must not exceed the cost (including a 'reasonable profit'); and if there has been no public procurement, it is necessary to determine the costs incurred by a private undertaking.[70]

The point of reference remained private companies. The setbacks experienced by some privatised companies have largely been ignored. The best example is British Railways, which was privatised in 1993, and has been plagued by recurring losses ever since. For example, the East Coast Main Line (the main line between London and Edinburgh) was operated by the government between 2009 and 2015, and also from 2018 to the present, with the government taking over from private companies when they failed. From an economic point of view, liberalisation has sometimes led to uncompetitive oligopolies. In other words, private neomercantilism has replaced public neomercantilism. Even in sectors where liberalisation was successful, such as air transport, the new operators sometimes benefited from state aid, such as low-cost carriers taking advantage of massively subsidised local airfields.

In conclusion, the Commission, in alliance with several member states, has encouraged a process of liberalisation in areas previously sheltered from competition. It has been the least effective in sectors organised around a costly physical network, such as energy and railways, in contrast to those where innovation created a supply-side shock, such as telecommunications, postal services, and air transport. This liberalisation has sometimes taken a neoliberal bent when threatening social protection, leading to a counter-offensive from a *solidarity*-driven coalition, and a difficult battle to gain recognition for 'services of general interest'.

8.3.3 The 'Modernisation' of Competition Policy as a Struggle between Ordoliberailsm and Chicago

The continent's competition policies were profoundly shaken up by the so-called 'modernisation' process carried out by the European Union in the 2000s.[71] This phenomenon originated firstly in an intellectual struggle between the second Chicago school and ordoliberals. The former criticised the latter for the ineffectiveness of their legal formalism and flaws in their economic analysis, which tended to protect a legalistic approach to competition rather that what really counts, 'consumer welfare'. This struggle among free marketeers began in the 1980s,[72] when European judges from the ECJ who studied in the US, such as René Joliet of Belgium, tried to promote this approach in Europe, in connection with the British academic Valentine Korah. The movement gained traction in the late 1980s, when American lawyers such as Barry Hawk also called for more economic expertise through academic articles, as well as the organisation of the transatlantic Fordham conferences bringing together competition policy experts from the Atlantic world, hosted at Fordham University in New York City.[73]

The other incentive to reform competition policy came from within institutions. In the 1990s and 2000s, the Court of Justice criticised the limited economic justification behind certain Commission decisions. For example, in 2002, the Court overturned two decisions prohibiting mergers.[74] Another argument for reform was the prospect of enlargement towards the east, which gave the Commission an incentive to streamline its decision-making process, and to focus on the most economically relevant cases. Transatlantic conflicts over the interpretation of competition rules increased, which heightened the need to find common assessment methods. The development of industrial economics provided a common toolbox, one that was adopted by the community of economists, and represented a step forward in the quest to objectify the harm caused to competition.[75]

In 1995, the top official in charge of competition at the Commission, Director General Claus-Dieter Ehlermann, pointed out that 'DG IV needs to focus on the essentials, what needs to be done at EU level. Everything else must be left to the member states or simply ignored.'[76] The cartel notification system overwhelmed the Commission with a huge number of cases, most of which were harmless. This prompted reflections on devolving powers to national authorities, with the Commission retaining intellectual leadership to ensure overall coherence in competition policy. In response to Ehlermann's note, his subordinate, Philip Lowe of the UK, who was the Director of the Merger Task Force, emphasised bolstering economic analysis in order to focus exclusively on the most problematic cases.[77] A debate arose regarding the establishment of an antitrust agency independent of the Commission in order to make the decision less politicised, which was inevitable when the discussion reached the stage of the College of Commissioners.[78]

The first major reform was the adoption of the 'leniency' procedure in 1996, following the example of the US (with a first US law in 1978, reformed in 1993). It granted an enterprise denouncing an illegal cartel (the most harmful cartels are usually secret) with reduced penalties and even complete immunity. Longitudinal studies of a large number of decisions tend to show increasing effectiveness on the part of competition authorities after adoption of the leniency procedure.[79] Due to its impact, this procedure was subsequently used by many European countries, such as France in 2001.

'Modernisation' was then implemented in earnest by Commissioner Mario Monti, the first trained economist to hold this post, with the help of Philip Lowe, who became Director General for Competition in 2002. Modernisation was both procedural (through partial decentralisation to national authorities) and substantive (through the adoption of a more economic approach).[80] It was first passed through a new cartel regulation adopted in 2003. It abolished the notification procedure and replaced it with an ex post control carried out by national authorities. The latter were brought together within a European Competition Network established under the Commission's supervision. The Commission deals with the most important cases, and ensures the harmonisation of case law. This regulation extends the Europeanisation of national competition policies. In 2004, a new regulation strengthened economic analysis in merger cases. Modernisation also led to the recruitment of a chief economist within the Directorate-General for Competition. This position is so important that when a US national was considered for the job in July 2023, official protests erupted among the French government and several commissioners (notably Thierry Breton of France), prompting the prospective candidate, Fiona Scott Morton, to withdraw.

Paradoxically, the 2003 regulation on cartels returned to the original interpretation of the Treaty of Rome defended by the French government in 1960, which is to say a system of ex ante control, whereas the German government had imposed its vision of ex post control in 1962. Many German actors, such as Commissioner Martin Bangemann and the lawyer Ernst-Joachim Mestmäcker, were critical, because the new procedure provided less legal certainty for businesses.[81] The more economic approach also led to adopting criteria similar to those applied in the US, although the Union preserved some distinctive features, such as the overarching goal of market integration.[82] This debate demonstrates the flexibility of the Treaty of Rome, which can be applied in different ways providing its overarching principles are respected (in this case establishing an efficient competition policy to ensure market integration).

8.3.4 Vestager: Towards a More Social Orientation (2014–24)?

Margrethe Vestager is the highest-profile commissioner in Danish history, and even inspired a character in the Danish television series *Borgen*. Her reputation is built on very strong activism, which can be measured through concrete aspects such as record fines for cartels, and sustained action against the digital multinationals (or GAFAM: Google, Apple, Facebook, Amazon, Microsoft). She was less aggressive towards national neomercantilism, except for the prohibition of the Alstom–Siemens merger in 2019. Like her predecessors, Vestager used abuse of dominant position provisions to target multinationals, but the fines she imposed have been unprecedented in size.[83] Between 2017 and 2019, she fined Google three times for a total of more than €8 billion. The Internet giant was accused of abuse of dominant position in connection with its Google search engine and Android operating software for smartphones, with a view to favouring its other products. In a more innovative approach, Vestager sued Apple for unfair tax aid. While the Commission has only very limited powers over taxation (this area is subject to unanimous decision-making at the Council), it can target discriminatory measures that would favour one actor at the expense of others. Under this rule, the Danish commissioner penalised a number of multinationals that benefited from preferential fiscal treatment in Luxembourg, the Netherlands, and Ireland. After Fiat and Starbucks in 2015 came Apple in 2016, and Amazon in 2017. The reimbursement of the aid from Apple amounts to €13 billion, the largest amount ever requested. A creative legal approach was also adopted in 2021 when the Commission condemned a cartel of three German car manufacturers seeking to delay the diffusion of automotive emission reduction technologies. Reference to the 2019 Green Deal was explicit in Vestager's statement accompanying that decision, whereas environmental factors did not play such a role previously.[84] The severity of Vestager's approach compared to that of her predecessors is visible in other respects as well. Joaquin Almunia wanted to conclude the Google case with an amicable compromise, prompting criticism from his colleagues.[85] Neelie Kroes, who now sits on the board of two overseas digital multinationals, Uber and Salesforce, has strongly criticised the Apple decision.[86]

Lastly, in 2022 Vestager obtained from the Council and Parliament the adoption of two new European regulations increasing the Commission's prerogatives: the Digital Market Act, which imposes specific competition obligations on dominant players in the sector, and the Digital Services Act, which regulates online content.[87] While the second law does not address competition policy in the strict sense, it is part of the same attempt to regulate a sector largely deregulated since its creation. Both pieces of legislation stemmed from the Commission's experience in its difficult proceedings against GAFAM, with the conviction that anti-competitive behaviour should now be prevented rather than corrected, hence a move from an ex post approach to an ex ante one. Legal uncertainty has been an additional argument for a strengthened legal framework, as European judges have at times overturned a few of the Commission's most spectacular decisions on appeal.

The importance of the Digital Market Act of 2022 is reflected by the outcry it generated among lawyers and economists specialising in competition policy.[88] Several of them voiced the fear of an 'antitrust hipster'; that is, an approach referring to criteria outside a strictly competition-based framework, such as notions of fairness, pluralism, and respect for environmental norms.[89] However, from a historical point of view, this new paradigm can be interpreted as a return to a mixed approach, which had already been applied before the ordoliberal shift under the name of 'public interest' (Chapter 3). In those days, the criterion of free competition was combined with social and industrial concerns. Some experts have also complained about the ex ante character of the legislation, which is more prescriptive for companies than an ex post approach. Here once again, historical records show that this solution has been applied before: when the Commission liberalised markets dominated by monopolies and oligopolies in the 1980s and 1990s, it largely shaped ex nihilo markets by favouring certain players (new entrants), and by putting others at a disadvantage (incumbents). Similarly, the first prescriptive competition legislation dates back to the mid-1960s, when the Commission promoted block exemptions to its cartel regulation.

This new policy borrows (on a limited scale) from the *solidarity* approach, as it includes environmental and redistributive elements (even if they are not central), and results in the transfer of large sums from multinationals to public coffers, whether they be those of the Union or national governments.

This practice echoes American debates of the late nineteenth century, when antitrust policy was erected against 'robber barons'. Today, competition policy is helpful as information technology has led to the rise of gargantuan actors benefiting from the winner-takes-all dynamic of the 'network effect'. For some US economists, this situation is a source of low productivity, regulatory capture, and inequality.[90] The economist Luigi Zingales of the US fears the emergence of a 'Medici vicious circle', in which private actors take control of the political structure, as in Florence in the time of the Medici.[91] A new Neo-Brandeisian approach has emerged, in reference to Supreme Court Justice Louis Brandeis (1919–39), who in 1914 denounced the 'curse of bigness', and defended more active antitrust policy against large companies.[92] Discussions have emerged among scholars over the need to strengthen an antitrust policy deemed too flexible under the Bush and Obama administrations, notably due to the permission granted to Facebook to acquire its competitors Instagram and WhatsApp in 2012–14. This approach has had influence in Washington under the Biden administration (2021–25).[93] Vestager's policy has contributed to this agenda by adding specific European concerns, such as defence of the Single Market, in addition to European values such as privacy, pluralism, and environmentalism.

Vestager's approach is not protectionist, because she targeted companies that do not have European competitors (the German software publisher SAP is one of the exceptions). Besides, both pieces of legislation sparked opposition within the Commission between Vestager and Thierry Breton of France, the Commissioner for the Internal Market. Breton defended a more vigorous DMA, with an ex ante approach and harsh sanctions, and reached a compromise with Vestager.[94] Vestager preferred to use the rhetoric of 'fair' competition.

To conclude, although competition policy has been guided by the approach of *liberty*, it has undergone four profound changes since its creation (see Table 8.1).[95] National competition policies largely pursued the multi-faceted objective of the public interest until the 1970s, except in Federal Germany, where ordoliberal influence was strong from 1957 onwards. This latter approach was largely but not exclusively (see Chapter 3) imposed in Brussels in 1962, before gradually giving way to the vision of the second Chicago School based on the absolute primacy of the consumer in the 1990s and 2000s. This movement also corresponds to the most intense phase of the fight against state aid and the liberalisation of new sectors, although close examination shows that accommodation with national neomercantilism was sometimes possible. Since the 2008 crisis in state aid, and the appointment of Vestager in 2014, a new approach has emerged in other sectors of competition

Table 8.1 The four dominant paradigms of European competition policy

Paradigm name	Public Interest	Ordoliberal (from 1962 onwards at the EEC level)	Second Chicago school (consumer welfare) (1990s)	Excess of market power (since 2014)
Market, solidarity or community	Blend of the three	Market	Market	Market and a bit of Solidarity
Criteria	Balance between competition and non-competition criteria	Protection of competitors	Protection of competition (consumer welfare)	Control of excess of market power, especially in the digital economy
Approach	Political balance	Legal formalism	More economic approach	Creativity in legal and economic reasoning
Non-competition criterion	Industrial, social, and regional policies		None	Protection of privacy, media pluralism, environmental protection

policy. It aims to curb an excess of market power on the part of multinationals, which stems from neoliberal globalisation and the winner-takes-all reality of the IT sector. To some extent, this approach is a return to an old 'public interest' approach.

8.4 The Euro: From Miracle to Greek Tragedy

While the birth of the euro was seen as miraculous, the eurozone crisis of 2010–15 culminated in a genuine Greek tragedy that threatened to undermine the very foundations of the Union before the implementation of major structural reforms.

8.4.1 The Miracle

The birth of the euro was miraculous for three reasons. First, its implementation followed the chronology laid out in the 1992 Maastricht Treaty: in 1999, the euro was born as a currency with the irrevocable fixing of parities, before becoming a fiat currency, with coins and notes, in 2002. In the meantime, the name 'euro' was adopted in 1995 at the request of the Germans, for whom 'Ecu' sounded like '*Die Kuh*' ('the cow') in German. Secondly, the eurozone immediately extended to Southern and Eastern Europe, consisting of eleven states when it was established in 1999, including Italy, Spain, and Portugal. It expanded to Greece in 2001 and the former communist country of Slovenia in 2007, before reaching twenty members in 2023. On the contrary, Northern European countries, whose economic performance would have enabled them to join the eurozone, refused to participate for political reasons (the UK from the very beginning, Sweden after its 2003 referendum, and Denmark). Third, the eurozone initially resulted in lower interest rates for weak-currency countries, as projected.

Such a rapid emergence of the euro was not anticipated by many observers.[96] Many North American economists had actually predicted its failure. In the early 1990s, Western Europe was experiencing a deep crisis, with low growth and high unemployment. The 1992 monetary crisis led to a sharp increase in fluctuation margins within the European Monetary System (from approximately 2.25 per cent to approximately 15 per cent), calling into question the idea of convergence towards monetary stability. At the same time, Delors had considered suspending the free movement of capital.[97] In 1996, only three countries, Denmark, Ireland, and Luxembourg, met the criteria set out in the Maastricht Treaty.

At the core of the euro lies the compromise between France and Germany, and more generally between countries emphasising solidarity, and those emphasising stability.[98] In 1995, the German Minister of Finance Theo Waigel called for a Stability Pact, namely stricter rules than those in the

Maastricht Treaty – with a 'medium-term objective' of a government deficit of 1 per cent instead of 3 per cent – in addition to stricter sanctions. Berlin wanted to ensure that common discipline was established after the creation of the euro. On the contrary, Paris proposed strengthening the 'economic government' of the future eurozone in order to counterbalance the European Central Bank, and insisted on including the concept of 'growth' alongside that of stability. Finally, the 1997 compromise took the form of the Stability and Growth Pact, which laid down criteria and sanction procedures, as well as the creation of the Eurogroup, a periodic meeting of finance ministers from the eurozone (rather than the entire Union). However, in 2003 both France and Germany violated the Stability and Growth Pact; the Commission initiated a sanctions procedure, but the Council cancelled it on 25 November 2003. Meanwhile, the president of the Commission himself, Romano Prodi of Italy, considered the Stability Pact to be 'silly' due to its rigidity.[99]

When the 2007 financial crisis erupted in the US, countries in the eurozone were affected by the recession, but the eurozone nevertheless appeared stable. Financial difficulties mainly affected several Central and Eastern European countries outside the eurozone, which were deprived of access to capital because of their weak currencies. This prompted Poland to consider joining the eurozone in 2009 in order to gain access to a stronger currency, and thereby to easier financing.[100] In the meantime, Hungary proposed, in alliance with Austria, creating a European support fund that would provide European solidarity in the event of a financial crisis, but the Union refused. Poland and Hungary were led at the time by pro-European governments, which were then replaced by much more Eurosceptic governments (Hungary in 2010, Poland in 2015), partly because of the lack of solidarity shown by the Union at that time. One-off financial aid was granted to Hungary, Lithuania, and Romania in exchange for austerity. The Union's participation was often secondary, with most of the funds being provided by the IMF, which is accustomed to managing financial crises.

8.4.2 *The Original Sin at the Outbreak of the Eurozone Crisis (2009–10)*

On 5 November 2009, the Greek Prime Minister Giorgos Papandreou, who had recently been elected, revealed that Greek deficit figures were twice as high as expected as the previous Greek government had manipulated its statistics. This type of fraud is rare, and dangerous between states sharing the same currency. This original sin prompted reservations among many Europeans towards massive solidarity measures towards Greece, and towards debtor countries in general. On the contrary, if the Greek crisis had been delayed by a few months, the eurozone crisis might have erupted in Ireland, a Northern European country considered virtuous (with a low budget deficit). If the crisis had originated in Ireland and not Greece, it may have been easier to express *solidarity*, because there would have been no 'original sin'.[101] Indeed, Ireland and Spain needed financial assistance during the eurozone crisis not because of excessive public spending before the crisis, but because of state expenditure to support ailing private banks. On 30 September 2008, the Irish government guaranteed €440 billion in potential losses from its banks, a sum greater than its national wealth, casting serious doubt on the state's fiscal credibility. Greece, Spain, Ireland, and Portugal were facing tremendous difficulty in the mid-2010s, and inherited the disgraceful nickname of PIGS, standing for 'Portugal, Ireland, Greece, Spain'.

This dual reality is at the origin of two complementary explanations for the eurozone crisis. In the first one, the financial difficulties stemmed from the competitiveness deficits of the southern countries (Greece, later Spain and Portugal), which engaged in excessive borrowing (public borrowing for Greece and private for Spain) thanks to the artificially low interest rates provided by the euro.[102] Under regular conditions, a lack of competitiveness can be compensated for by devaluating the currency, but this is impossible in a currency union. In the eurozone most of the adjustment took place with the migration of skilled workers from Southern Europe (notably Greece and Italy), and by internal devaluation (since the currency could not be devalued, then it was wages, pensions, and public spending that were curtailed).

The second explanation for the crisis is a neoliberal overconfidence in a self-regulating market.[103] It was private debt (notably of banks) that caused the crisis, not public debt, except for the original sin of Greek Government lie regarding its deficit. The financial crisis of 2007 was linked to underestimations of the risks of the US subprime market, as well as mismanaged regulation of the Irish and Spanish banking sectors. It was only massive government support for banks – and later for the whole economy as it plunged into recession – that created problematic holes in public spending (except, once again, in the Greek case).

Beyond those two interpretations, both of which are valid, the eurozone crisis shone a light on the loopholes in the 1992 Maastricht Treaty, which were incidentally mentioned in the 1989 Delors report: the absence of joint supervision of banks, of a large common budget, and a mechanism for crisis resolution. The Europeans strove to address these shortcomings.

8.4.3 *Between Solidarity and Ordoliberalism: A Crisis Painfully Resolved (2010–15)*

On 9 May 2010, on the sixtieth anniversary of the Schuman Declaration, the Union decided to help Greece – and any country facing financial difficulties in the future – in exchange for the implementation of austerity measures. The states established the European Financial Stability Facility (EFSF), an intergovernmental body to assist countries in crisis. At the same time, the ECB agreed to repurchase debt from countries experiencing difficulty on the secondary market. Governor Jean-Claude Trichet thus engaged in a creative interpretation of the Maastricht Treaty, which prohibits the purchase of debt on the primary market (directly from the states), but not when debt securities are sold on the secondary market. Furthermore, Article 122(2) of the Lisbon Treaty authorised financial assistance to a state in exceptional circumstances. After the aid package for Greece granted in May 2010, there quickly followed those for Ireland (2010), Portugal (2011), and Cyprus (2013), with Spanish banks also receiving aid (2012). These packages were accompanied by recommendations of austerity, which were monitored by the so-called Troika, an unprecedented coupling of the Commission, the ECB, and the IMF.

Moreover, after great hesitation, the Greek debt was reduced by 50 per cent in October 2011. In November 2011, the new ECB Governor, Mario Draghi, opened wide the gates of monetary creation, first for private banks in early December 2011, and then for states through a secondary market debt buyback programme in September 2012. These decisions were preceded by a famous speech delivered on 26 July 2012, in which the Italian central banker promised to do 'whatever it takes' to save the euro. This expression proved pivotal, because it restored market confidence in the sustainability of the euro. Like the US and Britain, the European Central Bank embarked on the unprecedented path of 'unconventional monetary policy', but did so somewhat later.[104]

Draghi acted because states agreed, at the same time, to strengthen mutual monitoring of their budgets via the Treaty on Stability, Coordination and Governance (TSCG),[105] as well as the ironically named Sixpack legislation, adopted in 2011. These decisions imposed strict austerity requirements, such as the inclusion in the constitution of the 'mandatory balanced budget rule', as well as rules strengthening sanctions ('strengthening of the excessive deficit procedure'), under which a member state may avoid a penalty only if it meets a qualified majority against it. The solidarity aspect of the deal was embodied by the creation of the ESM in 2012, which unlike the EFSF is permanent. In June 2012, member states also agreed to create a genuine 'banking union', which is to say unification of banking regulations at EU level, because the Maastricht Treaty did not provide for anything in this area. The aim of the banking union was to avoid the famous 'doom loop' (or vicious cycle), in which a banking crisis leads to massive public aid plans. A banking union was ultimately established, but remains incomplete: the ECB secured the power to supervise banks, and rules were established in the event of a banking crisis, but states have not agreed on European deposit insurance.[106]

After the turbulent period of 2010–13, the situation gradually normalised, except in Greece. In 2015, Greece's exit from the euro was envisaged, especially after a referendum held there on 5 July 2015 rejecting the European plan. However, Greek Prime Minister Alexis Tsipras negotiated a new plan, and, with the support of French President François Hollande, avoided Grexit, the country's exit from the eurozone (and even from the Union), a prospect explicitly mentioned in a Eurogroup document, and later defended by German finance minister, Wolfgang Schaüble.[107] The Greek tragedy unfolded, with massive wage and pension cuts coupled with a deterioration in the population's health indicators, as well as a political crisis.[108] In this cradle of democracy, the government disregarded the result of a referendum it had organised in 2015, since this was the only way to remain in the eurozone. Athens rejected the risk of Grexit, which was synonymous with potentially uncontrolled devaluation, high inflation, losses for all Greeks engaged in foreign trade, and enduring difficulties in securing international funds. Greece did not want to become the Venezuela of Europe.

The management of the eurozone crisis was particularly ordoliberal. The specific contribution of the ordoliberals was to refuse an early restructuring of Greek debt in the name of the original sin of fraud. However, debt restructuring is commonplace at the international level. During the eurozone crisis, the IMF often called for a greater reduction in Greek debt. Ken Rogoff, the IMF's Chief Economist from 2001 to 2003, who is regarded as a neoliberal, was also in favour of a greater reduction in Greek debt than the one granted.[109] Another neoliberal US economist, Ronald McKinnon, observed that Europeans 'provide too little, too late'.[110] A 2017 IMF report on the eurozone crisis lamented that the IMF was under pressure from the Union, and the ECB in particular, not to restructure Greek debt.[111] What is certain is that European financial assistance to Greece amounted to more than €250 billion between 2010 and 2018, higher than Greek GDP in 2011, which totalled approximately €200 billion.[112] Despite the partial debt forgiveness granted in 2011, the debt-to-GDP ratio increased as a result of the latter's decline (Greek GDP fell by 16 per cent between 2011 and 2015, and growth returned only in 2017). Aid to Greece was partly ineffective because it was provided too late.

The ordoliberal approach was present in Berlin, but not exclusively. The reference to the pioneers of ordoliberalism was explicit in the speeches of Wolfgang Schaüble, the German finance minister from 2009 to 2017, and Jens Weidmann, the president of the Bundesbank from 2011 to 2021.[113] Even the Polish liberal Donald Tusk, the president of the European Council, referred in 2015 to the positive influence of ordoliberalism in defending the Greek aid plan.[114] The ECB pursued a policy of higher interest rates and more restrictive financing of the economy, compared to the one pursued by its British and American counterparts, probably because it needed to establish the solidity of the euro, which was still a young currency. Quantitative easing and interest rate cuts came later in the eurozone, and the ECB even increased interest rates in 2011 in the middle of the crisis.

Other factors played out in this belated restructuring, such as the risk of moral hazard (incentivising reckless behaviour by rescuing the culprit), and the risk of massive losses among European private banks. Some banks, especially in France, had been encouraged by their governments to keep their Greek securities, so as not to exacerbate the crisis.[115] The memory of the crisis of the 1930s, which was aggravated by a powerful banking crisis in Austria and Germany, was still alive, especially after the run against the British bank Northern Rock in 2007, and the bankruptcy of Lehman Brothers in 2008. The chairman of the Federal Reserve at the time, Ben Bernanke (2006–14), had stigmatised the restrictive monetary policy pursued after the 1929 crisis in some of his academic work.[116] This memory of the 1930s banking crisis partly explains the widespread bailout of banks, as well as the reluctance between 2010 and 2012 to have them incur losses in debt restructuring.[117] Only Iceland was bold enough to do so: using capital controls and an IMF loan, Reykjavik imposed losses on the primarily foreign creditors of banks more than it did on Icelandic taxpayers.[118] But the Icelandic model was difficult to reproduce, for its banking sector was tiny; the IMF's lending capacity would have been unable to provide equivalent support to a medium-sized European country, and the bankruptcy of a single large European bank might have triggered an uncontrollable chain reaction.

8.4.4 Deep Trauma

The eurozone crisis has had dramatic consequences. From the economic point of view, the crisis stopped the convergence between Northern and Southern Europe, as illustrated in the Table 8.2. Four groups of countries can be distinguished in terms of the evolution of GDP per capita between 2009, the start of the eurozone crisis, and 2019, just before the Covid-19 pandemic. At the top, Ireland has experiencing strong growth well above the European average, after quickly rebounding thanks to European aid and the fiscal residence of US multinationals (which artificially inflates GDP). On the contrary, with the exception of Portugal, Southern Europe has been mired in crisis, Greece in particular. A third group consists of the continent's three most powerful economies, which have remained fairly stable in terms of relative wealth, although France and the UK have declined slightly relative to the EU average and Germany. Strikingly, France and Britain experienced a similar evolution, even though the former is in the eurozone, but not the latter. Finally, Eastern Europe has continued to gradually catch up with the European average. Poland and Slovenia, respectively the largest and richest economies of the former Soviet bloc, have surpassed Greece, and Poland has been described as 'Europe's Growth Champion'.[119]

Politically, the eurozone crisis led to a near-death experience for the Union: if Grexit had occurred in 2012 or 2015, Greece would have left not only the eurozone, but possibly the Union altogether. If that had happened, financial markets could have pressured Italy and Spain to do so as well, thereby breaking the eurozone for good, for rescuing these large economies far exceeded the financial assistance capacity of eurozone member states.

Table 8.2 *Evolution of GNP per population 2009–19*[120]

In current euros, purchasing power parity, base 100 = European Union at 27

	2009	2019
European Union 27	100	100
Eurozone at 19 (since 2015)	110	106
Ireland	130	193
Germany	118	120
France	109	106
United Kingdom	110	104
Italy	108	96
Spain	101	91
Greece	95	66
Portugal	60	73
Slovenia	86	89
Poland	60	73

Considerable powers were vested in three institutions independent of elected governments – the Commission, the IMF, and the ECB – with hardly any control from the European Parliament or from national parliaments.[121] The bailouts were influenced by the ECB, which could cut liquidity at any time to pressure struggling governments. In August 2011, Jean-Claude Trichet sent a letter to the Italian Prime Minister Silvio Berlusconi urging him to quickly adopt a series of reforms.[122] In July 2015, despite a negative popular referendum, the Greek government accepted another austerity plan in exchange for a new European assistance package. The European process admittedly remained democratic, because decisions are made either by elected national leaders or by the decision makers appointed by them, but the impression remains of a drift towards what the German philosopher Jürgen Habermas, a great defender of the European Union, called 'post-democratic executive federalism', one that is insufficiently based on collective deliberation.[123]

These traumatic events led to an identity crisis for the Union.[124] While the 2004 enlargement did not erase the East–West divide, the eurozone crisis rekindled the old North–South divide. The latter is based on the image of Protestant Northern Europeans who are disciplined and industrious, in contrast to disorganised and fickle Southern Europeans. The fact that Ireland, the only northern country receiving a rescue plan, recovered quickly only reinforced this representation. This negative view of Greece even spread to

Eastern Europe, notably Latvia, a country that experienced a sharp recession in 2007–09 due to the global crisis and the drastic recommendations of an IMF and EU aid plan, before rebounding strongly and joining the eurozone.[125] On the whole, thrifty Northern (and Eastern) Europeans have felt manipulated by inefficient Southern Europeans, who have benefited from massive funding transfers despite the no bailout clause of the Maastricht Treaty.

This prejudice is not entirely groundless, as evidenced by the manipulation of Greek statistics, the extent of tax evasion, the large sums spent on bailouts, and the considerable amounts of securities acquired by the ECB, which ultimately holds more debt from certain eurozone countries than their central banks did before the existence of the euro.[126] Many Germans and Eastern Europeans were also convinced that they made considerable efforts in the 1990s and 2000s to absorb reunification and liberalise their labour market in order to restore competitiveness, all while controlling deficits. However, this prejudice is clearly a misrepresentation: working time in Greece was higher than in Germany (because of low Greek productivity).[127] In 2015, Dieselgate revealed how massive fraud could occur at the very heart of the German system. Moreover, Germany has had a poor record of paying back its debt. In his book on public debt, the British academic Kenneth Dyson, a specialist on Germany, contrasted France and the UK, which have always paid what they owed, with Germany, which has often benefited from international agreements to reduce its public debt, especially via various conferences to reduce reparations (1924, 1929, 1932), the 1948 currency reform (which wiped out the domestic public debt), and the London Conference of 1953, which largely reduced the remaining external debt.[128]

As a matter of fact, many Germans did not indulge in such prejudices. In 2011, Jürgen Habermas criticised a policy of excessive austerity, which overlooked the partial debt forgiveness from which Germany benefited in 1953.[129] In 2012, in light of past experiences, Albrecht Ritschl, a German economic historian who had attributed part of the West German economic miracle to these debt cancellations, called for reducing Greek debt.[130] A year later, Ulrich Beck declared 'No to German Europe', while in 2016 Wolfgang Streeck drew attention to a 'crisis of democratic capitalism', in which Germany played a major role.[131] In 2018, the German Greens raised the question of German profits from lending to Southern Europe, while criticising a *Kaputtsparkurs* (destructive austerity).[132] This remark was consistent with several previous studies, which have shown that the stronger eurozone countries (such as Germany) have benefited from the crisis due to an inflow of capital, which has lowered their interest rates.[133]

The political consequences of these excesses of neoliberal federalism were dramatic, with the rise of the far right and the far left in both Greece and Germany. In 2013, Bernd Lucke, an economist at the University of Hamburg, called for pulling out of the euro, and created the Alternative Party for

8.4 THE EURO: FROM MIRACLE TO GREEK TRAGEDY

Germany (AfD). Since then, AfD has considerably expanded its audience by adopting a traditional far-right xenophobic discourse. The crisis also had a legal dimension: building on a long tradition of criticism regarding insufficiently democratic European institutions, dating back to the *Solange* ruling in 1974, the Federal Constitutional Court in Karlsruhe tersely criticised certain asset purchase programmes implemented by the ECB, on the grounds that they violated the European Treaties. The ECB even had to justify its monetary policy before the German Bundestag.

The old debates also resurfaced after the eurozone crisis. The Commissioner for Economic Affairs, Pierre Moscovici (2014-19) of France, joined with Southern European countries to promote a common European recovery plan akin to the 1978 'locomotive', whereas Northern European countries have remained focused on austerity. Jeroen Dijsselbloem, the Dutch minister of finance and president of Eurogroup, provocatively remarked about Southern countries: 'You cannot spend all the money on alcohol and women!'[134]

To conclude, faced with the prospect of a massive political crisis, eurozone members belatedly accepted revamping the architecture of the eurozone in three areas, drawing on long-standing ideas.[135] The projects are not strictly identical, as the context has changed, but the gist is the same. First, in terms of solidarity, the ESM is a possible embodiment of the 'European Monetary Fund' mentioned in the agreement establishing the EMS in 1978. Second, in terms of regulated liberalism, the banking union was the subject of Commission proposals in the 1970s,[136] as well as a mention in the 1989 Delors report. Third, enhanced coordination of national economic policy has been a constant theme since the plans of the French Commissioner Robert Marjolin in the 1960s, and the Werner Report in 1970. It is embodied in a more neoliberal version in the Fiscal Compact and the Sixpack legislation of 2011-12.

In hindsight, a better solution would have been to impose a faster and deeper reduction in Greek debt, in exchange for a certain degree of supervision over Greek policies (as is usual in all cases of financial assistance), and for ECB support for the Western banks affected by losses from this operation. Aid should also have been provided to the non-eurozone countries of Eastern Europe even before the eurozone crisis, thereby preventing the subsequent rise of populist governments. The 'concerted recovery' of 1978 could have been reactivated by more reflationary policies from the creditor countries of Northern Europe.

Major loopholes remain in the eurozone. The ESM has a limited mandate and power, and no financial solidarity is established in the case of the banking union, which remains incomplete. The ECB's power of intervention over the debt market is still curtailed by the provisions of the Maastricht Treaty, as well as the vigilance of the Federal Constitutional Court. The ECB is still largely beyond any democratic accountability, whereas other independent central banks are required to report more regularly to elected representatives. The debates from 1989-91 show that Delors and the socialist group in the European Parliament had considered alternative solutions for exerting greater political control over the future independent central bank (see Chapter 7).

All actors had to compromise. Germany had to abandon its ordoliberal vision of monetary policy in order to accept a reduction in Greek debt, massive assistance plans for Southern Europe, the accommodative monetary policy of the ECB, and the creation of a permanent stability mechanism (the ESM), in other words a series of concessions that would have been unthinkable at the beginning of the crisis. In exchange, membership in the euro has generally provided low interest rates for its members most of the time. It has successfully protected some fragile countries from financial crisis, in contrast to October 2022 when the UK almost experienced this under Liz Truss's ephemeral government, which ramped up spending projects and castigated the Treasury. The British example shows that even outside the euro, many European states would have opted for austerity, either willingly or due to the risk of financial crisis.

8.5 Conclusion

Since 1992, the neoliberal approach has gradually spread to all countries and fields, including sports and Internet.

The European Union has been one of the drivers of this neoliberal dynamic through enlargement, competition policy, the expansion of the Single Market, the threat of legislative Darwinism, and finally the ordoliberal characteristics of monetary union. Already visible in the 1990s with the UK government and British commissioners such as Leon Brittan, it reached its peak under the Barroso Commission (2004-14) – in connection with the Bolkestein directive and Court of Justice rulings deemed hostile to unions – and with the financial crisis of 2007, itself directly resulting from unregulated neoliberalism. The eurozone crisis (2010-15) showed the excesses of a more specifically ordoliberal vision, the misdeeds of which were denounced even in Germany and by the IMF. The Greek tragedy concerned the Greek people, along with the whole of the European Union project. In the end, while the sums spent on Greek assistance were massive, they came too late: earlier debt restructuring would probably have been less costly.

The period of the Barroso Commission (2004-14) and the Greek crisis (2010-15) can thus be read, in retrospect, as a culmination of federal neoliberalism. Federal mechanisms were visible with some decisions by the Commission, the ECB, and the Court of Justice, as well as with the considerable expansion of powers to impose penalties for deviations from stability policy. This led to what Habermas called 'post-democratic executive federalism'. The havoc unleashed by this excessive neoliberal and technocratic

8.5 CONCLUSION

federalism triggered a reaction.[137] It bolstered first euroscepticism and then illiberalism: the Bolkestein directive played a role in the French rejection of the Constitutional Treaty in 2005, and the Greek tragedy fuelled the rise of far-right and far-left parties in both Greece and Germany.

Central and Eastern European countries have been drivers of neoliberalism, as they abandoned gradualism in favor of rapid privatisation and Western investment, motivated by both economic reasons (such as access to capital and modernisation) and geopolitical considerations (notably as a safeguard against Russia). Once inside the EU, most of these countries continued to support neoliberal policies, though not uniformly across all areas, as they relied on funding from the cohesion policy and the Common Agricultural Policy, and more recently, on the joint procurement of Covid-19 vaccines.

More generally, the Europeans had always relied on a trinity of approaches – *liberty*, *solidarity*, and *community* – as well as historical precedents to inform their decisions. Drawing on long-standing reflections connected to the creation of a European monetary fund or banking union, they reformed the eurozone through creative interpretation of the Treaty, and by creating new institutions. Besides, it is difficult to say if the eurozone rules have limited social spending, through the implementation of Stability Pact rules, or facilitated it by diminishing the cost of borrowing for countries that had weak national currencies. In competition policy as well, the older approach of 'public interest' (which struck a balance between *liberty*, *solidarity*, and *community*) has made a comeback in a new guise under Commissioner Vestager, in what could be called an 'excess of market power' approach. Lastly, concerning the Single Market, neoliberal tendencies have clashed with a *solidarity* approach, as shown by the epic debates surrounding the Bolkestein directive and services of general interest. More generally, the *solidarity* approach has remained vibrant in these years, as Chapter 9 will illustrate.

9

Solidarity: Expanded and Contested Social and Environmental Action

Despite the neoliberal wave – or perhaps because of it – *solidarity* capitalism has remained important in Europe. Regulating neoliberal globalisation, which has increased inequality in the North as well as environmental damage worldwide, has been deemed a necessity.[1] Since it was impossible to tame capitalism globally (with the relative decline of the ILO and UNCTAD, the international organisations charged with this task), promoters of international *solidarity* turned to the European Union, and strove to strengthen its 'embryonic' welfare state developed in the 1980s (see Chapter 6).

This proved to be a Herculean task. The early 1990s brought a first peak of international awareness regarding environmental protection and interest in social Europe, but that was shattered by a neoliberal reaction from the mid-1990s to the mid-2010s. Since then, social and environmental policies have been on the rise again, only to be challenged by the Russo-Ukrainian War.

Three expressions of *solidarity* will be examined in this chapter. The first deals with the legal regulation of globalisation through social legislation and trade regulation. The second involves financial redistribution towards the neediest, with transfers to poor regions, and later with specific measures during the Covid-19 crisis (2020–21). The third addresses the rising importance of environmental regulation (Section 9.4) both in general and with regard to climate change (Section 9.5).

9.1 Social Europe: Neoliberal Flood and Ebb

Despite neoliberalism, national welfare states in Europe have continued to expand in certain areas such as the environment, the rights of women and LGBT people, extended periods for pursuing education, and reduced working time. Annual working time was roughly equivalent in Britain, France, Germany, and the US in 1980. It has since diminished by 15 per cent in Western Europe, but has remained the same in the US.[2] This dual dynamic has left its mark on the Union, characterised initially by the great social ambition of the Delors era, and later by the high-water mark of neoliberalism under Barroso, before a subsequent ebb.

9.1.1 The Delors Dynamic

A first period was characterised by continuing the efforts initiated by Jacques Delors, who served as Commission president until 1995.[3] Under the Conservative Major government (1990–97), the UK still remained social Europe's staunchest opponent. The Working Time Directive was adopted in 1993 despite British abstention. London mounted a legal challenge against the directive, albeit in vain, as the Court supported the Commission's interpretation.[4] The directive was updated in 2003, with minimum standards of a 48-hour workweek, and four weeks of annual paid leave. A directive on European works councils was adopted in 1994, with their number increasing sharply from 50 to 466 in the two years following the legislation.[5] Their power is nevertheless limited, as illustrated by the closure of the Renault factory in Brussels-Vilvoorde in 1997, which was pursued with no consultation of local staff representatives. The directive was reformed in 2009 to clarify the obligations of companies, but the constraints remain limited. Finally, Delors's emphasis on relaunching European social dialogue led to binding laws immediately after his departure from the Commission. Representatives for employers and workers – UNICE (now Business Europe) for private employers, CEEP for public employers, and the ETUC for employees – concluded three framework agreements, which were then implemented through directives (legally binding acts) pertaining to parental leave (1996), part-time work (1997), and fixed-term contracts (1999).[6] The fight against discrimination was broadened to include many areas (based on gender, race, faith, sexual orientation, etc.), and led to the adoption of numerous pieces of legislation.[7] One year later in 1998, member states launched the Bologna Process facilitating student mobility within the EU, doing so independently of the Commission.[8] Europe was actually rediscovering its medieval origins, as its universities were home to student and teacher mobility from the very beginning (an exchange facilitated by the common usage of Latin). The Bologna Declaration emphasised the university's multifunctional nature, including its civic, intellectual, and social role, in addition to academic freedom.

9.1.2 A Changing Mood

At the same time, in the mid-1990s, the environment changed with the rise of neoliberal ideas. Paradoxically, it coincided with what was referred to as 'Pink Europe', namely the simultaneous rise of left-wing governments in numerous European countries. Tony Blair, the new British prime minister (1997–2007), ratified the Social Charter that Thatcher and Major had refused. However, these left-wing governments remained divided. The French Prime Minister Lionel Jospin (1997–2002), and the short-lived German Minister of Finance Oskar Lafontaine (1998–99), defended a redistributive vision, whereas the

German Chancellor Gerhard Schröder and Blair promoted a more free market approach. Lafontaine soon left the government. Countries that used to be in favour of solidarity shifted to a more cautious position when centre-right governments returned to power. For example, at the Luxembourg Employment Summit in 1997, Spain (led by the conservative José Maria Aznar) admitted that it could not accept the ambitious social objectives that had been set, because the country had too many unemployed and too few resources to devote to them.[9] Later on, Italian Prime Minister Massimo d'Alema (1998–2000), a former communist, strove to change the Lisbon Strategy by adopting a more social approach, but the advent of the centre-right government led by Silvio Berlusconi (2001–06) changed Rome's position towards a more free market orientation.[10] More generally, social Europe was hampered by the advent of a new generation of leaders who were less enthusiastic towards European integration, such as Schröder in Germany (1998–2005), Chirac in France (1995–2007), Aznar in Spain (1996–2004), and Berlusconi in Italy (2001–06).

At the Commission, the active dynamic of the Delors era was fading.[11] The Commission chaired by Jacques Santer (1995–99) adopted a more modest profile. Instead of ambitious federal law, it promoted the open method of coordination (OMC), a non-binding effort to have national practices converge. His successor Romano Prodi was more ambitious, but had to focus on other priorities such as the euro, Eastern enlargement, and the revision of the European Treaties. In 2000, it adopted the Lisbon Strategy 'modernising the European social model by investing in human resources and creating an active social state', but the legislative tools remained weak, and its ideological foundation uneven.[12] In theory, Brussels wanted to promote the Danish model of flexicurity, a balance between labour market flexibility (especially redundancy facilities) and high unemployment benefits coupled with systematic training. This system required strong trade unions capable of negotiating collective agreements. However, unions have suffered a deep decline in Europe since the 1980s. They were weakened by the dismantling of industrial strongholds following the crisis of traditional manufacturing, as well as by subcontracting and rising international competition. Without strong unions, flexicurity proved to be no more than a free market policy. What is more, European social dialogue began to retract,[13] as the so-called new generation agreements were no longer followed by a legally binding Council directive. Consequently, the European laws that were passed (in 2002 on teleworking, in 2004 on harassment at work, etc.) were mere declarations of intent.

In terms of trade, since most customs duties on mainstream goods had already been removed in the 1990s, negotiations to stimulate free trade involved even more sensitive topics, such as harmonising legislation relating to services as well as social and environmental standards. As a result, in 1997 Jospin's new centre-left government in France opposed the conclusion of the

Multilateral Agreement on Investment launched in 1995 under the auspices of the OECD, which sought to attract international investment by providing guarantees to multinationals against state action. Jospin called for culture to be excluded from the agreement, for US legislation not to be extended abroad, and for compliance with European standards, particularly in social and environmental matters. Faced with the impossibility of having these conditions met, he suspended French participation in 1998, bringing negotiations to a halt.[14] In 2000 Paris succeeded in having the notion of cultural exception recognised in the Treaty of Nice.

To some extent, the European ambition to regulate globalisation by combining the dominant value of *liberty* with a modest degree of *solidarity* was promoted globally through the World Trade Organization (WTO), the new institution that emerged from the GATT in 1995. A string of top European officials who worked at the Commission went on to serve as Director-General of the GATT/WTO, including Peter Sutherland (1993–95), Renato Ruggiero (1995–99), and Pascal Lamy (2005–13). Several Europeans, in particular German-speaking lawyers, published a proposal in 1993 for a GATT Draft International Antitrust Code, an economically liberal regulation of globalisation.[15] The WTO launched working groups on this subject in 1996, but they stalled due to a lack of willingness on the part of member states to engage in binding regulations. Pascal Lamy, Delors's former right-hand man, exemplifies this idea of 'regulated globalisation'; he tried to revive global trade negotiations when he served as director general of the WTO from 2005 to 2013, but with little success.[16]

9.1.3 Barroso: High Neoliberalism

The period overlapping with José Manuel Barroso's (2004–14) two terms as Commission president was the apex of neoliberalism.[17] In Brussels Barroso defended minimal intervention on the part of the Commission – far removed from the ambitions of Delors – and was supported in this task by most member states. The 2004–07 enlargement to twelve poorer countries prompted wealthier countries to curtail the Union's spending. The negotiation of the 2005 European budget was marked by a joint letter calling for limiting EU expenditure drafted by the governments of Northern Europe (Germany, Austria, the Netherlands, Sweden, and Finland), but also from France.[18] The budget was smaller compared with the Delors period in terms of percentage of national wealth. With respect to the poorest states, the countries of the former Soviet bloc were in favour of intra-European redistribution, but not of progressive social legislation, because they feared losing a comparative advantage in their process of catching up with richer countries, and because socialism had been discredited by the Soviet experience.[19]

In terms of international trade, Barroso also defended a neoliberal agenda, but was hampered by the 2007 Lisbon Treaty, which gave Parliament the power to reject all trade agreements, and the right to be informed at all stages of negotiations. The rowdy and boisterous chamber in Strasbourg would have to be appeased. In 2012, under pressure from popular demonstrations and petitions, the Parliament rejected the Anti-Counterfeiting Trade Agreement (ACTA) pertaining to the enforcement of intellectual property rights.[20] In 2013, the debate shifted to the Transatlantic Free Trade Treaty, known by its English acronym TAFTA, whose name echoes the EFTA, the small UK-sponsored European Free Trade Area created in 1960.[21] The Commission insisted that culture and media be included within the negotiating mandate. In 2013, Barroso called the French demand for a 'cultural exception' as 'reactionary'.[22] However, the French government, with the support of other member states and Parliament, successfully opposed it. Paris also called for public consultation regarding the procedure for dispute resolution between investors and states, which became a highly contentious subject and fuelled a powerful globalist protest movement. Paradoxically, it took on greater importance in Germany than France,[23] although the negotiations ultimately came to an end.

Within the EU, the Lisbon Strategy was reformed along more neoliberal lines in 2005. The goal of combating unemployment was downgraded, with emphasis being placed on structural reforms to liberalise the labour market.[24] Similarly, the Bologna Process for higher education was reformed in 2005–06 according to a more market-oriented basis, with universities being considered exclusively as actors in the labour market.[25] Discussions surrounding a framework directive on public services, implementation of the equal treatment principle, and the revision of the Working Time Directive stalled.[26] Last but not least, the eurozone crisis led to massive cuts in welfare states, sometimes at the behest of the troika, especially in 2010–12 (see Chapter 9). Social Europe had reached its nadir.

9.1.4 A Progressive Social Revival since the Mid-2010s

In the mid-2010s, the pendulum of economic ideas swung in the other direction, away from neoliberalism. This evolution can be explained by the lessons learned from the 2008 financial crisis, which shattered the belief in self-regulatory markets, and from the botched management of the eurozone crisis in 2010–15. The balance of power shifted, with the advent of a socialist president in France (François Hollande, 2012–17), the Social Democrats in Germany (Merkel governed with them in 2013–21, Scholz government in 2021–25), and a more socially minded Commission president, the moderate Christian Democrat Jean-Claude Juncker (2013 to 2021). According to a survey of several European Commissioners and officials, between 2008 (the Barroso period) and 2014 (the Juncker period) the economic vision became less neoliberal and more favourable to corrective market interventions.[27] The growing isolation of neoliberal Britain under David Cameron (2010–16), further magnified by Brexit, also helped. Even the IMF became less neoliberal under the leadership of two French politicians, the socialist Dominique Strauss-Kahn (2007–11), and centre-right Christine Lagarde (2011–19). In 2012, the IMF accepted that capital controls could be justified in certain situations to ensure financial stability.[28] In 2017, one of its reports called for increasing the marginal tax rate for some countries in order to limit inequality.[29]

This led to a reorientation of economic policies. Tax cooperation has improved on the global level. In 2014, Switzerland partially lifted its banking secrecy in the face of intense pressure from the US. Discussions are ongoing regarding the taxation of multinationals and the financial transaction tax (the so-called Tobin tax). A first agreement was struck at the OECD in 2021, and was transposed in 2022 into an EU directive to take effect several years later. It set a minimal tax of 15 per cent on the profits of multinationals, which is seen as a concession by low-tax countries, and as an insufficient measure by many social activists.[30] The growing number of tax document leaks by whistle-blowers – in particular the 2013 offshore leaks and the 2014 Luxleaks – have led to major consultative work at the OECD, as well as subsequent EU decisions facilitating information exchange between governments and banks, with a view to limiting tax evasion.[31] The 2023 report of the EU Tax Observatory acknowledged that tax evasion by individuals had been reduced by two-thirds, but that tax evasion by multinationals remained high.[32] The decision-making process has been hampered by the requirement of unanimous voting for all EU tax decisions, and by the low-tax policy of several members (Ireland, Luxembourg, and the Netherlands are usually singled out).[33] Another obstacle to collective action is tax competition from non-EU countries, notably the Channel Islands and Switzerland, hence the importance of the OECD's work, although this institution is structurally weaker than the Union, for it relies on unanimity and soft law. Lastly, since 2025, the new Trump administration has opposed any deals on this issue.

In terms of trade policy, the negotiations surrounding new international agreements liberalising trade have become more difficult. In 2016, ratification of the Comprehensive Economic and Trade Agreement (CETA) between the EU and Canada was blocked by the Parliament of Wallonia, the French-speaking part of Belgium, and by its Minister-President Paul Magnette. Opposition was lifted only after publication of an interpretative declaration regarding the prerogatives of states and social norms.[34] A small region of 3.6 million inhabitants nearly derailed one of the most important trade treaties of recent decades. The conclusion of new trade agreements also stalled. In 2019, the Commission struck a deal to liberalise trade with the South American block Mercosur, but it has yet to be ratified. The French government opposed it before the ink was even dry, because under President Bolsonaro (2019–23) Brazil did not protect the Amazonian rainforest, thereby putting the country in breach of the Paris Agreement on climate change. Later on, despite Bolsonaro being replaced by the more avuncular Lula da Silva, France still strongly opposed the new agreement concluded in 2024, due to pressure from farmers protesting the potential import of cheap and substandard South American food products.

This shift towards more solidarity in the governance of European capitalism was also visible in Brussels. The Union once again actively pursued social policy beginning with the Juncker Commission (2014–19), and in 2017 adopted a European Pillar of Social Rights. In contrast to the Lisbon Strategy – especially since its revision under Barroso – this set of principles highlights traditional social rights more broadly than before. Reference is made to consultation with workers, thereby reconnecting with the spirit of the Vredeling directive. Gender equality is promoted in both principle and through more specific measures, such as early childhood care. Workers' rights are extended via the term 'workers' instead of 'employees', thereby enabling EU legislation to cover the precarious self-employed in the 'gig economy'. Finally, ambitious reforms are mentioned, such as the adoption of minimum wages across Europe, depending on the national context. This non-binding law was initially seen as lofty rhetoric, but it has gradually served as a lever for many supporters of social Europe.

Since 2014, the Union's solidarity policy has been visible in three areas. First, neoliberal laws have been corrected. The Pillar of Social Rights has been integrated into the European Semester, the regular review of national economic and social policies within the framework of the monetary union. Another example is the 1996 Posted Workers Directive. It ultimately proved ill-suited to the 2004–07 enlargement towards Eastern Europe, which considerably increased the number of low-paid mobile workers. The directive required that local standards for minimum wages and working hours be applied, but many loopholes remained. Furthermore, fraud has been facilitated by a lack of control and transnational cooperation. The Juncker Commission, and countries concerned with stricter rules, the French government in particular, successfully had the directive revised in 2018. It establishes the principle of equal pay for equal work in the same place. It also harmonises some ancillary benefits (but not social security contributions), and limits postings to one year. A European Labour Authority was created in 2019 to facilitate cooperation on labour mobility and to limit fraud.

Second, traditional social policies were revived, especially on gender equality, although the effort remains modest, and focused on female employment.[35] Social Affairs Commissioner Marianne Thyssen, a Belgian Christian Democrat, abandoned the old plan to strengthen the parental leave directive for women in order to reach agreement, in 2019, on a more comprehensive directive on work–life balance for working parents and caregivers. It granted minimum paid paternity leave, and limited the transferability of parental leave between parents.

Finally, new areas were explored, with the adoption of ambitious laws. In the field of competition, Commissioner Vestager launched a major offensive against large multinationals beginning in 2014, even moving into uncharted water, such as with state fiscal aid in the Apple case (see Chapter 8). In 2020, the Covid crisis prompted the Council to partially Europeanise national unemployment benefits with the SURE mechanism (Support to Mitigate Unemployment Risks in an Emergency), which relies on European loans to refinance national employment protection systems. The Commission assisted nine EU countries, and estimated the interest savings at €5.8 billion.[36] The Covid-19 crisis led to the joint distribution of a vaccine, as well as a global stimulus programme (see Sections 9.3.2 and 9.3.3). In 2022, the Union adopted a long-standing project on the minimum wage. Far from any effort at European harmonisation, it instead set minimal rules,[37] promoting expanded collective bargaining at the European level, in a clear nod to the Delors era. Last but not least, the Russo-Ukrainian War, which erupted in 2022, led to the generous welcome of refugees, in contrast to the hostility faced by non-European newcomers during the so-called migrant crisis in 2015. In this instance, the logic of *community* (the sense of sharing a common European identity with Ukrainians) was clearly combined with the logic of *solidarity*.

To conclude, the flanking European welfare state has gradually been reinforced after the backlash against high neoliberalism (1992–2014). It has benefited from the adoption of numerous reforms long under consideration, such as the inclusion of social rights in the examination of national economic policies, and the partial Europeanisation of minimum wages. But the Union remains predicated on neoclassical economics, with hardly any mention of reducing inequality as a goal in itself, and with strong opposition to any kind of social union from neoliberals, as well as those (such as Scandinavians) who prefer managing this issue at the national level.[38]

9.2 Redistribution: A Limited Transfer Union with an Impact on the Poor

Is the Union's sense of solidarity strong enough to proceed with massive financial transfers to its poorest members? Admittedly, Europe remains organised on the basis of financially independent nation states. The 1992 Maastricht Treaty establishing the monetary union excluded solidarity in terms of debt (Article 104). Income transfers are limited by the small size of the Community budget (roughly 1 per cent of the Union's GDP, and 2 per cent of its public expenditures). The Union's own resources (mainly customs duties and a share of consumer taxes) represents only one-third to one-quarter of its budget, the rest being covered by state contributions. This limited redistribution has had an impact on its poorest members, as it was combined with other tools such as the Single Market (which can boost exports and lower the price of imports, thereby increasing productivity), and a single currency (which lowered interest rates for poor countries before the eurozone crisis).

9.2.1 A Genuine Impact on Poor Countries

The first element of financial solidarity within the Union was Cohesion Policy, which grew out of Regional Policy in 1975. It has implemented continent-wide redistribution towards poor regions, mainly in Southern Europe, Eastern Europe, and Ireland. In Southern Europe, the period was marked by the co-financing of spectacular transport infrastructure, such as the longest bridge in Europe over the Tagus River in Lisbon, the completion of Venizelos Airport in Athens, and the high-speed Madrid–Barcelona train line. Southern European countries greatly benefited from these substantial financial transfers, which account for several points of GDP each year, but also from agricultural subsidies, tourist flows from the Single Market, the free movement of people (which allows emigration to rich countries and the inflow of tourists and pensioners), and finally economic and monetary union, which brought lower interest rates in the 2000s. These various elements triggered a process of convergence with wealthy countries from the 1980s up through the 2008 crisis.

Ireland represents an exemplary case with respect to economic development, with the country's per capita GDP surpassing the Union's average in the 1990s. The island has benefited from massive funding from Cohesion Policy, as well as its integration in a vast Single Market, where knowledge of English and cultural proximity has been an asset for many US multinationals (which based their primary European subsidiaries there).[39] Another advantage of European solidarity was the PEACE programme launched in 1994.[40] On 31 August 1994, the Irish Republican Army (IRA) proclaimed a permanent ceasefire in Northern Ireland. In response, the Delors Commission announced the release of extraordinary European funding to facilitate the peace process, drawing positive reactions from the governments of the UK and Ireland. Popular consultations were carried out to develop projects partly funded by the EU (urban renewal, social inclusion, tourism), especially those involving the two Catholic and Protestant communities in Northern Ireland. On the British government's own admission, this aid facilitated the conclusion of the Good Friday Agreement in 1998, which put an end to the most recent conflict between two EU members. The Union served as an honest broker, unable to negotiate peace, but willing to facilitate its implementation.

In the East, former communist countries had to catch up with the West in terms of economic development, and also build a liberal democracy and market economy from scratch.[41] At the Paris G7 Summit in December 1989, the G7 members (including non-EU members such as the US) tasked the Commission with providing aid to Central and Eastern Europe. The major instrument was the PHARE programme of 1989.[42] The acronym originally stood for Poland Hungary Aid for Economic Reconstruction, before being extended to most Central and Eastern European countries. In 1994, the Essen European Council explicitly linked EU funding to the enlargement process. It was meant to help these countries create an administrative and judicial apparatus capable of operating a liberal market democracy, and of implementing the large slate of '*acquis communautaire*', the collective body of Community legislation adopted for almost half a century.

Other actors have contributed to the East catching up, such as the European Bank for Reconstruction and Development (EBRD) established in 1990, along with private foundations. For instance, the Hungarian billionaire Georges Soros supported the development of liberal democracies in the East through his Open Society Foundations. He funded the creation of the Central European University (CEU) in Budapest, based on the Western Anglo-American model. He also created numerous scholarship programmes to Westernise young elites in Central and Eastern European countries. Even the Hungarian leader Victor Orbán – one of Soros's detractors, who forced the CEU to move to Vienna in 2018 – benefited from this programme during his own studies. Germany also played a role through massive transfers to the East.[43]

These transfers had a significant impact. They have been compared with the Marshall Plan, and have had the same dual effect: quantitative, with European allocations of around 2 per cent of the national wealth for the poorest countries (former Eastern bloc countries, Portugal, and Greece); and qualitative, with increased productivity and investment opportunity through foreign investment and integration in larger markets, as well as new management and production methods.[44] The level of funding was limited by the 'absorption capacity' of these countries (there were simply not enough actors capable of effectively spend European funds). For Poland, the amount of European funds is estimated at around €40 billion, or approximately €1,000 per Pole, an amount roughly equivalent to the €50 billion in private investment received by the country. Admittedly, Western firms established in this country have repatriated their profits, but not without creating jobs, paying taxes, and increasing productivity. On a more anecdotal level, the Austrian historian Philippe Ther, who has been travelling throughout Eastern Europe since the 1980s, observed that widespread corruption ended as it was no longer possible to avoid a speeding ticket by bribing a policeman.[45]

This dynamic favoured economic convergence between the Union's east and west, to the detriment of countries remaining outside. The comparison between Polish and Ukrainian living standards between 1990 and 2019 (before the Covid crisis and the Russo-Ukrainian War) is illuminating. According to World Bank data, Ukrainians were slightly richer than Poles in 1990 (measured in terms of GDP per capita respecting purchasing power parity). Thirty years later, Poles were 2.6 times richer than Ukrainians.

More generally, Table 9.1 shows the reality of this convergence process. In order to use the same measuring stick, the basis is not the EU average

Table 9.1 Convergence within the European Union: Changes in per capita wealth in seven countries[48]
Per capita GDP, basis 100 = France

	France	Spain	Greece	Ireland	Poland	Slovenia	Ukraine
1973	100	57	60	54	42	74	38
1989	100	67	58	63	33	72	37
2004	100	86	73	134	42	69	23
2018	100	82	61	168	71	76	25

(which changes depending on enlargements) but France, a country between Northern and Southern Europe, and whose GDP has been close to the UK's during that period.[46] Ireland is the most spectacular case, surpassing even France in the 1990s, taking full advantage of European funds, the Single Market, and globalisation. However, statistics for Irish national wealth are artificially inflated by the fact that the European subsidiaries of numerous multinationals are tax residents there.[47] The convergence of Southern Europe (Spain, Greece) was genuine until the eurozone crisis, and the dynamic has remained positive in former communist Europe.

9.2.2 A Belated and Frustrating Solidarity during the 2010s

The eurozone (2010–15) and migration (2015) crises faced by Europe led to increased solidarity, but only belatedly, and with a great deal of resulting frustration. During the eurozone crisis, five countries benefited from massive support plans, primarily Greece (in an amount exceeding its GDP), as well as Ireland, Portugal, and Cyprus. Spain received a proportionally smaller amount of EU funds considering its large size. A permanent system of assistance to countries in financial crisis, the European Stability Mechanism (ESM), was established in 2012. All eurozone countries subsequently benefited from the policy of quantitative easing implemented after 2012.

The overall outcome of this financial solidarity has been mixed. The Greek rescue plan and quantitative easing probably came too late (the UK and US authorities were more supportive of the economy in 2008–11). These rescue plans were massively financed by taxpayers.[49] Poverty increased significantly between 2008 and 2014 in all assisted countries.[50] Despite massive aid, the EU was unable to protect the most fragile during the crisis.

The so-called migration crisis of 2015 demonstrated a clear lack of solidarity, to the point that the very term 'migrant' became controversial.[51] According to the Dublin III Agreement of 2013, the first country encountering these migrants in the Union is responsible for handling them, and must quickly proceed with asylum claims.[52] This created two imbalances. First, from a geographical point of view, most immigrants arrive on Europe's southern shores (Spain, Italy, and Greece), but want to settle in richer Northern Europe. The issue was compounded by the eurozone crisis, which left Southern Europe's public finances in disarray. These migrants can travel fairly freely within the Union, as borders controls were largely removed in the 1990s. The second problem is that no common immigration policy exists. In short, the Europe of migration is based on solidarity for intra-European migrants, but not for extra-European ones. With respect to the latter, if we apply the prism of the trinity, Europe stands for *liberty*, as the free movement of people is ensured, but not *solidarity* (social aid is provided locally and nationally, and is often insufficient) or *community* (as no common definition of how to become a member of the community exists, since immigration policies are different).

In 2015, Europe faced an influx of millions of migrants fleeing the Syrian, Iraqi, Libyan, and Afghan civil wars, as well as dire living conditions in Africa. Europe as a collective body reacted with an utter lack of solidarity, the most appalling consequence being the drowning of thousands of people in the Mediterranean Sea. In Southern Europe, countries already weakened by the eurozone crisis faced a massive influx of people they could not handle. They allowed some to move freely towards the rest of Europe, which they saw as selfish, having in effect externalised their migration policy to countries on Europe's external borders.

Some sense of solidarity eventually emerged, but rather late. On 31 August 2015 the German Chancellor Angela Merkel boldly proclaimed 'We can handle this', as her country generously welcomed hundreds of thousands of migrants, including many refugees from the horrendous Syrian civil war. Among the 1.2 million first-time applicants for asylum recorded in 2015 in the EU, 35 per cent went to Germany (440,000), 14 per cent to Hungary (174,000), and only 6 per cent to France (70,000).[53] Paradoxically, while France has been a staunch supporter of social Europe, it has expressed far less solidarity towards migrants than Germany in 2015.

The Union then decided to reinforce the Frontex agency, which helps control the EU's external border, and more controversially to reallocate some of the migrants across Europe. However, this decision was made by a qualified majority of member states, against opposition from four Central European countries adamantly opposed to this decision (Hungary, Romania, Slovakia, and the Czech Republic). The minority eventually prevailed, as the legally adopted decision was not implemented. Some countries erected walls, such as Hungary on its border with Serbia. The crisis was eventually solved by an agreement between Europeans and Turkey concluded in 2016, according to which the latter would stop Syrian migrants on its soil in exchange for European aid. The backlash against migrants intensified later, including in Germany where Angela Merkel faced growing opposition from her own Christian-Democratic constituency for her bold decision. The Pact on Migration and Asylum adopted in 2024 imposed stricter rules to increase control at the EU border. The 2015 migrant crisis therefore increased *community* capitalism (by reinforcing border controls) to the detriment of *solidarity* capitalism.

9.3 Facing Covid-19 (2020–21): Towards a Transfer Union?

With the arrival of Covid-19 in 2020–21 – an unprecedented and highly contagious respiratory disease highly lethal for the elderly and those with fragile health – the world faced a massive human and economic challenge. The Union suffered over 1.1 million deaths from the disease (not including 200,000 in the UK).[54] An unprecedented solution was pursued to limit its spread, namely lockdowns that caused a deep economic recession in 2020, on average 6 per cent for the Union. European capitalism was on its knees, but reacted quickly to express greater *solidarity*, despite health not being one of the Union's competences.[55]

9.3.1 Health without Europe

International health cooperation has historically been pursued by global institutions. The International Office of Public Hygiene was born in Rome in 1907, while in 1923 the League of Nations created a Hygiene Committee, foreshadowing the World Health Organization (WHO) of 1948.[56]

The project of fostering European cooperation in health emerged only in 1950. On 24 September 1950, three months after the Schuman Declaration of 9 May 1950, the French Council of Ministers adopted the draft proposal by Minister of Health Paul Ribeyre to create a European Health Community, known as White Pool.[57] Ribeyre's project encompassed all three dimensions of the trinity – *liberty*, *solidarity*, and *community*. First, it sought to create an integrated market for medicine, medical equipment, and medical professions by facilitating free movement. Second, it provided funding for countries with the most inadequate equipment. Third, it proposed pooling hospital resources in order to promote their fullest use. A genuine industrial policy was planned, with the construction of joint research centres, as well as consultation on the production of medicine and medical equipment. To carry out this ambitious project, institutions were modelled on those of the European Coal and Steel Community.

The White Pool quickly failed because Ribeyre presented his project at the OEEC, a broad intergovernmental organisation including seventeen countries, some of which strongly opposed supranational institutions, such as the UK.

The international dimension ultimately prevailed, as the WHO still oversees health cooperation efforts. The Union limited itself to market integration, which proceeded in the 1990s through the free movement of medical products, enabled by a harmonised marketing authorisation procedure (mostly from 1993 onwards), the free movement of medical staff, and the free movement of persons seeking care.[58] Liberalisation has been very gradual. For example, the reimbursement of care received elsewhere in Europe has long been limited to emergency cases (thanks to the European Health Insurance Card), before the Court of Justice extended the free movement of patients in 1998, albeit with safeguards to avoid what has been referred to as 'medical tourism'.

9.3.2 The EU Facing the Outbreak of the Pandemic (2020)

When the pandemic struck in early 2020, the European response was initially national. Epidemics have always triggered a reflex of withdrawal into one's own community, for example, by closing the city's walls or by subjecting incoming vessels to quarantine. This phenomenon has also occurred within a nation state: in the US in 2020, state governors competed with each other and with the federal government to obtain medical equipment, and often restricted free movement from neighbouring states.[59] Even in smaller European countries, people were wary of those coming from the first region contaminated by the virus. The same reaction occurred in 2020 at the European level, with the free movement of people being interrupted by member states. Planes were grounded, and most countries kept their medical equipment (such as masks, gloves, and ventilators) for themselves. Local initiatives of solidarity occurred, with French patients being evacuated to German hospitals, but not on a massive scale.

The dimension of *solidarity* was more evident on the economic front. National governments massively supported companies to offset their losses resulting from lockdowns. In this respect, the Union's reaction was both faster and wider than during the 2007 crisis. It quickly reactivated the exemption clauses used during the preceding economic crisis. As early as March 2020, the Council adopted the Commission's proposals to suspend the Stability Pact's budgetary discipline rules, as well as to tolerate more state aid to enterprises.[60] The Central Bank announced a comprehensive plan to buy public and private assets, relaunching quantitative easing. Echoing the rhetoric of Mario Draghi in 2012, the new president of the ECB, Christine Lagarde of France, said: 'There are no limits to our support for the euro.'[61] These decisions were intended to facilitate the work of states, which spent huge sums to support the economy during lockdowns.

On 20 July 2020 the Union adopted a massive recovery plan of €750 billion, later dubbed NextGenerationEU (NGEU). In unprecedented fashion, it included grants and not just loans. The negotiations were tough, due to opposition from the 'frugal' group that replaced the UK as the primary opponent to European expenditure: Austria, the Netherlands, Sweden, Denmark, and Finland. Germany was initially hesitant, but the intensity of the crisis, the impossibility of blaming anybody for it (there was no 'original sin' as with the eurozone crisis), and a judgment by the German Federal Constitutional Court casting doubt on the legality of the ECB's action, forced Angela Merkel to act in order to prevent a new existential crisis for the Union.[62] As is often the case, a first French–German agreement, adopted on 18 May, laid the groundwork for a compromise, further refined by the Commission, and later amended by the 27. The other difficulty came from Poland and Hungary, which were both led by illiberal governments, and were careful regarding the linkage between fund allocation criteria and respect for the rule of law.

This historic decision reflects a powerful European sense of solidarity, which was more easily acceptable than during the eurozone crisis, because the number of victims and the scale of the recession could not be associated with governmental incompetence. One of the first regions in Europe affected by the virus, Northern Italy, is also one of the richest. Greece had fewer casualties in proportion to Northern European countries such as the UK or Sweden. Athens was nevertheless more economically affected by the pandemic, being more dependent on activities affected by transport restrictions, such as tourism.[63] The European aid plan aimed to partially offset this injustice. This decision was particularly welcomed in Spain, a country hard hit by the epidemic. Pablo Iglesias, the co-founder of the radical left-wing Podemos Party, spoke of a turning point after the neoliberalism of the eurozone crisis. The prime minister, the socialist Pablo Sanchez, welcomed it as a new 'Marshall Plan'.[64]

The stimulus package is indeed roughly similar to the Marshall Plan in terms of scale – it is not huge, but it is significant. Its €750 billion represents 5 per cent of the Union's national wealth, and therefore less than national recovery plans, which were massive. Its redistributive effect has been important for poor countries such as Bulgaria, Greece, and Croatia, which are expected to receive more than 10 per cent of their national wealth.[65] Over €1,000 per capita was provided for some Southern European (Italy, Spain, Portugal) and Eastern European (Slovakia, Croatia) countries. Moreover, the impact of the Marshall Plan hinged both on funding and related structural reforms, such as the adoption of new production methods, and the gradual opening up to free trade. Similarly, everything will depend on the recovery plan's implementation, which is to say whether funding will be allocated to the most efficient projects.

9.3.3 A Vaccination Campaign Based on Solidarity (2021)

In a second step, the 2021 vaccination campaign was made federal, with the EU centralising the procurement and allocation of vaccines. Its approach was market-driven, as it prioritised securing lower prices by grouping orders. It was also based on *solidarity* because the distribution by the Union put all Europeans – rich and poor, those benefiting from a national vaccine (mostly Germany) and those not – on equal footing. Without this common distribution of vaccines, poor countries would probably have received much fewer vaccines, and at higher prices.

However, the EU was accused of naivety in early 2021, as London embarked on a vigorous vaccination campaign. On the continent, caution on the part of governments delayed the start of the vaccination campaign, with many doubts being expressed about vaccines created in such great haste. Brussels focused on low prices and a social approach (hence the primacy of the precautionary principle, and insistence on greater responsibility for pharmaceutical companies than what London had agreed to). In contrast, the British were more protectionist, imposing a priority clause for delivery. In other words, Europe expressed *liberty* and *solidarity*, but not *community*.

Finally, the vaccination campaign quickly gathered pace in the spring of 2021. The main obstacle was the failure by AstraZeneca, the British drugmaker, to deliver its vaccine to the EU. If the doses purchased from the UK laboratory had been delivered on time and administered, the EU vaccination rate would have been significantly higher, at 29 per cent instead of 9 per cent on 22 March 2021, albeit behind that of the UK (41 per cent at that point).[66]

9.3.4 Conclusion: A 'Hamiltonian Moment' to Create a Transfer Union?

The 2020 decision to pursue a recovery plan of €750 billion, partly based on shared debt, was hailed as a 'Hamiltonian moment' by the most enthusiastic Europeans (the expression was coined by Olaf Scholz, the German Finance Minister at the time).[67] In 1790, Alexander Hamilton, the first Secretary of the Treasury of the United States, managed to convince the thirteen federated states to pool their debt, even though their respective debt levels were very different. Frugal states in the South accepted solidarity with their spendthrift neighbours to the North in exchange for moving the capital from New York to Washington. Hamilton created a market for Treasury funds, a bank, joint tax resources, customs duties, and even a police force responsible for making these taxes effective, the US Coast Guard. But Hamilton did not conjure up financial and banking solidarity overnight: state bankruptcies remained the norm until the early twentieth century, and the US federal bank (the Federal Reserve) was not established until 1907.[68]

Paradoxically, the metaphor of the 'Hamiltonian moment' was first invoked during the eurozone crisis in 2011 to criticise a Union unable to live up to the US example.[69] By contrast, mobilisation was much faster during the Covid-19 pandemic, initially with shared debt to finance massive solidarity, and then with the joint distribution of vaccines. It took over two and a half years for the Union to solve the eurozone crisis in 2009–12 (and much longer in the Greek case), whereas during the Covid-19 pandemic, it took no more than a few weeks to suspend the rules from the Stability Pact and on state aid control, and less than five months to agree on a massive stimulus package.

However, four elements must be considered before the metaphor of a 'Hamiltonian moment' can apply. First, the overall context for public finances has remained tense. The 2021–27 budget adopted in 2020 (in connection with the NGEU recovery plan) was marked by cuts obtained by the Frugal Four. Second, the NGEU is seen as an exceptional case by the Frugals, but by others as an example to emulate in creating a large permanent European budget. Third, as with other massive European aid programmes, the problem of absorption capacity arises. The Union can only finance projects that enhance competitiveness or solidarity, including those connected to the environment. In 2023, concerns arose over Italy's capacity to propose eligible projects, with several stadium renovations deemed inappropriate.[70] Fourth, the new tax resources envisaged in 2020 have been slow to materialise despite progress. Only the Carbon Border Adjustment Mechanism and the expansion of the CO_2 emissions trading system were adopted, while the financial transaction tax was again postponed.

Since February 2022, European financial solidarity has also been clearly present during the Russo-Ukrainian War, with Union contributions helping member states provide aid to Ukrainian refugees, as well as to finance the arms effort. Here too, the debate remains open as to whether these decisions are exceptional, or a first step towards a different union (see Chapter 10).

9.4 Rising Environmental Regulation and Backlash

The solidarity dimension of public policies has acquired a growing environmental dimension worldwide. Local and visible pollution (such as smoke emanating from a chimney's factory) have long been a source of concern, but the fight against diffuse pollution (such as water pollution from small doses of pesticides) and systemic pollution (such as global warming) started only in the late twentieth century. In terms of the governance of capitalism, the challenge is both substantial (how to offset neoliberalism through effective environmental legislation?) and institutional (how to ensure implementation despite diverse national approaches?). EU environmental regulation has developed to meet these two challenges, despite strong mobilisation by opponents.[71]

9.4.1 The Growing Importance of European Legislation

On the European continent, states have chosen to partly organise their environmental policy at the EU level in order to avoid conflicting measures creating different costs for companies. They were also motivated by the limitations of international organisations, which are hampered by institutional weakness (many countries involved, unanimous decision-making, weak enforcement). By contrast, the Union relies on directly applicable federal law, the power of sanctions, and since the 1992 Maastricht Treaty, the use of qualified majority voting at the Council, as well as the co-decision procedure with the Parliament. The latter is important, as it has often served as an echo chamber for environmentalist NGOs (and their opponents).[72] Besides, since the Commission is a small body, with few officials, it must rely on NGOs to gather information on environmental issues, and to monitor the implementation of its legislation. This is why the Commission has funded part of the operating costs for the Brussels office of several environmental NGOs, as they provide expertise and report violations, especially when national authorities are complacent or ineffective.[73] For example, in several documents from 1997 to 1998 published in association with the Commission, WWF Europe documented the insufficient implementation by member states of the 1992 Habitats directive on biodiversity. Even more radical NGOs not funded by the EC/EU, such as *Greenpeace*, played an indirect role, as their national protest movements put pressure on polluters to seek a European solution.[74]

European legislation has addressed a growing number of areas, starting with air and water pollution in the 1970s, and genetically modified organisms (GMOs), asbestos, and soil pollution disruptors in the 1990s.[75] Instead of a piecemeal approach, more comprehensive legislation has emerged, notably concerning biodiversity, water pollution, and chemicals. The protection of biodiversity and the right to information were addressed by the Habitat Directive of 1992, which requires impact assessments on all flora and fauna (rather than a particular species, as with the 1979 Birds Directive).[76] It prompted member states to create a network of 'special areas of conservation' called Natura 2000, which combine economic activity and environmental preservation. In terms of water quality, the sectoral directives of the 1970s and 1980s (on bathing water, drinking water, etc.) were replaced in 2000 by a European Water Framework Directive regulating all resources and uses. States must then establish integrated water resources management programmes within a geographically coherent basin, based on the polluter pays principle. In terms of chemicals, the 2006 REACH Directive reversed the burden of proof, requiring industries to prove the safety of all chemicals used (new and old). While this law has been challenged by environmentalists for its limitations (it concerns only certain chemicals), it was nevertheless adopted after an epic battle. An environmentalist coalition composed of Northern countries (Denmark, Sweden, the Netherlands) and Environment Commissioner Margot Wallström of Sweden (1999–2004) prevailed, but had to compromise with the three biggest European countries. Tony Blair of the UK, Gerhard Schröder of Germany, and Jacques Chirac of France sent a joint letter to Commission President Romano Prodi calling for future legislation to be more lenient, in order to preserve industrial interests.[77]

European legislation sometimes involved the implementation of less restrictive international agreements. The problem of international trade in hazardous waste became obvious in the 1980s, with numerous scandals related to European waste exported to poor countries in Africa or to Turkey.[78] Some European industrial actors, faced with more costly environmental regulations at home, saw illegal exports as a convenient way to dispose of their costly waste. Media attention and political action resulted in a three-pronged effort:

internationally with the two Basel Conventions on Hazardous Waste in 1989 and 1994; at the OECD with a scientific effort to classify such waste; and finally at European level, with several texts of increasing severity regarding the traffic of waste since the 1980s. Complementarity between these various international organisations emerged, with international soft law providing political impetus, a scientific effort at the OECD, and binding legislation with the EU.

The environmental approach has impacted agriculture. CAP reforms, especially those of 1999 and 2013, have encouraged the reorientation of aid to environmentally sound programmes. But their share of total agricultural aid remains low (75 per cent of aid is still tied mainly to production), and it depends on national contexts.[79] Since its creation in 1983, the Common Fisheries Policy emphasises species conservation by establishing fishing quotas, but they remained too high to effectively prevent overfishing, especially in the first two decades.[80]

Between 1992 and today, the evolution of European environmental policy has not been straightforward. It flourished around 1990, culminating with the 1992 Rio conference and the creation of the European Environmental Agency in 1994. Then came a backlash fuelled by neoliberal activism – for instance by the conservative UK government, which drew up lists of EU legislation to be repealed or watered down, albeit without success – and by the economic crisis (notably in Germany following the difficult reunification).[81] On the other hand, green parties secured positions in government for the first time in France in 1997, and Germany in 1998.

The context became slightly more favourable in the late 2010s, with the end of the eurozone crisis (and its logic of austerity), pro-environmental mobilisation by youth (notably by the Swedish activist Greta Thunberg, who organised the Fridays for Future youth protest movement in 2018), the worsening climate crisis (with a string of heatwaves), and Brexit (which removed a major obstacle to ambitious EU legislation).[82] An early study on the consequences of Brexit shows that far from implementing the 'green Brexit' hailed by Michael Gove, the Conservative UK government has actually downgraded environmental standards.[83] Even the Pope released an Encyclical with a strong focus on environmental protection.[84] After being appointed Commission President in 2019, Ursula von der Leyen made the 'green deal' a priority in her agenda. She was supported by the increased number of green MEPS after the 2019 election. In 2020–21, the Covid-19 crisis helped demonstrate the benefits of car-free towns in terms of air quality and noise, as well as the possibility of radically expanded remote working. Implementing the Green Deal fell to commissioner Franz Timmermans. In 2020–22, he successfully passed numerous pieces of legislation involving topics such as climate change (see Section 9.5), the fight against importing products causing deforestation, and expanding the green reporting obligations of enterprises.[85]

In the early 2020s, European environmental logic even had a marginal influence on bastions of free market thinking, such as monetary policy (especially in the policy pursued by its most recent president appointed in 2019, Christine Lagarde, who was bolder in green finance than her US counterpart),[86] finance (with regulation 2020/852 on the labelling of green investments), and trade (with several pieces of legislation linking trade and environmental standards, some denounced in the US as protectionist).[87] This demonstrates the contested nature of this issue.

9.4.2 Structural Barriers to Environmental Action

Environmental protection is challenging because this *solidarity* approach to capitalism conflicts with the two other poles of the trinity, *liberty* and *community*, which accept environmental regulation only if it does not hamper growth or competitiveness. Sometimes *solidarity* and *liberty* can be combined. The adoption of stringent environmental standards can favour a company if it benefits from a competitive edge in this domain. For instance, the German government advocated stringent environmental standards for cars in the 1980s and 1990s for environmental reasons, but also because its manufacturers had a technological lead in this area.[88] Later, the German Greens supported the liberalisation of energy markets in order to encourage the emergence of new renewable energy producers that could compete with incumbents using more polluting sources of energy (oil, gas, coal, and nuclear power).[89] They even supported the Commission's 2008–09 energy market liberalisation project, which their government opposed, out of opposition to dominant companies, accused of obstructing the market entry of renewable electricity producers. The French Greens sometimes used similar arguments when they entered the parliament in 1997.

Another obstacle is the division of the left and the centre-left between the Greens and others parties striving to protect certain jobs from costly environmental measures. For example, when the Commission discussed car emission standards in 2008, the Commissioner for the Environment, Stavros Dimas, a Greek conservative who favoured stricter standards, was opposed by the Commissioner for Enterprise and Industry Günther Verheugen, a German Social Democrat eager to protect carmakers.[90] Verheugen teamed with neoliberal Commission President Barroso to limit environmental standards. Regarding energy policy, German Social Democrats have been reluctant to close coal mines, as this sector has remained important both in terms of jobs and the SPD's identity.

A major obstacle is the difficulty of generating consensus among different countries. France, for example, is virtuous in terms of its carbon emissions because of its massive use of nuclear energy, but the plants pose other environmental problems, such as the severity of potential accidents, the cost of dismantling, the risk of proliferation of fissile material, and waste management. Divergence on this issue has increased, with Germany deciding to phase out its nuclear plants after the Fukushima nuclear accident of 2011, while countries such as France, Finland, and Poland chose to relaunch nuclear energy a few years later. In 2022, the pro-nuclear coalition (mainly France, Italy, Sweden, and most members of Central and Eastern Europe) even managed to have nuclear energy labelled a green investment in the official EU classification. French officials have been presenting nuclear energy as an environmentally friendly option since the late 1980s.[91]

Last but not least, economic crisis can weaken environmental policies. The two oil shocks (1973 and 1979) had a dual effect. At first they vindicated *The Limits to Growth* report and led to policies designed to save oil. Conversely, rising unemployment fostered the rise of business-friendly measures, and discredited robust measures against pollution. The severe economic crisis of 1992 also affected the dynamic in Europe. Neoliberalism was on the rise, and appeared less detrimental to the environment than state socialism, for during the early 1990s revelations emerged of the major environmental disaster that unfolded under the communist system, driven by the regime's productivist and authoritarian nature. This environmental backlash was particularly acute in Germany due to the cost of reunification. While Bonn had green credentials, Berlin was more hesitant. The historian Frank Uekötter has pointed out that in 1995, the weekly *Der Spiegel* reported on 'environmental madness', largely because of the economic difficulties resulting from reunification, whereas its coverage of environmental issues had been more moderate in the past.[92] The 2008 economic crisis impacted environmental policy, notably in countries most affected by austerity policies such as Spain, which was forced to slash its renewable energy subsidies.[93] Still, environmental policies have not been dismantled, proving fairly resilient.[94]

Another environmental backlash began in 2023 (with prodrome in 2019, in which Dutch farmers protested potential stringent measures to cut nitrogen emissions by drastically reducing livestock farming).[95] The Russo-Ukrainian War raging since 2022 has forced Europe to reduce its energy consumption, but coal-fired power plants have been relaunched to compensate for Russian gas supplies.[96] In a gesture of solidarity, the Union has facilitated the import of cheap Ukrainian agricultural products. Surging inflation, in particular for food prices, has led to increased protests by farmers against environmental legislation in 2023–24 (the French and German protests were sparked by a planned diesel tax increase for farmers, while Eastern European farmers were more concerned about Ukrainian imports). The anti-environmental backlash has spread beyond farmers: it started in Germany in the summer of 2023 with a contested law promoting heat pumps. This has impacted the European Parliament, where the adoption of green legislation had become more difficult since late 2023. The legislation to reduce the use of pesticides was shelved by the Commission in February 2024, after its rejection by the Parliament in November 2023. The legislation on car emissions in 2023 and on biodiversity in 2024 were both watered down, while the Commission announced measures to limit environmental standards for farmers.[97] The Greens suffered a setback during the 2024 European elections, and the Commission announced further measures to water down environmental legislation in 2025. The adversarial context is compounded by the Trump administration's direct attack against environmental legislation, repeal of the IRA, attacks on the EPA, and withdrawal from the 2015 Paris Agreement.

In short, the history of environmental policy was not characterised by continuous progress towards an enlightened future, but was more like a tidal wave, with substantial mobilisation (1973, 1988–92, and 2021–23) followed by environmental backlash. These latter episodes were characterised not by sheer 'policy dismantling', as the 'green state' proved relatively resilient,[98] but by less ambitious initiatives and laxer implementation.

9.4.3 *The Role of Industrialists: From Conversion to 'Merchants of Doubt'*

In addition to these structural barriers, some industrialists have been actively undermining environmental legislation. This was not the case for all companies, such as those for which environmental regulations represented a business opportunity (for instance the catalytic converter manufacturer that benefited from the ban on lead petrol, see Chapter 4). This has been documented by historians in both the Danish and German cases, for example.[99] For others, accepting a more environmentally friendly approach was simply a public relations gesture criticised as 'greenwashing'. An extreme case is that of the 'Merchants of Doubt', American industrialists who funded false scientific counter-expertise to cast doubt on the harmful nature of their products, such as tobacco, petroleum, pesticides, and so on.[100] The historian David Proctor coined the term agnogenesis in connection with the tobacco disinformation campaign, defined as 'ignorance as a deliberately engineered and strategic ploy'.[101] It is not the absence of knowledge that explains indecision, but the profusion of contradictory expertise sowing doubt. Companies appear to have been less militant in Europe. Between 1989 and 1994, the French oil giants Total and Elf joined the campaign led by the major US oil company Exxon against the proposed European carbon tax on hydrocarbons.[102]

The adoption of lenient measures was a second strategy for industrialists to mitigate the impact of environmental legislation. Instead of a tax or pollution thresholds, governments have increasingly resorted to market-based instruments since the 1990s because the older instruments, sometimes derided as 'command-and-control' (such as standards or emissions caps) were seen as too rigid and burdensome for business. For example, rules prescribing the use of the 'best available technology' led to endless discussions between companies and regulatory authorities. By contrast, market-based instruments (referred to as 'new economic policy instruments') are more flexible, and therefore considered more efficient.[103] They include the creation of a market for polluting rights, voluntary agreements by industrial actors to reduce pollution, and labels to help consumers and creditors identify the most virtuous industrialists. The use of market-polluting rights has been promoted by economists such as William Nordhaus since the 1970s (winner of the Nobel Prize for Economics in 2018 for his work combining economics and the environment).[104] These market-based instruments are not inherently less severe than the older instruments. Many environmentalists were won over by this approach, probably out of their distrust of government (often considered to be a dangerous behemoth by many Greens). The collapse of the USSR and the ensuing revelation of environmental disaster seemed to prove that a centralised command-and-control approach did not work.

The most ardent promoters of market-based instruments were certain multinationals and the International Chamber of Commerce, which defended them from 1990 onwards when global environmental tax plans multiplied.[105] The Commission has also been interested in these market tools, as they are in keeping with what a small institution can manage. As early as 1990, an internal note criticised the old 'command-and-control' tools (thresholds, standards), instead noting that 'more market related instruments could achieve better results for the environment'.[106] In the 2010s, this movement morphed with the rise of green finance, including significant initiatives such as the world's leading investment fund BlackRock supporting the adoption of best practices in environmental, social, and corporate governance (ESG) for its investments (which drew the ire of some US Republican politicians as soon as 2022). These efforts are in keeping with the formation of the Glasgow Financial Alliance for Net Zero in 2021, a group of investors supporting the fight against climate change.

Market-based tools are not inherently good or bad for the environment. They can lead to greenwashing if the price set for pollution is too low, if green label standards are too lax, or if public authorities relinquish their responsibilities, leaving companies unregulated. For example, European car manufacturers agreed to a voluntary agreement to limit CO_2 emissions in 1998 because they feared Brussels would be pressured by the Parliament. The agreement was endorsed by the Commission in 1999.[107] However, voluntary agreements proved disappointing, and in 2008 the Commission returned to the old method of setting thresholds via legislation.

Since European institutions are weak, examples of fraud are legion. They must rely on national inspection bodies, as well as standards bodies sometimes partially funded by industry. For example, in fisheries, compliance with quotas has long been theoretical, because local authorities have sometimes turned a blind eye to overfishing.[108] In the automotive sector, Dieselgate – German carmaker Volkswagen's admission in 2015 to fraud in complying with diesel emissions standards – demonstrated the limits of EU action, especially since the fraud was discovered by US authorities (see Chapter 8). Finally, since the EU acts through directives, if member states delay the transposition of legislation into national law, or do so imperfectly, or do not conduct inspections, the standard remains ineffective. This explains the 1996 reform of the Seveso Directive on the control of hazardous industrial sites, which added the requirement of regular inspections by national authorities.

Overall, European legislation has offered greater environmental protection than in North America, whereas the opposite was true before 1990.[109] The enforcement of violations of European legislation by numerous member states (including the wealthiest) shows that European legislation brings added value, and has proven more restrictive than many national authorities.[110]

9.5 The New Paradigm of Global Warming: An Opportunity for Europe?

'Why is there no storming of the Bastille because of the environmental destruction threatening mankind, why no Red October of ecology?' asked the sociologist Ulrich Beck in 2010.[111] The fight against anthropogenic global warming has become the dominant paradigm of environmental action in the twenty-first century, but only at a slow pace. It seems surprising considering that scientific consensus has existed on human-induced global warming at the UN since the first report from the International Panel for Climate Change (IPCC) in 1990. How to account for this time-lag?

The challenge has been scientific, economic, geopolitical (in terms of North–South relations), and technical. Technical issues are particularly daunting: should the priority be CO_2 or methane, which emits more greenhouse gases, but stays in the atmosphere for a shorter period of time? The American chemist Susan Solomon, who chaired IPCC Group 1, considered this a 'Faustian dilemma'.[112] How should their interaction be managed? The ozone is beneficial at high altitude, creating a protective layer against solar rays, but harmful below. How to reconcile these new objectives with older environmental policies for air pollution? Diesel engines were favoured in the early twenty-first century because they emitted less greenhouse gases, but they also release more microparticles that are particularly harmful to health. Finally, climate change is predicated on a governance of capitalism based on numbers that are difficult to establish: how can we assess carbon sinks? How to measure the carbon imported by international trade, or the reality of carbon offsetting schemes? How can governmental declarations regarding their carbon balance be verified?

In Europe, the Union seized an opportunity to play a major role in this new area, doing so in three stages: the failure of the 1992 carbon tax; the Kyoto Protocol in 1997, complemented by the 2015 Paris Agreement, which resulted in the European Fit for 55 package; and the return of a more protectionist version of the carbon tax in 2022.

9.5.1 First Environmental Mobilisation (1992) and Ebb

The issue of anthropogenic global warming came to the fore with the 1979 Charney Report from the US National Academy of Sciences. A scientific consensus gradually emerged since the conference in Villach, Austria, organised in 1985 by the UN Environmental Programme (UNEP).[113] The UN then created the IPCC in 1988 to establish irrefutable global scientific expertise laying the foundation for collective action. The first IPCC report was issued in 1990. It stated that there has been global warming of human origin of '0.3 °C per decade in the 21st century', which indeed has proven to be the case.[114] The report was used to prepare for the 1992 United Nations Conference on the Environment in Rio.

In Europe, the Rhodes European Council held on 2–3 December 1988 recognised the importance of combating the 'greenhouse effect'. In March 1989, Western European leaders met at the Hague Conference at the initiative of Dutch Prime Minister Rudd Lubbers and Norwegian Prime Minister Gro Harlem Brundtland (who initiated the famous report on sustainable development bearing his name), with the support of French Prime Minister Michel Rocard (who had already written about CO_2 emissions in a 1987 book).[115] It recognised climate change and the crucial need for financial transfers between the North and South to ensure an energy transition. Rocard envisioned the creation of a 'new international authority' on environmental regulation to be called 'Globe'.[116]

The European Economic Community (EEC) became the framework for public action.[117] In 1989, even Margaret Thatcher's neoliberal administration considered some kind of international taxation as inevitable: 'The general Whitehall view is that some sort of environment tax (though not necessarily at the Community level – OECD would be far better) is inevitable before long.'[118] The notes emphasise 'Italian enthusiasm' for the project, on the part of Mario Ruffolo, the Italian Minister for the Environment. Ruffolo had worked as an economist at the OECD in the late 1960s, when the organisation was working, with the Club of Rome, to quantify the environmental challenge, an effort that led to *The Limits of Growth* report.[119] Finally, it was another Italian, the Commissioner for the Environment Carlo Ripa di Meana, who proposed a European carbon tax bill, and had it adopted by the Commission in 1992. On the other side of the Atlantic, in 1993 US President Bill Clinton launched – under the impetus of his Vice President Al Gore – a project for a targeted carbon tax known as the British Thermal Unit (BTU).

The proposed European carbon tax sought to impose a tax of $3 per barrel of oil to take effect in 1993, and rising to $10 in 2000, in order to reduce consumption and thereby emissions.[120] The plan was innovative because it encouraged polluters to reduce their environmental impact, all while leaving them free to use the instrument of their choice. It also provided public authorities with additional resources. Ripa di Meana, a former director of the Venice Festival, was a flamboyant personality. When member states refused to endorse his plan, he abruptly refused to participate in the 1992 Rio Summit.

The idea was difficult to promote for scientific reasons (human-induced climate change was still contested), economic reasons (putting European companies at a disadvantage internationally), and institutional reasons, as tax matters require unanimity at the EC Council. Some of the richest Northern European countries, such as Denmark and the Netherlands, supported it, whereas the poorest feared that such a tax would hinder their development (Spain rejected it). The most neoliberal, such as John Major's Britain, opposed it on principle. France and Germany had diverging positions, both welcoming the tax, but only if it excluded nuclear energy for the former, and only it if it included it for the latter. France relied on the largest network of nuclear power plants in Europe, while Germany relied – especially after reunification – on coal-fired power plants, some of which used dirty brown coal from the former GDR. At the same time, some CO_2-emitting companies mobilised to oppose the project, which quickly floundered (like the US BTU project).[121] Hence, several experts noted a 'Green backlash' in the 1990s.[122]

A few substitutes for the carbon tax survived. At EU level, a framework for taxing lorries for using certain infrastructure was adopted in 1999.[123] Some states have applied a carbon tax for heavy vehicles (Austria, Germany, etc.). Social consensus has nevertheless been difficult to build: in France, a 2008 law provided for such a tax, but was shelved in 2013 following a popular protest by the *bonnets rouges* ('red bonnets') in Brittany, an agricultural region highly dependent on road transport. A new carbon tax was proposed a few years later, but was scrapped once again after a much more massive social protest by the *gilets jaunes* (yellow vests) movement in 2018-19. The farmer protests connected to the environmental backlash in 2023-24 are also in keeping with this pattern of mobilisation against green taxation.

9.5.2 *European Leadership in Emissions Trading Schemes*

Instead of a tax, the Union used an emissions trading scheme to implement the 1997 UN Kyoto Protocol. Kyoto was a global breakthrough, the first international agreement to impose reductions in greenhouse gas emissions (CO_2, methane, etc.). Its critics noted that the CO_2 reduction targets were relatively modest (minus 33 per cent between 1990 and 2020 for the EU-27), given that industrial activity was declining in Europe (hence Europe imported products made with greenhouse gas emitted elsewhere). The most polluting companies, those situated in the former communist bloc, were shut down or replaced. Implementation was delayed until 2005, as the Protocol required the ratification of fifty-five countries representing at least 55 per cent of emissions. The US signed the Protocol under Bill Clinton, but the Republican Congress refused to approve it. His successor, George Bush, Jr, withdrew from the protocol, thereby delaying its ratification.

The protocol was also a watershed for the Union, because the US rejection boosted European leadership, and because the Kyoto Protocol was implemented by the Union, whereas each of its member states could have chosen to implement it on their own. In 2005, Brussels created an emissions trading system (ETS) for European companies to exchange emissions permits and contribute to compensation schemes.[124] However, the low price of these permits has limited its impact, as have the numerous exemptions granted (in particular at the request of Germany and countries in Central and Eastern Europe, which have remained highly dependent on coal).[125] Pro-business actors have stressed that high prices would simply lead to 'carbon leakage', which is to say the replacement of European products by non-European ones made at heavily polluting plants.

The 2015 UN Conference in Paris led to a new agreement, once again without US support, as President Trump refused to endorse it. It sought to limit global warming to 1.5 °C if possible, or 2 °C maximum, as well as to set the goal of net zero emissions by 2050. Each country must determine its own rate of emissions reduction. The recurring question of North–South solidarity was left unresolved.

To implement the Paris Agreement, the EU adopted a set of measures in 2022–23 known as the Fit for 55 package, with the objective being to reduce greenhouse gases by 55 per cent by 2030 compared with 1990 levels. It encompassed ambitious measures, such as the decision to ban petrol-powered cars by 2035 (subject to revision), the expansion of the emissions trading system to other sectors, integrating the Paris objectives into future EU trade agreements, as well as a new version of the carbon tax.

9.5.3 *The Return of a Neomercantilist Version of the Carbon Tax*

The carbon tax was eventually adopted by the Union in a completely different form as an extra levy on importing products detrimental to the environment. Instead of an internal tax, it has become a neomercantilist tool designed to protect European industry from unfair competition. It has a long history: as early as 1996, Dutch and Danish officials asked the Commission to study 'border tax adjustment' or 'eco-duties'.[126] However, its adoption was constantly delayed, as the Commission was very reluctant towards any instruments that could impair free trade until the Green Deal. To avoid the closure of its largest emitters of greenhouse gases, such as steel plants, the Union adopted the Carbon Border Adjustment Mechanism (CBAM) in 2022. The aim was to combat carbon leakage, as imports account for 28 per cent of greenhouse gas emissions.[127] The CBAM is compatible with the WTO's international free trade obligations, because it is proportionate: it imposes a levy amounting to the cost of European carbon quotas that European companies would have been required to purchase. Initially dubbed the 'carbon tax', it has become a trade 'mechanism' to ensure compliance with WTO rules, and to avoid unanimous voting at the Council (the prevailing procedure for tax-related issues). Five carbon-intensive sectors are concerned – steel, aluminium, cement, nitrogen fertilisers, and electric power generation. Revealingly, they are almost exactly the same as the 'basic sectors' targeted by the first French plan for reconstruction in 1946: despite the IT revolution, those sectors are still strategic.

Implementing the CBAM, which takes full effect in 2026, will probably be tricky. The first problem is that it only concerns raw products, not processed products. Consequently, non-European steel imported to Europe will be taxed, but not the automobile manufactured outside of Europe with this foreign steel. More generally, extending the mechanism to processed products would be complex. For example, Apple's iPhone includes components from eight different countries. For that matter, CO_2 emissions do not capture all environmentally damaging aspects, such as those relating to the potential risks of the nuclear industry, or those pertaining to heavily polluting mining operations (especially for the minerals used in electric vehicle batteries). The second problem is political, namely how to impose a trade penalty on a country without fear of retaliation? It seems unrealistic to impose such a tax on powerful countries, even if they do not have a carbon market or if their markets appear overly lax. In July 2021, Beijing protested about the Commission's recently proposed CBAM, equating it with disguised protectionism.[128] It remains to be seen whether the mechanism will actually be used, as in 2023 the World Bank identified seventy-three carbon markets or taxes worldwide, covering 23 per cent of emissions (as opposed to just 7 per cent a decade earlier).[129] African countries (such as Zimbabwe for its steel, and Mozambique for its aluminium) fear that their exports could fall victim to the CBAM, as they are too weak to deploy effective counter-measures.[130] All of the difficulties associated with the practical implementation of a European preference, already visible in the 1980s, have resurfaced. How can the production process be accurately controlled? The CBAM is nevertheless useful by its very existence, namely as a deterrent, as well as an incentive to increase the price of carbon among EU trading partners.

To conclude, the fight against global warming has emerged as a new category of public policy, one that increasingly structures the debate surrounding the governance of capitalism. Action has remained insufficient, for while the Paris Agreement set the objective of limiting warming to 1.5 °C, it seems that this threshold has already been reached in 2024.[131] Huge challenges loom, in particular the conversion of entire swaths of industry, including the electrification of the automotive sector, in which Europe must face Chinese competition, prompting calls since 2024 to delay the phasing out of fossil fuel vehicles in Europe. Europe is becoming less and less central; China has become the world's leading industrial powerhouse, including for environmentally friendly technology, as well as the largest emitter. In terms of cumulative emissions between 1850 and 2021, China ranks second behind the US, followed by Russia, Brazil, and Indonesia, with the first European country, Germany, being only sixth.[132] Lastly, the Russo-Ukrainian War has shown the aggressiveness of Russia, the major power that actually benefits from global warming (likely to increase cultivable land, and to make Siberian sea routes available).

9.6 Conclusion

The neoliberal wave was ambiguous, as the governance of European capitalism was also marked by the strengthening of its dimension of *solidarity*. Redistributive Europe has had some success in the East, with a rough equivalent to the Marshall Plan that benefited Western Europe seventy years earlier. But the neoliberal management of the eurozone crisis wiped out some of its benefits, first in the East (because Eastern Europeans countries affected by the 2007–08 crisis were not assisted), and then in the South (because EU aid came too late). Some instances of solidarity corrected previous neoliberal legislation, such as the new Posted Workers Directive, redistributive measures during the eurozone crisis, and mobilisation against certain free trade agreements. The European Parliament, whose institutional powers have grown since the 1992 Maastricht Treaty, has often been used as a springboard for socio-environmental protest movements, which have now fully integrated the European dimension within their influence strategy (unlike the weak transnational social mobilisation for the Vredeling directive in the early 1980s).

Even if the European welfare state is structurally limited by the size of the European budget, as well as by a relatively low sense of solidarity, the social field has embraced ever-broader areas, with measures pertaining to anti-discrimination, the minimum wage, and the creation of the European Labour Authority. The Covid-19 epidemic Europeanised some health policy. Envisaged in 1950 with the European Health Community, this process was limited to the creation of a common regulated market from the 1990s onwards. In the face of Covid-19, member states initially reacted with national lockdowns, and stimulus plans. The Union quickly followed, moving faster and more forcefully than during the financial crisis by suspending fiscal and competition rules, easing monetary policy, and launching a broad recovery plan. The vaccination campaign was also marked by a federal logic of solidarity, as it has allowed even the poorest Europeans to gain access to vaccines.

Environmental issues have increased in importance since most pollution is transnational in nature. The Union treated this issue by merging the *liberty* and *solidarity* approaches to capitalism, especially by using market tools believed to reconcile growth and environmental protection. At times the Union went beyond the mere logic of the 'flanking welfare state' (see Chapter 6) by providing added value to national welfare states, notably in environmental protection.

There has not been a gradual rise in social and environmental policy, but rather flows and ebbs. Multi-level mobilisation (national, European, international) on environmental protection (notably in 1973, 1988–92, and 2018–22) was followed by environmental backlash. The EU has become a global environmental leader, or at least this is how it likes to portray itself,[133] although this may perhaps be for a lack of serious competitors. After the ambitions of the late Delors period (1989–92) – such as Ripa di Meana's carbon tax project in 1992 – the tide has turned. Opponents of environmental legislation have mobilised effectively. The 'Pink Europe' of the late 1990s did not bring about changes to the European regulation of capitalism, even if national social legislation progressed in some countries. The lessons learned from the eurozone crisis, the change of Commission in 2014, and the 2015 Paris Agreement on climate change marked the return to a certain voluntarism. The adoption of the CBAM in 2022 was an attempt to balance the three poles of the trinity – *liberty*, *solidarity*, and *community*. By contrast, the strong environmental backlash that has ensued since 2023 has rekindled the association between neoliberalism and the *community* approach.

Developing solidarity capitalism on an international scale has remained fraught with pitfalls. In addition to the lack of political will (due to the weak sense of solidarity), obstacles also include economic crisis (the massive cost of reunification dented Germany's environmental credentials, while surging inflation after the 2022 Russo-Ukrainian War weakened the pro-environmental coalition), underdevelopment (the poorest states frown upon solidarity measures reducing their competitiveness advantage), and active mobilisation by opponents (campaigns by the 'Merchants of Doubt').

Finally, Brexit embodies the paradox at the core of Europe's *solidarity*-based regulation of capitalism: the working classes have largely voted to leave a Union associated with neoliberal globalisation, while British trade unions called to remain in a Union whose social legislation is considered as a safety net against Tory neoliberalism. But it was Brexit that enabled Europeans to improve the *solidarity* dimension of their capitalist governance. However, recent times have seen the return of *community* capitalism.

10

The Resurgence of the Community Approach in the Twenty-First Century

While the late twentieth century was characterised by the growing prominence of *liberty* capitalism, the second half of the 2010s has witnessed a resurgence of *community* capitalism. This trend is evident in the rise of protectionism, authoritarianism, nativism, and violent conflict. Before 2016, *community* capitalism had never entirely disappeared, but it had played a secondary role, primarily expressed through the notion of the European Union as a normative power (the 'Brussels Effect'). Changes in the international context have prompted Europe to gradually assert itself as a community, first with Brexit and the election of Trump for the first time in 2016, then during the Russo-Ukrainian War (2022–present), and more recently with the Trump II administration since 2025.

10.1 The Return of Community Capitalism in the World

The resurgence of a more assertive form of *community* capitalism has been particularly pronounced since Donald Trump's election as US President in 2016. Although *community* capitalism has always persisted, it existed in a far more subdued form prior to the mid-2010s. This resurgence is evident first in geopolitics, with the weakening of US-based liberal internationalism even before Trump's first election in 2016; second, in domestic politics, with the rise of new forms of authoritarianism promoted by China and Russia; and third, at the economic level, through an unprecedented combination of community capitalism and neoliberalism. Two events further accentuated this shift towards community capitalism: first, the Covid-19 crisis in 2020–21, and second, the second Trump administration beginning in 2025.

10.1.1 Geopolitics: The Weakening of US-Based Liberal Internationalism

Liberal internationalism sought to create a world order governed by law, freedom, and transparency rather than power relations and secret diplomacy. While liberal internationalism was never fully implemented (as shown by various forms of Western imperialism), it has nevertheless allowed the

European continent to flourish after 1945 through a rule-based liberal Atlantic order dominated by the US. The end of the Cold War revived liberal internationalism, with US President George Bush, Sr announcing a 'new world order' on 11 September 1990. Protectionist tensions between Europe and the US persisted, but remained within the framework of the liberal international system, notably through the World Trade Organization (WTO). For example, when Europeans threatened to complain to the WTO regarding two US laws in 1996 targeting companies trading with Cuba (the Helms–Burton Act) and with Iran and Libya in hydrocarbons (Amato–Kennedy law), Washington agreed to a compromise in 1998 that gradually lifted sanctions.[1]

However, the US began to lose faith in liberal internationalism. The turning point came in 2001, first with the 11 September attacks, and then with China's entry in the WTO three month later on 11 December. Initially celebrated, the event later sparked growing concern. US unilateralism expanded during the two terms of President George W. Bush, Jr, with the 2003 Iraq War being launched without the consent of the UN Security Council, and the failure to ratify both the Kyoto Protocol on climate change in 1997 and the Rome Statute of the International Criminal Court in 1998. Washington increasingly 'weaponised interdependence' by using the tools of the international liberal order to suit its geopolitical interest, such as using legal proceedings against private companies, financial regulation, or Internet regulation.[2]

The situation grew worse in 2016 with Brexit, the election of Donald J. Trump, and the US refusal to appoint new judges to the WTO's Appellate Body, thereby blocking the international legal mechanism for resolving trade disputes. From 2017 to 2021, President Trump toughened this unilateral stance. Washington withdrew from major international agreements it had previously accepted, including the Paris Climate Agreement from 2015, the Trans-Pacific Partnership Agreement (TTPA) from 2016 (not yet ratified by Congress), and the Iran Nuclear Agreement from 2015. Trump ended the North American Free Trade Area (NAFTA), which had been in force since 1994, and renegotiated it to obtain a more protectionist agreement concluded in 2018. Washington has imposed broad punitive tariffs on China, as well as on its Western partners in a more limited manner. President Trump's ambiguous stance towards Russia, as well as his vehement criticism of NATO, even cast doubt on the US commitment to defending the liberal West. President Joseph R. Biden (2021–25) re-established a more cooperative policy, but doubts remain about US leadership, especially after the reelection of Donald Trump in 2024.

A movement of 'slowbalisation' – a term coined by Adjieedj Bakas in 2015 – apparently brought an end to the inexorable rise of globalisation. Trade as a share of GDP grew from 39 per cent in 1990 to 61 per cent in 2008, before declining to around 55 per cent.[3] Foreign direct investment has undergone the same negative trend after peaking in 2014–15, especially in China. With the supply difficulties revealed by the China–US trade conflict and the Covid-19 pandemic, the trend in the 2020s has been towards 'de-risking', 'reshoring', or 'friend-shoring', which is to say transferring (or duplicating) major plants outside of China in friendlier southern countries.

Three driving forces of liberal globalisation seem to be coming to an end. First, the US no longer supports it. Second, from a technological point of view, the price of transport is no longer decreasing, especially due to more stringent environmental standards. Third, in terms of regulation, the more obvious barriers to trade, such as customs duties, have already been largely removed. Non-tariff barriers such as social, environmental, and health standards remain, and are much more difficult to harmonise. Besides, there is no global will to promote international high standards in this realm, even in the Global South.

In fact, the Global South has partly filled the vacuum left by the US. The Global South denotes the emergence of non-Western superpowers, but not a homogeneous camp. These countries are nevertheless united by a willingness to move beyond the old US-led world order. In the wake of the 2007–08 financial crisis, the G20 replaced the G7 for a time. Since 2009, non-Western powers have pursued the BRICs format (initially with Brazil, Russia, India, China, and since 2010 South Africa). The group was further enlarged in 2023. For certain members, notably Russia and China, the BRICS framework adopts an explicitly anti-Western stance, whereas for others, such as Brazil and India, it maintains a neutral position. Similarly, the Trans-Pacific Partnership refused by Washington was replaced by a new treaty in 2018, the Comprehensive and Progressive Agreement for Trans-Pacific Partnership (CPTPP), but without China. Reconnecting with an ancestral tradition based on a China-centred worldview,[4] Beijing has proposed its own regional organisations, such as the Shanghai Cooperation Organisation with Russia and Central Asian countries (2001), the One Belt One Road Initiative (2013), the Asian Infrastructure Investment Bank (AIIB, 2014), and an alternative payment system to the Western Swift. China has also supported the expanded use of the renminbi in international trade. It took advantage of Donald Trump's rejection of the TTPA to propose a new one, the Regional Comprehensive Economic Partnership (RCEP) signed in 2020, which associates China with ASEAN, along with close US allies such as Japan and Australia. This agreement is less comprehensive than the EU's Single Market, but it nevertheless facilitates trade by harmonising certain customs barriers, tariffs, and rules of origin, thereby strengthening China's role in Asian production chains (and thwarting 'reshoring'). China has also requested to join the Comprehensive and Progressive Agreement for Trans-Pacific Partnership (CPTPP), a more ambitious Asian trade agreement than the RCEP. It includes non-Asian Western countries such as Canada and Australia. The UK was one of the first non-Pacific states to declare its interest in participating in the capital of the AIIB, and even, in the post-Brexit context of 2021, acceding to the CPTPP.[5]

Another manifestation of the rise of the Global South is the resilience of Russia despite massive sanctions imposed by the West in 2022 following its attack on Ukraine. Moscow have been able to skirt Western sanctions by trading with non-Western countries, notably China and India. Many Western technological components whose export to Russia was forbidden by the West found their way to Moscow through friendly third countries.

In short, US-based liberal internationalism has sharply declined, primarily because of US unilateralism, but also thanks to the rise of an alternative to the Western world order. This is visible not only in geopolitics, but also in political institutions.

10.1.2 Internal Politics: The Rise of Illiberal Nationalism in China, Russia, and the West

Nationalism is a normal phenomenon for expressing the strength and ambition of a community. It can be associated with a certain degree of liberalism, as was the case in nineteenth-century Europe when national movements were often (but not always) combined with the democratic movement. But since the 2010s, nationalism has undergone a radicalisation. It has often been nicknamed as 'illiberal' for its disregard of the rule of law, and the emphasis on displays of brute force. Even liberal democracies have been exposed to the rising influence of illiberal demagogues, namely politicians eager to tinker with the election process (with new tools such as fake news on social media), and to then claim that their election prevails over any counterbalancing powers (such as parliaments, courts, international organisations, the media, etc.). Since political liberalism is predicated on a balance of power designed to prevent any form of authoritarian drift, such political practice is designated by the term 'illiberalism'.[6]

The combination of moderate *community* capitalism and progressive liberalisation was the path largely followed after 1945 by Japan, and later by South Korea and Taiwan. After adopting *community* capitalism to launch their industries (with protectionism and government subsidies), these countries gradually accepted more liberal rules, both economically and politically, with Japan becoming a democracy in 1945, South Korea in 1987, and Taiwan a few years later.

On the contrary, China has practised a less liberal and more nationalistic form of neomercantilism since 1979. Unlike other emerging countries, its size (with massive reserves of raw materials), political clout (a permanent member of the UN Security Council and a nuclear power), and effective economic reforms (it has massively reduced poverty since 1979) have allowed it to control its relationship to globalisation. The country bears the memory of a self-centred world – with its very name meaning 'Middle Country' in Chinese – as well as a period of Western and Japanese humiliation from 1842 to 1949. After the Maoist

10.1 THE RETURN OF COMMUNITY CAPITALISM 241

period, Deng Xiaoping imposed a different path based on stability in 1979, combining gradual openness to liberal capitalism and preservation of the communist dictatorship.[7] China resisted political liberalisation, but continued its process of freeing markets progressively, enjoying the implicit support of the Americans, who believed that Chinese democratisation was inevitable. For example the US secretary of state James Baker wanted to convince his Chinese interlocutors in 1991 that 'political change will inevitably be stimulated by [their] economic successes'.[8]

Any essentialism regarding the incompatibility between Chinese culture and liberal democratic values should be avoided. In the past, many decision makers tried to reconcile the two, especially during the May Fourth Movement (1919), and with figures such as Sun Yat-sen. In 1948, when the Universal Declaration of Human Rights was negotiated at the United Nations, it was the Chinese delegate Peng Chun Chang, a philosopher eager to build a bridge between the European Enlightenment and Confucianism, who influenced its drafting by inserting the notion of 'consciousness'.[9]

The reforms implemented since 1979 have combined progressive openness to free trade for goods with the preservation of numerous internal barriers. Initially, foreign investment had to be made in association with a Chinese company, and all production exported. The Chinese domestic market subsequently remained closed, in order to allow for the gradual adaptation of the Chinese economic fabric, which slowly opened up to private property and competition. Even after China joined the WTO in 2001, its radical form of *community* capitalism continued through the impossibility of acquiring Chinese companies, the obligation for foreign companies to partner with Chinese firms, the continuing risk of intellectual property theft, the inaccessibility of government procurement, and state control of the currency. In less than a decade, China has become the world's largest exporter and second largest economy. It was further strengthened by the 2007 economic crisis, which affected the West to a greater extent. The rise of the domestic market has further reinforced China's growth. The Middle Kingdom now has its multinational equivalents to North America's GAFA (Baidu for Google, Alibaba for Amazon, Huawei for Apple and Microsoft, Tencent for various web services), is a world leader in green energy, and offers its citizens better services than Washington in terms of electronic payment and high-speed trains.

Xi Jinping, who rose to power in 2012, reinforced the illiberal approach internally. Externally, the One Road One Belt Initiative (2013) – with its major loans and dispute mechanism based on Chinese standards – helped project Chinese influence. It has even appealed to EU countries, in both the East (Hungary, Poland, Bulgaria) and the South (Greece, Italy). To comply with EU austerity measures, Greece had to sell part of the Port of Piraeus to Chinese investors in two stages: a partial stake in 2008 at the beginning of the financial crisis, and a majority stake in 2016 at the end of the eurozone crisis. Soon after,

Athens blocked an EU position condemning Beijing's conduct in the South China Sea, and its record on human rights.[10] In 2014, thanks to a large scholarship programme, the number of African students studying in China surpassed the number studying in the US.[11] China's presence in Africa is also reflected through its participation in international counter-piracy operations off Djibouti, where Beijing established its first permanent military base abroad in 2017. President Trump's unilateral policy (2017–21, and since 2025) allowed Xi Jinping to present himself as a defender of multilateralism.

Russia is a second player challenging the US-centric liberal order, through an illiberal nationalism that combines economic neomercantilism with political authoritarianism. Russian revisionism feeds on the trauma of the 1990s, including the loss of 22 per cent of its territory after the fall of the USSR. The transition from communism to capitalism has been destructive, marked by hyperinflation, financial dependence, and the enrichment of a small minority of oligarchs. The traumatised Russian population has faced declining life expectancy. Both the population and national wealth have been halved between the USSR in 1991, and Russia in 2018.

Vladimir Putin's rise to power in late 1999 benefited from an economic recovery fuelled by rising oil prices (in contrast to China, which relied on an industrialisation strategy). Without being as harsh as China's, the Russian regime has become more authoritarian and chauvinistic (especially in terms of women and LGBT rights). From a geopolitical point of view, President Putin has pursued a more aggressive policy since 2007, including military interventions in Georgia (2008) and Ukraine (2014, 2022 to present), as well as a covert operation to influence elections in the West through the World Wide Web.[12]

The rise of China and Russia is part of the global trend of illiberalism. The share of the world's population living in autocracies rose from 46 per cent in 2012 to 72 per cent in 2021.[13] Even in the US, a failed coup occurred on 6 January 2021 to reverse the results of the presidential election. Two years later, the same phenomenon happened when the illiberal Brazilian president Jair Bolsonaro lost the election to Luiz Inácio Lula da Silva. Even within the Union, this turn towards a more illiberal nationalism has had some success since the 2010s, such as in Poland under the Law and Justice Party government from 2015 to 2023, and in Hungary under Viktor Orbán since 2010. These parties are openly hostile to liberal developments in politics and society, such as pluralism, an independent judiciary, and rights for sexual minorities. They conceive of immigration as a threat, especially since the crisis of 2015. The rule of law is undermined by legislation weakening the separation of powers, and creating tensions with the Union.

Hungary represents the most successful case of illiberalism, a term claimed by its leader Orbán, who has cited Singapore, Turkey, Russia, and China as examples.[14] His approach stems from a sense of historical injustice, in this case the Treaty of Trianon of 1920, which significantly reduced Hungarian territory (formerly part of the Austro-Hungarian Empire). Orbán, the Prime Minister since 2010, has pursued a policy of systematic concentration of power, coupled with strong criticism of liberal internationalist actors. This led to the Central European University moving from Budapest to Vienna in 2018. During an election speech in February 2019, he stated that 'Brussels bureaucrats' wanted to encourage non-Christian immigration in order to overwhelm the historical inhabitants of the Pannonian plain. Since 2025, US President Trump has played a prominent role to encourage illiberal leaders, including Viktor Orbán.

10.1.3 Economy: The Alliance between Community Capitalism and Neoliberalism

The recent developments of *community*-based capitalism have sometimes translated into an original combination with neoliberalism. During his first term (2017–21), US President Donald J. Trump simultaneously practised a highly protectionist and neoliberal economic policy, marked by tax cuts for the rich, an offensive against Obamacare – social security for the poor – and the elimination of many environmental legislation. A study carried out in May 2020, at the very beginning of the Covid-19 pandemic and after three years of the Trump administration, identified approximately 100 environmental measures that were cancelled.[15] The Reagan presidency (1981–89) was also marked by a combination of a neoliberalism (lower taxes, especially for the wealthy, etc.) and protectionism (the conflict with Europeans over steel), but with less intensity and more respect for its Atlantic partners. Reagan was a bulwark against the USSR, whereas Trump has constantly impaired the Atlantic alliance.

The second Trump administration (since 2025) has pursued a similar approach, exhibiting an even more aggressive vision that combines neoliberalism and nationalism. Neoliberal reforms have manifested in an unprecedented and early assault on the welfare state, notably through the dismantling of the US Aid Agency, the financial cuts to the Environmental Protection Agency, and the termination of numerous research projects. *Community* capitalism has emerged in the form of protectionist measures, as during Trump's first term, but also through territorial claims (against Panama, Canada, and Denmark) and strategic collaboration with digital corporations to consolidate political power.

Outside the Western world, this combination was also illustrated by some nationalist leaders elected in the 2010s. In Brazil, Jair Bolsonaro allowed massive development of the Amazon rainforest at the expense of both the environment and the local population. In India, some radical Hindu leaders took advantage of the Covid-19 outbreak to suspend many social laws (on working conditions and the role of trade unions).[16]

Even in Europe, *community* capitalism has sometimes been combined with neoliberalism, especially in Orbán's Hungary. In 2018, he passed a law allowing companies to impose overtime but to pay for it at a later time, prompting opponents to call it a 'slave law'.[17] More generally, his strategy of economic development is based on an aggressive search for FDI, primarily via massive subsidies to companies, including those from authoritarian countries: Hungary will be the first country to host a Chinese factory producing electric-powered cars, thanks to massive government support. As of June 2023, Hungary was the EU country with the highest share of state aid relative to GDP (under the Temporary Crisis and Transition Framework created in reaction to the Russo-Ukrainian War).[18] Orbán has also waged an aggressive anti-immigrant policy. The link between neoliberalism and *community* capitalism is also visible in the sequence of events: it was the detrimental consequences of high neoliberalism, especially the eurozone crisis (Chapter 9), that brought far-right and far-left parties to power, which often tend to opt for protectionism. More generally, far-right parties at the European Parliament (which received a sizeable share of the vote during the 2024 elections) usually oppose *solidarity* capitalism, with most refusing any social and environmental measures. In particular, far-right parties (among others) have fed the European environmental backlash (since 2023), and converted it into a broader opposition towards norms and standards.[19] While some standards may have less impact, others are essential to protecting the weak. In short, most far-right parties promote a nationalistic form of *community*-based capitalism, with restrictive immigration in particular, combined with opposition to a *solidarity*-based approach at the European level. If this vision is implemented, it could lead to the return of a free trade area, in other words a minimalistic European organisation devoted exclusively to the basic promotion of trade.

10.1.4 The Covid-19 Crisis as a Reassertion of State Intervention (2020–21)

The Covid-19 epidemic (2020–21) triggered an unprecedented form of state dirigisme through massive subsidies for companies and individuals affected by lockdowns. The notion of a lockdown is based on curtailing liberty of movement. The epidemic also laid bare vaccine nationalism, as major producers of vaccines and medical equipment such as the US (as of December 2020) and India (in March 2021) limited these strategic products exclusively to their populations.[20] Conversely, China and Russia massively distributed their vaccines to friendly countries – despite doubts surrounding their effectiveness (they were not subject to the traditional international verification process) – with a view to boosting their international influence.

Neoliberal globalisation was challenged by the pandemic, which appears to have originated from unregulated business practices such as live animal markets in China, and to have spread via global trading channels. The first area affected in Europe was Northern Italy, one of the continent's richest and most connected regions, probably through an employee of a multinational whose colleagues returned from China.

Dependence on China became starkly obvious: the Middle Kingdom produced 42 per cent of global exports for protective medical equipment in 2018,[21] and approximately 40 per cent of the antibiotics imported by Germany, France, and Italy. Meanwhile, US export restrictions on all vaccine components have disrupted production lines around the world. A debate subsequently emerged in Brussels in 2020: Josep Borrell, a Spanish socialist and Vice-President of the European Commission, and Bernd Lange, a German Social Democrat and Chairman of the Parliament's Committee on International Trade, considered the possibility of encouraging companies to relocate some strategic production to Europe.[22]

10.1.5 The Second Trump Presidency as the Final Blow to Liberal Internationalism

The return to power of Donald J. Trump in 2025 has precipitated a more forceful challenge to liberal internationalism. Beyond the predictable step of withdrawing from the 2015 Paris Agreement on climate change, the second Trump administration went further by making aggressive territorial claims against US allies, including Panama, Greenland, and even Canada. This level of assertiveness is unprecedented at least since the era of President William McKinley (1897–1901), whom Trump referenced in his inaugural address, and his immediate successor, Theodore Roosevelt (1901–09). These two presidents expanded US territorial holdings, incorporating regions such as the Philippines, Hawaii, and others.

In terms of trade, following a series of highly unbalanced trade agreements concluded in July 2025, the average US tariff is estimated to have risen to 18 per cent – eight times its level prior to the Trump II administration. This new system could be interpreted as a revival of 'imperial preference', as it is heavily skewed in favour of the United States, at least in the short term (without accounting for the potential effects of higher tariffs on inflation and productivity). In July 2025, several of the United States' most steadfast allies – including Japan, the United Kingdom, and the European Union – were compelled to sign agreements under which they accepted unilateral increases of 10–15 per cent in US tariffs on most goods (with certain exemptions), without any compensation or retaliatory measures, alongside unilateral reductions in tariffs on US-imported goods. Furthermore, the President of the European Commission, Ursula von der Leyen, was obliged to commit to purchasing $750 billion of US energy and to investing $600 billion in the United States. It remains uncertain whether this agreement will be fully implemented, as the Commission lacked the authority to mandate private investment.[23]

Europeans were compelled to accept such a severe agreement for three reasons: first, the EU ran a trade surplus with the United States, making the threat of even higher US tariffs in the absence of an agreement credible; second, the US had already concluded agreements with other partners (Japan and the United Kingdom) before engaging the EU, raising the risk of European isolation; and third, without a tariff agreement, Europeans feared that Washington might withdraw its support for Ukraine. This exemplifies a characteristic feature of the post-liberal international order: since international law carries limited weight, all issues are deeply interconnected. Trade matters are not governed solely by trade law and the WTO, but by global bargains encompassing multiple domains. Consequently, the implementation of certain EU legislation that might be perceived as adversarial towards the United States – such as the Digital Markets and Services Acts (DMA-DSA), the environmental and social regulations of multinationals, or the Carbon Border Adjustment Mechanism (CBAM) – is jeopardised by the assertiveness of the Trump administration, and are sometimes even targeted explicitly in the EU–US trade deal concluded on 21 August 2025.[24]

This policy is unprecedented in US history since the 1930s with respect to tariffs, and since the late nineteenth century in terms of territorial threats between liberal democracies. The assault on international norms has further strengthened China's role on the global stage. Following the tariff war initiated by US President Trump in 2025, the possibility of the European Union joining the Asia-centred Comprehensive and Progressive Agreement for Trans-Pacific Partnership (CPTPP) was raised.[25] If realised, the regulatory centre for international trade could shift from Brussels and Washington to Asia. More generally, traditional US allies, including European countries, Japan, and South Korea, would be less inclined to comply with US demands in the future and more likely to explore alternative measures for self-defence, potentially including nuclear capabilities. In response to this resurgence of *community* capitalism, Europe has endeavoured to reinvent itself.

10.2 A Liberal Form of Community Capitalism: Europe as a Normative Power

Structurally marked by a rules-based pacifist and multilateral logic, the Union has never developed a strong protectionist policy (with exceptions such as the early CAP), hence the failure of European industrial policies, and the success of a residual and liberal neomercantilism establishing Europe as a normative power.

10.2.1 *The Failure of European Industrial Policies*

Industrial policies have never been Europeanised due to the difficulty of defining the concept of European preference, the problem of fair return, opposition to the delegation of power, and little motivation from exporting states (which do not see the need for it). As a result, only a minimalist horizontal approach has prevailed, with the only European tools being subsidies for non-competitive research, environmental protection, and venture capital (notably through the European Investment Bank).[26]

This minimalistic approach was dominant during the period of 'high neoliberalism': European did not wage a comprehensive policy to support their solar panel industry, which was crushed by Chinese subsidies. The situation is even worse now, as China has emerged as a major competitor in all sectors where Europeans enjoyed a competitive edge, including information technology and even cars. China was a net importer of cars in 2020, but in 2023 it became the world largest exporter thanks to the electric vehicle revolution.[27] The Letta and Draghi reports from 2024 clearly underline Europe's lost competitive edge in industry, and call for more assertive (but not dirigiste) European industrial strategy.

European companies are logically the target of non-Western takeovers. In the automotive sector, the Indian company Tata purchased Jaguar and Land Rover in 2008, the jewels of the former colonial metropole, while the Chinese company Geely took over the Swedish company Volvo in 2010. In the steel industry, the Indian companies Mittal and Tata respectively bought Arcelor and Corus in 2006, the two European champions.[28] Even in the football industry, Abu Dhabi bought Manchester City club in 2008, while Qatar bought PSG in 2011. Of course, most of these companies stayed in Europe (football clubs cannot be offshored), but their leadership have moved outside of the Western world, making it more difficult for political leaders and the people they represent to exert influence over them.

In the international arena, European countries have been divided against China, with Southern countries willing to attract Chinese investment after the shock of the eurozone crisis. They have also been divided against Russia, especially before the Russo-Ukrainian War. In 2005, Gerhard Schröder's Germany chose to build the Nord Stream pipeline with Putin's Russia, at the risk of weakening Poland and Ukraine (Moscow could henceforth pressure these two countries by limiting their gas supplies while continuing to supply Western Europe). The building of North Stream 2 started in 2018, after Russia's invasion of Crimea. It was interrupted only by Russia's full-scale war against Ukraine. Lesser-known examples abound. For example, Cyprus tried to solve its banking crisis with Russian aid in 2013, before accepting the European bailout.[29] In Ukraine, the EU entered into an ambitious trade partnership in 2013, which some Europeans (especially in Poland) explicitly saw as a project to reverse Russian influence. But when the country needed financial assistance in 2013, the EU did not provide it. According to the historian Adam Tooze, this was one of the many elements that triggered the Orange Revolution of 2014, as it prompted Ukrainian President Viktor Yanukovych to hesitate between Moscow and Brussels.[30] Kiev obtained more emergency aid only after the Russian invasion of Crimea and Donbas. Finally, as in the eurozone crisis, the Union was obliged to lend more than it initially planned, because it had waited too long. The Union has confined itself to a liberal strategy based on commercial attraction, rejecting the *solidarity* and *community* approaches for wielding international influence.

10.2.2 The Persistence of National Champions and the Difficult Emergence of European Champions

National industrial policies have remained prevalent. This strategy has sometimes been associated with a Europeanisation of companies, but not always. Since US companies retain a competitive edge in many sectors, European firms often prefer to partner with them than with their European competitors. For example, a 2020 European study on R&D in Artificial Intelligence shows that European actors were involved in cooperation with non-European actors much more often than their US and Chinese counterparts.[31]

National champions have nevertheless proven resistant, pursuing one of two strategies. The Germans have adopted a low profile, with most German companies remaining untouched by foreign takeovers, a sign of the resilience of its *community* capitalism model, for they have been protected by a dense network of long-term financial participation, and special rules limiting foreign ownership (for example the 50+1 rule of the Bundesliga).

France has adopted a more visible stance in defending its national champions, using state intervention to protect against foreign takeovers, encourage mergers, and rescue strategic companies in the name of 'economic patriotism'.[32] In 2014, the government acquired a stake in the capital of Peugeot SA (PSA) to bolster the large car manufacturer, which had been weakened by the financial crisis. At the time, all governments were intervening massively to save their industries, including the US and Germany in the automotive (GM and Opel) and banking sectors. The European Commission acted to limit the German aid granted to Opel in 2009.[33] However, France kept its stake in Peugeot (now Stellantis), while Washington quickly sold off its stake. In Germany, the federal state of Lower Saxony still owns 12 per cent of the Volkswagen company (after long owning 20 per cent), while the French state owns 15 per cent of Renault. This public support may have helped both companies flourish and expand in Eastern Europe, where Volkswagen bought the Czech company Skoda, and Renault the Romanian company Dacia.

Some firms have constituted true European champions, in the sense that it is impossible to link them to a single state. The founding of the steel giant Arcelor from the French, Luxembourg, and Spanish steel industries in 2002 represented one such instance, but it was taken over by the Indian company Mittal in 2006. STMicrolectronics is a French–Italian semiconductor manufacturer that was once among the world's leaders (reaching the top five in 2001), and remains a mid-sized multinational. It benefited from European support in the late 1980s and 1990s (Eureka funding and an anti-dumping procedure against Japan), as well as from Brussels's tolerance of French and Italian state aid in the early 1990s.[34] The most emblematic European champion remains Airbus, formed in 1999 as the European Aeronautic Defence and Space Company (EADS), which combined the French Aerospace company Aerospatiale-Matra and the German DASA, with a smaller contribution from the Spanish CASA. It became Airbus Group in 2014. The French, German, and Spanish states still have a minority share in the capital, and a right to scrutinise many strategic decisions. Regular French–German bickering over Airbus shows that national governments never completely abandoned these strategic sectors. The refusal by the German government to let the Italian Bank Unicredit buy Commerzbank in 2024–25 is also telling. In the end, these examples confirm the lack of European industrial policy.

10.2.3 Europe's Normative Power: The 'Brussels Effect'

It is as a normative power that the Union has pursued a form of liberal neomercantilism.[35] Brussels has promoted its standards globally since the 1980s, moving from being a 'standard-taker' to a 'standard-maker' (see Chapter 6). The EU benefited from the establishment of the Single Market in 1993, and from its expansion to an ever-increasing number of countries. It also benefited from the fact that the Single Market is, to a certain extent, more integrated with respect to standards than other large national markets, such as the US and India. This provides a strong incentive for multinationals to promote European standards globally. European norms also have the advantage of being compromises struck between countries with different approaches, thereby making them more likely to be adopted by a wide range of countries.

The notion of the Brussels Effect was coined in 2020 by Anu Bradford, who documented cases where Brussels legislation influenced global standards in competition policy, digital technology, health, safety, and environmental protection.[36] In the digital sector, the Personal Data Protection Directive (Directive 95/46) in 1994, and the General Data Protection Regulation (GDPR, Directive 2016/679) in 1996, imposed new standards for protecting personal data. They influenced certain international laws, forcing US technology multinationals to comply with them. More recently, the 2023 Digital Markets Act (DMA) and Digital Services Act (DSA), have further strengthened this dynamic (see Chapter 8). The 2024 Artificial Intelligence Act (AI Act) is one of the first comprehensive laws setting international standards on AI, adopting a risk-based approach.

This assertion of Europe as a community of interest is based on a mix between *liberty* and *community* capitalism. The GDPR, DSA, and AI Act regulate the Internet with a view to promoting the rights of individuals.

They are predicated on the principle of non-discrimination, as European actors are subject to the same rules as non-European ones. They do not seek to protect European industry, in contrast to the Chinese 'state-driven model' and even the US 'market-driven' one (since US firms dominate the market).[37] The European model itself has been disputed. During the DMA-DSA negotiations (2020–22), Northern European prime ministers and the Danish Commissioner Margarethe Vestager have defined digital sovereignty as the ability to monitor the market rather than steer it, while the French Commissioner for Internal Market, Thierry Breton, has emphasised relocating production to Europe.[38]

Europe's normative power has also been strengthened by constant dialogue with the US, structured in particular by the first agreement in 1991 regarding cooperation in competition policy, and later by agreement in 2000 (International Safe Harbour Privacy Principles) on transatlantic data transfer, even if they were later invalidated by the Court of Justice of the European Union. The Union and the US Biden Administration (2021–25) also set up a Trade and Technology Council in 2021 to avoid wide legislative divergence.

Finally in agriculture, Southern European countries (France, Italy, Spain, Portugal, and Greece) secured protections for designations of origin from the Union in 1992, despite opposition from some countries in the North (the UK, Denmark), which saw them as unwelcome protectionism.[39] These standards combine food quality and geographical location, thereby bringing together market-based rules (the standard improves market information), social and environmental concerns (product quality), and the protection of local communities.

This European normative power is reflected in the free trade agreements of the twenty-first century, which henceforth primarily concern non-customs barriers to trade, since tariffs have already been significantly reduced. The EU–Canada Comprehensive and Economic Trade Agreement (CETA) concluded in 2016 reflects this dual dynamic. It offers export opportunities for Europe – through the protection of controlled designations of origin in the agricultural and food sector – reduced customs protection, and access to Canadian public procurement markets. Such an agreement entails broad regulatory convergence and confidence in the partner's ability to implement common rules. For instance, Canadians allow GMOs and antibiotics in certain animal products, which is forbidden in the EU. This implies that Ottawa must control the application of certain EU standards for Canadian products exported to the EU. As usual, much will depend on the agreement's implementation. On the whole, European normative power is the manifestation of a moderate form of *community* capitalism, one that is fully compatible with liberal internationalism.

Recently, the 'Brussels Effect' has been challenged by a reactionary 'Washington Effect', promoting regressive norms. In 2025, the second

Trump administration launched attacks on diversity and inclusion programmes, at times threatening European companies operating in Europe to abandon such practices.[40] The EU–US trade agreement of August 2025 explicitly addresses several landmark pieces of legislation concerning socio-environmental and information technology regulation. Moreover, amid concerns that Europe may be sidelined in the artificial intelligence (AI) race, European experts are increasingly focused on resolving the trade-offs between, on the one hand, safeguarding privacy and freedom of speech – as embodied in the GDPR, DSA, and AI Act – and, on the other hand, promoting European competitiveness.[41] Consequently, the 'Brussels Effect' can no longer be taken for granted.

10.3 A More Assertive Europe since 2016

Even before the Russo-Ukrainian War, the idea of creating a more assertive Europe has returned to the fore since 2016, which saw Brexit and the election of Donald Trump. This move is particularly visible in four areas: international trade, tolerance towards revived national protectionism in Europe, and a bolder approach with respect to industry as well as foreign and defence policy.

10.3.1 The Reaction to Global Protectionist Tensions

The return of community capitalism in a more aggressive form has been embodied primarily by the trade wars of President Trump (2017–21, 2025–), and by China's unprecedented domination of world markets thanks to a bold neomercantilist policy and to its sheer geopolitical clout.[42] The 'Chinese challenge' is therefore much more dangerous for European industries than the 'Japanese challenge' of the 1980s or even the 'American challenge' of the 1960s.

The Union's first collective response was to defend liberal internationalism. In 1920, Europe saved the Wilsonian project of the League of Nations by supporting the new organisation, which its primary promoter, the US, had ultimately rejected.[43] A century later, as a peaceful law-abiding actor, the Union has an interest in safeguarding the legal regulation of globalisation. The first response from Europeans was to respond to the trade offensive by relying on EU and WTO legal procedures.

The second approach was to compensate for the US leadership deficit by strengthening existing global institutions, such as the WTO or NATO, in the face of Washington's vacillation. The 2015 Paris climate agreement was preserved, and the retreat of the US did not prompt any further departures. The multilateral framework of international law was prioritised to avoid escalation, thereby facilitating the return of the US to more cooperative practices under President Joseph R. Biden (2021–25). Finally, the Union has sought to strengthen free trade by concluding new agreements, linking the elimination of trade barriers to regulatory convergence, notably with Canada (CETA, 2016), Japan (2018) and Mercosur (2024, pending confirmation). An agreement was even reached with China in late 2020, under the German presidency of the EU, on investment-related issues, although its implementation has been blocked by protests on human rights.

The Union's third response was to strengthen its commercial arsenal. Many laws have been adopted since 2018 to strengthen anti-dumping legislation (2018), control foreign investment (2019), ease export restrictions (2020) and trade sanctions (2021), promote reciprocity in opening up public procurement (2022), consider distorting foreign subsidies in competition cases (2022), and tax some polluting imports (2023 with the Carbon Border Adjustment Mechanism or CBAM, see Chapter 9). Most of these laws had been debated for a long time. Reciprocity in opening up public contracts was requested in 1984 in the Albert–Ball Report in connection with the debates on the Common Market.[44] The current International Procurement Instrument (IPI) regulation was proposed in 2012, but adopted only in 2022. It introduced a supranational procedure, enabling the Commission to investigate serious and recurring restrictions on access to the public procurement contracts of a third country. Similarly, the distortive Foreign Subsidy Regulation adopted in 2022 stipulates that the Commission can take foreign subsidies into account when applying competition policy, and therefore in its assessments of mergers, cartels, and public procurement. In 1988–89, French officials (notably Jean-Claude Trichet, the future President of the European Central Bank, who at the time was the Director of the French Treasury) requested that foreign competition be taken into account when the first regulation empowering the Commission to control mergers was negotiated.[45] However, it was adopted in 1989 without the French provision, which was seen as overly protectionist at the time. Lastly, the CBAM is partly inspired by the carbon tax adopted by the Commission in 1992.

These European protectionist tools should be put into perspective, for everything ultimately depends on how the Europeans will apply these measures especially as they face unprecedented protectionist threats from 2025 onward —from the United States, with its unilateral tariff war, and from China, with its restrictions on critical-mineral exports. Will the Europeans be willing and able to assertively defend European interests at the risk of countervailing measures?

10.3.2 Tolerating the Return of National Protectionism

National protectionist temptations reappeared in the West during the financial crisis (2008–12). All governments, even the most ardent advocates of free trade in Washington, London, and Berlin, granted massive aid to their struggling companies, with no European coordination other than regulatory tolerance. In Brussels, the Commission temporarily suspended its restrictive rules on state aid control. The Covid-19 crisis (2020–21) once again prompted the

10.3 A MORE ASSERTIVE EUROPE SINCE 2016

Commission to tolerate state aid to industry on an exceptional basis. The Russo-Ukrainian War that broke out in February 2022 forced the Commission to renew its lenient stance towards aid to industry, especially due to sharply increasing energy costs.

The more protectionist international context forced even the most ardent zealots of free trade, such as the Germans, to evolve. Following China's acquisition of German companies operating advanced technologies (notably Kuka, taken over by the Chinese Midea Group in 2016), the German government became more concerned. In 2016, the Minister of Economic Affairs, Sigmar Gabriel, blocked China's acquisition of two companies producing electrical and electronic equipment, Aixtron and Ledvance.[46] In 2019, following Commissioner Vestager's refusal of the merger between the French Alstom and the German Siemens, the French and German economic ministers, Bruno Lemaire and Peter Altmeier, issued a joint memorandum calling for a European industrial policy. It encapsulated two old French demands previously rebuffed by the Germans: reciprocity in opening up public procurement, and modifying competition policy to take account of international competition. Paris and Berlin believed that the Alstom–Siemens merger was rejected because of an underestimation of Chinese rail competition. Both countries also requested protection against certain foreign investments. This memorandum nevertheless did not garner consensus, with the CDU leader at the time, Anegret Kramp-Kambauer, rejecting it as being too interventionist. Since 2021, the German trade balance with China has become negative. The Middle Kingdom largely dominates the new electric car sector (BYD surpassed Tesla in 2025), while German brands continue to struggle. The Russo-Ukrainian War that erupted in 2025 has further increased German temptations to help its industries, as its previous advantages – exports to China's huge market, and imports of low-cost energy from Russia – have been disrupted.

The passage of the Inflation Reduction Act (IRA) in the US in 2022 has further revived national industrial policies. Based on massive subsidies for climate-friendly products (such as electric cars), it imposes a minimum of US content for products to be eligible for a public subsidy, thereby violating WTO rules. The IRA was also described, by Secretary of the Treasury Janet Yellen, a former central banker, as 'modern supply-side economics', an industrial policy with beneficial social and environmental effects.[47] This is a combination of *liberty*, *solidarity*, and *community* capitalism. A comparative study of the IRA and EU subsidies clearly shows the far more discriminatory nature of US measures.[48] In addition, aid to industry from US states has flourished.[49]

The Union reacted by further easing its control over state aid. Adopted for one year on 23 March 2022 in response to the Russo-Ukrainian War, the latest package in this area was supplemented on 9 March 2023 by a broad New Temporary Crisis and Transition Framework. If there is a real risk of investment being directed away from Europe, 'Member States may provide ... the amount of support the beneficiary could receive for an equivalent investment.'[50] There are looming fears of the return of a subsidy race, as private companies could encourage governments to overbid subsidies in order to attract them.

Unlike the late 1980s, when Bonn demanded greater state aid discipline, Berlin is now being targeted for its generosity. As the continent's central economic and industrial power, with low debt and deficits, the German government's ability to provide subsidies is unmatched in Europe. Between 2005 and 2019 (the year before Covid-19), the level of German state aid for the economy tripled.[51] Germany has risen from twentieth to fifth in the ranking of EU countries providing the most aid. While France granted 50 per cent more aid than Germany (as a proportion of GDP) in 2012, Berlin now grants 50 per cent more aid than Paris.

Lastly, the return of protectionism and of nativism is also evident in the increasing obstacles to the free movement of people both within the European Union and from abroad. Under the influence of more nationalist leaders such as Giorgia Meloni, the European Union has adopted a more restrictive approach to migration policy, exemplified by the 2024 Pact on Migration and Asylum, stricter controls at the EU's external borders, and agreements with non-European countries (notably with Turkey in 2016, Libya in 2017, Tunisia in 2024) designed to encourage them to retain migrants in exchange for financial aid. This policy has been very controversial from a human rights perspective.[52]

10.3.3 A Tentative European Industrial Policy

As a result of this more protectionist context, a European industrial policy of sorts is slowly emerging. Its most striking successes are two European companies, Airbus and Ariane. They were created outside the Union framework, although the Commission has defended Airbus against Boeing at the GATT/WTO since the 1980s. The Union has even entered the space industry by funding the Galileo satellite positioning programme, which was launched in 1999, relaunched in 2007 after delays (notably by French Transport Commissioner Jacques Barrot, 2004–08), and finally became operational in 2016. The programme has been mired not only in financial and industrial complications, but geopolitical ones as well, for some actors consider Galileo to be a purely commercial venture (China was invited as a partner), while others view it as one element in Europe's diplomatic clout.[53]

Beginning in 2014, the Juncker Commission pursued a more proactive vision.[54] It launched the Juncker Plan, which consists of a €21 billion guarantee providing leverage to finance economic development projects, especially for SMEs, with a target of at least €300 billion, which was achieved in 2018.[55] The scheme became Invest EU in 2021. Its impact is estimated at 4–10 per cent of the EU's investment volume, but it is difficult to assess whether the projects supported are new, or would have been financed anyway.[56] More generally, from 2015 onwards Jean-Claude Juncker explicitly praised the model of national investment banks, following the model of the European Investment Bank for the Union, the Caisse des Dépôts et Consignation in France, and the Kreditanstalt für Wiederaufbau in Germany (equivalent in size to its French counterpart).[57] These institutions epitomise a mix of *liberty* and *community* capitalism. They are state-owned banks whose purpose is to support active industrial policy by providing financing facilities to certain companies. This stands in contrast to a more sceptical discourse towards these institutions, which were suspected a few years earlier of obstructing competition.

The Commission has even promoted a more vertical industrial policy since 2014, with the Important Project of Common European Interest (IPCEI), which facilitates the acceptance of targeted state aid in particularly important cases.[58] This has allowed the Commission to authorise €3.2 billion in aid from a consortium of seven European countries to build factories manufacturing electric car batteries (which make up approximately 40 per cent of the price of electric vehicles).[59] Germany and France are the main funders of this 'Airbus of Batteries', followed by Italy and Poland. In the same vein, the European Chips Act adopted in 2023 facilitates the installation of semiconductor plants in Europe, within a broader context of dependence on production in East Asia. These measures will likely lead to massive financing for US, Taiwanese, and South Korean producers, thereby illustrating an original feature of the European industrial policy, namely its lack of preference for EU companies. Defence is the only area where an explicit European preference exists, as the European Defence Fund launched in 2021 only supports companies from the Union (and countries in the Single Market, such as Norway and Switzerland). In environmental industrial policy, European companies had to buy carbon credits abroad to compensate for their excess emissions: EU carmaker Stellantis planned to buy tens of millions of euros of carbon credits from the US carmaker Tesla in early 2025.[60]

The Covid-19 pandemic also forced Brussels to act. As early as April 2020, the Commissioner for Competition, Margrethe Vestager, stressed the risk that foreign powers such as China could pay discount prices for European firms in disarray due to the pandemic.[61] In June 2020, in conjunction with the Commissioner for Industry Thierry Breton, she proposed strengthening the procedures for controlling acquisitions of companies by non-European firms, and evaluating the negative impact of foreign subsidies.[62] Finally, the shortcomings of liberal globalisation in supplying masks and gloves – once considered basic, but suddenly scarce in an emergency – prompted the EU to adopt controls for certain trade flows. Regulation 2020/402 of 14 March 2020 made the export of certain products essential for combating the epidemic subject to authorisation. The Union was less protectionist than its primary trading partners, which instituted numerous export bans. The Union's economic liberalism was obvious during the EU–AstraZeneca dispute in early 2021, when the British–Swedish firm, which provided almost the entire first batch of vaccines to the Union, delivered only 30 million of the 120 million doses planned in the first quarter of 2021. Brussels was accused of having excessive faith in market rules, as the EU had exported 10 million vaccine doses to the UK between 1 February and mid-March, but received no doses itself. Furthermore, AstraZeneca explained that its contract with the British government required it to make priority deliveries to the UK, as London had provided massive funding for its research. This naïve EU commitment to free trade rules was shared by Germans: Berlin had financed the start-up BioNTech, which found one of the first vaccines, but it did not include a priority delivery clause. BioNTech partnered with the US multinational Pfizer, which certainly prevented any such provision. In contrast, on the other side of the Channel, according to journalist Dave Keating, there were plans for the Oxford laboratory that discovered the vaccine to partner with the US company Merck, but London imposed the alliance with the British AstraZeneca instead.[63]

The Union's protectionism was limited during the Covid-19 crisis. Regulation 2020/402 of 29 January 2021 made the export of vaccines subject to authorisation. It was used on 4 March 2021 by Italy, which blocked the departure of 250,000 doses of AstraZeneca vaccines destined for Australia, with the support of the Commission, but it was not much used afterwards. It was later replaced by a new and more sophisticated export control system, which allowed for donations of vaccines to poorer countries. The Union remained open to Russian and Chinese vaccine diplomacy. Hungary, the Czech Republic, and Slovakia voiced their intention to acquire non-Western vaccines, even if they did not adhere to the standard approval procedure due to a lack of verifiable data.[64] The Commission granted them the authorisation to do so, but the move soon fell through, for in April 2021 Chinese officials themselves recognised the limited effectiveness of their vaccine.[65]

10.3.4   Europe's Diplomatic and Military Power in the Making

The idea of shaping Europe as a diplomatic and military power re-emerged in four stages. The first was the Maastricht Treaty of 1991, which created the Common Foreign Security Policy (CFSP). The CFSP was a failure from the very beginning, given European impotence in the war in former Yugoslavia between 1991 and 1995. The second attempt came in 1998, when the French–British Saint-Malo declaration revived Europe-wide defence after renewed commitment to European integration by the new prime minister of the UK, Tony Blair. In 1999, the Berlin Plus agreement concluded at the NATO summit facilitated relationships between that organisation and the Union, granting it access to EU resources. That same year Javier Solana of Spain, the former NATO Secretary General, became the EU's top CFSP

10.3 A MORE ASSERTIVE EUROPE SINCE 2016

representative. The Europeans militarised Airbus by launching the A400M transport aircraft programme in 2001. The Germans departed from their pacifism by agreeing to deploy troops to Afghanistan. However, the Iraq War in 2003 shattered these efforts. At the Azores (Portugal) summit on 16 March 2003, the leaders of four European countries – José Manuel Barroso of Portugal, Tony Blair of the UK, José Maria Aznar of Spain, and Silvio Berlusconi of Italy – expressed their full support for the US intervention in Iraq without a UN mandate, despite popular demonstrations in their countries. Central and Eastern European countries also supported the Americans, while the German and French governments opposed it. As a permanent member of the Security Council, Paris exercised its veto, which eventually forced the Americans to intervene in Iraq without a UN mandate. It was at this time that the former Reagan administration official Robert Kagan drew a contrast between Mars – the US, intent on using hard power in an 'anarchic Hobbesian world' – and Venus, the Union, more peaceful and bent on negotiating living in Kant's 'Perpetual Peace'.[66]

A third attempt came in 2007 with the conclusion of the Lisbon Treaty, which created a more substantial Common Security and Defence Policy (CSDP). It included an article on mutual assistance in the event of armed aggression on its territory (Article 42-7), giving concrete expression to the idea of Europe as a community of shared destiny. However, military expenditure was still excluded from the European budget (Article 41-2). NATO was vindicated by France's return to the organisation's integrated command in 2009. The nature of the Union, essentially normative and peaceful, has not changed. In 2011, former Commission President Romano Prodi waxed lyrical: 'The rule of law has replaced the crude interplay of power ... by making a success of integration, we are demonstrating to the world that it is possible to create a method for peace.'[67] The Union's main external influence remained its ability to prompt neighbouring states wishing to join it to institute changes. An important exception was the 2015 agreement with Iran (Joint Comprehensive Plan of Action) to control its nuclear programme. The Union was a full-fledged signatory to the agreement (its High Representative for Foreign Affairs Federica Mogherini played a significant role at the end of the negotiation), alongside the three primary European countries (Germany, France, the UK), in addition to the major non-European powers of Russia, China, and the US.

President Trump's non-cooperative policy (2017–21) initiated a fourth turning point. His trade war, unilateralism (he pulled the US out of the agreement on Iran), and fierce criticism of NATO sowed doubt regarding the permanence of American engagement in Europe. In 2019, French President Emmanuel Macron feared that NATO was 'brain dead'. Without going that far, Chancellor Angela Merkel recognised that Europe needed to strengthen its autonomous defence capability, in a marked change of tone.

The discourse on Europe as a power evolved. In his speech at the Sorbonne on 26 September 2017, the newly elected Macron asserted the crucial importance of the Union stressing its 'sovereignty', including in new areas such as digital technology, the environment, as well as foreign and defence policy, in which he called for a 'capacity for autonomous action ... in addition to NATO'. Macron's ambitious rhetoric echoed past French projects, but in a more Europeanised manner, with some of its points being adopted by other Europeans. In the speech she delivered upon being appointed in 2019, Commission President Ursula von der Leyen of Germany encouraged her Commission to assert itself geopolitically. The March 2019 Communication on China broadened the traditional – and purely economic – perspective to include more strategic considerations, such as network security and monitoring foreign direct investment.[68] The Covid-19 pandemic and the Russo-Ukrainian War shifted the discourse towards the need to reduce the vulnerability of certain strategic production chains, especially those relating to medicine, computer equipment, and even armament. The vocabulary is certainly less self-centred than in Paris: the Commission, like Spain or the Netherlands, has insisted on the concept of 'open' strategic autonomy, with a view to avoiding any protectionist drift.[69] Even the German Chancellor Olaf Scholz, in his Prague speech in 2022, spoke of European 'sovereignty', albeit in a more moderate tone: Europe should be 'responsible for its own security' and promote its interests in the world.[70] While the vocabulary is different from that of Paris, the evolution from the traditional pacifist and normative vision of Europe is noteworthy.

Concrete decisions followed. On the military level, European countries agreed to support French interventions in Africa, whereas they were previously viewed with great suspicion as postcolonial adventures. In 2020, ten European countries agreed to support Operation Takuba, the French intervention against jihadists in Mali, which had been ongoing since 2013. However, only two countries, Estonia and the Czech Republic, took part in the military operations, and the largest troop contingent remained French. In 2022, all of the European troops left Mali after a pro-Russian military coup the previous year. From the financial point of view, in 2016 Commission President Jean-Claude Juncker launched two initiatives that led to the creation of two new funds, the European Peace Facility (set up in 2021), and the European Defence Fund (in 2017). The first is an intergovernmental mechanism that circumvents regulatory budgetary restrictions to finance military equipment. It includes an element of preference, as funding is reserved for European firms. The second is a more federal mechanism that funds cooperation between European industrial actors in defence R&D. The sums spent remained modest compared with national defence budgets, and did not involve the production of European weapons until the Russo-Ukrainian War. Besides, the European military sector was also marked by a sharp decline in military spending after the end of the Cold War, as well as by the emergence of new exporters such as China, South Korea, and Turkey. The mood has changed recently, with the outbreak of the Russo-Ukrainian War in 2022 and Trump's second term in 2025. However, European military spending has risen only slowly, and remains far below its Cold War average.

The 2001 decision to produce the A400M – the first military aircraft from the European company Airbus – reflects both the success and limits of Europeanisation, since the programme has experienced numerous delays, especially due to the differing needs of the various sponsoring armies. In addition, the A400M replaces an aircraft from the US, the Lockheed Hercules, but a French–German one as well, the Transall, whose programme was launched in 1958. Europeanisation had therefore already been present for a long time in connection with this type of transport aircraft. In particular, Franco-German cooperation in armament have been regular and often difficult despite a strong political impetus, for example, with the helicopter Tiger, which entered into regular service only in 2009 whereas the programme was launched in 1984.[71]

Another European company emerged in 2001 in the missile sector, the French–British MBDA. In 2017, Paris and Berlin launched two joint initiatives to create the tank and fighter jet of the future, but negotiations between industrial actors have proven very difficult. In 2022, at the beginning of the Russo-Ukrainian War, the President of the Italian Council of Ministers, Mario Draghi, lamented: 'Our security spending is about three times that of Russia, but it's divided into 146 defence systems. The United States only has 34.'[72] Although a European Defence Agency was set up in 2004 to facilitate European collaborative projects, it is estimated that only 18 per cent of the EU military budget is collaborative in nature.[73]

Structural barriers remain the same. On the one hand, the principle of fair return and safeguarding national defence industries prevents any effective sharing of the production process. On the other, Atlanticist logic remains prevalent. Despite these weaknesses, the constant strengthening of European institutions as well as defence funding have created habits and meetings between professionals in the sector, leading to a certain rapprochement between strategic and military cultures, although the role of the Union remains weak: it is a 'Europeanisation without Europe'.[74] Similarly, in terms of identity, a survey conducted in the summer of 2021 showed the emergence of a small majority in support of a European army within the Union (except in Germany and Scandinavia), but only as a complement to national armies.[75] The next logical step would be to share the production process at the European level, for example, with a clear division in French–German cooperation, with French leadership in fighter jets, and German leadership in tanks. For now, such a Yalta of the arms industry remains an illusion.

10.4 In the Face of Brexit (2016–20): Preserving the Community

Brexit, the UK's departure from the Union, was decided by referendum on 23 June 2016 by a vote of 51.89 per cent, and became effective on 31 January 2021. It was an earthquake for the Union, marking the first departure of one of its members.[76] A domino effect just after the Leave vote was anticipated by some observers, with far-right leaders calling for referendums that could lead to Nexit in the Netherlands or Frexit in France.[77] The contagion ultimately did not take place, because the complicated implementation of Brexit left that country divided, and because the choice chiefly grew out of British peculiarities. Brexit was nevertheless a challenge for the Union.

10.4.1 Managing the Identity Challenge

Beyond short-term factors, Brexit was structurally an assertion of distinctive British features.[78] All other European countries were occupied by armies of authoritarian regimes during the World War II, except for Britain, which resisted Hitler alone from June 1940 to June 1941. The legacy of the world's largest colonial empire allows London to project itself even today as an alternative space to the European continent, namely that of the Commonwealth and English-speaking countries.

More broadly, Brexit was also part of the international movement to reassert local identities. According to surveys conducted shortly after the vote, the main reason for the Leavers (those who voted to leave the Union) was to regain control over the country's borders and migration policy. Brexit supporters have sometimes expressed hostility to immigration they deem excessive, especially from Central and Eastern European countries. After joining the EU in 2004, the UK was one of the few countries that did not use the transitional clauses limiting free movement. This factor, combined with the Blair government's underestimation of future migration flows and weak labour regulations, led to strong immigration from the former Eastern bloc to the UK.

The exit from the Union was also supported by neoliberal elites in line with a Thatcherite tradition equating Brussels with a socialist bureaucratic beast. Boris Johnson, one of the leaders of the Leave campaign, was part of this dynamic. Kwasi Kwarteng, Dominic Rabb, Priti Patel, Chris Skidmore, and Elisabeth Truss, all of whom became ministers in the Johnson government in 2019, published a pamphlet in 2012 entitled *Britannia Unchained*, which called for radical neoliberal reforms. Through a rollback of social regulations, they hoped that the UK would become a 'Singapore-on-Thames'.[79] Rishi Sunak, who served as prime minister between 2022 and 2024, followed the same approach, reneging on environmental measures. Similarly, David Hannan, an influential voice in the Leave campaign, published 'The Case for EFTA' in 2005, with EFTA referring to the European Free Trade Area.[80]

Conversely, in 2016 trade unions defended the Remain vote in the name of preserving European social and environmental laws. Jeremy Corbyn (2015–20), the Labour leader at the time, insisted on preserving regulatory convergence with the EU in these areas when he voted on the EU exit agreements presented by the government in 2018–19. Conversely, as foreign minister (2016–18) and prime minister (2019–22), Johnson delivered contradictory speeches, some of which were clearly neoliberal, such as when he denounced European standards as bureaucratic hurdles preventing the conclusion of trade agreements, especially with the US. Washington has explicitly identified stricter European health standards as major obstacles to the conclusion of such an agreement.

10.4.2 Preserving the Single Market

In the face of Brexit, negotiated since 2016 and effective in 2020, the Union has pursued a strategy of safeguarding the integrity of the Single Market and its normative power. By contrast, the UK wanted continued access to the Single Market without being constrained by EC law. However, this would have seriously challenged the unity of the Single Market, and hence its interest: if one of its members could pick and choose the legislation it wanted to follow, then other members could do the same. In the end, nobody would follow the common legislation, with the Single Market ultimately dissolving into a mere free trade area. London also wanted to separate the four freedoms of movement, retaining those relating to goods, services, and capital, but rejecting the one concerning persons, but this would also have seriously undermined the identity dimension of the Single Market.[81]

The Union negotiator was a seasoned French and European politician, Michel Barnier, who focused on safeguarding the unity of the EU-27 and the Single Market (including its four liberties of movement) through regular visits to European capitals. This strategy strengthened Brussels, and neutralised the risk of Brexit contagion.[82]

Finally, the agreements concluded with the Johnson government in 2020 (on the withdrawal in January 2020, and the future relationship in December 2020) ended with an ambiguous compromise: the island of Great Britain would be free of Single Market standards, while Northern Ireland would have to remain in strong regulatory convergence with the Union. The price of maintaining the absence of border controls between Northern Ireland and the Republic of Ireland (and hence the Union) had to be paid by internal controls in the UK, particularly in the Irish Sea (between Great Britain and Northern Ireland). The implementation of the agreement sparked traffic disruptions within the UK, with product shortages in Northern Ireland in early 2021. Violent protests by Unionist Protestants fearing greater distance from London agitated the streets of Belfast. In February 2021, the Unionist party DUP announced its intention to launch legal action against the Irish protocol negotiated between London and Brussels, as it would be incompatible with the 1800 Act of Union, which provided for unfettered trade throughout the UK.[83] In response, in July 2021 Johnson threatened to restore controls at the Irish border if Brussels did not accept reduced internal controls in the UK, which the EU refused.[84] Accepting such a request would pose significant and increasing risks of fraud, with the importing via Ireland to the rest of the Union of products that do not comply with European standards. For the moment the risks are low, as legislation remains very close on both sides of the Channel, but differences will naturally increase in the future. A compromise was later reached between Brussels and the Sunak government in 2023, but the substantive problem remains.

10.4.3 Reorganising the Bilateral Relationship

Two scenarios could emerge in the long run. The British could opt for the neoliberal Singapore-on-Thames strategy and practise legislative Darwinism, lowering the standards in force in order to increase competitiveness vis-à-vis the continent. Projects to increase flexibility in labour law after the lifting of EC working-time constraints were revealed in January 2021.[85] Such decisions would be logical, as they would be in keeping with the constant opposition by conservative governments towards the European Working Time Directive. Similarly, adopting less stringent health standards would facilitate the import of North American agricultural products, and hence the conclusion of a trade agreement with the US. If such a race to the bottom materialised, then the temptation of fraud in Ireland (by importing cheaper products with lower standards from the UK to the Union) would be great, leading to simmering conflict between Brussels and London. This temptation remains present even with the return to power of a Labour government in 2024 under Keir Starmer's leadership. Confronted with a growing risk of trade war with the US under Donald Trump's second term, London still appears ready to negotiate with Washington on this issue. It struck a first tentative deal with the US in May 2025. Another solution would be for the UK to follow the path of Norway, Switzerland, and Iceland by rejoining the Single Market, probably with a special status. In any case, growing US isolationism and the threat to NATO posed by Trump's unilateralism certainly reinforce the case for stronger military cooperation on the European continent, including between EU and non-EU members. While it is difficult to determine what people really want, in June 2016 a majority of the British people voted either to remain in the Union or for what they anticipated to be a soft Brexit but in the end, they got a hard Brexit.

Conversely, in the EU, the departure of the British may lead to a more assertive European economic identity. The adoption of a more cautious approach towards China has been facilitated by the departure of David

Cameron, one of Europe's most enthusiastic proponents of Chinese investment, along with his British supporters in Brussels.[86] The former British representative in Brussels, Sir Ivan Rodgers, has indicated that the massive recovery plan adopted in 2020 to contend with the pandemic would have been vetoed by the UK if Brexit had not occurred.[87] At this point, Brexit has become a vexing but secondary topic for Europeans. While Brexit initially challenged the Union as a community, it has ultimately presented an opportunity to reassert it.

10.5 Facing the Russo-Ukrainian War: Europe as a Power, or as a Junior Partner?

The Russo-Ukrainian War, triggered by the Russian military invasion of its neighbour on 24 February 2022, is a major event for Europe, which is caught between a need to assert its 'hard power', and the fact that it is part of an Atlantic alliance dominated by the US.

10.5.1 A Major and Surprising Event

The Russo-Ukrainian War has four remarkable features with respect to the history of international relations. First, it is the first military aggression on European territory since the World War II, excluding the war in the former Yugoslavia, which was more local in nature. Even during the Cold War, the USSR respected the principle of the inviolability of borders reasserted at the 1975 Helsinki Conference.[88] The war marks the end of attempts to integrate Russia within a Western world order, as Moscow was irritated by NATO enlargement and the abandonment of the Partnership for Peace proposed by President Clinton in the 1990s as an alternative to enlargement, which proved illusory with the deteriorating situation in Russia.[89] Russia was not an international pariah at the time; for instance, it was Russia's ratification of the Kyoto Protocol in 2004 that allowed it to be implemented against US opposition.

Second, this war involves two major belligerents. Russia is one of the two major nuclear powers, the world's largest country in terms of surface area, and among the ten most populous and wealthiest countries. While Russia is no longer an ideological power like the USSR, its authoritarian and illiberal model is attractive to the far right in the West, and also generates some interest among far-left voters (notably the rising star of the German far left, the BSW created in 2024). Moscow has also waged a large-scale ideological offensive on the web to discredit the West.[90] Ukraine is the largest European country (after Russia), and one of the largest grain exporters in the world. The conflict is also massive in terms of death toll, with the number of Russian casualties surpassing that of the intervention in Afghanistan, which lasted ten years (1979–89).

Third, field operations have shown the importance of military dynamics that Europeans have long forgotten, notably the importance of having a large reserve of ammunitions, and most of all the power of national pride, which explains the heroic Ukrainian resistance, even as everyone expected a rapid collapse in February 2022. If Russian plans for a rapid Ukrainian conquest had been successful, Moscow would probably have threatened the Baltics and Moldova next (they remain Moscow's targets if Kiev is defeated).[91] Europeans have trimmed down their armies since the end of the Cold War; the most ambitious countries have kept small units for extra-European operations, but with no production capacity to supply a long and intense war without US support.

Fourth, this conflict has a strong ideological component.[92] If Ukraine were to lose, it could weaken Europe and its model of law-abiding liberal democracies. The invasion has already strengthened Russia territorially via the annexation of Crimea in 2014 and the Sea of Azov in the 2022, leading to a drastic reduction of the Ukrainian coastline. While the war could weaken Moscow economically in the long run – due to the exile of skilled Russians, trade sanctions, and greater difficulty accessing high-tech Western components – Russia has been able to find alternative suppliers in the Global South. As a matter of fact, a majority of non-Western countries remained neutral in the Russo-Ukrainian War (such as Turkey and India), or even pro-Russian. Moscow was able to maintain its oil exports despite the European embargo by massively increasing flows to Beijing and New Delhi. The Russo-Ukraine War thus forced Europe to react to avoid further decline.

10.5.2 *The Clarification of European Borders*

For Europe, the conflict has clarified the continent's limits as a community of destiny. It has drawn a clear border in the east and the south. In the east, the EU's military mobilisation against Russia, Russia's exclusion from the Council of Europe in 2022, and the fact that even a neutral country such as Switzerland took part in sanctions against Moscow, shows that Europe's border is now firmly set between Ukraine and Russia. In fact, fear of Russia – and of the USSR – has been a long-standing motivation for European integration. In his pioneering book from 1923 entitled *Pan-Europe*, Richard von Coudenhove-Kalergi pointed out that Russian expansionism was a constant feature, forcing Europe to unite lest it come under Russian influence, as could have occurred in 1915 if Nicholas II had won the war, or in 1918–20 if the Marxist revolution had succeeded in Germany through internal revolution or Lenin's military offensive.[93] The same fear motivated some Europeans, who believed that without US troops Stalin's forces would have advanced until Brest, in French Brittany (and not Brest-Litovsk in Belarus).

10.5 FACING THE RUSSO-UKRAINIAN WAR

In the south, the border with Africa and the Middle East has been reinforced, for both good and bad reasons. European solidarity with Ukrainian migrants stands in contrast to the tensions caused by the arrival of non-European migrants from Africa or Asia. Admittedly, the situation is not quite the same, as Ukrainian refugees are overwhelmingly women and children, a population that always tends to cause less rejection than migrant men. However, European governments have clearly identified with the Ukrainians by massively providing aid, with no strings attached. For the first time, the Union invoked the 2001 Temporary Protection Directive to provide temporary protection for refugees. The Union redirected certain European funds to help finance the directive, which facilitates movement, work, and access to social benefits.[94]

In the south-east, the rift between Turkey and the Union has deepened. While the country is still a candidate for EU membership, and remains one of NATO's main armies, its neutrality in the Russo-Ukrainian War conflict clearly brings it closer to the Global South. Its impartiality allowed it to secure a grain agreement between the two belligerents in July 2022.[95] Turkey appears as an ancient and self-centred empire, a world of its own, like Russia or China.

However, this clarification of the Union's borders does not mean that the enlargement process will stop soon. Thanks to Russian aggression, Ukraine and Moldova were admitted as candidates for EU enlargement in June 2022 (as well as Georgia in 2023), but with no guarantee that accession will come soon or at all. Since 2014, Ukraine has enjoyed a free trade agreement with the EU, the Deep and Comprehensive Free Trade Area (DCFTA), which helped reorient its trade from the East to the West. A referendum held in the Netherlands in 2016 rejected this agreement, albeit with a low turnout. Today, Ukraine's inclusion remains predicated on important reforms, in particular surrounding the rule of law and the fight against corruption.

The Russo-Ukrainian War lends more credence to the idea of a multi-speed Europe, with an integrated core consisting of the eurozone, then the European Union, and beyond it the whole continent. Proposed on 9 May 2022 by French President Macron, the European Political Community is now a forum for discussion across the continent's forty-seven countries. The initiative is notable because a similar French project was presented by President Mitterrand in 1991, the European Confederation, which was rejected because it was conceived as an alternative to the Union's enlargement towards the East (see Chapter 2). On the contrary, Macron explained that the creation of the European Political Community did not necessarily exclude further enlargement. The Forum met for the first time in Prague on 6 October 2022. It has helped bring the UK back on board with respect to European cooperation. On the whole, the clarification of Europe's border and the European Political Community could reinforce the Union's cohesion.

10.5.3 The Union's Unprecedented Mobilisation

The conflict has generated the Union's unprecedented mobilisation in four areas: welcoming Ukrainian refugees, sanctions against Russia, energy, and financial and military support. In terms of Russian sanctions, the EU made quick and radical decisions. On 27 February 2022, three days after the start of the invasion, the Union suspended most trade relations, excluded most Russian banks from the SWIFT interbank system, and froze Russian holdings in Europe, including those of the Russian Central Bank. Previously, sanctions were more targeted at companies or individuals.

The Union also made energy-related decisions that were unthinkable before the Ukrainian aggression, as it was heavily dependent on Russian hydrocarbons. At the beginning of the war the Union collectively spent €1 billion per day on Russian hydrocarbons. As a result, in early April 2022, it had already provided €35 billion to Russia through its imports, compared with just €1 billion in aid to Ukraine.[96] At first, coordination was difficult because Germany was very dependent on Russian gas, and because Hungary remained politically close to Russia. In the end, Moscow facilitated European coordination by gradually and unilaterally interrupting its gas deliveries in the summer of 2022. The Union decided to drastically reduce its imports of Russian gas and oil, but fell short of an embargo. It also capped the price of Russian oil at $60 per barrel on 3 December 2022.

On the military level, while no European soldiers have been sent to the front – European countries have always been careful not to be considered co-belligerents – the Union has made the unprecedented decision to deliver lethal weapons to a country at war. Admittedly, Brussels acted through its member states by reimbursing national contributions via the Peace Facility, doing so for significant albeit modest sums given the scale of the war effort (€3 billion as of year-end 2022 for the Facility, compared with €55 billion in European aid).[97] In May 2023 the Union also adopted the Act to Support Ammunition Production (ASAP) to mobilise €500 million from the EU's general budget to co-finance the production of arms in Europe, including ammunition. Denmark withdrew its thirty-year-old opt-out with regard to participation in the Union's defence programmes via a referendum held on 1 June 2022.

On the whole, the financial effort by Europeans was massive and unprecedented, and could lead to structural changes on the continent. From the financial point of view, while the US provided more help to Ukraine than the Europeans in 2022, the figure was reversed in 2023. In 2022–23, Europeans provided slightly less military aid, and much more financial and humanitarian aid (especially to millions of Ukrainian refugees).[98] According to the Kiel Institute, government support to Ukraine in 2022–24 totalled €132 billion for Europe and €114 billion for the US. The nomination of the outspoken

Russian critic Kaja Kallas (the former prime minister of Estonia) as the next High Representative of the Union for Foreign Affairs and Security Policy in June 2024 is another sign of Europe's determination, which will be further tested by Donald Trump's return to power.

In Germany, the Social-Democrat Chancellor Olaf Scholz announced the so-called *Zeitenwende* (epochal change) on 27 February 2022: faced with the scale of military threats, Berlin agreed to deliver weapons to a country at war, and to massively increase its military budget (through the creation of a special fund of 100€ billion). In 2025, the new Christian-Democrat Chancellor Friedrich Merz, representing the centre-right CDU, went further by obtaining an exemption from the 'debt brake' – a German constitutional provision that limits government deficits for military expenditure. Such measures would have been inconceivable prior to the Russo-Ukrainian War, as Germany had historically prioritised pacifism and stability. Beyond the German context, European states collectively agreed in early 2025 to substantially increase their military spending, in response to US President Donald Trump's threat to withdraw the American security umbrella.

Eurozone members have been discussing the possibility of excluding some military expenditure from the Stability Pact. This would amount to momentous change. To take just the example of France and Germany, between 2000 and 2022, their indebtedness diverged considerably. Both countries had the same level of public debt in 2000, but France's doubled in two decades, while Germany's remained almost flat. However, France spent 0.8 per cent more of GDP per year on defence than Germany, notably to fund its nuclear arsenal, which could be part of a European defence system.[99] This additional military expenditure represents one-third of the rise in French debt over the period. Consequently, the greater assertiveness of the European Union as a diplomatic and military power could also affect its internal economic rules.

10.5.4 Europe as a Junior Member of the Atlantic Community

However, this assertion of hard power in Europe is part of an Atlantic dynamic, in which Europe has remained a junior partner. Since the creation of NATO in 1949–50, born as a reaction to Russian aggression (Berlin in 1948–49, indirectly in Korea in 1950), Europeans have always counted on US military support (see Chapter 5). The end of NATO was envisaged in the early 1990s with the end of the Cold War,[100] but the Europeans never gave up on it.

Several factors attest to the primacy of an Atlanticist logic. First, Western military interventions are contingent upon US military support, which remains indispensable in domains such as intelligence gathering and nuclear capabilities. It is primarily the US nuclear umbrella threat that prevents Russia from using its own nuclear arsenal. In early 2024, several politicians in France, Germany, and Poland evoked the possibility of 'Europeanising' the French nuclear arsenal, perhaps by extending the guarantee of French deterrence (in exchange for European funding, as the French nuclear arsenal represents 20 per cent of French military expenditure), but no genuine discussions were launched.[101] In any event, both the French and British nuclear arsenals are ten to twenty times smaller than the US and Russian ones, with the British one also being intertwined with that of the US.[102] Even though the European defence budget has increased by 30 per cent since the start of the Russo-Ukrainian War (2022–24), Europe's total defence spending has still not exceeded 1990 levels in real terms, and is on a par with Russia in purchasing-power parity (in 2023).[103]

Second, the war has reinforced NATO, as Sweden and Finland have shed their neutrality to join the organisation. Europeans have coordinated with the US and other Western allies within the framework of the G7 and the Atlantic alliance. This explains their effectiveness. Third, before the Trump II administration, the American contribution to military aid was greater than that of Europeans both in terms of quality (notably intelligence) and quantity (either directly as aid to Ukraine, or indirectly as aid to European countries to replenish their stocks after their gifts to Kiev). On 4 September 2023, the Ukrainian Minister of Defence estimated the military assistance provided since the beginning of the conflict at $100 billion, 60 per cent of which came from the US.[104] This pre-eminence corresponds to US supremacy in terms of military spending: the US military budget is three to four times higher than the collective defence budgets of all EU countries combined.[105] What is more, US military expenditure is more efficient than its European counterpart because it is unified. Consequently, the meeting to coordinate arms deliveries took place in Germany, but did so under US leadership at its Ramstein military base. The first meeting was held on 26 April 2022, and was chaired by US Secretary of Defense Lloyd Austin.

Hence, the inauguration of a much more isolationist US administration under Trump II represents a formidable challenge for Europeans should they be required to ensure their own defence without the US nuclear umbrella. Trump's challenge goes much farther than the previous complaint of US presidents about the lack of European funding, which existed since Eisenhower (see Chapter 5). The only solution for Europeans to be more effective would be to closely coordinate their defence programmes and capabilities, on either a federal (as in Servan-Schreiber's call from 1967) or more probably on an intergovernmental basis. The European identity is too flimsy to support a full federalisation of this area. What is more, any progress in this area should include non-EU members such as the UK and Norway; Canada has even been mentioned after Trump's offensive against its neighbour in 2025. Concrete proposals have already emerged: in 2023, the then Estonian Prime Minister Kaja Kallas (who has served as the EU High Representative for

Foreign Affairs and Security Policy since 2024) proposed a joint European weapons procurement programme for Ukraine, as the Europeans did for vaccines during the Covid-19 pandemic.[106]

Third, the increase in military spending in Europe did not benefit the European arms industry alone. The famous German *Zeitenwende* resulted in significant purchases of US equipment, beginning with F-35 aircraft, and later Patriot missiles and Arrow-3 hypersonic ballistic missiles (the latter being Israeli-American) as part of the Sky Shield air-defence system. Launched by Germany in October 2022 in response to massive Russian air attacks on Ukraine, Sky Shield is shared by nineteen European countries (including Switzerland). In addition to these American and Israeli-American missiles, it also includes German-made IRIS-T missiles. The French and Italians did not participate because they jointly produce a different anti-aircraft missile, the Aster. Berlin also conditioned its deliveries of Leopard tanks on US willingness to send their Abrams tanks first. Similarly, when Warsaw delivered some of its tanks to Ukraine in 2022, it replaced them with South Korean ones because they were cost-effective, and because South Korean factories were the only ones ready to deliver them quickly.[107]

Fourth, the Union is far from being united in its stance on the Russo-Ukrainian War. Diplomatically, the Union remains divided between a few players who are attracted by the illiberal Russian model, such as the Hungarian government; a hesitant majority (Germany, France, Italy); and Central and Eastern European countries, which are sometimes fiercely anti-Russian. There are also simmering French-German tensions: President Macron has often chastised other leaders for their lack of support for Ukraine, even as France ranks low compared with other European countries for aid provided (far below Germany and the UK),[108] while German Chancellor Scholz (2021–25) has often appeared hesitant, paralysed by a bickering coalition (with Greens supporting Kiev, several social democrats being more pacifist, and liberals focused on austerity).[109] With regard to the relationship with NATO and the US, Paris has always remained more critical and willing to assert Europe's independence than Berlin.

Beyond this traditional French–German difference, divisions among Europeans are important because they have undermined support for Ukraine. Since unanimity is required for the most important decisions, Hungarian reluctance has delayed the adoption of sanctions. Even Poland has wavered. A staunch supporter of Ukraine due to its cultural and geographical proximity (and fear of being the next country targeted by Russia), Warsaw nevertheless imposed an embargo on Ukrainian wheat, and on 20 September 2023 even on certain arms deliveries, in retaliation for what it described as dumping. The difficulty of exporting grain via the Black Sea forced some Ukrainian wheat to transit through the Union. Warsaw subsequently accused Kiev of using the circumstances to sell wheat in transit countries such as Poland, much to the displeasure of Polish farmers. The quarrel has abated, but it shows the limits of Europe's community spirit.

To conclude, the Russo-Ukrainian War has had mixed consequences on Europe asserting itself as a diplomatic and military power. On the one hand, Europe has been more assertive as a community. At the start of the war on 22 February 2022, the prospect of Ukrainian resistance and European influence in the conflict was low. Russia was expected to win quickly. Instead, Ukrainians have resisted fiercely, and cast their fight as a struggle between European democratic civilisation and Russian authoritarianism. They have enjoyed somewhat hesitant but generally steady support from the West. Such a scenario would have been inconceivable had Trump been in office in 2022. Ukraine now has a prospect of joining the Union, which was unthinkable before. The Union's old instruments of trade, support for refugees, and targeted funding have been reoriented to massively support Ukraine's war effort. The Union is now fully embracing military and strategic issues. While military aid initially came predominantly from the US, Europe eventually caught up with Washington, and has provided more overall support.

However, most operational military decisions are still taken by member states and coordinated by NATO under US leadership. Besides, the US commitment to NATO and to supporting Ukraine is dwindling under the Trump administration. In addition, geopolitical divisions have remained strong within the Union, although they are not surprising, because they can be found within each Western country, with the far right and the far left often remaining much more pro-Russian (with exceptions such as Giorgia Meloni's pro-US Fratelli d'Italia). Finally, from a geopolitical point of view, it is not yet clear whether the enlargement to Ukraine will happen soon, and whether it will strengthen the EU as a power, or dilute it into a vast free trade area.

10.6 Conclusion: From 'Soft Power' to 'Assertive Power'?

The return to the logic of *community* forced the European Union to morph from a 'soft power' into a more assertive power, without being a fully-fledged 'hard power'. The concepts of 'soft power' and 'hard power' were coined by Joseph Nye in 1990 to differentiate between influence through norms, culture, and economy on the one hand, and coercion through force on the other.[110] While the 'Brussels Effect' flourished during the liberal international order of the late twentieth century, it became insufficient in a twenty-first century marked by the return of the state and of *community* capitalism, which was largely the result of the detrimental consequences of the period of 'high neoliberalism': austerity measures and regressive social policies fuelled social discontent, while the lack of internet regulation facilitated the radicalisation of political debate and the rise of illiberalism.

European capitalism was forced to adapt by being more assertive in three areas: in trade, by adopting more protectionist tools; in industrial policy, by tolerating (or even encouraging) state subsidies, and to a limited extent even European preference; and by increasing European coordination in domains that were until recently a monopoly of the nation state, namely health, foreign policy, and military affairs. States and international organisations such as the WHO, the UN, and NATO have nevertheless remained the dominant actors in the field.

European capitalism has embraced solutions that were previously refused as too protectionist, such as European preference (implemented in limited fashion for military products), free trade contingent on adhering to social and environmental norms (the 2016 CETA agreement and the CBAM were steps in this direction), European subsidies to industry for strategic reasons, and competition policy decisions based on reciprocity. Some of these ideas were long defended by France. Germany previously criticised them, but has embraced some in trade since 2016, and others in diplomacy and foreign policy since 2022. The Commission evolved from neoliberalism under Barroso (2004–14) to greater emphasis on social and industrial concerns under Juncker (2024–19), and finally to the 'geopolitical' assertiveness under von der Leyen.

Crisis weakened the Union in 2005–15, but later served to strengthen it. The management of Brexit (since 2016) has reaffirmed the basis of European soft power – the 'Brussels effect' – that depends on the unity of the Single Market. The Covid-19 pandemic (2020–21) forced the Union to act in the new strategic domain of health by adopting protectionist and interventionist measures, in keeping with the rest of the world. The Russo-Ukrainian War has led Europeans to adopt strong sanctions packages, as well as enabling the Union's foray into military matters, which were previously the monopoly of NATO. But the Europeans still remain heavily dependent on the US for defence. Donald Trump's return to power in 2025 unleashed an unprecedented form – at least since 1945 – of aggressive *community* capitalism, characterised by the imposition of unilateral tariffs, threats of territorial annexation directed at allies, a pervasive disregard for international organisations and norms, and the conflation of disparate issues that compelled Europeans to compromise on trade in order to secure continued US support in the war in Ukraine. It has forced Europe to think harder about organising *community* capitalism.

It remains to be seen whether these crises will mark a turning point towards a more *community*-based approach to European capitalism. The structural shortcomings of the Union remain, with limited resources, strong reluctance towards any forms of protectionism (including any kind of European preference akin to US 'Buy American' rules), comfortable dependence on the US alliance, and, above all, a lack of political will for coordination. With Donald Trump's return to power, Europe (including Britain) is at a crossroads: it can either implement an efficient form of *community* capitalism, namely via more efficient coordination of its industrial and defence policies, or primarily remain a regulated market with elements of *solidarity* capitalism.

Conclusion: Chronology, Alternatives, and Current Challenges

> *These dinky little European States can not live in an airplane civilization. Today they have the alternative of submerging their national hatreds and national prides sufficiently to unify the continent or of destroying themselves completely and handing Europe over to the Bolsheviks.*
>
> *(William Bullitt, US Ambassador to France, 1936)*[1]

The 'dinky little European States' have not succumbed to self-destruction. Close study of their attempts to create new forms of capitalist governance since 1945 has revealed three key findings.

First, since 1945, the governance of capitalism in Europe has been structured around four main periods, each delineated by critical junctures at which alternative paths were abandoned, leading to the emergence of a distinctive form of European capitalism. Second, Europeans have invented an original system to reach compromise between both states and the three types of capitalist governance. Although imperfect and cumbersome, this system has nonetheless provided a degree of choice for Europeans. Far from the image of a neoliberal technocratic dictatorship, the European Union can be protectionist and/or socio-environmentalist if Europeans want it. Within this system, Germany has been influential but not dominant. Third, the trinity of capitalist governance points to three alternatives that were – and still are – present, including the recent challenge posed by the return of *community* capitalism, even though *community* capitalism has never completely disappeared.

The chronology of post-war European capitalism has been marked by a handful of turning points, moments when long-term structural choices were made, and alternatives not pursued (see Table 11.1). Four phases unfolded after 1945: 1) embedded liberalism; 2) global attempts at mixed capitalism; 3) high neoliberalism; and 4) the return of *community* capitalism. This gave rise to a distinctive form of European capitalism (5).

1 Embedded Liberalism (1945–73)

During the first period spanning from 1945 to 1973, capitalism was characterised by the values of *solidarity* and *community* at the national level, and an expanding role for *liberty* at the international level. This compromise was aptly named 'embedded liberalism' by John Ruggie, and is neatly encapsulated by the expression: 'Keynes at home, Smith abroad'.[2] As a matter of fact, Keynes's reflections from 1919 heralded the post-1945 settlements, with almost no reparations from Germany, inter-allied debts replaced by a US loan, and the creation of a free trade zone in Europe. Under the pressure from the Cold War, Europeans took part in the OEEC in 1948, which combined *liberty* and *solidarity* capitalism (with the Marshall Plan).

A small number of European countries decided, with full support from the US, to regulate economic tensions among them by creating the ECSC in 1951, a common market with semi-federal regulation of trade. While it alleviated tensions between French and German versions of *community* capitalism, it remained weak, and was just one of several European organisations alongside the OEEC, the Council of Europe, and NATO. Given the increasing pressure since 1955 for a return to international free trade, European integration could have perfectly remained quite modest in scope. Under this scenario, the governance of European capitalism would have been managed by Western international institutions, such as the GATT for trade, the IMF for monetary policy, and the ILO for work-related issues.

The year 1958 was a major turning point, with the EEC emerging as a central actor in organising European capitalism. The Treaty of Rome that created the EEC had been signed the previous year, but the organisation's primacy was not self-evident in 1957. Without Charles de Gaulle's return to power in May 1958, his rejection of the British project of a free trade area, and his firm commitment to respect France's free trade obligations, the Treaty of Rome would not have been fully implemented in France. It could have been rejected, like the European Defence Community Treaty before it, or remained an agreement of secondary importance, in which case the British free trade area would have established another governance of European capitalism, leaning more towards *liberty*. Without de Gaulle, the Algerian crisis could have mired France in a financial and political crisis, but with the reestablishment of French authority, European integration acquired a French flavour, with elements of both *community* and *solidarity* capitalism in several areas (agriculture, aid to former colonies, targeted legislative harmonisation). Italy was also influential in enhancing *solidarity* capitalism through the free movement of workers (an issue that transitioned from the ILO to the EEC), but it failed to develop a regional policy.

At the same time, de Gaulle's intergovernmentalism limited European developments in these areas, curtailing French projects for organising *solidarity* and *community* capitalism at the European level for tax harmonisation, and coordinated industrial policy, among others. The main exceptions were Airbus and the European Space Agency, which were developed outside the EEC framework. The period was still characterised by the robust development of the national welfare state and industrial policy, including in supposed free market bastions such as West Germany. Hence, *solidarity* and *community* capitalism were still prevalent at the national level. The EEC could not intervene in this area, as its competition policy remained weak at the time.

From the mid-1960s onwards, the global foundations underpinning this period began to unravel, as US dominance was contested due to the Vietnam War and its balance-of-payments difficulties. Non-communist left-wing alternatives flourished, notably a new kind of internationalism (promoted in particular by Willy Brandt in Germany and Olof Palme in Sweden), environmentalism, and reflections on a post-colonial organisation of world trade, which peaked with the call for a New International Economic Order in 1973.

2 Global Attempts at Balancing Capitalism (1973–92)

A new period subsequently began with the 1973 oil crisis, which dramatically curtailed growth and increased unemployment across the European continent. It sparked severe financial crises in Britain and Italy, and vindicated the West German model, with Bonn preserving a surplus in its trade balance. The first European response was not a general conversion to neoliberalism, but the exploration of many possible paths, including a coordinated Western relaunch (the 1978 Locomotive), a more neomercantilist worldwide organisation for raw materials markets, environmentally friendly planning, and the democratisation of multinationals. In other words, numerous projects seeking to foster *solidarity* and *community* capitalism on a European or on an international basis were initiated. Most of the endeavours launched at the international level failed, but some that were on a European scale enjoyed modest success, such as the 1975 Lomé convention to organise North–South trade, in addition to a handful of European decisions concerning social, regional, and environmental policies.

The 1979 oil crisis eliminated some of these alternatives. The joint recovery plan, to which Germany agreed after much hesitation in 1978, collapsed when Bonn experienced balance of payments difficulties in 1980–81, a largely forgotten episode that was nevertheless central for German leaders. At the same time, Margaret Thatcher's rise to power, the Volcker Shock, and Ronald Reagan's election one year later drove a neoliberal transformation. The European proposal in 1980 to democratise multinationals came too late, five years after most of the debates had been held on a national level. Lastly, 1979 also marked the strong commitment of both Germany and France to a form of European monetary cooperation based mainly on *liberty* capitalism, as Bonn and even Paris refused to create a European fund.

The year 1979 was also transformational outside of Europe.[3] The intervention in Afghanistan was, in retrospect, an essential stage in Soviet decline and the emergence of violent Islamic fundamentalism. The Iranian Revolution and the taking of hostages at the Great Mosque in Mecca confirmed this dynamic, and implicitly showed the waning of more secular ideologies, such as Pan-Arabism. The boat people crisis completed Marxism's loss of credibility. Finally, Deng Xiaoping's rise to power triggered China's gradual opening to free markets. If we also consider the intensifying anti-nuclear protests linked to the Three Mile Island nuclear accident, 1979 clearly marks the end of the post-war world, namely that of the debate between neo-classical economics, Keynesianism, and Marxism, a debate that would soon be replaced by the competing trio of neoliberalism, environmentalism, and identity politics.

The years between 1979 and 1992 were nonetheless still marked by attempts to promote a multifaceted form of capitalist governance. The Delors Commission (1985–95), with the support of most member states, launched many policies of *solidarity* capitalism, including social dialogue, cohesion policy, high standards, and environmental policy directives, culminating in the project for a European carbon tax. Thatcher's protests against social Europe in her 1988 Bruges speech – along with the significant legal disputes surrounding non-application of EC environmental law in many countries – show that the upward harmonisation of legislation was not a complete illusion. But the project to organise *community* capitalism at the European level failed, due to opposition from neoliberals (in member states and within the Commission), to the difficulty of organising a pan-European social movements, and to divisions among its promoters (Delors wanted to empower the Commission, while Paris preferred a non-EEC venture such as Eurekâ). The dirigiste steel policy pursued by the European Commission in the early 1980s remained an exception. Moreover, actors in the business world were often more interested in national or international cooperation (with the US and even the Japanese) than in cooperation with their primary European competitor. 'Fortress Europe' remained a dead letter (except in agriculture with the CAP and the 'Protected designation of origin' set up in 1992).

The organisation of European capitalism around *liberty* was decisively reinforced by the Single Market and monetary union (decided in 1985 and 1992 respectively), both of which were long-standing projects conceived before the crises of the 1970s. They stemmed from a conscious choice made by European leaders (except the British and Scandinavians with respect to fully-fledged monetary union). Many of them were not necessarily very enthusiastic or federalist, but they chose the European option because other alternative paths had failed, whether they were national (reconquest of the French domestic market), bilateral (French–German dialogue), or international (via the GATT, as sought by London and Bonn).

3 High Neoliberalism (1992–2016)

The year 1992 was a neoliberal turning point with the Maastricht Treaty (not entirely neoliberal, but largely interpreted as such), the disappearance of the USSR, and the compromise announcing the end of the GATT Uruguay Round. All previous protectionist agreements (the CAP, multifibre agreements, voluntary export restraints for Japanese cars) disappeared or were watered down. The most ambitious projects for social and environmental regulation were at their height in 1988–92, before ultimately fading away. In addition, the Community expanded to become a Union, with designs to absorb the entire continent. These various elements demonstrate that the process of European integration cannot be reduced to a simple consequence of the Cold War.[4]

The year 2005 was the height of a simultaneously neoliberal and federalist period, marked by the successful implementation of the euro despite predictions of its failure, along with a major enlargement. In addition, many non-Western countries were experiencing difficulties at that time, with Russia and Asia still reeling from the 1997–98 crisis. The leaders of the European Union sought to ratify a constitution, all while drifting towards a large free trade area: enlargement to include Turkey was envisaged, and numerous markets were opened up to competition. Any remaining elements of *solidarity* and *community* capitalism were targeted (Bolkestein directive, competition policy hostile to intra-European mergers, Court decisions against trade unions, etc.). Neoliberalism impacted ever more varied domains, including football as part of the Bosman ruling, with archives revealing the Commission's central role in negotiations with the UEFA. The free movement of people was established, but without any comprehensive agreement to cooperate on police and migration policies. The only element of *community* capitalism that remained was one compatible with free markets: the 'Brussels effect' of promoting EU standards.[5]

Neoliberalism also triumphed on the global level. Many countries, including the former communist ones from Europe that joined the EU in 2004–07, adopted neoliberal policies that went even further than those in the West. China joined the WTO in 2001, but the WTO Doha Round collapsed in 2003–06. The World Wide Web emerged without any stringent regulation. Any attempt to regulate neoliberal globalisation appeared doomed for failure, and the system appeared to work on the surface, as East Asian poverty declined, and 2005 saw the lowest number of casualties from state conflict.[6] A few years later, the US-centred neoliberal global order was shattered by the global financial crisis that began in 2007, by increasingly uncooperative behaviour of Russia, US decline (mired in Iraq and Afghanistan), and the rise of the Global South. In retrospect, the twenty-first century started on 11 September 2001, when the terrorist attacks distracted the US from its competition with China, as well as its reliance on international norms.

In Europe, the turning point came in 2005, with the rejection of the constitutional treaty in France and the Netherlands. It initiated the period of 'crises' that deeply challenged the Union: crisis of EU legitimacy, the Great Recession, the eurozone and migrant crises, and political tensions from rising illiberal governments.[7] Sometimes one crisis fuelled another: in the early 2000s, Poland and Hungary were led by pro-European governments, which were then replaced by much more Eurosceptic governments (2010 in Hungary, 2015 in Poland), partly due to the EU's lack of solidarity during the Great Recession.[8] The harsh neoliberal treatment inflicted during the eurozone crisis contributed to the rise of far-right and far-left parties in both creditor (the AfD in Germany) and debtor countries.

4 The Return of Community Capitalism (since 2016)

Neoliberalism nevertheless lingered on until 2016, which marked a decisive break with the vote for Brexit in the UK, and for Donald J. Trump in the US, both of which were in keeping with a return of *community*-based capitalist governance.[9] For Eastern Europeans, the brutal return to the *community* logic started even earlier, with the Russian invasion of Crimea in 2014. The year 2016 ultimately crystallised what 2015 had revealed – with Grexit avoided at the last minute, and the suspension of the Schengen Agreement due to the 'migrant crisis' – namely that European integration via the Union is not inevitable. In the wake of Brexit, far-right leaders called for Frexit and Nexit; the European Union appeared under threat.

However, the Union has bounced back during each of the subsequent upheavals: Brexit (2016–20), Trump's first presidency (2017–21), the Covid-19 pandemic (2020–21), and the Russo-Ukrainian War (since 2022). The departure of Britain has certainly simplified the pursuit of *solidarity* and *community* policies within the European Union. Since Brexit, the Union has sometimes implemented long-envisioned reforms, albeit often in modest fashion, such as a European Monetary Fund, a transfer union, a preference for European products, competition policy taking foreign protectionism into account, and a carbon tax. The 2019 Green Deal marked the peak of environmental policy. Simply put, *solidarity* capitalism was combined with *community* capitalism thanks to heightened awareness of neoliberalism's detrimental effects on both inequality and the environment (symbolised by Greta Thunberg's *Fridays for Future* starting in 2018).

In 2022, the Russo-Ukrainian War marked a final turning point, as it fuelled inflation and revived European integration in new areas (defence, more aggressive external economic policies via sanctions against Russia), while simultaneously contributing to an environmental backlash and increasing national state aid. Community capitalism has been on the rise on both the member state and European level, with less *solidarity* as a result. The re-election of Donald Trump in 2024 (and Narendra Modi in India) confirmed the return of *community* capitalism, which is also visible in the rising role of multinationals closely connected to the state in China, Russia, and even in the US since 2025.

A Peculiar Brand of European Capitalism?

When compared with other forms of capitalism in large countries (the US, China, or Russia), the European brand of capitalism has been marked by four features: i) the choice to Europeanise the management of *liberty* capitalism (trade, currency); ii) the development of strong national welfare states (especially compared with the US) with targeted elements of intra-European solidarity; iii) a belated but now quite forceful (again, compared with the USA) environmental policy which has been strongly Europeanised; and iv) a large variety of elements of *community* capitalism at national level, whose conflicts have been mediated by European institutions through competition policy and single market rules. The missing element is European *community* capitalism, which only began to take shape following the global resurgence of *community* capitalism since 2016, with some notable exceptions (Airbus and ESA).

Reaching Compromise in the European Governance of Capitalism

Europeans have been constantly negotiating compromises between different forms of capitalist governance because European institutions have been relatively flexible. This sub-chapter will develop this argument in three stages. First, the conditions within European institutions for changing capitalist governance are complex, but they do exist. Second, while Germany has often been very influential, European integration has never been dominated by a single country. Third, a peculiar form of European capitalism has gradually emerged, with specific institutional and socio-economic features.

The Conditions for Change within European Institutions

EU institutions are marked by inertia, but they are also conducive to exploring alternatives. They offer political opportunities for a wide range of actors, including groups that are marginalised on the national level, such as certain environmental NGOs or companies. They can influence public policy on the European level, especially for new issues such as competition policy, environmental protection, and regulating digital technology. Paradoxically, the

Table 11.1 Chronology of post-war European integration and globalisation

Form of capitalist governance	European integration	Political forces in the EEC/EU	Phase of globalisation
1945–73: Embedded liberalism (Strong national *community* and *solidarity* capitalism, combined with a slow return of international free trade)	1948–58: focus on managing national *community* capitalism through various combinations (OEEC, ECSC, EDC, EEC)	- Domination of pro-European Christian Democratic networks - Conservatives, Social Democrats, and socialists divided between a pro-European wing (Mollet) and a more nation-oriented one (Erhard) - Strong anti-European communism in France and Italy	- US domination - Bretton-Woods system - Progressive return to free trade within a Western framework
	1958–73: Regulating free trade through the Common Market	- Rise of different types of left-wing alternatives in the late 1960s, such as internationalism (Brandt, Palme) or environmentalism	Rising contestation of the US and the Bretton-Woods system in the 1960s, leading to the 1971–73 crisis
1973–92 Attempts at an international form of mixed capitalist governance	1973–79: Modest expansion towards socio-environmental policies	- Apogee of left-wing alternatives	Domination by the Triad (US, Japan, Western Europe), which absorbed rising protectionist tensions
	1979–92 'Relaunch' of solutions based on a balance between the dominant goal of liberty, as well as solidarity and community (EMS, Single Market, EMU)	- Failure of the global left-wing alternatives. In Europe, slow rise of environmentalism and of social policies. - Expanded neoliberal influence	- Globalisation still dominated by the Triad – Failure of the Eastern socialist bloc - Rise of East Asia, notably China

Table 11.1 (cont.)

Form of capitalist governance	European integration	Political forces in the EEC/EU	Phase of globalisation
1992–2016 High neoliberalism	1992–2005 Domination of neoliberal policies, albeit with rising environmental policies Curtailment of national *community* capitalism by the EU	- Failure of the centre-left alternative (Pink Europe) - Strong neoliberal coalition - Environmental momentum combined with an environmental backlash in 1992	- Rise of China, concealed by apparent US dominance (wars in Afghanistan and Iraq that appeared successful at first) - Rise of East Asia and other countries of the Global South, fuelled by the dwindling cost of communication
	2005–16 more contestation - EU referenda in 2005 - Eurozone crisis (2010–12) - 'migrant crisis' (2015) - Brexit (2016)	- Strong neoliberal coalition until 2012, more divided afterwards	- Decline of the US (quagmire in Iraq and Afghanistan) - Rising role of the Global South, China in particular - Non-cooperative Russian behaviour since 2007 - Globalisation persists despite a return of protectionist tensions since the Great Recession
2016: return of *community* capitalism	2016–22: - more industrial and social policy - Green Deal (2019)	- Rise of identity politics - Rise of the far right and of illiberalism	
	2022 Russo-Ukraine War - Emphasis on defence and foreign policy - Environmental backlash	- Same, plus decline of the Greens	

European leaders most sceptical of supranational European integration, such as de Gaulle and Thatcher, had a major influence. De Gaulle provided a decisive contribution to European integration by strongly supporting the beginnings of the Common Market between 1958 and 1962; Thatcher supported economically liberal orientations in the 1980s, blocked all advances in social matters, and inspired numerous imitators in Britain and abroad, in particular in Central and Eastern Europe.[10] Future historians may view Giorgia Meloni as another influential leader who shaped the course of European integration – this time by reorienting its migration policy towards a more restrictive approach.

The Europeans have always had a choice: not just being for or against Europe,[11] but also deciding on the kind of capitalist governance they wanted. The *Cassis de Dijon* ruling of 1979 did not automatically trigger a vast dynamic of harmonisation based on mutual recognition. Concrete advances did not come until states and the Commission converged towards the Single European Act in 1986.[12] Similarly, the Maastricht Treaty of 1991 was interpreted in different ways: in a neoliberal and ordoliberal vein with the destructive austerity imposed on Greece; and in a more social one, with the massive financial transfers belatedly put in place during the eurozone crisis, and rapidly expanded during the Covid-19 epidemic. Finally, environmental policy developed despite no reference to the matter in treaties until the Single European Act of 1986, and the fact that such issues could be addressed in other frameworks, as demonstrated by the Montreal Protocol of 1987 (protecting the ozone layer), or the Basel Convention of 1989 (on international movements of hazardous waste).[13] The most striking example of this inversion in the interpretation of legal rules is the treatment of cartels: while the 1962 regulation introduced a system of ex ante control based on prohibition, the 2003 regulation imposed the opposite approach, ex post control connected to the logic of abuse.[14]

The careful study of decision-makers, including non-state ones, reveals the role of trade unions and environmental NGOs on the one hand, and employers on the other, for instance in the early 1980s with IBM, or during the Vredeling Directive contest. In the latter case, enterprises were much more efficient in their lobbying strategy than trade unions.[15] Environmental concerns have enjoyed a growing audience since the 1970s, although 'Merchants of Doubt' with an interest in the status quo have successfully delayed policy decisions by decades.[16] The decision-making process is complicated by the internal division of non-state actors. Some companies support environmental legislation if it offers new business opportunities. Facing new costly regulations, two companies with the same business interests can have different reactions, with one being open and the other engaging in lobbying (see the contrasting positions of Renault and Peugeot on car emission regulations). Environmental NGOs have been split between the most radical, such as

Greenpeace, and those that cooperate closely with European institutions, and are sometimes even funded by them. As a result, the European arena offers a vast space of opportunity for various actors in capitalist governance.

For all that, legal obligations – such as Treaty provisions, the veto power, and the inertia of some institutions (such as the Court of Justice)[17] – limit the options available. Changing the course of the Union is hard, as it requires three conditions: 1) a convincing political project; 2) a strong transnational coalition; and 3) an institutional opportunity. These three factors were aligned in the progressive reinforcement of European competition policy, in specific areas of social and environmental policy (gender equality, biodiversity, etc.), and in the reinforcement of cohesion policy. As a result, *solidarity* and *community* capitalism remained relatively underdeveloped at the European level – not due to institutional constraints imposed by European bodies, but rather because the political and social coalitions advocating such models lacked sufficient strength. Left-wing parties and trade unions were often either openly hostile or largely indifferent to the European integration project. At the same time, many firms preferred to interact with national governments – whose concessions they could more easily influence – or to collaborate with non-European partners, rather than embed themselves within emerging European industrial policy frameworks.

Too Simple a Story: From German Europe to Italian Europe

If European integration is examined through the lens of large nation-states, it becomes tempting to conflate the process with the preference of its largest actor: Germany, and its so-called hegemony.[18] Germany certainly played a dominant role during the eurozone crisis, but also exerted discreet influence over European integration before it. This is due to Germany's sheer size: in a democratic system, it is logical that the most populous actor wields the most influence. Paradoxically, it is also predicated on Germany's relatively modest aims. German officials were not keen on delivering a grand vision for European integration like the French, or even the British (as Thatcher did in Bruges in 1988), except via a vague commitment to a federal Europe in the (very) long term. More moderate than the neoliberal British and dirigiste French, they have often been in line with the compromises struck in Brussels, namely those of a free market economy preserving its high social and environmental standards, as well as its peculiar form of *community* capitalism (codetermination, *Landesbanken*). Germany has evolved, sometimes being more favourable towards European forms of *solidarity* capitalism (in Brandt and Merkel's final years), and sometimes leaning towards neoliberalism (Hartz IV reform, eurozone crisis). It has been reinforced by the end of the Cold War, which has enlarged it and put it at the heart of a reunified Europe.

An alternative nation-centred reading could underscore France's strong influence at the start, for Britain was not a part of European integration until 1973 (and was politically weak until 1979), and Germany was beset by Nazi war crimes. France's capitalist governance was hampered by high military, colonial, and overseas spending. Its agriculture was competitive on the world market, but its industry had a mixed record. Its substantial social spending and often-ineffective social dialogue left the country vulnerable to inflation and high interest rates. As a result, Paris successfully pushed for the CAP, a favourable trade agreement with its former African colonies, and monetary agreements aimed at lowering interest rates (in 1979 and 1992). Many projects for pan-European *solidarity* and *community* capitalism were proposed but almost never pursued in earnest, with French officials being wary of supranationalism: they neither endorsed the creation of a European Monetary Fund, nor did they fully support Delors's project for social and industrial policy.

Britain became more influential under Thatcher. While she suffered setbacks in the 1980s, complaining about the European Monetary Union and Delors's Social Europe, she successfully instilled neoliberalism, often in association with like-minded Northern European countries, which were often less neoliberal than she but supported her on specific measures. While her influence was mixed in the 1980s, it became paradoxically more important when she left power, with neoliberalism peaking in the 1990s and early twenty-first century (Chapter 8).

After Brexit and the return of *community* capitalism in 2016, France's brand of European capitalism has been more visible, with expanding *solidarity* (a large stimulus plan and the Green Deal) and more industrial policy at the European level. The rise of the far right has threatened this legacy. Italy's government, led by the far-right Georgia Meloni since 2022, appears to be one of the strongest in Europe after the 2024 European and US elections, both of which bolstered its position. Has Europe finally acquired an Italian flavour?

While this nation-centred story has a kernel of truth, it is too simplistic. The example of Italy, a country whose influence has for decades been linked to supranational actors (Spinelli, Padoa-Schioppa, Monti, Draghi), shows that the concept of 'national influence' is a tricky one. Nationals from one country can be influential through different channels, both national and supranational, and in different ways, as shown by the contrast between Spinelli and Meloni.

Moreover, the influence of the three larger countries has always been predicated on their ability to forge national and supranational alliances. The French–German motor was certainly the most stable and influential alliance (notably in 1956–58 to secure the Treaty of Rome, 1979 on the EMS, 1991–92 on Maastricht, 2010–15 to preserve the eurozone, and 2020 during Covid). This is another unique feature in world history, as no such pairing between former arch-enemies exists: no one talks of a Korean–Japanese motor, or of an

Indian–Pakistani couple. But the French–German motor was not exclusive. In 1962, Gaullist France secured the CAP thanks to an improbable alliance with the Netherlands and the Commission. In 1992, it obtained the Monetary Union because many countries with weak currencies desperately wanted it. France secured exemptions for agricultural and cultural products because it teamed with other countries (mainly from Southern Europe). Conversely, Germany successfully imposed its ordoliberal vision of the monetary union during the negotiations surrounding the Maastricht Treaty negotiations, and then during the eurozone crisis, because most Northern (and later Eastern) European countries also supported it. In addition, countries squeezed (such as France) between the Northern creditors and the Southern debtors did not want to be associated with the latter, and therefore drew closer to the former.

In other words, German ideas were influential because they were close to an acceptable compromise for the majority of European citizens who supported a European capitalism based mainly on *liberty*, with only residual elements of *solidarity* and *community*. And Britain was often less isolated than its prime ministers have generally asserted for their domestic audience (with self-portrayals as 'freedom fighters' against statist continentals). Britain initially teamed with Italy to push through regional policy during its protectionist period, and then benefited from the neoliberal wave of the late twentieth and early twenty-first century. Most especially, it carved out a series of tailored exemptions for itself. Britain has been at the core of Europe without realizing it.

Lastly, other large countries have played a role, such as Spain under Felipe Gonzalez (1982–96) to support the 'relaunch of Europe', or more recently Poland since the Russo-Ukrainian War. Even some small countries have been influential: either as a broker between larger neighbours (such as the Benelux countries),[19] or as a veto-wielder (tax havens are preserved by the fact that all decisions involving taxation require unanimity) or to delay decisions (such as Hungary for sanctions against Russia). By teaming up, they can have considerable influence, such as the so-called Frugal Four (Austria, Denmark, the Netherlands, and Sweden, together making up roughly 10 per cent of the EU's population) during the negotiations over a concerted stimulus during the Covid crisis.

A Specific European Governance of Capitalism

European institutions have managed to become major players by prevailing over other European and international organisations, and even over states in many areas. This process has not been a smooth one, and it could be reversed in the future. Overall, the EC and later the EU have prevailed over their competitors, because they have represented a balance between federal and intergovernmental features acceptable to many, providing both credible commitments thanks to its federal law, as well as the possibility of preserving peculiar national features of capitalism. Overall, European integration has been driven by two central dynamics: i) the ability of member states to assert their national interest through European integration and to control its overall direction and ii) the influence of supranational and transnational actors, notably in what appeared at first as peripheral issues such as competition policy and environmental policy.

One of the main specific features of European capitalism is the pivotal role of EU institutions. The Commission plays a particularly important role thanks to its monopoly over proposing legislation, and its shared power to implement them and to control member states. But the Commission has not always been influential. Some commissioners have indeed wielded considerable influence when they managed to combine ambition, technical skills, and political clout to secure a majority in the College of Commissioner, the Council, and increasingly the European Parliament. For instance, the flamboyant federalist activist Spinelli was less effective than the former Belgian diplomat Davignon. The Commission's influence was not one-sided: Delors strove to promote *solidarity* and *community* capitalism, whereas Brittan was neoliberal, and Vestager somewhere in-between. The Commission should neither be considered a technical and depoliticised body, nor a government in making, but rather an indispensable stage director. It interprets the laws drafted by others (the Treaties, secondary law, jurisprudence) and coordinates their implementation, taking into account all involved, from the touchy lead actors (i.e. Britain, France, or Germany among others) to secondary characters (which often end up stealing the show).

Beyond the Commission, the other EU institutions are also important and peculiar: the European Parliament has allowed marginal constituencies to voice their claims (regarding environmental issues for example), the European Court of Justice has supported a rather federal interpretation of *liberty* capitalism, and the European Council is more than a juxtaposition of states.[20] Transnational actors, including environmental NGOs, gender advocacy groups, and multinational corporations, have also sought to shape this complex institutional landscape.

Historical accounts of the decision-making process reveal alternatives that were given serious consideration in the past, and that could potentially be revived in one form or another in the future.

The Ever-Present Neoliberal Alternative

The fact that there is a neoliberal alternative to European integration probably comes as a surprise to those who already consider the EU as the epitome of neoliberalism, but things could have been even worse! First, many so-called neoliberal reforms were in reality old-fashioned market-based policy. The fact that several countries adopted prudent macro-economic policies to restore their competitiveness and to ease their financial constraints is not a peculiarity of the late twentieth century. France did just that in 1959 after experiencing a financial crisis, as did Britain in the 1960s. Communist Eastern countries were also affected by growing financial constraints after 1973, although they could hardly be described as neoliberal. The neoliberal orientation is particularly evident in the extreme austerity measures that led to substantial reductions in welfare provisions, such as those implemented under Thatcher or in Greece during the eurozone crisis, as well as in the extensive deregulation of numerous sectors – likely exceeding what many individual member states would have undertaken independently.

Second, without the EC/EU, free trade dynamics could have been even harsher. In 1956–58, the British wanted to replace the Common Market with a free trade area that had no elements of *solidarity* or *community*. Later on, Thatcher and the new generation of neoliberals promoted expansive deregulation. German neoliberals such as Ludwig Erhard were also tempted by the free trade area, and by worldwide trade liberalisation. As a major exporter (notably outside Europe), Germany could have lived perfectly well without European integration. Bonn could have joined the ECSC and the EEC to satisfy its US protector, and then let it wither away like so many other international organisations. The country could also have adopted a more neutral stance after 1989, neglecting the EEC and NATO, a development feared at the time by some of its allies in both the US and Europe.[21]

Third, this neoliberal alternative still exists today. The Singapore-on-Thames project of some Brexiters, who came to power under Boris Johnson (2019–22), is a neoliberal strategy. It is national in scope, but could influence the Union by virtue of its legal Darwinism: if one of the major competitors to EU countries curtails its social and environmental legislation, that would certainly influence the debate in Brussels. This would be especially true if the UK were to retain access to the Single Market without conforming to the same standards. Neoliberal Europe could also come from within, as the rise of far-right parties means growing opposition to social and environmental standards on the European level, and sometimes on the national one as well (for environmental norms in particular). Most of these far-right parties would like to reduce Europe to a free trade area, without any federal, *solidarity*, or *community* features. They could effectively hollow out the Union from within.

The Ebb and Flow of Socio-environmental Alternatives

Many projects emphasising *solidarity* were devised but ultimately shelved (tax harmonisation, controlling multinationals, planning), amended (regulating international trade), or adopted belatedly (environmental protection, cohesion policy, carbon tax, stimulus plan). European *solidarity* capitalism has been marked by ebbs and flows, with a favourable period (1945–50, 1968–73, 1987–92, 2017–22) followed by a backlash, often caused by economic crisis. More generally, supporters of *solidarity* must overcome three specific difficulties.

First, the intellectual hurdle is high, for solidarity measures are perceived as being more costly than free market rules, because they involve redistribution (such as cohesion policy) or impose costs on companies (such as social and environmental standards). Free market rules also have distributive consequences, but they are less visible in the short term, or are more diffuse: the cost of a depolluting device is immediate, but the cost of pollution is hard to estimate. Many health issues were recognised only after decades of scientific disputes (such as the harm caused by tobacco or asbestos). Even mitigating climate change must still be justified despite constant heatwaves and raging brush fires.

Second, the *solidarity* coalition (left-wing parties, trade unions, green NGOs) was for a long time not particularly interested in European integration. This is logical because *solidarity* capitalism (in particular redistribution) has remained mostly national, and because the issue (whether it be inequality or pollution) is international in nature, and not just European. By contrast, Christian Democratic networks long ago engaged in cooperation within Carolingian Europe.[22] The *solidarity* coalition was quite late in using European institutions. The European Trade Union Confederation (ETUC) was formed twenty years after the first European business organisation. It was active in the European arena during the 1970s, but with no genuinely EC-based influence strategy. When it began to roll out such a strategy in the 1980s, it was already too late, as the neoliberal revolution had already swept through Britain.

What is more, the *solidarity* coalition has been divided by communism, with some Social Democrats being profoundly anti-communist, especially the West Germans who were appalled by the execution of their compatriots trying to cross the Berlin Wall. Paradoxically, some French and Italian communists supported Europe, as demonstrated by the reflections of the French minister Rigout in 1982, or the actions of Spinelli. The environmentalists have also been divided between advocates of de-growth and supporters of sustainable growth.

Third, it is more difficult to organise transnationally for actors representing the weak, who are often less powerful than those representing the business community. The records of trade unions, environmental NGOs, and certain international solidarity organisations such as the ILO often reveal their financial fragility. Multinationals are more powerful and can even capture the regulators, such as in the *Dieselgate* scandal.

As a result, for a long time there have been no efficient transnational coalitions in favour of a European integration based on *solidarity*. The

British and Scandinavians were often opposed to social Europe, refusing any form of interference with their welfare states. The poorest countries were favourable towards redistributive policies, but not to harmonising social legislation, which would eliminate their competitive advantage. The French government sometimes defended the principle of *solidarity* at the European level, especially under socialist governments (since Mollet), but also with moderate centre-right ministers (such as Robert Boulin), but did not do so systematically, balking at the cost (of regional policy and some environmental regulation, such as unleaded petrol) and the spectre of greater supranationalism. Germany has defended some environmental regulations, in addition to some targeted measures of solidarity (notably in 2015 with asylum seekers), but has generally accepted the solidarity elements of the European governance of capitalism under pressure from its partners.

The future of social Europe largely depends on the ability of its promoters to build coalitions between the North and the South, as well as with the East. In 2018, the revision of the Posted Workers Directive based on upward harmonisation of social standards was made possible by dialogue between Western, Central, and Eastern European governments. Overall, *solidarity* has often progressed when an efficient coalition has emerged in association with the *liberty* and *community* coalition, for example, with cohesion policy. Environmental measures in keeping with the *liberty* approach include market-based mechanisms for reducing pollution. Targeted protectionism (such as the Carbon Border Adjustment Mechanism) combines environmentalism and *community* capitalism.

Since 2022, the socio-environmental alternative has been on the defensive. Its progress depends on implementing already-existing measures. At the same time, old projects are being revisited (such as international taxation on certain exchanges), and others are emerging, notably to address new sources of pollution, from nanoparticles to the data centres powering AI.

The Challenge of Community *Capitalism*

Community capitalism has been ubiquitous in post-war Europe, and it is making a comeback after a decline under the 'high neoliberalism' period. All countries have adopted strategies to promote their own community, either to protect sectors that are non-competitive but essential to political stability, such as agriculture, or to foster the development of new industries. The archives show that even Thatcher supported a select number of ailing companies, and that the Germans actively supported its farmers and Airbus for economic reasons. Even actors considered to be liberal, such as Schlecht or Bangemann, envisaged targeted measures of industrial policy.

Enterprises frequently resort to such non-competitive practices. Examples from the archives demonstrate this, although they are rare, for it is difficult to access primary sources on cartels. The few accounts that emerge, such as Scandinavian cartels for paper, or the cartel involving electrical equipment manufacturers in Brazil, show the hidden reality of how markets function. Sometimes, as with steel or synthetic textiles around 1980, public authorities establish or tolerate crisis cartels. Cartels have therefore been part of industrial policy.

Industrial policy has always been limited on the European level, with the exception of steel in the early 1980s. European cooperation was primarily developed in high technology, due to its prohibitive cost, mainly in military cooperation and aerospace. It was done on an intergovernmental basis, although the Commission slightly increased its competence in these areas even before the Russo-Ukrainian War. Attempts by Delors to Europeanise industrial policy in high technology failed, with his neoliberal colleague Commissioner Brittan strongly opposing the merger of ATR/De Havilland. Even the implementation of preference in public markets proved impossible.

The examples of Airbus and the European Space Agency show that a successful industrial policy revolves around a dual balance. First, state authorities must both provide long-term financial and legal stability (usually for strategic reasons, including for Germany), all while preserving flexibility for industrial actors to pursue a business-oriented approach. State authorities should be able to 'pick the winner', but also to 'let the loser go'.[23] Second, a successful European industrial policy must combine intergovernmentalism (with long-term state subsidies and a favourable legal environment to avoid hostile foreign takeovers) and federalism (in terms of an integrated industrial and commercial structure, as well as the Commission's involvement to defend the company in case of trade conflict). Such projects work best in a new sector with high development costs, no dominant national actor, and a limited number of countries, thereby limiting the problem of fair return.

By contrast, subsidies for the French–British Concorde airplane were fairly inefficient due to bad luck (the oil shock), protectionism, and an approach based more on political prestige than business opportunity. Other counter-examples include the consortia established by political authorities, which bring together European companies engaged in fierce competition with one other. They often prefer to partner with US firms (which provide technical know-how and access to new markets) rather than with European neighbours.

The Airbus model is difficult to reproduce, and illustrates the economic and political difficulties associated with developing European industrial policy. Economically, many countries consider European industrial policy to be unnecessary (if their trade balance is already in surplus), and even detrimental, for promoting European preference could lead to retaliatory trade measures and a subsidy race. Politically, many promoters of European industrial policy are reluctant to accept the delegation of power that such policy would entail. Paris has often defended an intergovernmental logic, for instance with the

Eurekâ project in 1985. The logic of 'fair return' has often paralysed the debates. In the end, *community* capitalism requires a genuine political 'community', a stable and cohesive group that is still lacking in the European Union. This is true even though the EU is the heir to the European 'Community' set up in 1957, but it has been a community with no communitarianism, failing to establish any kind of European preference.

The Union has reacted to the return of *community* capitalism since 2016 by finally adopting measures that had been under discussion for decades, but always refused in the past: targeted protectionist schemes in trade policy, European preference (only in the weapons industry), and tolerance on subsidies to enterprises. Moreover, while this study has documented numerous instances of EU–US tensions over trade and NATO, as well as a multitude of international protectionist agreements up to the late 1980s, the Trump II administration has presented unprecedented challenges since 2025, featuring protectionist measures unseen since the 1930s and territorial threats reminiscent of the pre–World War I era.

Therefore two challenges remain. First, will Europeans create an effective *community* capitalism by moving beyond the fair return principle, and by linking economic and security matters in their foreign policy? This does not mean that Europeans should federalise their industrial and security policy, but that they should probably coordinate their policies in those areas more effectively if they want to play a role in a world increasingly dominated by more nationalistic dynamics. The second challenge will be combining a rising *community* approach with *liberty* and *solidarity*: fostering assertive European industrial policy runs the risk of sparking a subsidy race, which would fuel protectionism and deprive the government of resources for social and environmental policies.

The Trinity of European Capitalism in the Future

If the European Union does not disappear, the trinity of capitalism will be helpful in distinguishing several scenarios for the future (see Figure 11.1). The three poles of the triangle all lead to an 'ideal-type' of Europe: a free trade area with no regulation (similar to what Hayek envisaged in 1939); 'fortress Europe' with assertive power (in terms of trade, migration, and defence); and the European welfare state. Depending on one's perspective, the latter can be seen either as a paradise or a catastrophe. For British Eurosceptics, it conjures up an apocalyptic vision: in his dystopian novel *The Aachen Memorandum*, published in 1995, the Thatcherite Andrew Roberts imagined a semi-authoritarian Union limiting working time to thirty-two hours a week, and applying a top European tax rate of 95 per cent![24]

The future will most likely be some combination of the three. Continuing momentum around a regulated market could lead, as advocated in the 2024

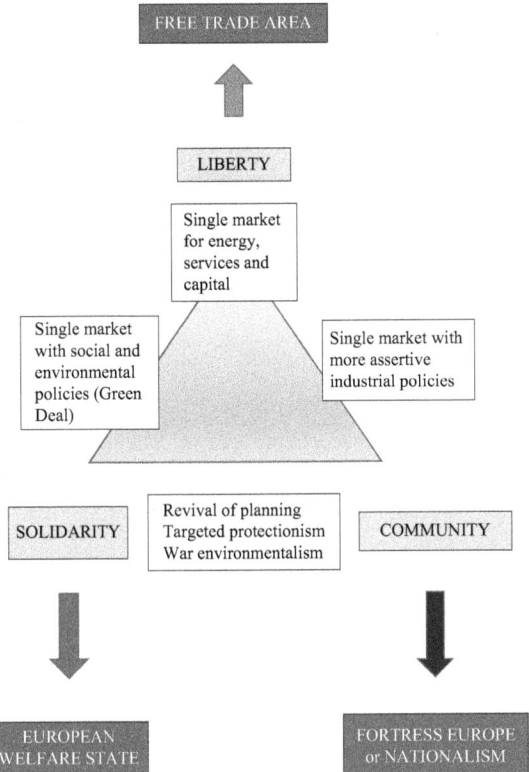

Figure 11.1 Scenarios for the future of Europe

Draghi and Letta reports, to a deepening of the Single Market (for example for financial markets or infrastructure). A push to the far right would combine *community* Europe (with respect to migration) and neoliberalism (because of the far right's opposition to high European social and environmental standards).[25] It could lead to the transformation of Europe into a mere free trade area, and the return of nationalistic tensions. The Russo-Ukrainian War could lead to an assertion of European diplomatic and military clout (a genuine 'Fortress Europe'), or conversely to the reassertion of the national dimension, or to the continuity of the post-war compromise in which Atlantic logic plays a dominant role. *Community* and *solidarity* approaches could come together as part of a so-called war environmentalism.[26] For example, developing renewable energy and integrating national energy grids in Europe would reinforce the Union's autonomy and reduce its dependence on external suppliers of hydrocarbons. Developing local production chains could diminish industry's carbon footprint and reduce dependence on China, whose domination in so many areas of manufacturing is unparalleled in history. But these solutions are costly in the short term, and could potentially lead to inflation and a trade war. Protectionism needs to be carefully calibrated to avoid a 1930s-like escalation. As always, European integration must manage the tensions around *community* capitalism, albeit in unprecedented fashion.

NOTES

Introduction

1 Lauren Collins, 'Banksy was here', *The New Yorker*, 7 May 2007.
2 This trinity is explained below, and in more detail in Chapter 1.
3 The book is focused mainly on the European Union (set up in 1992) and its predecessor the European Economic Communities (set up in 1951 and in 1957). It includes also other European forums, the first one being the Organisation of European Economic Co-operation (OEEC) created in 1948.
4 Erik Jones, 'Towards a theory of disintegration', in *Journal of European Public Policy*, 25, 3, 2018, 440–451; John Gillingham, *The EU: An Obituary*, Verso Books, 2018; Ben Rosamond, 'Theorising the EU in crisis: De-Europeanisation as disintegration', in *Global Discourse*, 9, 1, 2019, 31–44.
5 Such a claim is fairly commonplace for a historian. To take a recent example, Emma Rotschild states in the introduction to her famous book on acid rain: 'without past knowledge of how societies have dealt with environmental pollution, we have little chance of improving upon these efforts ... An important caveat: ... no historical period will ever be a perfect laboratory to model how the future will unfold .... With that said, we have no better options'. Emma Rothschild, *Poisonous Skies. Acid Rain and the Globalization of Pollution*, Chicago University Press, 2019, 5.
6 Three major monographs have already connected the two albeit somewhat differently, notably on the late 1940s and the 1950s: Ernst B. Haas, *Uniting of Europe: Political, Social, and Economic Forces, 1950–1957*, University of Notre Dame Press, 2020 [1958]; Alan Milward, *The Rescue of the Nation-State*, Routledge, 1992; on the years between 1955 and 1992, but without recourse to archival documents: Andrew Moravcsik, *The Choice for Europe: Social Purpose and State Power from Messina to Maastricht*, Cornell University Press, 1998. For a more general perspective, see: Harold James, *Europe Contested. From the Kaiser to Brexit*, Routledge, 2019. Edited volumes have tackled this issue using a more multiperspectival approach. See, for example, Aurélie Andry, Emmanuel Mourlon-Druol, Haakon Ikonomou and Quentin Jouan (eds.), *Rethinking European Integration History in Light of Capitalism*, Routledge, 2022. See the last section of this introduction for further detail on the historiography.
7 See below in Footnotes 48 and 49; on varieties of capitalism: Peter A. Hall, David Soskice (eds.), *Varieties of Capitalism. The Institutional Foundations of Comparative Advantage*, Oxford University Press, 2001. On international political economy: Kevin O'Rourke, 'Economic history and contemporary challenges to

globalization', *Journal of Economic History*, 79, 2, 2019, 356–382; Thomas Piketty, *Capital in the Twenty-First Century*, Harvard University Press, 2014.

8 Among the most incisive books in this field, with a logical focus on the UN and the US (and the anti-US reaction): Mark Mazower, *Governing the World: The History of an Idea*, Allen Lane, 2012 (the EU is mostly covered in pages 406–415); Sandrine Kott, *A World More Equal. An Internationalist Perspective on the Cold War*, Columbia University Press, 2024. See also: Glenda Sluga and Patricia Clavin (eds.), *Internationalisms: A Twentieth Century History*, Cambridge University Press, 2017.

9 On European integration and international organisations: Lorenzo Mechi, Guia Migani and Francesco Petrini (eds.), *Networks of Global Governance: International Organisations and European Integration in a Historical Perspective*, Cambridge Scholar Publishing, 2014; Garavini Giuliano, *After Empires European Integration, Decolonization, and the Challenge from the Global South 1957-1986*, Oxford University Press, 2012; Emmanuel Mourlon-Druol and Federico Romero, *International Summitry and Global Governance. The Rise of the G7 and the European Council, 1974–1991*, Routledge, 2018.

10 Jürgen Kocka, *Capitalism and Its Critics: A Long-Term View*, Leibniz Information Centre for Economics, 2018, 72–73; Jürgen Kocka, *Capitalism: A Short History*, Princeton University Press, 2016.

11 Jürgen Kocka has also used the term 'industrial capitalism', which began in the eighteenth century in Great Britain, and in the nineteenth elsewhere. See the seminal article: E. P. Thompson, 'Time, Work Discipline, and Industrial Capitalism', in *Past & Present*, 38, 1967, 56–97.

12 Sarah Bauerle Danzman, and Sophie Meunier, 'The EU's geoeconomic turn: From policy laggard to institutional innovator', in *JCMS*, 62, 4, 2024, 1097–1115; Sophie Meunier, and Kalypso Nicolaidis, 'The geopoliticization of European trade and investment policy', in *JCMS*, 57, 2019, 103–113; Milan Babić, Adam D. Dixon, and Imogen T. Liu (eds.), *The Political Economy of Geoeconomics: Europe in a Changing World*, Palgrave, 2022; Robert D. Blackwill and Jennifer M. Harris, *War by Other Means: Geoeconomics and Statecraft*, Harvard University Press, 2016; Daniel W. Drezner, Henry Farrell, and Abraham L. Newman (eds.), *The Uses and Abuses of Weaponized Interdependence*, Brookings Institution Press, 2021; on deglobalisation: O'Rourke, 'Economic history'; Kathleen R. McNamara, 'Transforming Europe? The EU's industrial policy and geopolitical turn', in *Journal of European Public Policy*, 2023, 1–26; 'Special report: Homeland Economics', *The Economist*, 2 October 2023; Luuk van Middelaar, 'Brexit as the European Union's "Machiavellian moment"', *Common Market Law Review*, 55, 3, 2018, 3–28; on 'statecraft' see also Draghi report: *The Future of European Competitiveness: Report by Mario Draghi*, 2024, 3.

13 Eric Helleiner, *The Neomercantilists: A Global Intellectual History*, Cornell University Press, 2021.

14 On this 'economic lawfare': Cornelia Woll, in *Corporate Crime and Punishment: The Politics of Negotiated Justice in Global Market*, Princeton University Press, 2023; see also: Nicholas Mulder, *The Economic Weapon: The Rise of Sanctions as a Tool of Modern War*, University Press 2022; Christopher R. W. Dietrich (ed.), *Diplomacy and Capitalism: The Political Economy of US Foreign Relations*, University of Pennsylvania Press, 2022.

15 Fabio Buffone, Tibur Ergen, Manolis Kalaitzake, 'No strings attached: Corporate welfare, state intervention, and the issue of conditionality', in *Competition & Change*, 27, 2, 2023, 253-276.
16 On the construction of markets: Polayni, *The Great Transformation*, 141; Alec Stone Sweet, Wayne Sandholtz, and Neil Fligstein (eds.), *The Institutionalization of Europe*, Oxford University Press, 2001; Bernard Jullien and Andy Smith (eds.), *The EU's Government of Industries: Markets, Institutions and Politics*, Routledge, 2015.
17 See Chapter 10. Kathleen McNamara has defined industrial policy as 'the use of public powers to actively shape markets for the interests and values of a bounded political community'. It is a break from 'neoliberal market governance', which was 'framed as neutral'. 'Today's EU industrial policy, in contrast, makes politically explicit the distributional choices over the sectors and activities being privileged'; McNamara, 'Transforming Europe?'.
18 See Chapter 3 on Keynes, and Chapter 8 on Hayek.
19 See Chapter 2 and: Jeffrey Checkel and Peter Katzenstein (eds.), *European Identity*, Cambridge University Press, 2009; Aline Sierp, *History, Memory, and Trans-European Identity: Unifying Divisions*, Routledge, 2014; Viktoria Kaina, Pawel Karolewski, and Sebastian Kühn (eds.), *European Identity Revisited: New Approaches and Recent Empirical Evidence*, Routledge, 2016; Robert Frank, 'Cultural, memorial and reference sphere, public sphere and European democracy, in Wilfried Loth (ed.), *Experiencing Europe*, Nomos, 2009, 152-168; Hartmut Kaelble, *The European Public Sphere*, Max Weber Lecture, EUI, 2007.
20 While the transparency of the EU should be improved (see the 2022 Qatargate scandal and the role of lobbying), it is certainly greater than in most countries in the world, including many of its own member states.
21 On member states' differences: Hussein Kassim and Adriaan Schout (ed.), *National Government Narratives of the EU: 'Official Stories' of Belonging*, Palgrave Macmillan, 2025.
22 On the impact of EU trade regulations, see Chapters 6 and 10; Anu Bradford, *The Brussels Effect: How the European Union Rules the World*, Oxford University Press, 2020.
23 For the broader institutional argument, see Chapter 2 on European institutions.
24 To borrow the vocabulary of Andrew Moravcsik, member states have engaged in interstate bargaining based on asymmetrical interdependence. They accept institutional delegation in order to ensure credible commitments. See: Moravcsik, *The Choice for Europe*; Milward, *Rescue*; Christopher Bickerton, Dermot Hodson, and Uwe Puetter (eds.), *The New Intergovernmentalism: States and Supranational Actors in the Post-Maastricht Era*, Oxford University Press, 2015; Luuk van Middelaar, *The Passage to Europe: How a Continent Became a Union*, Yale University Press, 2013.
25 The dates mentioned are those for Spinelli's terms in office, first as European Commissioner (1970-1976), later as a member of the Italian Parliament (1976-1983), and finally as a member of the European Parliament (1979-1986). Andrew Glencross and Alexandre Trechsel, *EU Federalism and Constitutionalism: The Legacy of Altiero Spinelli*, Lexington books, 2010.
26 In her speech from 21 May 1980, Thatcher asserted: 'There is no real alternative [to neoliberal policies]'; Jan-Werner Müller, *What Is Populism?* University of

Pennsylvania Press, 2017; Erik Jones, 'Populism in Europe', in *SAIS Review of International Affairs*, 27, 1, 2007, 37–47.

27 Samuel Moyn, *Not Enough: Human Rights in an Unequal World*, Harvard University Press, 2018; On Europe, see for example an analysis of the popular vote on Brexit, which is explained by cultural, educational, and economic issues: Sasha O. Becker, Thiemmo Fetzer, and Dennis Novy, 'Who voted for Brexit? A comprehensive district-level analysis', in *Economic Policy*, 32, 92, 2017, 601–650.

28 These three values echo the Preamble to the United States Constitution, which evokes 'Liberty', 'the general Welfare', and 'the common defense', as well as the motto of the French state since 1880: 'Liberty, Equality, and Fraternity'.

29 The call to fuse these approaches is widely shared among historians: Patricia Clavin, 'Defining transnationalism', in *Contemporary European History*, 14, 4, 2005, 421–439; Kiran Klaus Patel, 'An emperor without clothes? The debate about transnational history twenty-five years on', in *Histoire@Politique*, 26, May 2016, 191–206; David Reynolds, 'From the transatlantic to the transnational: Reflections on the changing shape of international history', in *Diplomacy & Statecraft*, 24, 1, 2013, 134–148.

30 Karl Polanyi, *The Great Transformation: The Political and Economic Origins of Our Time*, Beacon Press, 1985 [1944],135 on the 'birth of the liberal creed' and the 'evangelical fervour' of its supporters. See also: Peter A. Hall (ed.), *The Political Power of Economic Ideas: Keynesianism across Nations*, Princeton University Press, 1989. On European integration history: Craig Parsons, 'Ideas and power: Four intersections and how to show them', in *Journal of European Public Policy*, 23, 3, 2016, 44–463.

31 John Maynard Keynes, *The General Theory of Employment, Interest and Money*, Macmillan, 1936, 379. Strikingly, Keynes himself was both a theorist and a practitioner, notably a currency trader: Olivier Accominotti, David Chambers, and James Morrison, 'The speculative consequences of the peace', in Patricia Clavin and al. (eds.), *Keynes's Economic Consequences of the Peace after 100 Years: Polemics and Policy*, Cambridge University Press, 2024.

32 Giovanni Capoccia, 'Critical Junctures', in Orfeo Fioretos, Tulia Falleti, Adam Sheingate (eds.), *Oxford Handbook on Historical Institutionalism*, Oxford University Press, 2016, 95–108.

33 For example, on the limitations of the archives for the Court of Justice of the European Union, see: Fernanda Nicola, 'Waiting for the Barbarians: Inside the Archive of the ECJ', in Claire Kilpatrick, and Joanne Scott (eds.), *New Legal Approaches to Studying the Court of Justice: Revisiting Law in Context*, Oxford University Press, 2020; Veera Fritz, 'Judge Biographies as a Methodology to Grasp the Dynamics inside the CJEU and Its Relationship with EU Member States', in Michael Rask Madsen, Fernanda Nicola, and Antoine Vauchez (eds.), *Researching the European Court of Justice: Methodological Shifts and Law's Embeddedness*, Cambridge University Press, 2022, 209–234.

34 Kiran Klaus Patel, 'Provincializing European Union: Co-operation and integration in Europe in a historical perspective', in *Contemporary European History*, 22, 4, 2013, 649–673.

35 Frederick Cooper, 'Provincializing France', in Ann Laura Stoler, Carole McGranahan, and Peter C. Perdue (eds.), *Imperial formations*, Currey, 2007, 341–377.

36 Antonio Varsori, *La cenerentola d'Europa. L'Italia e l'Integrazione Europea dal 1947 a Oggi*, Rubbetino, 2010; Antonio Varsori and Benedetto Zaccaria (eds.), *Italy in the International System from Détente to the End of the Cold War: The Underrated Ally*, Palgrave Macmillan, 2018; for examples in the archives of political leaders disregarding the importance of Italy, see: BR-NA, PREM19/133, steering brief, 22 November 1979; AAPD/1983, doc. 338, note on a Kohl–Thatcher meeting of 9 November 1983; AAPD/1984, doc. 29, note on a Kohl–Mitterrand meeting of 2 February 1984; James Baker archives (Princeton USA), box 111, folder 6, note for James Baker, 30 June 1992.

37 Many examples are provided in this book, notably of the usual suspects (i.e. the Benelux states of Belgium, Luxembourg and the Netherlands) but also of Ireland, Greece, Scandinavian as well as Central and Eastern European states.

38 Philipp Ther, *Europe since 1989. A History*, Princeton University Press, 2017; Ferenc Laczo and Vera Scepanovic, 'Eastern Europe in the history of European integration: From the periphery to the centre?', in Brigitte Leucht, Katja Seidel, and Laurent Warlouzet (eds.), *Reinventing Europe. The History of the European Union, 1945 to the Present*, Bloomsbury, 2023, 281–298.

39 Andy Smith, 'Why European Commissioners matter', in *JCMS*, 41, 2003, 137–155; Mark Pollack, *The Engines of European Integration. Delegation, Agency, and Agenda Setting in the European Union*, Oxford University Press, 2003; Hussein Kassim and Brigid Laffan, 'The Juncker Presidency: The political commission in practice', in *JCMS*, 57, 1, 2019, 49–61; Frédéric Mérand, *The Political Commissioner: A European Ethnography*, Oxford University Press, 2021; Michelle Cini and Nieves Pérez-Solórzano, *European Union Politics*, Oxford University Press, 2022.

40 See Chapter 2 and: Karen Alter, *The European Court's Political Power: Selected Essays*, Oxford University Press, 2009; Antoine Vauchez, *Brokering Europe. Euro-Lawyers and the Making of a Transnational Polity*, Cambridge University Press, 2015; Fernanda Nicola and Bill Davies (eds.), *EU Law Stories. Contextual and Critical Histories of European Jurisprudence*, Cambridge University Press, 2017; Billy Davies and Morten Rasmussen, 'Introduction: Towards a new history of European law', in *Contemporary European History*, 21, 3, 2012, 305–318; Peter Lindseth, *Power and Legitimacy: Reconciling Europe and the Nation-State*, Oxford University Press, 2010. For a critical approach: Morten Rasmussen and Dorte Sindbjerg Martinsen, 'EU constitutionalisation revisited: Redressing a central assumption in European studies', in *European Law Journal*, 2019, 1–22. On the history of the European Parliament, see recently: Mechtild Roos, *The Parliamentary Roots of European Social Policy: Turning Talk into Power*, Palgrave Macmillan, 2021; and: Berthold Rittberger, 'The creation and empowerment of the European Parliament', in *JCMS*, 41, 2, 2003, 203–225; Yves Mény (ed.), *Building Parliament: 50 Years of European Parliament History 1958-2008*, Office for Official Publications of the European Communities, 2009.

41 Pepper Culpepper considers that business tends to have more influence on policymaking regarding topics that are technical: Pepper Culpepper, *Quiet Politics and Business Power: Corporate Control in Europe and Japan*, Cambridge University Press, 2011.

42 On the dynamism of the field: Sven Beckert, 'The new history of capitalism', in Jürgen Kocka and Marcel van der Linden (eds.), *Capitalism. The Reemergence of a Historical Concept*, Bloomsbury, 2016, 235–249.

43 To name but just four classics: Polanyi, *The Great Transformation*; Piketty, *Capital*; Joseph Stiglitz, *Globalization and Its Discontents Revisited: Anti-globalization in the Era of Trump*, Norton & Company, 2018; Dani Rodrik, *The Globalisation Paradox: Democracy and the Future of the World Economy?*, Norton & Company, 2012.

44 Kevin O'Rourke, 'Globalisation', in Jeffery Jenkins and Jared Rubin (eds.), *Oxford Handbook of Historical Political Economy*, Oxford University Press, 2024; Michael Huberman, *Odd Couple. International Trade and Labor Standards in History*, Yale University Press, 2012.

45 Contribution with a broad perspective on the relationship between companies and environmental policy include: Ann-Kristin Bergquist, 'Renewing business history in the era of the Anthropocene', in *Business History Review*, 93, 2019, 3–24; Sandra Bott, Sabine Pitteloud, and Janick Marina Schaufelbuehl, *Environmental Regulation and the History of Capitalism: The Role of Business from Stockholm 1972 to the Climate Crisis*, Routledge, 2025; Ben Huf, Glenda Sluga, and Sabine Selchow, 'Business and the planetary history of international environmental governance in the 1970s', in *Contemporary European History*, 31, 2022, 553–569; Naomi Oreskes and Eric M. Conway, *Merchants of Doubts. How a Handful of Scientists Obscured the Truth on Issues from Tobacco Smoke to Global Warming*, Bloomsbury, 2010; Robert Proctor, 'Agnotology: A missing term to describe the cultural production of ignorance (and its study)', in Proctor Robert and Schiebinger Londa (eds.), *Agnotology. The Making and Unmaking of Ignorance*, Stanford University Press, 2008, 1–35.

46 Helleiner, *The Neomercantilists*; Mariana Mazzucato, *The Entrepreneurial State: Debunking Public vs. Private Sector Myths*, Anthem Press, 2013; Fred Block, 'Swimming against the current: The rise of a hidden developmental state in the United States', *Politics & Society*, 36, 2, 2008, 169–206.

47 See Chapter 1 on the notion of an efficient industrial policy, based on: Reka Juhasz, Nathan J. Lane, and Dani Rodrik, *The New Economics of Industrial Policy*, NBER working paper 31538, 2023.

48 Hall and Soskice (eds.), *Varieties of Capitalism*; David Hope and David Soskice, 'Growth models, varieties of capitalism, and macroeconomics', in *Politics & Society*, 44, 2, 2016, 209–22.

49 Bob Hancké, Martin Rhodes, and Mark Thatcher (eds.), *Beyond Varieties of Capitalism: Conflict, Contradictions, and Complementarities in the European Economy*, Oxford University Press, 2007; Sven Steinmo, *The Evolution of Modern States: Sweden, Japan, and the United States*, Cambridge University Press, 2010; Orfeo Fioretos, *Creative Reconstructions. Multilateralism and European Varieties of Capitalism after 1950*, Cornell University Press, 2011; Kathleen Thelen, *Varieties of Liberalization: The New Politics of Social Solidarity*, Cambridge University Press, 2014; Lucio Baccaro and Harry Jonas Pontusson, 'Rethinking comparative political economy: The growth model perspective', in *Politics & Society*, 44, 2, 175–207.

50 Notable exceptions include: Vivien Schmidt and Mark Thatcher (eds.), *Resilient Liberalism in Europe's Political Economy*, Cambridge University Press, 2013; Manuela Moschella, Lucia Quaglia, and Aneta Spendzharova (eds.), *European Political Economy: Theoretical Approaches and Policy Issues*, Oxford University Press, 2023; Joachim Becker, Johannes Jäger, 'Integration in crisis: A regulationist perspective on the interaction of European varieties of capitalism', *Competition & Change*, 16, 3, 2012, 169–187.

51 This book was influenced by Peter Gourevitch's approach, which differentiates between five types of economic policy: classical liberalism, socialisation and planning, demand stimulus, protectionism, and mercantilism: Peter Gourevitch, *Politics and Hard times: Comparative Responses to International Economic Crises*, Cornell University Press, 1986.
52 Kiran Klaus Patel, 'Widening and deepening? Recent advances in European integration history', in *Neue Politische Literatur*, 64, 2, 2019, 327–357.
53 A topic already touched upon from an economic history perspective in: Kevin O'Rourke, 'Why the EU won', Ideas-Repec working paper, 2011.
54 For example with GATT: Coppolaro Lucia. *The Making of a World Trading Power: The European Economic Community (EEC) in the GATT Kennedy Round Negotiations (1963-67)*, Routledge, 2016; or with the CSCE: Angela Romano, *From détente in Europe to European détente: How the West Shaped the Helsinki CSCE*, Peter Lang, 2009.
55 On 'Europeanisation', see: Theofanis Exadaktylos and Claudio Radaelli, 'Europeanisation', in Kennet Lynggaard, Ian Manners, and Karl Löfgren (eds.), *Research Methods in European Union Studies*, Palgrave Macmillan, 2015, 206–218.
56 See Chapter 2 on the European political system. The book will build on inspiring recent monographs that have covered some of this book's topics: Grace Ballor, *Enterprise and Integration: Big Business and the Making of the Single European Market*, Cambridge University Press, 2025; Piers Ludlow, *The European Community and the Crises of the 1960s: Negotiating the Gaullist Challenge*, Routledge, 2006; Kiran Klaus Patel, *Project Europe: A History*, Cambridge University Press, 2020; Emmanuel Mourlon-Druol, *Federal Anathema: How European Policymakers Shelved Economic Union in the Making of the Euro*, Cornell University Press, 2025.
57 See Chapter 2. Moravcsik, *The Choice for Europe*; van Middelaar, *The passage to Europe*; Bickerton, Hodson and Puetter (eds.), *The New Intergovernmentalism*; Sebastian Rosato, *Europe United: Power Politics and the Making of the European Community*, Cornell University Press, 2011; Ulrich Krotz and Joachim Schild, *Shaping Europe: France, Germany, and Embedded Bilateralism from the Elysee Treaty to Twenty-First Century Politics*, Oxford University Press, 2015.
58 See Footnote 40. On transnational networks: Wolfram Kaiser, Brigitte Leucht, and Morten Rasmussen (eds.), *The History of the European Union. Origins of a Trans- and Supranational Polity, 1950-1972*, Routledge, 2009; for a detailed history of the European Commission, see the three volumes of *The European Commission. History and Memories of an Institution*s (1958-72, 1973-86 and 1986-2000) available on the 'Publications Office of the EU' website; on supranational institutions, see above.
59 To name but a few: Perry Anderson, *Ever Closer Union? Europe in the West*, Verso Books, 2021; Alan W. Cafruny and Magnus Ryner (eds.), *A Ruined Fortress? Neoliberal Hegemony and Transformation in Europe*, Rowan & Littlefield Publishers, 2003; John Gillingham, *European integration, 1950-2003: Superstate or New Market Economy?* Cambridge University Press, 2003; Dieter Plehwe, Bernhard Walpen, and Gisela Neunhöffer (eds.), *Neoliberal Hegemony. A Global Critique*, Routledge, 2006; Hagen Schulz-Forberg and Bo Strath, *The Political History of European Integration: The Hypocrisy of Democracy-through-Market*, Routledge, 2010; Wolfgang Streeck, *Buying Time: The Delayed Crisis of*

Democratic Capitalism, Verso, 2017. See also Fritz Scharpf's argument, which is discussed in Chapter 2.

60 To put this debate in perspective, see: Michele Di Donato, 'The European Social Democrats: Neoliberalism or internationalism?', in Michele Di Donato, Silvio Pons (ed.), *European Integration and the Global Financial Crisis Looking back on the Maastricht Years, 1980s–1990s*, Palgrave Macmillan, 2023, 139–160.

61 Stephanie Lee Mudge, 'What is neoliberalism?', in *Socio-economic Review*, 6, 2008, 703–731; Quinn Slobodian, *Globalists: The End of Empire and the Birth of Neoliberalism*, Harvard University Press, 2018.

62 Examples of archive-based studies of business in English include: Ballor, *Enterprise and Integration*; Eric Bussière, Michel Dumoulin, and Sylvain Schirmann, 'The Development of Economic Integration', in Wilfried Loth (ed.), *Experiencing Europe*, Nomos, 2009, 45–102; Alexis Drach, 'An early form of European champions? Banking clubs between European integration and global banking (1960s–1990s)', in *Business History*, 66, 1, 2024, 287–310; Aleksandra Komornicka, 'Stable support, scant initiative: European business associations and Economic and Monetary Union, 1946–1992', in *Business History*, 67, 4, 2024, 1021–1042; Sabine Pitteloud, 'Let's coordinate! The reinforcement of a "liberal bastion" within European industrial federations, 1978–1987', in *Business History*, 65, 2, 2023, 345–365; Sigfrido Ramírez Pérez, 'Embedding the market during times of crisis: The European automobile cartel during a decade of crisis (1973–1985)', in *Business History*, 62, 5, 2020, 815–836; Liane Hewitt, 'Monopoly menace: The rise and fall of cartel capitalism in Western Europe, 1918–1957', *Enterprise & Society*, 25, 4, 2024, 992–1014.

63 Neil Rollings and Laurent Warlouzet (eds.), 'Business history and European integration: How EEC competition policy affected companies' strategies', in Special issue of *Business History*, 62, 5, 2020, 717–742.

64 Bastiaan van Apeldoorn, *Transnational Capitalism and the Struggle over European Integration*, Routledge, 2002. See more recently: Benjamin Bürbaumer, 'TNC competitiveness in the formation of the Single Market: The role of European business revisited', in *New Political Economy*, 26, 4, 2020, 631–645.

65 See Chapters 4 and 9. On the historical literature regarding trade unions: Aurélie Andry, *Social Europe: The Road Not Taken: The Left and European Integration in the Long 1970s*, Oxford University Press, 2022; Andrea Ciampani and Pierre Tilly, *National Trade Unions and the ETUC: A History of Unity and Diversity*, ETUI, 2017; Christophe Degryse and Pierre Tilly, *1973–2013: 40 Years of History of the European Trade Union Confederation*, ETUC, 2013; Roos, *The Parliamentary Roots*; Sigfrido Ramírez Pérez, 'European Trade Unions from the Single European Act to Maastricht: 1985–1992', in *Studi storici*, 62, 1, 2021, 211–245.

Chapter 1

1 Max Weber, Essais sur la théorie de la science. Premier essai: 'L'objectivité de la connaissance dans les sciences et la politique sociale', *Plon*, 1965.

2 Marc Bloch, *Apologie pour l'histoire ou Métier d'historien*, Dunod, 2020 [1949], 233–237. Bloch also called on historians to be more rigorous in their definition of concepts, and did not reject what he referred to as the effort of 'nomenclature'.

3 This trinity is of course not the same as the Christian one ('Trinity, in Christian doctrine, [means] the unity of Father, Son, and Holy Spirit as three persons in one Godhead' according to the *Britannica Encyclopedia*), or the three orders of medieval society – those who fight, those who pray, and those who labour – which relates to the trifunctional hypothesis of Georges Dumézil concerning Indo-European people.
4 Frank Bösch, 'Krisenkinder. Neoliberale, die Grünen und der Wandel des Politischen in den 1970er und 1980er Jahren', in Frank Bösch, Thomas Hertfelder, Gabriele Metlzer (eds.), *Grenzen des Neoliberalismus. Der Wandel des Liberalismus im späten 20. Jahrhundert*, Franz Steiner Verlag, 2021, 39–60.
5 Giovanni Gozzini, 'Italian Communism', in Norman Naimark, Silvio Pons, and Sophie Quinn-Judge (eds.), *The Cambridge History of Communism*, Cambridge University Press, 2017, 597–600.
6 Polanyi, *The Great Transformation*, 141; Neil Fligstein, *The Architecture of Markets*, Princeton University Press, 2001.
7 Paul Pierson, *Dismantling the Welfare State? Reagan, Thatcher and the Politics of Retrenchment*, Cambridge University Press, 1994.
8 The facts cited hereafter are from the following reference works: Adam Tooze, *The Wages of Destruction: Formation and Ruin of the Nazi Economy*, Allen Lane, 2006; and Tim Schanetzky, *Kanonen statt Butter. Wirtschaft und Konsum im Dritten Reich*, Beck, 2015.
9 'TechnoMAGA', *The Economist*, 23 November 2024.
10 Emma Rothschild, *Economic Sentiments: Adam Smith, Condorcet and the Enlightenment*, Harvard University Press, 2001; on Adam Smith see also: Polanyi, *The Great Transformation*, 111: 'wealth was to him merely an aspect of the life in community, to the purposes of which it remained subordinate'.
11 Marc-William Palen, *Pax Economica: Left-Wing Visions of a Free Trade World*, Princeton University Press, 2024.
12 Jenny Andersson, *Between Growth and Security: Swedish Social Democracy from a Strong Society to a Third Way*, Manchester University Press, 2013.
13 William Davies, 'Neoliberalism: A Bibliographic Review', *Theory, Culture and Society*, 31, 7, 2014, 309–317; Pierson, *Dismantling*; Monica Prasad, *The Politics of Free Markets: The Rise of Neoliberal Economic Policies in Britain, France, Germany, and the United States*, University of Chicago Press, 2006; Colin Hay, 'The normalizing role of rationalist assumptions in the institutionalist embedding of neoliberalism', *Economy and Society*, 33, 2004, 500–527; Dieter Plehwe, Bernhard Walpen, Gisela Neunhöffer (eds.), *Neoliberal Hegemony. A Global Critique*, Routledge, 2006.
14 Angus Burgin, *The Great Persuasion: Reiventing Free Markets since the Depression*, Harvard University Press, 2012, 73–81; more generally: Daniel Stedman Jones, *Masters of the Universe: Hayek, Friedman, and the Birth of Neoliberal Politics*, Princeton University Press, 2012; Aaron Major, *Architects of Austerity: International Finance and the Politics of Growth*, Stanford University Press, 2014.
15 See also on this point: Julian Germann, *Unwitting Architect: German Primacy and the Origins of Neoliberalism*, Stanford University Press, 2021, 169.
16 Marion Fourcade-Gourinchas and Sarah Babb, 'The rebirth of the liberal creed: Paths to neoliberalism in four countries', *American Journal of Sociology*, 108, 3, 2002, 533–579.

17 For Hayek and Friedman on Chile and South Africa, see Slobodian, 179; for Alan Walters: BR-NA, PREM 19/928, note, Alan Walters, 26 October 1982.
18 On these: Melinda Cooper, *Family Values: Between Neoliberalism and the New Social Conservatism*, MIT Press for Zone Books, 2017; Wendy Brown, *In the Ruins of Neoliberalism. The Rise of Antidemocratic Politics in the West*, Columbia University Press, 2019, 96–108.
19 Enoch Powell's speech in Morecambe, 11 October 1968, available at www.enochpowell.info.
20 Ian Bruff, 'The rise of authoritarian neoliberalism', *Rethinking Marxism* 26, 1, 2014, 113–129.
21 Tobias Rupprecht, 'Formula Pinochet: Chilean lessons for Russian liberal reformers during the Soviet collapse, 1970–2000', *Journal of Contemporary History*, 51, 1, 2016, 165–186.
22 In 2009, Peter Thiel declared: 'I no longer believe that freedom and democracy are compatible.' Peter Thiel, 'The education of a libertarian', Cato Institute, 13 April 2009.
23 See for example: Stephanie Lee Mudge, 'What is neoliberalism?', *Socio-economic Review*, 6, 2008, 715–716; more generally: Josef Hien and Christian Joerges (eds.), *Ordoliberalism, Law and the Rule of Economics*, Bloomsbury Publishing, 2017.
24 Wilhelm Röpke, *Solution to the German Problem*, New York, Putnam's sons, 1946, 259–261, quoted in John R. Gillingham, 'The German problem and European integration', in Desmond Dinan (ed.), *Origins and Evolution of the European Union*, Oxford University Press, 2006, 59.
25 Friedrich Hayek, 'The economic conditions of interstate federalism', in Friedrich Hayek, *Individualism and Economic Order*, Chicago University Press, 1958 [1948], 255–272 (258–260 in this case), originally published in 1939 in *The New Commonweath Quarterly*, V, 2, September 1939, 131–149.
26 Friedrich Hayek, *The Road to Serfdom*, Routledge, 1944.
27 Quinn Slobobian, *Globalists: The End of Empire and the Birth of Neoliberalism*, Harvard University Press, 2018, 184–216.
28 Roberto Ventresca, 'Neoliberal thinkers and European integration in the 1980s and the early 1990s', *Contemporary European History*, 2021, published online: https://doi.org/10.1017/S0960777321000199.
29 Antoine Acker, 'What could *Carbofascism* look like? A historical perspective on reactionary politics in the Covid-19 pandemic', *Journal for the History of Environment and Society*, 5, 2020, 135–148.
30 Bruno Latour, *Where to land? Comment s'orienter en politique*, La Découverte, 2017; François Jarrige, Thomas Le Roux, *La contamination du monde: Une histoire des pollutions à l'âge industriel*, Seuil, 2017.
31 Günter Wallraff, *Lowest of the Low*, Mandarin, 1988 (original in German, *Ganz Unten*, 1985).
32 See Chapter 4 and: Christoph Mauch, *Slow Hope. Rethinking Ecologies of Crisis and Fear*, Rachel Carson Center, 2019.
33 Joachim Radkau, *Nature and Power: A Global History of the Environment*, Cambridge University Press, 2008, 3, 260–265.
34 Amartya Sen, *Commodities and Capabilities*, North Holland, 1985.
35 Eva Oberloskamp, 'Energy and the Environment in Parliamentary Debates in the Federal Republic of Germany, United Kingdom and France from the 1970s to the

1990s', in Éric Bussière, Anahita Grisoni, Hélène Miard-Delacroix, and Christian Wenkel (eds.), *The Environment and the European Public Sphere: Perceptions, Actors, Policies*, The White Horse Press, 2020, 205-219.

36 See Chapters 4 and 9. The term 'merchants of doubt' comes from the title of the seminal book by Naomi Oreskes and Erik Conway, who studied several American examples from the 1980s, such as acid rain, the ozone layer, smoking, global warming, and DDT pollution: Naomi Oreskes and Eric M. Conway, *Merchants of Doubt: How a Handful of Scientists Obscured the Truth on Issues from Tobacco Smoke to Global Warming*, Bloomsbury, 2010.

37 Gertrud Neuwirth, 'A Weberian outline of a theory of community: Its application to the "Dark Ghetto"', *The British Journal of Sociology*, 20, 2, 1969, 148-163. The Weberian notion of 'community' encompasses both Tönnie's concepts of *Gemeinschaft* (community) and of *Gesellschaft* (society).

38 Francis Fukuyama, *Political Order and Political Decay: From the Industrial Revolution to the Globalization of Democracy*, Straus and Giroux, 2014, 27.

39 Jeffrey Checkel and Peter Katzenstein (eds.), *European Identity*, Cambridge, Cambridge University Press, 2009; Thomas Risse, *A Community of Europeans?: Transnational Identities and Public Spheres*, Cornell University Press, 2015.

40 Céline Spector, *No Demos? Souveraineté et démocratie à l'épreuve de l'Europe*, Seuil, 2021, 69 and 82; Céline Spector, 'Reclaiming Rousseau: National and European Identity', *Paradigmi. Rivista du critica filosofica*, XL/3, 2022, 487-502.

41 Derek Philipps, *Looking Backward. A Critical Appraisal of Communautarian Thought*, Princeton University Press, 1993; see Michael Walzer, *Thick and Thin*, Notre Dame University, 1994.

42 Joint review of Amitai Etzioni (ed.), 'New Communitarian Thinking: Persons, Virtues, Institutions, and Communities', by Antonin Wagner, Rudolph Bauer, Jon Van Til, and Costanzo Ranci, *Voluntas: International Journal of Voluntary and Nonprofit Organizations*, 8, 1, 1997, 64-88.

43 Hence this book's original title in French: Laurent Warlouzet, *Europe contre Europe. Entre liberté, solidarité et puissance*, Paris, Cnrs éditions, 2022.

44 Eric Helleiner, *The Neomercantilists: A Global Intellectual History*, Cornell University Press, 2021.

45 Juhasz, Lane and Rodrik, *The New Economics of Industrial Policy*.

46 Van Apeldoorn, *Transnational Capitalism*, 80.

47 'Corporate welfare' is widespread but difficult to gauge, especially as to whether it is conditional or unconditional: Fabio Bulfone, Tibur Ergen, and Manolis Kalaitzake, 'No strings attached: Corporate welfare, state intervention, and the issue of conditionality', *Competition & Change*, 27, 2, 2023, 253-276; see also: Kevin Farnsworth, *Social versus Corporate Welfare: Competing Needs and Interests within the Welfare State*, Palgrave, 2012; James T. Bennett, *Corporate Welfare: Crony Capitalism That Enriches the Rich*, Routledge, 2015; and a famous book by the consumer activist Ralph Nader: Ralph Nader, *Cutting Corporate Welfare*, Random House, 2000. On quantitative easing as corporate welfare: Clement Fontan, 'Frankfurt's double standard: The politics of the European central bank during the eurozone crisis', *Cambridge Review of International Affairs*, 31, 2, 2018, 162-182. On recent UK housing, industrial and pension policy: Craig Berry, 'The substitutive state? Neoliberal state interventionism across industrial, housing and private pensions policy in the UK', *Competition & Change*, 26, 2, 2022, 242-265.

48 The economist Carl-Ludwig Holtfrerich has argued that between 1951 and 1956, West Germany developed a policy that can be referred to as 'mercantilist', because it was based on encouraging exports through low wages and low inflation. However, one of the experts he cites, Alec K. Cairncross, who at the time was at the OEEC, more aptly called this policy 'deflationary', thus equating it with a neoclassical practice; Carl-Ludwig Holtfrerich, 'Monetary policy in Germany since 1948: National tradition, international best practice or deology', in Jean-Philippe Touffut (ed.), *Central Banks as Economic Institutions*, Edward Elgar, 2008, 34–36.

49 Philippe Minard, Pierre Gervais, and Judith Le Goff, 'Colbertism continued? The inspectorate of manufactures and strategies of exchange in eighteenth-century France', *French Historical Studies*, 23, 3, 2000, 477–496.

50 Kocka, 'Capitalism and Its Critics', 77–78.

51 Helleiner, *The Neomercantilists*.

52 Patricia Clavin, *The Great Depression in Europe, 1929–1939*, St Martin's Press, 2000, 133; Robert Boyce, *The Great Interwar Crisis and the Collapse of Globalization*, Palgrave Macmillan, 2009, 230–237 and 314–323.

53 Albert Hirschmann, *National Power and the Structure of Foreign Trade*, University of California Press, 1945, 3.

54 AAPD, 1982, doc. 211, note on a meeting between Schmidt and British Ambassador Taylor, 14 July 1982; HAEU, speech collection, Caspari's speech in Cologne, 14 October 1981.

55 Fris Bolkestein, 'Let the market choose Europe's champions', *Financial Times*, 14 June 2004.

56 Johanna Bockman, 'Socialist globalization against capitalist neocolonialism: The economic ideas behind the new international economic order', *Humanity: An International Journal of Human Rights, Humanitarianism, and Development*, 6, 1, 2015, 109–128; Mauro Boianovsky, 'The Economic Commission for Latin America and the 1950s' debate on choice of techniques', *Review of Political Economy*, 25, 3, 2013, 373–398.

57 Alice Amsden, *The Rise of 'the Rest': Challenges to the West from Late-Industrializing Economies*, Oxford University Press, 2003.

58 Catherine Schenk, *Hong Kong as an International Financial Centre. Emergence and Development, 1945–1965*, Taylor & Francis, 2001.

59 Marc Levinson, *An Extraordinary Time: The End of the Postwar Boom and the Return of the Ordinary* Economy, Basic Books, 2016, 160.

60 Mariana Mazzucato, *The Entrepreneurial State: Debunking Public vs. Private Sector Myth*, Anthem Press, 2013; Mariana Mazzucato, 'Innovation, the State and Patient Capital', *The Political Quarterly*, 86, 1, 2016, 98–118. The acronym DARPA stands for Defense Advance Research Project Agency.

61 Hubert Zimmerman, *Money and Security: Troops, Monetary Policy, and West Germany's Relations with the United States and Britain, 1950–1971*, Cambridge University Press, 2002.

62 Woll, *Corporate Crime*.

63 On the European Commission and GAFA, see Chapter 7; on BNP's profits: 'En repli de 26,4%, le bénéfice net de BNP Paribas en 2013 déçoit', *La Tribune*, 13 February 2014.

64 Concerning relief and the availability of domesticated species: Jared Diamond, *Guns, Germs and Steel. The Fates of Human Societies*, Norton, 1999; on the availability of cheap coal as one factor explaining the 'Great Divergence' between England and China's richest region: Kenneth Pomeranz, *The Great Divergence: China, Europe, and the Making of the Modern World Economy*, Princeton University Press, 2000.
65 Daron Acemoglu and Simon Johnson, 'Unbundling institutions', *Journal of Political Economy*, 113, 5, 2005, 949–995.
66 Hall and Soskice, *Varieties of Capitalism*.
67 On the contrast between Germany's export-led growth and the UK (and Italy)'s wage-led growth model over the period 1944-2007: Lucio Baccaro and Harry Jonas Pontusson, 'Rethinking comparative political economy: The growth model perspective', *Politics & Society*, 44, 2, 2016, 175–207.
68 Edwin Williams, *Made in Germany*, William Heinemann, 1896.
69 Sebastian Haffner, *Geschichte eines Deutschen: die Erinnerungen 1914–1933*, Pantheon Verlag, 2000.
70 Tooze, *The Wages of Destruction*.
71 Barry Eichengreen and Albrecht Ritschl, 'Understanding West German Economic Growth in the 1950s', *Cliometrica*, 3, 2009, 213–214; Tamás Vonyó, *West Germany's Growth Miracle after 1945*, Cambridge University Press, 2018.
72 Hall and Soskice, *Varieties of Capitalism*; Peter Katzenstein, *Policy and Politics in West Germany: The Growth of a Semisovereign State*, Temple University Press, 1987.
73 Denis Cogneau, *Un empire bon marché. Histoire and économie politique de la colonisation française, XIXe-XXIe siècle*, Seuil, 2023.
74 Jean Monnet, *Memoirs*, Doubleday, 1978 [p. 306 in the French version].
75 Henry G. Overman and Alan Winters, 'Trade and Economic Geography: The Impact of EEC Accession on the UK', January 2006; http://personal.lse.ac.uk/overman/research/shockloc18_dp.pdf (accessed 24 January 2025).
76 Peter Katzenstein, *Small States in World Markets. Industrial Policy in Europe*, Cornell University Press, 1985.
77 Rothschild, *Economic Sentiments*.
78 Immanuel Kant, *Perpetual Peace: A Philosophic Essay* [German: *Zum ewigen Frieden. Ein philosophischer Entwurf*], 1795.
79 Yaman Kouli, Léonard Laborie, *The Politics and Policies of European Economic Integration, 1850–1914*, Springer, 2023.
80 Kott, *A World More Equal*.

Chapter 2

1 The quotation comes from: Jean Monnet, *Memoirs*, Institut Jean Monnet, 2025, p. 417; for a fuller account of the history of European integration, see: Brigitte Leucht, Katja Seidel, and Laurent Warlouzet (eds.), *Reinventing Europe: The History of the European Union, 1945 to the Present*, Bloomsbury, 2023, and Dermot Hodson, *Circle of Stars: A History of the EU – and the People Who Made It*, Yale University Press, 2023.
2 See Keynes's reflections of 1919 in Chapter 3. On the ideas of European integration before 1950, see: Mark Hewitson, *European Integration since the 1920s: Security*,

Identity, and Cooperation, Oxford University Press, 2024; Mathieu Segers, *The Origins of European Integration: The Pre-History of Today's European Union, 1937–1951*, Cambridge University Press, 2023.

3 Filippo Occhino, Kim Oosterlinck, and Eugene N. White, 'How much can a victor force the vanquished to pay? France under the Nazi boot', *Journal of Economic History*, 68, 1, 2008, 1–45.

4 Angus Maddison, *Statistics on World Population, GDP and Per Capita GDP, 1–2008 AD*, 2008; www.ggdc.net/maddison/oriindex.htm. 'Western Europe' in Angus Maddison's typology does not correspond to the European Economic Community, as it includes Germany, Belgium, Austria, Denmark, Finland, France, Italy, Norway, the Netherlands, the United Kingdom, Sweden, and Switzerland.

5 Geir Lundestad, '"Empire by invitation" in the American century', *Diplomatic History*, 23, 2, 1999, 189–217.

6 Patel, 'Provincialising European Union.'

7 Kott, *A World More Equal*; Segers, *The Origins*.

8 Sylvain Kahn, *Histoire de la construction de l'Europe depuis 1945*, PUF, 2018, 318–319.

9 Mathieu Leimgruber, Matthias Schmelzer (eds.), *The OECD and the International Political Economy since 1948*, Palgrave Macmillan, 2017; Matthias Schmelzer, *The Hegemony of Growth. The OECD and the Making of the Economic Growth Paradigm*, Cambridge University Press, 2016.

10 Giuliano Garavini, 'The battle for the participation of the European Community in the G7 (1975–1977)', *JEIH*, 12, 1, 2006, 141–158.

11 Oriane Calligaro, *Negotiating Europe: EU Promotion of Europeanness since the 1950s*, Palgrave Macmillan, 2013.

12 Piers Ludlow, 'Not a wholly new Europe: How the integration framework shaped the end of the Cold War in Europe', in Frédéric Bozo, Andreas Rödder, and Mary Elise Sarotte (eds.), *German Reunification. A Multinational History*, Routledge, 2017, pp. 133–152; Kenneth Dyson and Kevin Featherstone, *The Road to Maastricht: Negotiating Economic and Monetary Union*, Oxford University Press, 1999; Michael Geary, Carine Germond, and Kiran Klaus Patel, 'The Maastricht Treaty: Negotiations and Consequences in Historical Perspective', *JEIH*, 19, 1, 2013.

13 Ludlow, 'Not a wholly new Europe', 141.

14 On this project: Frédéric Bozo, *Mitterrand, the End of the Cold War, and German Unification*, Berghahn Books, 2009, ch. 7.

15 Mark F. Imber, *The USA, ILO, UNESCO and IAEA: Politicization and Withdrawal in the Specialized Agencies*, Palgrave Macmillan, 1989.

16 Ann-Kristin Bergquist and Thomas David, 'Beyond planetary limits! The International Chamber of Commerce, the United Nations, and the invention of sustainable development', in *Business History Review*, 97, 3, 2023, 481–511; Iris Borowy, *Defining Sustainable Development for our Common Future: A History of the World Commission on Environment and Development (Brundtland Commission)*, Routledge, 2013.

17 Matthieu Leimgruber and Matthias Schmelzer (eds.), *The OECD and the International Political Economy since 1948*, Palgrave Macmillan, 2017; Sandrine Kott and Joëlle Droux (eds.), *Globalizing Social Rights: The International Labour Organization and Beyond*, Springer, 2013.

18 Steen Rynning, *NATO. From the Cold War to Ukraine, a History of the World's Most Powerful Alliance*, Yale University Press, 2024; Timothy Andrew Sayle, *Enduring Alliance. A History of NATO and the Postwar Global Order*, Cornell University Press, 2019; Harold James, *International Monetary Cooperation since Bretton Woods*, Oxford University Press, 1996.

19 Walter Mattli, *The Logic of Regional Integration. Europe and Beyond*, Cambridge University Press, 1999; Laurien Crump and Simon Godard, 'Reassessing Communist international organisations: A comparative analysis of COMECON and the Warsaw Pact in relation to their Cold War competitors', in *Contemporary European History*, 27, 1, 2018, 85–109; regarding Mercosur, according to *The Economist*: 'intra-block exports have fallen as a share of members' total exports from a peak of 24% in 1998 to around 11% in 2023'; reference: 'Mercosur's new nadir', *The Economist*, 13 July 2024.

20 Nathalie Brack and Nicholas Startin, 'Introduction: Euroscepticism, from the margins to the mainstream', in *International Political Science Review*, 36, 3, 2015, 239–249.

21 For a synthesis of the three primary approaches to European integration theory, see: Liesbet Hooghe and Gary Marks, 'Grand theories of European integration in the twenty-first century', *Journal of European Public Policy*, 26, 8, 2019, 1113–1133.

22 Middelaar, *The Passage to Europe*; Mourlon-Druol and Romero, *International Summitry*.

23 For contrasting views of this process, see: Karen Alter, *Establishing the Supremacy of European Law: The Making of an International Rule of Law in Europe*, Oxford University Press, 2003; Vauchez, *Brokering Europe*; Rasmussen and Sindbjerg Martinsen, 'EU constitutionalisation revisited'.

24 For a precise study on the different forms of power wielded by the Commission: Mark Pollack, *The Engines of European Integration. Delegation, Agency, and Agenda Setting in the European Union*, Oxford University Press, 2003.

25 O'Rourke, 'Economic history and contemporary challenges to globalization', 369.

26 Bruno De Witte, Andrea Ott, and Ellen Vos (eds.), *Between Flexibility and Disintegration: The Trajectory of Differentiation in EU law*, Edward Elgar, 2017; Frank Schimmelfennig and Thomas Winzen, *Ever Looser Union? Differentiated European Integration*, Oxford University Press, 2020.

27 AAPD, 1984, doc. 137, note on the Genscher–Dumas talks, 15 May 1984.

28 EPP archives, 17/2, letter from EPP President Piet Bukman, 11 June 1985.

29 Francis Cheneval and Kalypso Nicolaïdis, 'The social construction of demoicracy in the European Union', *European Journal of Political Theory*, 16, 2, 2017, 235–260.

30 Liesbet Hooghe and Gary Marks, 'A Postfunctionalist Theory of European Integration: From Permissive Consensus to Constraining Dissensus', *British Journal of Political Science*, 39, 1, 2009, 1–23; Giandomenico Majone, *Dilemmas of European Integration: The Ambiguities and Pitfalls of Integration by Stealth*, Oxford University Press, 2009; Claudia Sternberg, Kira Gartzou-Katsouyanni, and Kalypso Nicolaïdis, *The Greco-German Affair in the Euro Crisis: Mutual Recognition Lost?*, Palgrave Macmillan, 2018.

31 Jan-Werner Müller, *Contesting Democracy: Political Ideas in 20th Century Europe*, Yale University Press, 2011.

32 EPA, PE2 AP RP/ECON.1984 A2-0129/87, *Niveau de puissance acoustique admissible des tondeuses à gazon*, report by Heinz Schreiber, 1984.

33 Milward, *Rescue*; Moravcsik, *The Choice*; Bickerton, Hodson, and Pütter, *The New Intergovernmentalism*.

34 For a comprehensive analysis of the 'integration-through-law' approach, including its divisions and shortcomings: Robert Schütze, '"Integration-through-Law": Grand theory, revisionist history', *European Law Open*, 4, 2, 2025, 162–200.

35 On the role of historical institutionalism in better understanding the rise of competition policy, see Chapter 3 and: Laurent Warlouzet, 'The centralization of EU competition policy: Historical institutionalist dynamics from cartel monitoring to merger control (1956–91)', *JCMS*, 54, 3, 2016, 725–741; on historical institutionalism in EU studies: Paul Pierson, 'The path to European integration: A historical institutionalist analysis', *Comparative Political Studies*, 29, 2, pp. 123–163. See Chapter 5 on the 1991 ATR/De Havilland affair. Within the European institutional framework, national decision-makers are especially constrained by the partial autonomy of supranational institutions, the multiplicity of technical issues to master, the limited time-horizons of national decision-makers and their shift in policy preferences.

36 For example, when polled about the advent of 'United States of Europe', 65 per cent of French people responded that it would a good idea in October 1950 (Anne Dulphy and Christine Manigand, 'Du Plan Schuman à la CECA: les perceptions de l'opinion française', in Andreas Wilkens (dir.), Le Plan Schuman dans l'histoire. intérêts nationaux et projets européens, Bruxelles, Bruylant, 2004, pp. 244–267); 77% per cent of respondents to a 2024 Eurobarometer survey support a common defence and security policy among EU Member States; EU, *Standard Eurobarometer 101 – Spring 2024*.

37 Zbigniew Brzezinski, *The Grand Chessboard: American Primacy and Its Geostrategic Imperatives*, Basic Books, 1997, 61.

38 It started with the 'Solange' case of 1974: Billy Davies, *Resisting the European Court of Justice: West Germany's Confrontation with European Law, 1949–1979*, Cambridge University Press, 2012.

39 Simon Bulmer, *The Domestic Structure of European Community Policy-Making in West Germany*, Garland, 1986, 255–277.

40 Warlouzet, *Governing Europe*, 187; Alexandre Bernier, *La France et le droit communautaire 1958–1981: histoire d'une réception et d'une coproduction*, PhD, University of Copenhagen, 2017.

41 BR-NA, FCO 98/948, note 'The second UK presidency', 22 July 1980; Stephen George, *An Awkward Partner. Britain in the European Community*, Oxford University Press, 1994.

42 Wolfram Kaiser and Johan W. Schot, *Writing the Rules for Europe: Experts, Cartels, and International Organizations*, Palgrave Macmillan, 2014; Yaman Kouli and Léonard Laborie, *The Politics and Policies of European Economic Integration, 1850–1914*, Palgrave Macmillan, 2022.

43 AAPD, 1980, doc. 60, note from Rufhus, London, 24 February 1980.

44 AAPD, 1981, doc. 71, note Elder von Braunmühl, 16 March 1981; doc. 74, note Zeller, 17 March 1981; see also: AAPD, 1980, doc. 85, note von Staden, 18 March 1980.

45 AAPD, 1980, doc. 62, note on a meeting Genscher–Carington, 26 February 1980.

46 Warlouzet, 'De Gaulle as a father of Europe: The unpredictability of the FTA's failure and the EEC's success (1956–1958)', *Contemporary European History*, 20, 4, 2011, 419–434.

47 AAPD, 1984, doc. 122, note on a meeting Kohl–Thatcher, 2 May 1984.
48 See Chapters 3 and 8, and: Laurent Warlouzet, 'Britain at the centre of European cooperation (1948-2016)', *Journal of Common Market Studies*, 56, 4, 2018, 955-970.
49 Fritz W. Scharpf, The Double Asymmetry of European Integration, or Why the EU Cannot Be a Social Market Economy, MPIfG Working Paper 09/12, 2009.
50 Giandomenico Majone, 'The regulatory state and its legitimacy problems', *West European Politics*, 22, 1, 1999, 1-24.
51 Laurent Warlouzet, 'Towards a fourth paradigm in European competition policy? A historical perspective (1957-2022)', in Adina Claici, Assimakis Komninos, and Denis Waelbroeck (eds.), *The Transformation of EU Competition Law: Next Generation Issues*, Kluwer, 2023, 33-52.
52 The most famous typology, on which the table is partly based, is from: Bela Balassa, *The Theory of Economic Integration*, Allen & Unwin, 1961.
53 McNamara, 'Transforming Europe?'

Chapter 3

1 John Maynard Keynes, *The Economic Consequences of the Peace*, Macmillan, 1919, chapter 7, part 1.
2 Keynes, *The Economic Consequences*.
3 Kiran Klaus Patel and Wolfram Kaiser, 'Continuity and change in European cooperation during the twentieth century', in *Contemporary European History*, 27, 2, 2018, 165-182.
4 Note from Jean Monnet of 5 August 1943, Algiers, available on the website Cvce; on Monnet in English, see: François Duchêne, *Jean Monnet, The First Statesman of Interdependence*, WW Norton & Company, 1994.
5 Alan S. Milward, *The Reconstruction of Western Europe, 1945-1951*, Routledge, 1984.
6 On the British: Alan S. Milward, *The Rise and Fall of a National Strategy, 1945-1963*, Whitehall History Publishing, 2002, 247; on Erhard and the ordoliberals: Slobodian, *Globalists*.
7 On the ECSC, see in English: John Gillingham, *Coal, Steel, and the Rebirth of Europe, 1945-1955. The Germans and French from Ruhr Conflict to Economic Community*, Cambridge University Press, 1991; Milward, *The European Rescue*.
8 On the ECSC and cartelization: Liane Hewitt, 'Monopoly Menace: The Rise and Fall of Cartel Capitalism in Western Europe, 1918-1957', in *Enterprise & Society*, 25, 4, 2024, 992-1014.
9 On the support of these left-wing leaders for competition policy, see: Laurent Warlouzet, *Europe contre Europe. Entre liberté, solidarité et puissance*, CNRS éditions, 2022, 230-232.
10 Yves Mény and Vincent Wright (eds.), *The Politics of Steel: Western Europe and the Steel Industry in the Crisis Years (1974-1984)*, De Gruyter, 1987.
11 Laurent Warlouzet and Tobias Witschke, 'The difficult path to an economic rule of law: European competition policy, 1950-91', in *Contemporary European History*, 21, 3, 2012, 437-455.
12 CVCE, Memorandum of the Netherlands Ministry of Foreign Affairs on European Integration (11 December 1952); Memorandum of the Netherlands Government on the European Community (5 May 1953).

13 The example of the Soviet Union was cited as a justification for the Common Market in a French newsreel from 3 July 1957, Pathé-Journal, www.cvce.lu.
14 Patel, *Project Europe*; Enrico Serra (ed.), *The Relaunching of Europe and the Treaties of Rome*, Bruylant, 1989.
15 On the negotiations surrounding the Free Trade Area, see, on the British side: Wolfram Kaiser, *Using Europe, Abusing the Europeans. Britain and European Integration, 1945-63*, Macmillan Press, 1996; Milward, *The Rise and Fall*; James Elisson, *Threatening Europe*, Palgrave Macmillan, 2000. On the European issues: Laurent Warlouzet, 'De Gaulle as a father of Europe'.
16 Laurent Warlouzet, *Le choix de la CEE par la France. L'Europe économique en débat de Pierre Mendès-France à Charles de Gaulle*, Cheff, 2011, 45-47.
17 On the first point: Archives of the ELEC [thereafter AELEC] 654, Letter from Robert de la Forteille to Baron Boel, 15 February 1958; on the second: AELEC 653, minutes of the meeting of 7 October 1957.
18 Neil Rollings, *British Business in the Formative Years of European Integration, 1945-1973*, Cambridge University Press, 2007, 103.
19 For Oliver Daddow, Britain was first a 'saboteur' and then a 'rival' of the European Communities: Oliver Daddow, 'Interpreting the outsider tradition in British European policy speeches from Thatcher to Cameron', in *JCMS*, 53, 1, 2015, 73-78.
20 Bernhard Löffler, *Soziale Marktwirtschaft und administrative Praxis*, Franz Steiner, 2002, 232-233, 563.
21 Warlouzet, *Le choix de la CEE*, 159.
22 Warlouzet, *Le choix de la CEE*, 103.
23 Frances Lynch, 'De Gaulle's first veto: France, the Rueff plan and the free trade area', in *Contemporary European History*, 9, 1, 2000, 111-135; Warlouzet, 'De Gaulle as a Father of Europe...': De Gaulle used the expression 'traité de commerce'.
24 Alan S. Milward, *Politics and Economics in the History of the European Union*, Routledge, 2005.
25 Wilhelm Röpke, *International Order and Economic Integration*, Reidel, 1959, 261-269.
26 GER-NA, B 136, 2553, letter from Erhard to Adenauer on 10 January 1961; note from Alfred Müller-Armack on 5 December 1960; Warlouzet, *Le choix de la* CEE, 357-358.
27 FR-FAA, DECE 1484, note MAE/CAP, 28 August 1979.
28 BR-NA, PREM 19/1222, note by David Williamson, 22 June 1984.
29 European Commission, *Completing the Internal Market*, Com 85, 310, 14 June 1985, 220.
30 Lucia Coppolaro, *The Making of a World Trading Power. The European Economic Community (EEC) in the GATT Kennedy Round Negotiations (1963-1967)*, Aldershot, 2013.
31 On the negotiation of the Treaty of Rome with respect to competition: Warlouzet *Le choix de la CEE*, 273-276; Laurent Warlouzet, 'The Centralization of EU Competition Policy: Historical Institutionalist Dynamics from Cartel Monitoring to Merger Control (1956-91)', in *JCMS*, 54, 3, 2016; on the history of EEC/EU competition policy more generally, see: Warlouzet, 'Towards a fourth paradigm'.
32 David J. Gerber, *Law and Competition in XXth Century Europe. Protecting Prometheus*, Oxford, 1998; on ordoliberalism, see also chapter 1.

33 HAEU archives, CM3/236, note by the secretariat, 'Common Market Group', debates of 7 September 1956; note of 5 November 1956 by Meyer-Cording; GER-NA, B 102/ 134644, note of 3 October 1960; B 102/ 134647, note Epphaardt, 15 June 1961.
34 On Regulation 17/62: Warlouzet, 'Towards a Fourth Paradigm'; Sybille Hambloch, *Europäische Integration und Wettbewerbspolitik. Die Frühphase der EWG*, Nomos, 2009, 79–126; Sigfrido Ramirez, Sebastian van der Scheur, 'The Evolution of the Law on Articles 85 and 86 EEC. Ordoliberalism and its Keynesian Challenge', in Kiran Klaus Patel and Heike Schweitzer (eds.), *The Historical Foundations of EU Competition Law*, Oxford University Press, 2013, 19–53.
35 Bernhard Löffler, *Soziale Marktwirtschaft und administrative Praxis*, Stuttgart, Franz Steiner, 2002, 548–552.
36 GER-NA, B 102/259100, note BMWi, EA4, 1 June 1965; Commission decision of 23 September 1964 on a procedure under Article 85 of the Treaty.
37 GER-NA, B 102/259100, notes BMWi, Everling, 14 July 1965 and 7 October 1965.
38 'Opinion of Advocate General Karl Roemer, delivered on 27 April 1966'; judgment of the Court of 13 July 1966, Joined Cases 56 and 58–64.
39 Niklas Jensen-Eriksen, 'Creating clubs and giants: How competition policies influenced the strategy and structure of Nordic pulp and paper industry, 1970–2000', in *Business History*, 62, 5, 2020, 763–781.
40 HAEU, BAC 31/1984/768, note DG V/B-3, 19 December 1963, 'Öffentlich-rechtliche Markteregelungen'; Warlouzet, *Le choix de la CEE par la France*, 233–235; Vay, *La mise en problème*, 109–123.
41 GER-NA, B 102/12619, note of 22 August 1958.
42 BR-NA, T 390/283, Memorandum received 17 May 1978; UKREP telex, Council of 2 May 1978; FCO 30/3819, Callaghan letter, 30 January 1978; T 390/284, UKREP telex, COREPER of 25 May 1978; European Commission document of 17 May 1978; UKREP telex, 1 June 1978.
43 *Why Positive Adjustment Policies?*, OECD, 1979.
44 BR-NA, FCO30/3819, note Franklin, 20 January 1978; FR-NA, 19900452/17, note SGCI, 8 September 1980 and note MAE, 9 September 1980; FR-FAA, DECE1298, note, 25 April 1978.
45 Michelle Cini, Lee Mc Gowan, *Competition Policy in the European Union*, Palgrave, 1998, 11–40.
46 This principle was applied for the first time against Belgium in April 1984, in a case upheld by the Court of Justice in 1986: decision no. 84/496/EEC of 17 April 1984; judgment of the Court of 10 July 1986, 'Kingdom of Belgium v. Commission of the European Communities', Case 234/84.
47 BR-NA, MAF 333/68, note of Tolladay, 10 April 1980.
48 HAEU, BAC 131/1996/135, note DG XVI.A.2.JVG, 20 March 1981; *Fourteenth Report on Competition*, Brussels, European Commission, 1985, 146 and 155–156.
49 BR-NA, PREM 19/1325, note from Gregson to Thatcher, 27 July 1983.
50 BR-NA, PREM 19/1325, note from Sparrow to Thatcher, 26 July, 1983.
51 GER-NA, B 102/375364, memo BMWi, EA1, 7 December 1981; memo BMWi, EA1, 3 December 1981; on the proceedings against West Germany: memo BMWi, IC2, Paulssen, 26 November 1981; memo BMWi, EA1, Müller-Thuns, 1 December 1981; memo BMWi, IC2, 8 June 1982.

52 Case 84/82; *Fourteenth Report on Competition*, Luxembourg, European Commission, 1985, 126–127.
53 Astrid Eckert, 'West German borderland aid and uropean state aid control', *Jahrbuch für Wirtschaftsgeschichte*, 58, 1, 2017, 107–136; on the concern in Bonn about Andriessen: GER-NA, B 102/375364, note BMWi, EA1, Müller-Thuns, 1 December 1981.
54 GER-NA, B 102/375364, note BMWi, EA1, 1 June 1982; FR-FAA, DECE 1896, note from the French Embassy in Germany, 7 February 1983.
55 Commission, *First survey of State aids in the European Community*, SEC(88)1981, 13 December 1988, 20 and 25; on the 1982–85 conflicts between Brussels and Paris, see: Warlouzet, *Governing* Europe, 170–172.
56 FR-FAA, DECE 1898, note DAEF, PM, 20 April 1983.
57 FR-FAA, DECE 1897, note DAEF, SL, 14 January 1982.
58 FR-FAA, DECE 81–83, 1897, telegram, REP, 19 October 1982; FR-NA, 5AG4/PM/50/1, note from the Industry Minister's cabinet, Lorino, 29 November 1982.
59 On the relaunch: Piers Ludlow, 'From deadlock to dynamism. The European Community in the 1980s', in Desmond Dinan (ed.), *Origins and Evolution of the European Union*, Oxford University Press, 2006, 218–232; Moravcsik, *The Choice*, 314–379.
60 Piers Ludlow, *Roy Jenkins and the European Commission Presidency 1976–1980: at the Heart of Europe*, Palgrave, 2016, 199–230.
61 Maria Green Cowles, 'Setting the agenda for a new Europe: The ERT and EC 1992', in *JCMS*, 33, 4, 1995, 501–526.
62 Warlouzet, *Le choix de la CEE par la France*, 26–35.
63 GER-NA, BArch, B 102/12619, note of 22 August 1958.
64 BR-NA, BT298/595, note, 27 March 1974; see also: BR-NA, PREM 16/852, note, Cabinet Office, 31 March 1976; Alan Dashwood, 'Hastening slowly: The community path towards harmonization', in Helen Wallace, William Wallace, and Carole Webb (eds.), *Policy-Making in the European Communities*, John Wiley & Sons, 1983, 179.
65 FR-FAA, DECE 1833, note SGCI of May 1981, 'technical barriers to trade'; DECE 2061, note SGCI, 20 November 1981: 'deepening'.
66 See Ulrich Everling's reluctance towards a federal orientation for European law when he was still a German civil servant: Billy Davies, 'Meek Acceptance? The West German Ministries' Reaction to the Van Gend en Loos and Costa decisions', in *JEIH*, 14, 2, 2008, 67; and as a judge: Grégoire Carasso, *Entre neutralité et concurrence fiscales: la Commission européenne et l'imposition des entreprises au sein du marché commun*, PhD, University of Geneva, 2021, 303.
67 For all these examples except René Joliet, see: Vay, *La mise en problème*, 81, and 207–208; for René Joliet: Warlouzet, *Governing Europe*, 163.
68 Dashwood, 'Hastening Slowly', 183; Fritz W. Scharpf, 'The Double Asymmetry of European Integration, or Why the EU Cannot Be a Social Market Economy', in *MPIfG Working Paper*, 09/12, 2009, 12 and 16–17.
69 Karen J. Alter and Sophie Meunier-Aitsahalia, 'Judicial Politics in the European Community. European Integration and the Pathbreaking *Cassis de Dijon* Decision', *Comparative Political Studies*, 26, 4, January 1994, 540–543, see also: Moravcsik, *The Choice for Europe*, 354.
70 HAEU, BAC 91/94/56, note of 23 January 1980, DG III, P. Cecchini.

71 Laurent Warlouzet, 'The role of the European Parliament in the Single Market Programme: The cost of non-Europe and the Car Emission Directive (1983-89)', in *JEIH*, 27, 1, 2021, 21-36; Laurent Warlouzet, *Completing the Single Market: The European Parliament and Economic Integration, 1979-1989*, Bruxelles, European Parliament Research Service, 2020.

72 European Commission, *Europe 1992. The Overall Challenge*, Com(88) 524, 13 April 1988; see an archival-based study of this report in Pierre Alayrac, *Une noblesse d'Europe. Socio-histoire de l'autorité des économistes de la Commission européenne (1958-2019)*, PhD, EHESS, Paris, 2022.

73 Alexis Drach, 'Reluctant Europeans? British and French commercial banks and the Common Market in banking (1977-1992)', *Enterprise and Society*, 21, 3, 2020, 768-798; on some of them being 'defensive': Grace Ballor, *Enterprise and Integration: Big Business and the Making of the Single European Market*, Cambridge University Press, 2025; on the division of the ERT: Bastiaan van Apeldoorn, *Transnational Capitalism and the Struggle over European Integration*, Routledge, 2002.

74 FR-NA, 5AG4/EG/36, Benelux Memorandum on the Internal Market, 17 October 1983.

75 AAPD, 1983, doc. 13, note on a discussion between Kohl and Mauroy, 20 January 1983, 72.

76 GER-NA, B 102/299774, draft note (EA3) for Ambassador Cornelio Sommaruga, 29 July 1982.

77 GER-NA, B 102/315414, Sekretariat der Wirtschaftsministerkonferenz, 3 June 1982 and 18 June 1982, Länder Economic Ministers' Conference of 10-11 June 1982; B 102/342256, note on the Länder Economic Ministers' Conference, 24 November 1983; BR-NA, FV 8/51, brief, London meeting, 22 April 1983.

78 See archival evidence from the British national archives in: Warlouzet, *Europe contre Europe*, 91-92.

79 GER-FAA, ZW/124.419, note AA/Steinkühler, 29 January 1982; on the debates of 1981-1984, see archival evidence from the French National Archives in: Warlouzet, *Europe contre Europe*, 92-94. See also: Kenneth Armstrong and Simon Bulmer, *The Governance of the Single European Market*, Manchester University Press, 1998.

80 Warlouzet, *Governing Europe*, 185-186.

81 GER-FAA, ZW/124.454, note for Karkow, 18 May 1983; AAPD, 1983, doc. 143, note on a Kohl-Mitterrand meeting in Paris, 16 May 1983; doc. 148, note on a Franco-German meeting on 18 May 1983.

82 FR-NA, 5 AG4/ EG 38, note by the SG of the SGCI, 22 June 1984; note by the SGCI on the CAP, 21 June 1984. On the agricultural front, France obtained the progressive dismantling of positive compensatory amounts, which constituted additional subsidies for producers in countries with strong currencies, such as West Germany.

83 Conclusions of the Fontainebleau European Council (25 and 26 June 1984).

84 FR-NA, 5AG4/EG 34, summary note by Attali for Mitterrand, 3 December 1983.

85 'The thrust of Commission policy. Statement by Jacques Delors, President of the Commission, to the European Parliament. Strasbourg, 14 and 15 January 1985', in *Bulletin of the European Communities*, 1985.

86 *Completing the Internal Market*, Com (85) 310, 14 June 1985; on standardisation: Ballor, *Big Business and Integration*.

87 HAEU, JD-3, Official report of the Milan European Council, 28 and 29 June 1985.

88 AAPD, 1985/311, minutes of the Kohl–Delors talks, 11 November 1985.
89 S. K. Vogel, *Freer Markets, More Rules: Regulatory Reform in Advanced Industrial Countries*, Cornell University Press, 1996.
90 Michelle Egan, *Constructing a European Market*, Oxford University Press, 2001.
91 Council Directive 89/552/EEC of 3 October 1989 (OJ L 298, 17.10.1989, 23); Sophie Meunier and Philip Gordon, 'Globalization and French cultural identity', *French Politics, Culture & Society*, 19, 1, 2001, 22–41.
92 For VAT: Council Directive 92/77/EEC of 19 October 1992; see also: HAEU, interview with Christiane Scrivener, 20 April 2016; for excise: Council Directive 92/84/EEC of 19 October 1992 and Council Directive 92/12/EEC of 25 February 1992.
93 Gilles Grin, *The Battle of the Single European Market. Achievements and Economic Thought, 1985–2000*, Paul Kegan, 2003, 155–157.
94 On the free movement of people, see: Emmanuel Comte, *The History of the European Migration Regime: Germany's Strategic Hegemony*, Routledge, 2017; Simone Paoli, 'Migration in European integration: Themes and debates', *JEIH*, 22, 2, 2016, 279–296; Bastian Matteo Scianna, 'Abgeordnete ohne Grenzen? Das Europäische Parlament und die Entstehung des Schengener Abkommens', *JEIH*, 28, 2, 2023, 247–268.
95 Warlouzet, 'Towards a fourth paradigm'.
96 HAEU/AO, HistCom2, interview with Peter Sutherland by Laurent Warlouzet, 8 September 2011.
97 FR-FAA, DECE 2305, notes on the SGCI meetings of 9 October 1986 and 28 November 1986.
98 FR-FAA, DECE 2305, letter from Madelin to Sutherland, 23 April 1986 and DECE 2302, note SGCI of 2 June 1986, minutes of the Madelin–Sutherland interview of 26 May 1986; AN, 5AG4 / 3113, note Boublil, 11 June 1986.
99 For details regarding this controversy: Laurent Warlouzet, 'The collapse of the French shipyard of Dunkirk and EEC state-aid control (1977–86)', *Business History*, 62, 5, 2020, 858–878.
100 Nicholas Colchester and David Buchan, *Europe Relaunched: Truth and Illusions on the way to 1992*, The Economist Books, 1990, 151.
101 Mark Thatcher, *Internationalisation and Economic Institutions: Comparing the European Experience*, Oxford University Press, 2007.
102 Hussein Kassim and Handley Stevens, *Air Transport and the European Union. Europeanization and Its Limits*, Palgrave Macmillan, 2010, 86–87.
103 HAEU, BAC 104/1993/61, Legal Service Note, 20 May 1981.
104 Judgment of the Court (Second Chamber) of 10 June 1982, 'Nicholas William, Lord Bethell, v Commission of the European Communities', Case 246/81.
105 Judgment of the Court of 22 May 1985, 'European Parliament v. Council of the European Communities', Case 13/83.
106 FR-FAA, DECE 2302, letter from Sutherland to Auroux, 31 October 1985; FR-FAA, DECE 2302, reasoned opinion of the European Commission, doc. C (85) 1267 of 19 August 1985; Kassim and Stevens, *Air Transport*, 82 and 93.
107 Judgment of the Court of 30 April 1986, *New Frontiers*, joined cases 209 to 213/84; Council Regulations 3975/87 and 3976/87 of 14 December 1987.
108 Kassim and Stevens, *Air Transport*, 98–101.
109 Thatcher, *Internationalisation*, 166–168.

110 Commission Directive 88/301/EEC of 16 May 1988 on competition in the markets for telecommunications terminals.
111 Judgment of the Court of 19 March 1991, 'French Republic v Commission of the European Communities. Competition in the markets for telecommunications terminals', Case C-202/88.
112 Jean Joana and Andy Smith, *Les commissaires européens: technocrates, diplomates ou politiques?*, Presses de sciences-po, 2002, 132.
113 Judgment of the Court of 17 November 1987, *British-American Tobacco Company Ltd and R. J. Reynolds Industries Inc. v. Commission*, Joined Cases 142 and 156/84. This judgment is considered the major element of the negotiation in Tim Büthe and Gabriel T. Swank, *The Politics of Antitrust and Merger Review in the European Union: Institutional Change and Decisions from Messina to 2004*, Center for European Studies Working Paper Series, 142, 2007; Pollack, *The Engines*, 284–291.
114 This account of the negotiations surrounding the 1989 merger regulation is based on: Laurent Warlouzet, 'The centralization of EU competition policy', 725–741.
115 AFDP, A 49-272, Fax BMWI-ABT I, Janicki, meeting of 25 October 1989; note of 7 November 1989; doc. Zweites Kartte-Papier von 2.11.89.
116 FR-NA, 5AG4/EG/79/3, note sent on 10 November 1988.
117 GER-NA, B 136/17859, note AA, Referat 421, 10 November 1982.
118 FR-NA, 19900452/29, Trichet for the Minister, note of 4 October 1989.
119 George Ross, *Jacques Delors and European Integration*, Polity Press, 1995, 133–134.
120 On this episode and the 1984 memorandum, see: Warlouzet, *Governing Europe*, 189.
121 BR-NA (FOIA request), MWB.021/1, note to Robert Armstrong, received on 21 May 1984.
122 BR-NA (FOIA request), MWB.021/1, note from Unwin (Treasury) to Julian Bullard (FCO), 24 May 1984; MWB.021/1, note from Gray (DTI) to Julian Bullard (FCO), 24 May 1984; note from Westmacott (European Community Department) to Renwik, received on 31 May 1984.
123 The memorandum was published in *JCMS*, 28, 1, 1984, 73–81.
124 BR-NA (FOIA request), MWB.021/1, note from Fairweather to Renwick, 14 June 1984.
125 BR-NA (FOIA request), MWB.021/1, note from A. Leslie to P. J. Westmacott, 23 August 1984; note from Christopher to Miss Neville-Jones (Planning Staff), 23 July 1984 (doc no. 94); note from Paul Le Breton (Information Dpt) to Barrington, 13 August 1984.
126 BR-NA, CAB 193/455, Dutch note on deregulation in the European context, 11 February 1985.
127 BR-NA, CAB 193/455, note Cabinet Office, David Barclays to Williamson, 27 February 1985; note Guy Stapleton to Williamson, date partly erased, presumably 5 March 1985.
128 BR-NA, CAB 193/455, note Cabinet Office, Private Secretary, Charles Powell, 2 March 1985.
129 BR-NA, CAB 193/455, note JS Wall, European Community Department, FCO, 6 March 1985; note, Cabinet Office, meeting chaired by Williamson, 15 March 1985; CAB 193/464, meeting between Mr R. Q. Braithwaite, and Dr Posthumus Meyjes, FCO, 15 March 1985; note J. A. Shepherd, FCO, 9 May 1985.

130 BR-NA, CAB 193/455, Cabinet Office note on a meeting chaired by Williamson, 8 March 1985; note, Health and Social Security, Kathleen E. W. Blunt, 12 March 1985.
131 BR-NA, PREM 19/1490/2, note from Goulden to Powell, 29 March 1985.
132 BR-NA, PREM 19/1490/1, 'The creation of wealth and employment in the Community', European Council of Brussels, 29–30 March 1985.
133 BR-NA, PREM 19/1490/2, telex UKREP, 1 April 1985; Cabinet Office note, Williamson, 1 April 1985.
134 BR-NA, PREM 19/1751, note from David Williamson to Charles Powell, 27 November 1986; letter from the Paymaster General (then Kenneth Clarke), to Thatcher, November 1986.
135 BR-NA, PREM 19/1751, letter from Howe (Foreign Secretary) to Thatcher, 6 October 1986.
136 See the drawing by Richard O'Toole, Peter Sutherland's Chief of Staff, in Laurent Warlouzet, 'The internal market and competition', in Vincent Dujardin et al. (eds.), *The European Commission, 1986-2000. Histories and Memories of an Institution*, Publications Office of the European Union, 2019, 257–280.
137 BR-NA, PREM 19/1751, note from Charles Powell (Private Secretary) to Thatcher, 3 January 1986.
138 'Le Club 89 et le Club de l'Horloge publient un rapport commun sur l'Europe sociale', *Le Monde*, 2 May 1989.

Chapter 4

1 *Social Insurance and Allied Service: A Report by William Beveridge*, Cmd. 6404, 1942.
2 This definition is ad hoc, for even specialists on the welfare state tend to avoid the delicate question of its definition and boundaries: Nicholas Barr, *Economics of the Welfare State*, Oxford University Press, 2012, 7–12.
3 See below and: Milward, *The Rescue*; Lucia Coppolaro and Lorenzo Mechi (eds.), *Free Trade and Social Welfare in Europe: Explorations in the Long 20th Century*, Routledge, 2020; Andry, *Social Europe*; Amandine Crespy, *Welfare Markets in Europe: The Democratic Challenge of European Integration*, Palgrave Macmillan, 2016; Stephan Leibfried and Paul Pierson, *European Social Policy: Between Fragmentation and Integration*, Brookings Publications, 1995.
4 With the exception of European monetary cooperation, see Chapter 7.
5 Marcel van der Linden et al. (eds.), *ILO Histories. Essays on the ILO and Its Impact on the World during the Twentieth Century*, Peter Lang, 2010; Daniel Maul, *The ILO: 100 Years of Global Social Policy*, De Gruyter, 2019.
6 Paul Finet of Belgium (a former metalworker, President of the International Confederation of Free Trade Unions) and Heinz Ponthoff of Germany (a former mechanical fitter and member of the German trade union confederation DGB). On the ILO and the ECSC: Lorenzo Mechi, 'Economic regionalism and social stabilisation: The International Labour Organization and Western Europe in the early post-war years', *The International History Review*, 35, 4, 2013, 844–862.
7 Lorenzo Mechi, 'Managing the labour market in an open economy: From the International Labour Organisation to the European Communities', *Contemporary European History*, 27, 2, 2018, 221–238; Nicolas Verschueren, 'From steel house to mass housing for the working class', *JEIH*, 22, 2, 2016, 249–262.

8 Lise Rye, 'The rise and fall of the French demand for social harmonisation in the EEC, 1955-1966', in Katrin Rücker and Laurent Warlouzet (eds.), *Which Europe (s). New Approaches in European Integration History*, Peter Lang, 2006, 155-169; Warlouzet, *Le choix de la CEE*, 43-49.
9 Warlouzet, *Le choix de la CEE*, 77-78 and 87-93.
10 Mechi, 'Managing'.
11 GER-FAA, note AA, 25 November 1970; Warlouzet, *Governing Europe*, 38-39; Andry, *The Road*.
12 Degryse and Tilly, *40 years; Ciampani, Tilly, National*.
13 Michele Di Donato, *I comunisti italiani e la sinistra europea: il PCI ei rapporti con le socialdemocrazie (1964-1984)*, Carocci editore, 2015.
14 AAPD, 1977, doc. 264, note on a meeting between Schmidt and Mitterrand, 29 September 1977.
15 Warlouzet, *Governing Europe*, 50-52; Andry, *The Road*.
16 Jasmien van Daele, Magaly Rodriguez Garcia, and Geert van Goethe, *Writing ILO Histories. Essays on the International Labour Organization and Its Impact on the World during the Twentieth Century*, 2011, Peter Lang, 29.
17 ILOA, 110.472, note from the ILO Board, 17 January 1978.
18 ILOA, 111.348, report of the Board, 22-26 September 1980, 26-28.
19 See the subchapter below: 'The illusion of well-developed social and fiscal harmonisation'.
20 On Delors's influence see: Alessandra Bitumi, '"An Uplifting Tale of Europe", Jacques Delors and the Contradictory Quest for a European Social Model in the Age of Reagan', *Journal of Transatlantic Studies*, 16, 3, 2018, 203-221; Helen Drake, *Jacques Delors: Perspectives on a European Leader*, Routledge, 2000; Ken Endo, *The Presidency of the European Commission under Jacques Delors. The Politics of Shared Leadership*, Palgrave Macmillan, 1999.
21 See below on the Maldague Report. On the European Parliament see: EPA, Interventions of Jacques Delors in plenary sessions of the European Parliament on 15 January, 15 November, and 2 December 1980.
22 AAPD, 1981, doc. 290, meeting Schmidt-Mitterrand in Latché, 8 October 1981; BR-NA, FCO 33/4478, note P. C. Petrie, 24 September 1981, conversation with Pierre Achard (SGCI).
23 Etienne-Jeannette, *Penser et construire l'Europe sociale. Les conseillers de François Mitterrand et l'intégration européenne, 1981-1989*, unpublished masters' dissertation, Sorbonne Université, 2013, 86; ACFDT, 8 H 1896, Note CFDT-International, 7 December 1981.
24 Claude Didry and Arnaud Mias, *Le moment Delors. Les syndicats au cœur de l'Europe sociale*, Peter Lang, 2005.
25 ETUC 2099, note on the first Val Duchess Meeting, 31 January 1985.
26 Etienne-Jeannette, *Penser*, 133-136.
27 For the environment see below; for health and safety see: Volker Eichener, *Social Dumping or Innovative Regulation? Processes and Outcomes of European Decision-Making in the Sector of Health and Safety at Work Harmonizationn*, Florence, EUI working paper Sps 92/28, 1992; Aude Cefaliello, *Towards an Improvement of the Legal Framework Governing Occupational Health and Safety in the European Union*, dissertation in law, University of Glasgow, 2020, 41-47.
28 On the active support of the German DGB for Delors's agenda: Marvin Schnippering, The German Trade Union Confederation's European Policy, 1969-1992:

An alternative to a market-driven Europe, unpublished PhD diss., University of Glasgow, 2022, 124–161.

29 George, *An Awkward Partner*, 193; see the hostile reaction to the speech by Jacques Delors at the TUC Congress: AAPD 1988, doc. 349, note on the Kohl–Thatcher meeting, 2 December 1988.

30 Etienne-Jeannette, *Penser*, 146.

31 Etienne-Jeannette, *Penser*, 171–211.

32 AAPD, 1988, doc. 332, note on a meeting between Helmut Kohl and Ciriaco De Mita, 22 November 1988; AAPD, 1989, doc. 109, note Schönfelder, 21 April 1989; on Blum: AAPD 1989, doc. 410, note Schürmann, 15 December 1989.

33 Philippa Watson, *EU Social and Employment Law: Policy and Practice in an Enlarged Europe*, Oxford University Press, 2009, 56.

34 AAPD, 1989, doc. 410, note of Wilhelm Schürmann, 15 December 1989.

35 Ballor, *Enterprise and Integration*, chapter 6.

36 Frédéric Bozo, 'In search of the Holy Grail: France and European monetary unification, 1984–1989', in Michael Gehler and Wilfried Loth (eds.), *Reshaping Europe. Towards a Political, Economic and Monetary Union, 1984–1989*, Steiner, 2020, 283–330; Varsori, *La Cenerentola*, 366–367.

37 Commission européenne, *Croissance, compétitivité, emploi*, Com (93) 700, 5 December 1993; Fabio Masini, *European Economic Governance: Theories, Historical Evolution, and Reform Proposals*, Palgrave Macmillan, 2022; Mathieu Fulla, 'The "Nordicisation" of the European Socialist Employment Policy in the early 1990s', in Alan Granadino, Stefan Nygard, and Peter Stadius (eds.), *Rethinking the History of Post-War European Social Democracy*, 2022, 48–66.

38 Giubboni, *Social Rights*, 85.

39 Simone Paoli, 'Erasmus', in Vincent Dujardin et al. (dir.), *The European Commission 1986–2000. Histoire et mémoires d'une institution*, Publications Office of the EU, 2019, 446–447.

40 Pauline Ravinet, 'La Commission européenne et l'enseignement supérieur. La néolibéralisation du discours comme ressort de pouvoir?' *Gouvernement et action publique*, 2, 2014, 81–102.

41 Éliane Gubin, 'La grève des ouvrières de la Fabrique nationale d'armes à Herstal (1966): un tournant?', in Anne-Laure Briatte, Éliane Gubin, and Françoise Thébaud (eds.), *L'Europe, une chance pour les femmes? Le genre de la construction européenne*, Éditions de la Sorbonne, 2019, 115–126.

42 Paul Pierson, 'The path to European integration: A historical-institutionalist analysis', in Wayne Sandholtz and Alec Stone Sweet (eds.), *European Integration and Supranational Governance*, Oxford University Press, 1998, 51–53.

43 Gubin, 'La grève des ouvrières', 123.

44 The first directive expanded the article's scope from the notion of 'equal work' to 'work of equal value'. The second focused on equal access to employment, professional training, and promotions, in addition to equivalent working conditions. Finally, the third addressed equal treatment with respect to social security. See: Elizabeth Vallance and Elizabeth Davies, *Women of Europe. Women MEPs and Equality Policy*, Cambridge University Press, 1986.

45 BR-NA, PREM 19/1751, note from Charles Powell (private secretary) on a meeting between Thatcher and Delors, 27 November 1986; Ben Jackson, 'Free markets and

feminism: The neo-liberal defence of the male breadwinner model in Britain, c. 1980-1997', *Women's History Review*, 2018, 297-316.
46 Didry, Mias, *Le moment Delors*, 18.
47 On Seveso and waste control: Liesbeth van de Grift, 'Representing European Society. The Rise of New Representative Claims in 1970s European Policies', *Archiv für Sozialgeschichte*, 58, 2018, 263-278; Koen van Zon, Liesbeth van de Grift, *The European Parliament and the Origins of Consumer Policy*, European Parliamentary Research Service, 2024.
48 BR-NA, PIN 34/520, note HindMarchh: brief for Vredeling visit on 24 January 1977; note on a meeting with Vredeling, 24 January 1977; brief for the meeting with Vredeling on 12 July 1979.
49 BR-NA, PIN 34/817, telex UKRep, Bruxelles, 17 May 1983 and 2 June 1983.
50 Jarrige, Le Roux, *La contamination du monde*, 305.
51 On the impact of human activity on the environment: John R. McNeill and Peter Engelke, *The Great Acceleration: An Environmental History of the Anthropocene since 1945*, Harvard University Press, 2014; on the change in public policy: Rüdiger Graf, 'Die Ökonomisierung der Umwelt und die Ökologisierung der Wirtschaftseit den 1970er Jahren', in Rüdiger Graf et al. (eds.), *Ökonomisierung: Debatten und Praktiken in der Zeitgeschichte*, Wallstein Verlag, 2019, 188-212; Grift, 'Representing'.
52 Donella H. Meadows, Dennis L. Meadows, Jørgen Randers, and William W. Behrens III, *The Limits to Growth*, Universe books, 1972.
53 Meg Jacobs, *Panic at the Pump: The Energy Crisis and the Transformation of American Politics in the 1970s*, Hill and Wang, 2016.
54 Christophe Bonneuil and Frédéric Thomas, *Semences: une histoire politique. Amélioration des plantes, agriculture et alimentation en France depuis la Seconde Guerre mondiale*, éditions C. Léopold Mayer, 2012, 117.
55 AUN, Geneva, G.X.33/1, Background note, 26 June 1980, and letter of 10 March 1977; Rothschild, *Poisonous Skies*.
56 Jan Van der Harst, 'Sicco Mansholt: courage and conviction', in Michel Dumoulin (ed.), *The European Commission, 1958-1972: Histories and Memories*, Publications Office of the EU, 2007, 165-180.
57 Jan-Henrik Meyer, 'Pushing for a greener Europe: The European Parliament and environmental policy in the 1970s and 1980s', *JEIH*, 27, 1, 2021, 57-78.
58 On the history of EEC/EU Environmental policy, in addition to Jan-Henrik Meyer's contributions, see: Laura Scichilone, *L'Europa e la sfida ecologica. Storia della politica ambientale europea (1969-1998)*, il Mulino, 2009; Nigel Haigh, *EU Environmental Policy: Its Journey to Centre Stage*, Routledge, 2016; Andrew Jordan and Viviane Gravey, *Environmental Policy in the EU. Actors, Institutions and Processes*, Routledge, 2021.
59 Jan-Henrik Meyer, 'Green activism: The European Parliament's Environmental Committee promoting a European Environmental Policy in the 1970s', *JEIH*, 17, 1, 2011, 73-86.
60 Henning A. Arp, *The European Parliament in European Community Environmental Policy*, EUI Working Paper EPU no. 92/13, Florence, 1992.
61 BR-NA, PREM 19/1490/1, steering brief and brief on Environmental Issues, 26 March 1985.
62 On Volker Hauff see chapter 7; on the Brundtland Report: Borowy, *Defining Sustainable Development*.

63 Borowy, *Defining Sustainable Development*, 147 and 205–207. On its influence on the EEC: Eelke Seefried, 'Developing Europe: The formation of sustainability concepts and activities', in A.-K. Wöbse and P. Kupper (eds.), *Greening Europe: Environmental Protection in the Long Twentieth Century: A Handbook*, De Gruyter Oldenbourg, 2021, 389–418.

64 Ann-Kristin Bergquist and Thomas David, 'Beyond planetary limits! The International Chamber of Commerce, the UN and the invention of sustainable development', *Business History Review*, 97, 3, 2023, 481–511; Ben Huf, Glenda Sluga, and Sabine Selchow, 'Business and the planetary history of international environmental governance in the 1970s', *Contemporary European History*, 31, 2022, 553–569.

65 On power plants: Alexandre Lauverjat, 'One atmosphere, yet twelve energy policies: The Community's struggle against air pollution from power stations (1983–1988)', *JEIH*, 2026; on the negotiations surrounding car emissions: Grace Ballor, *Liberal Environmentalism: The Public–Private Production of European Emissions Standards*, Cambridge University Press, 2023; Samuel Klebaner and Sigfrido M. Ramírez Pérez, 'Managing technical changes from the scales of legal regulation: German clean cars against the European Pollutant Emissions Regulations in the 1980s', *Management & Organizational History*, 14, 4, 2019, 442–468; Mattias Näsman and Sabine Pitteloud, 'The power and limits of expertise: Swiss–Swedish linking of vehicle emission standards in the 1970s and 1980s', *Business and Politics*, 24, 3, 2022, 241–260; Laurent Warlouzet, 'The Role of the European Parliament in the Single Market Programme: The Cost of non-Europe and the car emission directive (1983–89)', *JEIH*, 27, 1, 2021, 21–36.

66 Birgit Metzger and Laurent Schmit, 'Shades of Green: Ökologische Modernisierung im deutsch-französischen Vergleich (1970–1990)', in Martin Bemman, Birgit Metzger, and Roderich von Detten (eds.), *Ökologische Modernisierung. Zur Geschichte und Gegenwart eines Konzepts in Umweltpolitik und Sozialwissenschaften*, Campus Verlag, 2014, 271–272.

67 On the 'merchants of doubt', see Chapters 1 and 9; FR-NA, 5 AG4/ EG 26, note from the ministry of Industry, 2 December 1983.

68 FR-NA, 19880071/62, note Jean Desley, 3 August 1983; Isabelle Roussel, 'La pollution atmosphérique entre santé et environnement (1958–1996)', in *Écologie & politique*, 58, 2019, 35–52; FR-NA, 19880070/2, letter from Huguette Bouchardeau to François Mitterrand, 26 May 1984; AN, 5AG4/39, note SGCI, 29 November 1984.

69 HAEU, BAC 127/95/28, note, 20 April 1989.

70 Geoffrey Jones and Christina Lubinski, 'Making 'Green Giants': Environment sustainability in the German chemical industry, 1950s–1980s', *Business History*, 56, 4, 2014, 623–49; Geoffrey Jones, *Profits and Sustainability: A History of Green Entrepreneurship*, Oxford University Press, 2019; David Wallace, *Environmental Policy and Industrial Innovation: Strategies in Europe, the US and Japan*, Routledge, 1995.

71 Milward, *La reconstruction*, 140. See the German debate between Werner Abelshauser (sceptic) and Anthony James Nicholls (who believed the Marshall Plan had an important role among other factors): Werner Abelshauser, *Deutsche Wirtschaftsgeschichte seit 1945*, Beck, 2004; Anthony James Nicholls, *Freedom with Responsibility: The Social Market Economy in Germany, 1918–1963*, Clarendon Press, 1994.

72 Dutch memorandum of 11 December 1952 and of 5 May 1953, available on the CVCE website.
73 Lorenzo Mechi, 'Formation of a European society? Exploring social and cultural dimensions', in Wolfram Kaiser and Lorenzo Mechi (eds.), *European Union History: Themes and Debates*, Palgrave Macmillan, 2010, 150–168.
74 George, *An Awkward Partner*.
75 FR-NA, 5AG3/914, note from the Treasury, 29 November 1978; FR-NA, 5 AG3/916, notes of Panafieu, 19 June 1979 and 28 November 1979; Helen Wallace, 'Distributional politics: Dividing up the community cake', in Helen Wallace, William Wallace, and Carole Webb (eds.), *Policy-Making in the European Communities*, John Wiley & Sons, 1983, 93.
76 For details on the French position: Warlouzet, *Europe contre Europe*, 139–140.
77 BR-NA, PREM 16/398, German memorandum, 12 November 1975.
78 FR-NA, 5AG4/EG 96/3, German memorandum, 12 September 1983.
79 BR-NA, PREM 19/1026, general brief, European Council in Athens, 4/6 December 1983.
80 *Réussir l'Acte unique, une nouvelle frontière pour l'Europe*, Com (87) 100, 15 February 1987; Nicolas Jabko, *Playing the Market: A Political Strategy for Uniting Europe, 1985-2005*, Cornell University Press, 2006, 121–146.
81 Jabko, *Playing the Market*, 127–129.
82 AAPD, 1988, doc. 15, note on a cabinet discussion, 14 January 1988; doc 36, note Trumpf, 27 January 1988; doc. 59, Note Ungerer, 15 February 1988.
83 The share of the ERDF (and the Cohesion Fund beginning in 1993) rose from 5.6 per cent of the EC budget in 1985 to 14.9 per cent in 1995; the share of the CAP's most productivist component (the 'guaranteed' rather than 'orientation' portion of the budget) decreased from 68.4 per cent to 50.4 per cent of the EC budget over the same period; source: EU budget 2008, *Financial Report, Luxembourg, Publication Office of the European Union*, 2009, annex, 79–84.
84 European Commission, *Growth, Competitiveness, Employment*, 15.
85 Kiran Klaus Patel, *The New Deal. A Global History*, Princeton University Press, 2016.
86 On this project and its partial application see: Alexander Nützenadel, *Stunde der Ökonomen. Wissenschaft, Politik und Expertenkultur in der Bundesrepublik 1949-1974*, Vandenhoeck & Ruprecht, 2005, 222–228; Warlouzet, *Le choix de la CEE*, 339–356; Hugo Canihac, 'Un marché sans économistes? La planification et l'impossible émergence d'une science économique européenne (1957–1967)', *Revue française de science politique*, 69, 1, 2019, 95–116.
87 Shonfield, *Modern Capitalism. The Changing Balance of Public and Private Power*, Oxford University Press, 1965, 122: in addition to France and Great Britain, Italy, Belgium, the Netherlands, Austria, Sweden, and Norway had indicative planning systems at the time.
88 ACNPF, 72 AS 1412, *Business Week*, May 25, 1963; John H. McArthur and Bruce R. Scott, *L'industrie française face aux plans, Harvard ausculte la France (Industrial planning in France)*, Paris, Organisation, 1970.
89 Paul Samuelson, *Economics*, 8th ed., 1970; quoted in Piketty, *Le Capital*, 218.
90 Warlouzet, *Le choix de la CEE par la France*, 342–356; Laurent Warlouzet, 'The EEC/EU as an evolving compromise between French dirigism and German ordo-liberalism (1957–1995)', *JCMS*, 57, 1, 2019, 77–93.

91 Andry, *Social Europe*, 165–171.
92 European Commission, *Report of the Study Group 'Problems of Inflation'*, 3 March 1976. The European Commission acknowledged that it was an influential document (see note 93).
93 Commissioner Willy Haferkamp, a German Social Democrat, circulated a document criticising the report's excessive emphasis on planning: HAEU, Collection de documents SEC, SEC(76)4165, note DG II of 22 novembre 1976.
94 BR-NA, T 390/283, doc RE 961/January 1977, Stuart Holland, note of the Labour Party, NEC/ EEC Study group, received at the Treasury on 20 January 1977.
95 Jacques Delors, 'The decline of French planning', in Stuart Holland (ed.), *Beyond Capitalist Planning*, Basil Blackwell, 1978, 25–27.
96 Delors, 'The decline of French planning', 32.
97 Stuart Holland, 'Introduction' and Franco Archibugi, Jacques Delors, and Stuart Holland, 'Planning for development', in Holland (ed.), *Beyond Capitalist Planning*, 9 and 184–202.
98 Norbert Wierzcorek, 'Perspectives for planning', in Holland (ed.), *Beyond Capitalist Planning*, 110–115.
99 BR-NA, T 390/98, ETUC, note for the 9 February 1977 meeting.
100 BR-NA, PREM 19/462, *ETUC Manifesto for Employment and Economic Recovery*, 5 May 1981.
101 Stuart Holland, 'Out of crisis: International economic recovery', in James Curran (ed.), *The Future of the Left*, Polity Press, 1984, 243–264; Kevin Featherstone, *Socialist Parties and European Integration. A Comparative History*, Manchester University Press, 1988, 64.
102 BR-NA, PREM 19/1751, letter from Mathias Hinterscheid (ETUC) to Margaret Thatcher (President of the EC Council), 19 November 1986.
103 Warlouzet, *Le choix de la CEE par la France*, 34.
104 Mechi, 'Du BIT...', 26.
105 Warlouzet, *Le choix de la CEE par la France*, 39–40.
106 Carasso, *Entre neutralité*, 160; on the German initiative from June 1965: 110; on Debré: 128 and 156.
107 Catherine Schenk, 'The Regulation of International Financial Markets from the 1950s to the 1990s', in Stefano Battilossi and Jaime Reis (eds.), *State and Financial Systems in Europe and the USA*, Routledge, 2016, 149–166.
108 BR-NA, PREM 16/850, joint statement by the Tripartite Conference, 24 June 1976; T 390/98, note Moore (Employment) to Thorp (Treasury), 6 April 1977.
109 BR-NA, FCO 30/395213, note UKREP, 25 September 1978.
110 BR-NA, PIN 34/520, brief for the meeting with Vredeling, 12 July 1979.
111 FR-NA, 5AG3/915, note DAEF, 12 March 1979; DECE 1484, note, Ministry of Foreign Affairs, 4 January 1979; DECE 1489, note DAEF/SCE/JG, 6 March 1979.
112 FR-NA, 5AG3/915, note on the EEC meeting of 9–10 March 1979; note of Olivier Fouquet, 12 March 1979.
113 FR-FAA, DECE 1490, note SGCI 22 May 1979; DECE 1422, opinion of the ESC on working time, 26 October 1979.
114 FR-NA, 5AG3/916, note SGCI, Pierre Achard, 29 May 1979.
115 BR-NA, PREM 19/51, note Department of Employment, 13 June 1979; on the outcome of the debate: FR-FAA, DECE 1491, note SCGI, 19 June 1980; FR-NA, 5AG3/916, note Panafieu, 28 November 1979.

116 AAPD, 1981, doc. 331, note Zeller, 19 November 1981.
117 Warlouzet, *Governing Europe*, 51.
118 ILOA, 238.121, note on the ETUC Congress in Munich, 14–18 May 1979; FR-FAA, DECE 1490, note from the Labour Ministry, 12 June 1979; Featherstone, *Socialist Parties*, 30 and 156–60.
119 FR-FAA, DECE 81-83/1835, note from the Labour Ministry, 25 August 1981.
120 Etienne-Jeannette, *Penser*, 61 and 78–79.
121 FR-FAA, DECE 81-83/1835, note DGRST, 26 August 1981; note from the Ministry of Economics and Finance, 14 September 1981; note from the Labour Ministry of 24 June 1981, 25 August 1981, and 16 September 1981.
122 Warlouzet, *Governing Europe*, 45.
123 AAPD, 1984, doc. 122, note on a meeting between Kohl and Thatcher, 2 May 1984; Andreas Wirsching, *Abschied*.
124 AOIT, 238.121, note on the ETUC meeting of 9–11 May 1983.
125 AETUC 1485, telex, 1 June 1984; FR-NA, 5 AG4/ EG 38, note SGCI, 21 June 1984.
126 FR-FAA, DECE 2023, note SGCI for the meeting of 27 April 1982; note DAEF/ Guy Legras, 10 November 1982; AETUC 1483, note ETUC, 11 November 1982 and 20 October 1982; AETUC 1485, note ETUC, 3 May 1984.
127 Degryse and Tilly, *40 years*, 32.
128 Robert Marjolin, *Le travail d'une vie, 1911–1986*, Robert Laffont, 1986; Jacques Delors, *Mémoires*, Plon, 2004.
129 Wallace Oates, *Fiscal Federalism*, Harcourt, 1972.
130 BR-NA, PREM 16/1253, telegram UKREP, 23 March 1977.

Chapter 5

1 Marc Trachtenberg, 'France and NATO, 1949–1991', *Journal of Transatlantic Studies*, 9, 3, 2011, 184–194.
2 Michael Creswell, 'Between the bear and the phoenix: The United States and the European Defense Community, 1950–54', *Security Studies*, 11, 4, 2002, 89–124.
3 Geir Lundestad, 'Empire by Invitation? The United States and Western Europe, 1945–1952', *Journal of Peace Research*, 23, 3, 1986, 263–277; see also on France and the EDC: Victor Gavin, 'Power through Europe? The case of the European Defence Community in France (1950–1954)', *French History*, 23, 1, 2009, 69–87.
4 Iris Glockner and Berthold Rittberger, 'The European Coal and Steel Community (ECSC) and European Defence Community (EDC) Treaties', in Finn Laursen (ed.), *Designing the European Union: From Paris to Lisbon*, Palgrave, 2012, 16–47.
5 Charles de Gaulle, speech on 22 July 1947. The two stages represented the distance between Eastern France and Czechoslovakia. On the French EDC quarrel: Craig Parsons, *A Certain Idea of Europe*, Cornell University Press, 2003.
6 FRUS 1958–60, Western European integration vol VII, part 1, doc 164, Memorandum of Conversation, 12 December 1958, 371.
7 Georges-Henri Soutou, *L'alliance incertaine: les rapports politico-stratégiques franco-allemands, 1954–1996*, Fayard, 1996, 55–121; Jenny Raflik, 'France and the abandoned dream of a European bomb, 1954–58', in Nicolas Badalassi and Frédéric Gloriant (eds.), *France, Germany, and Nuclear Deterrence: Quarrels and Convergences during the Cold War and Beyond*, Berghahn Books, 2022.

8. On Euratom: Gunnar Skogmar, *The United States and the Nuclear Dimension of European Integration*, Palgrave Macmillan, 2004.
9. Marc Trachtenberg, *A Constructed Peace: The Making of the European Settlement, 1945-1963*, Princeton University Press, 1999, 201-247.
10. Götz Neuneck, 'The atomic bomb reveals the political responsibility of science', in Lutz Castell and Otfried Ischebeck (eds.), *Time, Quantum and Information*, Springer, 2003, 50-51.
11. On the MLF, see: Trachtenberg, *A Constructed Peace*, 297-321.
12. 'Le Marché commun, 160 millions de clients', *Journal Les Actualités Françaises*, 23.01.1957, www.Ina.fr.
13. Charles de Gaulle, press conference of 23 July 1964; Moravcsik, *The Choice for Europe*, 177-225.
14. Marc Trachtenberg, *A Constructed Peace: The Making of the European Settlement, 1945-1963*, Princeton University Press, 1999. On Adenauer: Hans-Peter Schwarz, *Adenauer: Der Staatsmann: 1952-1967*, Deutsche Verlags-Anstalt, 1991, 285-307.
15. Frédéric Gloriant, 'De Gaulle's Nuclear Policy, West Germany and the Second Berlin Crisis: A Historiographical Reappraisal, 1958-63', in Badalassi and Gloriant (eds.), *France, Germany, and Nuclear Deterrence*.
16. Angela Romano, *From détente in Europe to European détente: How the West Shaped the Helsinki CSCE*, Peter Lang, 2009.
17. Eva Oberloskamp, 'The European TREVI Conference in the 1970s: Transgovernmental Policy Coordination in the Area of Internal Security', *JEIH*, 22, 1, 2016, 29-46.
18. Piers Ludlow, 'Solidarity, sanctions and misunderstanding: The European dimension of the Falklands Crisis', *The International History Review*, 43, 3, 2021, 508-524.
19. Robert Hayden, *From Yugoslavia to the Western Balkans: Studies of a European disunion, 1991-2011*, Brill, 2012; Branislav Radeljic, *Europe and the Collapse of Yugoslavia: The Role of Non-state Actors and European Diplomacy*, Bloomsbury Publishing, 2016.
20. The Lockheed F-104 (introduced in 1958) was produced in Italy and Germany; the General Dynamics F-16 (introduced in 1978) was produced in Belgium, the Netherlands, and Turkey; and the Lockheed Martin F-35 (introduced in 2015) is currently produced in partnership with the UK, Italy, the Netherlands, Denmark, and Norway. More generally, see: Frédéric Mérand, *European Defence Policy: Beyond the Nation State*, Oxford University Press, 2008.
21. David Burigana, 'The European search for aeronautical technologies, and technological survival by co-operation in the 1960s-1970s ... with or without the Americans?', *Humana.Mente Journal of Philosophical Studies*, 16, 1, 2011, 69-103.
22. AAPD 1985, doc. 198, note by Oesterhelt, 16 July 1985.
23. Guido Thiemeyer, 'The failure of the green pool and the success of the CAP: Long term structures in European Agricultural integration in the 1950s and the 1960s', in Kiran Klaus Patel (ed.), *Fertile Ground for Europe? The History of European Integration and the Common Agricultural Policy since 1945*, Nomos Verlag, 2009, 47-60.
24. Patel (ed.), *Fertile Ground for Europe?*; Ann-Christina Knudsen, *Farmers on Welfare: The Making of Europe's Common Agricultural Policy*, Cornell University Press, 2009.
25. Gunnar Myrdal, 'Economic nationalism and internationalism', *Australian Outlook*, 11, 4, 1957, 3-50, quoted by: Elmar Rieger, 'The Common agricultural policy', in

Helen and William Wallace (eds.), *Policy-Making in the European Union*, Oxford University Press, 1996, 105.
26 Gordon Wright, *Rural Revolution in France: The Peasantry in the Twentieth Century*, Stanford University Press, 1964, 167-168; see also: Laurent Warlouzet, 'The Deadlock: The choice of the CAP by de Gaulle and its impact on French EEC policy (1958-69)', in Patel (ed.), *Fertile Ground for Europe?*, 101-103.
27 Kiran Klaus Patel, 'Veto player N°1? Germany and the creation of the EEC's Common Agricultural Policy, 1957-1964', in Michael Gehler (ed.), *From Common Market to European Union Building: 50 years of the Rome Treaties 1957-2007*, Böhlau, 2009, 349-370.
28 Jean Rebuffat, '52 images Belges', *Le Soir*, 21 April 1999.
29 Warlouzet, 'The Deadlock', 111-114.
30 FR-NA, 5AG3/921, notes by J. P. Dutet, advisor to the President of the Republic, for the President, 22 October 1974 and 27 November 1975; FR-NA, 5AG3/922, note by Guy de Panafieu, advisor to the President of the Republic, for the President, 6 November 1980.
31 Winfried von Urff, 'The CAP', in Carl-Christoph Schweitzer and Detlev Karsten, *The Federal Republic of Germany and EC Membership Evaluated*, Pinter, 1990, 81-82.
32 FR-NA, 5AG3/916, note by Guy de Panafieu, advisor to the Presidency of the Republic, 28 November 1979; BR-NA, PREM 19/133, Treasury note, 26 November, 1979; BR-NA, PREM 19/1221, note for Edwards, 26 September 1983.
33 FR-NA, 5AG3/916, note on the meeting between Giscard d'Estaing and Jenkins of 23 November 1979; note Rodocanachi, 28 November 1979.
34 FAA-FR, DECE 2064, note from the Ministry of Agriculture, 'CAP financing', 10 June 1983; note DAEF, 10 June 1983, note 'CAP financial situation'; FAA-FR, DECE 2065, note DAEF/GL, 30 May 1983.
35 Ulrich Kluge, *Vierzig Jahre Agrarpolitik in der BDR*, Paul Parey, 1989, 251.
36 AAPD, 1978, doc. 329, note on a Schmidt-Jenkins interview, 27 October 1978; AAPD 1979, doc. 26, note on a Schmidt-Giscard d'Estaing interview, 31 January 1979.
37 AAPD, 1983, doc. 270, note on a Kohl-Thatcher discussion, 21 September 1983; AAPD, 1983, doc. 271, note on a Kohl-Craxi meeting, 23 September 1983.
38 AAPD, 1983, doc. 134, note on an interministerial meeting chaired by Kohl, 11 May 1983.
39 Eckart Gaddum, *Die deutsche Europapolitik in der 80er Jahren, Interessen, Konflikte und Entscheidungen der Regierung Kohl*, Shöningh, 1994, 155.
40 On CAP reform: Mark Pollack, *The Engines of European Integration: Delegation, Agency, and Agenda Setting in the European Union*, Oxford University Press, 2003, 265-281; Gerry Alons, 'Farmers versus ideas: Explaining the continuity in French agricultural trade policy during the GATT Uruguay Round', *Journal of European Public Policy*, 21, 2, 2014, 286-302; Katja Seidel, 'Contested fields: The common agricultural policy and the common fisheries policy', in Vincent Dujardin et al. (eds.), *The European Commission, 1986-2000. History and Memories of an Institution*, Publications Office of the European Union, 2019, 347-352.
41 Total aid to farmers between 1989 and 1991 was bn63 écus compared with bn27 écus for the US, and bn25 for Japan. The average amount of aid by farmers was 9,000 écus per year in the EEC, 17,000 in the US, and 11,000 in Japan. The average

EEC farm encompassed 18.4 ha, compared with 179.6 ha in the US. HAEU, BAC/ 1998/286/62, note from the Commission on the Uruguay Round, November 1992.

42 Frances Lynch, 'A treaty too far? Britain, France, and Concorde, 1961–1964', *Twentieth Century British History*, 13, 3, 2002, 253–276.

43 Burigana, 'The European search'; Bill Gunston, *Airbus: The Complete Story*, Haynes Publishing, 2010.

44 BR-NA, PREM16/1263, telegram from Bonn, 22 June 1977, T384/44, note from Hunt to the Prime Minister, 12 October 1977.

45 BR-NA, T390/284, note Bowder, 4 June 1978.

46 AAPD/1983/145, note on a meeting Kohl–Mitterrand in Paris, 17 May 1983; 1983/270, note on discussions Kohl–Thatcher, 21 September 1983; 1984/30, note on discussions Mitterrand–Kohl, 2 February 1984.

47 GER-FNS, A 49-64, FDP Bundestagfraktion, meeting of 8 November 1989.

48 Ahrens, 'The importance of being European'.

49 Richard Baldwin and Paul Krugman, 'Industrial policy and international competition in wide-bodied aircraft', in Richard Baldwin (ed.), *Trade Policy Issues and Empricial Analysis*, University of Chicago Press, 1987, 50.

50 Marcel Chillaud, *Les champions industriels français et l'Europe (1980–1992)*, unpublished dissertation, Paris Sorbonne Université, 2025.

51 On the ESA: Sara Venditti, 'Europeanization of Space: The Ariane Project between Europeanization and Independence', *Annali della Fondazione Luigi Einaudi*, 53, 1, 2019, 121–140; John Krige, Arturo Russo, and Lorenza Sebesta, *A History of the European Space Agency, 1958–1987*, ESA Publications Division, 2000.

52 For these failed European industrial programmes, see: Warlouzet, *Europe contre Europe*, 210–212.

53 Nicolas Verschueren, 'Crises et intégration européenne: Experts et pratiques de la restructuration industrielle durant les années 1960', *Vingtième Siècle*, 4, 2019, 52–64.

54 Elisabetta Bini, Giuliano Garavini, and Federico Romero (eds.), *Oil Shock: The 1973 Crisis and Its Economic Legacy*, Bloomsbury Publishing, 2016.

55 Henning Turk, *Energiesicherheit nach der Ölkrise. Die Internationale Energieagentur 1974–1985*, Nomos, 2023.

56 FR-NA, 5 AG3/ 911, note by J.-P. Dutet, advisor to the President of the Republic, 26 November 1976; note by the technical advisor to the Minister of Foreign Affairs, 6 December 1976; FR-NA, 5AG3/917, note by Guy de Panafieu, advisor to the President of the Republic, 22 April 1980.

57 Gabrielle Hecht, *The Radiance of France: Nuclear Power and National Identity after World War II*, MIT press, 2009.

58 Michael Bess, *The Light-Green Society: Ecology and Technological Modernity in France, 1960–2000*, University of Chicago Press, 2003.

59 Vivien A. Schmidt, *From State to Market? The Transformation of French Business and Government*, Cambridge University Press, 1996, 3.

60 For archival evidence on the dilemmas facing French leaders under Giscard d'Estaing and Mitterrand, see: Warlouzet, *Governing Europe*, 200–201.

61 Schmidt, *From State to Market?* 125. The five groups were: CGE, Saint-Gobain, Pechiney, Thomson, and Rhône-Poulenc.

62 FAA-GER, ZW/122.3315, note BMWi, IVA1, 10 November 1976.

63 FR-NA, 1990.0452/17, note on the FRG, 23 April 1980, note K. D. Jacoby; FR-NA, 1990.0452/17, note Marseteau, 1978, distributed by SGCI on 29 November 1979.

64 NEDC, *UK Competitors' Official Policies towards the Electronics Industries*, 4 December 1980.
65 Ralf Ahrens, 'Sectoral subsidies in West German industrial policy: Programmatic objectives and pragmatic applications from the 1960s to the 1980s', *Jahrbuch für Wirtschaftsgeschichte*, 58, 1, 2017, 59–82; Wolfgang Neumann, Henrik Uterwedde, *Industriepolitik: Ein deutsch-französischer Vergleich*, Leske, 1986.
66 Katzenstein, *Policy*, 15; Fioretos, *Creative Reconstructions*, 142–143.
67 Fritz Franzmeyer, 'Mehr gemeinsamer Markt bei verschärftem Aussenschutz der EG. Die Bundesrepublik im Handelspolitischen Dilemma?', in Rudolf Hrbek and Wolfgang Wessels (eds.), *EG-Mitgliedschaft: ein vitales Interesse der Bundesrepublik Deutschland?*, Europa Union Verlag, 1984, 82; see also in shipbuilding: Bo Strath, *The Contraction of the West European Shipbuilding Industry: The Politics of De-Industrialization*, Croom Helm, 1987, 29–30.
68 Franz Fendel, *Industriepolitik der Europäischen Wirtschaftsgemeinschaft. Entwicklungen, Bestimmungsfaktoren und Beispielfälle: Stahl (EGKS), Schiffbau und Kunstfaser*, Peter Lang, 1981, 250–251; Fritz W. Scharpf and Volker Hauff, *Modernisierung der Volkswirtschaft*, Europäische Verlagsanstalt, 1975; in contrast, Friedrichs published a more liberal book: Hans Friderichs, *Mut zum Markt: Wirtschaftspolitik ohne Illusionen*, Verlag Bonn Aktuell, 1975.
69 GER-NA, B 102/151161, note BMWi, for the Parlamentarischen Staatssekretär Grüner, 29 April 1977; B 102/251162, note BMWi, Tietmeyer to Schlecht, 5 August 1977.
70 Neumann and Uterwedde, *Industriepolitik*, 66 and 167.
71 FR-NA, 1990.0452/17, note on public shareholdings in West Germany, 23 April 1980.
72 GER-NA, B 102/277171, note BMWi, Tietmeyer (Leiter der Abteilung I), 26 July 1979; B 102/342254, note, Landeswirtschaftsministerkonferenz am 3. Dezember 1981; GER-NA, B 102/342254, note BMWi, Pietsch, IA4, 30 November 1981, for ‚Parlamentarischen Staatssekretär' Grüner.
73 GER-NA, B 102/277171, note BMWi, Tietmeyer, 26 July 1979.
74 GER-NA, B 102/342254, letter from the Land of Lower Saxony, 13 January 1981; also: B 102/277171, note BMWi, IC1, Nehring, 20 June 1979; note BMWi, Tietmeyer, 26 July 1979.
75 He was Deputy Chief of Staff and Chief of Staff to Hans von der Groeben, the first Competition Commissioner (1961–63), then Director General of Competition (1967–70), and finally Minister-President of the CDU of Lower Saxony (1976–90).
76 GER-NA, B 102/315414, note BMWi, IA4, for Parliamentary State Secretary Grüner, 2 July 1982; B 102/342254, note, Wirtschaftsministerkonferenz am 7. Juli 1982 in Hannover, der 12. Juli 1982.
77 Gérard Bökenkamp et al. (eds.), *'30 Jahre Lambsdorff-Papier'*, Friedrich-Naumann-Stiftung für die Freiheit, 2012, 20–31.
78 See contributions on the British, Italian, Spanish, and Swedish examples in: Christian Grabas and Alexander Nützenadel (eds.), *Industrial Policies in Europe*, Palgrave Macmillan, 2014.
79 Ben Jackson and Robert Saunders, 'Introduction: Varieties of Thatcherism', in Ben Jackson and Robert Saunders (eds.), *Making Thatcher's Britain*, Cambridge University Press, 2012; Peter Hall, *Governing the Economy: The Politics of State Intervention in Britain and France*, Oxford University Press, 1986; Keith

Middlemas, *Power, Competition and the State. Volume 3*, Macmillan, 1991, 357–369; Stephen Wilks, *Industrial Policy and the Motor Industry*, Manchester University Press, 1988.

80 David Parker, *The Official History of Privatisation. Vol. 1, 1979–1987*, Routledge, 2009, 49.
81 *Industrial Policy in the UK*, memorandum by the Director General, NEDC (82) 25, 11–12; on high-tech: Esposito, 501 and 543.
82 Hall, *Governing the Economy*, 112.
83 John Vickers and Vincent Wright, 'The politics of industrial privatisation in Western Europe: An overview', *West European Politics*, 11, 4, 1988, 13, quoted in: Mélanie Vay, *La mise en problème européen de l'économie publique: Socio-histoire des mondes de l'entreprise publique au contact de la politique européenne (1957–1997)*, Dalloz, 2021, 302–303.
84 Karel Van Miert, *Le marché et le pouvoir. Souvenirs d'un commissaire européen*, Racine, 2000, 51–52.
85 Commission, *First survey of State aids in the European Community*, SEC(88) 1981, 13 December 1988, 14; FR-NA, 5AG4/ 3113, rapport au Parlement sur les aides à l'industrie, 1987; Commission, *Mesures fiscales et financières en faveur de l'Investissement*, Com (83) 218, 18 April 1983; Commissariat général au Plan, *Défis à l'économie française. Les dossiers du Groupe: Perspectives économiques à moyen terme*, Documentation française, 1986, 178; Robert Ford and Wim Suyker, 'Industrial Subsidies in the OECD Economies', *OECD Economic Studies*, 15, 1990, 37–81.
86 FR-NA, 1990.0452/17, note Trésor, Alain Marseteau, 1978, distributed by SGCI on 29 November 1979.
87 FR-NA, 5AG4/4341, notes from Christian Sautter, 23 January 1984; see also the notes of 9 and 25 January 1984; FR-NA, 5AG4 / 3113, note SGG, 3 May 1985.
88 FR-NA, 5AG4 / 3113, note SGG, 3 May 1985.
89 FAA-FR, DECE 2225, note from the French Embassy in Germany, JCR, 28 August 1985.
90 Elie Cohen, *L'Etat brancardier: Politiques du déclin industriel (1974–1984)*, Calmann Lévy, 1984, 25–68 and 200–214.
91 *Resolutions adopted by the European Movement at the Westminster Conference (20–25 April 1949)*, www.cvce.Eu, accessed 10 July 2024.
92 Jean-Jacques Servan-Schreiber, *Le défi Américain*, Denoël, 1967; in English: *The American Challenge*, Atheneum, 1969.
93 Servan-Schreiber, *Le défi Américain*, 185; on Michel Albert's participation: AEU/ AO, interview with Michel Albert, 18 December 2003.
94 Laurent Warlouzet, 'Towards a European industrial policy? The European Economic Community (EEC) debates, 1957–1975', in Christian Grabas and Alexander Nützenadel (eds.), *Industrial Policy in Europe after 1945*, Palgrave Macmillan, 2014, 213–235; Lorenzo Mechi and Francesco Petrini, 'La Comunità europea nella divisione internazionale del lavoro: Le politiche industriali, 1967–1978', in Antonio Varsori (ed.), *Alla origini del persente: L'Europa occidentale nell crisi degli anni '70*, Franco Angeli, 2006, 251–283; Veera Mitzner, *European Union Research Policy Contested Origins*, Palgrave Macmillan, 2020.
95 HAEU, Spinelli private papers (Florence), AS 270, letter from Altiero Spinelli to François-Xavier Ortoli, 24 October 1974.

96 Michel Albert, James Ball, *Toward European Economic Recovery in the 1980s. Report to the European Parliament*, Praeger, 1984; On its echo: Warlouzet, 'The Role of the European Parliament'.
97 Warlouzet, *Europe contre Europe*, 219–223.
98 AAPD, 1982, doc. 180, note by Steinkühler, 11 June 1982.
99 FAA-GER, ZW/130.620, note AA/414, 9 November 1984.
100 BR-NA, PREM 19/1025, note on the inter-ministerial meeting, 2 December 1983.
101 *Europe: The Future*, submitted to the Fontainebleau European Council on 25–26 June 1984.
102 BR-NA, PREM 19/750, brief on Information technology, 17 March 1982; PREM 19/1030, brief FCO, 9 June 1983; BR-NA, PREM 19/1028, brief on Innovation and Industrial Policy for the March 1983 European Council in Brussels; PREM 19/1026, general brief for the European Council in Athens, December 4/6 1983; AAPD, 1984, doc. 64, minutes of Kohl–Thatcher discussions of 28 February 1984.
103 Georges Saunier, 'Eurêka: un projet industriel pour l'Europe, une réponse à un défi stratégique', *JEIH*, 12, 2, 2006, 57–74; Wayne Sandholtz, *High-Tech Europe: The Politics of International Cooperation*, University of California Press, 1992.
104 FAA-FR, DECE 2498, note from the Minister's office (Jean Vidal), 8 June 1985.
105 BR-NA, PREM 19/1491, letter from Howe to Thatcher, 25 June 1985; PREM 19/1491, note from Williamson to Powell, 27 June 1985; note from C. R. Budd (Private Secretary) to C. D. Powell, 27 June 1985.
106 BR-NA, PREM 19/1491, note by Charles Powell, 26 June 1985.
107 Saunier, 'Eurêka', 74; Sandholtz, *High-Tech Europe*, 294: an assessment at the end of 1989 shows France's participation in 130 projects, the largest number, followed by West Germany with 101, Italy with 88, Spain and the UK with 85.
108 FAA-FR, DECE 2225, note SGG, minutes of the interministerial meeting of 3 May 1985.
109 Arthe Van Laer, 'Research: Towards a new common policy', in Eric Bussière et al. (eds.), *The European Commission, 1973–86. History and Memories of an Institution*, Publications Office of the European Union, 2014, 289–290.
110 AAPD, 1985/79, note on Kohl–Delors meeting on 25 March 1985; FAA-FR, DECE 2498, note on Stresa conference, 10 June 1985.
111 Mazower, *Governing the World*.
112 George Ross, *Jacques Delors and European Integration*, Polity Press, 1995, 117–124.
113 Ross, *Jacques Delors*, 133–134.
114 Frédéric Jenny, 'Droit européen de la concurrence et efficience économique', *Revue d'économie industrielle*, 63, 1993, 202–203; Fabrice Fries, *Les grands débats européens*, Seuil, 1995, 203–206.
115 HAUE/AO, oral recording of Laurent Warlouzet's interview with Helmut Schröter in Brussels, 30 September 2016.

Chapter 6

1 Quoted by Lucia Coppolaro, 'Globalizing GATT: The EC/EU and the Trade Regime in the 1980s–1990s', *JEIH*, 24, 2, 2018, 344.
2 Jean-Christophe Graz, 'The Havana Charter: When state and market shake hands', in Erik Reinert, Jayati Ghosh, Rainer Kattel (eds.) *Handbook of Alternative Theories of Economic Development*, Edward Elgar, 2016, 281–290.

3 The 'trade openness index', or the relation between total exports and imports to GDP, rose in 1973 to approximately 30 per cent, the level reached in 1913: Esteban Ortiz-Ospina, Diana Beltekian, and Max Roser, 'Trade and Globalization', 2018. Retrieved from: 'https://ourworldindata.org/trade-and-globalization' [Online Resource, accessed 6 March 2023].
4 See more archival evidence on the negotiations surrounding multinationals in: Warlouzet, *Governing Europe*, 57–77.
5 Katzenstein, *Policy and Politics*, 134–144; Karl Lauschke, *Mehr Demokratie in der Wirtschaft. Die Entstehungsgeschichte des Mitbestimmungsgesetzes von 1976*, Hans-Böckler-Stiftung, 2006.
6 Keith Middlemas, *Power, Competition and the State – Volume 3: The End of the Postwar Era: Britain since 1974*, Macmillan, 1991, 180–182. On the HAEUW's opposition see: ACFDT, 8 H 1896, note on the meeting CFDT-TGWU, 3–4 June 1978; Andry, *Social Europe*, 172–176 and 305–306.
7 AETUC, 2211, note of 7 February 1975.
8 FR-NA, 5 AG3/ 1785, note Fourquet, 19 April 1978.
9 Matthieu Fulla, *Les socialistes français*, 351.
10 Featherstone, *Socialist Parties*; Escalona, *La reconstruction*.
11 Benedetto Zaccaria, 'Learning from Yugoslavia? Western Europe and the myth of self-management (1968–1975)', in Michel Christian, Sandrine Kott, and Ondrej Matejka (eds.), *Planning in Cold War Europe: Competition, Cooperation, Circulations (1950s–1970s)*, De Gruyter, 2018, 213–236.
12 HAEU, BAC 42/1988/612/91, letter from Louis Phillips, Trade Dpt, to Edoardo Volpi (DG XI), 13 August 1976; BAC 42/1988/612/180, letter from Robert Coleman (DG XI) to Louis Phillips, 17 November 1976; on Chrysler: Frederick M. Rowe, Francis G. Jacobs, and Mark R. Joelson (eds.), *Enterprise Law of the 80s: European and American Perspectives on Competition and Industrial Organization*, American Bar Association, 1980, xii.
13 Margarita Fajardo, *The World That Latin America Created. The United Nations Economic Commission for Latin America in the Development Era*, Harvard University Press, 2022; John Toye and Richard Toye, *The UN and Global Political Economy: Trade, Finance, and Development*, Indiana University Press, 2004, chapters 5–8.
14 *Declaration on the Establishment of a New International Order*, UN, 1 May 1974, part III.C; on the link between the NIEO and Europe: Garavini, *After Empires*; on the linkage between Prebisch ideas and the NIEO: Johanna Bockman, 'Socialist globalization against capitalist neocolonialism: The economic ideas behind the new international economic order', *Humanity*, 6, 2015, 109–128.
15 Harold James, *International Monetary Cooperation*, International Monetary Fund, 1996, 317–319.
16 AAPD, 1983, doc. 208, note Steinkühler on CNUCED VI, 7 July 1983.
17 On the UN debate on multinational control: Kott, *A World*, 147–149; more generally: Jennifer Bair, 'Taking aim at the new international economic order', in Philip Mirowski and Dieter Plehwe (eds.), *The Road from Mont Pèlerin: The Making of the Neoliberal Thought*, Harvard University Press, 2015, 367–374.
18 UNCTAD, *The History of UNCTAD, 1964–1984*, UN, 1985, 113–115.
19 Antoine Compagnon and Caroline Moine, 'Pour une histoire globale du 11 September 1973', *Monde(s)*, 8, 2015, 17–18.

20 AUN/ CNUCED, 1882/ 428, note Perrin, 20 July 1976.
21 AUN/CNUCED, 1882/ 428, Brazilian study on multinational companies in electrical equipment industry, August 1976.
22 UNCTAD archives, UN1842/ 93, note UNCTAD by Cato Adrian, 10 December 1985; draft resolution of 11 December 1990.
23 AOCDE 398, note, 16 June 1970; OECD, *Guidelines for Multinational entreprises, national treatement, international investment incentives and disincentives, consultation procedures*, OECD, 1976; HAEU, BAC 104/1993/283/19, note DG III, 8 September 1978.
24 ILOA, 151.307, letter from the French minister of Social Affairs, 18 May 1983.
25 BR-NA, PREM 15/1503, note on the Heath–Brandt meeting on 7 October 1973; note on the Heath–Pompidou meeting on 17 November 1973; note on a Heath–Brandt meeting on 2 March 1973.
26 *Tindemans Report*, 29 December 1975; Benedetto Zaccaria, 'Personalism and European integration: Jacques Delors and the legacy of the 1930s', *Contemporary European History*, 33, 3, 2024, 988–990.
27 See Chapter 4 for the Maldague Report and its ramifications; AETUC 2066, doc. ETUC, Walter Braun, 25 October 1974; BR-NA, PREM 16/850, joint statement by the Tripartite Conference, 24 June 1976, Luxembourg.
28 Andry, *Social Europe*.
29 BR-NA, FCO 30/395213, note UKREP, 25 September 1978.
30 On the Vredeling directive: Warlouzet, *Governing Europe*, 67–77; Francesco Petrini, 'Demanding democracy in the workplace: The European Trade Union Confederation and the struggle to regulate multinationals', in Wolfram Kaiser and Jan-Henrik Meyer (eds.), *Societal Actors in European Integration: Polity-Building and Policy-Making, 1958-1992*, Palgrave Macmillan, 2013, 151–172; Andry, *Social Europe*.
31 HAEU, BAC 42/1988/1610, minutes of the Commission meeting of 2 April 1980, 23 July 1980, and 1 October 1980.
32 BR-NA, PREM 19/1032, brief for the meeting with Tugendhat on 19 February 1983; GER-AN, B 102/287544, note BMWi, Everling, for Schlecht, 19 September 1980.
33 GER-NA, B 102/287544, note BMWi, Everling, for Schlecht, 19 September 1980.
34 His administration did initiate the first law of decentralisation giving more power to local authorities, but remained fairly centralised in its approach to social policy; FR-FAA, DECE 1833, notes SGCI, May 1981, 'droit des sociétés' and 'politique sociale'; DECE 1835, note Michel Praderie, 16 September 1981.
35 BR-NA, PIN 34/817, telex UKRep, 11 January 1983.
36 ACFDT, 8H1896, note CFDT-International, 7 December 1981.
37 GER-NA, B 102/287544, note BMWi, EA1, Lichte, 10 June 1980; telegram BMWi to REP, 16 June 1980; note BMWi, Faust, 6 November 1980; note BMWi, Kemper, 17 November 1980, note BMWi, IS2, Faust, 18 November 1980, note BMWi, Schaal, 8 December 1980.
38 GER-NA, B 102/287544, letter from the Ministry of Social Affairs, 16 February 1981; note BMWi, Faust, 24 February 1981.
39 Petrini, 'Demanding Democracy', 159–160.
40 ACBI, 3/DDG6/37, note from Liam Connellan (CBI) to Bryan Rigby, 30 September 1980; letter from Amédée Turner to the CBI, 17 September 1980; letter from to Esso (20 July 1981), Shell (5 May 1982), ICI (13 July 1982) and

Barclays (29 July 1982); letter from Bryan Rigby (CBI) to Hugo Herbert-Jones, 6 February 1981; lettre from M. D. M. Franklin à B. Rigby (CBI), 9 July 1981; letter from CBI to Bryan Rigby, 28 May 1982.
41 AETUC 2212, note DGB 18 May 1982; see also: AETUC 2212, note DGB, 26 May 1981.
42 HAEU, BAC 42/1988/1613, note SEC (79) 1494, 28 September 1979, meeting Commission-ETUC; AETUC 1481, note Peter Coldrick, 16 November 1981; note ETUC, 8 March 1982; ETUC press release, 25 March 1982.
43 AETUC 2200, note on the meeting of 12-13 May 1980; notes Piehl, ETUC, 13 October 1980 and 7 January 1981; AETUC 1487, decision of the Executive Committee on 4 December 1980; AETUC 2211, note CGT-FO, Marc Blondel, 15 May 1981.
44 AETUC 2212, DGB press release, 26 May 1981.
45 Petrini, 'Demanding Democracy', 160.
46 HAEU, BAC 42/1988/1613, note Braun for Narjes 17 March 1982; HAEU, minutes of the Commission meeting, 15 June 1983.
47 FR-FAA, DECE 2432, COREPER report of 6 December 1984; AETUC 1487, note Rath, 8 February 1985; HAEU, BAC 42/1988, 1613, brief Niessen for Cockfield, 22 May 1985
48 Henry G. Overman and L. Alan Winters, 'Trade and Economic Geography: The Impact of EEC accession on the UK', 2006, http://personal.lse.ac.uk/overman/research/shockloc18_dp.pdf; accessed on 13 August 2021.
49 BR-NA, CAB 193/206, summary of the Rambouillet Meeting by HJH Maud, 28 November 1975.
50 Citation taken from the French meeting minutes: FR-NA, 5 AG3/ 911, note from the cabinet, Ministry of Foreign Affairs, 6 December 1976; broadly confirmed in the English archives: BR-NA, PREM 16/851, 'draft record of the European Council, The Hague, 29 November 1976'.
51 FR-NA, 5AG3/912, from the cabinet, Ministry of Foreign Affairs, 5 July 1977; note Dutet, 28 June 1977; note SGCI, J. R. Bernard, 27 June 1977; AAPD, 1977, doc. 114, note on the London Summit, 8 May 1977.
52 Middlemas, *Power, Competition and the State*, 155.
53 James Tobin, 'A Proposal for International Monetary Reform', *Eastern Economic Journal*, 4, 3, 1978, 153-159.
54 Citation from 1980 reported by *Spiegel*, and attributed to Helmut Schmit regarding Willy Brandt.
55 *Tenth Report of the Commission's activities, 1976*, Brussels, EEC, 1977, points 111-112; *Eleventh Report of the Commission's activities, 1977*, Brussels, EEC, 1978, points 122-123.
56 Guia Migani, 'Europe, decolonisation and the challenge of developing countries', in Mathieu Segers and Steven van Hecke (eds.), *The European Union. Vol. I*, Cambridge University Press, 2024, 78-105.
57 Martin Rempe, *Entwicklung im Konflikt. Die EWG und der Senegal 1957-1975*, Böhlau, 2012.
58 Megan Brown, *The Seventh Member State: Algeria, France, and the European Community*, Harvard University Press, 2022.
59 On STABEX: Migani, 'Europe'.
60 Alice Milor, 'Ownership Matters: French Governments and Automotive Industrialists Facing the Japanese Challenge, 1974-1986', *Business History*

Review, 96, 4, 2022, 833–855. For the German cartel: Alice Milor, Construire l'automobile, conduire l'Europe Industriels, consommateurs et responsables politiques (1972–1998), unpublished PhD diss., Sorbonne Université, 2021, 192, quoting an interview of a Commission official from 1992. See also this dissertation for the connection with the GATT negotiations.

61 Milor, Construire; Hitoshi Suzuki, *Japanese Investment and British Trade Unionism: Thatcher and Nissan Revisited in the Wake of Brexit*, Palgrave Macmillan, 2020; Grace Ballor, 'Liberalisation or protectionism for the single market? European automakers and Japanese competition, 1985–1999', *Business History*, 65, 2, 2023, 302–328.

62 EC at Nine. Commission, *Report on the Textile and Clothing Industry*, Com(88)653, 1988, 30–34.

63 BR-NA, FCO98/948, note 'The Second UK Presidency', 22 July 1980; note Cooper, 4 August 1980; FCO98/948, note Department of Trade, 3 November 1980; BR-NA, BT241/2925, note 17 December 1979; FR-NA, 5AG3/921, note Dutet, 25 May 1977; FR-FAA, DECE1833, note SGCI, May 1981, 'arrangements multifibres'.

64 AMAE-RFA, ZW/124418, note Steinkühler, 3 April 1981; ZW/124419, note Steinkühler, 8 January 1982; ZW/122449, note BMWi, 3 March 1981; note sur une réunion avec Lambsdorff 26–27 October 1981; ZW/124417, note Boll, 29 October 1981; AAPD, 1982, doc. 198, note de Steinkühler, 1 July 1982; NA-RU, PREM16/1264, brief, 'French ideas on international trade', 27 June 1977.

65 European Commission, *The Situation and Prospects of the Textile Industry*, Com (81)388, 27 July 1981, 10.

66 Christian Marx, 'A European structural crisis cartel as solution to a sectoral depression? The Western European fibre industry in the 1970s and 1980s', *Jahrbuch für Wirtschaftsgeschichte*, 58, 1, 2017, 163–197.

67 BR-NA, FG5/486, *Industrial Policy in the EEC*, draft, 9 June 1981; NA-GER, B102/278120, note Stahl, 1 February 1978; NA-GER, B102/278120, note, 1 February 1978.

68 NA-GER, B102/ 278120, note Kartte, 2 February 1978; note Nehring, 9 February 1978; note Stahl, 17 February 1978; note Nieß, 15 February 1978; GER-FAA, ZW/ 122331, memorandum zur Strukturpolitik in der EG, 24 April 1978.

69 GER-NA, B 102/278124, note Obernolte, 1 August 1978; letter from Kartte to Schlieder, 2 August 1978; B 102/278126, note BMWi, IB5, 26 September 1978.

70 GER-NA, B 102/278126, note BMWi, 26 September 1978.

71 GER-NA, B 102/278122, note 6 June 1978; B 102/278124, note Groger, 27 July 1978; note Büchner-Schöpf, 28 July 1978; B 102/278126, notes 5 December 1978 et 12 April 1979; AEU, minutes of the Commission meeting, 8 November 1978 and 29 November 1978; on the new agreement in 1982: Christian Marx, 'A European structural'.

72 For more details on this sub-chapter: Laurent Warlouzet, 'When Germany accepted a European industrial policy: Managing the decline of steel from 1977 to 1984', *Economic History Yearbook*, 1, 2017, 137–162. See also: Yves Mény and Vincent Wright (eds.), *The Politics of Steel: Western Europe and the Steel Industry in the Crisis Years (1974–1984)*, De Gruyter, 1986; Dimitri Zurstrassen, 'EU industrial policy in the steel industry: Historical background and current challenges', in Jean-Christophe Defraigne, Jan Wouter, Edoardo Traversa, and Dimitri Zurstrassen (eds.), *EU Industrial Policy in the Multipolar Economy*, Edward Elgar, 2022, 270–303.

73 BR-NA, PREM 19/220, note Paul Lever (FCO) on a meeting Thatcher–Schmidt, 12 June 1980.
74 Zurstrassen, 'EU industrial policy', 281.
75 Geoffrey Dudley and Jeremy Richardson, 'Competing advocacy coalitions and the process of "frame reflection": A longitudinal analysis of EU steel policy', *Journal of European Public Policy*, 6, 2, 1999, 225–248.
76 Adam Smith, *An Inquiry into the Nature and Causes of the Wealth of Nations*, Electronics Classics Series Publication, 2005 [1776], 417. For more archival references on this sub-chapter, see: Laurent Warlouzet, 'The collapse of the French shipyard of Dunkirk and EEC state-aid control (1977–86)', *Business History*, 62, 5, 2020, 858–878.
77 ANORMED, volume 724, ACF report for the Board, 1976 and 1980; volume 37, note on CSCN meeting of 17 December 1981, note of the meeting of 23 July 1981.
78 ANORMED, 1988006/2, note 'charte', 15 March 1978; note Chauchat, 22 March 1978; note on the meeting of 4 April 1978.
79 BR-NA, PREM16/1255, brief EEC/Japan, 17 March, 1977.
80 Warlouzet, 'The collapse'.
81 Warlouzet, 'The collapse'.
82 O'Rourke, 'Economic history'.
83 Guia Migani, 'The road to Cancun: The birth and death of the North–South Summit, 1978–1982', in Emmanuel Mourlon-Druol and Federico Romero (eds.), *Summitry at the Dawn of the Global Era: Historical Enquiries into the Rise of the G-7 and the European Council*, Routledge, 2014, 174–197.
84 BR-NA, PREM 19/1028, brief on 'North–South', European Council of March 1983; FR-FAA, DECE 2065, note DAEF, Nina-Sylvia Stantcheva, 14 June 1983.
85 Coppolaro, 'Globalizing GATT, 339; BR-NA, PREM 19/749, Speaking note for the PM, European Council 29–30 March 1982, letter from Thatcher to Martens, 26 March 1982; PREM 19/749, telegramme from Fretwell, 25 March 1982.
86 GER-FAA, ZW/124.419, note, Steinkühler, 8 January 1982; AAPD, 1982, doc. 180, note, Steinkühler, 11 June 1982; FR-FAA, DECE 2063, note DREE, 11 March 1983; note DAEF, Guy Legras, 16 March 1983: 'relations CEE/Etats en matière Agricole'.
87 AAPD, 1985, 112, note on Brühl, 3 May 1985; Gerry Alons, 'European external trade policy: The role of ideas in German preference formation', *Journal of Contemporary European Research*, 9, 4, 2013, 509–511.
88 GATTA, doc. C/M/1987, note on the Council of 30 April–1 May 1985; BR-NA, CAB 193/464, note, J. A. Shepherd, FCO, 9 May 1985.
89 On the end of the Uruguay Round: Pollack, *The Engines*, 274–280; Alons, 'European external trade policy', 513–515.
90 Coppolaro, *The Making of a World Trading Power*.
91 For details regarding the many different trade conflicts, see the work of: Julien Barbaroux who is working on a PhD project entitled: "Les Commissions Delors et les Etats-Unis (1985–1995) Lundestad, *Empire by Invitation*.
92 Angela Romano, 'G7 summits, European Councils and East–West economic relations (1975–1982)', in Emmanuel Mourlon-Druol and Federico Romero (eds.), *International Summitry and Global Governance*, Routledge, 2014, 214–238; Warlouzet, *Governing Europe*, 88.
93 BR-NA, PREM 19/751, telegrams, British Embassy in Bonn, 24 and 25 June 1982; AMAE-RFA, ZW/124.420, teleram AA/Steinkühler, 23 July 1982.
94 BR-NA, PREM 19/752, note of 23 June 1982.
95 Chillaud, *Les champions*.

96 FR-NA, AG3/921, note Dutet for the Président, 17 November 1976; BR-NA, PREM 16/851, draft record of the European Council, The Hague, 29 November 1976; AAPD, doc. 357, note Engels, 8 December 1977.
97 FR-NA, 5 AG3/ 911, note Dutet, 23 March 1977; AN, 54G4/PM/50/1, note from the Ministry of Industry, 28 July 1983.
98 BR-NA, PREM 19/750, brief on trade relations with US and Japan, 23 March 1982; PREM 19/752, note 23 June 1982, 'External Trade Issues (Except US)'; FV 90/20, record of a conversation Keith Joseph / Giraud, 14 September 1979; PREM 19/1223, brief on consumer electronics and Japan, 3 December 1984; AAPD, 1982, doc. 316, note on a meeting Kohl–Thatcher, 23 November 1982, 1651.
99 Suzuki, *Japanese Investment and British Trade Unionism*.
100 FR-FAA, DECE 2064, note DREE before the Stuttgart summit, 1983, 'Relations CEE–Japon'.
101 BR-NA, PREM 19/1027, general brief on European Council, FCO, 7 March 1983; AMAEF, DECE 2063, note SGCI, 17 March 1983.
102 Warlouzet, *Governing Europe*, 130–132.
103 HAEU/AO, interview of Jean Dubois by Laurent Warlouzet, 16 February 2011.
104 HAEU/AO, interview of Frans Andriessen by Arthe van Laer et Laurent Warlouzet, 14 October 2010.
105 Arthe Van Laer, 'Liberalization or Europeanisation? The EEC Commission's policy on public procurement in information technology and telecommunications (1957–1984)', *JEIH*, 12, 2, 2006, 111.
106 BR-NA, PREM 19/750, brief on Information technology, 17 March 1982; ANF, 5AG4/EG/34, note from Michel Camdessus (Treasury), note date, probably between October and December 1983.
107 FR-NA, 5AG4/PM/51, note SGCI, 7 October 1983; see also FR-NA, 5AG4/EG/26, note HD, 19 December 1983.
108 FR-NA, 5AG4/96/3, letter for President Mitterrand, 7 January 1985, de W. Dekker, Philips.
109 FR-NA, 5AG4, EG 77/ 1, note from the Prime Minister Jacques Chirac to Elisabeth Guigou, 14 January 1988.
110 Alexis Drach, 'Reluctant Europeans? British and French commercial banks and the common market in banking (1977–1992)', *Enterprise & Society*, 21, 3, 2020, 768–798; Grin, *The Battle*, 138; Jabko, *Playing*, 65–73; Célia Burgdorff, '"Une Europe passoire" ou une "Europe forteresse"? Imaginaires, débats et politiques autour du régime migratoire européenne', unpublished PhD Univ. Paris 1-LMU Munich, 2022.
111 Rawi Abdelal, *Capital Rules: The Construction of Global Finance*, Cornell University Press, 2007, 15.
112 François Duchêne, 'The European Community and the uncertainties of interdependence', in Wolfgang Hager and Max Kohnstamm (eds.), *A Nation Writ Large? Foreign-Policy Problems before the European Community*, Palgrave Macmillan, 1973, 1–21.
113 Zaki Laïdi, *Norms over fForce: Tthe eEnigma of European Power*, Palgrave Macmillan, 2008; Kazuto Suzuki, 'The EU: Regulatory Influence in the Global Market or "Regulatory Empire"?', The 21st World Congress of the International Political Science Association, Santiago, Chile, 2009; Anu Bradford, *The Brussel Effect: How the European Union Rules the World*, Oxford University Press, 2020.

114 Anu Bradford, *The Brussels Effect: How the European Union Rules the World*, Oxford University Press, 2020.
115 Burgdorff, *Une Europe passoire*, 107.
116 James Baker archives (Princeton), box 289, folder 2, note James Baker, 26 November 1991.
117 Andy Smith, 'A constructivist-institutionalist approach to EU Politics: The case of Protected Geographical Indications for Food', in Jay Rowell and Michel Mangenot (eds.), *A Political Sociology of the European Union*, Manchester University Press, 2010, 149–152; Council Regulation (EEC) No. 2081/92 of 14 July 1992 on the protection of geographical indications and designations of origin for agricultural products and foodstuffs.
118 Sophie Meunier, *Trading Voices: The European Union in International Commercial Negotiation*, Princeton University Press, 2005.
119 Arthe Van Laer, 'The European Community and the paradoxes of US economic diplomacy: The case of the IT and telecommunications sectors', in Kiran Patel and Kenneth Weisbrode (eds.), *European Integration and the Atlantic Community in the 1980s*, Cambridge University Press, 2013, 127.
120 GER-FAA, ZW/130.620, note AA/414, 9 November 1984.
121 BR-NA, PREM 19/2152, letter from Geoffrey Pattie to Margaret Thatcher, 12 November 1986.
122 BR-NA, PREM 19/2152, note from Ricky Verral (Industry Dpt.), to C.D. Powell, private secretary to the PM, 7 September 1987; Léonard Laborie, 'Concurrence et changement technique. De la norme au marché, la trajectoire unique de la téléphonie mobile en Europe depuis les années 1980', *Histoire, Economie et Sociétés*, 2008, 1, 91–102.
123 Werner Bührer et Laurent Warlouzet, 'Regulating markets: Peak business associations and the origins of European competition policy', in Wolfram Kaiser et Jan-Henrik Meyer (éd.), *Non-state Actors in European Integration 1958–1992*, Palgrave Macmillan, 2013, 59–83.

Chapter 7

1 Pierre du Bois, *Histoire de l'Europe monétaire, 1945–2005. Europe qui comme Ulysse...*, PUF, 2008; Kenneth Dyson and Ivo Maes (eds.), *Architects of the Euro: Intellectuals in the Making of European Monetary Union*, Oxford University Press, 2017; Kenneth Dyson and Kevin Featherstone, *The Road to Maastricht: Negotiating Economic and Monetary Union*, Oxford University Press, 1999; Michael Gehler and Wilfried Loth (eds.), *Reshaping Europe: Towards a Political, Economic and Monetary Union, 1984–1989*, Nomos, 2020; Harold James, *Making the European Monetary Union*, Harvard University Press, 2012; Kathleen McNamara, *The Currency of Ideas: Monetary Politics in the European Union*, Cornell University Press, 1998; Emmanuel Mourlon-Druol, *A Europe Made of Money: The Emergence of the European Monetary System*, Cornell University Press, 2012; Mourlon-Druol, *Federal Anathema*; Amy Verdun, 'The role of the Delors Committee in the creation of EMU: An epistemic community?', *Journal of European Public Policy*, 6, 2, 1999, 308–328.
2 Robert Mundell, 'A theory of optimum currency areas', in *American Economic Review*, 1961, 53, 4, 661–662.

3 On the project for European monetary cooperation in the 1960s, see: Dyson and Maes (eds.), *Architects*; Mourlon-Druol, *Federal Anathema*.
4 On Marjolin, Monnet and Triffin: Warlouzet, *Le choix de la CEE*, 194–202 and 356–370.
5 Laurent Warlouzet, 'L'Europe monétaire face au dollar: l'offensive Debré (1966–68)', in *Histoire@Politique*, 19, 2013, 114–127.
6 Catherine Schenk, *The Decline of Sterling: Managing the Retreat of an International Currency, 1945–1992*, Cambridge University Press, 2010.
7 For a long-term perspective on this franco-german debate: David Howarth and Joachim Schild, 'France and European macro-economic policy coordination: From the Treaty of Rome to the euro area sovereign debt crisis', *Modern & Contemporary France*, 25, 2, 2017, 171–190.
8 Note by Willy Brandt on the creation of a European reserve fund (Bonn, 10 November 1969) reproduced on the website www.cvce.eu.
9 Lars Magnusson and Bo Strath (eds.), *From the Werner Plan to the EMU: In Search of a Political Economy for Europe*, Peter Lang, 2001; Elena Danescu and Susana Muñoz (eds.), *Pierre Werner and Europe: His Approach, Action and Legacy*, Peter Lang, 2015.
10 James, *Making the European Monetary Union*, 117 and 121–122.
11 BR-NA, ETUC note for the meeting of 9 February 1977; PREM 16/393, note P. J. Weston, 18 July 1975; CAB 193/206, note HJH Maud, 28 November 1975; PREM 16/852, note John Hunt for the Prime Minister, 15 March 1976; for Callaghan: PREM 16/851, draft record of the European Council, The Hague, 29 November 1976; PREM 16/ 1253, FCO, 21 March 1977; note Roy Denman, 18 March 1977; FR-NA, 5 AG3/ 911, note from Foreign Affairs Ministry, 6 December 1976; Warlouzet, *Governing Europe*, 144–145; Mourlon-Druol, *Federal Anathema*.
12 Robert Boyce, *The Great Interwar Crisis and the Collapse of Globalization*, Palgrave Macmillan, 2009, 324.
13 BR-NA, PREM 16/853, record, European Council, Luxembourg, 1976.
14 BR-NA, PREM 16/851, draft record, European Council, The Hague, 29 November 1976; FR-NA, 5 AG3/ 911, note from the technical advisor to the cabinet of the Minister of Foreign Affairs, 6 December 1976.
15 BR-NA, PREM 16/853, record, European Council, Luxembourg, 1976.
16 BR-NA, PREM 16/1254, note PC Petrie (private secretary), 28 March 1977; AAPD, 1977, doc. 79, note by Engels, 28 March 1977; BR-NA, PREM 16/1263, record, European Council, June 29–30, 1977, London; AN, 5AG3/913, note SGCI, concluding statement of the preparatory meeting of 17 March 1978, 20 March 1978.
17 Dino Knudsen, *The Trilateral Commission and Global Governance*, Routledge, 2016.
18 AAPD, 1977, doc. 13, note of 24 January 1977, p. 76.
19 AAPD, 1978, doc. 225, note, Bokk, 20 July 1978; GER-NA, B 136/24006, note on talks between Schmidt and Robert, 10 November 1978.
20 Gaddum, *Die deutsche Europapolitik*, 63.
21 AAPD, 1980, doc. 178, note Oehms, 18 June 1980; AAPD, 1980, doc. 184, note on the Venice summit, 22/23 June 1980; BR-NA, PREM 19/462, draft record, European Council, Luxembourg, 29–30 June 1981.
22 Jürgen Bellers and Markus Porsche-Ludwig, *Auß enwirtschaftspolitik der Bundesrepublik Deutschland, 1950–2011. Ein Handbuch zu Vergangenheit und Gegenwart*, Lit Verlag, 2011, p. 488.

23 ABB, B 330/11165, 575. Zentralbankrats der Deutschen Bundesbank, 19 February 1981: ABB, B 330/11166, 576. Zentralbankrats der Deutschen Bundesbank, 5 March 1981.

24 ABB, B 330/11166, 576. Zentralbankrats der Deutschen Bundesbank, 5 March 1981.

25 Plehwe, Walpen, and Neunhöffer (eds.), *Neoliberal Hegemony*; Richard Cockett, *Thinking the Unthinkable: Think-Tanks and the Economic Counter-Revolution, 1931-1983*, Harper Collins, 1994; Slobobian, *Globalists*.

26 Marion Fourcade-Gourinchas and Sarah Babb, 'The rebirth of the liberal creed: Paths to neoliberalism in four countries', *American Journal of Sociology*, 108, 3, 533-579; Schmelzer, *The Hegemony of Growth*.

27 Odd Arne Westad, *The Global Cold War. Third World Interventions and the Making of Our Times*, Cambridge University Press, 2005.

28 On Sweden: Marc Levinson, *An Extraordinary Time. The End of the Postwar Boom and the Return of the Ordinary Economy*, Basic Books, 2016, 205-207.

29 Levinson, *An Extraordinary Time*, 189.

30 Marc Buggeln, 'Taxation in the 1980s: A five-country comparison of neo-liberalism and path dependency', in Marc Buggeln, Martin Daunton, and Alexander Nützenadel (eds.), *The Political Economy of Public Finance: Taxation, State Spending and Debt since the 1970s*, Cambridge University Press, 2017, 123-125.

31 Quoted in: Ian Bruff, 'The rise of authoritarian neoliberalism', *Rethinking Marxism. A Journal of Economics, Culture & Society*, 26, 1, 2014, 118.

32 Ronald Inglehart, *The Silent Revolution: Changing Values and Political Styles Among Western Publics*, Princeton University Press, 1977; Samuel Moyn, *Human Rights and the Uses of History*, Verso, 2014.

33 Mark Blyth, *Great Transformations. Economic Ideas and Institutional Change in the Twentieth Century*, Cambridge University Press, 2002, vii.

34 On transatlantic dynamics: Giovanni Arrighi, *The Long Twentieth Century*, Verso, 1994, 301-304.

35 ACFDT, 8 H 1898, CFDT note, eco action sector, 2 January 1979.

36 Stefan Eich and Adam Tooze, 'The Great Inflation', in Anselm Doering-Manteuffel, Raphaël Lutz, and Thomas. Schlemmer (eds.), *Vorgeschichte der Gegenwart. Dimensionen des Strukturbruchs nach dem Boom*, Vandenhoeck & Ruprecht, 2016, 181.

37 ETUC archives, 2066, ETUC note sent by Walter Braun on 25 October 1974; 1480, ETUC declaration, Luxembourg European Council, 1-2 December 1980, note 19 November 1980.

38 For example the French socialist leader François Mitterrand: Matthieu Fulla, *Les socialistes français et l'économie (1944-1981)*, Presses de Sciences po, 2016, 306.

39 Source for 1984-1988: OECD, *Economic Outlook No. 46*, Paris, OECD, December 1989, 17. Source for 1972-1983: P. Muller & R. W. Price, 'Structural budget deficits and fiscal stance', in *OECD Economics Department Working Papers*, 15, OECD, 1984.

40 Warlouzet, 'De Gaulle as a Father of Europe'; on the cautious policy of the Banque de France: Éric Monnet, *Controlling Credit Central Banking and the Planned Economy in Postwar France, 1948-1973*, Cambridge University Press, 2019, 186-205.

41 Stephen Kotkin, 'The Kiss of Debt. The East Bloc Goes Borrowing', in Niall Ferguson, Charles S. Maier, Erez Manela, and Daniel J. Sargent (eds.), *The Shock*

of the Global. The 1970s in perspective, Harvard University Press, 2011, 80–93; more generally on the absence of an alternative to debt in the East: Etienne Peyrat and Kristy Ironside, 'The Communist World of Public Debt (1917–1991): The Failure of a Counter-Model?', in Nicolas Barreyre and Nicolas Delalande (eds.), *A World of Public Debts*, Palgrave Macmillan, 2020, 317–345.

42 Aleksandra Komornicka, 'From "economic miracle" to the "sick man of the socialist camp": Poland and the West in the 1970s', in Angela Romano and Federico Romero (eds.), *European Socialist Regimes' Fateful Engagement with the West. National Strategies in the Long 1970s*, Routledge, 2021, 78–106; Christophe Starzec and François Gardes, 'Inflation in Poland in the 1970s between official figures and the reality', in Michel-Pierre Chélini and Laurent Warlouzet (eds.), *Calmer les prix. Inflation in Europe in the 1970s*, Presses de Sciences po, 2016, 191–213.

43 André Steiner, 'State price policy in the German Democratic Republic in the 1970s and 1980s', in Chélini and Warlouzet (eds.), *Calmer les prix*, 169–190.

44 Tim Schanetzky, *Wirtschaftspolitik, Expertise und Gesellschaft in der Bundesrepublik 1966 bis 1982*, Akademie Verlag, 2007, 273; Dieter Grosser (ed.), *Der Staat in der Wirtschaft der Bundesrepublik*, Leske Verlag, 1985, 53–54.

45 Hartmut Soell, *Helmut Schmidt. 2: 1969 bis heute. Macht und Verantwortung*, Deutsche Verlags-Anstalt, 2008, 628–629.

46 Reimut Zohlnhöfer, *Die Wirstchaftspolitik der Ära Kohl. Eine Analyse der Sclüsselentscheidungen in den Politikfeldern Finanzen, Arbeit und Entstaatlichung, 1982–1998*, Leske, 2001, 71–81; Gerard Bökenkamp et al. (eds.), '*30 Jahre Lambsdorff-Papier*', Friedrich-Naumann-Stiftung für die Freiheit, 2012.

47 Schnippering, *The German*, 120.

48 Michel Crozier, 'Western Europe', in Michel Crozier, Samuel P. Huntington, and Joji Watanuki, *The Crisis of Democracy. Report on the Governability of Democracies to the Trilateral Commission*, New York University Press, 1975, 11.

49 Schenk, *The Decline of Sterling*, 371–378.

50 Keith Middlemas, *Power, Competition and the State. Volume 3*, 350; Alec Cairncross, *The British Economy since 1945*, Blackwell, 1995, 245.

51 Francesco Petrini, 'The politics of inflation and disinflation: The Italian case', in Chélini and Warlouzet (eds.), *Calmer les prix*, 128–135.

52 On the creation of the EMS: Mourlon-Druol, *A Europe Made of Money*.

53 Mourlon-Druol, *A Europe Made of Money*, 205, 239–240.

54 Mourlon-Druol, *A Europe Made of Money*, 196.

55 Mourlon-Druol, *A Europe Made of Money*, 258; James, *Making the European Monetary Union*, 180.

56 James, *Making the European Monetary Union*, 174.

57 FR-NA, 5AG3/914, note by J.-P. Ruault, advisor to the President, 4 December 1978; Commissariat général au Plan, *Quelle stratégie européenne pour la France dans les années 80*, Documentation française, 1983, 37.

58 BR-NA, PREM 16/1644, minutes of discussions of the Brussels European Council on 4–5 December 1978.

59 FR-NA, 5 AG3/922, note by de Boissieu for de Panafieu, 24 October 1979; note by de Panafieu for the President, 6 February 1980; 5AG3/914, note by Paye, Barre's advisor, 21 December 1978; note by the advisor to the Presidency of the Republic, G. de Panafieu, 14 December 1979.

60 James, *Making the European Monetary Union*, 178.

61 FR-FAA, DECE 1835, French memorandum, transmitted 9 December 1981.
62 FR-FAA, DECE 1835, Draft Memorandum 'Recovery', 9 November 1981.
63 AAPD, 1980, doc. 213, note on Schmidt–Werner interview, 15 July 1980.
64 BR-NA, PREM 19/750, brief, EMS, 23 March 1982.
65 On the French crisis of 1981–83: Warlouzet, *Europe contre Europe*, 283–288; Mathieu Fulla, 'The neoliberal turn that never was: Breaking with the standard narrative of Mitterrand's tournant de la rigueur', in *Contemporary European History*, 33, 2, 2024, 763–784.
66 BR-NA, ETUC Paper on Unemployment, note for the meeting of 9 February 1977); ACES 1480, ETUC statement, European Council Luxembourg, 1–2 December 1980, note, 19 November 1980.
67 Michael Loriaux, *France after Hegemony: International Change and Financial Reform*, Cornell University Press, 1991, 233–235.
68 Matthieu Tracol, *La rigueur et les réformes. Histoire des politiques du travail et de l'emploi du gouvernement Mauroy (1981–1984)*, PhD, Université Paris 1, 2015, 533.
69 Pierre Favier and Michel Martin-Roland, *La décennie Mitterrand. 1. Les Ruptures (1981–1984)*, Seuil, 441–443.
70 Mathieu Fulla, 'Quand Pierre Mauroy résistait avec rigueur au "néolibéralisme" (1981–1984)', in *Vingtième siècle. Revue d'histoire*, 138, 2018, 49–63.
71 GER-FAA, B2/249, letter from Mitterrand to Kohl, 16 March 1983.
72 GER-FAA, ZW/178.875, note from the head of the chancellery, 18 March 1983.
73 AAPD, 1983, doc. 110, letter from Kohl to Mitterrand, 21 April 1983.
74 AAPD, 1983, doc. 74, Steinkühler note, 23 March 1983.
75 Thomas Piketty, *Le Capital*, 429; and: 'In the case of France, specifically 1968–1983, let me make it very clear, and I think I make it very clear in the book, the rise of the minimum wage probably was excessive'; Thomas Piketty (Paris School of Economics), interview with Emmanuel Comte (European University Institute of Florence) in Florence, added to YouTube on 27 January 2015; accessed 17 July 2019.
76 BR-NA, PREM 19/1025, note on a conversation with Chirac, 30 November 1983.
77 On Delors's ideas: Drake, *Jacques Delors*; Endo, *The Presidency*; Ross, *Jacques Delors*.
78 AAPD, 1985, 19, note on a Genscher–Delors interview on 23 January 1985; AAPD, 1985, 79, note on a Kohl–Delors interview on 25 March 1985; AAPD, 1985, 311, note on a Kohl–Delors interview, 11 November 1985.
79 FAM-FR, DECE 2499, 'Prime Minister', note on the IGC, probably a note from the SGCI in late November 1985.
80 Tommaso Padoa-Schioppa (ed.), Mervyn King, Michael Emerson, and Jean-Claude Milleron (collab.), *Efficiency, Stability, Equity: A Strategy for the Evolution of the Economic System of the European Community*, Economica, 1987.
81 Quoted in Rawi Abdelal, *Capital Rules. The Construction of Global Finance*, Cornell University Press, 2007, 77, referring to: Hobart Rowen, '... Of European Unity', *Washington Post*, 25 October 1990.
82 Monnet, *Controlling Credit*, 198.
83 James, *Making the European Monetary Union*, 228–229; David Howarth, *The French Road to European Monetary Union*, Palgrave Macmillan, 2001; Jabko, *Playing the Market*, 155 and 159.
84 AAPD, 1985, 313, note on Kohl–Santer interviews, 13 November 1985.

85 Drach Alexis, 'Removing obstacles to integration: The European way to deregulation', in Alexis Drach and Youssef Cassis (eds.), *Financial Deregulation: A Historical Perspective*, Oxford University Press, 2021, 83–85.
86 James, *Making the European Monetary Union*, 245–53; Dermot Hodson, 'Jacques Delors: Vision, revisionism, and the design of EMU', in Kenneth Dyson and Ivo Maes (eds.), *Architects of the Euro: Intellectuals in the Making of European Monetary Union*, Oxford University Press, 2016, 212–232; Mourlon-Druol, *Federal Anathema*.
87 Dyson and Featherstone, *The Road to Maastricht*, 364.
88 AAPD, 1989, doc. 189, note Trumpf, 23 June 1989; doc. 280, note Jelonek, 20 September 1989; doc. 380: note Schönfelder, 24 November 1989.
89 AAPD, 1989, doc. 399, note of 7 December 1989. By contrast, other business groups mobilised for European monetary Union: Aleksandra Komornicka, 'Stable support, scant initiative: European business associations and Economic and Monetary Union, 1946–1992', *Business History*, 2024, 1–22; Marco Vianelli, 'L'Azione di Confindustria a favore dell'Unione monetaria europea', *Ventunesimo Secolo*, 55, 2, 2024, 117–138.
90 James, *Making the European Monetary Union*, 314–315.
91 On Italy: Varsori, *La Cenerentola*; Antonio Varsori, 'The Andreotti governments and the Maastricht Treaty: Between European hopes and domestic constraints', *JEIH*, 19, 1, 2013, 23–43; on France: Georges Saunier, 'La négociation de Maastricht vue de Paris', *JEIH*, 19, 1, 2013, 45–66.
92 Bozo, 'In search of the Holy Grail', 283–330.
93 Mourlon-Druol, *Federal Anathema*.
94 James, *Making the European Monetary Union*, 279–280.
95 HAEU, Florence, GSPE 79/468, Political report of the Socialist Group, 10–14 April 1989.
96 James, *Making the European Monetary Union*, 282.
97 AAPD, 1985, doc. 19, note on a Genscher–Delors meeting on 23 January 1985.
98 Isabella M. Weber, *How China Escaped Shock Therapy: The Market Reform Debate*, Routledge, 2021, chapter 3.

Chapter 8

1 Aristotle, *Poetics*, section 1, part 6, ca. 350 BCE, available at: http://classics.mit.edu/Aristotle/poeticfors.html.
2 Neil Fligstein, *Euroclash: The EU, European Identity and the Future of Europe*, Oxford University Press, 2008, 117.
3 On the history of Internet regulation: John Palfrey, 'Four phases of internet regulation', *Social Research: An International Quarterly*, 77, 3, 2010, 981–996.
4 David Vallat, 'An alternative to state-market dualism: The sharing economy: Practical and epistemological questions'. SASE 28th Annual Conference entitled Moral Economies, Economic Moralities, 2016. Available at https://shs.hal.science/halshs-01331107/.
5 Helen Margetts and Patrick Dunleavy, 'Data science, artificial intelligence and the third wave of digital era governance', *Public Policy and Administration*, 2023.
6 Timothy Snyder, *The Road to Unfreedom: Russia, Europe, America*, Vintage, 2019.
7 See Chapters 6 and 9.

8 Ther, *Europe since 1989*, 82; Vera Šćepanović, 'National interests and foreign direct investment in East Central Europe after 1989', in Stefan Berger and Thomas Fetzer (eds.), *Nations and Nationalism in Economic Perspective*, Central European University, 2019.
9 Isabella Weber, *How China*.
10 On the various national paths: Dorothee Bohle and Bela Greskovits, *Capitalist Diversity on Europe's Periphery*, Cornell University Press, 2012.
11 Laczo, Šćepanović, 'Eastern Europe in the history of European integration'.
12 Šćepanović, 'National interests'.
13 Philipp Ther, *Europe since 1989*, 139.
14 'Middle-class malaise', *The Economist*, 23 November 2024.
15 See the ongoing 'Single Markets project' led by Craig Parsons and Andy Smith; Michelle Egan, *Single Markets: Economic Integration in Europe and the United States*, Oxford University Press, 2015.
16 'Migration in India: Immobile republic', *The Economist*, 23 March 2024.
17 Michelle Egan, *Constructing a European Market: Standards, Regulation, and Governance*, Oxford University Press, 2001; Gilles Grin, *The Battle of the Single European Market. Achievements and Economic Thought, 1985–2000*, Paul Kegan, 2003.
18 Jean Joana and Andy Smith, *European Commissioners*, 108–109.
19 AUE, oral archives, interview with John Mogg by Piers Ludlow, 17 January 2017.
20 *Report of the group of independent experts on legislative and administrative simplification*, Com (95) 288, 21 June 1995.
21 AUE, BAC 254/2006/248, note from DG XXIV, 10 September 1999, quoted in: Laurent Warlouzet, 'The Internal market and competition', in Vincent Dujardin et al. (eds.), *The European Commission*, 272.
22 AUE, BAC 254/2006/248, note from the French Government, 2 September 1999 and British note (DTI), 7 September 1999; cited in Warlouzet, 'The Internal Market', 270.
23 AUE, BDT 220/2009/50, note from the Secretariat-General of 23 June 1987 on the meeting of Chefs de cabinet on Monday 22 June 1987; handwritten note from Perrisich to Braun stapled to a note in German of 1 February 1989; note from the Secretariat-General for Lamoureux, 25 January 1989.
24 AUE, BDT 220/2009/50, note DG III of 20 January 1992.
25 Judgment of the Court of 15 December 1995, Case C-415/93; William Gasparini and Jean-François Polo, 'The European Football Area: Institutional dynamics and social constructions', *European Policy*, 36, 2012, 9–21.
26 Padraig Flynn of Ireland was the Commissioner for Social Affairs, and a member of Fianna Fail (liberals); Marcelino Oreja of Spain was the Commissioner for Culture, and a member of the Conservative Party; AUE, BAC 424/1999/171, note from Padraig Flynn's cabinet preparatory to a meeting with UEFA, 30 January 1996, quoted in Warlouzet, 'The internal market', 273.
27 Paragraphs 71 and 81 of the Bosman Ruling of 15 December 1995, Case C-415/93.
28 AUE, LAC 189/2000/499, minutes of the College of Commissioners' meeting, 7 February 1996, quoted in Warlouzet, 'The internal market', 273.
29 AUE/AO Kinnock by Piers Ludlow, 25 October 2016; on his neoliberalism, see also: Gillingham, *European Integration*, 468.

30 The Bolkestein episode is comprehensively examined by Amandine Cresy. See among other publications: Amandine Crespy, 'When "Bolkestein" is trapped by the French anti-liberal discourse: A discursive-institutionalist account of preference formation in the realm of European Union multi-level politics', *Journal of European Public Policy*, 17, 8, 2010, 1253-1270; Amandine Crespy, 'The vanishing promise of a more "social" Europe: Public services before and after the debt crisis', in Amandine Crespy and Georg Menz (eds.), *Social Policy and the Eurocrisis*, Palgrave Macmillan, 2015, 119-121.
31 Alter, *The European Court*; Vauchez, *Brokering*.
32 Kalypso Nicolaïdis, 'The Cassis legacy: Kir, banks, plumbers, drugs, criminals and refugees', in Fernanda Nicola and Bill Davies (eds.), *Contextual and Critical Histories of European Jurisprudence*, Cambridge University Press, 2017, 288; Pollack, *The Engines*, 299-320.
33 Pollack, *The Engines*, 333.
34 Judgment of the ECJ of 12 September 2006, Cadbury Schweppes plc, Case C-196/04; Carasso, *Entre Neutralité*, 317.
35 Judgment of the Court (Grand Chamber) of 11 December 2007, 'International Transport Workers' Federation and Finnish Seamen's Union v Viking Line ABP and OÜ Viking Line Eesti', Case C-438/05.
36 Judgment of the Court (Grand Chamber) of 18 December 2007, 'Laval un Partneri Ltd v Svenska Byggnadsarbetareförbundet, Svenska Byggnadsarbetareförbundets avdelning 1, Byggettan and Svenska Elektrikerförbundet', Case C-341/05.
37 Judgment of the Court (Second Chamber) of 3 April 2008, 'Dirk Rüffert v Land Niedersachsen', Case C-346/06.
38 Judgment of the Court (First Chamber) of 19 June 2008, 'Commission of the European Communities v Grand Duchy of Luxembourg', Case C-319/06.
39 For the first opinion: Peter Lindseth, 'Viking's semantic gaps', in Nicola and Davies (eds.), *Contextual*, 498-501; for the second: Robert Schütze, 'Judicial Majoritarianism revisited: "We, the other court?"', *European Law Review*, 2018, 43, 2, 269-280. More generally, 'The CJEU is more than a court; it is a storyteller, a battleground, and a mirror of European society's struggles' according to: Fernanda Nicola, 'Is a distributive analysis enough? A critical take on the case law of the European Court of Justice', *Transnational Legal Theory*, 2024, pp. 1-25.
40 Lindseth, 'Viking's Semantic Gaps', 503.
41 See contrasting view of the Court's political impact in: Michale Blauberger and Susanne K. Schmidt, 'The European Court of Justice and its political impact', *West European Politics*, 40, 4, 2017, 907-918; Alec Stone Sweet, *The European Court of Justice and the Judicialization of EU Governance* (2 April 2010), available at SSRN: https://ssrn.com/abstract = 1583345; on human rights: Aurelia Ciacchi, 'The direct horizontal effect of EU fundamental rights', *European Constitutional Law Review*, 15, 2, 2019, 294-305.
42 Friedrich Hayek, *Law, Legislation and Liberty: A New Statement of the Liberal Principles of Justice and Political Economy*, Routledge, 1998 [1973], 23.
43 Amendment adopted on 6 December 2017 in the PANA Commission on Panama Papers.
44 Giandomenico Majone, 'The regulatory state and its legitimacy problems', *West European Politics*, 22, 1, 1999, 11-16.
45 'Systematic fraud by the world's biggest carmaker threatens to engulf the entire industry and possibly reshape it', *The Economist*, 26 September 2015.

46 Seidel, 'Contested fields', 352–354.
47 For an assessment: Agnès Bénassy-Quéré, Guntram Wolff, Clemens Fuest, and Vincent Aussilloux, *Making the Best of the European Single Market*, Brueguel report, 2 February 2017.
48 Laurent Warlouzet, '"Towards a fourth paradigm in European competition policy?" A historical perspective (1957–2022)', in Adina Claici, Assimakis Komninos, and Denis Waelbroeck (eds.), *The Transformation of EU Competition Law: Next Generation Issues*, Kluwer, 2023, 33–52.
49 SEC(95)1713, *Competition Policy and Competitiveness of European Industry*, 13 October 1995.
50 Commission Decision of 14 March 2000, Case COMP/M.1663 – *Alcan v Alusuisse*; Commission Decision of 29 September 2003, Case COMP/M.3225 – *Alcan v Péchiney (II)*.
51 See paragraph 33 of: Judgment of the Court (Grand Chamber) of 16 July 2009, *Commission of the European Communities v Schneider Electric SA*, Case C-440/07 P.
52 Sebastian Billows, Sebastian Kohl, and Fabien Tarissan, 'Bureaucrats or ideologists? EU merger control as market-centred integration', *JCMS*, 59, 4, 762–781.
53 European Commission, *State Aid Action Plan. Less and Better Targeted State Aid: A Roadmap for State Aid Reform 2005–2009*, COM(2005) 107, Brussels, 2005.
54 Barbara Curli, 'The "vincolo europeo": Italian privatization and the European Commission in the 1990s', *JEIH*, 18, 2, 2012, 296–297.
55 Eiko R. Thielemann, '"Institutional limits of a Europe with the Regions": EC state-aid control meets German federalism', *Journal of European Public Policy*, 6, 3, 1999, 399–418.
56 Commission decision of March 2005, confirmed by the Court of Justice in 2007 (Judgment of the Court (Grand Chamber) of 23 October 2007, *Commission of the European Communities v Federal Republic of Germany*, Case C-112/05), and subsequently in 2013 (Judgment of the Court (Grand Chamber) of 22 October 2013, *European Commission v Federal Republic of Germany*, Case C-95/12).
57 Karel Van Miert, *Le marché et le pouvoir: Souvenirs d'un commissaire européen*, Racine, 2000, 223.
58 Billows, Kohl, and Tarissan, 'Bureaucrats or Ideologists?'; Anu Bradford, Robert J. Jackson Jr, and Jonathan Zytnick, 'Is EU merger control used for protectionism? An empirical analysis', *Journal of Empirical Legal Studies*, 15, 1, 2018, 165–191.
59 See Chapter 7 and: Mark Thatcher, *Internationalisation and Economic Institutions: Comparing the European Experience*, Oxford University Press, 2007, 179–191.
60 Wolf Sauter, *Coherence in EU Competition Law*, Oxford University Press, 2016, 234; Thatcher, *Internationalisation*.
61 Thatcher, *Internationalisation*, 182.
62 Vay, *La mise en problème*, 400–403 and 403–414 for the following developments.
63 David Buchan, 'Energy policy: Sharp challenges and rising ambitions', in Helen Wallace, Mark Pollack, and Alasdair R. Young (eds.), *Policy-Making in the European Union*, Oxford University Press, 2010, 361–366.
64 Vay, *La mise en problème*, 385–386; on the reserves of Monti, Brittan, and Van Miert, see: 483.
65 Amandine Crespy, *Welfare Markets in Europe: The Democratic Challenge of European Integration*, Palgrave Macmillan, 2016; Vay, *La mise en problème*; Adrienne Héritier, 'Market integration and social cohesion: The politics of public

services in European regulation', *Journal of European Public Policy*, 8, 5, 2001, 825-852.
66 AUE, Philip Lowe Fund (PL) 11, Note from Claus-Dieter Ehlermann on Structural Priorities of DG IV (1995-2000), 5 January 1995.
67 Van Miert, *Le marché et le pouvoir*, 102.
68 Vay, *La mise en problème*, 517-579.
69 AUE, BAC 527/1998/16, note from DG IV, 14 August 1997, mentioned in Warlouzet, 'The internal market'.
70 Judgment of the Court of 24 July 2003, *Altmark Trans GmbH and Regierungspräsidium Magdeburg v Nahverkehrsgesellschaft Altmark GmbH*, Case C-280/00.
71 David J. Gerber, 'Two forms of modernization in European competition law', *Fordham International Law Journal*, 31, 5, 2007, 1235-1265.
72 Warlouzet, *Governing Europe*, 162-163.
73 Barry Hawk, 'The American Antitrust Revolution: A lesson for the EEC?', *Quarterly Review of European Law*, 1989, 5-44. On transatlantic legal dialogue, see also: Julie Bailleux and Antoine Vauchez (eds.), *Exploring the Transnational Circulation of Policy Paradigms: Law Firms, Legal Networks and the Production of Expertise in the Field of Competition Policies*, European University Institute of Florence, 2014; Angela Wigger and Andreas Nölke, 'The privatisation of EU business regulation and the erosion of Rhenish capitalism: The case of antitrust enforcement', *JCMS*, 45, 1, 2007, 487-513.
74 Air Tours/First Choice (decision of 6 June 2002) and Schneider/Legrand (22 October 2002).
75 A pioneering book being: Jean-Jacques Laffont and Jean Tirole, *A Theory of Incentives in Procurement and Regulation*, MIT Press, 1993.
76 AUE, Philip Lowe Fund (PL) 11, Note from Claus-Dieter Ehlermann for Deputy Director General and Directors on Structural Priorities of DG IV (1995-2000), 5 January 1995.
77 AUE, Philip Lowe Fund (PL) 11, Lowe's Note to Ehlermann, 15 December 1994.
78 Claus-Dieter Ehlermann, 'Reflections on a European cartel office', *Common Market Law Review*, 32, 2, 1995, 471-486.
79 José Manuel Ordóñez-De-Haro, Joan-Ramon Borrell, and Juan Luis Jiménez, 'The European Commission's fight against cartels (1962-2014): A retrospective and forensic analysis', *JCMS*, 56, 5, 2018, 1087-1107.
80 Gerber, 'Two forms of modernisation'.
81 Catherine Prieto and David Bosco, *Droit européen de la concurrence: Ententes et abus de position dominante*, Bruylant, 2013, 208.
82 Prieto and Bosco, *Droit européen de la concurrence*, 207-209. On the difficult integration of economic logic among lawyers specialising in competition law, see: Lola Avril, *The Costume under the Dress. Lawyers in Multi-Card Professionals of the European Regulator State: Geneva, Consolidation, Contestations (1957-2019)*, PhD in political science, University Paris 1, 2019, 364-377.
83 The dismantling of a cartel on truck prices among several European manufacturers over the course of fourteen years resulted in a record fine of EUR 2.9 billion in 2016. For a summary of M. Vestager's policy, see: Warlouzet, 'Towards a fourth paradigm'.
84 'EU fines German car makers EUR 875 million for colluding on car emission control systems Access to the comments', *Euronews*, 8 July 2021.

85 'The Google case is stirring up the Commission', *Euractiv*, 8 April 2014.
86 Neelie Kroes, 'Why EU state aid is not the right tool to fight tax avoidance', *The Guardian*, 1 September 2016.
87 Michelle Cini and Patryk Czulno, 'Digital single market and the EU competition regime: An explanation of policy change', *Journal of European Integration*, 44, 1, 2022, 41–57.
88 See the debates in: Adina Claici, Assimakis Komninos, and Denis Waelbroeck (eds.), *The Transformation of EU Competition Law: Next Generation Issues*, Kluwer, 2023.
89 On the 'Hipster Antitrust': Niamh Dunne, 'Fairness and challenge of making markets work better' *Modern Law review*, 84, 2, 2020, 230–264.
90 Thomas Philippon, *The Great Reversal. How America Gave up on Free Markets*, Harvard University Press, 2019.
91 Luigi Zingales, 'Towards a political theory of the firm', *Journal of Economic Perspective*, 31, 3, 2017, 113–130.
92 Louis Brandeis, *Other People's Money: And How the Banker Uses It*, Stokes, 1914; on Brandeis: Patrice Bougette and Frédéric Marty, *Information Exchange among Firms: The Coherence of Justice Brandeis' Regulated Competition Approach*, GREDEG Working Paper No. 2020-56, available at SSRN.
93 Lina M. Khan, 'Amazon's antitrust paradox', *The Yale Law Journal*, 126, 3, 2017, available at SSRN.
94 Catherine Hoeffler and Frédéric Mérand, 'Digital sovereignty, economic ideas, and the struggle over the digital markets act: A political-cultural approach', *Journal of European Public Policy*, 31, 8, 2024, 2121–2146.
95 The four categories in the table are based on: Warlouzet, 'Towards a fourth paradigm'.
96 Verdun Amy, 'Why EMU happened? A survey of theoretical explanations', in Patrick Crowley (ed.), *Before and beyond EMU. Historical Lessons and Future Prospects*, Routledge, 2002, 71–98.
97 Abdelal, *Capital Rules*, 81.
98 David Howarth, *The French Road*.
99 Andrew Osborne, 'Prodi disowns "stupid" stability pact', *The Guardian*, 18 October 2002.
100 Adam Tooze, *Crashed: How a Decade of Financial Crises Changed the World*, Viking, 2018, 233.
101 Mark Blyth, *The History of a Dangerous Idea*, Oxford University Press, 2015; Jean Pisani-Ferry, *The Euro Crisis and Its Aftermath*, Oxford University Press, 2014.
102 Alison Johnston, *From Convergence to Crisis. Labor Markets and the Instability of the Euro*, Cornell University Press, 2016.
103 Mark Blyth, *Austerity: The History of a Dangerous Idea*, Oxford University Press, 2013; Tooze, *Crashed*; Ben Clift, *The IMF and the Politics of Austerity in the Wake of the Global Financial Crisis*, Oxford University Press, 2018.
104 Manuela Moschella, *Unexpected Revolutionaries: How Central Banks Made and Unmade Economic Orthodoxy*, Cornell University Press, 2024.
105 Also called the Fiscal Compact. It was adopted in March 2012, and concerns only eurozone countries.
106 Mathias Dewatripont, Lucrezia Rechlin, and André Sapir, 'Urgent reform of the EU resolution framework is needed', Bruegel Blog, 16 April 2021.

107 'Donald Tusk interview: the Annotated transcript', *Financial Times*, 16 July 2015.
108 On the health effect of the crisis on Greek people: Alexander Kentikelenis et al., "Greece's health crisis: from austerity to denialism", The Lancet, 383, 2014, pp. 748–753.
109 Matthew Belvedere, 'The Original Sin threatening the euro: Ken Rogoff', CNBC.com, 8 July 2015; www.cnbc.com/2015/07/08/the-original-sin-threatening-the-euro-ken-rogoff.html, accessed 29 August 2021.
110 Stanford Ronald McKinnon, 'Oh, for an Alexander Hamilton to save Europe!', *Financial Times*, 18 December 2011.
111 'An investigation denounces the management of the Greek crisis by the IMF', *EurActiv*, 29 July 2016.
112 Review of assistance to Greece on the EU Council website: www.consilium.europa.eu/fr/infographics/financial-assistance-to-greece-2010-2018/; Greek GDP statistics 2011 on Eurostat website, accessed 27 September 2021.
113 Josef Hien and Christian Joerges, *Dead Man Walking: Current European Interest in the Ordoliberal Tradition*, EUI Working Paper, Law 2018/03, 2018.
114 'Donald Tusk interview: the Annotated transcript', *Financial Times*, 16 July 2015.
115 For the French case: Clément Fontan and Sabine Saurugger, 'Between a rock and a hard place: Priority training in France during the Eurozone crisis', in *Political Studies Review*, 18, 4, 2020, 507–524.
116 Ben Bernanke, *Essays on the Great Depression*, Princeton University Press, 2000.
117 Clément Fontan, 'Frankfurt's double standard: The politics of the European Central Bank during the Eurozone crisis', *Cambridge Review of International Affairs*, 31, 2, 2018, 162–182; Christakis Georgiou, 'Corporate power and the resolution of the Eurozone crisis', *European Politics*, 77, 2022, 66–115.
118 Blyth, *Austerity*.
119 Marcin Piatkowski, *Europe's Growth Champion. Insights from the Economic Rise of Poland*, Oxford University Press, 2018.
120 Eurostat, consulted on 26 August 2021.
121 Clément Fontan, 'Frankenstein in Europe: The impact of the European Central Bank on the management of the euro area crisis', *European Policy*, 42, 2013, 25–45.
122 Letter from Jean-Claude Trichet to Silvio Berlusconi, 5 August 2011, available at: www.ecb.europa.eu
123 Jürgen Habermas, *Zur Verfassung Europas. Ein Essay*, Suhrkamp, 2011.
124 On the Greek–German relationship: Claudia Sternberg, Kira Gartzou-Katsouyanni, and Kalypso Nicolaïdis, *The Greco-German Affair in the Euro Crisis: Mutual Recognition Lost?*, Palgrave Macmillan, 2018.
125 Heather Stewart, 'If Latvia is a bailout success story, be very scared of failure', *The Guardian*, 11 December 2011; Joanna Berendt, 'Little sympathy for Greece in Eastern Europe', *New York Times*, 8 July 2015.
126 Eric Monnet, *La Banque-Providence. Démocratiser les banques centrales et la monnaie*, Seuil, 2021, 52.
127 Working time in Greece was higher than in Germany because of low Greek productivity: Stanislas Jourdan, 'Les Grecs travaillent-ils trop?', *La Tribune*, 29 December 2011.
128 Kenneth Dyson, *States, Debt, and Power: 'Saints' and 'Sinners' in European History and Integration*, Oxford University Press, 2014; 'Albrecht Ritschl, Economic historian "Germany Was Biggest Debt Transgressor of 20th Century"', *Spiegel*, 21 June 2011.

129 Jürgen Habermas, 'Habermas: Warum Merkels Griechenland-Politik ein Fehler ist', *Süddeutsche Zeitung*, 22 June 2015.
130 Eichengreen and Ritschl, Understanding West German'; Albrecht Ritschl, 'Germany, Greece and the Marshall Plan. A comment on Professor Hans-Werner Sinn', *The Economist*, 15 June 2012; 'Albrecht Ritschl, economic historian "Germany was biggest debt transgressor of 20th century"', *Spiegel*, 21 June 2011.
131 Ulrich Beck, *No to German Europe: Towards a European Spring?*, Otherly, 2013; Wolfgang Streeck, *How Will Capitalism End? Essays on a Failing System*, Verso, 2016.
132 Claire Stam, 'Germany earned EUR 3 billion from Greek debt', *Ouest France*, 22 June 2018.
133 Claudia Broyer, Ann-Katrin Petersen, and Dr Rolf Schneider, 'Impact of the euro crisis on the German economy', Allianz, Working paper N°154, 25 September 2012.
134 Frédéric Mérand, *The Political Commissioner: A European Ethnography*, Oxford University Press, 2021, 211.
135 Erik Jones, Daniel Kelemen, and Sophie Meunier, 'Failing forward? The euro crisis and the incomplete nature of European integration', *Comparative Political Studies*, 49, 7, 2016, 1010–1034.
136 Emmanuel Mourlon-Druol, 'Banking Union in Historical Perspective: The Initiative of the European Commission in the 1960s–1970s', *JCMS*, 54, 4, 2016, 1–15.
137 Maurizio Ferrera, *Politics and Social Visions. Ideology, Conflict and Solidarity in the EU*, Oxford University Press, 2024; Michael A. Wilkinson, *Authoritarian Liberalism and the Transformation of Modern Europe*, Oxford University Press, 2021. Laurent Warlouzet, 'The Surprising Alliance of Illiberalism and Neoliberalism', *Journal of Modern History*, 23, 4, 2025, 17–22.

Chapter 9

1 On neoliberal globalisation's impact on rising inequalities in Northern countries in the 1990s and 2000s: Piketty, *Capital in the 21st Century*; Branko Milanovic and Christoph Lakner, *Global Income Distribution: From the Fall of the Berlin Wall to the Great Recession*, World Bank, Policy Research Working Paper No. 6719, 2013; Joseph Stiglitz, *The Price of Inequality*, Norton & Co, 2012. More generally, on the 'political trilemma of the world economy', see: Dani Rodrik, *The Globalization Paradox: Democracy and the Future of the World Economy*, Norton & Co, 2011.
2 See the working time statistics available on the OECD website: https://stats.oecd.org/. Average annual hours actually worked per workers in France, Germany, the UK, and the USA, in 1980: 1,806, 1,746, 1,619, and 1,859; in 2023: 1,500, 1,343, 1,524, and 1,799.
3 Stephan Leibfried and Paul Pierson (eds.), *European Social Policy. Between Fragmentation and Integration*, The Brookings Institution, 1995.
4 Mark Pollack, *The Engines of European Integration: Delegation, Agency, and Agenda Setting in the European Union*, Oxford University Press, 2003, 330–335.
5 Romuald Jagodzinski, 'The EWC directives and the SE legal framework: Symbiosis and mutual reinforcement brought to a stop?', in Michael Stollt, Jan Cremers, and Sigurt Vitols, *A Decade of Experience with the European Company*, ETUI, 2013, 273–290; Council Directives 94/45 of 22 September 1994; Directive 2009/38 of the European Parliament and of the Council of 6 May 2009.

6 Framework agreement on parental leave, adopted by a 1996 Directive (96/34/EC), the same for the Directive on part-time work (97/81/EC) and the Directive on fixed-term work (99/70/EC); Didry and Mias, *Le Moment Delors*; Crespy, *Social Europe*, 136–138.
7 Crespy, *Social Europe*, 82–84.
8 See Pauline Ravinet's work on the Bologna Process, especially: Pauline Ravinet, 'From voluntary participation to monitored coordination: Why European countries feel increasingly bound by their commitment to the Bologna Process', *European Journal of Education*, 43, 3, 2008, 353–367.
9 Jean-Claude Barbier, *La longue marche vers l'Europe sociale*, PUF, 2008, 63–103.
10 Maurizio Ferrera and Elisabetta Gualmini, *Rescued by Europe? Social and Labour Market Reforms in Italy From Maastricht to Berlusconi*, Amsterdam University Press, 2004, 106–108.
11 Stephan Liebfried and Paul Pierson, 'Social policy', in Helen and William Wallace (eds.), *Policy-Making in the European Union*, Oxford University Press, 1996; Stephan Leibfried, 'Social policy: Left to judges and the markets?', in Helen Wallace, Mark A. Pollack, and Alasdair R. Young (eds.), *Policy-Making in the European Union*, Oxford University Press, 2010, 253–281.
12 Thierry Berthet, Bernard Conter, Tommaso Pardi, and Andy Smith, 'Employment policy: "Desperately seeking a flexibility-security equilibrium"', in Bernard Jullien and Andy Smith (eds.), *The EU's Government of Industries: Markets, Institutions and Politics*, Routledge, 2015, 190–215.
13 Crespy, *Social Europe*, 138–140.
14 Philip Gordon and Sophie Meunier, *The New French Challenge: France Facing Globalisation*, Odile Jacob, 2002.
15 Laurent Warlouzet, 'La contribution européenne aux projets de régulation mondiale de la concurrence (1945-2005)', in Éric Bussière (ed.), *Régionalisme européen et gouvernance mondiale au XXe siècle*, Cahiers de l'IRICE, 2012, 105–116.
16 Sophie Meunier, 'Managing globalization? The EU in international trade negotiations', *JCMS*, 45, 4, 2007, 905–926.
17 The Barroso turning point is highlighted in: Philippe Pochet, *A la recherche de l'Europe sociale*, PUF, 2019; Amadine Crespy, 'Social policy: Is the EU doing enough to tackle inequalities?', in Ramona Coman, Amandine Crespy, and Vivien A. Schmidt (eds.), *Governance and Politics in the Post-Crisis European Union*, Oxford University Press, 2020, 199.
18 Kahn, *Histoire de la construction européenne*, 232.
19 On this strategy from the standpoint of Central and Eastern European countries: Georg Menz, 'What happened to social Europe? The three-pronged attack on European social policy', in Amandine Crespy and Georg Menz (eds.), *Social Policy and the Eurocrisis*, Palgrave Macmillan, 2015, 57.
20 *The European Parliament Rejects ACTA*, press release of the European Parliament, 4 July 2012.
21 TAFTA stands for Transatlantic Free Trade Area. The project is also known as the TTIP: Transatlantic Trade and Investment Partnership.
22 Antoine Vauchez, *Démocratiser l'Europe*, Seuil, 2014, 63.
23 Sophie Meunier and Rozalie Czesana, 'From back rooms to the street? A research agenda for explaining variation in the public salience of trade policy-making in Europe', *Journal of European Public Policy*, 2019, 1–19.

24 Amandine Crespy and Pierre Vanheuverzwin, 'What "Brussels" Means by Structural Reforms: Empty Signifier or Constructive Ambiguity?', *Comparative European Politics*, 17, 1, 2017, 92–111.
25 Pauline Ravinet, 'La Commission européenne et l'enseignement supérieur. La néolibéralisation du discours comme ressort de pouvoir ?', in *Gouvernement et action publique*, 2, 2, 2014, 95.
26 Crespy, *Social Europe*, 94.
27 Hussein Kassim, Michael W. Bauer, Sara Connolly, and Andrew Thompson, 'From here to Eternity? Assessing the stability of the beliefs and values of individual bureaucrats', paper given at the EUSA conference in Miami, 4–6 May 2017, paper available at: www.eustudies.org, accessed 27 August 2021.
28 'Special report: The World Economy', *The Economist*, 1 October 2016.
29 IMF, *IMF Fiscal Monitor: Tackling Inequality*, October 2017.
30 See a critique by the EU Tax Observatory, led by Gabriel Zucman: Global Tax Evasion Report 2024, www.taxobservatory.eu/.
31 Directive 2022/2523 and 2021/2101.
32 Global Tax Evasion Report 2024, EU Tax Observatory, 22 October 2023.
33 See the failure of Commissioner Thierry Moscovici's efforts to adopt legislation in this area: Mérand, *The Political Commissioner*.
34 Wallonia includes all French-speaking Belgians except the Brussels area, which has a bilingual status. Paul Magnette shared this experience in a book: Paul Magnette, *CETA Quand l'Europe déraille*, Luc Pire, 2017.
35 Sophie Jacquot, 'Gender equality policy', in Samuel B. H. Faure and Christian Lequesne (eds.), *The Edgar Companion to the European Union*, Edwar Elgar, 2023, 285–297. Two additional laws were adopted in 2022–23: directive 2022/2381 on gender balance among directors of listed companies, and directive 2023/970 on transparency, which forced companies to share information regarding their gender pay gap, and includes fines for major violations.
36 The savings are from the lower interest rates secured by the Union compared with those that member states could have obtained on their own. European Commission, *Report confirms SURE's success in protecting jobs and incomes*, 22 March 2021.
37 Directive (EU) 2022/2041 of the European Parliament and of the Council of 19 October 2022 on adequate minimum wages in the European Union; Thorsten Schulten and Torsten Müller, 'A paradigm shift towards Social Europe? The proposed Directive on adequate minimum wages in the European Union', *Italian Labour Law e-Journal*, 14, 1, 2021, 1–19.
38 Amandine Crespy, 'Social and health policy', in Samuel B. H. Faure and Christian Lequesne (eds.), *The Elgar Companion to the European Union*, Edward Elgar, 2024, 271–284.
39 Dorothée Bohle and Aidan Regan, 'The comparative political economy of growth models: Explaining the continuity of FDI-led growth in Ireland and Hungary', *Politics & Society*, 49, 1, 75–106.
40 Piers Ludlow, 'The Peace Programme for Northern Ireland', in Dujardin et al. (eds.), *The European Commission, 1986–2000*, Publications Office of the EU, 2019, 442–444.
41 Ther, *Europe since 1989*; Laczo and Scepanovic, 'Eastern Europe'.
42 Julien Barbaroux and Paul-Antoine Tugayé, 'Négocier sa position à l'international: la Commission européenne des années Delors (1985–1995)', *Histoire Europe Relations Internationales*, 6, 2025.

43 Estimated at somewhere between DM 600–1,000 billion for the period between 1991 and 1995 alone; Georg Koopmann, Christoph Kreienbaum, and Christine Borrmann. *Industrial and Trade Policy in Germany*, Nomos-Verlag, 1997, 121.
44 Ther, *Europe since 1989*, 146 for comparison with the Marshall Plan and figures on Poland. More generally on this comparison: Benedicta Marzinotto, *The Growth Effects of EU Cohesion Policy: A Meta-analysis*, Bruegel Working Paper, No. 2012/14, 11. According to Jakub Iwaniuk: 'Deducting its contribution to the European budget, the country has received a net value of €170 billion under the cohesion policy and the common agricultural policy', Jakub Iwaniuk, 'Twenty years after Poland's successful entry into the EU, its relationship with Europe has shifted', *Le Monde*, 1 May 2024.
45 Ther, *Europe since 1989*, 143.
46 See also Table 9.1, which details the evolution between 2009 and 2019.
47 Patrick Honohan, 'Is Ireland really the most prosperous country in Europe?', *Economic letter of the Central Bank of Ireland*, Dublin, Irish Central Bank 2021, 7. It concludes: 'There is less consumption per capita than in the United Kingdom, and on this metric we are closer to New Zealand, Israel and Italy, than to the United States, Switzerland or Norway (which is where the GDP comparison would put Ireland).'
48 *Maddison Project Database*, version 2020. Jutta Bolt and Jan Luiten van Zanden, '"Maddison style estimates of the evolution of the world economy": A new 2020 update', *Journal of Economic Surveys* 2020; source: www.rug.nl/ggdc/historicaldevelopment/maddison/releases/maddison-project-database-2020; accessed 26 August 2021. Irish GDP figures are overestimated because the European subsidiaries of numerous multinationals are tax residents there.
49 The concept of 'lease-in' (making private creditors pay) has subsequently advanced, notably in the context of the bailout of Cypriot banks in 2013.
50 '40% of Spanish children below the poverty line', *Euractiv*, 18 April 2017.
51 The term migrant is used here in its original meaning, as a person 'who changes his or her country of usual residence, irrespective of the reason for migration or legal status' (UN) [https://refugeesmigrants.un.org/definitions, accessed 9 October 2023].
52 Regulation (EU) No 604/2013 of the European Parliament and of the Council of 26 June 2013; on migration policy: Andrew Geddes, Leila Hadj-Abdou, and Leiza Brumat, *Migration and Mobility in the European Union*, Bloomsbury Publishing, 2020.
53 Eurostat newsrelease, *Record number of over 1.2 million first time asylum seekers registered in 2015*, 44/2016, 4 March 2016.
54 Figures of excess death between January 2020 and October 2022 according to the OECD: OECD, 'COVID-19 mortality and excess mortality', in *Health at a Glance: Europe 2022: State of Health in the EU Cycle*, OECD Publishing, 2022.
55 Lucia Quaglia and Amy Verdun, 'The COVID-19 pandemic and the European Union: Politics, policies and institutions', *Journal of European Public Policy*, 30, 4, 2023, 599–611.
56 Kouli and Laborie, *The Politics*.
57 Alban Davesne and Sébastien Guigner, 'La Communauté Européenne de la Santé (1952–1954)', *Politique Européenne*, 41, 2013, 40–63.
58 Scott L. Greer, 'The three faces of European Union health policy: Policy, markets, and austerity', *Policy and Society*, 33, 1, 2014, 13–24.

59 J. David Goodman, 'N.Y. will impose quarantine on visitors from states with big outbreaks', *New York Times*, 24 June 2020; 'The White House v covid-19', *The Economist*, 11 April 2020.
60 The decision was taken for a year, renewed in March 2021: Council Decisions of 17 March 2020; European Commission, *Communication from the Commission to the Council on the Activation of the Derogation Clause of the Stability and Growth Pact*, com(2020) 123, 20 March 2020.
61 Stella Ladi and Dimitris Tsarouhas, 'EU economic governance and Covid-19: policy learning and windows of opportunity', *Journal of European Integration*, 42, 8, 2020, 1041–1056.
62 This change with the German government is explained by several factors: Laura Pierret and David Howarth, 'To play or not to play the "moral hazard card": Germany and the European Union's response to the Covid-19 crisis', *Journal of European Public Policy*, 31, 4, 2024, 1075–1099; Amandine Crespy, Tom Massart, and Vivien Schmidt, 'How the impossible became possible: Evolving frames and narratives on responsibility and responsiveness from the Eurocrisis to NextGenerationEU', *Journal of European Public Policy*, 31, 4, 2024, 950–976.
63 On this argument, see details and figures in: Laurent Warlouzet, 'European integration and economic crisis up to Covid-19: From reconstruction to the twin neoliberal and neomercantilist challenges', *H-Soz-Kult*, 11 November 2020. Available online: www.hsozkult.de/searching/id/diskussionen-5096.
64 Jean-Baptiste François, 'Europe, un accord forgé dans l'alliage des compromis', *La Croix*, 22 July 2020; interview with Pablo Iglesias in *Le Monde*, 21 July 2020.
65 'A giant leap forward', *The Economist*, 3 April 2021.
66 Author's calculation based on the John Hopkins Coronavirus Resource Center.
67 Federico Fabbrini, *EU Fiscal Capacity: Legal Integration after Covid-19 and the War in Ukraine*, Oxford University Press, 2022; Christakis Georgiou, 'Europe's 'Hamiltonian moment'? On the political uses and explanatory usefulness of a recurrent historical comparison', *Economy and Society*, 51, 1, 2022, 138–159.
68 Peter Conti-Brown, and David Skeel (eds.), *When States Go Broke: The Origins, Context, and Solutions for the American States in Fiscal Crisis*, Cambridge University Press, 2012.
69 Stanford Ronald McKinnon, 'Oh, for an Alexander Hamilton to save Europe!', *Financial Times*, 18 December 2011.
70 'The EU's covid-19 recovery fund has worked, but not as intended', *The Economist*, 15 February 2024.
71 Nigel Haigh, *EU Environmental Policy: Its Journey to Centre Stage*, Routledge, 2016; Andrew Jordan and Viviane Gravey (eds.), *Environmental Policy in the EU. Acts, Institutions and Processes*, Routledge, 2021; on the impact on national legislation: Rüdiger Wurzel, *Environmental Policy-Making in Britain, Germany and the European Union*, Manchester University Press, 2006; Kenneth Hanf and Alf-Inge Jansen, *Governance and Environment in Western Europe: Politics, Policy and Administration*, Routledge, 2014.
72 Jan-Henrik Meyer, 'Pushing for a greener Europe: The European Parliament and environmental policy in the 1970s and 1980s', *JEIH*, 27, 1, 2021, 57–78.
73 Andrea Lenschow, 'Environmental policy: Contending dynamics of policy change', in Helen Wallace, Mark A. Pollack, and Alasdair R. Young (eds.), *Policy-Making in the European Union*, Oxford University Press, 2010, 319. Nathalie Berny estimates

that in 2002, the European Commission funded 50 per cent of the operating costs for the Brussels office of Friends of the Earth and Birdlife International, and 35 per cent of the WWF's European Policy Office: Nathalie Berny, 'Le lobbying des ONG internationales d'environnement à Bruxelles', *Revue Française de Science Politique*, 58, 1, 2008, 110.

74 For example with legislation on dumping of acid waste in the sea in the 1980s and 1990s: Frieda Ottmann, 'Navigating Europe's Waters: The Struggle of Greenpeace and the TiO2 Industry', *JEIH*, 32, 2026, forthcoming.

75 For details pertaining to European environmental legislation, see in particular: Haigh, *EU Environmental Policy*; Jordan and Gravey, *Environmental Policy*.

76 See Chapter 4 on the Birds Directive. On the Habitat Directive and its difficult implementation: Doug Evans, 'The habitats of the European Union habitats directive', *Biology and Environment: Proceedings of the Royal Irish Academy*, 106, 3, 2006, 167–172.

77 Williams, E. Spencer, Julie Panko, and Dennis J. Paustenbach, 'The European Union's REACH regulation: A review of its history and requirements', *Critical Reviews in Toxicology*, 39, 7, 2009, 553–575; Jean-Noël Jouzel and Pierre Lascoumes, 'Le règlement Reach: Une politique européenne de l'incertain. Un détour de régulation pour la gestion des risques chimiques', *Politique Européenne*, 33, 2011, 185–214.

78 Anthony Zito, *Creating Environmental Policy in the European Union*, Basingstoke, 2000, 133–146.

79 See for example the debate on the 2013 reform: Gerry Alons, 'Agriculture and environment: Greening or greenwashing?', in Ramona Coman, Amandine Crespy, and Vivien A. Schmidt (eds.), *Governance and Politics in the Post-crisis European Union*, Cambridge University Press, 2020, 140–158.

80 Katja Seidel, 'Creating a "blue Europe": The common fisheries policy', in Éric Bussière et al. (eds.), *The European Commission, 1986–2000. History and Memories of an Institution*, Publication Office of the EU, 2014, 313–336.

81 In 1992, the UK government suggested weakening EU legislation on biodiversity, waste, and water quality: Viviane Gravey and Andrew J. Jordan, 'Policy dismantling at EU level: Reaching the limits of "an ever-closer ecological union"?', in *Public Administration*, 98, 2, 2020, 353–354; on Germany: Frank Uekötter, *The Greenest Nation? A New History of German Environmentalism*, MIT Press, 2014, 141; Christoph Knill and Duncan Liefferink, 'The establishment of EU environmental policy', in Andrew Jordan and Viviane Gravey (eds.), *Environmental Policy in the EU: Actors, Institutions and Processes*, Routledge, 202, 23–31.

82 On the difficult situation before the mid-2010s: Charlotte Burns, Peter Eckersley, and Paul Tobin, 'EU environmental policy in times of crisis', *Journal of European Public Policy*, 27, 1, 2019, 1–19.

83 On UK environmental policy and Brexit: Viviane Gravey and Jordan Andrew, 'Simultaneously de-Europeanising, disengaging and (re)-engaging?', *Journal of European Public Policy*, 30, 11, 2023, 2349–2371.

84 Pope Francis, *Laudato Si*, 2015.

85 Estelle Brosset and Laurent Warlouzet, 'Environnement et agriculture', Eurolab, *Bilan de la 9e législature du Parlement européen (2019-2024)*, Ceser, 2024, 32–40.

86 Nicolas Jabko and Nils Kupzok, 'Indirect responsiveness and green central banking', *Journal of European Public Policy*, 31, 4, 2024, 1026–1050.

87 Regulation 2023/1115 on the ban on imports of products resulting from deforestation; directive 2022/2464 on sustainability reporting (based on Environmental, Social, and Corporate Governance criteria) for all multinationals operating in the Union sparked an outcry from Republican members of Congress in the United States, who denounced protectionism; Viktoria Dendrinou, 'Yellen says US is concerned about EU's ESG supply chain rules', *Bloomberg*, 13 June 2023.
88 See Chapter 4 on unleaded petrol.
89 Eva Oberloskamp, 'Energy and the environment in parliamentary debates in the Federal Republic of Germany, United Kingdom and France from the 1970s to the 1990s', in Éric Bussière et al. (eds.), *The Environment*, 205-219; David Buchan, 'Energy policy', 363.
90 Andrea Lenschow, 'Environmental Policy: "Containing dynamics of policy change"', in Helen Wallace, Mark A. Pollack, and Alasdair R. Young (eds.), *Policy-Making in the European Union*, Oxford University Press, 2010, 313; Viviane Gravey and Andrew J. Jordan, 'Policy dismantling at EU level: Reaching the limits of "an ever-closer ecological union"?', *Public Administration*, 98, 2, 2020, 355.
91 Alexandre Lauverjat found a first trace of this strategy in 1987: Lauverjat, 'One atmosphere'; Kate Abnett, 'EU parliament backs labelling gas and nuclear investments as green', *Reuters*, 6 July 2022.
92 Frank Uekötter, *The Greenest Nation? A New History of German Environmentalism*, MIT Press, 2014, 141.
93 Nathalie Berny, 'Lectures', *Politique européenne*, 53, 4, 2016, 142-146.
94 Viviane Gravey, *Does the European Union Have a Reverse Gear? Environmental Policy Dismantling, 1992-2014*, PhD, University of East Anglia, 2016.
95 Paul Tullis, 'Nitrogen wars: The Dutch farmers' revolt that turned a nation upside-down', *The Guardian*, 16 November 2023.
96 Pierre Bocquillon, 'Climate and energy transitions in times of environmental backlash? The EU "Green Deal" from adoption to implementation', *JCMS*, 62, 1, 124-134.
97 On this anti-environmental backlash at the European Parliament: Brosset and Warlouzet, 'Environnement et agriculture', 36-39.
98 Gravey, *Does the European Union Have a Reverse Gear?*
99 Niklas Olsen & Sebastian Lundsteen Nielsen, 'The pollution-industrial complex and the making of Denmark as an environmental frontrunner, 1965-1975,' *The International History Review*, 2025, 1-19; Stephen Gross, *Energy and Power: Germany in the Age of Oil, Atoms, and Climate Change*, Oxford University Press, 2023.
100 Oreskes and Conway, *Merchants of Doubt*. This is a burgeoning field of study: Kristoffer Ekberg, Bernhard Forchtner, Martin Hultman, and Kirsti M. Jylhä, *Climate Obstruction: How Denial, Delay and Inaction Are Heating the Planet*, Routledge, 2022; Keetie Sluyterman, 'Royal Dutch Shell: Company strategies for dealing with environmental issues', *Business History Review*, 84, 2, 2010, 203-226.
101 Proctor, 'Agnotology'.
102 Christophe Bonneuil, Pierre-Louis Choquet, and Benjamin Franta, 'Early warnings and emerging environmental accountability: Total's responses to global warming, 1968-2021', *Global Environmental Change*, 71, 2021, 102386.
103 Andrew Jordan, Wurzel Rüdiger, Zito Anthony, and Brückner Lars, 'European Governance and the Transfer of "New" Environmental Policy Instruments

(NEPIs) in the European Union', *Public Administration*, 81, 3, 2003, 555-574; Christoph Knill, 'Implementation', in Jeremy J. Richardson (ed.), *European Union, Power and Policy-Making*, Routledge, 2006, 351-375; Laurent Warlouzet, 'The European Community's Environmental Policy and the Rise of Market-based Instruments (1973-1992)', *JEIH*, 32, 2026, forthcoming.

104 On the rise of environmental economics see: David Pearce, 'An Intellectual History of Environmental Economics', *Annual Review of Energy and the Environment*, 27, 1, 2002, 57-81.

105 Dominique Pestre, 'Les entreprises globales face à l'environnement, 1988-1992. Engagements volontaires, management vert et labels', *Le Mouvement Social*, 271, 2020, 83-104; Andrew J. Hoffman, *From Heresy to Dogma: An Institutional History of Corporate Environmentalism*, Stanford University Press, 2011; Jennifer Clapp, 'The privatization of global environmental governance: ISO 14000 and the developing world', *Global Governance*, 4, 1998, 295-316; Hartmut Berghoff and Adam Rome (eds.), *Green Capitalism?: Business and the Environment in the Twentieth Century*, University of Pennsylvania Press, 2017.

106 HAEU v Commission, BDT 111/95/5, Commission response on Brundtland report, draft, 2 March 1990.

107 Alice Milor, *Building Automotive, Leading Europe Industrials, Consumers and Policymakers (1972-1998)*, PhD, Sorbonne University, 2021, 720-753.

108 Testimony of an expert from the Commission, François Benda, in: AHEU, Oral Archives, interview with François Benda by Katja Seidel on 2 November 2010.

109 David Vogel, 'The hare and the tortoise revisited: The new politics of consumer and environmental regulation in Europe', *British Journal of Political Science*, 33, 2003, 557-580.

110 The environment accounted for the largest share of proceedings for violations of European law: Andrea Lenschow, *Environmental Policy*, 322; on France: Raphael Romi, *L'Europe et la protection de l'environnement*, PUF, 2004, 141-156.

111 Ulrich Beck, 'Climate for change, or how to create a green modernity?', *Theory, Culture & Society*, 27, 2010, 254.

112 Quoted in Stefan C. Aykut and Amy Dahan, *Gouverner le climat? 20 ans de négociations internationales*, Presses de Sciences Po, 2015, 34.

113 Aykut and Dahan, *Gouverner le climat*.

114 Christophe Bonneuil, 'Genèse'. The IPCC has included many representatives of industries of government hostile to any meaningful action to tackle climate change: Jean-Baptiste Fressoz, *More and More. An All-Consuming History of Energy*, London, Allen Lane, 2024.

115 Michel Rocard, *Le Coeur à l'oeuvre*, O. Jacob, 1987, 241-242, quoted in Bonneuil, 'Genèse'.

116 BR-NA, PREM 19/2652, note Powell to Thatcher, 26 January 1989.

117 Fabienne Jouty: 'The rise and fall of the European carbon tax project: Study of a European Commission's approach to EU climate policy, 1988-1992', *JEIH*, 32, 2026, forthcoming.

118 BNA, FCO 30/7783/58, note from Richard Powell, FCO European Community Dpt, 6 December 1989.

119 Serge Audier, *L'âge productiviste: hégémonie prométhéenne, brèches et alternatives écologiques*, La Découverte, 2019, 607.

120 Zito, *Creating Environmental Policy*, 88-110.

121 On the French example (Total, Elf, Saint-Gobain, etc.) see: Bonneuil, 'Genesis'.
122 Matthew Paterson, 'Understanding the green backlash: Review article', *Environmental Politics*, 8, 1999, 183–187.
123 Directive 1999/62/EC of the European Parliament and of the Council of 17 June 1999.
124 A. Denny Ellerman, Frank J. Convery, and Christian de Perthuis (eds.), *Pricing Carbon: The European Union Emissions Trading Scheme*, Cambridge University Press, 2010.
125 Buchan, 'Energy policy', 375–376; WWF, *Where Did All the Money Go?*, Report of 29 November 2022.
126 BR-NA, AT 83/473, note UK, 19 April 1996.
127 'EU's consumption (final demand of goods and services) caused 3.2 billion tonnes of global CO_2-emissions, which is about 9 per cent of worldwide emissions. Of these, some 0.9 billion tonnes originated from non-EU countries e.g. through imports into the EU', in European Commission, Greenhouse gas emission statistics – carbon footprints, 29 January 2024 (Eurostat website).
128 'China says EU's planned carbon border tax violates trade principles', *Reuters*, 26 July 2021; Jiarui Zhong and Jiansuo Pei, 'Carbon border adjustment mechanism: A systematic literature review of the latest developments', *Climate Policy*, 24, 2, 2024, 228–242.
129 'Free exchange: The perfect carbon price', *The Economist*, 3 June 2023.
130 'CBAM will force change in carbon-intensive sectors', *The Economist*, 27 December 2023.
131 World Meteorological Organization (WMO), *State of the Climate 2024, Update for COP29*, 2024, 3; 'The January – September 2024 global mean surface air temperature was 1.54 °C (with a margin of uncertainty of ±0.13°C) above the pre-industrial average'.
132 Source: 'Carbon brief. Climate is changing. Hot Tempers', *The Economist*, 26 November 2022.
133 Andrea Lenschow and Carina Sprungk, 'The myth of a green Europe', *JCMS*, 48, 1, 2010, 133–154.

Chapter 10

1 Stefaan Smis and Kim Van der Borght, 'The EU-US compromise on the Helms-Burton and D'Amato acts', *American Journal of International Law*, 93, 1, 1999, 227–236.
2 Henry Farrell and Abraham L. Newman, 'Weaponized interdependence: How global economic networks shape state coercion', *International Security*, 44, 1, 2019, 42–79; Cornelia Woll, *Corporate Crime and Punishment: The Politics of Negotiated Justice in Global Markets*, Princeton University Press, 2023.
3 Esteban Ortiz-Ospina, Diana Beltekian, and Max Roser, 'Trade and globalisation', 2018. Published online at OurWorldInData.org. [Online Resource, accessed 6 March 2023].
4 Odd Arne Westad, *Restless Empire: China and the World since 1750*, Basic books, 2012.
5 Agence France-Presse, 'Après le Brexit, Londres demande à rejoindre le traité commercial transpacifique', 1 February 2021.

6 On illiberalism, which is a contested notion (such as 'populism'), see the synthesis in: Helena Rosenblatt, 'The history of illiberalism', in András Sajó, Renáta Uitz, and Stephen Holmes (eds.), *The Routledge Handbook of Illiberalism*, Routledge, 2021, 16–32.
7 Isabella M. Weber, *How China Escaped Shock Therapy*.
8 Private archives of James Baker, Princeton University (USA), 8C, notes JAB 15 November 1991; see also the notes on 5 June 1989 and on 25 February 1992.
9 Sumner Twiss, 'Confucian ethics, concept-clusters, and human rights', in Marthe Chandler and Ronnie Littlejohn (eds.), *Polishing the Chinese Mirror: Essays in Honor of Henry Rosemont, Jr.*, Global Scholary Publications, 2007, 60–62.
10 'Where to from here?', *The Economist*, 9 September 2023.
11 Victoria Breeze and Nathan Moore, 'China has Overtaken the US and UK as the top destination for English-speaking African students', *Quartz Africa*, 30 June 2017.
12 Timothy Snyder, *The Road to Unfreedom: Russia, Europe, America*, Crown, 2018.
13 V-Dem Institute Gothenburg, cited in: 'China's latest attempt to rally the world against Western values', *The Economist*, 27 April 2023.
14 'Orbán says he seeks to end liberal democracy in Hungary', *Bloomberg*, 28 July 2014.
15 Including for automotive emissions and the regulation of mercury emissions from power plants: Nadja Popovich, Livia Albeck-Ripka, and Kendra Pierre-Louis, 'The Trump administration is reversing 100 environmental rules: Here's the full list', *New York Times*, 20 May 2020.
16 Guillaume Delacroix, 'Coronavirus: L'esclavage fait son retour en Inde, qui sape son droit du travail', *Le Monde*, 12 May 2020.
17 'Briefing, Hungary', *The Economist*, 31 August 2019. However, nativists also have a social agenda, notably via higher child benefits to boost the birth rate.
18 European Commission, *Competition State Aid Brief*, February 2024, 2.
19 'The global backlash against climate policies has begun', *The Economist*, 11 October 2023; Nathalie Brack, *Opposing Europe in the European Parliament: Rebels and Radicals in the Chamber*, Palgrave Macmillan, 2018.
20 'Vaccine exports', *The Economist*, 27 March 2021: the US as of December 2020, and India as of March 2021.
21 'Globalisation: Torn apart', *The Economist*, 16 May 2020.
22 Josep Borrell, 'Covid-19: The next world is already here', *Foreign Policy*, 2, 2020, 9–23; Bernd Lange, 'International trade after the corona-crisis: Business as usual or systemic change?', 28 April 2020, website: https://media.business-humanrights.org/media/documents/files/International-trade-after-the-corona-crisis-Bernd-Lange-EN-27042020.pdf, accessed 27 August 2021.
23 Which is why the Nobel-winning economist Paul Krugman estimated that Trump was tricked by von der Leyen: Paul Krugman, 'Fossil Fool. How Europe Took Trump for a Ride', blog, 30 July 2025. https://paulkrugman.substack.com
24 European Commission, Joint Statement on a United States-European Union framework on an agreement on reciprocal, fair and balanced trade, 21 August 2025, point 10 on the EU Deforestation Regulation, point 11 on the CBAM, point 12 on the CSDDD and the CSRD, point 13 on telecommunication regulation.
25 'America's bullied allies need to toughen up', *The Economist*, 15 March 2025.
26 See Chapter 5. On minimalistic European industrial policy: European Commission, *The Competitiveness of European Enterprises in the Face of Globalisation: How to Encourage It*, Com (1998) 718 final of 20 January 1999.

27 'The German economy: Beyond repair?', *The Economist*, 23 November 2024.
28 Arcelor was a French–Spanish–Luxembourgish company established in 2002, while Corus was a British–Dutch company founded in 1999.
29 'The Cypriot deal: Second time unlucky', *The Economist*, 30 March 2013.
30 Tooze, *Crashed*, 495.
31 Riccardo Righi et al., 'The AI techno-economic complex System: Worldwide landscape, thematic subdomains and technological collaborations', in *Telecommunications Policy*, 44, 6, July 2020.
32 Ben Clift and Cornelia Woll, 'Economic patriotism: Reinventing control over open markets', *Journal of European Public Policy*, 19, 3, 2021, 307–323.
33 Jim Brunsden, 'Commission gets tough with Germany over Opel', Europeanvoice.com, 1 October 2009.
34 Christophe Lécuyer, 'Conception, production et souveraineté chez STMicroelectronics', in Clotilde Druelle-Korn, Patrick Fridenson, Pascal Griset, and Laurent Warlouzet (eds.), *Industrie, développement et souveraineté*, Igpde, 2025, 243–266.
35 Ian Manners, 'Normative power Europe: A contradiction in terms?', *JMCS*, 40, 2, 2002, 235–258.
36 Bradford, *The Brussel Effect*. On environmental protection, she especially mentions the GMO standard, the control of chemical substances through the REACH directive, and carbon emissions.
37 Anu Bradford differentiates between Europe's 'rights-driven' approach, Chinese 'state-driven model' and the US 'market-driven' model: Anu Bradford, *Digital Empires: The Global Battle to Regulate Technology*, Oxford University Press, 2023.
38 See the open letter from the prime ministers of Germany (Angela Merkel), Denmark (Mette Frederiksen), Finland (Sanna Marin), and Estonia (Kaja Kallas) to Ursula von der Leyen on 1 March 2021: 'Digital sovereignty is about building on our strengths and reducing our strategic weaknesses, not about excluding others or taking a protectionist approach'; source: https://openfuture.eu/wp-content/uploads/2022/04/210301DE-DK-FI-EE-Letter-to-COM-President-on-Digital-Sovereignty.pdf; on Thierry Breton: 'Europe: the keys to sovereignty', www.linkedin.com, 11 September 2020. Benjamin Farrand and Helena Carrapico, 'Digital sovereignty and taking back control: From regulatory capitalism to regulatory mercantilism in EU cybersecurity', *European Security*, 31, 3, 2022, 435–453; Michelle Cini and Patryk Czulno, 'Digital Single Market and the EU Competition Regime: An Explanation of Policy Change', *Journal of European Integration*, 44, 1, 2022, 41–57.
39 Regulation 2081/92; see: Andy Smith, 'A constructivist-institutionalist approach to EU Politics: The case of protected geographical indications for food', in Jay Rowell and Michel Mangenot (eds.), *A Political Sociology of the European Union*, Manchester University Press, 2010, 146–163.
40 Mathieu Rosemain and John Irish, 'US orders French companies to comply with Trump's diversity ban', *Reuters*, 29 March 2025. See also above on the EU–US trade deal of August 2025.
41 Anselm Küsters and Cecilia Emma Sottilotta, 'How Europe Can Navigate the Regularoty Tightrope. Trade-Offs and Risks in EU Digitial Policy', Centrum für Europäische Politik, 2025.
42 The UK also dominated global industrial goods manufacturing at the start of the Industrial Revolution, although globalisation (in real and relative terms) was much less extensive.

43 Although private US actors were influential in the League: Ludovic Tournès, *Philanthropic Foundations at the League of Nations: An Americanized League?*, Routledge, 2022.
44 Michel Albert and James Ball, *Toward European Economic Recovery in the 1980s. Report to the European Parliament*, Praeger, 1984, 107.
45 NA-FR, 1990.0452/28, SGG note: inter-ministerial meeting of 16 November 1988; NA-FR, 19900452/29, note Trichet for the Minister, note of 4 October 1989.
46 Klaus Larres, 'China and Gemany: The honeymoon is over', *The Diplomat*, 16 November 2016.
47 'Industrialising America', *The Economist*, 4 February 2023.
48 David Kleimann, Niclas Poitiers, André Sapir, Simone Tagliapietra, Nicolas Veron, Reinhilde Veugelers, and Jeromin Zettelmeyer, *How Europe should answer the US Inflation Reduction Act*, Bruegel, 23 February 2023.
49 Melike Arslan and Chase Foster, *Beyond Smokestack Chasing: Toward a New Typology of Subnational Investment Subsidies in the United States*, working Paper, 2024.
50 European Commission press release: *State Aid: Commission Adopts Temporary Crisis and Transition Framework to Further Support Transition towards Net-Zero Economy*, 9 March 2023.
51 European Union, *State Aid Scoreboard*, accessible on Eurostat.
52 Theresa Hartl, 'Europe places its own values in jeopardy', *Friedrich Ebert Stiftung*, 3 July 2025, post on their website: www.fes.de.
53 Kazuto Suzuki, *Policy Logics and Institutions of European Space Collaboration*, Routledge, 2019.
54 Daniela Felisini and Paolo Paesani, 'Industrial policy and its funding at the frontier of European integration: Lessons from the past and present challenges', *Enterprise & Society*, 2024, 1–26.
55 Vincent Lequeux, 'What is the Juncker plan', *All Europe*, 20 September 2018, www.touteleurope.eu/institutions/qu-est-ce-que-le-plan-juncker/, accessed 27 August 2021.
56 A study by Bruegel from 8 June 2016, at the beginning of the Juncker Plan, argues that the latter has financed projects that would otherwise have been supported by the EIB, but the study acknowledges that the available sources do not make it possible to assess the risk profile of the investments (Grégory Claeys and Alvaro Leandro, *The Juncker Plan Needs to Be Turned on Its Head*, Brueguel, 8 June 2016).
57 Daniel Mertens, Matthias Thiemann, and Peter Volberding, 'Introduction: The making of a European field of development banking', in Daniel Mertens, Matthias Thiemann, and Peter Volberding (eds.), *The Reinvention of Development Banking in the European Union: Industrial Policy in the Single Market and the Emergence of a Field*, Oxford University Press, 2021, 1–32.
58 Communication from the Commission, Criteria for the analysis of the compatibility with the internal market of State aid to promote the implementation of important projects of common European interest (OJ C 188, 20.6.2014, 4).
59 State aid: Commission approves €3.2 billion public support by seven Member States for a pan-European research and innovation project in all segments of the battery value chain, EU press release, 9 December 2019.
60 'Automakers to pool CO_2 emissions with Tesla, Polestar to meet EU 2025 rules', *Reuters*, 7 January 2025.
61 'Is China winning?', *The Economist*, 18 April 2020.

62 Jorge Valero, 'The EU wants to defend itself better against foreign subsidies', *Euractiv*, 19 June 2020.
63 Dave Keating, 'L'Union paye sa naïveté et son absence d'offensive sur les contrats vaccinaux', *Le Grand Continent*, 20 March 2021.
64 Jilian Deutsch, 'Commission's Breton: "It's fine if EU countries buy vaccines from Russia, China"', *Politico*, 4 March 2021; Aneta Zachová, 'Czech Republic orders Chinese vaccine Sinopharm', *Euractiv*, 4 March 2021.
65 'Covid-19: la diplomatie du vaccin de la Chine prise à revers', *Le Monde*, 13 April 2021.
66 Robert Kagan, 'Power and weakness', *The Hoover Institution*, 1 June 2003; Robert Kagan, *Of Paradise and Power: America and Europe in the New World Order*, Vintage, 2003.
67 Speech by Romano Prodi at Sciences-po, Paris, 29 May 2001, available on the European Commission's website: https://ec.europa.eu/commission/presscorner/detail/en/speech_01_244 [accessed 2 March 2025].
68 Pierre Haroche, 'A "geopolitical commission": Supranationalism meets global power competition', *JCMS*, 61, 4, 2023, 970–987.
69 Haroche, 'A geopolitical commission'.
70 Discourse of Bundeskanzler Scholz an der Karls-Universität, 29 August 2022, Prague.
71 Ulrich Krotz, *Flying Tiger: International Relations Theory and the Politics of Advanced Weapons*, Oxford University Press, 2011.
72 Speech by Mario Draghi, President of the Italian Council, to the European Parliament on 3 May 2022.
73 'A year of war', *The Economist*, 25 February 2023.
74 Samuel Faure and Andy Smith, 'Differentiated integrations: Lessons from political economies of European defence', in *European Review of International Studies*, 6, 2, 2019, 3–17; see Chapter 5 on the industrial dominance of the US in combat aircraft; Catherine Hoeffler and Samuel Faure, 'Introduction. L'européanisation sans l'Union européenne: Penser le changement des politiques militaires', *Politique européenne*, 48, 2015, 8–27.
75 Fondapol, *Libertés: l'épreuve du siècle*, Paris, January 2022, p. 54. The answer was no in Germany and the Scandinavian countries.
76 Although two other marginal cases exist: Algeria in 1962, and Greenland in 1985, also after a referendum: Patel, *Project Europe*, 10. For systematic study of the different aspects of Brexit: Patrick Diamond, Peter Nedergaard, and Ben Rosamond (eds.), *The Routledge Handbook of the Politics of Brexit*, Routledge, 2019.
77 Olivier Faye, 'Marine Le Pen exulte et réclame un "Frexit"', *Le Monde*, 23 June 2016.
78 Some commentators blame the tepid Remain campaign of Corbyn and Cameron, while others point to at Russia's involvement on social media.
79 Kwasi Kwarteng, Priti Patel, Dominic Raab, Chris Skidmore, and Elizabeth Truss, *Britannia Unchained: Global Lessons for Growth and Prosperity*, Palgrave Macmillan, 2012.
80 David Hannay, *The Case for EFTA*, Bruges Group, 2005.
81 Mérand, *The Political Commissioner*.
82 Thierry Chopin and Christian Lequesne, 'Disintegration reversed: Brexit and the Cohesiveness of the EU27', *Journal of Contemporary European Studies*, 29, 3, 2021, 419–431.

83 'Brexit: The DUP Unionist Party launches a legal action against the Northern Irish Protocol', *Euractiv*, 22 February 2021.
84 'EU rejects British plan to rip up Brexit deal', *Financial Times*, 21 July 2021.
85 'UK workers' rights at risk in plans to rip up EU labour market rules', *Financial Times*, 14 January 2021. The article cites rules on working time, rest time, and leave calculation. These reflections sparked official protests from Labour.
86 Thim Summers, 'Brexit: Implications for EU–China relations', *Chatham House*, May 2017; Hugo Meijer, *European Foreign and Security Policies toward the People's Republic of China*, Oxford University Press, 2022.
87 'Charlemagne, The benefits of Brexit', *The Economist*, 30 May 2020.
88 'The inviolability' of frontiers should be distinguished from the 'intangibility' of frontiers, which allows for modifying them by mutual agreement, such as during German reunification in 1990, or the Czech–Slovak partition in 1992.
89 Mary E. Sarotte, *Not One Inch: America, Russia, and the Making of Post-Cold War Stalemate*, Yale University Press, 2022.
90 Snyder, *The Road to Unfreedom*.
91 See the interview of one of Putin's main advisors, Nikolaï Patrushev: 'L'Ukraine pourrait cesser d'exister cette année', *Grand Continent*, 14 January 2025.
92 The president of the European Parliament, Roberta Mensola, asserted that the 'extraordinary heroism by Ukrainians ... showed the world that our way of life is worth defending', President Roberta Metsola's Speech to Plenary, 1 March 2022.
93 Richard de Coudenhove-Kalergi, *Pan-Europe*, Pan-Europa Verlag, 1923.
94 Council Directive 2001/55/EC of 20 July 2001 on minimum standards for giving temporary protection in the event of a mass influx of displaced persons. Sergio Fabbrini, Federico Fabbrini, *EU fiscal capacity: Legal Integration after Covid-19 and the War in Ukraine*, Oxford University Press, 2022, 131.
95 Concluded under the auspices of the UN and Turkey, the agreement allows Kiev to export grain by sea without fear of having its ships sunk by the Russian Black Sea fleet.
96 'EU has spent EUR 35bn on Russian energy since the war began and just EUR 1bn on aid to Ukraine – Borrell', *Euronews*, 6 April 2022. This was an estimation by Josep Borrell, the High Representative of the European Union for Foreign Affairs and Security Policy.
97 *The Ukraine Support Tracker: Which Countries Help Ukraine and How?*, Working paper no. 2218, Kiel Institute for the World economy, February 2023, 25.
98 *Ukraine Support Tracker*, website of the Kiel Institute for the World Economy, accessed 26 February 2025.
99 Calculations were made using the SIPRI Military Expenditure Database and Eurostat figures. Between 2000 and 2022, military expenditure as a share of GDP stood at 2 per cent for France and 1.2 per cent for Germany. Over the same period, French debt rose from 59.7 per cent to 111.2 per cent, while German debt rose from 59.2 per cent to 65 per cent.
100 Kenneth Waltz, 'The emerging structure of international politics', *International Security*, 1993, 76: 'NATO's days are not numbered, but its years are'.
101 'Unionspolitiker kritisieren Diskussion um mögliche EU-Atomwaffen', *Zeit Online*, 14 February 2024; on the French arsenal: Bruno Tertrais, 'La dissuasion nucléaire française', *Cahiers français*, 427, 2022, 8–14.

102 According to SIPRI (Stockholm International Peace Research Institute), the total number of warheads (as of January 2023) was: 4,489 for Russia, 3,708 for the US, 290 for France, and 225 for the UK.
103 On the increase: *Defence Data 2024-2024, European Defence Agency*, 2024. 'Can Europe defend itself without America', *The Economist*, 24 February 2024: 'Europe's total defence spending will reach around $380bn – about the same as Russia's, after adjusting for Europe's higher prices'.
104 Deutsche Welle, *Ukraine aktuell*, 4 September 2023. See below for military aid figures in 2022-24.
105 World Bank, military expenditure in current US$ in 2022: $258 bn for the EU; $876 bn for the US. Accessed 25 September 2023.
106 Kaja Kallas, 9 February 2023, quoted in Pierre Haroche, *Arsenal Europe*, Institut Jacques Delors, 2023. See also: 'One option would be for Europeans to pool their resources. For the past sixteen years, for instance, a group of twelve European countries have jointly bought and operated a fleet of three long-range cargo aircraft – essentially a timeshare programme for airlift. In January Germany, the Netherlands, Romania and Spain teamed up to order 1,000 of the missiles used in the Patriot air-defence system, diving down the cost through bulk.' 'Can Europe defend itself without America', *The Economist*, 24 February 2024.
107 Since that country has been in a state of war with its northern neighbour since 1950, despite the 1953 Armistice. Hyonhee Shin, 'South Korea, Poland sign $5.8 trillion tank, howitzer contract', *Reuters*, 27 August 2022.
108 According to the Kiel Institute for the World Economy, France ranks eleventh in terms of government support to Ukraine (financial, humanitarian, and military) among European countries (including non-EU countries such as the UK). Source: www.ifw-kiel.de. Table: Government support to Ukraine, commitments 24 January 2022 to 15 January 2024.
109 'German coalition cracks deepen over Ukraine policy', *Euractiv*, 18 March 2024.
110 Joseph Nye, *Bound to Lead: The Changing Nature of American Power*, Basic Books, 1990.

Conclusion

1 Letter from William Bullitt, US ambassador to France, to President Franklin D. Roosevelt, 24 November 1936, FDR library, available at: www.fdrlibrary.marist.edu/_resources/images/psf/psfa0287c.pdf [accessed 1 November 2023]. Quoted in: Eric Roussel, *Jean Monnet*, Fayard, 1996, 234.
2 Ruggie, 'International regimes'.
3 On 1979 as a global turning point: Odd Arne Westad, *The Global Cold War: Third World Interventions and the Making of Our Times*, Cambridge University Press, 2005; Christian Caryl, *Strange Rebels: 1979 and the Birth of the 21th Century*, Basic Books, 2012; Frank Bösch, *Zeitwende 1979: Als die Welt von heute begann*, Munich, Beck, 2019.
4 Mark Gilbert, *European integration: A Political History*, Rowman & Littlefield, 2020.
5 Bradford, *The Brussels Effect*.
6 The percentage of the global population killed by state-based conflict hit a post-war low of 0.0002 per cent in 2005. 'The new economic order', *The Economist*, 11 May 2024.

7 Leonard Seabrooke and Eleni Tsingou, 'Europe's fast- and slow-burning crises', *Journal of European Public Policy*, 26, 3, 2018, 468–481. On the decline of EU law enforcement by the Commission: Daniel Kelemen, and Tommaso Pavone, Tommaso, 'Where have the guardians gone? Law enforcement and the politics of supranational forbearance in the European Union', *SSRN*, December 2021.
8 Tooze, *Crashed*.
9 Although Brexit cannot be reduced exclusively to *community* capitalism. See Becker, Fetzer, and Novy, 'Who voted for Brexit?'.
10 Such as Vaclav Klaus, the Czech Prime Minister from 1993 to 1997 and President from 2003 to 2013.
11 Moravcsik, *The Choice for Europe*.
12 A point recently reasserted by Robert Schütze: Schütze, 'Integration-through-law'.
13 See Chapters 4 and 9.
14 See Chapter 8; Warlouzet, 'Towards a Fourth Paradigm'. On the long-term reversal of competition policy regimes, see a US and French perspective in: Erik Peinert, 'Monopoly politics: Price competition, learning, and the evolution of policy regimes', *World Politics*, 75, 3, pp. 566–607.
15 See Chapter 4.
16 See Chapters 4 and 9; Oreskes and Conway, *Merchants of Doubt*.
17 Scharpf, *The Double Asymmetry*.
18 The concept of 'hegemony' is different from that of 'empire': Emmanuel Comte and Fernando Guirao (eds.), *Discussing Pax Germanica: The Rise and Limits of German Hegemony in European Integration*, Routledge, 2024; Simon Bulmer and William E. Paterson, *Germany and the European Union: Europe's Reluctant Hegemon?*, Red Globe Press, 2019; Mathieu Dubois, *L'économie sociale de marché à la conquête de l'Europe: la diplomatie allemande et le modèle européen (1953-1993)*, Pur, 2024; Joachim Schild, 'The myth of German hegemony in the euro area revisited', *West European Politics*, 43, 5, 2020, 1072–1094; Germann, *Unwitting Architect*.
19 Examples of the major influence of the Benelux countries on European integration include the 1952 Beyen Plan, the 1955 Benelux memorandum, the 1956 Spaak Report, the action of the Commissioners Sicco Mansholt (one of the creators of the CAP) and Etienne Davignon (with respect to cooperation in foreign policy and industrial policy), as well as of several Commission Presidents (Jean Rey, Gaston Thorn, Jacques Santer, Jean-Claude Juncker).
20 Luuk van Middelaar has called it a 'third sphere': van Middelaar, *The Passage to Europe*, 2013.
21 See Chapter 10.
22 Wolfram Kaiser, *Christian Democracy and the Origins of European Union*, Cambridge University Press, 2007.
23 This argument is in line with a recent influential study: Reka Juhasz, Nathan J. Lane, and Dani Rodrik, *The New Economics of Industrial Policy*, NBER working paper 31538, 2023.
24 Andrew Roberts, *The Aachen Memorandum*, Weidenfeld and Nicolson, 1995.
25 Laurent Warlouzet, 'The surprising alliance of illiberalism and neoliberalism', *Journal of Modern European History*, 2025. Both the far-right ideology and neoliberalism are inegalitarian in nature.

26 Translated from: Pierre Charbonnier, *Vers l'écologie de guerre. Une histoire environnementale de la paix*, La Découverte, 2024; Ben Judah, Shahin Vallée, and Tim Sahay, *Escaping the Permanent Suez: Navigating the Geopolitics of European Decarbonization*, Atlantic Council/Europe Center, 2024; Dani Rodrik, *Shared Prosperity in a Fractured World: A New Economics for the Middle Class, the Global Poor, and Our Climate*, Princeton University Press, 2025.

PRIMARY SOURCES (ARCHIVES AND INTERVIEWS)

Interviews Available

In addition to these 33 interviews, those which are not publicly available are not mentioned here.

oral archives available on the website of the historical archives of the European Union: two former European commissioners (Frans Andriessen, Peter Sutherland), one former French minister (Elisabeth Guigou) and twelve former European officials (Jean-Louis Cadieux, Jean Dubois, Claus-Dieter Ehlermann, Jonathan Faull, Anne Houtman, Michel Petite, Martine Reicherts, John Temple-Lang, Jean-François Vestrynge, Claude Villain, Paul Waterschoot, Heinz Zourek).

oral archives available at the Comité d'histoire du ministère français des Finances (cheff): one former European commissioner (Jacques Delors), two former French ministers (Clement Beaune, Alain Lamassourre), three former French officials (Christian Babusiaux, Armand Saclé, Jean-Claude Trichet).

oral archives available at the European Parliament archives: 10 former member of the European Parliament, or MEP collaborator, or EP officials (François Bayrou, Paul Collowald, Alfredo De Feo, Nicole Fontaine, André Fourçans, Françis Jacobs, Gérard Laprat, Benjamin Patterson, François Roelants du Vivier, Karl von Wogau).

Archives of National Governments

Archives of the Bundesbank (Frankfurt am Main).
Archives of the French Ministry for Foreign Affairs (La Courneuve).
Archives of the French Ministry for the Economy and Finances (Savigny-le-Temple).
Archives of the German Ministry for Foreign Affairs (Politischesarchiv Berlin).
British national archives (London/Kew): series CAB (Cabinet), FG (National Economic Development Council), FO (Foreign Office), FV (Trade and Industry), MAF (Agriculture and Food), PREM (Prime Minister), T (Treasury).
French national archives (Pierrefitte): series 5AG1 to 5AG4, SGCI, Ministry of Industry.

366   PRIMARY SOURCES (ARCHIVES AND INTERVIEWS)

German national archives – Bundesarchiv – (Coblence): series for the Chancellery (B136) and the Ministry for Economic Affairs (B 102)

Archives of European and International Organisations

Archives of the European Parliament (Luxembourg).
Archives of the European People's Party (EPP) and the European Parliament (Brussels and Luxembourg).
Archives of the GATT (Geneva): available online on the Stanford website (http://gatt.stanford.edu).
Archives of the International Labour Organization – ILO – (Geneva).
Archives of the OECD (Paris): series RBP.
Archives of the UN / UNCTAD series (Geneva).
Historical archives of the European Union: series for the European Commission, private series (François Lamoureux, Philip Lowe, Emile Noël, Altiero Spinelli, Peter Sutherland, Pierre Uri), series for socialist and liberal groups in the European Parliament (Florence, some series for the European Commission are also available in Brussels).

Archives of Non-state Actors

Archiv des Liberalismus, Friedrich-Naumann-Stiftung (Gummersbach): archival series for the FDP.
Archives of the Confédération démocratique du travail – CFDT – (Paris).
Archives of the Confederation of British Industry – CBI – (Warwick).
Archives of the European League for Economic Cooperation (Louvain-la-Neuve).
Archives of the European Trade Union Confederation – ETUC – (Amsterdam).
Archives of the Fondation Jean Monnet (Lausanne): series Jean Monnet and Robert Marjolin.
Archives of the Fondation nationale des Sciences Politiques (FNSP, Paris): Michel Debré series.
Archives of the Monde du travail (Roubaix): series for the Normed shipyard.

Acknowledgements

This book stems from more than twenty years of research. I started examining protectionism, industrial policies, cartels, and their connection to international tensions and welfare states in 2002. At the time, during the period of 'high neoliberalism', these topics were deeply unpopular, and even considered slightly seditious. Today they have come back to the fore in dramatic fashion.

After my PhD on European history, I made a foray into global history with my book *Governing Europe,* and by co-founding the first journal of global history, *Monde(s).* The study of South American, African, and Asian history showed me that what I believed to be a regional phenomenon – European integration – actually had global relevance through its influence on the global economy (and increasingly on its politics), and the fact that it has no counterpart. As a result, 'provincialising Europe' does not mean that focusing on Europe is pointless, but that the continent's experience is a case study that is instructive for all, not just Europeans.

This book is therefore the product of those two decades of enquiry. It is an enriched translation of a work originally published in 2022 in French by CNRS éditions under the title *Europe contre Europe. Entre liberté, solidarité et puissance.* It has been updated (to include the Russo-Ukrainian War and recent developments in environmental and trade policy up to August 2025), expanded (to include foreign and defence policy), and largely overhauled. While the French expression '*Europe puissance*' has a specific recognised meaning, its strict English translation, 'Europe as a Power', is confusing. Preference has instead been given to the notion of *community* for this third category. The full list of references has not been reproduced in the print version of the book, but is available on the publisher's website, as well as my personal site.

The English version grew out of the lively debates sparked by presentations of *Europe contre Europe* in various academic seminars around the world. While I feel a certain degree of flight shame, I am nevertheless convinced that direct and frank discussions with colleagues over coffee or beer are irreplaceable. It would be hard for me to understand how my American, Japanese, or Chinese colleagues view Europe and the world while comfortably remaining on the banks of the Seine, gazing at the Sainte-Chapelle from my office window.

ACKNOWLEDGEMENTS

I would like to express my deepest gratitude to those who have invited me to discuss *Europe contre Europe*, and more generally to all those who provided thoughtful feedback: Ralf Ahrens, Pierre Alayrac, Jenny Andersson, Nicolas Badalassi, Sebastian Billows, Estelle Brosset, Megan Brown, Éric Bussière, Alain Chatriot, Michelle Cini, Ramona Coman, Amandine Crespy, Nicolas Delalande, François Denord, Michele di Donato, Pierre-Yves Donzé, Mathieu Dubois, Ken Endo, Olivier Feiertag, Maurizio Ferrera, Orfeo Fioretos, Mark Gilbert, Pierre-Cyrille Hautcoeur, Alan Hervé, Liane Hewitt, Haakon Ikonomou, Erik Jones, Wolfram Kaiser, Tomoya Kuroda, Karl Lauschke, Christian Lequesne, Brigitte Leucht, Michel Mangenot, Kathleen McNamara, Lorenzo Mechi, Frédéric Mérand, Guia Migani, Jan-Werner Müller, Philipp Müller, Alexandre Nützenadel, Francesco Petrini, Thomas Piketty, Jan Pomarek, Sigfrido Ramirez-Perez, Andreas Rödder, Eric Roussel, Elke Seefried, Katja Seidel, Glenda Sluga, Céline Spector, Kazuto Suzuki, Mark Thatcher, Philipp Ther, Guido Thiemeyer, Blaise Truong-Loï, Antoine Vauchez, Nicolas Verschueren, Scott Viallet-Thévenin, Blaise Wilfert, and Cornelia Woll.

For the most insightful comments on the main argument of the book, I would like to extend my special thanks to Antoine Acker, Grace Ballor, Benjamin Bürbaumer, Mathieu Fulla, Giuliano Garavini, Hussein Kassim, Sandrine Kott, Justine Lacroix, Piers Ludlow, Sophie Meunier, Andrew Moravcsik, Emmanuel Mourlon-Druol, Craig Parsons, Kiran Klaus Patel, Sabine Pitteloud, Morten Rasmussen, Vera Scepanovic, and Andy Smith. I am also grateful for the perceptive comments from several of my PhD students, including Adeline Afonso, Julien Barbaroux, Fabienne Jouty, Alexandre Lauverjat, Liupeng Wang and Marco Vianelli. More generally, I would like to thank all of my students who helped shape my current approach over the course of two decades of teaching in three different countries. This book was made possible by collecting archival sources in eight countries, for which I would like to express gratitude to archivists as well as my interviewees.

As this project is also a capitalist venture, I acknowledge here the various sources of funding that have enabled this research, in addition to the publication and translation of the book: Sorbonne University, the SIRICE research centre, the GIS EUROLAB, the ANR (through the ANR-DFG ELEMENT project) and the European Union for its funding of the Jean Monnet Chair GreenEUHist. The usual disclaimer applies, for these sources of funding did not interfere with the publication in any way. The book was largely translated and corrected by Arby Gharibian, the translator of Sandrine Kott's *The World More Equal*, published by Columbia University Press, one of the few individuals able to understand the intricacies of academic research in this field in both languages. Some chapters were also linguistically corrected by Don Stoudt.

Last but not least, I would like to thank my family for their indispensable support, as well as the late Michel Albert – a pioneer of the 'varieties of capitalism' literature – who was kind enough to write a preface to my first book in 2011. His masterpiece *Capitalism against Capitalism*, a book still widely cited today, inspired this book.

INDEX

Aachen Memorandum, The, 290
AAPD, *See* Akten zur Auswärtigen Politik der Bundesrepublik Deutschland (AAPD).
Abu Dhabi, 247
Acker, Antoine, 21
ACP countries, 137, 174
Act to Support Ammunition Production (ASAP), 266
Adenauer, Konrad, 50, 104–105
AEG, 120
aerospace industry, 69, 71–72, 106–107, 110–112, 113, 117, 120, 123–125, 151, 185, 259, 269
Aerospatiale-Matra, 249
AfD, *See* Alternative Party for Germany (AfD).
Afghanistan, 106, 218, 238, 257, 263, 275, 277, 280
Africa, 42, 135, 136–137, 218, 224, 234, 242, 258, 265, 283
Africans, 137, 242
agriculture, 40, 51–53, 54, 61, 107–108, 110, 144, 145, 148–149, 273, 275
AI, *See* articifial intelligence.
aid, 52, 58–60, 117, 119, 137, 140, 141–142, 214, 225, 253–255, 268, 273
Air France, 70, 185
air transport, deregulation of, 69
Airbus, 27–28, 110–113, 115–116, 121–125, 145, 151, 185, 249, 254, 288–289
 aircraft
  A300, 111, 113
  A320, 111
  A400M, 257, 259

aircraft, *See* aerospace industry.
Aixtron, 253
Albert, Michel, 63, 120–122
Albert-Ball Report, 67, 121, 252
Alcan, 184
Alfa Romeo, 119
Algeria, 105, 137, 273, 360
Algiers Conference of Non-Aligned Countries, 130
Alibaba, 241
Allende, Salvador, 130
Almunia Joaquin, 183, 192
Alstom, 184–185
Alstom, Siemens merger, 191, 253
Alternative Party for Germany (AfD), 203, 277
Altmeier, Peter, 253
aluminium, 184, 234
Alussuisse, 184
Amato, Giuliano, 167
Amato-Kennedy law, 238
Amazon (company), 185, 191, 241
Amazon (rainforest), 21, 211, 243
Amsterdam, Treaty of, xi, 188
Andreatta, Beniamino, 184
Andreotti, Giulio, 164
Andriessen, Frans, 59, 70, 143, 147
Anti-Counterfeiting Trade Agreement (ACTA), 210
antitrust policy, 15, 51, 192–193, *See also* cartels and competition policy
Apeldoorn, Bastian van, 13, 25
Apollo lunar program, 112
Apple, 28, 173, 185, 191, 234, 241
Arab-Israeli conflict, 106
Arcelor, 247, 248

370

Archibugi, Franco, 93
Ariane program, 110, 113, 124–125, 151, 254
Aristotle, 173
Arrow-3 missile system, 269
Artificial Intelligence Act, 249
asbestos, 86, 224, 287
ASEAN, *See* Association of Southeast Asian Nations (ASEAN).
Asian Infrastructure Investment Bank (AIIB), 239
Association of Southeast Asian Nations (ASEAN), 38, 239
AstraZeneca, 222, 256
AT&T, 70
Atlantic Alliance, *See* NATO.
ATR, 72, 123
Attali, Jacques, 65, 122
Aubry, Martine, 128
Auroux, Jean, 128
Austin, Lloyd, 268
Austria, 196, 200
authoritarianism, 20, 35, 92, 127, 141, 158, 227, 237, 240, 242, 255–256, 260, 263
automobile industry, 29, 30, 59, 89, 144, 146, 151, 226, 233–234, 247
  Dieselgate scandal, 182, 202, 230, 282
  electric-powered vehicles, 244, 253
automotive industry, unleaded petrol, 89–90, 281, 288
Aznar
  José Maria, 208, 257
Aznavour, Charles, 158
Azores summit, 257

Baidu, 241
Bakas, Adjieedj, 238
Baker, James, 149
Baldwin, Richard, 112
Ball, Albert, 63
Balladur, Édouard, 167
Ball-Albert Report, *See* Albert-Ball Report.
Bangemann, Martin, 111, 123–124, 191, 288
banking, 30, 116–117, 148, 157, 169, 183, 197, 199–200, 211, 222, 255
Banque de France, 93, 154, 166–167

Bardot, Brigitte, 88
Barnier, Michel, 261
Barre, Raymond, 87, 116, 141, 163, 164
Barroso, José Manuel, 180, 181, 206, 209–210, 212, 226, 257, 271
Basel Conventions on Hazardous Waste, 225, 281
Basel-Nyborg Agreement, 167
basketball, 173
Beck, Ulrich, 202, 230
beer, 65, 76, 110
Beer Purity Decree, 65
Belgium, 50, 52, 53–54, 79, 85, 95–96, 102, 119, 136, 138, 141, 144, 311
Benelux countries, 50, 52, 63, 73, 76, 135, 146, 284, 363
Bérégovoy, Pierre, 60, 97, 165, 166, 167
Bergman, Ingrid, 158
Bergougnoux, Jean, 187
Berlin crisis, 53, 105
Berlusconi, Silvio, 201, 208
Bernanke, Ben, 200
Bethell, Nicholas William, 69–70
Beveridge, William, 22, 78
Beyen, Johan Willem, 51, 91
Bhopal disaster, 88
Biden, Joseph R., 193, 238, 251
BioNTech, 256
Birds Directive (1979), 224
Bismarck, Otto von, 22
BlackRock, 229
Blair House Agreement, 110
Blair, Tony, 178, 207, 224, 256–257
Bloch, Marc, 14
Blum
  Norbert, 83
Blum, Léon, 51
Blyth, Mark, 158
Boeing, 28, 69, 111–112, 254
Boersma, Jacob, 88
Bolkestein directive, 177, 179–180, 204–205
Bolkestein, Frits, 27, 179
Bologna Process, 207, 210
Bolsonaro, Jair, 21, 176, 212, 242, 243
Borrell, Josep, 245, 361
Bosman, Jean-Marc, 179
Bouchardeau, Huguette, 89–90
Boulin, Robert, 96–97, 99, 128, 131, 288

Boussac, 120
Bradford, Anu, 149, 249
Brandeis, Louis, 193
Brandt, Willy, 7, 80, 99, 131, 135–136, 155, 274, 279, 282
Brazil, 130, 138, 150, 176, 211, 235, 239, 243, 289
Breit, Ernst, 82
Bresciani, 141
Breton, Thierry, 187, 191, 193, 250, 255
Bretton-Woods system, 154, 279
Breuel, Birgit, 117
Brexit, 36, 38, 44, 47, 211, 225, 236, 238, 260–271, 277, 283, 286
Britannia Unchained, 260
British Aerospace, 68
British Budget Question, 61
British Leyland, 118
British Railways, 189
British Shipbuilders, 118
British Telecom, 70, 118, 119
Brittan, Leon, 41, 68–69, 71–72, 74, 76, 123–124, 148, 149, 178, 179, 183, 187, 204, 285, 289
Brittan, Samuel, 71
Bruges Group, 75
Brundtland report, 88
Brundtland, Gro, 88
Brussels effect, 148–149, 237, 249, 250–251, 270–271, 276
Brussels Pact, 103
Brzezinski, Zbigniew, 42
BSC, 140, 141
BSE (bovine spongiform encephalopathy) crisis, 44, 182
Bukman, Piet, 40
Bulgaria, 221, 241
Bull (company), 123
Bullitt, William, 272
Bullock, Alan, 128
Bundesbank, xi, 57, 117, 154, 157, 163, 165–166, 167, 171, 176, 199
Bundeskartellamt, 57
Bush
 George H. W., 37, 238
 George W., 185, 233, 238
Butler, Michael, 73

Cadbury Schweppes, 181
Caisse des Dépôts et Consignation, 255
Centre Européen des Entreprises Publiques (CEEP), 188, 207
Callaghan, James, 135, 156, 161
Cameron, David, 210, 262
Canada, 36, 113, 162, 211, 243, 245, 252, 268
CAP, See Common Agricultural Policy.
capitalism, trinity of, 2, 5, 7, 16, 44, 153, 174, 290
car industry, See automobile industry.
carbon dioxide, 223, 229, 230–233, 234
carbon tax, 11, 228, 231–234, 252, 275, 277, 287
Cardoso, Antonio, 187
Carey, Henry, 26
Carington, Peter, 43
cartels, 3, 16–17, 24–25, 45, 56–57, 58, 130–131, 138–139, 142, 150, 190–191, 289
 notification system, 58, 190
 regulation, 190, 192
Carter, Jimmy, 69, 129, 156, 163, 171
Caspari, Manfred, 27
Cassis de Dijon ruling, 62–63, 76, 281
Catalonia, 34
catalytic converters, 89, 281
CBI, See Confederacy of British Industry (CBI).
CDU, See Christian Democratic Union (CDU).
Cecchini, Paolo, 63
CEEP, See Centre Européen des Entreprises Publiques.
Central European University (CEU), 215, 243
CEPT, 66
CETA, See Comprehensive Economic and Trade Agreement (CETA).
CFDT, xi, 10, 132–133, 159
CFM, 113
Chaban-Delmas, Jacques, 82, 93
Chang, Peng Chun, 241
Channel Islands, 211
Channel Tunnel, 123
Charney Report, 231
Chernobyl accident, 114
Chernobyl disaster, 88

Chevènement, Jean-Pierre, 165
Cheysson, Claude, 121
Chicago school, 45, 119, 189, 193–194
Chicago school of economics, 21, 157, 189 See also neoliberalism
Chile, 20, 130, 157
China, 20, 35, 38, 173–174, 175, 176, 234–235, 237–242, 244–247, 251–254, 257–259, 264, 276–280
  dependence on, 245, 292
Chinese capitalism, 176
Chinese vaccine diplomacy, 256
Chirac, Jacques, 70, 86, 148, 161, 166, 208, 224
Christian Democratic Union (CDU), 76, 110, 161, 253, 267
Chrysler, 28, 129
Churchill, Winston, 43
CIEC (Conference on International Economic Cooperation), 130
CLEAR campaign, 89
Clinton, Bill, 233, 263
Clinton-Davis, Stanley, 70
Club 89, 75
Club de l'Horloge, 75
CNPF, 10
CO_2, See carbon dioxide.
coal, 6, 30–31, 50–51, 57, 102, 114, 118, 127, 226, 233
Cockfield Report, 56, 65–67, 74, 149
codetermination, 83, 127–128, 132, 134, 282
Colbert, Jean-Baptiste/Colbertism, 26, 27, 115, 124
Cold War, 36, 50, 53, 75, 81, 101, 144, 170, 173, 174, 238, 259, 263–264, 276, 282
Colonna di Paliano, Guido, 121
Commerzbank, 249
Committee of Permanent Representatives (COREPER), x
Common Agricultural Policy (CAP), 61, 65, 87, 92, 107–110, 124–125, 141, 144, 275–276, 283, 284, 288
Common Fisheries Policy, 225
Common Foreign and Security Policy (CFSP), 10, 106, 256

Common Market, 46–47, 48, 52–55, 61–62, 68, 69, 75–77, 97–98, 105, 136, 141, 146, 252, 281
Common Security and Defence Policy (CSDP), 257
Commonwealth of Nations, 53–54, 260
Communication Decency Act (US 1996), 173
Communist Party of France (PCF), 15
community capitalism, 1, 3–5, 7–8, 13, 14, 15, 16, 17, 18, 21–26, 36–37, 43–44, 58, 63, 74, 124, 125, 154, 220, 237, 243–244, 270, 271, 274, 276, 285, 288
  balance with other forms of capitalism, 1
  British Empire, 31
  challenges, 7–8, 288–290
  China, 176
  in combination, with both, 127, 129, 205, 219, 253
  combined with other ideal types, 17
  ECSC and, 273
  EEC and, 274
  environmental protection and, 226, 236, 288
  ethical valence, 8
  European Community and, 100, 126, 178
  European institutions and, 44
  European integration and, 5, 13
  France, 283
  globalisation and, 150
  historical context, 26–29
  migration and, 218
  monetary union and, 153
  Nazism as extreme version of, 17
  neoliberalism and, 243–244, 276
  neomercantilism and, 24
  normative power and, 151, 250
  overview, 3
  protectionism and, 4
  solidarity capitalism and, 45
  South East Asia, 240
  Trump administration as example, 1, 18
  UEFA, 179
community principle, 4, 25, 27, 107, 140, 146, 148

competition policy, 41, 45–46, 49, 51, 56–57, 60–61, 67–68, 183, 186, 189–194, 204–205, 249–250, 278–282
Comprehensive Economic and Trade Agreement (CETA), 211, 250, 252, 271
Concorde, 111, 116, 289
Confederation of British Industry (CBI), xi, 10, 133
Conference on Security and Cooperation in Europe, x, 87
Confucianism, 241
Corbyn, Jeremy, 261
COREPER, See Committee of Permanent Representatives (COREPER).
Corn Laws, 31
Cotonou Agreement, 174
Coudenhove-Kalergi, Richard von, 264
Council for Mutual Economic Assistance, 38
Council of Ministers, 39–40, 45, 64, 65, 70, 73, 97, 134, 170, 219, 259
Court of Justice, See European Court of Justice (ECJ).
Covid-19 pandemic, 200, 213, 220–221, 222, 243, 252, 255, 258, 263, 269, 270–271, 277, 284
Crimea, 247, 264
CSCE (Conference on Security and Co-operation in Europe), x, 87
CSDP (Common Security and Defence Policy), 257
Cuba, 28, 238
cubism, 8
customs barriers, 25, 63, 239
customs duties, 26, 38, 51, 53, 54, 56, 61–62, 208, 213, 222, 239
Cyprus, 36, 198, 217, 247

Dacia, 248
Daimler-Benz, 71, 112, 118
d'Alema, Massimo, 208
DASA, 249
Dasault Rafale, 107
Dassault, 113
Dassault Mercure, 113

Davignon, Étienne, 12, 132, 133, 138–142, 146, 151, 285, 363
De Havilland, 72, 123, 148
de Michelis, Gianni, 82
Debré, Michel, 95, 109, 154
Debunne, George, 97
Deep and Comprehensive Free Trade Area (DCFTA), 265
Defense Advanced Research Projects Agency (DARPA), 7, 28
Defrenne, Gabrielle, 85
Dekker, Wisse, 148
Delors Commission, 74, 98, 166, 214, 275
Delors, Jacques, 12, 37, 40, 63, 65–66, 74, 76–77, 81–84, 91, 93–94, 96, 98–99, 122–124, 128, 132, 148–149, 165, 166–167, 168, 170, 178, 184, 207, 209
Delors Report, 168, 169–170, 197, 203
Deng Xiaoping, 241, 275
Denmark, 36, 40, 55, 83, 158, 162, 195, 220, 224, 232, 243
deregulation, 18, 45, 70, 73–75, 161, 178, 286
d'Estaing
   Valéry Giscard, 61, 142
Deutsche Telecom, 186
deutschmark, 30, 157, 163, 165–166, 168, 169–170
DGB, See German Trade Union Confederation (DGB).
Dieselgate scandal, 182, 202, 230, 282
Digital Markets Act (DMA), 192, 249
Digital Services Act (DSA), 192, 249
Dimas, Stavros, 226
DIN standards, 64
dioxin, 86
Director General for Competition, 184, 188, 190
Djibouti, 242
dollar (currency), 4, 120, 143–144, 153–154, 163, 170
Donbas, 247
Draghi, Mario, 10, 184, 198, 220, 259, 283, 291
Dublin III Agreement, 217
Duchêne, François, 148
Dumas, Roland, 40, 60

INDEX 375

Dutch East India Company, 26
Dyson, Kenneth, 202

East Asia, 135, 255
East Coast Main Line (UK), 189
East India Company, 127
EBRD (European Bank for Reconstruction and Development), 215
EC, *See* Euroean Community.
ECAC (European Civil Aviation Conference), 70
ECSC Treaty, 51, 79, 140, 151
Eden, Anthony, 103
EDF (European Development Fund), 136
EDF Energy, 119
education, 6, 16, 24, 37, 41, 78, 84, 93, 175, 188, 206, 210, 302
EEA (European Economic Area), 177
EEC, *See* European Economic Community (EEC).
EFSF (European Financial Stability Facility), 197-198
EFTA, *See* European Free Trade Association.
Ehlermann, Claus-Dieter, 184, 188, 190
EIB (European Investment Bank), 91, 247, 255
Eisenhower, Dwight D., 28, 103, 104, 105, 124, 268
ELEC (European League of Economic Cooperation), xi, 54
electricity generation, 29, 114, 187
Elf, 228
Elizabeth II of the UK, 110
embedded liberalism, 33, 272-273, 279
EMEP (European Monitoring and Evaluation Programme), 87
EMU (economic and monetary union), x, 46, 169, 279
energy, 12, 50, 52, 95, 114, 116, 124, 145, 177, 186-187, 226
  low-cost, 253
  nuclear power, 42, 113-114, 116, 119, 226-227, 232, 263
  renewable, 291
environmental legislation, 89, 182, 223, 227-228, 236, 281, 286

environmental NGOs, 5, 8, 16, 224, 278-287
environmental policy, 78, 88, 223, 227-228, 230, 236, 274, 277-282, 285, 290
  regulations, 13, 40, 90, 206, 223, 224, 226, 228, 231, 276, 288
Environmental Protection Agency (EPA), xi, 182, 228
environmentalism, 15, 22, 24, 89, 193, 224, 229, 274-275, 287-288
EPA, *See* Environmental Protection Agency.
EPC (European Political Cooperation), 106
EPP, *See* European People's Party.
EPU, *See* European Payments Union.
Erasmus programme, 37, 67, 84
ERDF, *See* European Regional Development Fund (ERDF).
Erhard, Ludwig, 54, 108, 279, 286
ESA, *See* European Space Agency.
ESF (European Social Fund), 79-80, 91
ESM, *See* European Stability Mechanism.
ESPRIT programme, 65, 122-123, 150
Essen European Council, 215
Estonia, 175, 181, 258, 267
ETS (emissions trading system), 233
ETUC, *See* European Trade Union Confederation.
Etzioni, Amitai, 23
EUI, *See* European University Institute.
Eurafrica, 136-137
Euratom, x, 39, 104, 114
Eurekâ project, 122, 125, 249, 275, 290
euro (currency), 40, 172, 195-196, 197, 198-199, 201-202, 204, 208, 220, 255, 276
Euro-Arab dialogue, 106, 114
Eurofighter Typhoon, 107
Eurogroup, 196, 199, 203
Euromarkets, 95
Euromissile crisis, 97
European Adaptation Fund, 91
European Aeronautic Defence and Space Company (EADS), 249
  See also Airbus

European army, 100, 101–102, 107, 125, 259
European Bank for Reconstruction and Development (EBRD), 215
European Central Bank (ECB), 72, 167, 169–170, 184, 196, 197–199, 201–204, 220, 252, 303
European Chips Act, 255
European Civil Aviation Conference (ECAC), 70
European Coal and Steel Community (ECSC), x, 39, 50–52, 54, 56–57, 79, 102, 114, 139, 219, 286
European Commission, 6, 29, 41, 53, 76, 93, 95–96, 123, 178, 248, 275
European Community (EC), 21, 36–38, 43–44, 49, 55, 57, 91–92, 105–108, 125, 129, 131, 133–134, 135, 136–140, 147–149, 153, 162, 166
European Competition Network, 190
European Confederation, 37, 265
European Conference of Postal and Telecommunications Administrations, 66
European Council, 39, 74, 83, 92, 96, 131, 142, 157, 168, 199, 285
European Court of Justice (ECJ), x, 10, 12, 41, 42, 44, 58, 60, 62, 70, 85, 177–180, 188–189, 204, 285
European Currency Unit, 163
European Defence Agency, 259
European Defence Community (EDC), x, 101–103, 125, 154, 279
European Defence Fund, 255, 258
European Democrats group, 133
European Development Fund (EDF), 136
European Economic Area (EEA), 177
European Economic Community (EEC), x, 6, 36–39, 45–46, 52, 55–56, 93–94, 100, 121–122, 136, 144–145, 154, 231, 273–274, 279, 286
European Environmental Agency, 225
European Financial Stability Facility (EFSF), 197–198
European Free Trade Area, x, 210, 260

European Free Trade Association (EFTA), x, 36, 46, 55–56, 210, 260
European Health Community, 219, 235
European Health Insurance Card, 219
European industrial policy, 13, 115, 120, 122, 125, 150, 249, 253–254, 289
European Investment Bank (EIB), 91, 247, 255
European Monetary Fund (EMF), 154, 164, 203, 205, 277, 283
European Monetary Snake, 155, 163
European Monetary System (EMS), x, 40, 43, 162–167, 171–172, 195, 203, 279, 283
European Parliament, 34, 39–40, 41, 63, 69–70, 81, 133–134, 170, 228, 244, 285
European Payments Union (EPU), x, 50, 154
European Peace Facility, 258
European People's Party (EPP), 40
European Political Community, 102–103, 265
European Political Cooperation (EPC), 106
European recovery plan, 203
European Regional Development Fund (ERDF), 91, 321
European Round Table for Industry, 25, 63, 148
European Social Fund (ESF), 79–80, 91
European Space Agency (ESA), 112–113, 121, 274, 289
European Stability Mechanism (ESM), 198, 203–204, 217
European Strategic Program for Research and Development in Information Technology, *See* ESPRIT programme.
European Technological Community, 121
European Trade Union Confederation (ETUC), xi, 10, 80, 82, 94, 95–98, 131, 133–134, 151, 155, 159, 164, 181, 188, 207, 287
European treaties, 45, 86, 203, 208

European Water Framework Directive, 224
European Working Time Directive, 262
Euroscepticism, 38, 73, 75, 77, 90, 97, 196, 205, 237, 277
Everling, Ulrich, 58, 62

F-104 Starfighter, 107
F-16, 107
F-35, 107, 269
Fabius, Laurent, 64, 89, 97, 165, 166
Fabrique Nationale (FN), 85
Facebook, 191, 193
Falklands conflict, 106
Fanfani, Amintore, 121
Federal Republic of Germany, *See* German Federal Republic.
Federal Reserve, 200, 222
Fiat, 63, 191
Finland, 58, 209, 220, 227, 268
Fiscal Compact, 203
Fischler, Franz, 182
fisheries, 24, 177, 225, 230
flanking policy, 78, 92, 98
Flynn, Padraig, 179
Fokker, 113
Fontainebleau summit, 61, 65, 73
football, 173, 178–179, 247, 276
Fordism, 90, 134
foreign aid, 65, 200, 218, 221, 266
Fortress Europe, 1, 146, 148, 271, 275, 290–291
Fouchet, Christian, 105
Fouchet Plan, 105–106, 125
franc (French currency), 154–156, 163–165, 167
France
  aerospace industry, 107, 111
  agricultural policy, 109–110, 250
  agricultural sector, 61, 65
  automobile industry, 89
  as basis of wealth convergence assessment, 217
  Colbertism, 26, 27
  competition policy, 57–59, 72
  defence policy, 102
  EC presidency, 83, 97, 103, 149
  economy
    1957–1958 financial crisis, 160
    1959 financial crisis, 286
    1968 financial crisis, 154
    1983 financial crisis, 119, 154, 163, 164–166
    inflation, 57
    monetary policy, 144, 153, 154, 163
    protectionism, 137
    public debt, 267
    trade balance, 31, 64
  environmental policy, 87, 89–90, 226, 232
  European council presidency, 97
  European institutions and
    Common Marker treaty, 52–53
    European Commission, 60
    European confederation, 37
    French attitude to Europe, 42
  European integration and, motivations for, 35
  European organizations and, European Health Community, 219
  European states and
    Belgium, 54
    United Kingdom, 54
  European treaties, Constitutional Treaty (2005), 205
  European treaty negotiations
    Free Trade Area, 53–56
    Treaty of Rome, 57
  exports, 30
  foreign affairs
    Algerian war of independence, 54
    ambitions as European power, 104–106
    colonial conflicts, 30
    decolonization, 103
    development funds, 136
    Euro-Arab dialogue, 114
    military interventions in Africa, 258
    Germany and, 27, 51, 103, 107, 110–111, 112, 113, 119, 125, 156, 163, 184, 186, 227, 253, 259, 269, 273, 276, 283–284
    bilateral agreements, 108
    dispute over non-tariff barriers, 65
    war reparations, 35

France (cont.)
  immigration to, 218
  industrial policy, 27, 112, 115–116, 121
    automotive idustry, 89
    coal, 50
    European industrial policy and, 122
    German criticism of, 27
    indicative planning, 30, 78, 92, 116, 118
    market liberalisation, 68, 70, 76
    national stakes in companies, 248
    neomercantilism, 72
    opposition to harmonisation, 68
    privatisation, 120
    protectionism, 30
    state aid, 59, 60–64, 120
    See also Airbus.
  influence on Europe, 283
  international organisations and, NATO, 102, 257
  labour laws, 79
  labour relations, 96
    trade unions, 80
  Marshall Plan and, 90
  monetary policy, 161
  nuclear industry, 114
  nuclear power, 227, 232
  nuclear programme, 103–104
  nuclear weapons, 115
  planning system, 93
  political ideologies, far right extremism, 75
  political ideology, 14
  social policy, 94
    working time, 95, 206
    working time legislation, 97
  trade policy, 136
    'economic patriotism', 248
    Japanese imports, 64, 145–146
    legislative harmonisation, 61
    protectionism, 64
    rejection of FTA, 36
    tarrifs, 53
  treaty negotiations
    Common Market, 94
    Maastricht Treat, 83
    Multilateral Agreement on Investment, 208
    Rome Treaty, 85
  United Kingdom and
    proposal for French Commonwealth membership, 53
    UK admission to EC, 43
France Telecom, 186–187
France,competition policy, cartels, 142
fraud, 182–183, 196, 199, 202, 212, 229–230, 262
free movement, 177, 220, 260
  of goods, 76, 219
  of people, 219
free trade area (FTA), 36, 37–38, 43, 45–46, 48, 53–56, 244, 273, 276, 286, 290–291
Freedom of the Skies campaign, 69
French Community, 9
French Greens, 226
French Planning Board, 92, 93
French–German, 103, 107, 110–111, 113, 125, 156, 163, 259, 269, 276, 283–284
Friedman, Milton, 20, 155, 157, 175
Frontex agency, 218
Frugal Four, 284
Fukushima nuclear accident, 227
Fukuyama, Francis, 23

G20, 239
G7, 37, 73, 121–122, 135, 144, 156–157, 214, 239, 268
Gabriel, Sigmar, 253
Gagarin, Yuri, 93
Gaitskell, Hugh, 51
Galileo programme, 254
GATT, *See* General Agreement on Tariffs and Trade.
  Uruguay Round, 67, 149
Gaulle, Charles de, 30, 42, 43, 49, 55, 56, 273
gender, 22, 78, 84, 207
gender equality, 13, 85, 98–99, 212, 282
gender pay gap, 84
General Agreement on Tariffs and Trade (GATT), x–xi, 10, 32, 52, 56, 64, 126, 138, 144, 145–146, 147, 151, 174, 209, 273, 276

General Data Protection Regulation (GDPR), 249
General Electric, 113, 130
Genscher, Hans-Dietrich, 43, 111, 165, 166–167, 169
German Greens, 202, 226
German reunification, 36–37, 72, 168
German Trade Union Confederation (DGB), 82, 97, 127, 133–134, 159, 161
Germany, xi, 11, 15, 22, 28, 30, 31, 40, 42, 43, 51–52, 54, 57, 58, 59–60, 61, 62, 63, 65, 69, 70, 71, 72, 76, 80, 82, 83, 88, 90–91, 93, 95, 96, 97, 98, 103, 104, 108, 109, 111, 114–115, 116, 118, 122, 124, 125, 127, 132, 135, 136–137, 139, 140, 141, 144, 147–148, 150, 154–156, 157, 160, 161, 163, 165, 167, 168, 176, 185, 186, 202, 205, 227, 254, 256–257, 274, 276, 286, 304
  agriculture, 108–110
  banking sector, 188
  capitalist style, 29–30
  competition policy, 57, 71
  currency, 30, 157, 163, 165–166, 168, 169–170
  currency union and, 196
  defence policy, 267, 269
    nuclear weapons, 104
    rearmament, 102–103
  economy
    1923 hyperinflation, 159
    1973 oil crisis, 87
    balance of payments, 152, 156–157, 171
    currency, 155
    exports, 30, 82, 89
    fiscal harmonisation, 95
    fiscal policy, 167
    Marshall Plan and, 90
    monetary union, 170
    monetary union and, 83
    public debt, 202, 267
    trade balance, 253
  energy
    coal, 114
    natural gas, 145, 247
    oil policy, 114
  environmental policy, 89, 227, 230, 288
    automobile regulations, 191
    carbon taxes, 232
  EU presidency, 252
  European treaty negotiations, exchange rate mechanism], 163
  fiscal policy, 167
  foreign policy, legacy of Nazism and, 42
  France and, 103, 107, 110–111, 113, 125, 156, 163, 259, 269, 276, 283–284
    criticism of industrial policy, 27
    historical conflicts, 102
    historical rivalry, 35
    historical wars, 35
  Greek debt crisis and, 204
  health policy, 221, 256
  hegemonic status, 282
  immigration to, 22, 218
  industrial policy, 7, 116
    blocks on Chinese acquisition of German companies, 253
    codetermination, 127
    environmental legislation and, 89
    European Coal and Steel Community and, 51
    high-tech investment, 117, 123
    opposition to state aid, 60
    opposition to term, 14, 27
    regional aid, 68
    regulatory fraud, 182
    standardisation, 150
    state aid, 115, 117, 141, 248, 252, 254–255
    workers' rights, 83
  military bases in
    British, 43
    US, 102
  Nazi regime, 17
  ordoliberalism, 6, 20, 45, 57, 59, 168, 199, 284
  regional aid, 185
  reunification, 36–37, 168

380 INDEX

Germany (cont.)
  social policy, 22, 83
    legislative harmonisation, 95
    unemployment benefits, 175
  trade policy
    free trade, 135, 144, 146
    legislative harmonisation, 62
    non-tariff barriers, 64, 76
    support for free trade, 30
    treaty negotiations, Yaoundé Convention, 136
  US military bases, 28
gilets jaunes movement, 232
Giscard d'Estaing, Valery, 43, 109–110, 113, 116, 135, 141, 156, 163–164
Glasgow Financial Alliance for Net Zero, 229
globalisation, 11, 13, 126, 129, 143, 150, 151, 209, 217, 238, 240, 279
GMOs (genetically modified organisms), 224, 250
González, Felipe, 37, 91, 99, 284
Good Friday Agreement, 214
Google, 185, 191–192, 241
Gore, Al, 232
Gove, Michael, 225
GPS, 28
Gramsci, Antonio, 15
Great Britain, *See* United Kingdom.
Great Depression, 92
Greece, 21, 36, 91, 149, 195, 196–202, 205, 214, 215–217, 221, 241–242, 281
  debt crisis, 198–199, 202, 203–204
Green parties, 22, 226, 228, 280
  France, 226
  Germany, 202, 226, 269
Greenland, 245, 360
Greenpeace, 86, 115, 224, 282
Grexit, 198–199, 200, 277
Groeben, Hans von der, 58, 95
Grundig, 58, 72
GSM standard, 150
Guigou, Elisabeth, 121
GWB (Gesetz gegen Wettbewerbsbeschränkungen), 57

Haberler, Gottfried, 21
Habermas, Jürgen, 201, 202, 204
Habitat Directive (1992), 224
Haferkamp, Wilhelm, 134
Haffner, Sebastian, 29
Hague Conference, 231
Hall, Stuart, 158
Halliday, Johnny, 158
Hallstein, Walter, 40
Hamilton, Alexander, 222
Hannan, David, 260
Hansenne, Michel, 83
hard power, 257, 263, 267, 270
Harland & Wolff shipbuilders, 60, 143
Hartz IV reform, 175, 282
Harvard University, 92
Hass, Ernst, 47
Hauff, Volker, 88, 117
Hauglustaine, Charlotte, 85
Haussmann, Helmut, 71
Havana Charter, 126
Havel, Vaclav, 37
Hawk, Barry, 189
Hayek, Friedrich, 5, 20–21, 157, 173, 182, 290
Healey, Denis, 156
healthcare policy, 24, 41, 51, 62, 66, 82, 89–90, 181, 188, 219, 249, 271
Heath, Edward, 80, 91, 99, 118, 131
Hecht, Gabrielle, 114
Helms-Burton Act, 238
Helsinki Conference, 106, 263
Herstal strike, 85
High Authority, 39, 51, 57, 79, 114, 120
  See also European Commission
Hirschman, Albert, 4, 27
Hitler, Adolf, 17, 27, 30
Holland, Stuart, 93–94
Hollande, François, 198, 210
Honecker, Erich, 161
Honeywell, 185
Howe, Geoffrey, 73, 74
Huawei, 241
Hume, David, 32
Hungary, 43, 196, 218, 220, 241–244, 256, 266, 277, 284

IBM, 113, 147, 281
ICAO (International Civil Aviation Organisation), 70
Iceland, 177, 200, 262

IG Mettall, 97
Iglesias, Pablo, 221
IMF, *See* International Monetary Fund.
immigration, 3, 20, 22, 35, 51, 217–218,
  242–243, 244, 260, 280
Indonesia, 235
industrial policy, 16–18, 24, 27–28, 30,
  51, 68, 72, 115–121, 123–125,
  255, 274–283, 288–289, 295
Industriepolitik, 116
inflation, 4, 25, 29–30, 93, 134, 156,
  158–165, 169–171, 175, 277,
  283, 292
Inflation Reduction Act (IRA), 228, 253
Instagram, 193
Intel, 185
intellectual property, 144, 210, 241
Inter-Allied Board, 49
International Chamber of Commerce,
  133, 229
International Civil Aviation
  Organisation (ICAO), 70
International Criminal Court (ICC), 238
International Energy Agency, 114
International Labour Organization
  (ILO), x–xi, 10, 12, 32–33,
  37–38, 79, 80–81, 94, 98, 133,
  151, 273
International Monetary Fund (IMF), x,
  38, 119, 129, 154, 156, 161, 166,
  196, 198, 199, 200–202, 204,
  211, 273
International Panel for Climate Change
  (IPCC), 230–231
International Procurement Instrument
  (IPI), 252
International Safe Harbour Privacy
  Principles, 250
International Telegraph Union (ITU),
  32
Internet regulation, 173, 238
IPCC (International Panel for Climate
  Change), 230–231
IPCEI (Important Project of Common
  European Interest), 255
IPI (International Procurement
  Instrument), 252
Iran, 28, 238, 257, 275
Iran Nuclear Agreement, 238

Iraq War, 238, 257, 277, 280
Ireland, 40, 101, 110, 191, 196–198,
  200–201, 211, 214, 217, 262
Irish Republican Army (IRA), 214
IRIS-T missiles, 269
Islam, 280
Islamic fundamentalism, 275
Italy, 52, 80–81, 91, 101, 102–103, 104,
  112–113, 118–119, 141,
  145–146, 154–156, 160,
  162–165, 171, 196–197,
  256–257, 273–274, 283–284
Italy, Communist Party, 15

Jaguar, 247
Japan, 36, 64, 123, 137–138, 142–143,
  144, 145–147, 150, 156, 162,
  239–240, 249, 251–252,
  275–276, 325
Jenkins, Roy, 43, 109–110, 133, 163
Jobs, Steve, 173
Johnson, Boris, 260–262, 286
Joliet, René, 62, 189
Jones, Hywel Ceri, 84
Jospin, Lionel, 178, 207–209
Juncker Commission, 212, 254
Juncker, Jean-Claude, 43, 255, 258, 271,
  363
Juncker Plan, 254

Kagan, Robert, 257
Kallas, Kaja, 267, 268
Kangaroo Group, 63
Kant, Immanuel, 32, 257
Kantor, Mickey, 149
Keating, Dave, 256
Kennedy, John F., 104
Keynes, John Maynard, 5, 9, 15, 48–49,
  75, 156, 273
Keynesianism, 20, 159–161, 275
Khrushchev, Nikita, 53, 105
Kiechle, Ignaz, 110
Kiel Institute, 266, 362
Kinnock, Neil, 180
Klöckner, 141
Kocka, Jürgen, 2, 26
Kohl, Helmut, 37, 65, 73, 83, 92, 97,
  110, 111, 147, 165, 166–169, 188
Kok, Wim, 96, 133

Korah, Valentine, 189
Korean War, 101, 267
Kraft Durch Freude organization, 17
Kramp-Kambauer, Anegret, 253
Kreditanstalt für Wiederaufbau, 255
Kroes, Neelie, 69, 183–185, 192
Krugman, Paul, 112
Krupp, 141
Kwarteng, Kwasi, 260
Kyoto Protocol, 231, 232–233, 238, 263

labour law, 84, 85, 262
Lafontaine, Oskar, 207
Lagarde, Christine, 211, 220, 226
Laïdi, Zaki, 149
Lambsdorff, Otto von, 59, 117–118, 132, 140–141, 161, 165
Lamy, Pascal, 74, 209
Land Rover, 247
Landesbanken, 26, 30, 117, 188, 282
Lange, Bernd, 245
Larosière, Jacques de, 167
Latvia, 202
Law and Justice party (Poland), 38, 242
Lawson, Nigel, 146, 166
League of Nations (LoN), 32, 49–50, 54, 219, 251
Legrand, 184
Lehman Brothers, 200
Lemaire, Bruno, 253
Letta report, 247, 291
LGBT rights, 206, 242
liberty capitalism, 1–2, 4, 8, 46, 126, 236, 273, 275
  as basic form of European capitalist goverment, 284
  combined with other capitalisms, 167, 171, 253
  competition policy and, 15, 143, 205
  European institutions and, 45–46
  globalisation and, 150
  health policy and, 219
  legislative harmonization and, 45
  moderate forms, 12
  monetary union and, 153
  neoliberalism as extreme of, 4, 17
  See also neoliberalism.
  overview, 19–21
  solidarity capitalism and, 20, 22

Libya, 218, 238
Lingren, Astrid, 158
Lion, Robert, 165
Lippmann, Walter, 20
lira (currency), 155
Lisbon Treaty, 198, 209, 257
List, Friedrich, 26
lobbying, 11, 12, 22, 89–90, 111, 133–134, 151, 185, 281–282, 295
Lockheed Hercules, 259
Lomé conventions, 137, 274
LoN, *See* League of Nations.
London Conference (1953), 30, 202
Lowe, Philip, 190
Lower Saxony, 117, 181, 185, 248
Lubbers, Ruud, 73, 162, 180, 231
Lucke, Bernd, 202
Lufthansa, 111
Lula da Sivla, Luiz Inácio, 212, 242
Luxembourg, xi, 50, 52, 62, 102, 141, 181, 182, 187, 191, 195, 211, 248
Luxembourg Employment Summit, 208

Maastricht Treaty, 37, 88, 167–170, 172, 195–198, 223, 235, 256, 281, 283
Macdonald Commission, 162
Macmillan, Harold, 43, 53, 105
Macron, Emmanuel, 257–258, 265
MacSharry, Ray, 110
mad cow disease, *See* BSE.
Madelin, Alain, 68
Magnette, Paul, 211, 350
Maij-Weggen, Hanja, 88
Major, John, 232
Maldague Report, 81, 93, 94, 131
Mali, 258
Malthus, Thomas, 116
Man in Palermo theory, 62
Manchester City FC, 247
Mannesmann AG, 128, 133
Mansholt, Sicco, 87, 108, 363
Mao Zedong, 158
Marbella Paper, 161
Marcinelle mining disaster, 79
Margetts, Helen, 174
Marin, Manuel, 91

Marjolin, Robert, xi, 20, 92–93, 94, 98, 121, 154
Marshall Plan, 36, 49–50, 90, 154, 215, 221, 235, 273
Martens, Wilfried, 73
Marxism, 15, 22, 32, 129, 157–158, 264, 275
Matthöfer, Hans, 117, 157
Maudling, Reginald, 54–55
Mauritania, 137
Mauroy stimulus, 161
Mauroy, Pierre, 165
May Fourth Movement, 241
Mayrisch, Emile, 139
MBB, *See* Messerschmitt-Bölkow-Blohm.
MBDA, 259
McDonnell Douglas, 111–112, 185
McKinnon, Ronald, 199
Meadows Report, 87
medical tourism, 219
Medici vicious circle, 193
Medium-term Economic Policy Committee, 93
Meidner, Rudolph, 128
Meloni, Giorgia, 283
Mendès-France, Pierre, 103
mercantilism, 4, 24, 26–27, 299
Merck, 256
Mercosur, 38, 211, 252
Mercury Communications Ltd., 70
mergers, 41, 45, 51, 68, 71–72, 76, 118, 183–186, 189, 248, 252–253
Merkel, Angela, 218, 220, 282
Merz, Friedrich, 267
Messerschmitt-Bölkow-Blohm, 71, 112, 118
Mestmäcker, Ernst-Joachim, 59, 191
Microsoft, 185, 191, 241
Miert, Karel van, 119, 179
migration policy, 23, 33, 43, 79–80, 84, 98, 176, 197, 213, 217–218, 260, 265, 276–277, 290–291
Milan European Council meeting, 110, 122
Milward, Alan, 90
Mines de Potasse d'Alsace, 88
minimum wage, 166, 212–213, 235, 340
Mitbestimmung system, *See* codetermination.

Mittal, 247, 248
Mitterrand, François, 37, 40, 61, 62, 65, 80–81, 83, 96, 99, 111, 119, 121–122, 125, 144, 165
Modi, Narendra, 177, 278
Mogg, John, 178
Mogherini, Federica, 257
Moldova, 264, 265
Molitor, Bernhard, 178
Mollet, Guy, 51, 53, 79, 99, 103–104, 279, 288
monetary policy, 2, 4, 6, 16, 40, 45–46, 200, 203–204, 226, 236, 273
monetary union, 37, 83, 152–153, 155, 168–170, 172, 204, 212, 213–214, 275, 284
Monnet, Jean, xi, 30, 34, 49, 79, 102, 114, 148, 154
monopolies, 3, 6, 15, 25–26, 69, 71, 119, 186, 192, 271, 285
Montesquieu, 32
Monti, Mario, 10, 181, 183, 185, 187, 190, 283
Montreal Protocol, 89, 281
Mosar, Nicolas, 187
Moscovici, Pierre, 203
Mozambique, 234
Müller-Armack, Alfred, 55
Multi-Fibres Agreement, 138
Multilateral Agreement on Investment, 209
Multilateral Force (MLF), 104
Mundell, Robert, 154
Munich Congress, 96
Musk, Elon, 243
Myrdal, Gunnar, 108

NAFTA (North American Free Trade Area), 238
Nakasone Yakuhiro, 162
Narjes, Karl-Heinz, 59, 63, 134
nationalism, 3, 8, 27, 240, 243
nation-states, 6, 12, 23, 41, 53, 78, 104, 170, 213, 220, 271, 282, 324
NATO, 35, 42, 100–103, 104, 238, 251, 257–258, 262, 267–271, 273, 286
Natura 2000, 224
Necker, Tyll, 169

neoliberalism, 1, 4–5, 7–8, 15–21, 73–75, 170–172, 174–175, 181, 183, 204–205, 210–211, 243–244, 274–277, 282–283, 285–286
neomercantilism, 24–25, 27–28, 69, 72, 120, 240
Net Zero, 229
Netherlands, 50, 52, 69–70, 87–88, 93–96, 147, 162, 211, 224, 284, 324
New International Economic Order (NIEO), 129, 135, 150, 274
New Temporary Crisis and Transition Framework, 253
Nexit, 260, 277
NextGenerationEU (NGEU), 220, 222
Nice, Treaty of (2003), 209
Nicolaïdis, Kalypso, 41
Nissan, 146–147, 151
Nixon, Richard, 145, 153
non-tariff barriers, 56, 62, 64, 65, 82, 239
Nord Stream pipeline, 247
Nordhaus, William, 229
normative power, 23, 24, 46, 127, 143, 148–149, 151, 157, 222, 237, 244–246, 249, 250, 261, 270
  environmental, 192, 227, 271, 286
  inverse, 250
North American Free Trade Area (NAFTA), 238
North Atlantic Alliance, See NATO.
North Rhine-Westphalia, 117–118
Northern Ireland, 60, 143, 177, 214, 261
Northern Rock, 200
Norway, 55, 88, 177, 255, 262, 268, 324
NOx emissions controls, 89, 182
nuclear power, 42, 113–114, 116, 119, 226–227, 232, 263
nuclear weapons, 35, 101–102, 103, 104–105, 107, 115
Nye, Joseph, 270

Occupational Health and Safety Framework Directive, 82
OECD, See Organisation for Economic Co-operation and Development.

OEEC, See Organisation for European Economic Cooperation.
Oftel, 70
Ohlin, Bertil, 94
Ohlin Report, 94
oil, 31, 114, 120, 129, 226–227, 232, 266
oil crises
  1973, 17, 87, 111, 114, 135, 155, 274
  1979, 114, 116, 140, 157, 274
Olivetti, 123
One Road One Belt Initiative, 241
OPEC (Organization of the Petroleum Exporting Countries), 25, 129
Opel, 114, 248
Open Method of Coordination (OMC), 208
Open Society Foundations, 215
Orange Revolution, 247
Orbán, Viktor, 215, 242–244
Ordnungspolitik, 168
ordoliberalism, 20–21, 55, 57–59, 168–172, 189, 192, 193–194, 197, 199, 204, 281, 284
Oreja, Marcelino, 179
Organisation for Economic Co-operation and Development (OECD), x–xi, 9, 10, 12, 36–38, 59, 87, 119, 131, 132–133, 142, 151, 156, 157, 209, 211, 225, 231
Organisation for European Economic Cooperation (OEEC), x, 9, 35–36, 44, 50, 51, 53, 54–55, 92, 108, 154, 219, 273, 279, 304
Organization of the Petroleum Exporting Countries, See OPEC.
O'Rourke, Kevin, 40
Ortoli, François-Xavier, 59, 60, 96, 121, 132, 134
Ostrom, Elinor, 4, 24
Ottawa Agreements, 31
Ouchy Convention, 52

Padoa-Schioppa, Tommaso, 167, 283
Palme, Olof, 274, 279
Panama Papers, 182
pandemic, See Covid-19 pandemic.
Pannonian plain, 243
Papandreou, Giorgos, 196

Papandréou, Vásso, 83
Paris Agreement on climate change, 1, 103, 212, 228, 231, 233, 235, 236, 238, 251
Paris European Council (1974), 67
Paris G7 Summit (1989), 214
Paris Saint-Germain FC, 247
Paris Summit (1972), 80, 91
Patel, Kiran Klaus, 108
Patel, Priti, 260
Patriot air-defence system, 269, 362
Pattie, Geoffrey, 150
PEACE programme, 214
Péchiney, 184
Pescatore, Pierre, 62
Peugeot SA, 89–90, 248, 281
Pfizer, 256
Pflimlin, Pierre, 108
Philip Morris judgment, 71
Philips NV, 63, 113, 148
Piketty, Thomas, 166, 340
Pinochet, Augusto, 20, 130, 157
planning, 11, 13, 30, 78, 81, 92–94, 98, 116, 118, 286, 299
Pleven, René, 102
Pöhl, Karl-Otto, 164, 165, 168
Poiares Maduro, Miguel, 181
Poland, 160, 196, 200–201, 215, 220, 227, 241–242, 247, 255, 268, 269, 277
Polanyi, Karl, 9, 19
police, 6, 24, 41, 276
pollution, 19, 33, 48, 86, 87, 88, 98–99, 223, 227, 229, 287
  air, 89, 230
  automobile, 90
Polnareff, Michel, 158
Pompidou, Georges, 80, 116, 131
Poos, Jacques, 106
Porignaux, Adelin, 109
Portugal, 35–36, 40, 55, 61, 83, 91, 149, 180, 195, 197–198, 200–201, 257
Potsdam Conference, 51
Powell, Charles, 75
Powell, Enoch, 20
Prebisch, Raul, 28, 129
principle of community, *See* community principle.

Private–public partnerships, 25
Proctor, David, 228
Prodi Commission, 180, 183
Prodi, Romano, 196, 208, 224, 257
Progress Party (Denmark), 158
protectionism, 1, 2–5, 7–8, 10–11, 18, 27–28, 45, 76, 100, 115, 126, 137–138, 165, 237–238, 243–246, 250–253, 271, 277–280, 291–292
Prussia, 152
Putin, Vladimir, 242, 247

Qatar, 247
quantitative easing, 25, 199, 217, 220, 303
quotas, 24, 46, 50, 51, 53, 137–139, 140, 141, 149, 230, 234

Raab, Dominic, 260
Rainbow Warrior, 115
Rambouillet conference, 135
Reagan, Ronald, 17, 28, 64, 121, 129, 143–144, 145, 162, 243, 257, 274
Régie des Télégraphes et Téléphone (RTT), 119
Regional Comprehensive Economic Partnership (RCEP), 239
Rehn–Meidner model, 19
Reichsbank, 168
Reinheitsgebot, 65
Relaunch of Europe, 61, 63, 67, 76, 84, 90, 284
Renault, 90, 114, 185, 207, 248, 281
Rhodes European Council, 231
Ribeyre, Paul, 219
Richard, Ivor, 134
Ridley, Nicholas, 69
Rigout, Marcel, 96, 119, 287
Rio Earth Summit (1992), 89, 225, 231, 232
Ripa di Meana, Carlo, 231–232, 236
Ristchl, Albrecht, 202
Rocard, Michel, 231
Rodgers, Ivan, 263
Rodrik, Dani, 24
Roemer, Karl, 58
Rogoff, Ken, 199
Romania, 196, 218, 362

Rome Statute, 238
Röpke, Wilhelm, 21, 55
Rothschild, Emma, *293*
Rousseau, Jean-Jacques, 23
Roussel Report, 90
Rover, 68
Rueff, Jacques, 55
Ruffolo, Mario, 231
Ruggie, John, 273
Ruggiero, Renato, 209
Ruhrgas AG, 145
Russia, 175, 235, 237–240, 242, 247, 253, 263–270, 276–284
Russo-Ukrainian War, 236, 244, 247, 253, 258–259, 263, 264–265, 267–271, 277
Rüstow, Alexander, 20

Sabena, 85
Sacilor, 140
Saint-Gobain (glassmaker), 26
Saint-Malo declaration, 256
Samuelson, Paul, 92
Sanchez, Pablo, 221
Santer, Jacques, 168, 208, 363
SAP, 193
Sarkozy, Nicolas, 180, 185
satellite communications, 112
satellite rocket launcher, 104
Saudi Arabia, 165
Scharpf, Fritz, 44, 117
Schaüble, Wolfgang, 199
Schengen Agreement, 40, 67, 277
Schlecht, Otto, 71, 117, 288
Schlüter, Poul, 162
Schmidt, Helmut, 43, 80, 81, 96, 110, 120, 135, 156, 161, 163–164
Schmidt, Vivien, 115–116
Scholz, Olaf, 222, 258, 269
Schröder, Gerhard, 25, 175, 208, 224
Schuman Declaration, 36, 38, 49, 50–51, 79, 102, 105, 108, 197, 219
Schuman, Robert, 102, 121
Schwartz, Ivo, 62
Scott Morton, Fiona, 191
SDI (Strategic Defence Initiative), 121, 122
Sen, Amartya, 22

Senegal, 137
Sermon, Lucien, 54
Servan-Schreiber, Jean-Jacques, 120, 268
Set of Multilaterally Agreed Equitable Principles and Rules for the Control of Restictive Business Practices, 131
Seveso dioxin leak, 86
Seveso Directive, 86, 230
SGCI, 68, 331
Shalke 04, 179
Shell, 63, 179
shipbuilding, 26, 59, 68, 115, 118, 141–143, 150–151
Siemens, 113, 123, 130, 184
Silguy, Yves-Thibault de, 179
Single European Act (1986), 61, 66, 68, 69, 82, 88, 90, 99, 110, 167, 281
Single Market, 45–49, 61, 65–68, 71–72, 74–77, 81–82, 92, 123–124, 148–149, 177–178, 183, 204–205, 214, 249, 261–262
Skidmore, Chris, 260
Skoda, 248
slowbalisation, 238
Small Business Innovation Research (SBIR) programme, 28
Smith, Adam, 4, 19, 32, 142
Smoot-Hawley Tariff Act, 27
SNCF, 119
Snecma, 113
soccer, *See* football.
Social Darwinism, 182
Social Democratic Party (Germany), 51, 114, 117, 159, 226
social flank, 78, 83, 98
social policy, 13, 21, 51, 78, 79–80, 84, 93, 132, 212, 331
soft power, 270
Solana, Javier, 256
solidarity capitalism, 5, 17–24, 25, 33, 44, 45, 76, 84, 150, 152, 155, 164, 167, 170, 197, 206, 213, 219, 221–222, 223, 273, 274, 277, 282, 288
Brexit and, 277
in combination with other capitalisms, 129, 253

community capitalism and, 4, 8, 277, 284
environmental policy and, 226
European institutions and, 44–45, 53
European integration and, 288
far-right parties and, 244
France, 273–274
globalisation and, 209
Greek debt crisis and, 197–200
liberty capitalism and, 19, 179
Marxism and, 32
migration and, 217–218
monetary union and, 153, 172, 195–196, 213
overview, 22–26
principles, 3, 15–16
regulation and, 186
Russo-Ukrainian war and, 227
social policy and, 175, 212, 235
United States, 4
vaccination and, 221–223
solidarity coalition, 80, 287
Solomon, Susan, 230
Solzhenitsyn, Alexander, 158
Soros, Georges, 215
South Africa, 20, 239
South Korea, 28, 142, 240, 259, 269
Soviet Union, 28, 52, 101, 102–103, 105, 135, 145, 174–175, 242, 243, 263–264
Soylent Green, 86
Spaak, Paul-Henri, 52, 79
Spaak Report, 52–54, 76, 363
space sector, 112–113, 254
Spain, 40, 83, 91, 101, 112–113, 149, 197, 200–201, 208, 217, 221, 227, 256–257
SPD, *See* Social Democratic Party (Germany).
Spiegel, Der, 227
Spinelli, Altiero, 7, 10, 88, 121, 147, 283, 285, 287
Sputnik satellite, 28, 52, 93, 104
STABEX programme, 129, 150
Stability and Growth Pact, 196
Stalin, Joseph, 35, 53, 103, 158, 264
Star Wars, *See* Strategic Defence Initiative.
Starmer, Keir, 262
state aid, 25, 56–61, 68, 116–120, 140–141, 145–146, 183–186, 188–189, 193, 252–253, 253–255
steel, 50–51, 79, 102, 120, 127–128, 139–142, 145, 150–151, 234, 243, 248, 289
STMicroelectronics, 248
Stoltenberg, Jens, 110, 165
Strategic Defence Initiative (SDI), 121, 122
Strauss-Kahn, Dominique, 211
subsidies, 4, 24–25, 68, 110, 112, 116, 117, 142, 149, 184, 289–290
  agricultural, 214
Sudan, 28, 137
Sudreau report, 128, 132
Suez Crisis, 42, 53, 104–105, 114
Sun Yat-sen, 241
Sunak, Rishi, 260
supranational principle, 51, 53, 56, 62, 95, 252, 283
Sutherland, Peter, 68, 76, 85, 178, 209
Suzuki, Kazuto, 149
Sweden, 40, 55, 58, 87, 101, 158, 195, 220–221, 224, 227, 268
Swedish Trade Union Confederation, 128
SWIFT interbank system, 266
Switzerland, xvi, 55, 101, 112–113, 177, 211, 255, 262, 264, 269
Syrian civil war, 218
SYSMIN aid system, 137

TAFTA, 210
Taiwan, 28, 240
Takuba, Operation, 258
tariffs, 3, 4, 31, 32, 51, 53, 56, 110, 174, 238, 239, 250
Tata, 247
tax controls, 62
tax cooperation, 211
tax evasion, 158, 202, 211
tax havens, 32, 68, 182, 284
taxation, 20, 66–67, 95, 130, 136, 162, 166, 176, 191, 232–234, 243
  corporate, 68, 95
  diesel taxes, 227
  international, 231, 288

taxation (cont.)
  regressive, 15, 22
  financial transaction, 211, 223
Tebbit, Norman, 86
telecommunications sector, 69, 70, 76,
  119–120, 149, 184, 186, 187, 189
Temporary Protection Directive, 265
Tencent, 241
Tesla Inc., 28, 243, 253, 255
textile sector, 17, 45, 60, 120, 135,
  137–138, 144–145, 151
TGV (high-speed train), 116, 119
Thatcher, Margaret, 7–8, 17, 20, 31, 43,
  49, 67, 71, 72–75, 83, 85, 96–99,
  118, 122–123, 125, 134–135,
  140–141, 143–144, 146,
  150–151, 162, 231, 274, 281,
  282–283, 286
Thatcherism, 82, 150, 157–158, 166,
  260, 290
Ther, Philippe, 215
Thiel, Peter, 20, 302
Thomas, Albert, 123
Thunberg, Greta, 225, 277
Thyssen AG, 141
Thyssen, Marianne, 212
Tiananmen Square protests, 241
Tietmeyer, Hans, 117–118
Timmermans, Franz, 225
Tindemans, Léo, 131
Tobin, James, 136
Tobin tax, 136, 211
Tooze, Adam, 247
Tornado (aircraft), 107
Total, 228
Toyotism, 138
trade balance, 31, 62, 64, 274, 289
trade barriers, 4, 23, 56, 252
  removal of, 45–46
trade surplus, 135, 156
trade unions, 3, 5, 9–12, 30, 95–96, 118,
  128, 181, 183, 208, 276,
  281–282, 287
Transatlantic Free Trade Treaty, 210
transfer pricing, 130
Trans-Pacific Partnership, 38, 238–239
Treaty Establishing a Constitution for
  Europe (2004), 180, 205, 277
Treaty of Paris, 39

Treaty of Rome, 52–53, 54, 57–60,
  70–71, 73, 77, 79, 85, 179, 180,
  185, 191, 273
Trevi, 106
Trichet, Jean-Claude, 72, 198, 201, 252
Triffin, Robert, 154
Trump, Donald J., 1, 20, 38, 238–245,
  251, 262, 267, 268, 277–278
Truss, Liz, 204, 260
Tsipras, Alexis, 198
Tupolev Tu-144, 111
Turkey, 218, 224, 242, 259, 264–265,
  276, 324
Tusk, Donald, 199

UEFA, 178–179, 276
Uekötter, Frank, 227
Ukraine, 216, 242, 247, 263–270, 361,
  362
Ukrainian refugees, 223, 265–266
UN Environment Programme (UNEP),
  38, 89, 231
UNCTAD, *See* United Nations
  Conference on Trade and
  Development.
  session of, 130, 144
UNECE, x
unemployment, 97, 131, 133, 134, 159,
  171, 175, 195, 210, 227
unemployment benefits, 175, 208
UNEP (UN Environment Programme),
  38, 89, 231
UNESCO, 37
UNICE, 10, 80, 82, 133, 207
Unicredit, 249
Unidata, 113, 116
United Kingdom (UK), 53–56, 59, 65,
  68, 74, 83, 85, 91, 96, 98, 107,
  114, 121, 144, 146, 165, 182,
  185, 202, 222, 262–263, 265
  agriculture, BSE crisis, 182
  as awkward partner, 42
  Brexit, 260–261, 277
    leaves Single Market, 177
    Single Market and, 261–262
  Brexit referendum, 34
  budgetary contribution disputes, 44,
    61, 65, 141
  defence policy, 268

EC accession, 43, 105
EC membership application, 36, 42
economy
  IMF rescue (1976), 156, 171
  inflation, 161
  taxation, 158
  Truss crisis (2022), 204
education policy, 84
environmental policy, 110
European integration stance, 42–43
European relaunch and, 72–73
Euroscepticism, 75
fiscal policy, liberalisation of capital movements, 168
foreign policy, Suez crisis, 104, 114
free trade area, 53–56
GATT negotiations, 64
Germany and
  industrial output, 26
  support for rearmament, 102
health policy, Covid vaccines, 256
immigration to, 20
industrial policy, 124
  codetermination, 133
  Japan and, 146–147
  privatisation, 119–120
  shipbuilding, 142
  state aid, 59, 142, 143, 145
international treaties, Brussels Pact, 103
legislative harmonisation, 65
monetary union and, 195
nuclear weapons, 268
postcolonial legacy, 9
social policy
  trade unions, 80, 82
  working time, 95
telecommunications industry, 70
trade policy, 143
  Common Market and, 286
  free trade, 31, 138
  tariffs, 31, 135
transport policy, railways, 188
transportation policy, 69–70
treaty negotiations, Socal Charter, 207
troops stationed in West Germany, 43
United States and, 150

United Kingdom (UK), Brexit, EU relationship going forward, 262–263, 303, 324, 362
United Nations (UN), x–xi, 10, 12, 32–33, 98, 130–133, 151, 230–231, 257
United Nations Conference on Trade and Development (UNCTAD), x, 10, 129–131, 206
United Nations Relief and Rehabilitation Administration (UNRAA), 50
United Nations, Security Council, 42, 105, 238, 257
United States, xi, 4, 17, 28, 35, 42, 87, 101, 103–104, 145, 150, 170, 185, 193, 222, 238–239, 241, 248, 251–252, 259, 261, 262, 270, *293*
Universal Declaration of Human Rights, 241
unleaded petrol, 89–90, 281, 288
Usinor, 140
USSR, *See* Soviet Union.

Van Miert, Karel, 179, 183–184, 185, 187
van Theemaat, Verloren, 62
Vandenbroucke, Jean-Luc, 63
Varfis, Grigoris, 91
Verheugen, Günther, 226
Vestager, Margrethe, 12, 183, 185, 191–192, 193, 205, 213, 250, 253, 255, 285
Vetter, Heinz Oskar, 134, 161
VFW-Fokker 614, 113
Vietnam War, 86, 101, 274
Viking Line ferry company, 181
Vogel-Polsky, Eliane, 85, 99
Volcker, Paul, 162
Volcker Shock, 4, 143, 162, 274
Volkswagen, 17, 60, 89, 182, 185, 230, 248
Voluntary Export Restraint (VER), 137–138
Volvo, 247
von der Leyen, Ursula, 117, 225, 258, 271
Vredeling directive, 83, 133, 151, 212, 235

Vredeling, Henk, 86, 95–96, 97,
    131–132, 133, 134, 282

Wagenknecht, Sahra, 21
Waigel, Theo, 195
Wales, Jimmy, 173
Walesa, Lech, 175
Wallonia, 140, 211, 350
Wallraff, Günter, 22
Wallström, Margot, 224
Walters, Alan, 20
Wapping Dispute, 118
Wassenar Compromise, 162
Weber, Max, 4, 14, 23
Weidmann, Jens, 199
welfare states, 4–6, 17, 19–22, 73–74,
    78, 90–91, 98–99, 180, 206,
    235–236, 284–286
Werner, Pierre, 155
Werner Report, 155, 203
West Germany, *See* German Federal
    Republic.
Western European Union (WEU), 103
WhatsApp, 193
WHO, *See* World Health Organization.
Williams, Edwin, 29

Williamson, David, 56
Wilson, Harold, 121, 128, 135, 156
windfall effect, 25
work week, 80, 96–97, 207
worker participation, 128, 131
Working Time Directive, 181, 207, 210
World Bank, 144, 234
World Health Organization (WHO),
    86, 219, 238, 271
World Trade Organisation
    (WTO), x, 32, 209, 234, 238,
    241, 251, 276
World War II, 21, 35, 37, 43, 49, 53,
    101, 260, 263
Wright, Gordon, 108
Würzen, Dieter von, 63

Xi Jinping, 241–242

Yaoundé Convention (1963), 136–137
Yellen, Janet, 253
Yugoslavia, 106, 128–129, 175, 256, 263

Zeitenwende, 267
Zimbabwe, 234
Zingales, Luigi, 193

For EU product safety concerns, contact us at Calle de José Abascal, 56–1°, 28003 Madrid, Spain or eugpsr@cambridge.org.

www.ingramcontent.com/pod-product-compliance
Ingram Content Group UK Ltd.
Pitfield, Milton Keynes, MK11 3LW, UK
UKHW022146150326
469019UK00020B/1538